Space Programs
Outside the United States

Space Programs Outside the United States

All Exploration and Research Efforts, Country by Country

Daphne Burleson

McFarland & Company, Inc., Publishers

Jefferson, North Carolina, and London

Library of Congress Cataloguing-in-Publication Data

Burleson, Daphne, 1961–
Space programs outside the United States : all exploration and
research efforts, country by country / Daphne Burleson.
p.   cm.
Includes bibliographical references and index.

ISBN 0-7864-1852-4 (illustrated case binding : 50# alkaline paper)♾

1. Astronautics — Directories.
2. Aerospace industries — Directories.   I. Title.
TL788.3.B87   2005   629.4'025 — dc22   2004024053

British Library cataloguing data are available

Cover photograph ©2005 PhotoSpin

Manufactured in the United States of America

*McFarland & Company, Inc., Publishers
Box 611, Jefferson, North Carolina 28640
www.mcfarlandpub.com*

Acknowledgments

My thanks to the following people and agencies:

Frits de Zwann, European Space Agency (ESA); Tony McDonald, Enterprise/Space Ireland; Sune N. Lauritsen, Danish Space Research Institute; Dr. Frantisek Farnik, Czech Space Agency (CSA); Annika Benson, Swedish Space Corporation (SSC); Helen Westman, Swedish Space Corporation (SSC); Dr. Werner Balogh, Austrian Space Agency (ASA); Bettina Troestl, Austrian Aerospace GmbH; Dr. Michael Green, Space Licensing and Safety Office, Government of Australia; Dr. Allan Paul, University of Queensland, Hyshot Program; Sophie Berthier-Loiseu, CNES of France; Laura Sarrate, CONAE of Argentina; Dr. Martin Tajmar, MSS, ARC Seibersodorf Research GmbH Space Propulsion, Austria; Canadian Space Agency; Brazil Space Agency; NASDA; Tekes of Finland; K. P. Cheng, National Space Program Office (NSPO), Taiwan; Mavis Ho, National Space Program Office (NSPO), Taiwan; Dr. El' Both, Director, Hungarian Space Office; Jan Kolar, Czech Space Agency; DLR, German Aerospace Center and Space Agency; Stuart Grayson, British National Space Center; Marieke Hofhuis, EOS/SRON, The Netherlands

Contents

Preface

What is a space program? Many people think first of the United States' National Aeronautics and Space Administration (NASA) and its space shuttle — probably the most famous space program and space vehicle in the world. This book informs readers about the many space programs that exist outside the United States and their exciting, often technologically innovative, endeavors.

Returning to the question, "What is a space program?": it is most often a government-controlled entity assigned to perform activities and research related to the exploration of space. It can also refer to a nation's commercialization and development of space technology as well as medical research.

A space program can be either manned or unmanned, or both (NASA has the manned Space Shuttle program as well as the unmanned planetary missions out of the Jet Propulsion Laboratory).

This book comphrehensively covers 42 space programs around the world. The information for each country discussed is divided into separate discussions of that space program's projects or departments. Since many European countries also participate in programs through the European Space Agency (ESA), Europe gets an entry of its own.

I performed the majority of research for this project through direct contact with the agencies themselves, and, in the process, developed a rapport with the various space program representatives in order to compile the information presented. It helped considerably that I had initially made some of these contacts many years ago when I first began to develop an interest in space programs outside the United States.

Societies for Enthusiasts

There are some excellent membership societies that bring together space enthusiasts. Two of the most active in the United States are the National Space Society (NSS) and the Planetary Society, which was co-founded by Carl Sagan.

The National Space Society (NSS)
600 Pennsylvania Avenue SE, Suite 201
Washington DC 20003
(202) 543-1900
Website: www.nss.org
Email: members@nss.org

The Planetary Society
65 North Catalina Avenue
Pasadena CA 91106-2301
(626) 793-5100
Website: www.planetarysociety.org
Email: tps@planetary.org

ARGENTINA

Argentina National Commission on Space Activities (CONAE)

CONAE (Comisión Nacional de Actividades Espaciales), the National Space Agency in Argentina, was created in 1991. CONAE has concentrated its efforts on the generation of Space Information Cycles (CIE's), which are sets of information from space used in conjunction with other resources to have a relevant impact on the country's socio-economic activities. These activities include: agriculture and forestry, environmental studies, emergency management, oceanography, geology and mining, and internal revenue.

Argentina's space program involves a wide spread of the space data obtained from space for its processing and applications on land. This data helps the country expand its business scope, creating greater and better opportunities for employment in the production of goods and services.

Argentina's emphasis in space has been on the operation and development of orbital satellites. CONAE's Córdoba Ground Station (ETC) has been in operation since 1997, and receives data from 12 international satellites, including the Argentine SAC-C. The station also has capability for Telecommand, Telemetry and Control Stations (TT&C).

CONAE plans to set up a second ground station in Ushuaia, Province of Tierra del Fuego, at the southern tip of Argentina in the near future for collection of data on the Antarctic continent.

The Argentine National Space Program provides two satellite series which are both devoted to Earth Observation, one in the optical range (SAC) and the other in the microwave range (SAOCOM). In the SAC series, three satellites have been launched with strong international cooperation, including participation with NASA. SAC-A, SAC-B, and SAC-C were all successful. SAC-D is planned for launch in 2006.

The SAOCOM series involves the construction of two missions with a Synthetic Aperture Radar (SAR) as the main payload. These missions will be part of the Italian-Argentine System of Satellites for Emergency Management (SIASGE), together with the Italian COSMO-Skymed missions.

In the field of international cooperation, Argentina's partners include Belgium, Brazil, Canada, Denmark, France, Germany, Italy, the United States, Spain, Russia, Ukraine, the United Kingdom and the European Space Agency. Agreements with other space agencies are in negotiation.

SAC-A

The SAC-A was first in a series of satellite missions to conduct land observations and collect data on the Argentine environment. Specific objectives of SAC-A included:

Technological development testing. SAC-A served as a basis for technological testing of subsystems for future, more advanced missions such as SAC-C. SAC-A was used as a testing base for altitude control systems used for orientation of the satellite in orbit, telecommunications, and control and management of data on board the satellite. SAC-A acted as a precursor to the study of satellite operation in flight.

Global positioning systems (GPS) utilization. CONAE technicians chose to utilize GPS systems for SAC-A orbit and altitude. By incorporating GPS into the SAC-A mission, CONAE was able to test GPS capabilities before utilizing them more frequently in the navigation and control of more complex satellite missions.

Monitoring of the Southern Frank Whale. SAC-C, which followed SAC-A and SAC-B, was scheduled to carry a system of communications and remote sensors for the study of the habitats of the Southern Frank Whale portion of Argentina. This was part of the greater intent to study and monitor endangered species and the marine environment. SAC-A was equipped with a replica of the spatial segment of the Southern Frank Whale experiment.

Testing and Solar Qualification of Boards. SAC-A was built with solar panels which were mounted by the Argentine National Commission of Atomic Energy.

Observation and Geomagnetic Harvesting of Data. The SAC-A incorporated a geomagnetic data observation system to test the efficiency of these instruments for future missions. CONAE combined the data obtained with the information from the GPS systems.

Training and Development of Systems and Procedures for Operations Control. Another of SAC-A's objectives was to experimentally test telemetry, telecommand, and control. Operations control required examination of the efficiency of a team of engineers on the ground, manning the hardware and software used to control the satellite.

SAC-A was developed during a very brief, strict timeline, resulting in completion after only 11 months. CONAE was able to drastically reduce costs by eliminating excessive internal documentation and clearly assigning responsibilities to those involved on the design team.

The design of SAC-A required the construction of a delicate mechanism called the "wheel of inertia," which was a part of the altitude control subsystem, the assembly of the solar boards, and the telecommunications systems for linking with land by means of UHF and VHF. SAC-A was also equipped with a panoramic camera chamber for land observation.

SAC-A was a joint mission between CONAE and NASA, although the spacecraft was built by CONAE.

On December 14, 1998, SAC-A was launched and placed in orbit by NASA using the space shuttle mission Endeavor, STS-88. The launch took place at Kennedy Space Center, Cape Canaveral, Florida.

Once launched, CONAE was responsi-

ble for the operation, telemetry, telecommand and control of SAC-A.

SAC-A weighed 68 kg (150 lbs) with more than half of the weight dedicated to the altitude control systems, power and structure.

SAC-A was equipped with four antennas for the GPS system, an S-band antenna connected with its operations base, and VHF for the experimental monitoring of the Southern Frank Whale. The S-band and VHF antennas were linked to transmit telemetry and to receive commands.

Energy was supplied by NiCd batteries, providing 36 watts of power, and deployable GaA solar boards. The NiCd batteries were operational only when the solar boards were not powered by the sun.

SAC-A was placed in circular orbit at an inclination of $51.6°$ and an altitude of 389 km (242 miles). This was determined to be the best position to obtain images of Argentina and the largest cover of the terrestrial globe.

During the six-month orbit, enough time was allowed to test and qualify all the subsystems on board and to achieve mission objectives. However, CONAE operations suffered a setback when they experienced temporary loss of contact with the satellite. Contact was fully regained within five days to fulfill all mission objectives.

There were a number of instruments aboard the SAC-A including the magnetometer, the whales search experiment, the panoramic chamber, the GPS system, and the solar boards.

The magnetometer was designed to study the terrestrial magnetic field and the anomalies of localities. The information provided by the magnetometer was coordinated with data obtained from the GPS.

This instrument collected data at two levels of precision: readings with 10 and with 20 bits. The data of 10 bits obtained satisfactory results, which were utilized for the control of altitude (orientation) of the satellite. The data of 20 bits were compared with the 10. All information collected was made available to the experiment developers and the public through the Internet.

The whales search experiment was of critical importance to the Office of the Secretary of Environment of the National Government for environmental study purposes. The terrestrial segment of the experiment located whales at every position it targeted as well as the temperature of the sea in the location of the whale and its depth of immersion, while recording the data for future reference.

The panoramic chamber consisted of a Kodak DC-40, which was developed as an electromagnetic interface and an electronic means to collect digital images and send them to land bases. The images generated averaged 307 km by 198 km with a resolution of 400 m (1312 ft).

The first image captured by the chamber was on January 16, 1999, of the River of the Silver Zone. Capturing of this image constituted a milestone as being the first image of the national territory for the country of Argentina.

During March 1999, the satellite was rotated to orient it toward regions with more adequate lighting conditions. On March 4, the first photograph was taken. Nearly 600 photographs were taken of the earth, space, and the stars.

The GPS Trimble Trans Vector system was designed to measure the orientation of SAC-A in orbit. This application proved to be very useful in studying the spatial field and contributed to Argentina's technological advances in spatial engineering. GPS measurements were compared with those taken by the magnetometer.

SAC-A carried two experiments related to its solar boards. The solar boards consisted of two small boards with seven solar cells made of crystalline silicon. The experiments focused on the behavior of the cells in the spatial environment. Four individual cells, one in each, were placed on different faces of the satellite as angular sensors of position. These formed fundamental splits of the orientation system with regards to the sun. The solar boards were designed and manufactured in the laboratory of the Solar Energy Group of the National Commission of Atomic Energy (CNEA).

SAC-A was considered to be a complete success, yielding important data for scientists and environmentalists and supporting future

decisions on more effective land management in the country of Argentina.

SAC-B

The primary objective of the SAC-B mission was to advance the study of solar physics and astrophysics through the examination of solar flares, gamma-ray burst sources and the diffuse soft X-ray cosmic background. The SAC-B payload consisted of an Argentine instrument from the Institute of Astronomy and Space Physics to measure the temporal evolution of X-ray emissions from solar flares as well as non-solar gamma ray bursts, a NASA combined soft X-ray and gamma ray burst detector, a CCD diffuse X-ray background detector from Pennsylvania State University, and an energetic neutral particles detector, sponsored by the Italian Space Agency and provided by the Italian Istituto di Fisica dello Spazio Interplanetario (IFSI).

SAC-B was an international cooperative project between NASA and the Secretariat of State, Science and Technology of the Argentine Republic (SECYT). CONAE was responsible for the design and construction of the SAC-B satellite, and the Institute of Astronomy and Space Physics (IAFE) provided one scientific instrument. NASA provided two scientific instruments and launch services on a Pegasus XL vehicle.

Argentina also signed separate agreements with the Italian Space Agency (ASI) to provide the solar arrays made of Gallium Arsenide (GaA) cells, and with the Brazilian National Institute for Space Research (INPE) to provide the facilities for the system qualification tests of the satellite.

SAC-B was a 400-lb (191.5 kg) class spacecraft which was launched from NASA's Wallops Island facility on November 4, 1996. The satellite immediately began transmitting telemetry data following placement in orbit at a height of 550 km (341 miles) and an inclination of 37.97°.

SAC-B was designed with an orbital lifetime of three years and was to fulfill the following objectives: to observe the hard and soft X-ray emissions from solar flares to further the understanding of the interaction of accelerated particles with the ambient solar atmosphere; to observe gamma-ray bursts and correlate them with observations made by other similar detectors; to study the spectrum of the diffuse X-ray background for selected regions of the sky; and to provide an understanding of the location of the source plasma for auroral phenomena in the magnetosphere and the spatial and energy dependence of the ratio of oxygen+ to hydrogen+ as a function of time in order to clarify the transport between the magnetosphere and the ionosphere.

The satellite carried several scientific instruments on board, including the Hard X-Ray Spectrometer (HXRS) provided by the Argentine Institute of Astronomy and Space Physics (IAFE), which was to observe the hard X-ray spectrum between 20 and 320 keV of rapidly varying events on time scales as short as tens of milliseconds, and provide information on the temporal evolution of non-solar gamma-ray bursts; the Goddard X-Ray Experiment (GXRE), provided by NASA/Goddard Space Flight Center (GSFC) with two sets of detectors: the Soft X-Ray Spectrometer (SOXS) for performing coordinated observations with the HXRS by observing soft X-ray emissions from solar flares, and the Gamma Ray Burst Spectrometer (GRaBS) for providing time profiles of the X-ray emission from non-solar gamma-ray bursts in the energy range from 20 keV to greater than 300 keV; the Cosmic Unresolved X-Ray Background Instrument (CUBIC) using CCDs, provided by Pennsylvania State University for measuring the spectrum of the diffuse X-Ray background with unprecedented sensitivity and spectral resolution between 0.1 and 10.0 keV in selected areas of the sky; and the Imaging Spectrometer for Energetic Neutral Atoms (ISENA) for measuring neutral atoms at spacecraft altitudes.

The SAC-B spacecraft was 62 cm by 62 cm (2 ft by 2 ft) wide by 80 cm (2.6 ft), high equipped with four extended solar panels 62 cm wide by 76 cm long (2 ft x 2.5 ft). The HXRS and SoXS instruments were mounted on the sun-facing end of the spacecraft along with the Fine Sun Sensor with fields of view toward the sun. The GaA cells of the solar array panels also faced the Sun.

The SAC-B structure featured two pseudo-honeycomb panels. The inside of the aluminum sandwich structure was machined from solid material allowing solid bosses for fasteners. The bottom panel, or solar platform, interfaced with the Pegasus launch vehicle. Eight 6061-T6 aluminum beams bolted to this panel, connecting with the second sandwich panel, the equipment platform, and also with an open 6081-T6 aluminum angle frame at the top called the PSU frame. Load bearing 6081-T6 aluminum side panels were bolted to the two sandwich panels and the top frame and beams, forming a semi-monocoque structure.

The satellite power system was comprised of a solar array to collect power, batteries, a power distribution bus system, a battery charge system and power dissipating shunts. The four-panel solar array was covered with GaA cells, feeding power directly to spacecraft loads through a regulated 28 V primary bus.

All the instruments and electrical components on board were thermally controlled between -10° and +40° by a semi-passive thermal system using heaters and radiators. The batteries were thermally isolated from the rest of the spacecraft.

Unfortunately, contact was lost with the satellite, and CONAE was unable to regain contact after several attempts made from San Miguel, Bs Ace., Cordoba, Argentina, and Malindi, Kenya.

SAC-C

SAC-C was designed to advance Argentina's objectives in teleobservation, communications and basic sciences. It was the first satellite designed as a land observation satellite. SAC-C was launched November 21, 2000, by a Delta 7320 launcher from Vandenberg Air Force Base, California.

SAC-C was a successful mission, fulfilling its objectives of observing the earth and producing images of Argentine territory. Maps of Argentina are being utilized in agriculture to reckon crops, to evaluate the productivity of a field, to detect plagues, and in the study of the marine and terrestrial environment.

The data provided by SAC-C has been fundamental for the management, control and recovery of the areas affected in case of catastrophes such as fires, floods or discharges of contaminants in coastal water.

Argentina also obtained data that has proved useful in monitoring the temperature and water vapor content of the atmosphere, in measuring the terrestrial magnetic field, in studying the structure and dynamic of the atmosphere and ionosphere, and in determining long components of wave of the field land gravitation. New technological developments made with SAC-C will permit improvements of future spatial missions, such as the device to study the effects of the new generation spatial radiation electronic components, or the "chips" that will carry the next satellites.

The Control Center of SAC-C is located in the Earthly Station Cordoba of the Spatial Center Teófilo Tabanera (CETT). Data received on a daily basis was immediately made available to scientists.

SAC-C weighed 485 kg (1070 lb) with a height of 2.2 m (7.21 ft). It had a minimum life of four years. SAC-C had three chambers and seven instruments, including a multispectral chamber of average resolution (Multispectral Medium Resolution Scanner — MMRS) for monitoring agriculture, forest stations, coastal and interior waters; a panoramic chamber of high sensibility with a resolution of 35 meters (115 feet); an environmental data harvesting system (DCS) for obtaining information of numerous automatic stations which were distributed all over the country; a GPS receiver (GPS Occultation and Passive Reflection Experiment Blow) provided by the NASA-JPL to measure the gravitational land field and to map the profiles of temperature and humidity of the atmosphere; an assembly of magnetometers for measurements of the magnetic land field (Magnetic Mapping Payload — MMP), developed and built by a consortium formed by NASA-JPL and the Danish Space Research Institute (DSRI) with an antenna eight meters long which unfolded once the satellite was in orbit; a French instrument to determine the effect of particles of high energy in electronic components ("chips") of the latest generation (ICARE); and two instruments provided by Italy, the IST, experimental instrument of navigation that identified the altitude of the SAC-C, and the INES, an Italian instrument of navigation that worked with the world network of "global positioning" satellites and consisted of two subsystems: the GPS Tensor and the GPS Lagrange. There was also an Argentine experiment to determine the migratory route of the Southern Frank whale (Whale Tracker).

The capabilities of SAC-C included the sensibility of the multispectral chamber (MMRS) to the different bands of the infrared sensor, permitting knowledge on the health of plants and predicting the results of crops. SAC-C was also able to monitor the advanced desertation of floors affecting Argentina. The chamber of high sensibility (HSC) allowed observation of the terrestrial surface during the night as well as the detection of fire foci in remote forests. In the visible band of light, the SAC-C proved ideal for coastal studies of water contamination and floors. The satellite also evaluated hydroenergy, as water changed levels in the high basin of the Paraná or snow accumulated in the summits that fed the River Limay, which helped determine areas vulnerable to floods. In the high bands of visible light, SAC-C studied mining and geological resources.

The resolution of the Multispectral Chamber (MMRS) images was 175 meters (574 feet), with a wide sweeping of 360 kilometers (1,181,157 feet). The resolution of the SAC-C was ideal for the maritime and farm activities in Argentina, since it provided the quality of information which was necessary to study large extensions of territory, including coastal and field areas. The SAC-C was also able to obtain data during the solar cycle of activity similar to other satellites such as the GEOSAT.

At its completion, SAC-C obtained 2.7 billion pieces of telemetric data on the land and environment of Argentina, information which has proved valuable to the country's resource studies.

SAC-D

SAC-D is a joint satellite mission between CONAE and NASA-JPL to conduct land observation over Argentina. This mission will carry the JPL instrument Aquarius, which will be used to measure the salinity of the sea for the first time.

CONAE will develop an infrared thermal chamber that will detect high temperature foci in the terrestrial surface. Data firing risk maps in Argentina will be recorded. This chamber will also be used to measure the humidity of the sea floor in order to give early warnings of floods.

In determining the humidity of the sea floor, scientists will be able to provide recorded data to be used by agricultural cattle raisers as well. SAC-D/Aquarius instruments will be very useful in determining foci fires, which is extremely critical to Argentina's Federal System of Emergencies. Argentina will use this satellite system in the implementation of future emergency management.

The Aquarius instrument will be equipped with four infrared channels that will permit measurement of the oceans' salinity and record sea surface temperature from space. This information will be very useful for Argentina's fishing industry and will help the country's fauna conservation efforts, contributing to the expansion of knowledge on climactic change globally.

Aquarius will also record data on the detachment of ice in the polar zones. All information obtained will be made available to official agencies as well as to the national and international scientific community.

Using NASA-JPL provided design schemes, the construction and integration of Aquarius will be done entirely in Argentina by INVAP S.E., CONAE's primary contractor.

SAC-D will be launched in 2006 by a NASA provided vehicle.

SAOCOM 1-A

CONAE has developed a new satellite, SAOCOM 1-A, scheduled for launch in 2004. SAOCOM 1-A will be a new generation observation satellite based on radar technology.

This teleobservation by radar will allow the land and sea to be seen through clouds or smoke during day or night hours, a capability which is not possible with optical satellites.

SAOCOM 1-A was designed with a band microwave radar L and an infrared thermal chamber. The radar will be able to detect small objects on the terrestrial surface, as well as two meters beneath the surface. The satellite will contribute very useful information on the humidity and the geological structure of the terrain. The infrared chamber will be capable of detecting fires and eruptions. SAOCOM 1-A will add excellent benefits for the management of environmental emergencies and monitoring natural resources.

SAOCOM 1-A will weigh one ton, including a 10 meter antenna radar weighing more than 220 kilograms (440 lbs). It will be equipped with solar panels built in Argentina and four wheels of inertia for proper orientation of the satellite.

The primary objectives of SAOCOM 1-A will be to aid in the natural monitoring of disasters; evaluation, prevention, and support in the recovery phase; agricultural monitoring including land use, forests, the mining industry; exploitation of environmental floors; monitoring of ice, snow, and weather changes; monitoring of coastal and marine zones; mapping and topography; monitoring land infrastructure and urban zones; and providing support for search and rescue missions.

WSO/UV Satellite Project

The World Space Observatory (WSO) Project is a new space mission concept that has grown out of the needs of the astronomical community to have access to the ultraviolet range of the electromagnetic spectrum.

The physical diagnostics in this domain supply a richness of new experimental data unmatched by any other wavelength range in studies of the universe.

The WSO/UV satellite will consist of a single ultraviolet telescope in orbit which will incorporate a 1.7 m diameter (5.6 ft) mirror, feeding a UV spectrograph and UV imagers.

CONAE is working with an international team of scientists on the World Space Observatory Implementation Committee (WIC) to prepare WSO/UV for launch in 2007.

WSO/UV will study a number of fundamental problems in astronomy, including reaching a better understanding of the genesis and the behavior of the "discrete absorption" components in early stars; reaching a better understanding of symbiotic objects— most of which have been observed in the UV range only in the low dispersion mode; identifying the meaning of the abnormal intensity ratio of the Si IV and C IV features in some close binaries outside of the eclipse; extending the range of objects observed with high dispersion and high resolution in the UV; acquiring a better understanding of the UV of objects in galaxies other than the Milky Way; improving the understanding of the phenomenon of accretion onto compact stars in binary systems; identifying close binaries that may fall within the stage of rapid mass loss; analyzing the nuclei of planetary nebulae in the galaxy; investigating the presence of magnetic fields and zeeman patterns in early type stars; studying the resonance lines of metals that originate in the circumstellar material of early type stars; and studying the properties of newly born massive stars.

AUSTRALIA

CSIRO, Office of Space Science and Applications

Australia has had deep ties to space for many years. The country's Aboriginal society has continuously observed the heavens longer than any other culture.

Native Australians used the changing star patterns to guide them to seasonal food sources as well as to create stories which helped them interpret the relationship between humans and nature. When Captain Cook arrived along the East Coast in 1770 on his ship, the *Endeavor*, he was able to fulfill the real purpose of his journey — the observation of the passage of the planet Venus across the face of the sun to improve the accuracy of methods then used to calculate longitude. ,

In 1788, when Governor Phillip led the First Fleet to the new colony of New South Wales, he was accompanied by the first astronomer of the modern period of Australian history, Lieutenant William Dawes.

Dawes recorded many astronomical and chronological measurements from an observatory on the western side of Sydney Cove, including the earliest recorded Australian weather observations. This site later became prominent in the early intellectual life of the new colony.

As a pioneer in the science of radioastronomy, Australia has world-famous observatories such as the Australia Telescope National Facility. The Parkes radio telescope, in combination with seven small and newer radio telescopes at Narrabri and Sidling Springs, form the Australia Telescope Long Baseline Array, which collects signals from natural radio sources.

The Parkes radio telescope played a very prominent role in the discovery of the first quasar, and in tracking the 1986 encounter of the European space probe Giotto with Halley's comet.

Other astronomical facilities, which rely on optical observations rather than the detection of radiowaves, are also based in Australia. These include the Anglo-Australian Observatory, the UK Schmidt Telescope, and the Sidling Springs Observatory. Australian astronomers from these facilities have made valuable contributions to space observatory missions of other countries, including the U.S. Hubble Space Telescope and the European Hipparcos.

The country's launch complex for satellites and rockets is located in Woomera, in

Central Australia. On November 29, 1967, an Australian scientific satellite, WRESAT (Weapons Research Establishment Satellite), was launched using an American Redstone rocket, making Australia the fourth nation in the world, following Russia, the United States, and France, to launch a satellite into earth's orbit from its own territory.

WRESAT carried instruments aboard to measure properties of the earth's upper atmosphere, solar radiation, the temperature of the sun's outer atmosphere, or corona, and to study ozone concentrations at very high altitudes.

The Woomera range was also the launch site for the United Kingdom's Prospero scientific and engineering test satellite on a Black Arrow rocket on October 28, 1971.

One of the most common uses of space technology in Australia has been telecommunications. Satellites have been used to carry the majority of international telecommunications traffic from Australia, transmitting live features of overseas sporting and news events. The first live international television broadcast in Australia occurred in November 1966, to the United Kingdom via the Carnarvon Station of the Overseas Telecommunications Corporation (OTC).

Technologies and services developed in Australia have been exported by OTC to clients worldwide, including Antarctica, Malta, Vietnam, Laos, Cambodia, and the Pacific Islands.

Due to heavy demand, the Australian government created AUSSAT in 1979, one of the first national communications satellite systems in the world.

Today, Australia has a new satellite company, the Cooperative Research Centre for Satellite Systems (CRCSS), which has developed and launched FedSat, its latest scientific satellite.

In addition to accomplishments in satellites and rockets, Australia has had two of its citizens fly in space. In 1984, Australian-born U.S. citizen, Dr. Paul Scully flew on a mission. In 1997, Australian-born NASA astronaut, Dr. Andrew Thomas made his second space flight as an Australian citizen due to a change in citizenship rules.

From 1987 to 1996, Australia had an Australian Space Office which was closed following the termination of the U.K.'s Blue Streak project. The Cooperative Research Centre for Satellite Systems (CRCSS) is now considered the country's official national space agency.

Space Research

CSIRO, Australia's largest scientific and engineering research organization, carries out research and development work with the responsibility of assisting Australian industry, furthering the interests of the Australian community, and contributing to the national objectives and international responsibilities of the country's commonwealth. CSIRO maintains an active space research program, with emphasis in the fields of earth observation, space-related engineering, and radioastronomy.

The CSIRO Earth Observation Centre (EOC) was established in late 1995 with four primary focus areas: applications support, measurement models, data systems, and sensor systems. A group of 80 scientists spread throughout CSIRO are involved in earth observation and associated space activities.

The EOC has collaborated with NASA to evaluate and develop data from the EO1 experimental satellite system. EO1 has been in constellation orbit with Landsat 7 ETM, SAC-C, and the EOS TERRA satellites. While there it is advancing instruments onboard, including the first civilian Hyperspectral sensor to be deployed in space.

The Centre also fields data from the SEASTAR, Topex/Poseidon, Jason, ERS-1 and ERS-2 satellites, and the Tasmanian Earth Resources Satellite Station (TERSS).

The Forestry and Forest Products division continues to undertake a number of projects which utilize remote sensing data for forest inventory and biomass accumulation. The research studies the relationships between remotely sensed data and the structure, growth and health of native eucalyptus and plantation forests.

A number of projects have been conducted by this division, including prediction of forestation and diseases from hyperspectral remote, using imagery and the development of routine and generic methodologies that can be applied by forest plantation managers. It also uses high spatial resolution imagery and digitized aerial photography to automatically predict stem numbers in plantation forests; it uses ground based and airborne LIDAR to predict a range of forest inventory attributes; and it uses broad scale MIODIS and AVHRR imagery to predict biodiversity and forest production at a regional level in the United States, Canada and South America. It also predicts leaf biochemistry from satellite EO-1 HYPERION and airborne HYMAP imagery.

The remote sensing research group of the Division of Land and Water, Environmental Processes and Resources Program, has nearly 20 years of experience in the use and interpretation of remotely sensed data for environmental applications and resource mapping.

The group's main areas of expertise include hyperspectral remote sensing with emphasis on vegetation mapping, land use assessment, water quality and coastal zone mapping; ground-based field verification and use of hand-held spectroradiometers and related water quality, plant or forestry measurement methodologies; imaging radar remote sensing for assessment of soil moisture, vegetation structure and biomass; instrumentation development for ground-truthing and measurement during remote sensing projects; and time-series analysis and data integration for regional/continental resource assessment.

The Mathematical and Information Sciences Remote Sensing group has been pursuing the Land Monitor project, which involves the production of salinity and remnant vegetation maps over Southwestern Western Australia. Sequences taken from Landsat TM images, along with landform maps derived from digital terrain models, will be used to produce the output map products.

The Telecommunications & Industrial Physics division, formerly the divisions of Radiophysics and Applied Physics, has built and supplied an X-band transmit/receive feed system for a Department of Defense earth station.

Additions have been made to the Parkes radio telescope, including a 13-element multibeam feed and an associated receiver. This multibeam system operates in the 21 cm (8.3 inch) band and has 26 signal channels (13 beams by 2 polarizations) which required the development of an array feed system with minimal beam cross-coupling, a large-scale radio frequency, and cryogenic components.

Cooperative Research Centre for Satellite Systems (CRCSS)

The Cooperative Research Centre for Satellite Systems (CRCSS) was established on January 1, 1998, to carry out research and training in space technologies. Its primary objective is to develop Australian capability in the design and exploitation of small satellites.

The Centre operates on the rationale that satellite technologies are used daily to provide key services to Australia in areas such as weather forecasting, communications, environmental management, navigation, and resource navigation. It also takes into account the fact that a new "smaller, cheaper, faster" approach to satellite systems has begun to open space markets to a wider range of public and private sector players, and new small satellite technology is well within the capability of the Australian industry to produce.

CRCSS carries out research in the following primary areas: space science, satellite communications, remote sensing, satellite systems, and satellite engineering. In the area of space science, the program has the following objectives: to conduct basic research on the structure and dynamics of the ionosphere and exosphere using magnetic field observations and propagation delays of Global Positioning System (GPS) signals; to apply the results of this research to space weather and communications prediction models; to study the dynamics of field-aligned currents in the auroral zones and the equatorial current system; to study oscillating wave fields and their variability in the ionosphere and exosphere, including ELF ion cyclotron waves and ULF hydromagnetic waves in conjunction with ground station observations; to provide vector measurements for the mapping of the geomagnetic field over Australia and contribute to secular variation and solid earth studies; and to provide improved accuracy for GPS applications which will deliver benefits to the navigation and position services industries, including geomagnetic mapping and satellite communications.

The objectives of the satellite communications area are to develop new communications techniques for use in future small Low Earth Orbit (LEO) satellite communications and earth observation constellations; to develop innovative solutions to network management, and satellite tracking and control; to test applications in new series such as two-way paging, mobile computing and Internet access for uses in remote areas; and to find new solutions to the design of Low-Earth Orbit (LEO) satellite communications systems and networks that are robust in the face of interference and fading.

In the area of satellite systems, the primary objectives are to develop new techniques utilizing GPS receivers on board LEO satellites for real-time tracking and for high precision determination of satellite orbit and altitude; to develop techniques that would enable GPS corrections to be broadcast from LEO satellites to improve the accuracy of wide area global positioning systems; and to study the design of adaptable, high performance computing systems for use on board LEO satellites. Modular, reconfigurable structures will be developed along with formal verification techniques for satellite software systems.

The group will also be responsible for developing and implementing satellite flight and ground segments for Centre space projects.

The Centre's first major project was the FedSat experimental satellite, built to demonstrate Australian space capability. Launched in December 2002 by Japan's H2-A rocket from a remote island, the 58 kilogram (120 pound) FedSat has high-tech communication, space science, navigation, and computing equipment intended to bring broadband Internet services to remote parts of Australia.

FedSat carries several payloads including the GPS receiver to decode radio signals containing time and orbit-position codes, allowing accurate measurement of the satellite's position which will support the CRCSS study into methods of precisely determining satellite orbits. This receiver will also support space-science studies of the ionosphere, an electrically-charged layer of the atmosphere, allowing for the building of three-dimensional moving pictures of the ionosphere. CRCSS is the only organization studying the little-known southern region of the ionosphere in this manner.

Also aboard the FedSat is the NewMag magnetometer, a very sensitive rapid-sampling device for measuring the strength of the earth's magnetic field. The earth operates much like a big bar magnet, with magnetic field lines emerging from the poles and far out into space. FedSat's polar orbit will cross all these lines, allowing NewMag to effectively gain a window into the whole magnetospheric region. NewMag will also measure vibrations simultaneously with ground-based magnetometers, investigating the dynamics of the magnetosphere or changes in its shape due to variations in the sun, and it will study magnetospheric wave-propagation.

Prior research revealed this to be a complex region, with variations in the solar wind having a huge effect on the magnetosphere and space weather which can also affect ground infrastructure. FedSat data will help provide early warning systems against solar-magnetic events and space weather events, which damage satellites. NewMag is mounted away from the main satellite on a 2.5 m (8 ft) extendable boom.

NASDA, the National Space Development Agency of Japan, launched FedSat at no cost in exchange for the NewMag data.

The high performance computing payload aboard FedSat is the world's first use of reconfigurable computing technology in space. Reconfigurable computers allow changing of their physical circuits via software control. This way new physical circuits can be installed into a reconfigurable computer module by remote command. For spacecraft, this technology means that satellites can be rewired without having to retrieve them.

The FedSat payload is establishing the basics of working with these devices in space, including their susceptibility to radiation, which is of great interest to the international community, including NASA and John Hopkins University, who supplied the module.

If these devices are proved to work in space, it could mean a new species of reconfigurable and adaptable spacecraft which could eventually fix and modify their own circuits. This reconfiguring computing could open up new realms of spacecraft adaptability, including the re-use of old spacecraft.

The Ka-band transponder aboard FedSat was designed to handle the new experimental high-frequency and high-capability Ka part of the radio spectrum. The transponder processes signals to and from the ground in the frequency band using CRCSS-designed Gallium Arsenide (GA) monolithic microwave circuits, to be space qualified by FedSat for the first time.

The Ka-band transponder has been interfacing with the CRCSS-designed Kaband ground station to lead to new Australian-developed remote area communications applications.

The FedSat baseband processor provides on-board computer processing of the Ka- and UHF- band payloads. It was designed and built by CRCSS to operate as a low power single modem with flexible operation, and also to provide the channel for satellite operations commands. University students will also use the FedSat baseband processor to study and develop a variety of telecommunications protocols, including ground-satellite links and inter-satellite links.

The FedSat Ultra High Frequency band payload has introduced a new type of packet data service for LEO satellites to obtain environmental data. For example, ocean buoys may transmit data using this means to orbiting satellites, which are retransmitted back to the lab for analysis. This payload facilitates high speed transmission via a special multiple access scheme and error-control techniques. Built by CRCSS, the payload will also fly on Korean and other Asian satellites over the next few years.

FedSat has also been equipped with a compact disc mounted on its side containing the audio messages that members of the Australian public recorded from March to August 2000. The disc also carries a copy of the song "From Little Things, Big Things Grow" by Paul Kelly, with permission from the writers.

The CD will orbit the earth as long as FedSat does, about a century, making the recorded messages a time capsule about life in Australia in 2000. In the event that future historians cannot retrieve or play the FedSat CD, a duplicate is being held in the National Museum of Australia with a CD player.

The Australian Space Research Institute (ASRI)

The Australian Space Research Institute Ltd. (ASRI) is a non-profit organization formed out of the merger of the Australian Space Engineering Research Association Ltd. and the Ausroc Projects Group. ASRI was formally created in a merger May 17, 1993, to consolidate various non-profit space engineering research groups within the country into a focused, integrated national education program.

ASRI is currently undertaking research, development and educational programs in launch vehicle and satellite technology areas. The institute has been formed to fill a void in these research, development and educational disciplines within Australia. ASRI coordinates numerous space engineering projects at various universities to allow students and ASRI members to gain practical space engineering experience.

The objectives of ASRI include developing and advancing space science and technology; conducting, encouraging, and promoting research in the field of space science and technology; extending knowledge in the field of space science and technology, making available educational opportunities in the field; and conducting, coordinating and supporting advancement in related projects.

Projects at ASRI cover a broad range of space technology fields at various levels of complexity and involve students from the high school level through post-graduate level. The CARATEL is an experimental liquid-fueled vehicle, which is a 2.6 m (8.5 ft) liquid-fueled rocket based on the AUSROC I propulsion system also developed by ASRI, with a newly developed payload and improved aerodynamic surfaces. AUSROC II-2 is a liquid-fueled demonstration vehicle based on the original AUSROC II concept which suffered a launch failure in 1992 due to a faulty LOX valve actuator with redesigns. The AUSROC III, the third of the AUSROC series of liquid-fueled launch vehicles, is aimed at promoting space-based education through the development of launch vehicle technologies. It is a sounding rocket capable of lifting 100 kg (220 lbs) of useful scientific payload to an altitude of 500 km (310 miles), with a recovery capability, and is also to be used as a test bed for several technologies with direct application to satellite launchers, including regenerative liquid propulsion, composite structures, inertial navigation, three-axis vehicle guidance and control, telemetry and flight termination systems, ground support, tracking and range safety. The AUSROC IV is a satellite launch vehicle capable of placing a 20–4 kg (44–88 lb) microsatellite into a polar orbit. Programs also include the AUSTALIS-1 micro-satellite and the Hyshot scramjet project at the University of Queensland.

The AUSROC programs are the most well known and ambitious of ASRI. The ultimate goal of the programs is to develop a low cost micro-satellite launch vehicle, utilizing technologies that can be scaled up for use in heavier launch vehicles.

The programs are broken down into four stages, with each one significant as a proving platform for technologies and systems incorporated into its successor. There have been three rocket models.

AUSROC I was a small liquid-fueled rocket which used a hypergolic, spontaneously combusting, acid-alcohol combination as propellants. It served as an introduction to liquid-fuel rocket systems and the hazards involved. AUSROC I was successfully launched in 1989.

AUSROC II was a substantially more sophisticated vehicle in design that was intended to generate an experience base in the con-struction and operation of the rocket systems that are to be used in the AUSROC III and AUSROC IV vehicles. It was 6 meters (20 feet) long, 25 centimeters (9.8 inches) in diameter, and operated on a powerful combination of pressure fed liquid oxygen and kerosene.

Two AUSROC II rockets were built. The first was destroyed in a fire on the launch pad after the main liquid oxygen valve froze shut during unexpected launch delays. The second was successfully launched in 1995, gaining international acclaim and publicity through a British produced documentary.

The AUSROC III sub-orbital vehicle is the most recent to be developed with attention to the following objectives: navigation, guidance and control; liquid fuel propulsion; composite structures and materials; space qualified electronics; payload integration; range development and operation; project management; and systems engineering.

In order to carry out these ASRI programs, a broad range of scientific and engineering disciplines are being pursued by the institute. These include liquid, solid and hybrid rocket propulsion systems; guidance and control systems; composite and lightweight structures; telemetry systems; launch site development and operations; aerodynamic testing and analysis; flight safety systems; spacecraft structures; space-qualified electronics; supersonic airbreathing propulsion technology; and systems engineering methodologies.

Woomera Launch Range

In the late 1940s, the United Kingdom required a large area to serve as a test range for its long-range weapons program. The decision to build a rocket range was made in the postwar environment when the world was still recovering from the massive destruction and loss of life of World War II.

Initially, areas in Canada and Wales were considered, but were later ruled out in favor of the huge central Australian desert. In 1947, construction managed by the Long Range Weapons Board of Administration began at the site, including a small town. The launch range area was named "Woomera," the Aboriginal word for a short stick used to launch a spear.

Located 486 km (302 miles) north of Adelaide and positioned 165 m (541 feet) above sea level, Woomera is located in the middle of a desert terrain where the average annual rainfall is only seven inches.

In June 1946, a Dakota aircraft landed on the first temporary airstrip. A regular RAAF courier service was inaugurated, which provided travel, food, mail and supplies for people who were building the range. On April 1, 1947, Arcoona leased the land to the Department of Defense, and the Woomera village was surveyed and built.

From 1947 to 1970, Woomera was an important launch facility. Throughout the 1950s and 1960s a number of rockets were launched, culminating in the launch of the Prospero satellite in 1969. Woomera was used to test a variety of British rocketry projects such as the Blue Steel, Bloodhound and Thunderbird missiles, but its most important role was in the British and European space programs.

As early as 1953, the United States eyed Woomera and began running tests in 1957 that were either impossible or impractical to perform elsewhere. In 1958, NASA completed its first space tracking station at Woomera, with other stations built in support of such U.S. space projects as Gemini, Mercury, Mariner, and Apollo.

Between the years 1969 and 1972, NASA's station served as a vital communications link for Apollo 11, including when Neil Armstrong and Buzz Aldrin landed on the moon in July 1969.

In 1957, the first Skylark sounding rocket was launched from Woomera, while the base was also used to launch the Jindiviks, a jet powered target vehicle, and the Black Knight re-entry test rockets which were capable of delivering seven tons into outer space at 7,000 miles per hour. Throughout the 1960s, Woomera was used by the European Launcher Development Organization (ELDO) to test the Europa I launch vehicle, a 104 ton (229,278 lb) rocket developed to launch satellites independent of the great super powers at the time — the United States and Russia. The Europa I was designed with a long-range liquid-fueled missile, the Blue Streak, which was adapted to be used as the rocket's first stage.

The first Blue Streak first-stage launch was carried out at the Spadeadam site at Woomera on June 5, 1964. Four other first stage launches were carried out successfully, but the second and third stage launches were unsuccessful.

Following the Europa I, a Europa II rocket was developed and moved to an equatorial site at Kourou, French Guiana. In 1967, Woomera became a spaceport when a Redstone rocket purchased from the United States placed Australia's first satellite in orbit. This was followed in 1971 by the Black Arrow rocket launch of Prospero, the first British satellite.

Over the period that Woomera was fully operational, many missiles were launched from the complex including Europa I, Sparta, Black Arrow, Aero Mach, Jabiru, Black Knight, Skylark, Long Tom, R.T.V., Aero High, Aeolus, H.A.D., Koorigal, H.A.M, H.A.T., and H.A.E.C.

The Woomera range consisted of numerous facilities for weapons testing, the launch of high-altitude sounding rockets, and subsequently, the launch of satellites. The range was comprised of several launch areas (LAs). LA 1 at Range E was used for early surface to air point defense missile tests and was decommissioned in the late 1960s. LA 2 at Range E remains fully functional, having various rail launchers. LA 3 and 4 at Range E were last used for the Bloodhound and Thunderbird surface to air defense system trails, and decommissioned in the mid-1970s. LA 5 at Range E was used throughout the 1960s and '70s for testing the Black Knight and Black Arrow rockets, and it was the site of the Prospero satellite launch in 1971; it was also decommissioned in the late 1970s. LA 6 is located on the edge of the usually dry Lake Hart which was originally built for testing the British Blue Streak ICBM (Intercontinental Ballistic Missiles), but following that program's cancellation, it was converted for the use of the ELDO program, with only one launch facility, LA 6A, completed, resulting in ten launches occurring from 1964. It was last used on June 12, 1970, and later dismantled as a complex. LA 7, located near Lake Hart, was used in the 1960s for launching United States Redstone rockets as part of the Sparta program to test nose cone materials during re-entry. A space Redstone rocket was later used by Australia to launch its first satellite, WRE-SAT-1 in 1967. LA 8 was the area near Lake Hart once used to test some scientific rockets. Finally, LA 9 was the area near Range E used to test ship-launched, anti-aircraft Sea Dart and Sea Wolf missiles for Britain's Royal Navy. It is now used by the ASRI for Zuni rockets launched exclusively by volunteers.

Woomera also served as home to the first deep-space station established outside the United States by NASA. It was designated as a Deep-Space Station 41 (DSS 41). In February 1959, a survey team selected a location in a natural depression near the Island Lagoon dry lake bed, approximately 56 kilometers (35 miles) south of the rangehead of the Woomera Rocket Range. In August 1960, negotiations were completed for a United States–Australian agreement to operate NASA stations in Australia. Under the supervision of JPL engineer Floyd W. Stoller, a radio construction company crew erected a 26 meter (85 foot), polar-mounted antenna similar to the one at the Goldstone Pioneer station in California. From August to November 1960, JPL engineer Richard K. Mallis supervised a JPL-Collins Radio Company team that installed the electronics on the antenna.

The Deep-Space Station was operated by the Australian Department of Supply (DOS), whose Weapons Research Establishment (WRE) managed the Woomera range. The DOS/WRE appointed William Mettyear as the first station director. The facility employed more than 100 professional, technical and administrative staff who lived at neighboring Woomera Village. The Department of Supply gave the contract for operational and maintenance services to Amalgamated Wireless (Australia) Ltd.

The tracking station participated in various spacecraft projects which ventured more than 16,000 kilometers (9,942 miles) from

earth, including the first successful mission to another planet — the flyby of Venus by *Mariner 2* during December 1962, and the first successful flyby of Mars by *Mariner 4* in July 1965. It also played a key role in the Ranger and Lunar Orbiter missions which provided valuable information in the lead-up to the Apollo missions to the moon. The antenna was also made available to Australian astronomers for astronomical research between missions.

The Woomera station closed operations on December 22, 1972, as part of a consolidation of NASA station facilities. After the DOS determined that the cost of transporting the antenna to a new, more accessible location for radio astronomers would be prohibitive, the antenna was dismantled and sold for scrap in 1973.

The Island Lagoon area was also the site of a large Baker Nunn camera installed during 1958 as part of the International Geophysical Year (1957-58) activities. The camera could photograph orbiting satellites which had ceased transmitting, or gather more precise orbital data than was obtainable by electronic tracking. The Baker Nunn camera was equipped with an 81-centimeter (32 inch) diameter mirror and could photograph objects as faint as 15th magnitude, which is about 1/4,000th the brightness of the faintest stars visible to the average person. The camera was also used for astronomical observations of flare stars and comets.

By the 1970s, with the cancellation of various British space projects, Woomera went into a decline. However, on July 30, 2002, the Hyshot scramjet experiment, developed by the University of Queensland, had a successful launch of the world's first flight test of supersonic combustion, the process used in an air-breathing supersonic ramjet engine, known as a scramjet.

The United States company Kistler Aerospace is establishing two launch sites for operation of the fleet of K-1 aerospace vehicles, the world's first fully reusable aerospace vehicle designed to lift satellites into low-earth orbit. Spaceport Woomera is located in Woomera, South Australia, about 470 km (280 miles) north of Adelaide. Test flights and initial commercial operations will be conducted from Spaceport Woomera.

Launch Vehicles, Satellites and Rockets

Australia designed and built the first satellite to be put into orbit from Woomera. This was a result of the United States and Britain's use of Woomera launch facilities to conduct tripartite research into the physical effects of high-speed re-entry of warheads, an activity known as Project SPARTA.

Project SPARTA utilized three-stage launch vehicles. The first stage was the highly successful Redstone rocket, and the second and third stages were solid-propellant based.

Nine SPARTA launch vehicles and one spare were sent to Australia for use in the project. However, since no launch failures occurred, the spare SPARTA launch vehicle was not used.

Funding was secured for the project.

From the onset of the WRESAT project it was decided that for simplicity, WRESAT would be integrated directly into the SPARTA third stage. In order to achieve an accurate orbital insertion, the combined second and third stage was spun to approximately two revolutions per second. The WRESAT 'package' was a little over two meters (6.6 feet) long and weighed approximately 72.5 kg (160 lbs). WRESAT was battery powered, and could therefore only operate for a short period of time in space.

It is interesting to note about the WRESAT design that although WRESAT was spinning around its long axis at orbital insertion, this was not the preferred orientation for the scientific payload. Close inspection of the WRESAT schematic to the right shows an energy dissipater, which was a closed hydraulic loop of silicone oil which dissipated by the rotational energy as heat. The net result is WRESAT eventually tumbling around its short axis, thereby placing the axis of rotation pointing out into space.

WRESAT carried scientific instruments which were very similar to those carried on sounding rockets already being used at Woomera. These sensors were predominantly for upper atmospheric research. There were sensors to measure solar radiation, specifically three wavelengths which had the greatest impact on the temperature and composition of the upper atmosphere. The same sensors could also measure the temperature of the solar atmosphere and the density of molecular oxygen in the Earth's atmosphere. Additionally, there was a small telescope with a lithium fluoride lens which could measure the faint ultraviolet halo, referred to as the GeoCoronal, that surrounds the earth at night.

WRESAT was launched on November 29, 1967, atop the spare SPARTA launch vehicle from Woomera's Launch Area 8, the same pad that was used for the nine Project SPARTA launches. The launch track was polar, slightly east of due-north.

The launch was successful, with WRESAT entering an elliptical polar orbit and becoming operational. However, with only batteries to provide power, WRESAT was operational for only two weeks. WRESAT orbited the earth every 99.3 minutes. Cosmic ray data was transmitted to earth for five days. The low perigee of the orbit, 198 km, also meant that the orbit would degrade rapidly; WRESAT re-entered the atmosphere on January 10, 1968, and burned up. Accordingly, the first Australian satellite to orbit the earth, Australis-OSCAR 5, although it was actually built before WRESAT but not launched until 1970, lasted just 43 days in orbit.

Woomera volunteers recovered the first stage of the WRESAT launcher from the Simpson Desert in April 1990. The surprisingly intact, but battered, 45 kg (99 lb) vehicle is now on display at the rocket park opposite the Woomera Heritage Centre.

Nearly 40 types of launch vehicles have been either developed, flown in Australia, or used by Australian organizations. These include AEOLUS for Woomera range development and upper atmospheric research; Aerobee, Aero High, Aero Mach, ALV, AUSROC, Black Arrow, Black Brant, Black Knight, Blue Streak, Cockateil, Cockatoo, Corella, CTV, Europa, HAD, HAEC, HARP, HAM, HASP, HAT, HI-STAR, Jabiru, Koorigal, K-1, Kookaburra, Long Tom, Lorikeet, LPAA, Redstone, RTV, Sighter, Skua, Skylark, SLV, UAR, Zulu Squire, and Zuni. The first launches were in 1949 of an LPAA and an RTV 1X vehicle.

The Long Tom was Australia's first sounding rocket, which was first launched from Woomera in October 1957. It was developed initially to test the Woomera rocket range's instrumentation for the British Black Knight and other high-altitude flights.

The two-stage Long Tom was developed in the 1950s by the Weapons Research Establishment at Salisbury, South Australia. It measured 8.2 meters (27 feet) in length and was stabilized by three fins.

The first launch of Long Tom utilized the Skylark launcher, but the third launch caused damage to that facility, forcing the Long Tom team to build their own 3 meter (9.8 foot) long launching rail.

The peak flight altitude of Long Tom was approximately 120 kilometers (75.6 miles), making it capable for use as a research sounding rocket. The vehicle's first stage used three Mayfly motors with simultaneous burn times of 3.6 seconds. The second stage used a single Mayfly motor which ignited for 3.6 seconds some 20 seconds after launch. A total of sixteen Long Toms were fired.

The first Black Knight was launched into Woomera's skies from Launcher 5A on September 7, 1958, reaching an altitude of 225 kilometers (140 miles). The ballistic test vehicle was developed by Saunders-Roe Ltd. in collaboration with the Royal Aircraft Establishment in the United Kingdom to gather data as part of the development of Britain's Blue Streak ICBM program.

The single-stage Black Knight was powered by a Gamma Mk. 201 rocket engine. The vehicle could reach a burnout velocity of over 12,000 km (7457 miles) per hour at an altitude of close to 113 kilometers (70 miles). The nose cone then separated as the vehicle continued to coast to an altitude of approximately 800 kilometers (500 miles), and then re-entered the atmosphere before being recovered. Total flight times averaged 20 minutes.

On May, 24, 1960, the sixth Black Knight took to the sky as a two-stage version,

with the nose cone later recovered following a successful mission. The second stage increased the velocity of re-entry to that expected for a Blue Streak warhead. When the Blue Streak program was cancelled in 1960, the two-stage Black Knight version was used for the Gaslight program, which gathered data related to physical phenomena associated with high-speed re-entry into the earth's atmosphere.

A two-stage version was also used in Project Dazzle, a joint Anglo-Australian-U.S. program researching phenomena occurring during re-entry. The two-stage Black Knights used a more powerful Gamma MK. 301 rocket engine.

The single-stage Black Knight had an overall length of 10.16 meters (33 feet), while the two-stage version was 11.6 meters (38 feet) in length.

The Aeolus was a Long Tom second stage rocket boosted by seven 5-inch Light Alloy Plastic Star (LAPSTAR) motors in the first stage. Aeolus, the Latin derivation of the original Greek word *Aiolos*, was the mythical Greek god of the winds. The word Aiolos also means "quick moving," which was quite befitting for "quick winds," the Aeolus vehicle since it was a sounding rocket initially used to aid in the development of the Woomera Range, and later to study the upper atmosphere.

The Aeolus was made up of a boost motor cluster, or first stage, held at the rear by a light metal fairing, which also served as the base for the four rectangular fins, and at the front by an aluminum alloy nose casting which was faired down to the diameter of the second stage. Mating of the two stages was achieved by a small cone on the front of the boost nose casting, which picked up in the venturi of the second stage.

The Aeolus boost assembly was 16 in. in diameter and 67 in. long. The total weight of the first stage was 600 lb. The weight of the second stage varied between 520 and 650 lbs., which gave a total launch weight range of between 1120 and 1250 lbs. There were seven launches of the Aeolus from 1958 to 1961.

Project Skylark was the result of the desire to begin a program of Upper Atmospheric research. D.I. Dawton developed a single-stage vehicle which was to be capable of carrying approximately 45 kg (100 lbs) of instruments to heights in excess of 150 km (93 miles). His design relied on a then hypothetical motor which had to produce 50 KN of thrust for at least 30 seconds, or an lsp of approximately 1590 KNs.

The primary decisions on the size, weight and configuration of the rocket required for the research were made in mid-1955. Initially, the rocket was known as the CTV5 Series III, which was the last of these aptly named test vehicles.

By early 1956, official agreement was given to rename the vehicle from the CTV5 Series III to the more commonly known Skylark.

The first Skylark consisted of a single stage, which utilized a Raven solid rocket motor. The rocket had a diameter of 44 cm (17.3 in) at its thickest point and stood approximately 7.5 m (24.6 feet) high.

Skylark rockets were single-stage until April 1960, when the Skylark was converted to a two stage launch vehicle. The original Skylark was revamped to become the second stage and a quick-burning Cuckoo motor became the first stage.

After February 1968, the Cuckoo was gradually replaced by the more powerful Goldfinch.

The Skylark operated in flight unguided, pointed by small adjustments made to the launch toward the prevailing wind conditions at the time of launch. Although the Skylark is no longer launched from Woomera, it is still used at Esrange of Sweden, and Andoya of Norway.

Australia developed various other rockets. The LORIKEET, another type of upper atmospheric rocket, was an improved version of an earlier HAT rocket, with 11 launchings occurring between July 1973, and September 1976, to test wind speeds and turbulence at high altitudes using a lithium trail. The COCKATOO was an upper atmospheric vehicle. Seventy-three rockets of this type were launched between 1970 and 1976. Other rockets included the HI-STAR, with three launches in September 1974, and the BLACK

BRANT 5, rockets fitted with telescopes to check light rays, X-rays, and gamma rays looking at Super Nova 1970A, with six launches between 1987 through 1988.

In more recent years there has been Hyshot, using a two stage Terrier-Orion Mk70 rocket to boost the payload and the empty Orion motor while it remained attached to the payload, to an apogee of approximately 330 km (205 miles). As the spent motor and its attached payload falls back to earth, they gather speed, and the trajectory is designed so that between 35 km (22 miles) and 23 km (14 miles) they are traveling at Mach 7.6, or nearly eight times the speed of sound. It is during this part of the trajectory that the Hyshot team at the University of Queensland records measurements of supersonic combustion.

Pressure measurements will be the primary means for obtaining the correlation, with approximately 40 measurements made in and around the engine. Gaseous hydrogen will be used as the fuel. As the combustion process in the scramjet is dependant on the ambient pressure, a highly parabolic trajectory with a near vertical descent during the test time was chosen so that a correlation could be developed over an envelope of ambient pressures. In addition to the scientific merits, a vertical trajectory is also more cost efficient and there are less structural difficulties resulting from the lower heat and dynamic loads. The approach being taken by the University of Queensland is cutting-edge technology. If shown to be successful, it will open a new era in flight testing hypersonic air-breathing engines.

The Hyshot Program has been headed by Project Leader Dr. Allan Paul.

The American Kistler Corporation has been building a small fleet of light space trucks to transport satellites to low earth orbit. The goals of these space trucks, named K-1 vehicles, are to lower the cost of access to space, to broaden markets for commercial space activities, and to generate new space business opportunities.

The K-1 will be launched from Woomera Space Centre and powered by three NK-33 engines, giving it 1,020,000 lbs of lift-off thrust. At an altitude of 135,000 feet, 121 seconds following liftoff, the first and second stages will separate. The center engine will then restart and place the first stage on a controlled return trajectory. Para-chutes will then be deployed at 10,000 feet and airbags will also be deployed just prior to a soft touchdown. The first stage will then be prepared for another flight.

AUSTRIA

Austrian Space Agency

The Austrian Space Agency (ASA) was established by the Austrian government in Vienna in 1972, and serves as the coordinator of space activities in Austria. In addition to sponsoring its own programs, ASA has participated in a variety of joint cooperatives through the European Space Agency (ESA), of which it became a full member in 1987.

Many people may not be aware of Austria's very early origins in the area of space development. Several great space pioneers were born in this country and have made notable contributions.

Conrad Haas, born in Dornbach, which is now a part of Vienna, in 1509, composed literature on his innovative ideas in the field of rocketry. During the sixteenth century, he wrote what was known as the very first description of the principle of a multi-stage rocket. In his manuscript, he described the two and three stage bundling of rockets, stabilizing fins and the use of liquid fuels, accompanied by drawings. One drawing depicts a cylindrical housing on top of a rocket, which could have actually been an early model of a space station. It is interesting to note that within his manuscript, Haas warns against the use of his descriptions being used in war and asks that they instead be used for peaceful purposes.

Guido von Pirquet, born in 1880, into a distinguished Austrian family, with a distinguished world renowned physicist, Clemens, as his brother. He made important contributions in the field of rocketry, such as his article about the possible concepts of space travel in his book *Die Möglichkeit der Weltraumfahrt* (The Possibility of Space Travel) and his series of articles about interplanetary trajectories (to Venus, Mars, Jupiter and Saturn) in the journal *Die Rakete* (The Rocket) of the Verein für Raumschiffahrt (German Rocket Society), the world's largest rocket society at the time.

By using calculations of a rocket nozzle for a manned rocket to Mars, he concluded that the rocket needed to lift off directly from earth would be too large, the nozzle area of the first stage having to be about 1500 square meters to be technically feasible. He therefore concluded that a manned expedition to Mars could only be accomplished by building a space station in earth's orbit where the space ship for travel to Mars could be assembled. Interestingly enough, in his 1928 published work the calculated trajectory he used for a space probe to reach Venus was identical to the one used by the first Soviet interplanetary spacecraft to Venus in 1961.

Franz von Hoefft, born in Vienna in 1882, earned his doctorate in physical chemistry from Vienna University and founded the first space related society in Western Europe in 1926, the Wissenschaftliche Gesellschaft für Höhen-forschung (The Scientific Society for High Altitude Research). Hoefft, an expert of rocket fuels, proposed a detailed program of rocket development, with the first step being the development of a liquid-fuel sounding rocket called RH-I (RH meaning Repulsion Hoefft). The rockets were to be transported by balloons up to the height of 5 to 10 kilometers, where they would be launched with the purpose of being used for rocket mail and for photographic remote sensing of the earth. In one of the intermediate steps, the manned spacecraft RH-V would fly around the earth in ellipses. The special form of the RH-V would then be able to take off and land on water by skids, and fly within the atmosphere as an airplane and above the atmosphere as a rocket. RH-V could also be used as the upper stage of RH-VI to RH-VIII, which would be launched from a space station and could be used to reach other planets or even leave our solar system. Unfortunately, Hoefft never had the opportunity to promote his visionary program by practical contributions.

Franz Abdon Ulinski proposed the design of a spacecraft propelled by a jet of electrons, or ions. A year later, he published his ideas in a journal of aeronautics in Vienna in which he proposed two types of energy supply. The first used solar panels for energy accumulation and second, disintegration of atoms. His ideas for propulsion of a spacecraft were ahead of his time and were not taken seriously. This appears to be the first application of ion propulsion, which was developed for use by Deep Space One decades later.

Herman Potocnik, who was born in 1892 and later educated in a variety of military schools, worked out a detailed technical design of a space station and published it 1929 in a book called *Das Problem der Befahrung des Welstraums—der Raketenmotor* (*The Problem of Space Travel—The Rocket Motor*), under his pen name, Hermann Noordung. His space station consisted of up to three modules: the "Wohnrad" or the inhabitable wheel, the power station, and the observatory, which would be connected by cables. The inhabitable wheel has the form of a giant wheel and rotates to simulate gravity in the living areas. On top of the wheel there would be parabolic mirrors mounted to concentrate the solar radiation for the power supply through a heat engine power station. Later, a very similar concept of a space station design was proposed by Wernher von Braun in 1953.

Potocnik also described in his book how a satellite could be positioned such as to be visible all day long from a spot on earth, about 36,000 kilometers above the equator. Today satellites in this "geostationary" orbit play an important role for telecommunications and weather forecasting.

Perhaps more familiar was Hermann Oberth, who was also Austrian born, and is considered to be a great space pioneer and contributor. Oberth first became interested in space travel after reading Jules Verne's novels, and went on to develop a thesis on rocket propulsion.

Shortly afterwards he published his work as a small booklet, *Die Rakete zu den Planetenraumen* (*The Rocket into Interplanetary Space*), at his own expense. This book was a great success and in 1929, Oberth started to build a high altitude rocket for the occasion of the premiere of the movie *Die Frau im Mond* by the Austrian director Fritz Lang, for which he was scientific advisor.

Max Valier, born in 1895, wrote a book on space exploration with Hermann Oberth's help called *Der Vorsto in den Weltenraum* (*Advance into Space*), which was published in 1924. In it, Valier proposed an advanced rocketry program of four stages to include test bed experiments; rocket-powered vehicles such as cars, railcars, sledges, and gliders; rocket-assisted airplanes; and the increase of airplane performance up to rocket-propelled space ships. Unfortunately, after starting experiments in 1930, he died in an accident during one of the test-bed experiments on May 17, when the rocket combustion chamber exploded.

Friedrich Schmiedl, who was educated in civil engineering as well as science and technology, became known for conducting the world's first rocket launches for the purpose of transporting mail. His first experiments with solid-fuel rockets were made in 1918, and after several unsuccessful attempts, he started his Experimental Rocket No. 7 in 1931, which transported 102 letters from Schöckl, near Graz, to a small village about 5 kilometers away. It was remotely controlled and the landing was accomplished by a parachute.

Eugen Sänger also started out his education in civil engineering and then switched to aeronautics after reading Hermann Oberth's book on space travel.

In 1932, he established a test-bed for

rocket engines at the University of Technology in Vienna, where he worked as an assistant researcher and developed and experimented on various designs of combustion chambers.

In 1933, he published his famous book, *Raketenflugtechnik* (*Rocket Flight Engineering*), which was the first book on rocketry from an academic professional. His experimental success in designing rocket engines led to a post as head of his development center for jet engines in Germany in 1936. He continued to experiment with designs for combustion chambers providing a thrust of up to 100 tons, and together with his wife, Irene, worked out detailed plans for a horizontal take-off and landing rocket space plane, which could transport a one ton payload into orbit.

Called the "Silbervogel" (Silver Bird), Sanger's design turned out to be the prototype for a series of designs of horizontally starting and landing space planes, including the German proposed Sanger II, a next-generation space plane.

These men served as a foundation of Austrian space involvement and contributions to come.

Space Technology Transfer

The active involvement of the Austrian government in space began with the Spacelab program in the early 1970s. After Austria became a full member in the European Space Agency in 1987, it began to contribute to all major ESA programs in key areas of space technology covering a broad range of disciplines. Today there are at least ten companies with an equal number of research institutes working in conjunction with the Austrian Space Agency on a number of projects.

The Gamma-Met 100 Titanium Aluminide Sheet — Production and Component Fabrication research program is based on the conclusion that space vehicles require lightweight, heat-resistant structures which place high demands on the materials used for their construction. The gamma-titanium aluminide sheet is a material developed in Austria.

Gamma-titanium aluminide (γ-TiAl) is an alloy whose specific strength is similar to that of other superalloys, but with a substantially higher specific stiffness. It can be used to replace super alloys for high temperature applications in the range of 500 to 800°C. This material is available as a sheet or rod under the brand name Gamma-Met 100 and is quite unique because of its primary use for both propulsion and airframe components.

Gamma-Met 100 is suitable for fabricating components as small as 25 millimeters long in the form of turbine blades, or as large as 10 meters long for hot ducts used for rocket propulsion systems. Its chief advantages are that it is 15 percent higher than titanium alloys and more than 50 percent lighter than superalloys, and it can replace the superalloys used in propulsion systems, thus saving component mass by a factor of 20, which can add up to over a half a ton for today's typical aerospace vehicle.

Additional future applications include civil aviation and automobile designs such as commercial subsonic and future supersonic high capacity aircraft, and high performance, low emission automobiles. Gamma-Met 100 components have also been found effective for low-weight moving parts in racing engines. This revolutionary material is an important advance in technology which can pave the way to production of low cost space vehicles for the commercialization and industrialization of space.

The Austrian Research Centers, Seibersdorf, contractors for the Austrian Space Agency, are Austria's largest contract research enterprise with over 500 employees. Since 1989, ARCS has worked under contract to ESA on the development and application of materials for use in space.

Their studies emphasize the applications of metallic materials in the aerospace industry and include the examination of space-specific properties involving thermal cycling, cold welding, and friction in the space environment; thermo-physical properties such as thermal conductivity, thermal expansion, and specific heat; microstructural characterization such as the scanning electron microscope and glow discharge optical spectroscopy; mechanical properties (tensile, compression, creep, fatigue); chemical composition; and corrosion behavior.

Cluster of Three Indium. Field-emission-electric-propulsion thrusters firing in vacuum chamber. (ARC Seibersdorf research)

ARCS operates a test facility for space and aerospace materials for the aerospace industry, directly benefiting the European aerospace community as a whole.

Another Austrian space contractor, Magna International Development, produces cryogenic systems, specifically the feed line which supplies the European launch vehicle workhorse, Ariane 5, with liquid hydrogen and liquid oxygen for its main stage. The materials used for the fuel lines must be able to withstand extremely low cryogenic temperatures, as well as fulfill other stringent technical requirements with respect to strength, endurance, weight (minimal), compatibility with hydrogen and oxygen fuels, and thorough cleanliness.

They also work with slush hydrogen (SLH2), which is a mixture of the solid and liquid phase propellant obtained by subcooling the liquid hydrogen below its normal boiling point.

The use of slush hydrogen is particularly attractive because of its increased density and its increased heat capacity in relation to the normal boiling point of liquid hydrogen. Workers in the United States have greatly benefited from this technology, finding savings in the gross take-off weight of a launcher between 13 and 26 percent on average. Another advantage of using slush hydrogen is that it only requires minor modifications to the overall rocket engine architecture.

Cryogenic composite feed lines have been developed and tested here. For example, on board the Ariane 5, this technique has reduced mass by as much as a factor of four and heat losses by at least a factor of two with respect to metallic lines.

The future of slush hydrogen use is targeted for the automotive and aircraft industries. Slush hydrogen equipped aircraft and vehicles driven by low emission will aid in minimizing environmental pollution and may also serve as an alternative for future transportation systems.

The Active Surface Imaging System (ASIS) was developed in Austria under an ESA contract initiated in 1991. ASIS is a three dimensional active surface laser imaging system or device which uses a pulsed, direction-detection method. This allows an instrument to have excellent performance, low complexity and a flexible design configuration.

An ASIS sensor is comprised of an electronic unit, with an optical fiber to an opto-mechanical scanner which has an extremely wide field of view. A standard laptop computer runs the required special purpose software to display range information and intensity images in real time.

ASIS can be used for several space applications including meeting the demand for autonomous systems for earth orbits and for lunar and planetary exploration which has grown tremendously in recent years. Tasks which are performed by ASIS are rendezvous and docking for the International Space Station or planetary sample-return missions, pathfinding and obstacle detection for the navigation of a planetary tower, robot manipulation and real-time detection of targets, and three-dimensional site characterization and environment reconstruction.

There are also ground applications for ASIS technology which allow the building of a three-dimensional model of a real object, allowing for a digital representation of its surface. This can be useful in the mining industry for dynamic data capture and instant display of three-dimensional site models, the steel industry for volume measurements in steel converters, environmental control applications such as glacier avalanche forecasting, railroad and utility mapping and modeling, long-term monitoring of buildings, bridges or tunnels, and sensors for industrial robots.

Austria has developed Geocoding software for spaceborne remote-sensing image data through a geocoding system (GEOS). The GEOS was designed to provide terrain-corrected output images and a digital elevation model to represent the ground surface and information regarding layover and shadow areas. This technology has benefited the field of geometric processing of remotely sensed image data in general.

A GPS or Global Positioning System has been put in place in order to meet the growing trend to combine ground data with remote sensing applications, which makes the requirement of an accurate civilian satellite navigation system inevitable. Data taken from this type of system can provide the user with the precise geographical information he or she needs, such as the actual position to an accuracy of 30 m in the standard mode and 1 m in more advanced locations; and satellite imagery providing an excellent overview of an area with a ground resolution ranging from 30 m to 1 m.

This GPS of satellite images has resulted in a software package, Digisat, Digital Satellite Image Mapper, which has two main features — integration of ground-truth information into the system in geocode or real-time data such as that which is used in American Landsat satellites, and display of a selection of predefined combinations of bands that allow the user to highlight the required information on the image.

Digisat software provides an inexpensive way of generating maps directly from satellite images and can bring the benefits of satellite image processing to a larger user community.

Austria has an Automatic Identification of Weather Systems from Satellite Images program which has been developed in response to the increasing need for very short-range weather prediction. This program allows a methodological framework and a prototype system for the automatic, real-time analysis of weather satellite images and the identification of weather systems.

This program is the answer to what is referred to as "nowcasting" by meteorologists to denote the production of short-term weather forecasts for up to six hours ahead. The importance of nowcasting has increased dramatically because many hazardous weather events have a very short life cycle and they often cannot be predicted by conventional forecasting methods.

A critical problem of nowcasting is that a large amount of data must be processed within a very short operational response time. For example, every half hour an aviation forecaster receives an average of three satellite images and 70 different numerical weather prediction data, as well as dozens of charts and hundreds of text messages from airports and automatic weather stations. The forecaster only has typically less than a minute to digest all this and produce an accurate forecast for a specific region in response to a pilot's inquiry.

During the past four years, the Austrian space contractor, Gepard, has developed mathematical methods and prototype software which can be used for automatic identification of cloud and weather systems. This system only needs a few minutes to identify 30 different weather systems, including several types of warm and cold fronts, jet intensification, waves, lee cloudiness, and thunderclouds. It provides forecasters with a satellite image on which graphical overlay shows the names of the major weather systems in the image which enables the recognition of the weather events in the area of concern, resulting in a major increase in decision speed.

This system will also aid in the areas of water management and emergency networks, as well as search and rescue systems in the future.

Earth observation data collected from space by satellites for applications such as meteorology and climatology is of great importance. Signals received from navigation satellites for earth observation are also quite useful. However, overall mission costs can be drastically reduced if cost savings obtained by reusing signal sources can be complemented by an economical implementation. These processing techniques can also be applied to airborne and ground-based applications.

Various geophysical parameters of the earth's surface and its environment, such as roughness, variation of the sea surface, and atmospheric temperature, may be measured by analyzing the behavior of radio waves in relation to the medium under study. Most commonly, earth's satellites transmit sensing signals derived from sources on board, but other operational spacecraft such as navigation or communication satellites can also obtain these signals. These are referred to as signal sources of opportunity.

In an effort to make this process more efficient, Austria has developed Digital Receiver Technology for Spaceborne Earth Observation and Airborne Applications. This DPS system is a hardware building block based upon a space qualified 32-bit floating point TSCC21020 processor, which can be used to form single, dual and multiple processor architectures. The hardware runs at clock rates of up to 20 Mhz with a small size, low mass, power-consumption minimization features, high reliability, and good thermal characteristics. This is accomplished by use of only space qualified and radiation tolerant components.

Some practical applications with the DPS systems include atmospheric sounding which is done on ground using signals radiated by the Global Navigation Satellite as an opportunity source. This allows for cost-saving methods of determining the properties of a radio communications channel. Tracking these signals as they are reflected from the surface of a river or lake can provide useful data for monitoring and managing water systems.

For airborne use, an airborne receiver for determining surface wind speed at sea, which exploits navigation satellite signals reflected from the water surface, is currently under development. In fact, there are nearly 4,000 commercial aircraft in the air at any moment and this figure is expected to double within the next 10 years. This allows for the potential for widespread airborne measurements of surface wind speed which can bring sizeable benefits to numerical weather prediction.

Austrian Space has also developed a Satellite Multi-Media Communications System in response to the need for wide bandwidth transmission systems for many multimedia applications which are not readily available in many areas. In the SMMC system, access to the satellite network is provided by a versatile gateway with a scaleable architecture similar to a computer flowchart. Various network interfaces to local area networks, private automatic branch exchanges, the integrated digital services network and other devices are connected to the multiplexer.

Data from these sources are separated into fixed-length cells and assembled into transmission bursts by the burst assembly module which helps to guarantee the quality of service and provide high system reliability. Typical applications of this system are business communications such as linking branch offices or a bank in a remote area with limited land infrastructure; tele-education, where links between

classrooms in different locations support mixed media traffic; and tele-medicine, where high-quality voice and video services support telecommunications between experts and include the remote monitoring of on-going surgery and tele-training. This data also serves to support applications such as filmless radiology and the transfer of medical images such as X-rays.

Space Research

The Austrian Space Agency is responsible for coordinating projects in the field of space research and technology in Austria. It is also responsible for the promotion and training of specialists in the field of space research and technology, in cooperation with university institutes and research organizations within Austria and other countries.

Austria is a member of the European Space Agency (ESA), as well as the European Meteorological Organization, EUMETSAT. EUMETSAT programs concentrate on operational meteorology including the Meteosat Series of satellites, the second generation of geostationary meteorological satellites (MSG), now in orbit, and the European polar orbiting meteorological satellite system, EPS, currently under development for launch in 2005.

ASA participates in the field of remote sensing research as a member of the European Association of Remote Sensing Laboratories (EARSeL). It is also actively involved with cooperative research agreements with NASA and the UN Committee on the Peaceful Uses of Outer Space (COPUOS). Work with COPUOS focuses on the applications of remote sensing from space for the needs of developing countries, the future utilization of the geostationary orbit, the use of nuclear power sources in space, and the protection and monitoring of the environment including space debris.

In 1975, ASA co-organized a summer school at Alpbach with the Austrian Federal Ministry of Transport, which is co-sponsored by ESA, to conduct various programs of space research. The aim of the summer school was to offer advanced training and working experience to European graduates as well as postgraduate students and young scientists and engineers on subjects not commonly offered in academia.

At the school, students have participated in a series of workshops which teach them the basic skills necessary to become Europe's future space mission designers. Students are encouraged to develop ideas for scientific space missions.

Examples of past ideas include the Submillimeter N Observation of PolarimeterY (SNOOPY), which was an all-sky survey infrared astrophysics mission designed to fit into the framework of an established ESA mission. The cost-effective mission's primary objective would be the understanding of the Inner Stellar Matter (ISM) structure and detection of galactic magnetic field lines by measuring polarization effects in the infrared band of the spectrum.

Interferometer with 3 baselines, Mi-3, would be an ambitious, infrared interferometry mission comprised of four spacecraft, carrying three telescopes and beam combiner optics as payloads. This mission would provide high angular resolution and high resolution spectroscopy for imaging active and merging galaxies, as well as galactic and extragalactic star-formation processes to improve the understanding of the physics of accreting systems through the history of the universe.

Another idea was IniXS, an all-sky survey space mission in the X-ray band (2-80 keV) to detect obscured active galactic nuclei and measure the X-ray background radiation.

The Alpbach Summer School Telescope Realizing INterferometry X-Rays was a proposed X-ray interferometry mission using a revolutionary X-ray optics concept developed at the school to provide milli-arcsecond resolution.

Students at the summer school have also taken workshops examining telematics applications, futuristic applications of satellite navigation and their economic chances, and sounding the atmosphere with space-borne satellite navigation receivers. During the course of these workshops students came up with their own ideas for satellite navigation missions. These included PANIC, Personal Assistant for Navigation, Information and Communication, for use by pedestrians in urban areas. This system uses GPS and has a mapping system stored in a Processing and Display Unit (PDU) and options to subscribe to various information channels, such as news, weather, sports, restaurants, stock quotes, etc.

Traffic Solutions for the Future was a student project focusing on a navigation system for pedestrians in cities, a navigation and guidance system for the visually impaired, an intelligent guidance system to avoid congestion of the available infrastructure, and a flexible management system for public transportation.

The ACRONIM, Advanced Counter-Rotating Radio Occultation Neutral Atmosphere and Ionosphere Sounding Mission Project, was a student idea encompassing a low-cost test configuration of two satellites. ACRONIM mission objectives included sounding of the ionosphere, sounding of the neutral atmosphere, and measuring the electron density in the plasmasphere.

Affiliated with ASA is the Austrian Academy of Sciences' Space Research Institute, which participates in several interplanetary missions dedicated to the exploration of earth and its neighborhood. These missions include the Cluster and DoubleStar with objectives of exploring the space-time structure of the terrestrial magnetic field and the magnetospheric plasma in great detail; GOCE, to determine with very high resolution and accuracy the structure of the terrestrial gravitational field; Cassini/Huygens, missions to explore Saturn and its satellite system; and Rosetta, designed to investigate the coma and the nucleus of the comet P/Wirtanen.

Additional research being conducted by the institute includes studies in the field of geodynamics, which is the activity and forces inside the earth, by use of GPS. Austria has a permanent network of 15 stations for this purpose.

In the field of near-earth space, the institute is heavily involved in the Cluster Mission, which has yielded amazing data on the interaction between the solar wind and the terrestrial magnetic field. It has also made two very important contributions to the DoubleStar to be launched in June 2003. The institute contributed the Flux-Gate Magnetometer, FGM, to measure the magnetic field on DoubleStar's dual satellite, and the Active Spacecraft Potential Control (ASPOC), to control and reduce the electric potential of the equatorial spacecraft.

The institute also contributed to the Cassini/Huygens Mission to Saturn and its satellite, Titan, with several instruments including the PWA, Permittivity Wave and Altimetry, to investigate electrical properties and electric field fluctuations in the atmosphere and ionosphere of Titan below 170 km; the Cassini/RPWS instrument to detect lightening and discharges during close flybys; and a meteoritic ionization model for studying the ionization of metallic ions of Titan's atmosphere.

For the Rosetta mission to the comet P/Wirtanen, due for launch in January 2003, the institute contributed the MUPUS and ROMAP experiments to the Lander. The MUPUS is a collection of sensors for investigating the thermal and mechanical properties of the near-surface layer. ROMAP will measure the magnetic field during the Rosetta Lander's descent and its possible time variation after landing.

The institute made additional contributions to the Rosetta Mass Spectrometer, COSIMA, and to the Rosetta magnetometer, RPC-MAG.

The Micro-Imaging Dust Analysis System, MIDAS, will investigate the physical parameters of cometary dust with an atomic force microscope. MIDAS consists of a dust collecting mechanism and an "Atomic Force Microscope" which will provide three dimensional images of the dust particles. This is critical to the operation of the mass spectrometer COSIMA, Cometary Secondary Ion Mass Spectrometer.

RPC-MAG is a fluxgate magnetometer to measure the magnetic field in the vicinity of comet P/Wirtanen, and is based on a similar instrument flown aboard the Deep Space 1 mission which measured the magnetic field near the comet Borelly.

Cooperative Projects and Austrian Contributions

Austria joined the European Space Agency (ESA) as a full participating member in 1987, and the European Meteorological Satellite Organization, EUMETSAT, in 1994. Basic space research is of critical importance to this country, and it is a challenging focus for the development of new and advanced technologies, stimulating innovations for applied research for many other industrial applications.

As a small country, Austria sees cooperation in international organizations as the most effective means of accomplishing this. Its participation falls in a wide variety of areas: space science, space technology development, telecommunications and navigation, earth observation and meteorology, and space transportation. By contributing to ESA and EUMETSAT, Austria supports the basis for space activities in industry as well as in research institutions and universities.

The Austrian Space Agency serves as a focal point for space activities in Austria, establishing the link to international space activities and organizations and assisting the Austrian Ministry of Transport, Innovation and Technology in the process. ASA is responsible for coordinating Austrian industry and scientific institutions in playing key roles in international space related projects.

Since Austria joined ESA in 1987, Austrian companies under the leadership of ASA have made significant contributions to most of the major ESA programs, becoming recognized partners in a variety of technological areas including scientific instruments, electronics, software, and mechanical structures, in addition to space-related areas.

As an ASA contractor, Austrian Aerospace has provided products in several areas including the design, manufacturing and testing of on-board equipment in digital signal processing such as navigation, signal receivers, data compression units, and sensor signal processing units; the design, manufacturing and testing of on-board equipment requiring mechanisms such as thruster pointing mechanisms for electric propulsion, reversible or non-reversible, and light-weight deployment systems; the design, manufacturing, testing and integration of on-board thermal hardware such as Multi Layer Insulation (MLI), which can be manufactured in large quantities for both space and terrestrial cryogenic applications; and the design, manufacturing and testing of Electrical and Mechanical Ground Support Equipment (EGSE and MGSE).

Austrian Aerospace contributed projects to the Rosetta mission, which studied the fabric of the comet and landed a small probe, the Rosetta Lander, on its surface. Rosetta data is expected to provide a vital insight into the origins of the universe itself. Rosetta's onboard instruments will be able to carry out a variety of experiments and examinations on the destination comet. It will study the appearance of the comet's surface and its composition and temperature distribution, and analyze the gas and dust emitting from its nucleus. Austrian Aerospace designed Rosetta's MIDAS instrument, the Space Craft Multi Layer Insulation, TT&C Special Check Out Equipment, and Thermal Hardware for Experiment Boom.

For the MIDAS Instrument, Austrian Aerospace designed the signal conditioning electronics, a DC/DC converter, and drive electronics for the positioning table, as well as manufactured all instrument electronics. This instrument analyzes micro-dust particles in a cometary environment by means of an atomic force microscope, allowing survey of nonconductive structures with resolution down to subnanometer range.

The Spacecraft Multi Layer Insulation is a part of the thermal hardware in Rosetta. Austrian Aerospace designed and manufactured the blankets and was responsible for the integration of the tailored blankets onto the satellite.

The Rosetta TT&C Special Check Out Equipment is a high precision and fully automatic Telecommand, Tracking & Control (TT&C) communication subsystem for operating in the S- and X-frequency bands.

The X-Ray Multi Mirror Mission (XMM) is a telescope designed to detect and pinpoint the X-rays which pervade the universe that are generated under extreme conditions, from stellar coronae to distant galaxies.

The XMM will carry three advanced X-ray telescopes, each with 58 high-precision nested mirrors. The large collecting area of the three telescope system will allow observations of millions of X-ray sources. XMM will allow astronomers to peer into deep space and observe details of very hot objects created when the universe was very young.

The XMM is unique in that it is the biggest science satellite ever built in Europe. Its telescope mirrors are the most powerful ever developed in the world, and with its sensitive detectors, it will see infinitely more than any previous X-ray satellite.

The XMM was launched December 10, 1999, aboard an Ariane-5 launcher. Its working lifetime is expected to be 10 years. Austrian Aerospace contributed several projects to the XMM, including the Mirror Optical Doors (MOD), Telescope.

Sun Shield (TSS), Venting and Outgassing Doors (VOD), exit baffles, thermal hardware for the upper module, antenna boom, and a mirror hoisting device.

The Mirror Optical Doors (MOD) and Telescope Sun Shield (TSS) work in conjunction with each other. The MOD is a lightweight spring drive, non-reversible deployment mechanism for opening the XMM cover doors and deploying the TSS. The mechanism design is based on a redundant, self-lubricating bearing concept, redundant spring actuators and a hold down and release mechanism, actuated by non-explosive separation nuts.

The Venting and Outgassing Doors (VOD) were designed to fulfill the opening and closing function of the telescope tube.

The exit baffles are part of the mirror assemblies. The configuration consists of three equal baffles designed to minimize the challenging weight requirement and compensate for any distortion or buckling effects due to thermal or mechanical effects.

The thermal hardware consists of multilayer insulation covering the XMM Upper Module, which was designed and integrated onto the telescope structure by Austrian Aerospace.

Austrian Aerospace also designed the structural antenna boom consisting of an aluminum tripod carrying the Low Gain Antenna

of the satellite; and the mirror hoisting device, which allows the integration, lifting and assembly of the XMM Mirror Assembly.

ESA's new gamma-ray astronomy mission INTEGRAL, International Gamma-Ray Astrophysics Laboratory, launched October 17, 2002, will observe gamma-ray sources located within our galaxy and across the universe. The mission will explore the most energetic phenomena that occur in nature and sources including exploding stars, black holes, gamma-ray bursts, and pulsars. The instruments aboard INTEGRAL consist of a gamma-ray imager, gamma-ray spectrometer, X-ray monitor and optical camera.

Austrian Aerospace's contributions to INTEGRAL include the MLI, Multi-Layer Insulation, covering the spacecraft payload module, and the MGSE, Mechanical Ground Support Equipment, with satellite transport containers, integration trolleys, mechanical test equipment, and lifting devices.

The 2,297 pound Mars Express is a cooperative mission between ESA and NASA, scheduled for launch June 2003. The Express will explore the atmosphere and surface of Mars from polar orbit. The spacecraft will carry a science payload with some heritage from European instruments lost on the illfated Russian Mars '96 mission, as well as a communications relay to support lander missions. Mars Express will itself carry a small lander as well.

Mars Express consists of an orbiter with seven onboard scientific instruments that will probe the atmosphere of Mars as well as its structure and geology, looking for evidence of hidden water from orbit and delivering a lander to the Martian surface.

The spacecraft must protect the onboard instruments and equipment, which means keeping some parts of the spacecraft warm and other parts cold. Two instruments, PFS and Omega, have infrared detectors that need to be kept at very low temperatures by radiating excess heat into space. The sensors on the camera also need to be kept cool, while the rest of the instruments and onboard equipment must remain at room temperatures between 10 and 20°C. In order to accomplish this, the inside of spacecraft is kept at this temperature by encapsulating the entire thing in thermal blankets, cooling those instruments that need it. The thermal blankets were designed by Austrian Aerospace and were made from gold-plated aluminum-tin alloy. This is the Mars Express Multi-Layer Insulation covering the spacecraft payload module.

ESA and EUMETSAT are cooperating in the development of a series of polar-orbiting weather satellites that will replace the meteorological satellites currently being used in weather forecasting, beginning in the year 2003. The METOP, Meteorological Operational satellites, will carry instruments carried by ESA, EUMETSAT, NOAA, and the French space agency, CNES. METOP will have a mass of roughly 4.5 tons and will fly at 835 km altitude in a five-day repeat sun-synchronous orbit with an equator descending crossing time of 9:30 am. The satellite system is expected to last a period of at least 14 years.

Austrian Aerospace designed the IASI Data Processing Subsystem for IASI, the Infrared Atmospheric Sounding Interferometer, to perform novel measurements for meteorology and climactic research. This system acts as the core processing of the IASI. They also designed and manufactured the core signal processing element of a GPS receiver performing atmospheric sounding for meteorological purposes, the GRAS Electronics Unit.

Other features of METOP designed by Austrian Aerospace include the NOAA Instruments Interface Unit, a digital processing unit which performs data compression while interfacing signals from the NOAA-type instruments to the satellite bus; the system MGSE, Mechanical Ground Support Equipment, consisting of satellite transport containers, mechanical test equipment, and lifting devices; and the HRPT Antenna Boom, the High Rate Picture Transmitter antenna of the satellite.

The ENVISAT is an advanced polar-orbiting earth observation satellite which is providing measurements of the atmosphere, ocean, land, and ice over a five year period. It is a powerful earth-observation satellite that will help scientists to understand how changes to one climate may affect the others.

Launched in March 2001, Envisat is al-ready providing scientists with a wealth of data, supporting earth science research and allowing the monitoring of the evolution of environmental and climactic changes. Austrian Aerospace contributed the MWR Centralized Electronics Unit (CEU) of the Envisat Microwave Radiometer (MWR) instrument, used for measuring the content of water and water vapor of the atmosphere; the MWR Structure and MLI, the Microwave Radiometer (MWR), and Multi Layer Insulation; the Cross Strap Assembly (CSA) of the data subsystem for the Advanced Synthetic Aperture Radar (ASAR), which holds the measurements of the radar back-scatter from parts of the earth's surface; the Purge Trolley, which provides constant climactic conditions during environmental testing of the satellite; DC/DC Power Converter boards for the MERIS instrument, The Medium Resolution Imaging Specrometer Instrument, used to measure color in oceans and coastal areas; the GOMOS structure, Global Ozone Monitoring by Occultation of Stars, and MLI, which is the primary mounting structure, carrying the optical path components and steerable mirrors, telescope and optical units; and the complete secondary structure, which provides light tightness and stray-light protection to the GOMOS instrument.

METEOSAT Second Generation (MSG) is a series of three spacecraft launched in 2000 which will be instrumental in the gathering of global weather data until at least the year 2012. Operating from geostationary orbit, MSG generates multi-spectral imagery of the earth's surface and cloud systems every fifteen minutes, double the rate of the previous Meteosat. Austrian Aerospace contributed the Pyro Release Unit (PRU), which is an electrical power subsystem of the MSG satellite. This unit provides the driving circuits needed for the firing of pyro devices of the satellite with the emphasis on the reliability, failure tolerance, and safety of the equipment.

Austrian Aerospace also provided Multi-Layer Insulation covering the spacecraft, a Passive Cooling Assembly (PCA), and Remote Terminal Unit (RTU) test equipment, a simulation and measurement tool.

ABRIXAS, A Broadband Imaging X-ray

All-sky Survey, is a German national X-ray satellite with seven 27-fold nested Wolter-1 telescopes, sharing one CCD detector, which is a copy of the EPIC camera used for XMM, in focus. Launched on April 28, 1999, on a COSMOS rocket from Kapustin Yar, Russia, ABRIXAS was intended to perform the first complete all-sky survey with imaging telescopes in the medium energy X-ray range (0.5–15 keV), but unfortunately contact with the satellite was lost on May 5, 1999. Austrian Aerospace contributed the Multi-Layer Insulation system to the Abrixas thermal hardware.

Austrian Aerospace has also contributed test equipment and power converters to various telecommunication satellites including ASTRA, EUTELSAT, SIRIUS, ARABSAT, EURASIASAT, and HISPASAT, as well as a GPS Occultation Sensor to the National Polar Orbiting Environmental Satellite System (NPOESS). This sensor performs atmospheric sounding for meteorological purposes.

For the small satellite platform, Proteus, which was developed in a French national program, Austrian Aerospace designed the Pyro Release Electronics system. The Proteus platform is highly cost-effective for both scientific, earth observation, and telecommunication missions.

ARIANE 5 is the current launch workhorse for the European Space agency that is utilizing transport containers for parts of the solid rocket booster. These are specifically referred to as the JAV and the JAR, which build the upper core of the booster structure and the lower end of the booster, housing the booster nozzle inside, respectively.

Another Austrian Space Agency contractor, MID Austria Space Technology AG (Magna International Development), is the supplier for the feed line system of the ARIANE 5 main stage. They were responsible for the design as well as the production of the lines for liquid hydrogen and liquid oxygen, representing the connection between the tanks and the Vulcain-engine of the launcher.

This involves the use of special corrosive-resistant insulated stainless steel pipes with flanges, axial and angular compensators as well as titanium supports connecting the lines to the engine frame. The materials for the ergol feed lines must be functional in extreme cryogenic temperatures, and in addition fulfill severe technical requirements in respect to strength, endurance, weight optimization, compatibility with hydrogen and oxygen, as well as extreme cleanliness. Today, MID Austria Space Technology AG remains active in all the propulsion units of the ARIANE 5 rocket including the main stage, the upper stage, and the boosters.

Plansee AG is an Austrian subcontractor that provides advanced high temperature materials for combustion chambers and electrical use. These expand into the area of chemical propulsion and can be used in high power thrust chambers of the ARIANE 5 Vulcain. Electrical uses are also possible for electronic components operated at elevated temperature or those without convection cooling.

In the field of electric propulsion, Plansee has also developed a hollow cathode emitter which can be used as a stationary plasma thruster for future satellite programs.

Austrian Research Centers has examined the use of space lidars for use in several missions of the Austrian Space Agency. Lidar is a laser radar and an acronym for light detection and ranging. Lidars are used to measure a range of atmospheric properties by analysis of the part of the laser radiation which is directed back to the lidar. Since only part of the laser radiation is scattered or absorbed by the atmosphere, the remaining laser radiation emitted from the spacecraft is incident on the earth surface, where it may lead to injuries, especially to the eye, if certain limits are exceeded in exposure. Telescopes and binoculars can greatly increase the hazard for ocular damage by directing more laser energy into the eye than in the case of the unaided eye.

In its "Human Risk Analysis Simulator for Space Lidars" Project, Austrian Research Centers used testing to determine the likelihood that either an unaided-eye or an aided-eye, with a binocular or telescope, intercepts the beam, to calculate the ocular exposure with atmospheric scintillation effects included, and then predict the probability that an ocular injury from a space-borne lidar would occur. The risk model developed will be implemented in a flexible and user friendly software to facilitate the risk evaluation of future missions involving lidars.

Austrian Research Centers continues to be involved in the Space Materials Testhouse, which is a long term cooperative project with ESA and ESTEC that has been in place since 1989. ESTEC places orders to evaluate the physical, mechanical and corrosive properties of spacecraft materials. These materials and processes studied are developed by the aerospace industry using several advanced materials, such as fiber reinforced ceramics and metal matrix composites.

This testhouse offers expertise on aerospace materials and methodology and is equipped with complementary facilities for the development, characterization, and qualification of materials and technologies. Fields of analysis include space specific properties such as thermal cycling, sublimation, outgassing, cold welding, and friction under space environment; thermo-physical properties including thermal conductivity, diffusivity, expansion, specific heat, and emissivity; microstructure, including electron and ion microprobes; mechanical properties including tensile, compressions and bending tests, creep, and fatigue; corrosion behavior such as stress corrosion, salt spray or climactic tests; and chemical composition.

BRAZIL

National Institute for Space Research (INPE)

The National Institute for Space Research (INPE) was created out of a strong desire on the part of many Brazilians to participate in the conquest of space.

On August 3, 1961, the Brazilian president at the time, Jânio Quadros, signed a decree which created the organizing group for the National Commission on Space Activities (COGNAE) as a subdivision of the National Research Council (CNPq). This group gave rise to the current National Institute for Space Research.

COGNAE, which soon became known as CNAE and later INPE, began its activities by stimulating, coordinating and supporting studies in space related areas, as well as building a team of skilled researchers and establishing cooperation with leading nations in the space arena.

In its early days, the research program developed in the CNAE laboratories at São José dos Campos — SP, which serves as INPE's main campus today, was best known for its studies in the field of space and atmospheric sciences. These studies included ionosphere sounding in the upper atmosphere by means of ground devices and the use of scientific rocket payloads launched from Barreira do Inferno, Natal-RN.

On April 22, 1971, after COGNAE was phased out, the Institute for Space Research (INPE) was created under a decree which stated that INPE would serve as the main civilian organization for space research development in accordance with the directives of the Brazilian Commission for Space Activities (COBAE), an advisory organ of the Republic Presidency.

Subsequently, the agency commissioned and developed meteorological, communications, and earth observation satellites to meet Brazilian needs. Among the projects were MESA, used for the reception and interpretation of meteorological satellite images; SERE, to utilize satellite remote sensing techniques and aircraft earth resources monitoring; and SACI, for improving the educational system through broadcasting using a geostationary communications satellite.

During the late seventies, INPE entered

a new era when the federal government approved the complete Brazilian Space Mission (MECB); the institute then began to develop space technology.

On March 15, 1985, the Ministry of Science and Technology (MCT) was created, and INPE became a part of an independent entity of the direct administration, with increased financial and administrative autonomy.

During the 1980s, INPE continued to develop such programs as the Complete Brazilian Space Mission (MECB), the China-Brazil Earth Resources Satellite (CBERS), the Amãzonia Research Program (AMZ), and the Center for Weather Forecast and Climactic Studies. It also kept track of other countries' research in space applications, facilitating collaboration and partnership with them. During this period, INPE also established its Integration and Tests Laboratory (LIT) which develops highly specialized research activities essential to the Brazilian space program's success.

In the early 1990s, the first results of MECB were yielded. Brazil's first resource-data collecting satellite, SCD-1, was launched from Kennedy Space Center (KSC) in Florida.

In 1998, the second Brazilian satellite, SCD-2, was successfully launched, performing better than the first one. In recognition of INPE's strides in space technology, Brazil was invited to participate, along with 16 other countries, in the construction of the International Space Station (ISS), one of space history's greatest undertakings.

INPE is made up of several divisions — Space and Atmospheric Sciences, Meteorology, Space Engineering and Technology, Earth Observation, and Special Technologies.

The Space and Atmospheric Sciences division is primarily concerned with the study of physical and chemical phenomena that occur in the atmosphere and outer space. The Space and Atmospheric Sciences General Coordination (CEA) performs experiments and research in the fields of aeronomy, astrophysics and space geophysics.

The Meteorology division is charged with studying the physical and dynamical processes that control the atmosphere and the interaction of the ocean-atmosphere. This leads to a better understanding of the impacts of the meteorological phenomena on human activities, as well as helping with social and economic planning.

The Center for Weather Forecasts and Climate Studies (CPT) at INPE carries out research and activities in the fields of meteorological sciences, meteorological study through the use of satellites, weather forecasting and climactic studies. The weather forecast is performed by a supercomputer that provides accurate forecasts with an advance warning system.

The Space Engineering and Technology division develops space systems and technology covering a wide range of applications such as the project and construction of satellites and ground systems.

The Space Engineering and Technology General Coordination (ETE) has developed such programs as the Brazilian Complete Space Mission (MECB), the Chinese-Brazilian Earth Resource Satellite (CBERS), and Brazilian participation in the International Space Station (ISS). ETE also develops activities in the fields of space mechanics control, electronics for aerospace, and ground systems.

The Earth Observation division is concerned with scientific knowledge and technological development related to the fields of remote sensing, natural resources, and environmental data processing and monitoring.

The Earth Observation General Coordination (OBT) division conducts research, development and application activities in remote sensing and digital processing.

The Special Technologies division is in charge of basic research and technological development in various other fields and specialties.

The Center for Special Technologies (CTE) at INPE engages in activities in the fields of sensors and materials, plasma, computer science, applied mathematics, and combustion and propulsion.

Alcantara Launch Center (CLA)

Brazil has maintained a space launch center at Alcantara which is in the northeastern part of the country along its 4,603 mile-long Atlantic Coast, near Natal, not far south of the equator. This facility also has tracking ability and is located near the European Space Agency's Kourou, French Guiana, launch site, north of the equator.

The Alcantara Launch Center, Brazil's main site, is on the Atlantic Coast outside of São Luis. Natal, Brazil's other launch site, which is less utilized, is located close by.

Launch pads on the ground at Alcantara blast off Satellite Launch Vehicle (VLS) space boosters, Sonda sounding rockets, meteorological rockets and other science-related boosters.

Since the mid–1960s, Brazilian scientists have launched hundreds of sounding rockets from Alcantara, also known as CLA. Alcantara has a launch control center and blockhouse and it has been said that its location near the equator offers a launch advantage over the United States' Cape Canaveral.

The Brazilian government has spent close to $300 million on the development of Alcantara, which has proved capable of serving as a world class commercial spaceport.

Alcantara is exactly three degrees south of the equator, enabling a greater rotational speed of the earth at that latitude which gives each rocket an added boost, requiring less fuel to escape the earth's gravity.

Brazilian authorities estimate fuel savings of over 30 percent for launches into equatorial orbit, which puts Alcantara at a competitive advantage over today's most dominant commercial satellite launch facility, the Europeans' Kourou Spaceport.

The People's Republic of China has recently considered shipping Long March rockets to Brazil for launch from Alcantara because of its location on the equator.

Satellite Launch Vehicle (VLS)

The first Brazilian-made rocket was designed to carry Brazil's series of data gathering satellites, the SCD-2A, which were a part of its Complete Space Mission (MECB).

The 63-foot tall Satellite Launch Vehicle (VLS) rocket was a four-stage launcher. It was in the design stage for 15 years, but efforts to bring the vehicle to completion and launch were hampered by previous embargos against Brazil's military. This included the refusal by the world's seven richest nations, the G-7 nations, to export the necessary technology until Brazil signed the Missile Technology Control Regime (MTCR). The program also suffered budgetary constraints.

The Brazilian Air Force's Space Activities Institute built the 50-ton rocket with the capacity to place satellites weighing 220 to 770 pounds into orbits between 125 and 620 miles above earth.

Four VSL rockets valued at $6.5 million each were earmarked by the program. Brazil had high hopes for the VLS to carry scientific as well as commercial payloads.

In November 1997, Brazil made its first attempt to launch a VLS rocket into space that only lasted 65 seconds. One of the rocket's four engines failed to ignite, and for security reasons controllers decided to destroy the rocket after losing control. All parts of the rocket fell into a secure area, into the ocean, roughly two kilometers (1.2 miles) from the launch pad.

The launch, which was broadcast live over national television, appeared to be proceeding well, but the rocket was only visible for a few seconds before disappearing into clouds. Officials reported the VLS to be 9,700 feet in altitude when the decision was made to destroy it. Unfortunately, the VLS payload, the $5 million SCD-2A environmental and scientific satellite, was also lost, marking a significant setback for both the VLS and satellite data-gathering program.

Brazil's Role in the International Space Station (ISS)

There are a number of countries contributing to the International Space Station (ISS), including the United States, the United Kingdom, Russia, Canada, Japan, Belgium, the Netherlands, Denmark, Norway, France, Spain, Italy, Germany, Sweden, and Brazil.

The ISS will provide a microgravity environment for basic, applied and commercial research in physical, chemical and biological processes. It will also serve as an important means for engineering development, and as an observation platform for earth and space science research.

On October 14, 1997, Brazil signed an agreement with the United States, the Brazilian Space Agency — AEB, and NASA to become bilateral partners in the ISS project. Brazil made a commitment to provide $120 million worth of hardware in exchange for research and crew privileges aboard the United States' portion of the low-earth orbiting laboratory.

The hardware provided by Brazil included science equipment for long-duration exposure tests outside the station, an earth observation system, and a cargo carrier to be mounted inside the space shuttle's cargo bay.

The Express Pallet, ExPS, is an unpressurized external piece of equipment with an adapter mechanism to support external payloads. Each ExPS can accommodate up to six payloads weighing 225 kg (495 lbs) for a total launch of 1.36 tons.

ExPS adapters are fully compatible with external robotics operations (ERO) and with crew extravehicular activities (EVA).

ExPS units are also compatible with robotic operations for removal from orbital cargo bay and assembly. The units have a 10-year operational lifetime.

The Technological Experiment Facility (TEF) is an external hardware facility to accommodate and support exposed technological experiments to the harsh environment of low earth orbit (LEO). The TEF can accommodate masses from 50 kg (110 lbs) to 125 kg (275 lbs), depending on the position.

The TEF will provide a power supply and data transfer to the experiments, similar to the Express Pallet System. The TEF also has an orbit operational lifetime of 10 years.

WORF-2, the Window Observational Research Facility Block 2, is an internal ISS unit designed to be assembled inside a standardized ISS Express Rack. This rack is positioned over the earth facing a window in the U.S. lab to accommodate earth observation payloads.

The WORF-2 will fully support these payloads by providing structural, thermal, conditioning power supply and data transfer.

The Unpressurized Logistics Container (ULS) is an external unit serving as a means of transportation and cargo storage for the ISS.

The unpressurized cargo to be transported on the ULF will use an interface unit called CHIA which provides electrical and mechanical interfaces between the cargo and the ULC.

The Cargo Handling Interface Assembly (CHIA) is an external support unit which provides interfaces between the cargo items and the ULF in orbit during the maintenance operations of the ISS. The CHIA design consists of plates or boxes where cargo items can be stored.

The CHIA unit provides heating as well as a data bus to verify that the cargo items are in operational condition and within their safety margins.

The last piece of equipment Brazil provided for ISS is the Z1-ULC Attach System, an external unit to support the ISS truss while the two ULC units remain in orbit.

Research Programs

There are a number of research programs that have been undertaken by INPE. These include monitoring the Brazilian Amazon forest through a project known as PRODES (Estimate of Amazon Gross Deforestation Project), the China-Brazil Earth Resources Satellite (CBERS), the Cimex Experiment — CCD Imaging Instrument Experiment, the ECO-8 Equatorial Constellation Orbit Satellite, Geomagnetism, Electromagnetic Induction, Geomagnetic Variations, the Humidity Sounder for Brazil (HSB), Airglow Group "LUME," and the Brazilian Complete Space Mission.

Monitoring the Brazilian Amazon forest using space technology has proved to be a very important project for Brazil. The Brazilian Amazon is comprised of the states of Acre, Amapa,' Amazonas, Mato Grosso Pará, Ronônia, Roraima, Tocantins and portions of Maranhaõ and Golás, totaling an area of close to five million square kilometers (3,000,000 miles), large enough to accommodate all of western Europe.

Four million kilometers (2,400,000 miles) of the total area is covered with forest formations. The aim of the Brazilian government is to generate periodic estimates of the extent and rate of gross deforestation in the Amazon, a task which could never be conducted without the use of space technology.

Brazil carries out these forest assessments based on the analysis of Landsat images acquired and processed by INPE since 1994. The first complete assessment covered the years 1974 and 1978. Since 1988, annual assessments have been conducted by INPE through the PRODES project. The PRODES project may be considered the largest project of forest monitoring in the world.

The China-Brazil Earth Resources Satellite (CBERS) project is the result of an agreement signed in July 1988, when President José Sarney of Brazil visited China.

The two countries contracted for work on the CBERS Satellite project in order to establish a complete remote sensing system that is both competitive and compatible with ongoing international needs.

The Chinese Academy of Space Technology (CAST) holds responsibility for implementing the CBERS program in China in conjunction with INPE's management in Brazil.

There have been notable similarities between Brazil and China when the broad concept of science and technology is considered.

In relation to the space sector, Brazil has experienced moments of great expectation concerning the success of the Complete Brazilian Space Mission (MECB). There was also a high degree of interest by each country in directing the space activities to strengthen national industry and the economy.

China has achieved a solid background in the construction of satellites and launch vehicles. This development began in the mid–50s and led to the first launch of the Long March series of vehicles in 1964, the first scientific satellite launch in 1970, and the launch of twenty other satellites including the recoverable and geostationary orbit from launch vehicles, as well as bases and tracking and control stations.

China became interested in Brazil's stronger experience in electronics and electrical components which could be used in remote sensing and meteorological satellite technology.

Another key similarity between the two countries is the physical layout of each. Both Brazil and China have extensive land territories with large, uninhabited, hard to reach areas, as well as great agricultural emphasis. On this basis, Brazil and China conceived a satellite with sensors specially designed for the management of earth's resources, forests, geology and hydrology, as well as a modern system to monitor the environment.

The first CBERS satellite was launched on October 14, 1999, aboard the Chinese Long March 4B, from the Taiyuan Launch Center, province of Shanxi, roughly 750 kilometers (450 miles) southwest of Beijing. A second satellite, CBER-2 was launched in October 2001.

Both countries are constructing two more satellites in the CBERS series, CBERS-3 and CBERS-4, substituting the previously used CCD camera with another of 5 meters (16.5 ft) of resolution for future launch.

CBERS satellites are made up of two modules. The payload module houses the optical system (CCD-High Resolution CCD Cameras, IRMSS — Infra-Red Multispectral Scanner, and the WFI-Wide Field Imager) and the electronic system used for earth observations and data collecting. The service module incorporates the equipment to ensure the power supply, control, telecommunications, and all other functions needed for satellite operation.

1100 watts of electrical power ensure continued operation of the onboard equipment. This power is obtained through solar panels that are deployed when the satellite is in orbit and are continuously oriented towards the sun by automatic control.

The satellites are equipped with a sensitive altitude control system that is complemented by a set of hydrazine thrusters for use in satellite orbit correction maneuvers. This altitude control system provides stringent pointing accuracy needed by the sensor systems to take high resolution images from a distance of close to 800 km (480 miles).

The CBERS satellites are designed for global coverage and are equipped with cameras to make optical observations, and a data-collecting system to gather data on the environment.

They are unique systems due to the use of onboard sensors which combine features specially designed to resolve the broad range of space and time scales involved in our ecosystem.

The CBERS satellites have a sun-synchronous orbit at an altitude of 778 km (467 miles), completing about 14 revolutions per day. Since the local solar time at the crossing of the equator is always 10:30 A.M., the same solar illumination conditions for comparing images taken on different days applies.

The CBERS satellites have multi-sensor payloads with different spatial resolutions and data collecting frequencies.

The Wide Field Imager (WFI) has a ground swath of 890 km (534 miles), which provides a synoptic view with a spatial resolution of 260 m (858 feet). The earth is completely covered in five days in two spectral bands—0.66 µm (green) and 0.83 µm (near infrared).

The high-resolution CCD camera provides images of a 113 km (68 mile) strip with 20 m (66 feet) spatial resolution. Since the CCD camera has a sideways pointing capability of plus or minus 32 degrees, it can take stereoscopic images of a particular region. Any phenomenon detected by the WFI may also be "zoomed" by the oblique view of the CCD camera with a maximum lag of three days.

The CCD camera operates in five spectral bands that include a panchromatic band from 0.51 to 0.73 µm. The two spectral bands of the WFI are also present in the CCD camera to allow correlation of the data from the two types of remote sensing images. The complete coverage cycle of the CCD camera occurs in 26 days.

The Infrared Multispectral Scanner (IR-MSS) operates in four spectral bands such as to extend the CBERS spectral coverage up to the thermal infrared range. It images a 120 km (72 mile) swath with the resolution of 80 m (264 feet), 160 m (528 feet) in the thermal channel. In a 26 day period, complete earth

coverage is obtained that can be correlated with the images of the CCD camera.

The CBERS includes a data collection system for real-time retransmission of environmental data gathered on the ground and transmitted to the satellite by small autonomous stations. The data from thousands of these stations, located anywhere on earth, are directed at the same time to processing centers and to the end-users by transmissions in varying frequencies.

The CBERS operation and control are manned by Brazil and China from the XI-AN Satellite Control Center during the routine phase. This includes the adjustments to maintain the orbital phasing.

The functions related to the scheduling of the satellite camera operations in response to user requests are handled by the Mission Center. The central hub for all operations related to the CBERS satellite and its mission control is the Control Center.

The TT&C stations provide the link between the satellite controllers and the satellite. They also gather the raw data of the CBERS, collecting it in S-band.

The Satellite Control Centers receive a variety of information, keeping the controllers updated on the status of equipment units, assuring their proper functioning. Specially designed software for the Control Center computers exchange with the satellite computer, permitting the programming of satellite instruments by means of stored commands executed during many orbits of the satellite.

The CBER Ground Segment supports all the necessary activities for the control of the satellites, allowing remote sensing tasks. This includes means for satellite tracking, command and control, satellite reception, storage, and distribution of images.

The CCD Imaging Instrument Experiment, or Cimex Experiment, will use the new technology in the multi-spectral area by means of CCD devices operating in the medium infrared region.

With CCD technology, the construction of small imaging systems of low weight and low power consumption is possible and important to space applications.

Cimex will be installed in a cylindrical

pattern container called Hitchhiker, as a classification system aboard a U.S. space shuttle in cooperation with NASA.

The Hitchhiker will offer power supply and data telemetry systems. It will also offer telecommand channels, atmospheric conditions inside the containers, and complete environmental conditions data.

The Cimex payload will consist of electronic modules mounted in a single metallic box. Each electronic module is made of a single circuit board. The CEP payload functions include controlling Cimex operation, supplying the interface signals between Cimex and the space shuttle electronics, and turning on and controlling the OBDA (Optical Block and Detector Adapter) electronics.

The electronics of CEP include power, video processing, formatting, sequencing, and interfacing.

The Power module conditions the power for the Cimex, including the bus conversion from 28V to 15V, plus or minus 12V and 5V. It receives and processes the CIMEX operation signals that come from the space shuttle to change the operation mode, for example, turning it on or off, acquiring images, and controlling cooling.

The Video Processing module receives video signals from the OBDAs and CCDs. This module is responsible for amplifying, multiplexing, and converting data from analogic to digital. It uses two image processing modules, each containing 16 video channels supplied by a CCD.

The Sequencer module generates the clock signal necessary to synchronize the CIMEX operation, including temporizing the CCDs. It also supplies the necessary synchronization signals to format and convert the video signal.

The Formatting module implements the frame and formats the video signal to be transmitted to the earth.

The Interface module has several functions, including receiving and responding via communication serial interface with the space shuttle electronics, counting the time to date the images, counting the number of image lines, and supplying to the formatting module the date and number of lines of information to compose the video signal.

The Equatorial Constellation Orbit System, ECO-8, will provide fixed cellular wireless and mobile voice communication services and pagers. It is designed to fulfill the needs of the tropical zone characterized by remote and low density populated areas where the main markets are associated with rural activities.

In relation to local repeaters, it can be an ideal solution to provide telecommunications for small villages in remote areas.

Unlike a terrestrial cellular, the ECO-8 is interconnected with the existing fixed telecommunications network, allowing worldwide access through the Public Switching Telephone Network — PS7N.

The ECO-8 System will use 12 satellites, 11 operating and one backup at an altitude of 2000 km (1200 miles).

Studies of geomagnetism at INPE are based on measurements of temporal variations of the terrestrial magnetic field as observed on the earth's surface. The variations result from two different contributions: one of external origin which is considered primary and generated by electric currents flowing in the ionosphere and magnetosphere; and another of internal origin, which is secondary, induced by the external variations in conducting materials of the earth's interior.

The skill needed to separate external from internal contributions is a fundamental aspect of geomagnetism, as it allows it to be interpreted in part in terms of the physical processes involved in their generation and transmission. Therefore, individualization of the external part makes it possible to study different electrodynamic processes in ionized environments consisting of electronic current systems in the ionosphere and interaction between the solar wind and the terrestrial magnetosphere, generating under certain circumstances the so-called magnetic storms; whereas the internal part makes it possible to infer the distribution of the electrical conductivity in the crust and upper mantle, a basic knowledge in pure and applied geophysics.

The researchers at INPE take into account both approaches — geomagnetic variations through the MAGTE project, studying the primary part of the geomagnetic field; and

Electromagnetic Induction through the SOMAT project, studying the secondary part. Along with these activities, the researchers of the group are also involved in studies in connected areas emphasizing aeronomy, meteorology, and remote sensing.

The team involved in these studies has been composed of 16 members, of which eight are permanent employees of INPE (four researchers, two electronic engineers, and two technicians). The other members are two emeritus researchers, one specialist in informatics, two other technicians, and three graduate students. Since 1997, more than 50 papers have been published by the group in peer-reviewed scientific journals.

Studies of electromagnetic induction have been developed by the INPE's group of geomagnetism to get geophysical information on the distribution of the electrical conductivity in the crust and upper mantle under diverse Brazilian tectonic provinces. The methodology uses natural variations of the geoelectromagnetic field to infer the variations of the electrical conductivity in the subsurface: methods Magnetotelluric (MT) and Geomagnetic Deep Soundings (GDS).

Ongoing projects include studies in the southern border of the Paraná Basin (states of Santa Catarina and Rio Grande do Sul, south of Brazil), in the Pantanal Wetland (states of Mato Grosso and Mato Grosso do Sul, southwest of Brazil), in the borders south-southwest of the São Francisco Craton and the Alto Paranaíba Igneous Province (states of Minas Gerais and Goiás, center of Brazil) with implications in the diamond research in the region, and deep studies in the Amazon (north of Brazil), giving constraints for orderly regional mineral exploration.

All these works require very intensive study, with innumerable projects approved and funded by Brazilian scientific agencies and mineral exploration companies.

The geomagnetic field of internal origin as observed in Brazil has two main features — the magnetic equator with the associated ionospheric diurnal currents of the equatorial electrojet, which crosses the north and west-central regions of the country, and the South Atlantic Magnetic Anomaly, the region of

minimum intensity of the total geomagnetic field in the earth's surface that is presently centered in the state of Santa Catarina (south of Brazil) and characterized by precipitation of energetic particles from the inner radiation belts into the local atmosphere.

Studies of geomagnetic variations at INPE are directly related to both phenomena. The primary goal is to understand the propagation of the geomagnetic micropulsations (variations with periods from tenths to hundreds of seconds; amplitude from tenths to tens of nT) to the Brazilian low-latitude regions, their amplification in the equatorial region, and the possible generation of events associated with the intensification of particle precipitation in the atmosphere of the South Atlantic Magnetic Anomaly following magnetically disturbed periods.

Data is collected in permanent geomagnetic stations operated by INPE in eight different sites in Brazil and Antarctica, and then stored in a database that is available to the members of the group for detection of events and determination of their physical parameters such as amplitude, phase, characteristic period, and polarization. The operation of the stations, data processing and interpretation are funded by Brazilian agencies FAPESP, CNPq, CAPES, and INPE.

The Humidity Sounder for Brazil (HSB) is part of the EOS PM-1 Mission of the EOS — Earth Observing System Program. The PM-1, the first of a series of spacecrafts, will fly in an orbit that covers the earth every 16 days.

The EOS program will provide the comprehensive global observations necessary to understand how the processes that govern global change interact as part of earth's system. The HSB will be a significant contribution to the improvement of modeling efforts, numerical weather prediction and monitoring of climate variations and trends.

Airglow group "LUME" is one of the three research lines of the Aeronomy Division (DAE) of INPE. Main scientific topics of study are upper atmosphere physical processes (temperature, wind and wave propagation) and photochemical processes (ions, oxygen, hydrogen and ozone reactions) by means of airglow observation from 80 to 300 km of altitude. Routine observations of the airglow OI 557,7 nm and OI 630,0 nm, sodium NaD 589 nm, hydroxil OH (6,2) band at 835 nm and molecular oxygen O2 atm.(0,1) band at 866 nm are being carried out. Optical instruments, a multi-channel airglow photometer, two all-sky imagers and a Fabry-Perot interferometer are in operational form.

There are many other ongoing projects of the EOS program. Photometric studies are being conducted in the Antarctic region by project FOTANTAR under PROANTAR (CNPq), which entails the monitoring of the mesopause temperature of the Antarctic upper atmosphere by measuring the airglow OH spectra. The Equatorial Atmosphere Research Satellite (EQUARS) Project studies the dynamic, photochemical and ionospheric processes in the equatorial upper atmosphere, with special emphasis on energy transport in the middle atmosphere and the development of plasma bubbles in the ionosphere; with experiments onboard including an Airglow photometer for the O1577, O16300 and OH measurements, an Airglow imager for gravity wave study by O2b (0,0), and a GPS receiver for stratospheric temperature profiles and the total electron content. Temperature and termospheric wind observation is conducted using O1530.0 nm emissions and Project FABRY-PEROT.

The Brazilian Complete Space Mission (MECB) focuses on the development and operation in orbit of small satellites with applications in environmental data collection and remote sensing, directed to specific Brazilian needs.

The MECB was established to promote the progress of space technology in Brazil through the development and in-orbit operation of a family of small application satellites. The MECB program promotes the development of satellites selected to meet specific Brazilian needs — three for environmental data collection, two for remote sensing and one for communications. Two data collecting satellites, SCD1, launched in 1993, and SCD2, launched in 1998, are already in orbit.

In addition to the development of satellites, the MECB program included, in its initial phases, the construction of general purpose facilities — the Integration and Tests Laboratory (LIT) and the satellite Tracking and Control Center (CRC). Today, these facilities are being used by the satellites of MECB and other programs.

Another important goal of the MECB program is to involve the Brazilian industry. This involvement has increased in volume as well as complexity. The Brazilian industry started its participation in the program by manufacturing single flight equipment, and it has now become a subsystem supplier, aiming to supply complete systems in the near future.

SCD1, SCD2 and SCD3 satellites are included on the data collection mission. The aim of this mission is to provide Brazil with one environmental data collecting system supported by satellites and data collecting platforms (PCDs) distributed all over the country.

The PCDs are small, automated stations usually situated in remote sites of difficult access. Data acquired by the PCDs is transmitted to the satellites, which relays it to INPE ground stations located in Cuiaba and Alcantara. From these stations, data is then transferred to the mission center, in Cachoeira Paulista, for processing and immediate distribution to the users. Processed data is then made available on the Internet for registered users.

Data currently collected by SCD1 and SCD2 is used on applications such as input for CPTEC weather forecast models, studies on ocean currents, tides, atmosphere composition, and agricultural planning, among others. One important satellite application is the monitoring of hydrological basins using data collected through ANEEL PCDs that acquire river and rain data.

The data collection system is presently composed of the SCD1 and SCD2 satellites and by the data collection ground segment. Additional satellites with data collection payloads include CBERS 1 and CBERS 2, SCD3, and SACI-2, which was destroyed in a launch failure of Brazil's VLS-1 rocket.

The SCD1 satellite was a 110 kg (243 lb) data collection satellite. Altitude control was performed through spin imposed by the launch vehicle (about 120 rpm after launch, with no speed control capability). A nutation damper corrected deviations during separation. Altitude determination was achieved from solar sensors and one magnetometer.

Electrical power was generated by eight rectangular lateral and one octagonal top solar arrays composed of silicon cells. One power conditioning unit (PCU) received and directed generated power to all satellite subsystems. A nickel-cadmium battery stored energy for SCD1 operation during eclipse. The excess power generated was then dissipated on two shunt dissipaters located on the bottom panel. One DC/DC converter and one power distribution unit (PDU) completed the subsystem equipment.

The onboard supervision subsystem of the satellite was capable of being programmed from the ground. Consisting of two computers, the UPC (central processing unit) and the UPD/C (distributed processing unit), the system configuration allowed time-tagged commands, storing telemetry for transmission when in visibility from the ground stations.

The TT&C (Telemetry, tracking and command) subsystem was composed of two redundant S-band transponders and one telemetry encoder (Codir). Two quadrifillar antennas both in the same polarization, located on the satellite top and bottom panels, allowed access to SCD1 from the tracking stations and vice-versa.

The satellite structure was composed of one aluminum calandered central cylinder with three octagonal panels for equipment mounting. Stiffness was achieved with four inclined bars joining the central panel edges to the joint between the cylinder and the bottom panel. Eight lateral panels provided the satellite's final shape. Assembly to the launch vehicle was made through one interface flange, machined in aluminum.

The satellite thermal control was fully passive. Thermal tapes and coatings (paints) with required thermo-optical properties were used. Some highly dissipative equipment was thermally grounded, and others were insulated from the environment to reduce the operation temperature range in orbit.

The satellite payload was basically one data collection transponder (DCP transponder) that received data acquired and transmitted by the automated platforms on ground and retransmitted them in real time (no onboard storage) in S-band to the ground stations.

For development purposes, one solar cell experiment flew with the satellite. This experiment was produced wholly in Brazil in order to achieve technology and manufacturing capability of silicon cells.

SCD1 was launched using the United States company Orbital Sciences Corporation's Pegasus vehicle on February 9, 1993, and is still operating in orbit, in spite of the specified life expectancy of one year.

The SCD2 satellite, weighing 117 kg (258 lbs) and similar to the SCD1, has a main payload with one data collection transponder (DCP) to retransmit data received from the PCDs on the ground. The new altitude in orbit allows the elimination of reception antennas on the spacecraft bottom panel. There are only four UHF monopolies on the top panel.

Data transmission to the ground stations is more efficient, since reverse polarization was adopted for the S-band quadrifillar antennas located on the satellite top and bottom panels.

SCD2 was also spin stabilized. Due to two new magnetic torque coils, spin rate may be controlled at the 32 to 36 rpm range. All additional altitude control subsystems are similar to SCD1.

Power generation is performed using only lateral panels, due to the new satellite attitude in orbit. The silicon panels were already provided by the national industry. The subsystem general conception is basically the equivalent to SCD1.

The on-board supervision concept was optimized. All functions are now performed by one single computer, the OBC (onboard computer).

The TT&C subsystem is composed of one set of equipment equivalent to SCD1. One of the S-band transponders was supplied by a Brazilian manufacturer, and the telecommand decoder was manufactured at INPE.

Structure and thermal control subsystems

are also very similar to SCD1. There are slight differences due to layout variation between both satellites.

As development, SCD2 carries onboard one new and more sophisticated solar cell experiment and one reaction wheel prototype (ERR). The ERR, developed by INPE, will aim to achieve national qualification for space systems with lubricated movable parts connected to motors.

According to the nationalization index, the SCD1 received a 73 percent rating and the SCD2 received an 85 percent. In addition, the Brazilian industry engagement improved from nine percent on SCD1 to 20 percent on SCD2, fulfilling the INPE directive of technology transfer to the local industry.

On November 2, 1997, an SCD2-A was launched from the Alcantara Launch Center using the VLS (Satellite Launch Vehicle). However, an ignition problem in one engine of the VLS first stage prevented the satellite from being placed in orbit.

The SCD2 was launched via Pegasus rocket on October 22, 1998, and has since continued an orbital life performing data collection, giving continuity and improving SCD1 services.

BULGARIA

Bulgarian Aerospace Agency

The Bulgarian Aerospace Agency (BASA) has been heavily involved in remote sensing and related aerospace technologies since its inception. It is a non-profit organization which was established in December 1993, in order to promote the national policy in the field of aerospace and coordinate the efforts of the government, science and industry for the commercialization of space applications.

It is a member of several international aerospace bodies including the International Astronautical Federation and the Space Agency Forum among others. BASA has recently signed cooperative agreements with the Russian Aviation and Space Agency (RASA), the Romanian Space Agency (ROSA), and the National Aerospace Agency of the Republic of Kazakhstan (NAKA). Other agreements are being negotiated with the European Space Agency (ESA), the Austrian Space Agency (ASA), the Deutsches Zentrum fuer Luft- und Raumfahrt (DLR), the National Space Agency of Ukraine, Bundesverband der Deutschen Luft- und Raumfahrtindustrie (BDLI), and Agenzia Spaziale Italiana (ASI).

BASA has received visits from several entities involved with the United States space program including the U.S. Space Foundation president, Richard MacLeod, and the astronaut, Ronald Sega, who flew aboard the Space Shuttle Atlantis in March 1996.

Bulgaria's keen interest in remote sensing led the country to establish the Remote Sensing Applications Center (ReSAC) in 1998. A notable aerospace technology developed by the agency in collaboration with scientists from Russia is a portable UV-Indicator for personal use, in response to the continuing danger of exposure to harmful ultraviolet rays from the sun as a result of a thinning ozone layer. This device has already been marketed in several countries, with its demand rapidly increasing.

BASA has also been involved in the field of aerospace biomedical investigations. The Neurolab-B system and Svet greenhouse projects are current Bulgarian pursuits. The Neurolab-B system is designed for use onboard the Mir space station as a method for psycho- and physiological examination of the crews. It is the first of its kind onboard space equipment. The flight prototype of the equipment was successfully launched on a Proton rocket from the Baikonur space center on April 22, 1996, and is already operational onboard Spectar Modul, Mir station.

Neurolab-B was designed and created by Bulgarian specialists in cooperation with the German Space Agency (DARA) and the Russian Space Agency (RSA). It measures, amplifies and processes the following physiological signals and parameters: electro-cardiogram, electro-encephalogram, electro-myogram, electro-oculogram, temperature, breathing frequency, galvanic skin resistance, arterial blood pressure, basal tone speech and pulse wave.

The system is modular based and the user, via exchange of separate modules to meet specific requirements, can easily modify its configuration. The follow-up design for Neurolab-B will be Healthlab, which will be mounted onboard the International Space Station.

CANADA

The Canadian Space Agency (CSA)

It is a little known fact that shortly after the launch of the Soviet's Sputnik in 1957, Canada entered the space race with the launch of its own satellite, Alouette 1, in 1962. Other Canadian space milestones include the birth of John Herbert Chapman on August 28, 1921, in London, Ontario. He gained wide recognition as the father of the Canadian space program. Dr. Chapman was later instrumental in initiating and directing the extremely successful Alouette/ISIS scientific earth satellite program. On November 8, 1958, a Nike-Cajun sounding rocket was launched from the Churchill Range with the first Canadian science payload. On March 11, 1959, NASA approved a Canadian proposal, submitted by the DRB, to build the Alouette 1 satellite for the study of the ionosphere, and NASA agreed to launch this first Canadian satellite. On September 5, 1959, the first truly Canadian sounding rocket, the Black Brant 1, was launched at the Churchill Range. It was built by Bristol Aerospace of Winnipeg, Manitoba. On June 22, 1960, the U.S. navigation satellite Transit 2-A was launched with a cosmic noise receiver, the first ever Canadian hardware in space. On August 12, 1960, Echo 1, a U.S. satellite-balloon used as a passive communications satellite, was deployed. It was the first to provide a two-way telephone conversation. Echo 1, a 30-meter-diameter inflatable structure, orbited the earth at an altitude of 1600 km, and one of its receiving station was Prince Albert in Saskatchewan. On September 29, 1960, Canada became the third country after the USSR and the United States to have a satellite in space after a Thor-Agena B rocket, launched from Vandenberg Air Force Base in California successfully released science satellite Alouette 1 on an 80-degree-inclination orbit at an altitude of 1000 km. Designed with a one-year lifetime, the topside sounder will transmit useful data for more than ten years on the ionosphere, the electrically-charged layer of the upper atmosphere that affects, among other things, long-distance radio transmission. On December 21, 1963, the first weather photo was transmitted to Canada from U.S. satellite TIROS 8. On November 29, 1965, a Thor-Agena B rocket launched Canada's Alouette 2 from Vandenberg AFB to continue ionospheric research from space. This first of the ISIS (International Satellites for Ionospheric Studies) scientific satellites, which was designed and built by Canada but launched by NASA, compiled useful data on the ionosphere for almost 10 years.

On September 30, 1970, Telesat Canada signed an agreement with Hughes Aircraft of

California to build Anik 1, Canada's first communications satellite. November 9, 1972, marked the launching of the Anik A-1 communications satellite, making Canada the first country with a domestic communications satellite in geostationary orbit. On April 20, 1973, Anik A-2, Canada's second communications satellite, was launched to bring network radio, TV and improved telephone services to Canadians living in the North. May 7, 1975, brought the launch of Anik A-3 on a Delta rocket. With the launch, Telesat Canada accomplished another world first by teaming Anik A-3 with A-2 in the same orbital position to permit the still usable channels on each satellite to be operated as if they were onboard the same spacecraft. On December 15, 1978, Anik B, Canada's fourth communications satellite, was launched atop a Delta rocket. Anik B became the world's first dual-band communications satellite, not only replacing the Anik A series as a commercial satellite operating in the 6/4 GHz frequencies, but also continuing the promising Hermes experiments using six channels in the higher 14/12 GHz range.

In 1980, Canada signed an agreement with ESA to participate in the development and exploitation of Olympus, the largest ever hybrid communications satellite launched by Western countries. Canada, with an 11 percent stake in the Olympus program, supplied solar panels, amplifiers and hyperfrequency components; and supported assembly, integration and testing at the David Florida Laboratory of the $1 billion ESA spacecraft. On November 13, 1981, Unit 201 of the officially-designated Shuttle Remote Manipulator System (SRMS), dubbed Canadarm, was test-deployed out of Columbia's payload bay for the first time during this second test flight of the space shuttle (mission STS-2). On August 26, 1982, Anik D-1 was launched atop a Delta rocket. The more capable D series replaced the A and B series, and formed the backbone of Canada's domestic satellite communications system until the early 1990s.

June 22, 1983, brought the first operational use of the Canadarm when it deployed the SPAS-01 out of the cargo bay of shuttle Challenger four days into mission STS-7. Oc-

tober 5–13, 1984, astronaut Marc Garneau became the first Canadian in space when he participated with six other crewmembers on mission STS-41G aboard space shuttle Challenger. As a payload specialist, he was responsible for the CANEX-1 set of Canadian experiments. On this same mission, the Canadarm (Unit 302) was operated for the ninth time on a space shuttle flight.

On March 18, 1986, Canada invested $800 million into the design and development of a mobile servicing centre (that will eventually become the Mobile Servicing System, or (MSS) to help in the building and servicing of the permanently-manned space station project initiated by the United States. On March 1, 1989, the Canadian Space Agency was born. The new space organization was created out of space activities that, up until this day, had been carried out under National Research Council Canada (NRCC)'s Space Division auspices, as well as in-house at various federal departments such as science and technology, communications or energy, mines and resources. Professor Larkin Kerwin became the first president of the new agency.

In March 1990, Canada invested $15 million into the U.S. FUSE (Lyman Far Ultraviolet Spectroscopic Explorer) space telescope. Canada provided optical subsystems and contributed to the exploitation of data downlinked by the satellite. Late October of the same year, a Memorandum of Understanding was signed between Canada and the USSR detailing space cooperation between the two countries.

On March 19, 1992, at the White Sands range in New Mexico, a Canadian Black Brant 9 sounding rocket was launched carrying the CSAR-1 (Canadian Space Agency Rocket) microgravity payload. On December 8, 1994, the CSAR-2 (Canadian Space Agency Rocket-2) mission was launched on a 14-minute suborbital flight from White Sands, New Mexico. CSAR-2 consisted of five material processing experiments in microgravity. On November 4, 1995, the first Canadian earth observation satellite, RADARSAT-1, was launched from Vandenberg Air Force Base in California, atop a Delta 2 rocket. December 5 of the same year, in Beijing, the Canadian Space Agency signed an agreement with the China National Space Administration for an eventual cooperation in space science and technology between the two countries.

In the years up to the present, Canada has continued to remain actively involved in a wide variety of space efforts, including the International Space Station, the training and selection of space shuttle astronauts, and the development and launch of telecommunications and scientific satellites. Following an April 19, 2001, launch of the space shuttle Endeavour, STS-100, Canadian astronaut Chris Hadfield became the first Canada to walk in space.

Earth and Remote Sensing

Study of the earth and remote sensing has always had a strong emphasis in the Canadian space program. In 1989, CSA established the Canada Centre for Remote Sensing (CCRS) to specifically address this need. Since then, CCRS has led the way in developing a dynamic, large-scale program geared toward making earth observation data and information an operational tool for resource and environmental managers in Canada.

OSIRIS (OPTICAL SPECTROGRAPH AND INFRARED IMAGER SYSTEM)

In April 2001, Canada sent the OSIRIS (Optical Spectrograph and InfraRed Imager System) instrument onboard ODIN, a Swedish satellite. Whereas the Egyptian god Osiris presided over fertility, the agency's Dr. E.J. (Ted) Llewellyn's creation has enabled the measurement of ozone levels in a new way. With OSIRIS, scientists have been able to see how the ozone fares at various altitudes.

OSIRIS has observed how light interacts with the earth's atmosphere and how it is scattered. It also looks at the airglow, or the aurora. This has been accomplished as the array points at the earth's limb (image). The array is composed of two separate instruments—a spectrograph (views UV to visible light) and an infrared imager. The former looks at a 1 km (v) by 18 km (h) region, whereas the latter takes "images" of an area 110 km (v) by 2 km

(h). How does this help? By having a better view of the situation, we can better understand phenomena like the Antarctic's "hole." Preliminary results have shown an interesting picture indeed.

Interestingly, ODIN is not only an astronomy satellite; it is also an aeronomy (the study of the atmosphere) satellite. This concept uses similar instruments to understand both interstellar gases and our own environment. Unlike its mythological counterpart, the god of war and destruction, ODIN is also a symbol of international cooperation—a Swedish satellite incorporating technology from Canada, France and Finland; launched from Russia.

The project has a long history, which led to the building of the instrument by Routes AstroEngineering Ltd. of Kanata, with a new vision of how things should be done. Doug Degenstein, now an assistant professor of engineering physics at the University of Saskatchewan, was part of the industrial team while he was a graduate student. This allowed for more efficient and cost-effective collaboration between the scientific and industrial partners. The concept of a graduate internship also ensures that Canada is developing highly qualified personnel in an effective manner, and greatly enhances the transfer of technology between university and industry.

OSIRIS has been an integral part of the Canadian Space Agency's earth observation and space science strategies. Committed to leading the development and application of space knowledge for the benefit of Canadians and humanity, the Canadian Space Agency has been a driving force in initiatives where the skies are used to better understand and preserve our environment. Canada has had a long history of atmospheric investigations, from Sir Edward Sabine's magnetic observatory at the University of Toronto, established in 1839 to study the Northern Lights; to the launch of Alouette in 1962, which made Canada the third nation in space; to today's various projects. As a result, Dr. Llewellyn and his team at the University of Saskatchewan have continued to analyze the first years of data obtained from OSIRIS.

CANADIAN SPACE AGENCY'S TRACKING, TELEMETRY AND COMMAND (TT&C) ANTENNA

In Saint-Hubert, Quebec, there is quite a large satellite dish — the Canadian Space Agency's Tracking, Telemetry and Command (TT&C) antenna, adjacent to the agency's headquarters. It has a cousin, far away in Saskatoon; together they provide an important service to space agencies from around the world and keep an "eye" on their spacecraft.

In launching a spacecraft, particularly an unmanned one, it is of critical importance to keep track of where it's going and how it's doing, and to be able to send instructions to correct any problem. This is the job of the TT&C segment, who is responsible for keeping track of a spacecraft, receiving its telemetry (its life signs) and controlling it from the ground by sending instructions. This is done through a series of ground stations along the path of the spacecraft.

When an Ariane rocket launches from Kourou, French Guiana, to put a satellite on polar orbit, there is a "data gap" between the launch site instruments and the next station, which is in Norway. This is where the Saint-Hubert Control Centre of the CSA comes into play, by providing data on the rocket launcher and the satellite to help French engineers ensure that the satellite isn't in danger, which is of critical importance to the overall success of the mission.

Following an agreement with the French space agency (CNES), the CSA was first called into service for the launch of the ESA's EN-VISAT satellite in the spring of 2001; and more recently with SPOT-5. The TT&C station in Saskatoon is also being used to monitor satellites, as it did with CNES's SPOT-5 during its launch and early orbit phase. This phase started with the separation and release of the satellite from the launcher, followed by the deployment of a solar array that powers the satellite. The CSA continued monitoring the satellite for a period of two weeks until it safely reached its final orbit.

This tracking service, provided by the CSA since 1999, continues to allow Canadian government agencies and industry to remain leaders in the competitive market of satellite monitoring. The CSA has already put in place a new system that allows its engineers to receive data on the position of the launch vehicle in real time from Kourou. It also allows them to calculate with exact precision the pointing angles for the agency's antenna tracking system, although it has been limited to polar orbit launches.

NEXT-GENERATION RADAR SATELLITE TECHNOLOGY AND RADARSAT-2

A key priority of the Canadian Space Program's Earth Observation (EO) has been to respond to the challenge of monitoring the environment and managing the earth's natural resources. It was with the launch of RADARSAT-1 in 1995 that the CSA first entered the internationally competitive business of earth observation.

Scheduled for launch in 2004, RADARSAT-2 will be the most advanced commercial Synthetic Aperture Radar (SAR) satellite in the world. Providing data continuity to RADARSAT-1 users, it will strengthen Canada's leadership role in the design, deployment and operation of SAR technology, and will serve as a milestone in the continuing trend to privatize the earth observation business in Canada.

Representing a significant evolution from RADARSAT-1, the design of RADARSAT-2 will be the first commercial SAR satellite to offer multi-polarization — an important tool increasingly used to identify a wide variety of surface features and targets.

The satellite will carry a C-band remote sensing radar with a ground resolution ranging from three to 100 meters (9.8 to 328 feet). Swath widths may be selected in a range from 20 to 500 kilometers (12.4 to 311 miles).

RADARSAT-1-compatible beam modes will also be available to ensure continuity for existing users. Other key features of RADARSAT-2 include the ability to select all beam modes in both left and right looking modes, high downlink power, secure data and telemetry, solid-state recorders, an onboard

GPS receiver and a high-precision altitude control system.

With its state-of-the-art SAR technology, RADARSAT-2 will provide data continuity to RADARSAT-1 users over a planned lifetime of seven years. Moreover, it will contribute valuable new information on the earth's resources and the environment, especially in the fields of mapping and surveillance, which are estimated to comprise 60 percent of the total remote sensing market.

CSA has been committed to ensuring that the earth observation business in Canada develops into a world-leading, profitable and sustainable business. In the transition from a government-led activity (RADARSAT-1) to an industry-run business, RADARSAT-2 will be a major milestone. While the costs for RADARSAT-2 will be shared with the private sector, federal government investment, related to the follow-up RADARSAT missions, will continue to decrease until the program is completely privatized.

Canadians will benefit richly from the RADARSAT-2 project, which will stimulate manufacturing and competitiveness in the Canadian aerospace industry.

Responding to the specific needs of clients, RADARSAT-2 will contribute to strengthening the development of a Canadian infrastructure and services industry.

Industrial benefits in the space and earth observation sector resulting from this next-generation satellite have been estimated at $2 billion. The RADARSAT-2 program is also expected to generate nearly 3,500 person-years of employment and $1.2 billion in export sales, while spurring the growth of small- and medium-sized businesses as the Canadian infrastructure and services industry continues to grow.

The Canada Centre for Remote Sensing (CCRS) will capture data and maintain archiving systems for RADARSAT-2 imaging at their downlink facilities located in Gatineau, Quebec and Prince Albert, Saskatchewan.

MEASUREMENTS OF POLLUTION IN THE TROPOSPHERE (MOPITT)

CSA's Measurements of Pollution in the Troposphere (MOPITT) instrument will fly aboard NASA's Terra satellite to monitor the troposphere from space and provide scientists with a greater understanding of the atmosphere's most chemically complex and dynamic region.

MOPITT will be Canada's first major instrument to measure pollution of the earth's atmosphere from space. It is also the CSA's biggest contribution to the NASA earth observation system (EOS), the most ambitious study of the planet's environmental processes to date. During the scheduled five-year mission, MOPITT will continuously scan the atmosphere below it to provide the world with the first long-term, global measurements of carbon monoxide and methane gas levels in the lower atmosphere. Together with other EOS measurements, the data will help form the first long-term integrated measurements of the earth's land, air, water and life processes. The database will be used by scientists to predict long-term effects of pollution, understand the increase of ozone in the lower atmosphere, and guide the evaluation and application of shorter-term pollution controls.

MOPITT will divide the globe into approximately 1,000,000 individual cells, or "pixels," to make a measurement over each one every four days. Each pixel covers approximately 22 kilometers (14 miles) square, which is small enough to ensure that emissions from individual cities can be measured.

MOPITT will make measurements of infrared radiation originating from the surface of the planet, and isolate the energy being radiated from carbon monoxide and methane molecules by using a technique called gas correlation spectroscopy. Since the instrument will be capable of measuring infrared radiation, MOPITT will be able to collect data during the night as well as throughout the day. However, it will not be able to "see" through clouds, a limitation which will cause a gap in data for cloud-covered areas. Sophisticated models will be used to estimate values where there are data gaps due to cloud cover.

MOPITT measurements will then be analyzed and converted into maps of atmospheric composition for use by the MOPITT science team and other scientists. These maps will be produced on weekly, monthly, and annual time scales so that the effects of weather, seasons, and long-term changes can be studied and interpreted.

Space Sciences and Technology

Canada has been involved in space science research since the early 1950s. It has also been heavily involved in other scientific areas such as study of the atmospheric environment, space astronomy, space exploration and joint cooperation with the European Space Agency (ESA), as well as more recent projects geared towards the exploration and study of Mars.

SPACE LIFE SCIENCES

Space life science research in Canada began in the 1950s when scientists developed anti-gravity suits for fighter pilots. These pilots had occasionally lost consciousness during steep dives in jet planes.

In subsequent decades, Canadian scientists became experts in this type of research.

In 1983, Canada's first space experiments in life sciences were carried out in the reusable space shuttle laboratory, Spacelab.

Today, the Space Life Sciences division of the Canadian Space Agency's Space Science program studies the effects of the space environment on human physiology and other living organisms.

While artificial atmospheres are not new to human beings, as seen previously in submarines, for example, living in complete weightlessness certainly is. Under weightless conditions, the human body experiences a number of changes to the heart, circulatory system, muscles, bones, sensory systems, the system that controls balance, as well as the kidneys and regulation of body fluids.

Canada has conducted studies in calcium loss, human energy use, and muscle and bone loss in space, which has had an impact on the treatment of geriatric patients and those with cerebral palsy.

Once Canadians spend extended periods aboard the new International Space Station, space life science researchers will be able to extend their research over several months. It is expected that this will have a considerable impact on the quality of life on earth.

In preparation for these long-term space missions, as well as for possible future human expeditions to Mars, Canadian researchers are attempting to fully understand the many changes that occur in the body during space flight. These studies will prove tremendously helpful in developing methods of preventing, or minimizing, a number of the adverse physical changes experienced by astronauts.

Through clinical applications of this research, medical scientists are also making advancements in developing new methods of treating osteoporosis, muscular atrophy, balance and orientation disorders, sleep disorders and other common diseases. In addition, studies in space biotechnology will bring pharmaceutical companies closer to developing new drugs for these diseases.

ATMOSPHERIC ENVIRONMENT

Scientists have only recently come to appreciate the delicate balance that operates within the earth's atmosphere, which is chemically a very complex and dynamic region. They are also coming to understand how easily this balance can be threatened.

Life on earth depends heavily on the atmosphere and its well-being. The atmosphere provides oxygen for breathing, transports gases around the globe and protects life from too much ultraviolet radiation.

The Canadian Space Agency's Atmospheric Environment division of the Space Science program continues to participate in space-related atmospheric research and to supply the country's policymakers with accurate information in order to make informed decisions.

The Canadian government is working with the international scientific community to determine the extent and causes of atmospheric changes that threaten human health and safety. Sound and reliable data is essential to finding effective solutions to problems such as pollution, the depletion of the ozone layer and climate change.

Canadian space researchers study the earth's upper and middle atmosphere using ground- and space-based instruments in an attempt to understand the very complex processes at work in and around this region, including its chemical composition, varying winds and temperatures, and energy transfer. This is of critical concern to all Canadians in regard to the issue of pollution.

Although large urban areas have been struggling with the issue of increasingly poor air quality for some time, it now appears that rural areas are also threatened by atmospheric pollutants damaging crops and forests. Increasing populations and industrial activities have continued to erode air quality in the country.

Observed decreases in the earth's ozone layer, along with Canada's northern geography, make it one of the most vulnerable countries in the world.

A recent Canadian environmental report which reviewed the findings of Canadian ozone scientists stated that serious thinning of the Arctic ozone layer could become more frequent over the next 10 to 20 years despite international action taken to reduce ozone-destroying chemicals. Reduction in the ozone layer has been cause for alarm, since the layer is responsible for protecting us from harmful UV-B rays. Increased exposure to UV-B rays results in higher numbers of cases of skin cancer, eye damage, and weakened immune systems.

Ozone thinning continues to be a serious problem in Canada, with ozone values decreasing by an average of roughly six percent since the late 1970s, with even greater losses ranging between eight and 10 percent in the springtime. As a result of the thinning ozone layer, sunburning UV-B rays have increased by an average of about seven percent in Canada. These increased UV-B levels will affect human health, crops, forests and marine and freshwater ecosystems, and are expected to remain higher than normal for the next 30–40 years.

Canadian space scientists have been involved in a number of studies related to mon-itoring the earth's atmosphere from space. Recent projects have included Canada's participation onboard the first of NASA's new network of sophisticated multi-billion dollar satellites with an instrument that measures the global distribution of carbon monoxide and methane gases.

Canada has also been preparing to launch SCISAT-1, its first satellite in nearly 30 years, which is designed to take precise measurements of the ozone layer with a particular focus on the high northern-latitude regions.

SPACE ASTRONOMY

By placing instruments on satellites above the atmosphere, scientists can observe stars and other features of the universe by measuring light that cannot be detected on earth.

These space-based telescopes provide scientists with a whole new way of looking at the universe, allowing them to discover gas clouds, stars and aspects of planets never seen before. Astronomers have been able to discover highly energetic processes occurring in galaxies, and have been able to watch the emergence of new stars and other celestial formations using a wide range of methods to piece together evidence relating to the formation and origin of the universe.

CSA's Space Science program provides support through its space astronomy element for studies on subjects ranging from the birth of new stars to cosmic background radiation, which was found to be a direct result of the Big Bang some 15 billion years ago.

For example, in 1990, the Canadian rocket flight COBRA successfully obtained the most precise determination of the nature of this cosmic radiation using a novel and sophisticated instrument cooled to a few degrees above absolute zero.

The Space Astronomy division has also contributed scientific instruments to international astronomical satellites, providing Canadian scientists with access to scientific data in several important new areas.

In one such effort, FUSE, Canadian astronomers have been able to study ultra-violet light from distant stars, galaxies and interstellar space in order to study atoms, ions and molecules whose nature has provided critical data on the events associated with the early evolution of the universe. In conjunction with NASA, the FUSE telescope is expected to aid researchers in answering important questions about several astrophysical entities such as active galaxies and quasars, massive stars, supernovae, planetary nebulae, and the atmospheres of cool stars and planets.

The scientific instruments provided by Canada for this mission will guide the satellite to enable it to point in precisely the right direction to make exact scientific observations. Early Canadian observations related to this project were focused on the study of "hot stars," which are the massive stars that are responsible for recycling matter within their host galaxies, both from stellar winds and exploding stars called supernovae.

Another CSA collaborative project in astronomy is in the Japanese satellite program VSOP, which uses Canadian equipment to record and correlate radio signals from deep space on magnetic tape to determine the shape and location of the object transmitting those signals.

The satellite, which when used in conjunction with several large ground-based dishes will provide Canadian and other scientists with detailed pictures of stars and galaxies, uses radio waves rather than the more usual visible light.

The Canadian Space Agency will also participate in the upcoming Next Generation Space Telescope (NGST) project, led by NASA under its Origins program.

NGST will be an eight-meter (26.4 feet) class space-based telescope to be launched in the year 2010, intended to provide continuity and a new focus for research in astronomy following the success of the Hubble Space Telescope.

The primary objectives of NGST will be to study the birth of the first galaxies, the determination of the shape and fate of the universe, and the study of star and planet formation.

SPACE EXPLORATION

The Canadian Space Agency's Space Science program has its sights outward to the moon, Mars, and beyond through its newly-created Space Exploration division. Up until this time, Canada had only provided modest support for space exploration activities. However, with the newly-formed Space Exploration division, CSA now hopes to be a frequent partner in future international planetary missions.

CSA has begun the early phase of defining the scientific priorities of this new program in coordination with the scientific and technological communities across Canada. Interest in branching out into this area was brought about by the response to the growing and committed interest from this domain by numerous companies and organizations, as well as individual planetary scientists and space engineers.

Canada has recently become involved in its first interplanetary mission, an international collaboration, Destination Mars.

Canada's contribution to Mars exploration will consist of a sophisticated instrument, the Thermal Plasma Analyzer, onboard Japan's Nozomi spacecraft. The CSA instrument will explore the Martian upper atmosphere and its interaction with the solar wind, as well as the effect on this region of meteorological phenomena in the Martian lower atmosphere and its interaction with the solar wind. This region of meteorological phenomena in the Martian lower atmosphere consists of dust storms. The journey from earth will take four years, and upon arrival, the spacecraft will collect its data for one Martian year (two earth years) venturing as close as 150 km (90 miles) to the Martian surface.

Destination Mars

For the past several years, CSA has participated in programmatic and scientific planning groups (both international and NASA-led) related to Mars activities. Since Mac Evans and Dr. Marc Garneau, CSA's new president, first presented the CSA's desire to collaborate in Mars exploration to NASA in May 2001, the CSA Mars team has also been participating in NASA systems engineering teams and mission-specific planning teams.

A series of annual Canadian Space Exploration Workshops (CSEWs) have been held for the last three years, during which the scientific community has been provided with the opportunity to describe and coordinate their expertise and capabilities in the area of solar system exploration. Industry has also participated in these workshops and provided feedback on technology development and thrusts.

During the last workshop, CSEW3, held in Montreal in May 2001, Mars exploration was specifically discussed in the context of a major new Canadian Mars exploration initiative. Working groups were formed and goals and objectives were developed, presented, and summarized in a written report now available on the CSA website and published in the Canadian *Space Exploration Journal*.

Each major scientific discipline was represented at the workshop. Mars is a specific target in the solar system that fulfills a large number of scientific priorities with a wide range of disciplines. For example, the atmosphere of Mars, both neutral and ionized, gives insight into the evolution of the planet and may give us clues to predict the evolution of earth's environment. Characterizing the dust in the Martian atmosphere is interesting both scientifically and operationally, since predicting and identifying dust devils mitigates risk. The moons of Mars present a scientific mystery that harbors clues to the creation and evolution of the solar system.

The largest group represented at CSEW3 were the geologists, who joined with the astrobiologists and geophysicists. This amalgamated group developed scientific goals and investigations that demonstrated a strong Canadian interest in this discipline that lies beneath the surface of Mars. The top surface of Mars is very mobile and mixed; getting below the surface is necessary to provide a true geological characterization of the unit being studied.

The stratigraphy of the subsurface will reveal the climactic and geological history of Mars. At the higher latitudes, frozen water may exist in the relatively shallow surface. Below the oxidation layer of the surface of Mars, organic compounds may be present, indicating present or past life. Once a hole exists,

that hole can be used for studying the geophysics of the planet, to study the core and to study the seismology of Mars. The conclusions of the group were clear; drilling a hole, as deep as possible, and studying the material brought up from the depths of Mars is of the highest scientific value to the Canadian community.

The presence of the industrial community at the workshop, which includes space and non-space as well as the Canadian mining industry, was pivotal to related plans and discussions, since they were able to provide immediate feedback on the feasibility of the concepts being presented. This created a unique, self-organized partnership between science and industry, leading to concepts that benefit both communities.

Armed with these ideas, CSA began consulting with international partners, mostly focusing on NASA-led missions to Mars. A set of key potential Canadian scientific and technical contributions have been developed based on these consultations. NASA, JPL, and CSA were set up to begin a set of multilateral discussion meetings in order to begin identifying potential Canadian contributions.

Canadian astronaut Chris Hadfield has expressed great enthusiasm for possible future exploration of Mars, saying, "Since the very first vehicle landed on Mars and took some pictures sitting on the surface, Canada has in fact been involved in probes going to Mars and sensors of the Martian atmosphere and environment up there. The more we learn, I think, the more intriguing Mars is."

By 2010, robots will be roaming semiautonomously over the surface of Mars, picking up samples to be analyzed on the spot or assembling a very diverse collection to be sent back to earth so that scientists can do laboratory analyses. The robots of the Mars Smart Lander and of a hypothetical Mars Sample Return mission that NASA is planning to launch in 2009 and beyond will no doubt travel many kilometers during their useful life, exploring two or three geological zones in the course of a single mission. However, they will only be able to move over relatively flat, even terrain.

By 2020, networks of robots will explore riskier places where they stand a greater chance of finding traces of Martian life, existing or extinct. They will go down cliffs to examine the stratigraphic record and identify the subsurface geological environment. They will travel throughout the Martian landscape in search of traces of water. They may drift above the surface like hot-air balloons; this would significantly increase their range and their ability to explore various types of terrain. They may even travel in groups, joining forces to take seismic, meteorological or astronomical measurements.

It is hoped that by 2030, manned missions to Mars will begin. Robots will play a crucial role, preparing for the astronauts' arrival by building the necessary life-support infrastructure and mining the natural resources such as water, oxygen and fuel required for the return trip. They will also be valuable crew members, accompanying their human co-workers on their forays onto the Martian surface.

As an international leader in space robotics, Canada's anticipated participation in these missions seems a natural evolution of the Canadian Space Program, which will call for adaptation of existing skills and the development of new technologies. The Martian environment poses technical challenges quite different from those of the robotic operations Canada takes part in under the International Space Station Program.

The non-trivial lag in communication, which will be up to 40 minutes round-trip, makes remote guidance of robots on the Martian surface next to impossible. Because of the sheer size of the terrain to be explored, in comparison, the area of Mars is as great as the earth's entire land area, and on the rugged landscape, new approaches will be needed to keep the robotic Mars explorers moving across the planet.

With this in mind, Canada intends to develop a specific set of technologies for planetary robotics in order to steal a march on its international partners and be in a position to take advantage of the mission opportunities that are sure to come its way in years to come.

In order to orient the country's research activities in this area, a technology "roadmap" was created to identify the technologies necessary for the exploration of Mars. Six fields of research were identified: design, manipulation, locomotion, detection, intelligent systems and support technologies. For each of these fields of research, three system generations are planned, and the explorer robots are expected to grow in flexibility and autonomy with each generation. Most of the technologies needed in the short term are being developed in cooperation with Canada's aerospace and mining industries.

In consideration of national industry, the CSA has focused its internal research and development efforts on the technologies required for missions farther in the future. The Space Technologies sector has begun to undertake a research program to develop some of the technologies identified in the roadmap. These will include cooperation between a number of mobile robots to carry out a task, locating vehicles on the surface using signals from an orbiting satellite, manufacturing a robot that can go down cliffs, and using inflatable structures either to carry antennas and solar panels or to allow a robot to drift long distances on the winds of Mars.

These research and development activities will extend Canada's reputation as a leader in orbital robotics to the planetary sphere, making it an indispensable partner in the international Mars exploration program and enabling it to seize the opportunity for Canada to shine once again in space. The technologies spun from mere dreams will then be transferred to Canadian industry, which will come to fruition as the country begins to explore the Red Planet.

In September 2002, MacDonald, Dettwiler and Associates Ltd. (MDA) undertook an important feasibility study to support the CSA in defining Canada's contribution to European missions to Mars and the NASA-led Mars Science Laboratory mission. Allan Rock, minister of industry and responsible for the CSA, announced the awarding of a $400,000 contract to MDA for this study.

Landing safely on the Red Planet will be a critical element of any future Mars mission. The study performed by MDA included an assessment of the design, development and use of laser-based sensor technology to land spacecraft on the surface of Mars. As a world leader in robotic technologies, Canada will also be considering its role in the development of a robotic mining device that will extract samples of the planet's subsurface and prepare them for scientific study.

The results of this study will help define Canada's potential role in upcoming missions to Mars and will contribute to Canada's development of new knowledge and cutting-edge technologies. The MDA robotics group has studied smaller, lighter robotic technology that should provide considerable spin-off benefits to robotic applications here on earth.

CHINA

China National Space Administration (CNSA)

The People's Republic of China has come a long way in the development of rockets since its start 2,300 years ago when Chinese religious mandarins first tossed ceremonial bamboo tubes packed with gunpowder into festival fires to drive off evil spirits.

Between 300 B.C. and A.D. 1000, "fire arrows" were used in China, although historians are not sure if these were actually rockets or more conventional burning arrows. Eventually, however, firecrackers did evolve into rockets, with sulphur, saltpeter and charcoal, used in making gunpowder, forming the earliest known solid fuel for rockets. By 1045, gunpowder rockets became important weapons in China's military arsenal.

The Sung Dynasty improved gunpowder projectiles in the thirteenth century with new explosive grenades and cannons that were used to hold off growing Mongolian hordes. Fire arrows repelled Mongol invaders at the battle of Kai-fung-fu in 1232.

Old records show the huge Chinese gunpowder rockets carried iron shrapnel and incendiary material, and may have utilized the first combustion-chamber "iron pots" to direct thrust. The noise from the blast-off of a fire arrow was so powerful that it could be heard for 15 miles, and its impact demolished everything within half a mile.

China's first long-range military ballistic missiles, and later space rockets, were developed by Tsein Weichang, an immigrant to the United States from China. Tsein Weichang was educated in Canada. He later worked for the U.S. government at the Jet Propulsion Laboratory, Pasadena, California, only to be forced back to his homeland in 1949 in America's spasm of anti-communist witch hunting.

Mao Zedong revolutionized the ancient territory of China after his Communist victory in 1949. Mao's People's Republic of China (PRC) opened its first Missile and Rocket Research Institution on October 8, 1956. At that time the PRC was on friendly terms with the former USSR.

Hindered by what China today calls "technical blockades put in by the imperialist countries," there was very little in the way of rocket development until the 1960s, when experiments with liquid-fuel rockets picked up momentum. Satellites, and the space rockets needed to carry them to orbit, were designed.

The People's Republic of China launched its first satellite, which was known as China 1 or Mao 1, to earth orbit on its own Long March space rocket on April 24, 1970. The 390-lb. electronic ball floated around the earth playing the patriotic song "The East Is Red."

Since then, China has made scores of successful satellite launches. They have included remote sensing, communications and weather satellites for both civilian and military use. Satellites have also been launched for paying foreign owners.

In November 1975, the first Long March 2 rocket carried China's first homing satellite to orbit, making China the third nation capable of retrieving a satellite. Since then, China has sent a number of satellites to orbit with packages to be retrieved from space. The pace of China's space industry picked up in the 1980s and 1990s. In September 1981, the PRC successfully launched three satellites into orbit with one rocket.

In 1999, China launched and recovered an unmanned capsule designed to carry men and women into orbit in the twenty-first century. This capsule was named Shenzhou.

China's Satellites

The launch of China 1, or Mao 1, in 1970, made China the fifth nation with a space rocket. It is believed that before this first successful launch, the Chinese may have experienced a launch failure in 1969. They may have also suffered three failures in 1974 and another in 1979.

China, as a nation, has made scores of successful satellite launches since 1970. By the end of 2001, China had launched nearly 50 satellites, with a 90 percent success rate. The spacecraft have included remote sensing, communications and weather satellites for both civilian and military use.

In 1986, China started selling commercial space launches to foreign satellite owners during a time when U.S. shuttles and European rockets were grounded. Numerous satellites have been launched for paying foreign owners in several countries. China's commercial space launch firm is the Great Wall Industrial Corp.

China launched Pakistan's first satellite to a 375-mile-high circular orbit on July 16, 1990. The satellite, Badr-A, was launched aboard the maiden flight of the Long March 2E rocket from Xichang Launch Center in China. Following 146 days in space, Badr-A fell into the atmosphere and burned.

Western Union's Westar 6 satellite and the Indonesian satellite Palapa B2 were carried to orbit in 1984 by the space shuttle Challenger before the shuttle's destruction in January, 1986. Palapa and Westar were dropped off in orbits lower than planned, which resulted in failure for both satellites. Later that year, the pair were recaptured by astronauts spacewalking from the space shuttle Discovery. They were returned to earth and rebuilt later on the ground.

The retrieved Westar 6 was renamed AsiaSat and launched by China using a Long March rocket, becoming the first American satellite sent to orbit by a non–Western country.

In 2000, Beijing orbited its first high-resolution electro-optical imaging satellite, which relays its state-of-the-art digital pictures by radio to ground stations. In earlier history, Chinese satellites snapped pictures on photographic film, which then was dropped down to earth in canisters.

The resolution of the digital-imaging satellite has been less than the capability of the sharpest U.S. military reconnaissance satellites, but comparable to the sharp images produced by U.S. and European commercial satellites, which produce pictures with a resolution of about nine feet.

The Chinese satellite, named Ziyuan-2 (ZY-2), has been able to produce photographs showing objects ranging in size down to nine feet across — a resolution more than three times the capability of China's earlier earth sensing satellite, Ziyuan-1 (ZY-1). ZY-2 is lower in orbit than ZY-1, which also means the satellite can offer higher resolution. When this satellite was launched from the Taiyuan Satellite Launching Center in the northern Shanxi Province, the official Xinhua news agency called it the Ziyuan-2 (ZY-2) and described it as a civilian remote sensing spacecraft. Ziyuan means resource in Chinese.

Earth sensing satellites monitor environmental changes and explore for natural resources on the ground. Xinhua announced that the satellite would be employed mostly for territorial surveying, city planning, crop yield assessment, disaster monitoring and space science experimentation.

Ziyuan-2 (ZY-2) has secretly been designated by Chinese government officials as Jianbing-3. It is believed that this photo-reconnaissance satellite will be eventually used for planning combat missions, targeting missiles at U.S. forces in Japan, or preparing aircraft strikes on Taiwan, an island nation that Beijing claims as a province of China.

Jianbing-3 continues to complete an elliptical orbit around the earth every 94.3 minutes, at an altitude ranging from 294 to 305 miles.

Built by the Chinese Academy of Space Technology, the Jianbing-3 spacecraft is expected to work for two years in orbit.

China launched its first military communications satellite in January 2000, as part of a People's Liberation Army command-and-control network linking forces for combat. China plans to launch more high-technology space platforms, including even-higher-resolution imagery satellites, electronic signals intelligence (SIGINT) satellites and military communications satellites.

Today, however, Chinese satellite technology serves not only military purposes, but also many areas of the national economy. Future satellites are expected to be especially useful in developing the remote western areas of China.

Over the next five years, China is planning to launch at least 35 different science and application satellites, according to Xinhua News Agency. The satellites would be used for communications and direct-to-home broadcasting, meteorological and oceanographic observations, navigation and positioning, disaster mitigation, and seed breeding.

China Aerospace Science and Technology Corporation (CASC) is a large, state-owned enterprise that builds five different series of satellites as a space contractor for CNSA. These include Dongfanghong communications satellites, Fengyun weather satellites, Shijian science exploration satellites, Ziyuan remote sensing earth resource satellites, Beidou navigation satellites, retrievable satellites, and other types of satellites.

Another CNSA contractor, the Chinese Academy of Space Technology (CAST), has been working on some of the satellites, such as a polar-orbiting sun-synchronous weather satellite FY-1D, and the oceanographic satellite Haiyang-1, with others are in planning the

planning stages. These include a direct-broadcasting satellite (DBS) that is being prepared for launch in 2004. This particular satellite would provide television broadcasts and educational and information transmissions, as well as other services, to the vast expanse of western China.

China's National Satellite Meteorological Center (NSMC) has announced the nation's plans to launch six more Fengyun (FY) meteorological satellites from 2002–2007, before the Olympiad in 2008, according to the Beijing *Evening Post*.

Fengyun means wind and cloud in Chinese. The first of the six was the polar-orbiting sun-synchronous Fengyun-1D (FY-1D), which was launched in 2002 on a Changzheng-4 (Long March 4) rocket. Next, a geostationary weather satellite, FY-2C, has been scheduled for launch in late 2003.

The FY-3 series would be the next generation of polar-orbiting sun-synchronous weather satellites. FY-3A will be launched in 2004 with FY-3B and FY-2D in 2006, and FY-3C in 2008. These satellites were designed to work for two to three years in space.

NSMC is a scientific research and operational facility that is also affiliated with the China Meteorological Administration (CMA). It receives processes and distributes satellite weather data to users.

The new satellites will forecast conditions and monitor bad weather around the clock, particularly convective rainstorms, thunderstorms and hailstorms. They will also monitor developing sandstorms, as well as air quality, and provide early warnings. The satellites to be launched in 2006 and 2008 will help forecasters predict weather for the Olympics.

For China, meteorological satellites are important in predicting the weather, but also in oceanography, agriculture, forestry, hydrology, aviation, navigation, environmental protection and national defense. They continue to contribute to the national economy, and to preventing and mitigating disasters.

China refers to its communications satellites as Dongfanghong (DFH). Dongfanghong means "East is Red" in Chinese. China's next generation of large communications satellites will carry C-, Ku-, Ka- and L-band transponders. This increased capacity will help the nation meet a growing demand for educational and commercial television broadcasts, stationary and mobile telecommunications, and data, voice and video transmissions for businesses.

China's Haiyang (HY-1 and HY-2) oceanographic microsatellites will carry radar altimeters, microwave scatterometers, ocean color scanners, and multichannel microwave radiometers for realtime views of oceans and coastal zones for monitoring biological resources, pollution monitoring and prevention, and monitoring of estuaries, bays and navigation routes. Haiyang is Chinese for ocean.

Two satellites are scheduled for launch on Changzheng-4 (Long March 4) rockets into 500-mile-high circular sun-synchronous orbits, crossing the equator near noon local time and passing over places on earth every two to three days.

The Chinese have a very strong interest in seed-breeding satellites, to supplement the country's heavy dependence on agriculture. Chinese scientists claim that seeds exposed to cosmic radiation yield superior quality produce. They would like to cultivate seedlings in space and then grow them in the climate of western China to help develop agriculture there. China's first satellite dedicated to seed breeding may fly by 2004. The satellite will house a variety of seeds and expose them to radiation before returning them to earth. China refers to its remote sensing earth resource satellites as Ziyuan (ZY). Ziyuan means resource in Chinese. The first satellite in this series was the China-Brazil Earth Resources Satellite (CBERS-1 or ZY-1). Later models will be able to take higher resolution photos and work longer in space. Scientists plan to use the ZY satellites to survey national resources, monitor crop growth and yields, watch for disasters and environmental pollution, and evaluate project sites. They are used for city planning, surveying and cartography.

Other retrievable satellites are used to conduct experiments in space life science, space environment, and space materials and new technologies. China refers to its science exploration satellites as Shijian (SJ), which means practice in Chinese.

A key cooperative satellite project is the Double Star Satellite in conjunction with the European Space Agency (ESA), which will launch in 2003. A pair of Double Star Project (DSP) satellites will study the effects of the sun on the earth's environment.

Ten European instruments will be installed inside each of the two Chinese Double Star spacecraft. These will complement ESA's four Cluster spacecraft already in space. An additional eight science experiments will be provided by Chinese institutes.

One of the Chinese satellites will fly an equatorial orbit. The other will be in a polar orbit. They will make observations of the magnetosphere.

The ten European instruments in Double Star will be identical to those aboard the four Cluster satellites. Chinese and European scientists hope all six satellites will be operational at the same time so they can coordinate data received from Cluster and Double Star. Studies with similar instruments are expected to increase the scientific return.

The equatorial satellite DSP-1 will be launched on a Changzheng-2C (Long March 2C) rocket from Xichang in south Sichuan province sometime late 2003. Six months later, another Changzheng-2C will ferry the polar satellite DSP-2 from Taiyuan in the Shanxi province west of Beijing.

China also plans to launch a Space Solar Telescope. The one-meter aperture telescope will be sent into a sun-synchronous polar orbit in 2005 to observe phenomena on the sun during daytime hours.

The nation's space agency has also been planning a constellation of four optical and four synthetic aperture radar (SAR) microsatellites to carry out round-the-clock, all-weather surveillance of the environment and disasters.

Two optical satellites and one synthetic aperture radar (SAR) microsatellite will be launched as search and rescue satellites. They will fly over a place on the ground every 32 hours.

China also plans to launch its Beidou Navigation Test Satellites (BNTS). Beidou refers to the northern dipper, the celestial constellation.

Long March Launch Vehicles

Long March 1 (CZ-1) was the first rocket sent to space on April 24, 1970. The three-stage Long March 1, in service since 1970, is 97 ft. tall and 7 ft. in diameter. It can carry 661 lbs. to a circular 273 mile-high orbit. Long March 2 (CZ-2) was first fired on July 26, 1975. The two-stage Long March 2, used since 1975, is 107 ft. tall and 11 ft. in diameter.

Long March 3 (CZ-3) was first used on August 19, 1983. The three-stage Long March 3, in use since 1983, is 142 ft. tall and 11 ft. in diameter. It can lift a 3,086-lb. payload to a 120-mi. geosynchronous transfer orbit.

Long March 4 (CZ-4) was first launched on September 6, 1988. The Chinese have sustained several launch failures over the years.

Today, China's workhorse series of space boosters is the Long March 4. It can lift 11,000 lbs., or over five tons, to a low orbit, using the same first and second stages as a Long March 3. The Long March 4 uses a different third stage for shots to low and medium altitude orbits, carrying more than 8,000 lbs.

With 600,000-lbs. thrust, Long March 4 can lift 5,000 lbs. to stationary orbit. This is nearly double the previously-most-powerful Long March 3, in use since 1983. Long March 3 can lift 2,800 lbs. to stationary orbit, or 6,000 lbs. to a low orbit. A Long March 2 can ferry a satellite of less than 2.5 tons to a low-earth orbit.

China first used a Long March 4 to launch a heavy weather satellite to stationary orbit from Taiyuan in 1988. Great Wall Industrial Corporation, which sells launch services, uses the larger rocket to draw more foreign customers for commercial satellite launches.

On September 6, 1988, China achieved an interesting space achievement. This consisted of the inaugural use of a third space launch site in north-central China at Taiyuan, Shanxi Province, south of Beijing; the maiden voyage of a new heavy-lifting Long March 4 space booster rocket; and the first launch of a 1,650-lb. Feng Yun 1 weather satellite to a 560-mile-high polar orbit.

Similar to U.S. NOAA weather satellites,

Feng Yun 1 had infrared and visible light sensors. Feng Yun 1 was designed to communicate radio data on clouds, ocean surface temperatures, marine water color, earth's surface, vegetation growth, and ice and snow cover to ground stations around the world. It transmitted pictures to earth on a frequency of 137.78 MHz. Unfortunately, Feng Yun 1 encountered problems and tumbled out of control.

On December 19, 1988, China offered another launch for its record book when it hit a space double header. The PRC launched a new space rocket from a new space center on southern Hainan Island.

The new rocket, known as Weaver Girl 1, named after a Chinese legend, ferried a recoverable satellite to space. The payload remained in space two and a half hours, returning to earth 40 miles from the launch site. The blast off was the first time Chinese scientists had researched earth's atmosphere from a low-latitude equatorial launch site.

Weaver Girl 1 was developed by the Chinese Academy of Sciences and the University of Defense Science and Technology.

China, the world's most populous nation, launches its Long March rockets from four major space complexes. These include the Jiuquan launch site in the northern Gobi Desert in far-western China, not far from Mongolia; the Taiyuan launch site in Shanxi Province, 60 miles southwest of Beijing, in north-central China; the Xichang launch site in an isolated corner of Sichuan province in southern China, not far from Burma, Laos and Vietnam; and the Hainan Spaceport on Hainan Island off the southern coast of China, separating the South China Sea from the Gulf of Tongking. Only 19° north of the equator, it is southeast of Hanoi, Vietnam, across the Gulf of Tongking.

All of the sites are remote and usually closed to foreigners, although the press was taken to the Xichang Satellite Center in 1988 as China was pressing the United States for approval of its launch business.

The Hainan Space Base, only 19° north of the equator, is used for low-latitude, low-altitude space research launches. Initially, rockets blasting off from Hainan flew only to a height of about 74 miles above earth.

The Xichang Launch Center is in hilly farm country in an isolated corner of Sichuan province in southwestern China. China launched Pakistan's Badr-A satellite from Xichange in 1990, on the then-new Long March 2E rocket.

Long March 2E was designed to lift 15,000 lbs. to a low elliptical orbit ranging from 250 to 500 miles above earth. The rocket, also called Cluster Carrier, blasted off from a new pad built to launch bigger boosters. Long March 2E, with four boosters strapped on, carried a large Australian dummy satellite and the 150-lb. Badr-A.

In all, China has developed more than 10 kinds of launch vehicles, including the LM-2, FB-1, LM-2C, LM-2D, LM-2E, LM-2F, LM-3, LM-A, LM-3A, LM-3B, LM-3C, LM-4A, and LM-4B. Since 1970, China's launch vehicles have made more than 60 flights and sent over 70 satellites into space, including 27 foreign satellites. The success rate for launch has been 90 percent. Since 1996, the Long March launch vehicle family has made 23 consecutive successful flights, a record rare not only in the history of China's space industry, but also in the world's space launch arena.

Shenzhou Manned and Unmanned Spacecraft

China's development of its manned spacecraft technology began in the early 1990s and continues to today. On November 20, 1999, China's Shenzhou experimental spacecraft, named by President Jiang Zemin, made a successful maiden voyage into space and ventured to earth on November 21, 1999. It is now China's aim to become the third country to launch manned spacecraft, behind the United States and Russia.

The Chinese National Manned Space Program has been referred to by the Chinese as Project 921.

The spacecraft transport are called *Shenzhou*, which is said to mean in Chinese either sacred vessel, magic vessel, vessel of the gods, divine craft, divine mechanism, or divine vessel. Shenzhou may also be a play on the name *China*.

Dome-shaped in design, Shenzhou looks very similar to a Russian Soyuz capsule. The early Soyuz design of 1962 was likened to the General Electric Company's proposal for America's Apollo capsule. The Russian Soyuz is currently used to carry cosmonauts and astronauts to and from the International Space Station, Alpha.

The Shenzhou spacecraft consists of a forward orbital module, a re-entry capsule, and an aft service module. The orbital module has a hatch where the Chinese astronauts or "yuhangyuans," or "talkonauts," can exit for a spacewalk (EVA). Shenzhou is slightly larger than a Soyuz, which can seat up to three persons. China intends to use Shenzhou to carry up to four yuhangyuans.

Shenzhou spacecraft have flown in altitudes from 122 to 207 miles (196 to 334 km). They are built by the state-run China Aerospace Science and Technology Corporation, and may be used eventually for a Chinese manned space station.

Shenzhou spacecraft are blasted off from the isolated Jiuquan Satellite Launch Center in northwest Gansu province, located in the Gobi Desert, one thousand miles west of the capital city of Beijing.

Shenzhou launches and landings occur during northern hemisphere autumn and winter months when the seas are calmer for the Yuanwang tracking ships stationed on oceans around the world. In contrast, sea conditions are very poor during the southern hemisphere autumn and winter months.

There have been four unmanned Shenzhou flights via new Long March 2F (CZ-2F) rockets from the Jiuquan spaceport, with the last three staying in space for an average of seven days.

Shenzhou 1 was launched on November 20, 1999, and made 14 orbits around the earth. It carried a dummy yuhangyuan, experimental seeds, commemorative stamps, national flags, and a banner with signatures of participating engineers and scientists. The descent module landed on November 21, in inner Mongolia.

Shenzhou 2 lifted off on January 9, 2001, and completed 107 orbits around the earth. It carried a monkey, a dog, a rabbit, some snails, gamma ray burst detectors, and 64 scientific payloads. The spacecraft maneuvered in orbit three times, landing after seven days in inner Mongolia.

During its week-long voyage, experiments on space life environment, space materials, space astronomy and physics, as well as voice transmission had been conducted on the spacecraft.

Shenzhou 3 was launched on March 25, 2002. It completed 107 orbits around the earth carrying a dummy yuhangyuan, and landed after seven days in inner Mongolia. Life science experiments onboard included a box of eggs from a black-bone chicken, tightly packed two days after being laid. The eggs, which were of top quality breed free of industrial pollution, were hatched following their return to earth. Black-bone chicken has been a traditional breed of high economic importance to China. The experiment was aimed to study the influence of the space environment on embryo growth, inheritance and breed selection. Other experiments involving life sciences, space materials, astronomy, physics and microgravity research were completed aboard the spacecraft.

Shenzhou 4 was launched on December 29, 2002. It completed 108 revolutions around the earth carrying a dummy yuhangyuan and 52 science payloads. The craft landed seven days after liftoff in inner Mongolia. Before Shenzhou 4 was sent to the launch pad, Chinese astronauts had trained on it and helped to improve living conditions aboard the craft for future missions. Equipment aboard Shenzhou was also rearranged to make astronauts feel more comfortable to live and work in the capsule. Shenzhou 4 has been seen as the dress rehearsal for Shenzhou 5 which China has planned to send its first people into orbit.

Shenzhou 5 is scheduled for late 2003. This will be the first manned flight from the world's most populous nation, the People's Republic of China. The 12 yuhangyuans, who had been selected from 2,000 middle-ranking Air Force pilots, were on hand to witness the SZ-3 liftoff as well as to test an emergency bailout system on the pad.

This emergency exercise required testing of the ability of the yuhangyuans to quickly exit Shenzhou through the escape hatch. They then continued through to safety down the eight-story tunnel in order to reach a bunker under the pad in under one minute.

Shenzhou 5 is scheduled to carry the first Chinese astronauts selected from the Peoples Liberation Army (PLA), air force jet fighter pilots who have been training for the mission for several years.

CUBA

Cuba in Space

The first Hispanic man in space was Cuban cosmonaut, Arnold Tomayo Mendez, in 1980. He was a member of an eight-day mission to the Russian Salyut 6 station. The second non–Warsaw Pact and second third-world cosmonaut, his mission was to grow organic monocrystals in space from Cuban sugar.

Cuba has continued to develop its space-related activities in recent years in spite of the country's difficult economic conditions, and has managed to become a notable presence in space.

In the area of remote sensing and the environment, in collaboration with the European Space Agency (ESA), high-resolution radar space images from ERS-1 and ERS-2 have been processed to form part of the project entitled "Applications of the ERS-1 and ERS-2 radar satellite images at the research stations of the Golfo de Batabano-Isla de la Juventud-Archipielago de Los Canarreos." The digital processing of the satellite images was completed, along with others obtained by different means, for the purpose of producing satellite maps of the region under study. The satellite maps have been used to gather information of interest to the municipal geographic information system (GIS) being assembled on the Isla de la Juventud, as well as for other research purposes and thematic cartography.

A project in collaboration with Mexico incorporates remote sensing applications and GIS capabilities in the investigation and thematic cartography of the natural resources of the coastal zones and marine platform of Cuba and Mexico.

An operational system for sugar cane crop monitoring, called System pour d'observation de la Terre (SPOT), and radar satellite images of a specific agricultural area has been in place for the purpose of permitting subsequent coverage of the entire country.

The National Forestry Inventory of Cuba continues work on a methodology, based on satellite images, which permits the operation of an early warning system for forest fires.

Research has also been conducted for quantitative determination of the surface temperature of the sea and of marine chlorophyll concentration using satellite images, with a view to applying this technique in the fisheries industry as well as environmental research and conservation.

An extremely important role in weather forecasting and monitoring has been played by geostationary and circumpolar satellite images, which enable researchers to obtain information from zones in the Caribbean, the Gulf of Mexico and the Atlantic that lack meteorological stations. Satellite data, combined with ground observations, are used in daily weather forecasting and monitoring, information supply to cyclone watch organizations, and the issuance of special warnings by the Cuban Institute of Meteorology.

In the space sciences, Cuba has engaged in sun observation programs using optical and radio-astronomical methods, and the relaying of the data collected to centers throughout the world. This research focused on solar activity of a geo-effective nature through the determination and description of coronal mass ejections (CMEs), the working hypothesis proposed being the differentiated generation of solar protons. Results were compiled in a CME catalogue detailing the magnetic conditions in which such ejections originated, and establishing the dynamic characteristics of CMEs in relation to their origin. Manifestations of solar variability were studied according to climactic parameters recorded in Havana, yielding a high correlation between the behavior of average temperature and Soviet Socialist Republics space flight, a pressure in relation to the length of the solar cycle.

In commemoration of the twentieth anniversary of the joint Cuba-Union, a ceremony was held in September 2000. Cosmonaut Arnaldo Tamayo Mendez served as a keynote speaker.

CZECH REPUBLIC

Czech Republic in Space

Space research began in Czechoslovakia in 1968 with the Interkosmos program. On October 14, 1969, the first satellite with Czechoslovakian instruments, Interkosmos 1, was launched from the Kapustin Yar launch site. It carried instruments for solar soft-X measurement and observation of the aerosol layers in the atmosphere during sunset on the earth.

The first Czech X-ray photometer flew aboard Prognoz 5 in 1975. In 1985, seven of eleven instruments on board the Prognoz 10 satellite were from Czechoslovakia. Two others were from Russia, with the remaining serving as joint efforts between the two countries.

Shortly thereafter, Czech scientists and

Satellites have long been part of the Czech space program. Here is a computer-generated image of the MTI satellite in orbit. (Frantisek Farnik/Czech Space Agency)

engineers constructed the most complex space equipment ever made in Czechoslovakia, the automatic stabilized platform (ASP). Russian scientists used the ASP on their Vega probes during investigations of Halley's comet and Venus. In 1989, the ASP was installed on board the MIR space station.

In 1970, a laser for use in space geodesy was developed by the Czech Technical University. This laser enabled the transmission of reflected laser signals from geodesy satellites in orbit.

Three years later, the prototype of a mobile laser was completed and moved to Egypt following three months of measurements in Riga.

The 1980s brought the implementation of a new generation of mobile laser stations, which served around the world in countries such as South America, Asia, Hungary, and Russia.

Several space flight research projects were conducted at Czechoslovak medical and biological research institutes. The Slovak Academy of Sciences' Institute of Farm Animal Physiology examined the effects of weightlessness on the embryo development of birds.

The institute installed an incubator with the eggs of Japanese quails on the Russian Kosmos 1129 Satellite which spent several weeks in space in 1979. A few years later, the same experiments were repeated aboard the MIR orbital station.

In 1978, the first Czech man went into space. Vladimir Remek spent seven days on board the Russian Salyut 6 orbital station, making Czechoslovakia the third nation to have a citizen in space.

Remek took along several experiments, including one from the Trebon Laboratory, where algae cultures were expected to reproduce in space for the first time ever. The materials research laboratory of the Physics Institute of the Czechoslovak Academy of

Sciences contributed an experiment to study the effect of weightlessness on the process of solidification and the physical properties of new materials. A team of researchers at the Biophysical Institute of the Czechoslovak Academy of Sciences in Brno studied the sensitivity of living organisms in irradiation, developing an instrument called an oxymeter to measure the quantity of oxygen in the blood. A weightlessness experiment developed by researchers from Purkyne University in Brno observed the changes in the thin air layer surrounding the human body using a special instrument, an electric dynamic catathermometer.

Following political changes in the former Czechoslovakia in 1990, the country began to formerly participate in ESA and NASA programs. In November 1996, a formal agreement was signed between the Czech Republic and ESA which increased opportunities for the active participation of Czech scientists and researchers in international space activities.

These activities include astronomical studies, magnetospheric, ionospheric and atmospheric research, remote sensing with earth observation, microgravity research experiments, and small satellite construction.

The Institute of Atmospheric Physics (IAP) is a part of the Academy of Sciences of the Czech Republic, which cooperates with other research institutions in the field of space science. Formerly the Geophysics Institute, the main focus was on the processes taking place in the troposphere, the lowest, densest part of the earth's atmosphere in which most weather changes occur and temperature generally decreases rapidly with altitude. It extends from the earth's surface to the bottom of the stratosphere.

In 1994, the Geophysical Institute became the IAP and expanded its research domain to cover the entire atmosphere, from the boundary layer up to interplanetary space.

Main research topics now include study of the atmospheric boundary layer processes, their mathematical modeling and measurements; mesoscale meteorological processes; precipitation measurements and forecasting and atmospheric effects on radiowave propa-

gation; atmospheric processes affecting the operation of a wind turbine; climate variability and climate change; ozone depletion research and physics of the middle atmosphere; study of the ionosphere and magnetosphere; and space plasma physics and solar-terrestrial relations.

This research is being conducted by use of very small, scientific satellites designed to investigate the complex nature of the earth's magnetosphere and ionosphere and are commonly referred to as Magion (MAGnetospheric and IONospheric) satellites. Magion satellites are launched as piggyback spacecraft designed to carry out their experiments in conjunction with a mother satellite. Magion 1, with a mass of only 15 kg (33 lb), was launched in October 1978, with Interkosmos, to monitor low frequency propagation in Low Earth Orbit (LEO) from an initial orbit of only 400 km by 775 km (248 by 482 mi) using a high inclination of 83 degrees.

Magion 2 was launched in September 1989, with Interkosmos 24, to investigate very low frequency (VLF) propagations in the magnetosphere and their interaction with energetic particles in the earth's radiation belts at an orbit of 505 by 2,490 km (314 by 1547 mi) with an 83 degree inclination. Magion 2 also carried a Soviet Pulsar maneuvering system to regulate the distance between the sub-satellite and its companion spacecraft, although the mission did not succeed.

Magion 3 was launched in 1991 with Interkosmos 25 under the Active Plasma Experiment (APEKS) program. Nearly identical to Magion 2, Magion 3 recorded the effects in the magnetosphere of electron and Xenon ion beams injected by Interkosmos 25. The pulsar engine used performed well on this mission, lasting nine months at an orbit of 440 by 3,070 km with an inclination of 83 degrees.

The Magion satellites were a part of the Interball project. Magion 4 was placed in orbit in 1995 as the Interball Tail Probe Subsatellite at an altitude of 193,000 km (115,800 mi). Magion 5 was launched as the Interball Auroral Probe Subsatellite at an altitude of 20,000 km (12,000 mi) and went out of control shortly after, ceasing to transmit telemetry data due to a shortage of power.

Open Czech small satellite MIMOSA which contains only one scientific instrument, a microac-celerometer. (Frantisek Farnik/Czech Space Agency)

Both satellites were launched with simple analog cosine law sun sensors with Magion 5 still in orbit. These sensors were small, low mass, and equipped with photocell assemblies.

The Magion satellites were launched in cooperation with Austria, Hungary, Russia, and the Ukraine. Additional contributions of scientific instruments and sensors were made by the Czech Republic, Bulgaria, France, Hungary, Poland, Romania, Russia, and the Slovak Republic. The Institute of Atmospheric Physics (IAP) was the chief designer and producer.

The MIMOSA project entailed measurements of the effect of the atmosphere on the dynamics of a satellite using a micro-accelerometer for recording of satellite accelerations.

The cube-shaped accelerometer was developed by IAP in cooperation with specialists from the Czech army's optics division and was named MACEK (MikroAkCElerometer). It was 30 mm (1.18 in) and was completed in 1991.

The Taurus rocket which launched the MTI placing it in orbit. (Frantisek Farnik/Czech Space Agency)

MACEK underwent testing on board the Soviet satellite Resurs F15 during a three-week flight in 1992. The instrument then passed high-altitude rocket tests at the NASA Marshall Space Flight Center and flew aboard the space shuttle Atlantis Mission STS-79 along with United States accelerometers in September 1996.

The objectives of the experiment onboard the shuttle were to perform three-axial acceleration measurements. These measurements determined the action of atmospheric pressure while the crew was asleep.

The private Czech firm Space Devices is continuing to manufacture small MIMOSA (Micro Measurements of Satellite Acceleration) satellites designed to carry very sensitive accelerometers similar to the ones used in previous missions. The body will be 60 cm (24 in) in diameter and polyhedron in shape, weighing approximately 45 kg (100 lb).

The core of the experimental device will be an electrostatically compensated three-axial microaccelerometer with sensitivity reaching the 10^{-11} ms^{-2} level. The project will focus on the detailed study of dynamical effects of satellite surface forces.

The Czech accelerometer will also be used by Alabama University in the United States for determining vibrations onboard the International Space Station (ISS).

IAP is continuing to update its activities in the field of small satellite development and is developing new sensors, instruments and systems for future scientific projects. One is the MIMOSA 3 project, for which IAP will supply new sensors, housekeeping systems and ground station services. Other projects in the proposal stages include M2S, survey of anthropogenic electromagnetic radiation; EMEC, electromagnetic monitoring of the European continent; and COLLISA-2, small spacecraft for the interstellar atoms composition studies.

The M2S mission will be a study in response to the growing danger of exposure to environmental radiation from anthropogenic radiation sources. Assessment of radiation amounts, exposure monitoring, and mapping are among the mission's objectives.

Solar research is another interest of the Czech Space Agency. Here is the Czech-made hard X-Ray Spectrometer for solar research, which was launched onboard the U.S. Air Force satellite MTI, on March 12, 2000, and continued to operate until February 2003.

The Institute of Atmospheric Physics and PO Polyot (Russia) signed a contract to design, develop and launch five EMEC satellites to measure man-made disturbances in the ionosphere.

The COLLISA-2, Small Spacecraft for the Interstellar Atoms Composition Studies, is part of an astrophysical experiment that was carried out in cooperation with the Space Research Institute (IKI) of the Russian Academy of Sciences, for the purpose of directly studying the isotopic composition of two neutral components of interstellar matter — Helium, He, and Neon, Ne. This study is yielding new knowledge about processes that occur outside our Solar System.

DENMARK

Danish Space Research Institute (DSRI)

The Danish Space Research Institute (DSRI) is a descendant of the Ionosphere Laboratory at the Technical University of Denmark. In 1966, the laboratory was divided into two parts to include a department that later separated as DSRI, which was concerned with experiments in space, and a second part that dealt with ground-based studies of the ionosphere, becoming the Geophysics Department of the Danish Meteorological Institute (DMI).

During the first years of its existence, DSRI activities were directed towards cosmic ray research and magnetosphere physics. Studies in magnetosphere physics were carried out in a natural cooperation with DMI within those scientific areas that also could be studied by means of ground-based instrumentation. This principal division of the Danish space research into satellite, rocket, and ground-based experiments was confirmed by the decision of a governmental committee established in 1979. As a result, all space related instrumentation work, including the development of magnetometers for sounding rockets and satellites, was transferred to DSRI. DMI has continued to handle ground-based observations, supplemented by the research required to maintain the quality and scientific relevance of the monitoring programs.

Since then, the primary scientific focus of the DSRI activities has moved towards X-ray astronomy. Compared to the size and available resources of the institute, DSRI embarked on a very large project — the delivery of crucial parts of the largest instrument, SODART (Soviet-Danish X-ray telescope) of the Russian SPECTRUM RG mission. The resources needed for the Danish contribution to this ambitious project, combined with a decrease in basic funding for the institute in the beginning of the nineties, forced the former board of the institute to concentrate on astrophysics, and hence abandon the activities in plasma physics. The magnetometer development was, however, continued in cooperation with a group at the Technical University of Denmark.

Today, the key science areas of DSRI include the study of time variation of the emission of light from compact objects and the structure and development of galaxies and clusters of galaxies.

DSRI has a long and respected track record in the development of focusing X-ray optics and X-ray detectors. In 1999, an agreement between the ESA and DSRI was reached on the delivery of the mirror systems to the Planck Surveyor mission. As a result, DSRI continues to maintain access to new observations of the cosmic microwave background radiation and the sources in the foreground (galaxies and clusters of galaxies) that will result from the all-sky monitoring conducted by the Planck Surveyor satellite.

As a part of its solar systems research, DSRI has continued to conduct studies into magnetic fields around planets (including earth) and in the interplanetary space; the physics of the heliosphere, particularly the relationship between the solar surface processes and the electrodynamic properties of the environment of planets; and the magnetic properties of the surface of Mars.

Solar System Physics

Solar system physics has been a relatively new research area at DSRI, which feels it is of critical importance in the understanding of the physical processes in our sun-earth environment.

DSRI has actively continued to focus on waves, electric and magnetic fields and charged particles in the magnetosphere and in the ionosphere as demonstrated by the institute's strong involvement in experiments onboard the ESA's satellites ESRO 1, HEO 2, GEO 1 and 2, and Cluster; and the Swedish satellite, Viking.

DSRI has emphasized magnetometer development and cooperated with the Technical University of Denmark on advanced sensor technology based on stress-annealed amorphous magnetic metal. This collaboration has resulted in world leadership in high precision space magnetometry, illustrated by the success of the Orsted satellite and the inclusion of Danish instruments on board the Argentine-U.S. satellite, SAC-C, as well as the German CHAMP satellite.

Today, DSRI has a three-focus research strategy, including the study of magnetic fields around planets including earth, and in the interplanetary space; the physics of the heliosphere, particularly the relationship between the solar surface processes and the electrodynamic properties of the environment of planets; and the magnetic properties of the surface of Mars.

These three focus areas are most closely connected by their dependence on high quality measurements of the magnetic field.

PLANETARY MAGNETIC FIELDS

DSRI has developed the International Geomagnetic Reference Field (IGRF) for its

The Ørsted satellite in orbit. In the background: Europe. Launched in 1999, Ørsted became the first Danish satellite. The scientific purpose of the satellite is to measure the Earth's magnetic field. Although it was only designed to survive for 14 months in space, Ørsted is still doing well in its fifth year in orbit. The data from Ørsted has formed the basis for the current geomagnetic reference model — the most detailed mapping of the Earth's magnetic field. (Danish Space Research Institute)

Orsted satellite. The IGRF is a mathematical model describing the main field of the earth and its secular variation. It consists of a set of spherical harmonic expansion coefficients (also known as Gauss coefficients) in a series expansion of the scalar geomagnetic potential.

The IGRF model is built up from 120 expansion coefficients, which represent a compromise adopted to produce well-determined models of the core field while avoiding most of the contamination resulting from crust sources.

Standard models of the geomagnetic field, like the IGRF, can only describe the large-scale features of the magnetic field produced by internal sources in the core crust.

Conversely, comprehensive models of the near-earth magnetic field include sources in the core, the crust, the ionosphere and the magnetosphere.

Recently, DSRI has worked in collaboration with NASA's Goddard Space Flight Center to demonstrate the great advantage of modeling earth's main field and its secular variation simultaneously with ionospheric and magnetospheric contributions by means of a joint inversion of ground-based and satellite magnetic measurements. This has resulted in a comprehensive model that uses over 16,000 parameters to describe the different geomagnetic field contributions, derived from over 500,000 measurements.

SOLAR WIND AND MAGNETOSPHERIC PHYSICS

DSRI studies solar wind and magnetospheric physics, which concern the processes that control the transfer of energy and momentum from the solar wind to the magnetosphere and further into the near-earth space environment.

This research examines the dynamic changes and variations in the solar wind, as well as the time-scales involved ranging from seconds to hours to seasonal and solar cycle periods.

By generating detailed mapping of these currents and the tracing of their relations to processes in the solar wind, DSRI utilizes important methods to the understanding of the physical processes involved in the interaction between the solar wind and the magnetosphere.

DSRI activity in the study of the ionospheric electric field, and current distributions through magnetic and radar ground measurements has a natural focal point in the Greenland ground-based geophysical observations, conducted in conjunction with the Danish Meteorological Institute. Data yielded from the Danish geomagnetic satellite projects, Orsted and Orsted-2, will be critical to this research area.

MAGNETOMETER DEVELOPMENT

Denmark has had an established tradition for advanced magnetometry, beginning with the first magnetic observatory established in Copenhagen in 1842.

This tradition followed through with the classical and internationally famous La Cour instruments developed from the 1920s on, to the Greenland Observatories and modern electronic instruments launched in the 1970s onboard sounding rockets into the polar ionosphere.

Since 1980, more than 20 sounding rockets of scalar and vector magnetometers have occurred. In 1993, the Danish Orsted satellite mission to map the earth's magnetic field was approved.

Other subsequent magnetometer missions have flown since 1997, including Auroral Turbulence 2, a NASA sounding rocket launched March 1997, from Alaska as a test flight of three digital-feedback-loop magnetometers on the main craft and two ejected sub-payloads; DEOS 1, 2, and 3, magnetometers flown aboard three German-Indian sounding rockets launched from Shar, India on April 19, 21, and September 28, 1998,

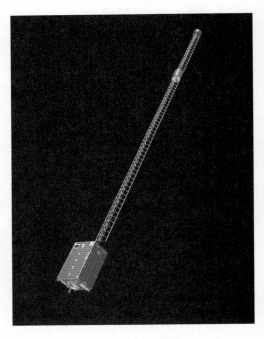

Ørsted's 8 meter boom carries two magnetometers, which measure the magnetic field. Ørsted is named after the Danish physicist H.C. Ørsted, who discovered that an electric current generates a magnetic field. (Danish Space Research Institute)

respectively; Astrid-2, a Swedish micro-satellite for ionospheric research launched December 10, 1998, which lost telemetry on June 23, 1999; and CHAMP, a German geopotentials satellite launched July 15, 2000, on a Russian Kosmos rocket.

THE ORSTED AND ORSTED-2 EXPERIMENTS

The Orsted satellite consisted of a compact spherical coil (CSC) with vector feedback magnetometer. The satellite was successfully put into orbit on February 23, 1999, as an auxiliary payload onboard a Delta-2 rocket, and on February 25, 1999, the CSC-magnetometer was successfully switched on for continued operation.

Since orbit, the CSC-magnetometer has measured the three components of the earth's magnetic field with 19-bit resolution.

The Orsted-2 mission, an enhancement of the Orsted, was equipped with a magnetic mapping payload (MMP) onboard the SAC-C, the joint Argentina-U.S. satellite.

The Orsted-2 was designed with a second generation star camera as well as a CSC-magnetometer.

Astrophysics Research Projects

DSRI's astrophysics group studies compact objects and the accretion flows associated with them, and the formation and development of galaxies and galaxy clusters and their cosmological implications.

In the future, the group plans to study the anisotropies of cosmic microwave radiation.

Recently, DSRI signed an agreement with the ESA to contribute the mirror system for its Planck Surveyor mission, currently scheduled for launch in 2007.

Research in X-ray astronomy began in 1978, with the design of a compact wide-field monitor for hard X-rays (WATCH). This instrument's primary purpose was for rapid localization of cosmic gamma-ray bursts. In the next 15 years, activities in the X-ray field increased considerably. The WATCH instrument was flown on two satellites, the Russian

INTEGRAL (International Gamma Ray Astrophysics Laboratory) is an X-ray and gamma mission led by the European Space Agency. The Danish Space Research Institute has contributed two advanced X-ray detectors to the mission. (Danish Space Research Institute)

GRANAT between 1989 and 1994, and the ESA EURECA from 1992 to 1993.

DSRI also invested heavily in the development of a major instrument complex for the Russian Spectrum X-Gamma Mission (SRG) during this period, and participated in a consortium responsible for the construction of an X-ray monitor for the ESA INTEGRAL mission which was launched in 2002.

Financial setbacks in the Russian space program have prevented Russia from completing the development of SRG and the launch data of this satellite remains uncertain.

The WATCH mission, however, has yielded significant results with dramatic developments in the gamma-burst field, leading to a new and more fruitful way of approaching this enigmatic phenomenon.

DSRI also contributed to ESA's Infrared Space Observatory (ISO), which successfully fulfilled its mission between 1995 and 1998, yielding data that is still being analyzed.

In an effort to compensate for the delays of the SRG mission, several projects have been initiated by DSRI including: INTEGRAL, Planck Surveyor, TopHat, a microwave background experiment, and HEFT, a hard x-ray experiment.

JEM-X

The JEM-X is an X-ray monitor instrument onboard the ESA gamma-ray astronomy satellite, INTEGRAL, which was launched on October 17, 2002.

The primary scientific objective of JEM-X on INTEGRAL is to investigate the emission at X-ray energies from the sources selected for study with the gamma-ray instruments. This objective is based on the fact that emission from sources powered by accretion onto compact objects may vary between different modes, where the balance between the X-ray and gamma-ray emission varies drastically.

JEM-X will also record accurate positions of new sources discovered by INTEGRAL.

JEM-X is equipped with a detector system consisting of two identical, high-pressure imaging microstrip gas counters. The diameters of these counters are 250 mm (10 in), corresponding to a collecting area of 500 cm² (80

The INTEGRAL satellite was launched in October 2002. It is expected to be operational until at least 2004. (Danish Space Research Institute)

in²). The detectors are filled with a mixture of xenon and methane to a pressure of three bar.

The primary energy of the JEM-X detector ranges from 3 to 35 keV. Above the xenon K-edge, the detector has reduced efficiency, although still retaining its imaging capabilities up to 60 keV. The detector position resolution is energy dependent, and 19 percent at an energy of 6 keV, which is sufficient to observe the astrophysics important in iron lines.

SPECTRUM-X GAMMA SATELLITE

The Spectrum-X Gamma Satellite, also known as the SRG satellite, is a large X- and gamma-ray astronomy satellite sponsored by the Russian Space Agency.

Setbacks in the Russian space program have delayed the SRG satellite launch from its original date in 1995 to sometime after 2003.

The SRG satellite is unique in comparison to other satellites such as Chandra and XMM-Newton in its ability to measure X-ray polarization by a very wide coverage, from the UV-region to hard X-rays, and by the fact that the satellite carries its own all-sky monitor.

SODART INSTRUMENT

The SODART is the largest instrument on board the SRG Satellite. It consists of two mirror modules, developed by DSRI in collaboration with Russia, an objective crystal spectrometer and eight focal plane instruments

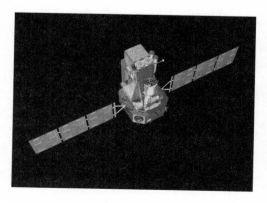

Close-up of the Danish-built X-ray detectors. The X-rays enter through the coded masks at the front of the satellite and are registered in the detectors in the back of the satellite. (Danish Space Research Institute)

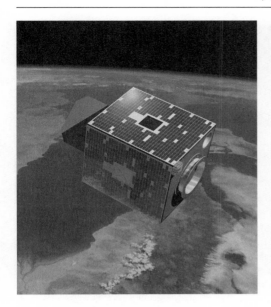

The Rømer satellite is to be the second Danish scientific satellite in space. The main purpose of the satellite is to do astroseismology: to measure oscillations in nearby stars. The satellite is still under development. (Danish Space Research Institute)

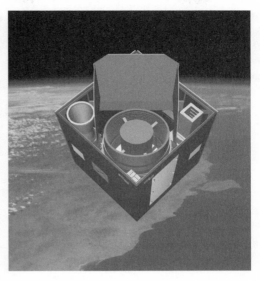

During its two year mission in space, Rømer will observe 20 select stars — each for about a month — and measure how the light from these stars vary in color and intensity. These observations can reveal the age, temperature and inner composition of the stars. (Danish Space Research Institute)

placed on two sledges; one for each focal plane of the mirror modules.

The eight components of the SODART are two sets of the Danish-developed HEPC and LEPC detectors (microstrip proportional counters), two sets of the Russian-developed KFRD proportional counters, a U.S.-developed X-ray polarimeter, SXRP, and a Finnish solid-state X-ray detector, SIXA.

SODART provides high-throughput foil telescopes with reliable throughput up to energies exceeding 10 keV.

The SODART instrument consists of two unique units never flown before: the Bragg-crystal spectrometer and the X-ray polarimeter.

The SODART Mirror Modules are two foil telescopes, designed as conical approximations to the Wolter-I X-ray telescope geometry. The outer diameter of the mirror modules is 600 mm (24 in). The focal length is 8 m (26.4 ft). Each mirror module has a 43 mm (5.72 in) closely nested mirror foil which completely fills the opening.

The SODART was designed with four interchangeable detectors mounted in the

focal plane. Imaging detectors, LEPC and HEPC, based on microstrip gas counter-technology, were installed.

The LEPC detector covers the X-ray energy band from 0.2 to 8 keV. The HEPC detector covers the range between 2 and 8 keV. The field of view of both detectors is 30 and 60 arc-min, respectively.

SODART will be useful in examining the X-ray emissions from clusters of galaxies, which are the largest gravitationally bound objects in the universe. The instrument can detect these emissions in X-rays at cosmological distances, opening up the possibility of direct studies of the formation and chemical evolution of clusters of galaxies.

SODART will also be able to study the diffuse X-ray background emission, since it is capable of obtaining broad-band spectroscopy at energies above 2 keV.

ESA PLANCK SURVEYOR MISSION

The main objective of the ESA Planck Surveyor Mission is to study the cosmic

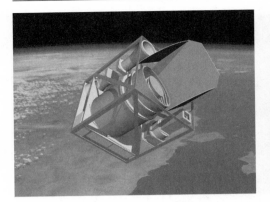

An inside look at Rømer. The main telescope is placed in the middle of the satellite. (Danish Space Research Institute)

This telescope will also be able to detect subtle variations in the light from a star which may indicate that a planet is passing in front of the star — another shot of Rømer satellite in operation. (Danish Space Research Institute)

microwave background radiation (CMBR) with precision sensitivity and angular resolution. DSRI has participated actively in Planck since inception of the project.

The institute's carbon fiber test mirror has been installed in the surveyor, demonstrating Danish capability to produce the optical elements of the required quality. The Planck Surveyor is scheduled for launch in the first quarter of 2007.

THE BALLERINA EXPERIMENT

As part of DSRI's Danish Small Satellite Program, an experiment called Ballerina is aimed at the enigmatic issue of the origin of the cosmic gamma-ray bursts.

The primary objectives of the Ballerina experiment are to obtain fast, arc-minute localization of gamma-ray burst sources and to study the detailed X-ray spectra of the early afterglow emissions following the gamma-ray bursts.

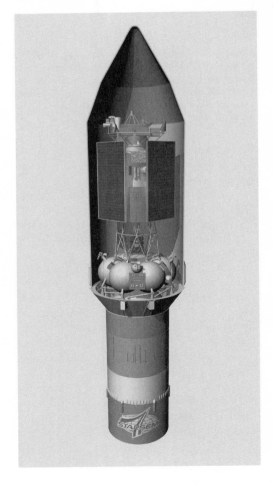

Inside the Rømer satellite telescope. (Danish Space Research Institute)

The Ballerina experiment will consist of four WATCH instruments provided by DSRI and an X-ray telescope provided by the Max Planck Institute in Garching, Germany.

The four WATCH units will be mounted in a tetrahedron configuration allowing all-sky coverage. The rotating WATCH modulators will double as momentum wheels, enabling satellite execution of a 180° repointing operation in less than one minute. This capability is based on the principle that the gamma-ray bursts are initially detected and coarsely located within a degree by WATCH and then the satellite is re-oriented to allow the X-ray telescope to study the early X-ray spectrum and to refine the source position.

TopHat Balloon Project

TopHat is a balloon project for cosmic microwave background radiation (CMBR) research. The project name was conceived from the location of a part of the instrument package located on top of the balloon.

The TopHat consists of two versions: the pointer and the spinner. The spinner was launched January 2001, and flew around the South Pole on a balloon for one week, yielding useful scientific data. The pointer has yet to be launched.

The High Energy Focusing Telescope (HEFT)

The High Energy Focusing Telescope (HEFT) was a balloon experiment designed to perform imaging and focusing at X-ray energies between 20 and 100 keV. The HEFT project was a cooperation between the California Institute of Technology, Columbia University and DSRI.

The scientific objectives of the HEFT mission demonstrated the performance of significant extra-galactic astrophysics based on balloon measurements for the first time.

During a six-hour exposure, HEFT reached a 40 keV flux threshold, 11 times lower than that achieved during a daylong observation by the most sensitive satellite instruments recently in operation.

The main scientific objective of the HEFT mission was to map the Ti-44 emission

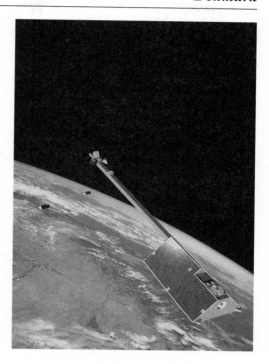

Swarm is the name of a multi-satellite Earth observation mission proposed by an international consortium led by the Danish Space Research Institute. Swarm is currently in development and is competing with two other proposed missions to be launched as part of the European Space Agency's Earth observation program. The scientific purpose of the Swarm mission is to study the variations of the Earth's magnetic field in time and space. (Danish Space Research Institute)

at 68 and 78 keV9 in Cas-A, and to provide the corresponding maps of the non-thermal continuum to energies above 40 keV in young supernova remnants. HEFT also observed cyclotron lines at 60 keV from accreting neutron stars.

The CdZnTe Detector

In the study of the potential of X-ray and gamma-ray detectors based on heavy element, semi-conductor materials, one of the most promising materials has been the CdZnTe (CZT). The principal advantage of CZT semi-conductor material is the high-quantum efficiency and the ability to operate at near-room temperatures. These properties make the

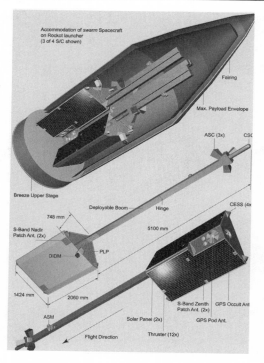

The Swarm satellites may be launched on board a Rocket launcher. Here is an illustration of how the four satellites can fit into the Rockot fairing. (Danish Space Research Institute)

CZT-detector particularly useful to space applications and ideal for a smaller satellite.

In 1996, DSRI began a program to develop detectors based on CZT, with plans to eventually develop focal plane detectors for the novel-type hard X-ray telescope.

In 1997, DSRI's CZT-detector research resulted in a new technique—the drift strip method, which led to considerable advances in achieving resolution, even for crystals containing charge trapping defects.

The Mars Polar Lander Shadow Model

The University of Copenhagen has participated in NASA's Mars exploration program by supplying a Magnetic Properties Experiment on the Mars Pathfinder Mission and also on the Mars Polar Lander. The purpose of the experiment is to identify the magnetic mineral that is contained in the dust on the surface of Mars. The experiment was based on a number of small magnets of varying strength that attract dust containing magnetic minerals in different proportions. By taking pictures of the collected dust at different times, information

The four Swarm satellites will circle the Earth in two different orbits. (Danish Space Research Institute)

about the grain size and probable composition of the magnetic material was obtained, which was important in understanding the evolution of the planet.

In September 1999, the Mars Climate Orbiter spacecraft was lost during Mars orbit insertion. The spacecraft was intended to act as a communication link between earth and the next Mars Lander — the Mars Polar Lander. Three months later, in December 1999, the ill-fated Mars Polar Lander (MPL) was supposed to land near the South Pole of Mars. Extensive preparations were performed in order to avoid the effects of the loss of the communication link. This meant that very meticulous planning of all science operations on the surface of Mars had to be performed in order to minimize the data volume to be downloaded.

One of the tools for planning image sequences of surface features was referred to as the Mars Polar Lander Shadow Model. The model was designed to show the shadows from the sun projected unto the lander deck and surface of Mars, as well as solar reflections from instruments on the lander deck. An exact model of the MPL was made with a 3D-modeling tool implementing all major instruments and lander configurations. The exact position of the sun at the expected landing site on Mars (76S, 165W) was derived with the use of NASA's solar ephemeris calculation algorithm on a computer at the NASA AMES Research Center in California. The algorithm derived the position of the sun every five minutes for the first three months of the mission. A ray-tracing program then calculated the projected shadows and reflections on the lander deck and surface of Mars.

The model was especially useful in timing the sequences for taking images of the magnetic properties experiments and the radiometric calibration target. A very important consideration when analyzing these instruments has been to detect whether a uniform illumination is present. By using the MPL shadow model, it was possible to take a single image with the optimal illumination, instead of a series of images, thereby minimizing the amount of data volume to be downloaded.

Another important scientific discovery was the detection of morning frost and CO_2-ice on the ground. At the time of the supposed landing, the sun would never set and frost detection would have been most probable under the lander deck after a long time in shadow. Here the MPL shadow model was used to determine the time for optimal imaging.

In the future, the MPL shadow model can easily be modified to simulate Mars missions as the deck, leg structure and scientific instruments are defined as interchangeable modules. New modules and solar Ephemeris for the landing site are the only key points that would need to be defined.

EUROPE

European Space Agency (ESA)

The European Space Agency (ESA) was formed in 1975, replacing the satellite and launcher organizations ESRO and ELDO. It is made up of 15 member states, including Austria, Belgium, Denmark, Finland, France, Germany, Ireland, Italy, the Netherlands, Norway, Portugal, Spain, Sweden, Switzerland and the United Kingdom. Canada has special status and participates in some projects under a cooperation agreement.

ESA's projects are designed to find out more about the earth, its immediate space environment, the solar system and the universe, as well as to develop satellite-based technologies and promote European industries.

One of the ways in which ESA's programs benefit Europe and its citizens is in keeping Europe at the forefront of scientific discovery on our solar system and the universe, which has also led to breakthroughs in other scientific areas. The program also improves medical science — many of the scientific discoveries that originated in space research are helping people live longer, healthier lives. Two examples include recent advances in detecting cancers and new treatments for heart disease. ESA generates new technology from space that can also be adapted for other uses, for example, the flame-resistant textiles used for protective clothing, which are the result of research to protect electric circuits in rockets. European industry has benefited from the award of ESA contracts and also puts the technical experience gained from taking part in ESA's programs to other uses. It promotes industrial development satellites that have been used to discover new mineral or oil deposits, and it protects the earth by the use of observation satellites which provide data used to safeguard the environment and to monitor environmental change and damage. The program assists agriculture by use of remote sensing, which provides information for geographical information systems (GIS) that are also used to improve land cultivation and conduct elaborate agricultural statistical evaluations at both European and national levels. The program also develops more accurate weather forecasts, which benefits agriculture as well as navigation and leisure activities; improves communications so that television broadcasts can now be beamed all over the world; uses satellites for cellular phones, as well as for intercontinental voice and data exchange; creates accurate maps to improve town planning; improves navigation by means of satellites which provide the navigation systems increasingly used in cars, trains, planes and ships; increases employment — the European space industry employs 40,000 people directly and 250,000 indirectly through its subcontractors; and prevents a brain drain by the use of innovative space-related science.

Ariane 511, Flight 145 at Kourou Space Center, Guiana. (ESA/CNES/ArianeSpace, 2002)

There are ten challenges that exist now for Europe in space. These include: Navigation satellites. Space navigation systems are indispensable for science and industry, and are even being used in some cars. But in critical areas such as air travel, applications have been restricted because the existing American and Russian systems are under military control. The operators deliberately degrade the services during a crisis, causing dismay that will be expressed by the European Union. In response, ESA is now diligently creating the civilian navigation satellites needed for European autonomy.

Easier spaceflight. Present methods of launching satellites, astronauts and supplies into space with conventional chemical rockets have proved to be somewhat cumbersome for the Europeans, as well as time-consuming and expensive. While ESA continues to sponsor improvements to the Ariane series of launching rockets, it is also continuing to develop a new, small launcher called Vega. ESA has also been examining new methods of propulsion for spacecraft. These include solar-electric engines already under development, and possibly the use of solar wind to push interplanetary spacecraft along.

Nanosatellites. The first U.S. satellite, Explorer 1 (1958), weighed only eight kg, yet it discovered the earth's radiation belt with a simple Geiger counter. Spacecraft of hundreds or thousands of kilograms have since become the norm, but now there is interest in small but very clever machines of less than 10 kg. Europe's first nanosatellite, developed by a U.K. university, went into space in June 2000. SNAP-1 weighed seven kg and has taken advantage of four decades of progress in microelectronic and micro-mechanical technologies since Explorer 1. Whether as single spacecraft for quick inexpensive missions, or for earth-observing swarms, the nanosatellites offer small countries, small companies and institutes a chance to compete with the aerospace giants.

Market share. The dramatic success of Europe's Ariane rockets in capturing a large part of the market in commercial launches of satellites has not been matched in the manufacture and sale of satellites for commercial purposes. Non–European telecommunications services, for example, still prefer American suppliers. In comparison, the U.S. space industry benefits from large public funding and technological stimulation from the military space sector, which is relatively small in Europe. ESA has been looking for more effective ways of supporting Europe's commercial space industry, for example by demonstrating new technologies in small, quick experiments in space.

Climate control. Intense diplomatic efforts are now calling for worldwide policies to moderate climate change. ESA's satellites for earth observation and research have helped to verify the scientific basis of these policies and to check up on their implementation and results.

Cosmic impacts. In 1996, the Council of Europe called for greater effort to detect "asteroids and comets potentially dangerous to humankind." Impacts of asteroids and comets have caused regional and global disasters in the past, and the search is on for inconspicuous

Ariane 504/Flight 119 collage at Kourou Space Center, Guiana, launched October 12, 1999. (ESA/CNES/AraineSpace, 1999)

objects in potentially dangerous orbits. ESA sponsors Spaceguard out of Rome, which coordinates 80 asteroid-hunting centers worldwide. Rosetta, a future ESA science spacecraft mission, will give a better understanding of the physical nature of the threat. Two projects under study by ESA promise to be excellent asteroid hunters: BepiColombo, which is intended to go to the heart of the solar system to examine the planet Mercury; and GAIA, a new star-mapping spacecraft.

Raw materials and energy in space. The moon and asteroids are rich in materials that could very well be quarried for manufacturing uses or to produce oxygen and water. The difficulties of working in space are partly offset by the weak gravity of such bodies, compared with the earth's. In the long run, large space stations or interstellar rockets, for example, might be more easily built in a low-gravity environment. ESA continues to encourage Europe's engineers and scientists to think along these lines, and also to keep under review the possibility of supplying the earth with clean energy from space. Another future long-term idea is that stations in orbit might generate power from sunlight or the natural electricity of the space environment and beam it to the ground.

Robots or astronauts? A memorable mission in 1993 to repair the defective NASA-ESA Hubble Space Telescope, in which the ESA astronaut Claude Nicollier played a part, helped to silence the critics of manned spaceflight. However, unmanned spacecraft and robots become more advanced in capability every year, without the life-support system or the return ticket to earth that a human being needs. Judging the respective roles of robots and astronauts in space stations, moon bases or the exploration of Mars is therefore a delicate strategic issue for space planners. ESA remains fully committed to manned spaceflight in the International Space Station, as well as development for the project of a robotic arm and an automated transfer vehicle to illustrate an even-handed support for the robots. Meanwhile, ESA's science program continues to develop robotic spacecraft capable of complex operations under autonomous control far from the earth.

Staying in front in the area of launcher development. Even while Ariane 4 was proving its success as the launcher of the 1990s, ESA was already developing the more powerful Ariane 5. An upgraded Ariane 5, capable of lifting 9.5 tons into orbit, is ready for launch, and will be followed in 2006 by an Ariane 5 launcher capable of carrying 12 tons into geostationary orbit.

Since its inception, ESA has become a major player in the space industry. The turning point came in 1986 when ESA's Giotto spacecraft, carrying the instruments of Europe's scientists and launched by Europe's rocket, made the most daring visit to Halley's comet attempted by any of the world's space agencies.

Some other highlights from ESA's accomplishments include: Ariane rockets developed by ESA now command the commercial market in space launches, especially for communications satellites, despite intense competition from the United States, Russia, China and Japan. This is now a billion–Euro industry.

Arianne 5 Assembly Kourou Space Center, Guiana. (ESA/CNES/ArianeSpace, 1998)

Global standards for the present generation of telecommunications satellites are based on techniques demonstrated by ESA, and over 50 telecom satellites have been built by European aerospace companies — another billion–Euro industry.

ESA currently leads the world in monitoring the ozone hole, ice sheets, ocean winds and currents, and other health checks for our planet. Meteosat and MSG, which provide the familiar daily films of the weather in Europe and Africa, were also developed by ESA.

Scientific spacecraft built by ESA have earned a leading role in the study of the sun and its effects on the earth, in investigating comets, in mapping the stars from space, and in unveiling the universe by infrared light and X-rays.

ESA's own astronauts have flown in space in 12 U.S. shuttle missions and spent several hours aboard the Russian space station Mir. They have also taken part in four missions to the International Space Station, to which ESA contributes as a full partner.

Ariane 503 integration at Kourou Space Center, Guiana, in preparation for mission to launch ARD (Atmospheric Reentry Demonstrator), a vehicle to demonstrate atmosphere reentry technologies.

There are a number of spacecraft of ESA that are either operational now or due for launch before the end of 2004, representing more than 20 projects in all. They are as follows:

Hubble Space Telescope (NASA and ESA), 1990; European astronomers benefit from guaranteed use of this famous visible-light space telescope, as a result of ESA's partnership and practical contributions to the project.

Ulysses (ESA and NASA, built in Europe), 1990; the first spacecraft ever to fly over the poles of the sun has transformed scientists' knowledge of the solar wind and its magnetism, which fill the space around us.

ERS-2, 1995; ERS-2 has carried a new instrument to observe the ozone hole, while continuing the valued work of ERS-1 in examining the earth by radar, microwaves and infrared light.

SOHO (ESA and NASA, built in Europe), 1995; the Solar and Heliospheric Observatory (SOHO) has made many discoveries about the sun's interior and explosive atmosphere, and it continues to monitor solar storms 24 hours a day.

Huygens (ESA's contribution to the NASA Cassini mission), 1997; in November 2004, Cassini-Huygens will parachute through the hazy atmosphere of Titan, Saturn's largest moon, and reveal the chemical secrets of this strange alien world.

XMM-Newton, 1999; this mission is made up of three amazing telescopes, each with 58 carefully shaped mirrors nesting inside one another, make this the most sensitive space observatory ever built for X-ray astronomy.

Cluster (ESA and NASA, built in Europe), 2000; Cluster comprises four satellites operating in company to give an unprecedented 3-D view of the battle between the solar wind and the earth's magnetic field, and accompanying space storms.

Artemis (ESA and Japan), 2001; this innovative telecommunications satellite will demonstrate direct links to mobile users on the ground, gather data from other satellites by laser beams, and broadcast navigation information for EGNOS.

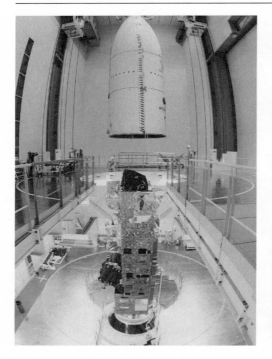

Servicing of Ariane 5 for launch of Envisat satellite at Kourou Space Center, Guiana. (ESA/CNES/ArianeSpace, 2002)

Integration of the Integral satellite at Kourou Space Center, Guiana. (ESA/CNES/Ariane-Space, 2002)

Envisat, 2002; Europe's newest remote-sensing satellite, launched in spring 2002, is watching over the earth with advanced versions of instruments used in ERS-2, and with several important new ones.

Integral, 2002; XMM-Newton's sister spacecraft uses its own ingenious telescopes and sensitive detectors to observe the gamma-rays coming from very violent events in cosmic space.

MSG-1 (ESA and EUMETSAT), 2002, and MSG-2, fall 2003; the Meteosat second generation satellites will give far sharper weather information than what was obtained from the Meteosats, which have operated over the equator since 1977.

SMART-1, 2003; this small experimental spacecraft will demonstrate the use of solar-electric propulsion and carry a set of scientific instruments to inspect the moon.

Rosetta (ESA, plus German/French-led lander), 2003; Rosetta will fly in company with a comet for many months, observing it from a close orbit and depositing a lander on its surface.

Mars Express (ESA, plus UK-led lander), 2003; during the most detailed scrutiny of the Red Planet yet attempted, Mars Express will look for hidden water or ice, and drop a lander sensitive to signs of life.

CryoSat, 2003; as the first of ESA's new Earth Explorer series, CryoSat will use twin radars to chart changes in the world's ice sheets and sea ice more accurately than ever before.

Metop-1 (ESA and EUMETSAT), 2003; while Meteosat and MSG observe the weather from above the equator, METOP will fly over the poles with advanced instruments for sounding the atmosphere.

Automated Transfer Vehicle, 2004; this ingenious ferry will carry cargo to the International Space Station, dock there automatically, correct the station's orbit, and finish as an incinerator.

European Robotic Arm, 2004; this is one of ESA's contributions to the International Space Station, intended for mounting on the Russian module but useful for European projects on the station.

EGNOS, to be in service by 2004; The European Geostationary Navigation Overlay Service (EGNOS) will use payloads on three geostationary satellites and a network of ground stations to make United States and Russian navigation systems more accurate and reliable.

Galileo, 2004–2008; the first few satellites of Europe's own navigation system, Galileo, are due to become available in 2006, while the full constellation of 30 satellites will be operational by 2008.

Columbus, 2004; ESA's largest piece for the International Space Station is a cylindrical laboratory 6.7 meters (22 feet) long where astronauts will supervise hundreds of experiments every year.

Europe's spaceport is located in Kourou, French Guiana. Created and operated by the French space agency CNES, Europe's spaceport was greatly expanded under ESA sponsorship for Ariane launches, both developmental and commercial. CSG is perfectly

located on the northern coast of South America for safe launches over the Atlantic Ocean. It also provides a great launch advantage of the earth's rotation near the equator to gain 10 percent or more in liftable satellite mass compared with Cape Canaveral in the United States.

Earth Observation

Over the last 20 years, earth observation from space has uncovered startling evidence of man's detrimental effect on the natural environment, and satellites are now being recognized as a key to helping us manage and monitor resources.

International initiatives within the world's scientific and political communities are tackling critical environmental issues such as climate change, CO_2 emissions and ozone depletion. Europe has continued to play a leading role in this research through the work of ESA's ongoing Earth Observation Program.

Assembly of the Cryogenic third stage of Ariane 42P at Kourou Space Center. (ESA/CNES/ AraineSpace, 2002)

Ariane 42P on launch table at Kourou Space Center, Guiana, just prior to launch on May 3, 2002 to place land spot 5 into orbit. (ESA/ CNES/ArianeSpace, 2002)

From the invention of its Ariane launcher back in the early sixties, ESA has been an instrumental force in science, telecommunication, earth observation and manned space missions.

The first significant contributions from ESA's Earth Observation Program came in 1977, when the first of seven Meteosat meteorological satellites was launched to monitor the weather of Europe and Africa from a vantage point over the equator.

The success of this and subsequent missions led to the formation of the European Organization for the Exploitation of Meteorological Satellites (EUMETSAT), which has since worked alongside ESA on an ongoing program of weather monitoring and climate change studies.

Over the years, climate monitoring has become a key element of the Earth Observation Program, based on the fact that nearly every change in our natural environment is reflected in our weather patterns. Meteorological satellites have played their part in identifying long-term trends, and it is estimated that improved weather forecasting has saved industries and the European public millions of euros every year.

Meteosat images of weather patterns are an everyday feature on European television and are used by national meteorological services to provide increasingly more accurate weather forecasting. As a continuation of this vital work, ESA and EUMETSAT have been working on the Meteosat Second Generation (MSG).

The first of three MSG spacecraft was launched in August 2002, and has been providing meteorologists with much improved imagery and data. A further development will come in the shape of Metop-1, which is scheduled to be launched in 2005 as part of a joint European–United States polar satellite system.

The first of a series of three similar satellites developed by ESA and EUMETSAT, Metop-1 will operate in unison with a similar United States spacecraft, producing high-resolution images, detailed temperature and humidity profiles of the atmosphere and temperatures of the land and ocean surfaces. Instruments on board will also monitor ozone

levels in the atmosphere and wind flow over the seas.

As a polar-orbiting satellite, Metop-1 will fly at a lower altitude than its geo-stationary Meteosat and MSG counterparts and will, therefore, be able to provide different and complementary kinds of meteorological information.

Since the beginning of the 1990s, ESA has taken earth observation to new heights through the work of its ERS satellites. ESA's ERS-1 spacecraft was launched into space by an Ariane 4 in 1991, followed by ERS-2 in 1995.

At the time, these two satellites, which carried highly advanced radar instruments, were the most sophisticated earth observation spacecraft ever developed in Europe. For the first time scientists were able to create accurate radar images of the earth's surface, giving us new eyes on our world.

They have since collected a wealth of information on the earth's land surfaces, oceans, sea ice and polar caps, and their contribution towards our understanding of world environmental issues has been invaluable.

On a global scale, the ERS program has increased understanding of the interaction between the oceans and atmosphere, ocean currents and changes in Arctic and Antarctic ice, giving climatologists more confidence in predicting changes in our climate and helping us to monitor environmental pollution.

Work in the field of earth observation has led to the development of the world's most ambitious earth observation satellite — Envisat. Envisat, which was launched on March 1, 2002, involved nearly 10 years of work by some of Europe's most respected scientists and engineers. Onboard the spacecraft are 10 highly sophisticated instruments, all of which will collect crucial environmental data over the five-year mission period.

Envisat will serve as one of the earth's most important sources of environmental information and will further establish ESA's position as a major authority on world environmental issues.

ESA's strong concern on the health of our planet has led to development of its future project, the Living Planet Program, the next generation of satellite missions. This program, which will be phased in over the next few years, will involve the use of smaller satellites on shorter, cheaper and more focused missions. Utilizing a new approach for ESA, it will encourage industry partnerships and increased dialogue with the scientific research and political communities within Europe.

ERS 1 AND 2

Every day the fine and delicate balance of our planet's natural ecological system is gradually being changed by many of the normal activities associated with modern daily life that we all take for granted.

Therefore, we now have an urgent need to monitor and understand both man-made and natural changes to our atmosphere, the land and the oceans in every part of the world.

In many cases, satellites have proven to be the only way to obtain suitable data. Satellites orbiting the earth have been able to gather comprehensive information, but visual systems that rely on daylight and clear conditions to "see" the surface have a distinct disadvantage in that they stop functioning when it is cloudy or dark.

With this in mind, European engineers, under the direction of ESA, have developed a special instrument called a Synthetic Aperture Radar (SAR). As one of the key instruments on the ERS-1 and -2 satellites, the SAR is a high-resolution, wide-swath imaging radar producing high quality images of the oceans, coastal zones, polar ice and land regions, irrespective of weather conditions and cloud coverage, or whether it is day or night.

SAR works by bouncing microwaves off the earth's surface and measuring the reflected radiation. A SAR also has five different modes of operation, allowing a variety of image types and giving us a new and permanently open window on the world.

The first SAR was launched into space by Europe's Ariane 4 rocket in July 1991, as one of three main instruments on ESA's ERS-1 spacecraft. It was later followed by a second on ERS-2 in 1995.

At the time, the two ERS satellites were the most sophisticated earth observation spacecraft ever developed and launched in Europe.

ERS-1 completed its operation in 1999, overlapping with the new ERS-2 launched in 1995. These highly successful ESA satellites have collected a wealth of valuable data on the earth's land surfaces, oceans, and polar caps. They have been programmed to monitor natural disasters such as severe flooding or earthquakes in remote parts of the world.

On a global scale, they have significantly added to our understanding of the interaction between the oceans and the atmosphere, ocean currents and changes in the Arctic and Antarctic ice, giving climatologists more confidence in assessing climate trends. The ERS satellites have also kept a close eye on agricultural areas, forests, coastlines and marine pollution.

By detecting land-use changes such as the destruction of tropical rain forests, ERS data has helped governments around the world police a broad range of local and global environmental problems.

In the area of satellite environmental data, the ERS spacecraft have brought significant benefits to Europe and the rest of the world. These benefits have ranged from improved public services such as weather forecasting and crop monitoring, to the creation and sharing of commercial and industrial enterprises, and helping European scientists to excel in key areas of environmental research.

Today, several hundred research groups worldwide, involving at least 2,000 scientists, use ERS data to further their studies. Much of this research has been used by several international entities, with countries across the globe working together to combat environmental problems.

Perhaps the most significant of these is the Inter-Governmental Panel on Climate Change (IPCC), which has led to the Montreal Protocol for worldwide reduction in the production of aerosol gases, or chlorofluorocarbons (CFCs).

Currently, the ERS-2 satellite circles the earth at a height of 800 km (497 miles) and completes an orbit every 100 minutes, crossing each pole in the process. The special orbit, known as a polar orbit, means that the earth is gradually rotating beneath the spacecraft.

By this method, on each different orbit a slightly different part of the ground is seen and the ERS-2 can, therefore, cover the entire globe in just three days.

Both ERS satellites were built with a core payload of two specialized radars and an infrared imaging sensor. The two spacecraft were designed as identical twins with one important difference — ERS-2 included an extra instrument designed to monitor ozone levels in the atmosphere. The following are the instruments aboard the ERS satellites:

The Active Microwave Instrument is the largest onboard system and combines the functions of a Synthetic Aperture Radar (SAR) and a wind scatterometer (SCATT). The AMI has three modes of operation: image mode and wave mode (performed by the SAR); and wind mode (by the SCATT). In image mode, the SAR produces highly detailed images of a 100 km wide strip of the earth's surface day and night and in all weather conditions. In its wind and wave modes, the instrument continuously measures global ocean surface wind speeds and directions, and provides information on the direction and shape of ocean wave patterns.

The Radar Altimeter measures variations in the satellite's height above sea level and ice with an accuracy of a few centimeters, and helps provide data to know the satellite's exact orbital position. As well as contributing data on the position of ice flows below, the instrument produces ocean surface wave height and wind speed information for climatologists.

The Along-Track Scanning Radiometer (ATSR) consists of two instruments, an Imaging Infrared Radiometer (IIR) and a passive Microwave Sounder (MS). The infrared sensor provides detailed maps of the temperature at the surface of the seas and oceans with an accuracy of more than 0.5°C. It also measures cloud top temperatures, cloud cover and land surface temperatures that has proven to be very useful in monitoring forest fires. For ERS-2, the infrared capability was enhanced with the addition of visible channels which enable the estimation of vegetation cover. The Microwave Sounder is a passive radiometer providing measurements of the total water content of the atmosphere within a 20 km (12 mile) footprint.

The Global Ozone Monitoring Experiment (GOME) was added to the ERS-2 payload in light of the increasing concern about atmospheric ozone levels. This ultraviolet and visible light spectrometer provides information on ozone, CFCs and trace gas levels. A more advanced version of GOME will be carried on the Metop spacecraft series, which consists of three polar orbiting satellites currently under development. These will produce high-resolution images, detailed vertical temperature and humidity profiles and temperatures of the land and ocean surface on a global basis.

Additional instruments to the core payload on both ERS-1 and 2 include:

The Precise Range and Range Rate Equipment (PRARE), an all-weather microwave ranging system designed to provide measurements used for highly precise orbit determination and geodetic applications, such as movements of the earth's crust.

The Laser Retroreflector, an optical device operating in the infrared that has been used as a target by ground-based laser ranging stations to determine the precise altitude of the spacecraft.

Near the end of 1993, it was becoming clear that ERS-1 was still in very good condition technically and operationally, even though it was coming to the end of its original lifespan. ESA saw the advantage, in terms of both scientific research and technological achievement, in overlapping the work of ERS-2 with the remaining few months of life of ERS-1 by flying the two satellites together in a tandem mission.

Shortly after the launch of ERS-2 in 1995, ESA decided to link the two spacecraft in the first ever tandem mission, which lasted for nine months. During this time, the increased frequency and level of data available to scientists offered a unique opportunity to observe changes over a very short space of time, as both satellites orbited earth only 24 hours apart.

In 1999, the ERS-1 satellite finally ran out of fuel. It had far exceeded its planned lifetime. ERS-2 is expected to continue operating for several more years.

ERS satellites have proven to be invaluable in understanding and addressing environmental concerns. Volcanic discharges and forest fires are just a few of the natural causes of change to our environment. Man's everyday activities have also been speeding up the effects of change and altering the delicate ecological balance of our world. Pollution from the cars we drive, the power stations that generate our electricity and the industrial processes that release toxins into the air has been altering our atmosphere at an unprecedented rate.

Data generated from ERS-1 and ERS-2 has helped scientists understand and begin taking steps to stop any further damage to the environment. Using the technology of the ERS satellites, scientists have been able to observe all these elements on a daily basis, building up a library of information from which to learn and act upon.

An example of this has been El Niño, the weather phenomenon responsible for some of the world's most drastic and devastating disasters. From summer droughts in Australia, Africa, Brazil, Asia and Central America to milder winters and severe flooding in other parts of the world, El Niño has been recognized by scientists as one of the world's most serious environmental threats.

Monitoring particular aspects of the environment can provide answers to many of the mysteries surrounding El Niño. ERS onboard instruments have been able to measure changes in sea temperature and levels — two key environmental changes associated with the El Niño event.

The many pieces of satellite-generated data now available to scientists ensures that they are more able to understand the signs and causes of this extraordinary natural phenomenon and are better able to help governments and communities predict and prepare for the future.

Observation of our polar ice caps plays an important role in helping us assess changes in our climate. Fears of melting ice in polar regions have been well-founded. This phenomenon would result in widespread flooding across the globe with many of our coastal cities disappearing beneath rising sea levels.

Fortunately, ERS data has helped scientists to see whether ice is melting or accumulating. Detailed maps of the ice sheets can be drawn up on a continuous basis to watch for emerging adverse patterns or trends.

Oil has been one of man's most valuable resources. We use it to power our cars, create our electricity and produce many of the plastic and cosmetic products that we all rely on. A key element of our modern world, it has proven to be both our savior and our enemy.

As we become increasingly reliant on oil to drive our economies, we have been finding it more and more difficult to find new sources. The ERS-2 Radar Altimeter has produced topographic maps of the sea floor to help us identify new oil supplies.

At the other end of the spectrum, ERS monitoring continues to help prevent the devastation that oil pollution can bring to our coastal, sea and marine environments. The highly sophisticated Synthetic Aperture Radar (SAR) can detect oil spills on the ocean surface. Thanks to ERS satellite monitoring, oil pollution monitoring has now been well established. Even illegal discharges, principally from ships clearing their tanks at night, can be identified and the offenders prosecuted.

The ozone layer is a composition of atmospheric gases above the earth's surface that acts like a sunscreen, filtering all the harmful rays of the sun and preventing the planet from overheating. Since the early 1990s, scientists around the world have been concerned about the number of holes appearing in this protective layer. If the earth continues its warming trend, and essentially becomes too warm, agricultural crops could fail, water supplies could become scarce, and diseases and conditions such as skin cancer could increase.

In an effort to monitor these effects, ERS-2 has been equipped with an ultraviolet and visible light spectrometer, the GOME, for atmospheric ozone level research. By maintaining ongoing information on ozone levels, scientists can help us to prevent further damage to the environment by restricting offending chemicals and pollutants or finding alternatives.

ENVISAT

Launched in February 2002, Envisat is the most powerful European earth observation satellite. It will make the most complete set of observations of our planet that any satellite has ever made. Envisat will monitor land, oceans, atmosphere, and ice caps. It will help scientists understand how changes to one, say climate, affect the others. Envisat was established as a key element of ESA's plans for the next decade to monitor earth's environment.

Envisat has its roots in a time in the late 1980s when the philosophy within space agencies around the world was to develop large multi-purpose missions. At the time, satellite and launcher technology were less sophisticated and flexible than they are today, small economies undermined greater thinking about technological development in general, and whatever thinking that existed was that a broad range of applications were needed to justify any space project.

Since then, space technology has grown in proportions and there is increasing emphasis worldwide on small, flexible missions that can be developed quickly and cheaply. One of Envisat's strengths is that it could very well provide data for seven to 10 years, which would allow continuity of observation over slowly changing environmental phenomenon.

Envisat will help to answer questions important for the future of all humanity. Scientists and policy makers need the kind of data that Envisat and other earth-observing satellites collect so that they can continue to make informed decisions about how to protect earth's environment.

The earth's ocean, the land with its plant and animal life, the ice covered regions, known as the cryosphere, and all levels of the atmosphere including the troposphere, stratosphere and mesosphere, are all parts of an interconnected system. A change in any one part affects what happens elsewhere in the system.

Envisat has been equipped with instruments to collect information that will help scientists understand each part of the earth system and to predict how changes in one part will affect others.

Many of Envisat's instruments have been based on the technology that flew on the ESA's earth-observing missions of the 1990s (ERS-1 and -2). This means that scientists have observations stretching back over 10 years, which make it possible to make comparisons between conditions observed during Envisat's lifetime and those recorded during the past 10 years.

The instruments on Envisat include the Global Ozone Monitoring by Occultation of Stars (GOMOS) which will observe the concentration of ozone in the stratosphere; the Scanning Imaging Absorption Spectrometer for Atmospheric Cartography (SCIAMACHY) which will measure trace gases and aerosol concentrations in the atmosphere; the Michelson Interferometer for Passive Atmospheric Sounding (MIPAS) which will collect information about chemical and physical processes in the stratosphere, such as those that will affect ozone concentration in the future; the Medium Resolution Imaging Spectrometer which measures radiation in 15 different frequency bands that give information about ocean biology, marine water quality, vegetation on land, cloud and water vapor; the Advanced Synthetic Aperture Radar (ASAR) which allows all-weather, day or night radar imaging; the Advanced Along Track Scanning Radiometer (AATSR) which measures sea-surface temperature, a key parameter in determining the existence and/or extent of global warming; the Radar Altimeter (RA-2), which measures the distance from the satellite to earth, as well a sea-surface height, an important measurement for monitoring El Niño; the Microwave Radiometer (MWR), which allows corrections to be made to radar altimeter data; the Doppler Orbitography and Radio Positioning Integrated by Satellite (DORIS) which gives Envisat positioning in its orbits to within a few centimeters, crucial to the understanding of all the instruments measurements; and the Laser Retro-Reflector (LRR) which reflects pulsed laser to ground stations to help determine the satellite's exact position in its orbit.

Envisat will have many specific applications. Some of the satellite's observations will help to solve basic science questions such as how the topography of the ocean changes with time, and how can this information be used to predict ocean circulation. Ocean circulation has a major impact on weather patterns and climate.

Other questions will have more immediate relevance to the political and commercial worlds. For example, how Envisat's observations can help in monitoring compliance with environmental treaties, or the selection of wind farm locations at sea.

Envisat will also help the Canadian satellite, Radarsat, monitor the ever changing ice patterns, making navigation of Canada's primary commercial shipping channel safe. Like Radarsat, Envisat carries a synthetic aperture radar (ASAR). The instrument provides images that permit the Canadian Ice Service to release frequent ice maps to the masters of ice breakers and visiting ships.

Wind energy has proven to be one of the most promising renewable energy sources currently available. Currently, wind turbines contribute significantly to electricity generation in Europe. In Denmark, for example, wind farms now meet roughly 15 percent of the country's electricity demand. In the future, the percentage of electricity generated by wind farms will increase, helping to meet a European Union target to increase the amount of energy generated by renewable sources from 14 percent in 1997 to 21 percent in 2010. Many wind farms around the world will be at sea.

Envisat's synthetic aperture radar has the potential to help planners decide on the optimum location for wind farms at sea. The aim is to find out where the wind energy is greatest from season to season so that wind farms can be sited where they will generate the maximum amount of energy.

METOP

Metop will be Europe's first polar-orbiting satellite dedicated to operational meteorology. It is a new cooperative venture with the United States that will provide data to be used to monitor our climate and improve weather forecasting.

A new generation of European instruments offering improved remote sensing capabilities to both meteorologists and climatologists will be carried with a set of heritage instruments provided by the United States. The new European instruments will enable increased accuracy in measurements of temperature and humidity, wind speed and wind

Spot 5 satellite integration. (ESA/CNES/ArianeSpace, 2002)

direction, especially the ocean, and profiles of ozone in the atmosphere.

Metop will be a series of three satellites to be launched sequentially over 14 years, starting in 2005, and forms the space segment of EUMETSAT's Polar System (EPS). Metop is a part of a European polar orbit satellite system which will fulfill a combined operational meteorological and climate monitoring mission.

Metop consists of two major modules, the service module and payload module.

The service module (SVM) design was largely derived from SPOT 5/Envisat program technology. It provides the main satellite support functions, including command and control, communications with the ground, power, attitude and orbit control, and propulsion. It also interfaces with the launcher. The SVM is box shaped, interfacing with both the launch vehicle and the payload module.

The SVM will provide the standard service functions, including altitude and orbit control, which is required to maintain accurate earth-pointing during the various operational modes. It is also needed in order to perform orbit acquisition and maintenance. This includes propulsion, for orbit and dedicated maneuvers, as well as propellant storage.

The SVM will derive its power from electrical generation through the solar arrays, storage compartments, conditioning, and overall distribution.

The command and control of the service module provides distribution of on-ground and onboard generated commands, and collection of housekeeping telemetry data for transmission to ground through the S-band link.

SVM ground communication will use central onboard software for telemetry generation, telecommand processing, and various application functions such as thermal control, onboard surveillance, and automatic command sequencing.

The SVM structure consists of the propulsion module ring, a machined aluminum alloy plate, used to support the four

Launch of Land Spot 5 on board Ariane 42P, flight 151 on May 4, 2002. (ESA/CNES/Ariane-Space, 2002)

propellant tanks and to interface with both the PLM and the SVM central structure. The central structure is a carbon fiber reinforced plastic (CFRP) sandwich construction cone featuring bonded aluminum alloy upper and lower rings. The box structure, centered around the CFRP cone, with upper and lower floors as well as external walls, forms a rectangle with shear walls that links the central cone to the external rectangular box structure, all of which are made of aluminum alloy sandwich panels.

The SVM battery compartment includes the assembly of the battery support plate and five equally-spaced radial stiffeners.

The SVM flat solar array drive mechanism (SADM) mounting structure is a set of local support structures (brackets and panels) for Attitude and Orbit Control Subsystem (AOCS) sensors, actuators, harness and antennas.

The service module thermal control consists of four main areas. These include the main body, where all the heat dissipating units are installed on the side and floor panels. The external radiators have been finished with silvered FEP Teflon tape. Multi-Layer-Insulation (MLI) blankets cover all the other faces of the main body to minimize the heat flow. Internally, the panel and the electronics units have been painted black in order to maximize the radiation exchanges. The batteries have been directly mounted on a radiator plate and enclosed in a compartment which has been thermally insulated from the rest of the spacecraft. The propulsion equipment has been conductively insulated from the spacecraft; the tanks and piping are temperature controlled using MLI and heaters. The solar array will provide its own thermal control, using passive means such as MLI and adequate thermal finishes, once it has been deployed. Active thermal control heaters are used only during the period after the separation of the spacecraft from the launcher and up to the completion of the solar array deployment.

The service module electrical power system consists of power generation, storage, distribution and control. Electrical power is generated by an eight-panel solar array. Five batteries store energy, allowing power supply during the launch and early orbit phase (LEOP), the eclipse and contingency mode, and the temporary power peak demand above the solar array capability during sunlight. The primary power bus will be unregulated, distributing power to the service module (SVM) and payload module (PLM) units. The 28 V power needed by the American instruments will be provided by a dedicated power control unit (PCU) located in the PLM.

Power in the unit will be controlled by a dedicated unit, the RSJD, that monitors the balance among the power provided by the solar array, spacecraft power demand and the power need to recharge the batteries, the distribution of several power buses, managing the batteries' thermal control, and providing switch-off lines for the satellite management in case of failure conditions.

The solar array was based on the technology utilized in the Environment Satellite (ENVISAT). It has a single wing, flat pack design solar array. It was designed with eight hinged rigid solar cell panels (each one by five m), and equipped with BSR type solar cells. The solar array cant angle is 20° and the generated power capability is 3900 W end of life.

The satellite commands and monitors solar array deployment while continuing to monitor deployment progress, position indicators, and temperature of the deployment motors and panels.

The array electrical power will be transferred through a cable harness along the primary deployment arm up to the Solar Array Drive Mechanism (SADM) mounted on the spacecraft side of the interface. The SADM will then rotate in order to hold the solar array correctly orientated towards the sun.

The PLM was based on design used in the ENVISAT. It contains the Metop instruments and associated payload support equipment, including data management, communications, and electrical distribution.

The Payload Module (PLM) will provide the main supporting structure for both the payload instruments and the payload support systems. Instrument sensors and antennas have been mounted on the external panels, while most of the electronics units are

accommodated inside the PLM. The payload module was developed and integrated by Astrium GmbH, Friedrichshafen (D).

The PLM will serve as the main supporting structure for the complement of instruments and various deployable features. The internal design of the PLM allows these instruments to work optimally.

The thermal control of the PLM maintains all electronics and instruments in predefined operational and non-operational temperature limits.

Scientific data acquisition, formatting, encryption and storage will be controlled by a dedicated unit to adapt the National Oceanic and Atmospheric Administration (NOAA) interfaces to European standards for the American instruments.

Each unit or instrument will be powered through a switchable and protected line, provided by specific PLM units. Unregulated power will be distributed to the European instruments while another unit will provide the American instruments with regulated 28 V power.

A dedicated data bus, based on the European Onboard Data Handling Standard (OBDH), will be used by the PLM. The Payload Module Computer (PMC) receives commands from the SVM and interfaces with the European Instrument Control Units (ICUs) and Microwave Humidity Sounder Protocol Conversion Unit (MPU), as well as with a specific PLM unit for the American instruments (NIU).

The Metop PLM structural design concept was based on the Environmental Satellite (Envisat) and consists of a box shape structure with a central cylinder as the main structural load path to the Service Module (SVM). The PLM structures can be categorized as being primary or secondary structural elements. Primary structural elements, which transfer the main loads and provide the overall rigidity, will include the central cylinder, shear walls, and horizontal floors.

Secondary structural elements, which have been fixed on the primary structure and ensure the interface to the PLM equipment, units and instruments include 16 removable external panels including thermal doublers, balcony including support webs, solar array (SA) hold-downs for stowed configuration, instrument support and interface brackets (for SEM-MEPED, HIRS and AVHRR), harness connector brackets, instrument radiators' sun shields, lifting and handling points including necessary reinforcements (MGSE beam), and connector bracket cut-out covers (including venting baffles).

Thermal control of the PLM was designed as a passive system consisting of radiators supplemented with heaters. Its main elements include Multi-Layer Insulation (MLI), flexible second surface mirror radiators, thermal doublers to spread the heat of high dissipating units, black paint on inner side of PLM panels, hardware controlled heaters, software controlled heaters, and monitoring thermostats.

Hardware controlled heaters will use thermostats to maintain minimum non-operating temperatures to allow immediate activation of the payload module computer (PMC), thermal control unit (TCU), power distribution unit (PDU), and the power control unit (PCU).

Software controlled heaters will be controlled by the PMC on the basis of thermostat readings, and defined temperature limits. They will be used for warm-up and for control of operational temperatures.

Most instruments have been designed with their own thermal control and thermal de-coupling from the PLM structure. Baseplate temperatures will be controlled by the PLM for the Advanced Very High Resolution Radiometer (AVHRR), High Resolution Infra-Red Sounder (HIRS) and the Search and Rescue Repeater (SARR) instruments.

Each Metop satellite will carry a set of 12 complementary instruments that have been provided by the ESA, EUMETSAT, NOAA and the French space agency, CNES.

The Metop payload will provide high-resolution images, detailed vertical temperature and humidity profiles, and temperatures of the land and ocean surface on a global basis. The Metop will also be equipped with instruments for monitoring ozone levels in the atmosphere and wind flow over the oceans. Meteorologists and many other scientists, par-

ticularly those studying the global climate, will use this data.

The Advanced Data Collection System (A-DCS), also known as ARGOS, will be one of the complement of American instruments provided by NOAA to fly on Metop-1, 2 and 3. The A-DCS will provide a worldwide in-situ environmental data collection and Doppler-derived location service with the basic objective of studying and protecting the earth's environment. A-DCS was provided by Centre National d'Études Spatiales (CNES), Toulouse, France, and developed by Thales Elancourt.

The Advanced Microwave Sounding Unit—A1 (AMSU-A1) and AMSU-A2 are two of the American instruments provided by the NOAA to fly on Metop-1, 2 and 3. The AMSU instruments will measure scene radiance in the microwave spectrum. The data from this instrument will be used in conjunction with the High-resolution Infrared Sounder (HIRS) instrument to calculate the global atmospheric temperature and humidity profiles from the earth's surface to the upper stratosphere, approximately at two millibar pressure altitude (48 km or 28 mi). The data will also be used to provide precipitation and surface measurements including snow cover, sea ice concentration, and soil moisture.

ASCAT will be Metop's Advanced SCATterometer. Its primary function will be to provide measurements of wind velocity over the world's oceans using radar.

The instrument will be the enhanced successor to the highly successful scatterometers flown onboard ESA's ERS-1 and ERS-2 satellites. Its use of six antennas allows the simultaneous coverage of two swaths on either side of the satellite ground track, allowing twice the information of the earlier instruments. On an experimental basis, ASCAT will also provide measurements at a higher than nominal resolution. In addition, ASCAT will find future roles in areas as diverse as land and sea ice monitoring, soil moisture, snow properties and soil thawing.

The instrument was developed under ESA/EUMETSAT contract by Astrium GmbH. Its wide array of hardware and software components were produced by space companies in nine of the European Space Agency's member states.

The Advanced Very High Resolution Radiometer (AVHRR/3) will be another American instrument provided by the NOAA to fly on Metop-1, 2 and 3. The AVHRR/3 will scan the earth's surface in six spectral bands in the range of 0.58–12.5 microns. It will provide day and night imaging of land, water and clouds, and measure sea surface temperature, ice, snow and vegetation cover.

The Global Ozone Monitoring Experiment-2 (GOME-2), a spectrometer, will collect light arriving from the sun-illuminated atmosphere of earth, or a direct view to the sun, and then decompose it into its spectral components. The recorded spectra will be used to derive a detailed picture of the atmospheric content and profile of ozone, nitrogen dioxide, water vapor, oxygen and oxygen dimmer, bromine oxide and other gases.

ESA and EUMETSAT have been jointly developing GOME-2 for operational meteorology and climate monitoring on the Metop satellite as an enhanced successor to GOME-1, which was launched on ESA's second European Remote Sensing Satellite (ERS-2) in 1995.

The Global Navigation Satellite Systems radio occultation (GNSS) Receiver for Atmospheric Sounding (GRAS) was designed as a GPS receiver that will operate as an atmospheric-sounding instrument. The GRAS will provide a minimum of 500 atmospheric profiles per day by a process of GPS radio occultation, as well as atmospheric soundings of the temperature and humidity of the earth's atmosphere. In addition, GRAS will provide navigation solutions of the Metop satellite position along its orbit. These profiles will then be incorporated into numerical weather prediction (NWP) models.

The High Resolution Infrared Sounder (HIRS/4) will be one of the instruments provided by the NOAA that will be flown on Metop. It is a 20 channel radiometric sounder that measures radiance in the infrared (IR) spectrum within its field of view of the earth. Data from HIRS/4 will be used in conjunction with data from the Advanced Microwave Sounding Unit (AMSU) instruments to calculate the atmosphere's vertical temperature

profile and pressure from the earth's surface to about 40 km (23.3 mi) altitude.

HIRS/4 data will also to be used to determine ocean surface temperatures, total atmospheric ozone levels, perceptible water, cloud height and coverage, and surface radiance (albedo).

HIRS/4 will fly on Metop-1 and 2. On Metop-3, HIRS/4 tasks will be taken over by the Infrared Atmospheric Sounding Interferometer (IASI) instrument.

The Infrared Atmospheric Sounding Interferometer (IASI) will consist of a Fourier transform spectrometer with an imaging system. This instrument's design was based on a Michelson interferometer to measure the infrared spectrum emitted by the earth.

IASI will provide improved infrared soundings of the temperature profiles in the troposphere and lower stratosphere, moisture profiles in the troposphere, as well as some of the chemical components playing a key role in climate monitoring, global change and atmospheric chemistry.

The Microwave Humidity Sounder (MHS) was designed to collect information on various aspects of the earth's atmosphere and surface, in particular, atmospheric humidity and surface radiation (temperature). The MHS consists of a five channel, self-calibrating, total power, microwave scanning radiometer. The data from these five channels provides information on humidity at various altitudes in the atmosphere, including atmospheric ice, cloud cover and precipitation (rain, snow, hail and sleet). Temperature information at the earth's surface will also be determined.

The Search and Rescue Processor (SARP-3) was provided by NOAA to fly on Metop-1 and 2. SARP-3 will receive and processes emergency signals from the 406 MHz beacons of aircraft and ships in distress. It will determine the name, location and time of the signal. The pre-processed data will then be fed in real time to the Search and Rescue Repeater (SARR) instrument for immediate transmission to SARSAT (Search and Rescue Satellite) distress terminals on the ground.

This will enable a 406 MHz beacon to send a distress message that can be sent to the appropriate authorities from anywhere on earth 24 hours a day, 365 days a year.

The SARR will receive and down-link emergency signals from aircraft and ships in distress. It will also provide a down-link for data received by the Search and Rescue Processor (SARP-3). The SARR will receive distress beacon signals on three separate frequencies, translate them to L-band and retransmit them to Local User Terminals (LUTs) on the ground. These terminals will then process the signals, determine the location of the beacons, and forward this information to a rescue Mission Control Centre (MCC).

The Space Environmental Monitor (SEM-2), a spectrometer, will provide measurements to determine the intensity of the earth's radiation belts and the flux of charged particles at the satellite altitude. It will provide data on solar terrestrial phenomena, and also provide warnings of solar wind occurrences that may impair long-range communication, high-altitude operations, damage to satellite circuits and solar panels, or cause changes in drag and magnetic torque on satellites.

METEOSAT SECOND GENERATION (MSG)

Images of real sequences of clouds moving across Europe have graced the country's daily TV weather forecasts for the past 25 years. Now, however, the satellites that delivered them are about to be replaced. Out with Meteosat First Generation; in with Meteosat Second Generation (MSG).

When the new satellites take over sometime after the first launch in August 2002, the images will be even clearer and sequences of cloud development will be smoother and more realistic. The improved images will allow meteorologists to provide more accurate medium and short-term weather forecasts.

MSG will take images at more wavelengths and at shorter intervals than its parents, making it particularly suitable for short-term forecasting of sudden troublesome weather phenomena such as snow, thunderstorms and fog. Televised weather bulletins will be able to advise Europeans with considerable accuracy about whether to take an um-

brella or avoid a particular stretch of road because bad weather is expected later in the day!

MSG is a joint project between ESA and EUMETSAT, the organization set up in 1986 to establish, maintain and operate a European system of meteorological satellites. Three satellites have been planned so far, as well as a ground segment. ESA was responsible for designing and developing the first satellite, and for procuring the other two on behalf of EUMETSAT. EUMETSAT has defined payloads based on user needs, managing the ground segment and launchers, and operating the system.

With the launch of MSG-2, at any one time, two MSG satellites will be functional in geostationary orbit, the operational one being at zero degrees longitude, which is above equatorial West Africa, the other being on stand-by with 10 degrees of separation.

The first satellite, MSG-1, was launched on board an Ariane 5 launcher in August 2002. MSG-2 has been scheduled for launch

Ariane 513, Flight 155 collage at Kourou Space Center, Guiana. Launched on August 28, 2002, Ariane placed the MSG-1 Atlantic Bird 1 Satellite in orbit. (ESA/CNES/ArianeSpace, 2002)

approximately 18 months later. MSG-3 will be built and put in storage until it is required to take over as MSG-1 nears the end of its life. Each satellite will have a nominal seven-year lifetime. A fourth MSG satellite of the same design is foreseen to ensure continuity of service until the end of the next decade.

The MSG satellites will all offer weather forecasters and climate modelers more sophisticated images and data than their predecessors, the first generation of Meteosats. The MSG camera, called the Spinning Enhanced Visible and Infra-red Imager (SEVIRI), will store images of the earth's surface and cloud cover in 12 different wavelengths once every 15 minutes, compared with three wavelengths once every 30 minutes for the camera on Meteosat. The images will also be sharper — SEVIRI will pick out structures as small as 1 km (0.6214 mile) in the visible compared with 2.5 km (1.55 miles) for Meteosat. In the infrared, SEVIRI will resolve features three km across compared with five km (3.0 miles) for Meteosat.

By doubling the rate of image taking, MSG will be able to keep closer track of cloud development and so be more sensitive than its predecessor to rapid changes in weather patterns. Four of the 12 imaging channels will look at sunlight reflected from the earth's surface and clouds, compared with only one channel on the Meteosat camera. The remaining eight channels will detect thermal infrared wavelengths, compared with just two on Meteosat. Four of these will measure the temperature of clouds, land and sea surfaces, and the other four will detect wavelengths emitted by water vapor, carbon dioxide and ozone in the atmosphere. Climate modelers will be able to keep track of the constituents of air masses, and so construct a three-dimensional view of the atmosphere.

SEVIRI will be the main instrument on board the MSG, and it will be accompanied by another instrument with a scientific research purpose. The Geostationary Earth Radiation Budget (GERB) experiment will contribute to climate change studies by measuring the amount of radiation arriving on earth from the sun and the amount leaving as heat, and scattered and reflected solar radiation. Two further items of the payload will also provide

services: a communications package and a transponder for search and rescue. The communications package will be particularly sophisticated because of the need to receive and transmit data between the ground station and the users.

Similar to Meteosat, MSG will monitor a large portion of the earth and its atmosphere from its position in geostationary orbit at zero degrees longitude, 35,800 km (22,246 miles) above the Gulf of Guinea off the west coast of equatorial Africa. MSG-1 will move into position 10 degrees west of the last Meteosat for up to six months before swapping places to take over as the operational satellite in the zero degree position.

MSG will transmit raw atmospheric data to the EUMETSAT control and processing center in Darmstadt via the primary ground station. The raw data will consist mainly of images generated by the camera, the spinning enhanced visible and infrared imager, and the geostationary earth radiation budget experiment onboard the satellite. Once processed, the data will be sent back to the satellite for broadcasting to users. The data collection platforms on ships, balloons, aircraft and ground–based platforms will also send meteorological data such as local temperature, wind speed and humidity directly to users via the satellite.

The primary ground station will send the processed data to users via the satellite at a high and a low rate. High Rate Information Transmission (HRIT) will contain the full volume of processed, compressed image data, and Low Rate Information Transmission (LRIT) will contain a reduced set at lower resolution. In addition, the EUMETSAT Control and Processing Center, with support from other satellite applications facilities throughout Europe, will extract information from the processed data and turn it into products of particular use to meteorologists and climatologists such as wind field diagrams, maps of upper tropospheric humidity and analyses of cloud shape and height.

MSG has also been equipped with a transponder to relay SOS messages at 406 MHz to a central reception station in Europe, from which they will be sent to the appropriate rescue organizations. This system continues to be run by the COSPAS-Sarsat organization, which achieves global coverage by having several search and rescue transponders on geostationary and other satellites.

The MSG satellite system carries the following instruments: The SEVIRI (Spinning Enhanced Visible and Infrared Imager), a radiometer which is the main instrument on board MSG. It provides images of the earth disc with cloud, land, ocean, snow and other information made visible by day and by night. It has been able to take one full resolution image every 15 minutes, thus illustrating the weather in motion. Its operating principle has been based on collecting the earth's radiation by means of a telescope and focusing it on detectors sensitive to 12 different bands of the electromagnetic spectrum. This is followed by the electronic processing of the signals provided by the detectors.

The GERB (Geostationary Earth Radiation Budget) experiment is a broadband, three-mirror telescope housed in the instrument optical unit. It views the earth with a

Geostationary Meterological Satellite MSG-1 antennas at Kourou Space Center, Guiana. (ESA/CNES/Arianespace, 2002)

black wide-band detector array, providing measurements of the earth's output radiation in a total band and a short-wave band. The long-wave band is obtained by subtraction. The Earth Radiation Budget (ERB) is the balance between the radiation coming from the sun and the outgoing reflected and scattered solar radiation, plus thermal infrared emissions, to space. GERB will work in conjunction with the SEVIRI sensor on MSG.

The MCP (Meteorological Communications Payload) is a highly reliable communications system for data transmission. The various antennas and transponders provide downlink of SEVIRI and GERB data to the Primary Ground Station (EUMETSAT), up to three megabits per second reception and transmission at one megabit per second of processed meteorological data and images to the user stations, and telemetry, tracking and command for the satellite monitoring and control.

The S&R (Search and Rescue) transponder is a 4066 MHz transponder carried by the MSG satellites that will detect and relay distress signals transmitted by distress beacons to an international rescue network developed by Canada, France, the United States and Russia, designed to assist worldwide search and rescue operations.

Navigation and Telecommunications

The Applications Directorate of the European Space Agency is responsible for navigation and telecommunications. Pursuit of these two elements is necessary to help the directorate achieve its main mission — to use satellite technology to improve our daily lives.

Many of the new telecommunication services which are in daily use depend heavily on the existence of efficient space technology. ESA has been a major player in this massive communications network.

Since the launch of an orbital test satellite in the late 1970s, ESA has both pioneered and influenced new technologies, contributing to the birth of the European telecommunications industry, which is able to play a key role in the world market.

Four European communications satellites launched between 1983 and 1988 revolutionized the communications industry by bringing cable TV, telephone communications, Eurovision transmissions and other specialist services to the entire European continent.

In 1989, ESA's Olympus satellite became the largest civilian communications satellite in the world. Its direct-to-home TV broadcasting payload allowed programs to be captured on antenna dishes as small as 30 cm (12 in) in diameter.

Today, ESA continues to play an instrumental role in developing satellite communications technology through its new telecommunications satellite, Artemis, which was launched in 2001; and the Artes program that supports the development of new communications systems, technologies and services for users in Europe and all over the world.

In the area of navigation, ESA has been working with the European Commission (EC) to develop Galileo, a civilian global satellite navigation system under European control. Galileo will be comprised of approximately 30 satellites circling the earth in medium earth orbit, starting in 2006, to reach full capacity in 2008.

ESA and the EC have also joined forces with the European Organization for the Safety of Air Navigation (Eurocontrol) to develop EGNOS, a system to complement the U.S. Global Positioning System (GPS) and the Russian Global Navigation Satellite System (GLONASS).

EGNOS will apply these military-controlled services to several civilian applications. The EGNOS signal will be generated by a sophisticated network of ground stations and broadcast by means of transponders installed on geostationary satellites by 2004.

EGNOS and Galileo will contribute greatly to Europe's global navigation system, making air travel, road traffic systems, maritime tracking and emergency services faster, more accurate and more reliable.

GALILEO

Galileo will be Europe's global navigation satellite system, providing a highly accurate, guaranteed global positioning service under civilian control. With Galileo in operation, a user will be able to take a position with the same receiver from any of the satellites in any combination.

By offering dual frequencies as standard, Galileo will deliver real-time positioning accuracy down to the meter range, which is unprecedented for a publicly available system. Galileo will guarantee availability of the service under all but the most extreme circumstances, and will inform users within seconds of a failure of any satellite. This will be particularly useful in applications where safety is crucial, such as running trains, guiding cars and landing aircraft.

Galileo is a joint project of the ESA and the European Commission (EC). The EC will be responsible for the political dimensions and the high-level mission requirements. The EC conducted studies on the overall architecture of Galileo that addressed the interoperability of local architectures and signals and frequencies.

ESA's role has been essential in the definition, development, and in-orbit validation of the space segment and related ground segment.

Development of Galileo technology has included high precision clocks to be installed onboard the satellites, which will apply rubidium and passive hydrogen maser frequency standards, onboard timing units for steering the individual clocks to a common Galileo System Time, and signal generators to produce the positioning signals that the Galileo spacecraft will broadcast. This will include power amplifiers, radio-frequency multiplexers and antennas, and telecommand/telemetry transponders.

ESA has also started work on the technologies needed for Galileo receivers, including the first version of the Galileo System Test Bed (GSTB VI), which will allow engineers to validate Galileo-specific control algorithms such as clock adjustments and procedures for predicting individual satellite orbits, before the full system goes into operation.

Galileo's satellite navigation system will include rubidium clocks based on oscillations at the atoms level, under development at the

Observatoire de Neuchatel and Temex Neuchatel Time, which are both located in the center of the Swiss clock industry.

These clocks, which will keep time to within a few hundred millionths of a second per day, can resolve a position anywhere on the earth's surface to within 45 cm (18 in).

Each of the 30 satellites in the Galileo system will have two clocks onboard, one based on the Rubidium atomic frequency standard and the other using a passive hydrogen maser. Although both clocks use different technologies, they make use of the same principle — if you force atoms to jump from one particular energy state to another, it will radiate the associated microwave signal at an extremely stable frequency. This frequency will range at around 6 GHz for the rubidium clock and at 1.4 GHz for the hydrogen clock. The generated broadcast signals will also provide a reference by which the less stable user receiver clocks can continuously reset their time.

Galileo will be positioned in three circular medium earth orbit (MEO) planes 23,616 km (14, 170 miles) above the earth at an inclination of the orbital planes of 56 degrees, with reference to the equatorial plane.

Once properly positioned, the Galileo system of 30 satellites (27 operational and three active spares) navigation signals will provide coverage even at latitudes of up to 75 degrees north, which corresponds to the North Cape and beyond. The use of a large number of satellites, together with the optimization of the constellation, and the availability of the three active spare satellites, will ensure that the loss of one satellite has no noticeable effect on the user.

The first experimental satellite, part of the Galileo System Test Bed (GSTB), will be launched in late 2004. After this initial test of critical technologies, four operational satellites will be launched between 2005 and 2006 in order to establish the basic Galileo space and ground related segment.

Once the in-orbit validation (IOV) phase has been completed, the remaining satellites will be launched to reach the full operational capability (FOC) in 2008.

Launch of Ariane 510, Flight 142 from Kourou Space Center, Guiana, to place Artemis satellite BSAT 2B in orbit, July 12, 2001. (ESA/CNES/ Arianespace, 2001)

ARTEMIS

Artemis, ESA's advanced relay and technology mission, was launched in July 2001. It has been demonstrating wide-coverage mobile communications-satellite services and testing direct satellite-to-satellite communications systems, including a revolutionary laser link known as SILEX.

Although Artemis was initially placed in an incorrect orbit, careful analysis and planning enabled a series of orbit maneuvers to successfully raise the spacecraft to a safe, temporary circular orbit at 31,000 km (18,600 miles) altitude.

Two in-orbit test results were performed in which the large inner-orbit link antenna used to relay data between Artemis and a "user" spacecraft in low-earth orbit demonstrated its ability to track the user in either pre-programmed pointing or auto tracking mode, and SILEX functionality was also successfully demonstrated with the perfect transmission of SPOT-4 images — a world first.

Human Spaceflight

ESA's main project in the area of human spaceflight has been the Automated Transfer Vehicle (ATV), which is anticipated to be one of the indispensable supply ships serving the International Space Station (ISS). The ISS has the need for regular deliveries of experimental equipment and spare parts as well as food, air and water for its permanent crew, which will be fulfilled by use of the ATV.

Every 12 months, the ATV will haul 7.5 tons of cargo from its Kourou launch site in French Guiana to the station located 400 km (240 miles) above the earth. An onboard high precision navigation system will guide the ATV on a rendezvous trajectory towards ISS, where it will automatically dock with the station's Russian service module.

The ATV will remain docked as a pressurized and integral part of the station for up to six months until its final mission — a fiery one-way trip into the earth's atmosphere to dispose of up to 6.5 tons of station waste.

The exterior of the 20-ton ATV is an eggshell-colored cylinder, 10.3 meters (34 feet) long and 4.5 meters (15 feet) in diameter. The outer structure of the ATV is covered with an insulating foil layer on top of anti-meteorite panels. The ATV's unique X-shaped extended solar arrays look very much like metallic blue wings. The interior of the ATV consists of two modules, the propulsion spacecraft and the integrated cargo carrier which docks with the ISS.

The ATV pressurized cargo section is based on the Italian-built Multi-Purpose Logistics Module (MPLM), which is already in service as a shuttle-carried space barge, transporting equipment to and from the station.

The ATV, which is equipped with its own propulsion and navigation systems, is a multi-functional spaceship combining both the full automatic capabilities of an unmanned vehicle with the human spacecraft safety requirements. Its mission in space can be likened to the relation of a tugboat to a river barge.

Onboard, the 45 m³ (158 ft³) pressurized section has room for up to eight standard racks, which are loaded with modular storage cargo elements. The integrated cargo carrier

also holds several tanks containing up to 840 kg (378 lbs) of drinking water, 860 kg (387 lbs) of refueling propellant for the station's own propulsion system and 100 kg (45 lbs) of air (oxygen and nitrogen). The cargo section nose contains the Russian-made docking equipment and several types of rendezvous sensors.

The ATV spacecraft module navigates with four main engines, 490 N in power, plus 28 smaller thrusters, 220 N, for altitude control. After docking, the ATV can perform ISS altitude control and debris avoidance maneuvers, and boost the station's orbit to overcome the effects of atmospheric drag. In order to perform this maneuver the ATV uses up to 4.7 tons of propellant.

The typical mission scenario of an ATV will begin when the craft is launched into a 300-km (180 mile) orbit atop an Ariane-5 from the French Guiana equatorial launch site. The ATV will then separate from Ariane navigation systems and activate under the European control center in Toulouse, France. Thrusters will fire to boost the ATV into the transfer orbit to the ISS.

Following three days of orbit adjustments, the ATV will come within sight of the ISS and will begin relative navigation from about 30 km (18 miles) behind and 5 km (3 miles) below the station. The cargo ship's computers commence final approach maneuvers over the next two orbits, closing with ISS at walking pace.

The actual docking of the ATV will be fully automatic, although a computerized back-up system can trigger a pre-programmed sequence of anti-collision maneuvers, if need be, that can be compared to the action of an airbag activating in a car.

Once the ATV is securely docked, the station's crew can enter the cargo section and remove the payload, including maintenance supplies, science hardware, and parcels of fresh food. Meanwhile, the ATV's liquid tanks will be connected to the station's own plumbing and discharge their contents.

The station crew will manually release air components directly into the ISS's atmosphere. For up to six months the ATV, mostly in a dormant mode, will remain attached to the ISS with the hatch open. The crew will steadily fill the cargo section with the station's waste. Every 10 to 45 days, the ATV's thrusters will be used to boost the station's altitude.

Once its re-supply mission has been fulfilled, the ATV, filled with waste, will be closed by the crew and automatically separated. Its thrusters will use their remaining fuel to de-orbit the spacecraft on a steep flight path in order to perform a controlled destructive re-entry high above the Pacific Ocean.

The first operational flight of the ATV is set for autumn of 2004. ESA plans to build eight additional ATVs depending on the operational lifetime of the space station.

European Launchers

Europe has a very strong launch program flagged by its Ariane launcher family. In July 1973, ESA's Member States made the decision to begin development of the Ariane launcher in an effort to give Europe independent access to space at an affordable cost. It has since proved to be a highly reliable and successful method of transportation into space.

Ariane first flew in December 1979 primarily as a method for putting telecommunications satellites into orbit two at a time in order to reduce launch costs.

As satellite size increased, Ariane 1 gave way in 1984 to the more powerful Ariane 2, and then the Ariane 3. All were later surpassed by Ariane 4 in 1988.

Although Ariane 2, 3 and 4 belonged to the same family of vehicles, they had certain differences. The first and third stages became extended in length, while liquid or solid propellant strap-on boosters were added for extra power and stability.

Ariane 4's arrival in June 1988 brought an increased payload capacity that would allow for placement in geostationary orbit by nearly three times, from 1700 to 4800 kg (3740 to 10,560 lbs).

In order to meet varying market demands, it was made available in six versions — one bare and the others fitted with two or four solid or liquid strap-on boosters, depending on the mass to be placed in orbit.

Ariane 4 also had a choice of widened fairings designed to house larger and heavier satellites, while using a special support structure, or Spelda, for launching two satellites at a time.

Ariane 4 has since been upgraded and replaced by Ariane 5, which has the ability to launch larger satellites, increase the use of low orbits for servicing the International Space Station, and reduce costs while maintaining a high reliability.

The first successful launch of Ariane 5 occurred on October 30, 1997, while its first operational flight with payload occurred in December 1999.

The European commercial launcher family will grow with the addition of Vega, a new vehicle scheduled to enter operation in mid–2006 for flights with small- to medium-sized satellite payloads.

Vega will be designed as a single-body vehicle consisting of three solid-propulsion stages, an additional liquid-propulsion upper module, and a fairing for payload protection.

Ariane 509 launch on March 8, 2001, of Flight 140, with BAF (Building Assembly Final) at Kourou Space Center, Guiana.

EUROPE'S SPACEPORT

The spaceport used by ESA is located at Kourou, French Guiana. In 1964, the French government chose Kourou as a base from which to launch its satellites. Later in 1975, when ESA was established, the French government offered to share its satellite launch center, Centre Spatial Guyanais (CSG), with ESA. ESA agreed to upgrade the launch facilities to prepare the spaceport for the Ariane launchers that were under development.

In addition to the spaceport, French Guiana has a very colorful history, including its sinister distinction as a former penal colony that was established in 1852. French convicts and deportees were imprisoned in Saint Laurant de Maroni, as well as on the islands of Royal and St. Joseph, while political prisoners were kept on Devil's Island.

Devil's Island was made notorious by the book *Papillion*, which was written by one of its last inmates, Henri Charrière. The infamous penal colony was finally closed in 1947.

Kourou lies at a latitude of 5°3', located 500 km (300 miles) north of the equator. Its location makes it ideal for launches into geostationary transit orbit as its close proximity to the equator means fewer changes have to made to a satellite's trajectory.

Also beneficial has been the "slingshot" effect, which is the energy created by the speed of the earth's rotation around the axis of the poles. This slingshot increases the speed of the launcher by 460 m (1,518 feet) per second. Both factors help to save fuel and money as well as to prolong the active life of satellites.

Europe's spaceport also offers a launch angle of 102°, which permits a wide range of missions from east to north. In addition to ESA, the spaceport at French Guiana has also been used by the United States, Canada, Japan, India and Brazil.

THE ARIANE FAMILY

The first Ariane launcher blasted into the sky on Christmas Eve, 1979. Ariane 1 was primarily designed to put two telecommunications satellite at a time into orbit, enabling a reduction of costs. As the need for larger satellites arose, Ariane 1 gave way to the more powerful Ariane 2 and Ariane 3 launchers.

Eleven Ariane 1 launches occurred between 1979 and 1986. Five successful Ariane 2 flights took off between 1987 and 1989. Ariane 3 made eleven flights from 1984 to 1989.

All three launchers varied slightly in design. The first and third stages of Ariane 2 and 3 were longer than those of Ariane 1. Ariane 3 also differed in that it had strap-on boosters carrying liquid or solid propellant, giving it the ability to launch a payload of 1.7 tons.

Ariane 4 has been known as the workhorse of the Ariane family. It has made over 113 successful launches since its maiden flight on June 15, 1988.

Ariane 4 has launched satellites for communications and earth observation, as well as for scientific research. Ariane 4 captured 50 percent of the commercial satellite launch market during its operational lifetime.

There were six versions of Ariane 4, including Ariane 40, with a maximum payload of 2,800 kg (6,160 lb); Ariane 42P, with a maximum payload of 3,063 kg (6,739 lb); Ariane 44P, with a maximum payload of 3,577 kg (7,869 lb); Ariane 42L, with a maximum payload of 3,572 kg (7,958 lb); Ariane 44LP, with a maximum payload of 4,330 kg (9,526 lb); and Ariane 44L, with a maximum payload of 4,947 kg (10,883 lb).

Ariane 5 was designed to meet several requirements — the ability to launch larger satellites, the increasing use of low orbits for

Ariane launch operations with six versions of Ariane four and one version of Ariane 5. (ESA/Illustrated by David Ducros, 2001)

Ariane 511 Vulcain Motor at Kourou Space Center, Guiana. (ESA/CNES/ArarineSpace, 2002)

Integration of EPS (Etage Propergols Stockable) Ariane 512 launcher at Kourou Space Center, Guiana.

servicing the International Space Station and the need to reduce costs while maintaining a high launch rate.

Its first successful launch occurred on October 30, 1997. It has since been used to launch satellites for communications, earth observation and scientific research into geostationary orbits and sun-synchronous orbits.

Ariane 5 has a simple and robust architecture consisting of a main cryogenic core stage, two solid booster stages, and an upper stage.

The main cryogenic stage is 30 m (100 ft) tall, operating on non-toxic cryogenic propellant for just under 600 s. Its Vulcain engine is ignited seven seconds prior to launcher liftoff, allowing for full monitoring during start up and stabilization of thrust.

The solid booster stage stands more than 30 m (100 ft) tall, consisting of two solid boosters which deliver more than 90 percent of the total launcher's thrust at the start of flight.

The storable propellant stage, or EPS, is

the first upper stage that was developed for Ariane 5. It propels the launcher's payload to its final orbit, providing an accurate orbital injection.

Ariane 5 is an evolving vehicle, with future plans to undergo modifications to the main cryogenic stage and solid boosters which will increase performance and meet the demands of a changing market.

Ariane 5 ESC-A, which began service in 2002, has enabled Ariane 5 to place 10,000 to 10,500 kg (22,000 to 23,100 lb) into geostationary orbit (GTO).

Ariane 5 ESC-B, powered by a new Vinci engine, will increase GTO payload performance to 11,000 to 12,000 kg (24,200 to 26,400 lb), starting in 2006.

Ariane 5 Versatile, which entered service in late 2001, has increased GTO payload lift capability to 7,300 to 8,000 kg (16,060 to 17,600 lb).

A variety of large payload fairings enable Ariane 5 to launch all satellites currently in service, as well as those in development. These include the internal structure for dual launches, Sylda 5, allowing dual-payload missions, accommodating satellites with a maximum height of 2.9 to 4.4 m (9.57 to 14.52 ft); the external structure for dual launches, Speltra, also for dual-payload missions, carrying satellites up to 6.1 m (20.1 ft) tall; and the Ariane Structure for Auxiliary Payloads, ASAP, which carries mini- or microsatellites as secondary payloads.

FUTURE VEGA

Vega is the European Space Agency's answer to the need for a small launcher to put 300 to 2000 kg (660 to 4400 lb) satellites into polar and low-earth orbits economically, for scientific and earth observation missions.

Vega was named after the second brightest star in the northern hemisphere, and will make access to space easier, quicker and cheaper.

Development of the Vega launcher started in 1998 and the first launch is expected in 2006.

The launcher will be 27 m (89.1 ft) in height and 3 m (10 ft) in diameter, with a payload mass of 1500 kg (3300 lbs) and a liftoff mass of 128 tons.

Vega will consist of three solid stages to perform the injection of the upper composite into a low-altitude orbit.

The liquid upper module, called AVUM (Altitude and Vernier Upper Module), will be used to improve the accuracy of primary injection, the compensation of solid-propulsion performance scatter, in order to circularize the orbit and perform the de-orbiting maneuver.

The AVUM will also provide roll control during the third-stage boost phase and three-axis control during the ballistic phases and before payload separation.

The first stage will be powered by a P80 advanced solid propellant motor. It will feature a novel filament-wound casing structure.

The second and third stages will consist of Zefiro solid-rocket motors. The second stage, Zefiro 23, will have a propellant mass of 23.8 tons. The third stage, Zefiro 9, will have a propellant mass of 9 tons.

The AVUM will be responsible for roll control during third and fourth stage flight; altitude control during coasting flight and the in-orbit phase; correction of axial velocity error due to solid-rocket motor performance scatter; generation of the required velocity change for orbit circularization; satellite pointing; satellite-release maneuvers; and empty-stage de-orbiting.

Total propellant loading will be between 250 and 400 kg (550 and 880 lb), depending on the mission to be performed. It will utilize a liquid bipropellant system for primary maneuvers, running on nitrogen tetroxide (NTO) as oxidizer and unsymmetrical monomethyl-hydrazine (UDMH) as fuel, which will both be fed by gaseous helium under pressure, and a cool-gas system (GN2) for altitude control.

Vega's first qualification flight has been scheduled for 2006, and will be followed by launches at a rate of three to four missions per year.

Space Science Missions

ESA, as an agency, has always placed heavy emphasis on space science exploratory missions. In addition to a number of cooperative projects with the United States, ESA has launched several European projects, including COS-B, the first ESA mission to study gamma-ray sources; Exosat, a high-energy mission to observe and detect X-ray sources; Giotto, the comet flyby mission; Hipparcos, to pinpoint the stars, their motion and distance; Infrared Space Observatory (ISO), to probe the cool and hidden universe; and the International Ultraviolet Explorer (IUE), for the ultraviolet observation of cosmic objects from comets to quasars.

COS-B

COS-B, ESA's first satellite dedicated to a single experiment, was launched on August 9, 1975, from Western Test Range, California.

Its scientific objective was to study in detail the sources of extra-terrestrial gamma radiation at energies above 30 MeV. This study included the spectrum and distribution of extragalatic gamma-ray emission, while investigating some known point sources in the gamma-ray range and searching for new point sources.

Data obtained was stored in the 2CG Catalogue with 25 gamma-ray sources out of 30 observations made during the first three years. COS-B studied a binary system, Cygnus X-3, containing a pulsar and gamma-ray emitter. Two other objects, the Crab and Vela sources, yielded a light curve.

The first full gamma-ray map of the galactic plane was created along with detection of the first gamma-ray AGN (active galactic nucleus) 3C 273.

Another major accomplishment of COS-B was the compilation of a catalogue on the spectrum of Geminga, one of the brightest gamma-ray sources recorded, and the location of it to within 0.25 degrees, allowing counterpart searches.

COS-B was powered by 9480 silicon solar cells, occupying nearly the entire outer surface of the satellite cylinder. The power outputted by the cells was 60 watts. A backup battery was also available to allow for the satellite to operate while in the earth's shadow.

COS-B was originally planned for a functional duration of two years. However, the spacecraft well exceeded that estimate and was finally switched off on April 25, 1982, after six years and eight months of operation.

EXOSAT

Exosat was the European Space Agency's first three-axis stabilized spacecraft. It was launched on May 26, 1983, from Vandenburg Air Force Base in California, and switched off April 9, 1986.

The spacecraft was equipped with three instrument packages, including the low-energy (LE) imaging telescopes with a Channel-multiplier Array (CHM) and PSD (position sensitive proportional counter); the medium-energy (ME) instrument consisting of four independently-movable quadrants, each equipped with two proportional counters — two of which remained on target, while the other two offset to observe adjacent areas of empty sky; and the Gas Scintillation Proportional Counter (GSPC)

with stronger spectral resolution than ME, but a smaller effective area.

Exosat was able to discover the quasi-period oscillations in LMXRB and X-ray pulsars, provide a comprehensive study of AGN variability, observe LMXRG and CV over many orbital periods, measure iron lines in galactic and extra-galactic sources, and obtain low-energy, high-resolution spectra.

During its operation, Exosat made 1,780 observations in the X-ray band of many classes of objects, including active galactic nuclei, white dwarfs, stars, Supernova remnants, clusters of galaxies, cataclysmic variables and X-ray binaries.

Exosat was able to achieve a highly eccentric orbit with an apogee of 190,000 km (114,000 miles), a perigee of 350 km (210 miles) and an orbital period of 90 hours.

Among its many discoveries, Exosat achieved the detection of quasi-periodic oscillations (QPO) in the radiation from GX 5-1, which are now known to be common in low-mass X-ray binaries; observations of the pulsing X-ray nova EXO 2030 + 375 revealed for the very first time in a single system, with changes in pulse period and shape as the luminosity changed by a factor of 100, providing new insights into the accretion dynamics and beaming of accreting neutron stars; the detections of Doppler variations in the Fe-line from SS433, showing thermal emission with a rest energy of 6.7 keV, arising from the near-side jet; the discovery of the spectacularly short eleven minute period in the globular cluster X-ray burster XB 1820-30; a spectral survey of 48 Seyfert galaxies over two decades of energy (0.1–10 keV), showing many examples with a "soft" X-ray component, supporting an accretion disk model for Active Galactic Nuclei and the discovery that there is a lack of X-ray luminous clusters at z > 0.1, indicating that cluster evolution has been strong and continuing.

GIOTTO

Giotto was ESA's first planetary mission, with a number of achievements including the first close-up images of a comet nucleus; the first spacecraft to encounter two comets —

Halley's and Grigg-Skjellerup; and the first deep space mission to change orbit by returning to earth for a gravity assist. The Giotto also discovered the size and shape of Halley's comet's nucleus; it made the closest comet flyby to date by any spacecraft coming to within 200 km (124 miles) of Grigg-Skjellerup Comet; it discovered a black crust and bright jets of gas on the nucleus of Halley's comet; it measured the size, composition and velocity of dust particles near the two comets; and it measured the composition of gas produced by the two comets.

The mission was launched on July 2, 1985, via an Ariane 1 rocket. The spacecraft was named after the famous medieval Italian artist, Giotto di Bondone, who lived from 1266 to 1337.

The Giotto spacecraft was based on the GEOS earth-orbiting research satellites, which were built by British Aerospace. The most prominent addition was a buffer to protect it from a battering by high speed dust particles during the comet encounter.

The spacecraft was a modest 960 kg (0.96 tons), and it consisted of a short cylinder 1.85 m (6.07 ft) in diameter by nearly 1.1 m (3.6 ft) in height. It was equipped with three interior platforms — the top platform, 30 cm (12 in) thick; a main platform, 40 cm (15.7 in); and an experiment platform, also 30 cm (12 in). Each of these held a disc within the cylinder, on which were mounted various subsystems and science experiments. The main rocket motor was located in the center of the cylinder with the nozzle protruding from the bottom.

Giotto traveled at a rate of 245,000 km/h (152,243 miles/h), the equivalent to crossing the Atlantic Ocean in eleven minutes! It was equipped with solar arrays which were made up of 5,032 silicon cells wrapped around its cylindrical exterior. These cells provided 190 watts of power during the first comet encounter. Four silver-cadmium batteries were carried as back up and for use while the spacecraft was in shadow mode.

When the spacecraft was spin-stabilized, it rotated at a speed of 15 rpm. During the Halley's encounter, the spacecraft approached with its dust shield and spin axis pointing towards the nucleus, while its dish antenna continually pointed towards the earth to ensure non-stop communications.

Giotto carried ten scientific instruments, including a narrow-angle, multicolor camera to obtain pictures of the nucleus; three mass spectrometers to measure gas and dust composition; a dust impact detector to measure the mass of dust particles striking the shield; two plasma experiments to study the solar wind and charged particles; an energetic particles analyzer to study electrons, protons and alpha-particles; a magnetometer to study changes in the magnetic field; an optical probe to study the brightness of the coma; and a radio science experiment to investigate the electron environment.

During the Halley's comet flyby, Giotto was able to obtain 2,112 images. Detailed analysis of the data confirmed that the comet had formed 4.5 billion years ago from ices condensing onto grains of interstellar dust, and has since remained almost unaltered in the cold, outer regions of the solar system.

Important results from Giotto included the following revelations: water accounted for about 80 percent by volume of all of the material thrown out by the comet, including substantial amounts of carbon monoxide (10 percent), carbon dioxide (2.5 percent) methane and ammonia. Traces of other hydrocarbons, iron and sodium were also found. The surface of the nucleus was very dark — blacker than coal — which suggested a thick covering of dust. The nucleus surface was very irregular, with hills and depressions. The nucleus also had a porous texture, with a density as low as 0.3 g/cc (one third the density of water). Seven jets were identified which threw out three tons of material per second. These jets gave the comet a strange, wobbling rotation which seems to be stable over centuries or even millennia; and most of the dust was no larger than specks of cigarette smoke. The largest grain detected was 40 mg, though the large particle that knocked the spacecraft out of alignment was estimated to be from 0.1 to 1 gram.

Two major classes of dust particles were found by Giotto. One was dominated by the light CHON elements — carbon, hydrogen, oxygen and nitrogen. The other was rich in mineral-forming elements — sodium, magnesium, silicon, iron and calcium.

All of the comet's light elements (except nitrogen) were found in the same relative abundance as the sun, which indicated that Halley's comet consists of the most primitive material known in the solar system.

During the flyby of comet Grigg-Skjellerup, the eight operational experiments (including the radio science investigation) provided a surprising wealth of exciting data. Conditions inside the comet's plasma or ionized gas cloud were significantly different than that found with Halley. The first cometary ions (charged particles) were detected 440,000 km (273,416 miles) from the nucleus, about 12 hours before the closest approach.

Scientists were surprised when an abrupt shock wave, that had apparently been caused when the supersonic solar wind slammed into plasma around the comet, was detected on Giotto's outbound leg, but not clearly identified on the inward journey.

The strangest discovery of all was unusual magnetic waves, each about 1000 km (621 miles) apart, near the comet. Activity rose and fell for nearly 70 seconds and increased in strength as time went by. The waves were generated by pick-up ions — charged particles created from the break up of water molecules around the comet — as they moved in the magnetic field created by the solar wind.

HIPPARCOS

Hipparcos was the first European space mission for measuring the positions, distances, motions, brightness and colors of stars for astrometry. Launched in 1989 and operational until 1993, the satellite pinpointed more than 100,000 stars 200 times more accurately than ever before.

In addition to giving a previously unprecedented three-dimensional picture of the distances and movements of stars in the vicinity of the sun and the earth, Hipparcos helped to predict the impacts of comet Shoemaker-Levy 9 on Jupiter; identified stars passing close to the sun; established the distances of stars possessing planets; cut the distance of the Pleiades cluster; discovered that the Milky

Way is changing shape; identified a group of stars that invaded our galaxy when it was young; altered the cosmic distance scale, making the universe larger and younger than previously expected; and confirmed Einstein's prediction of the effect of gravity on starlight.

The 1.4 ton Hipparcos satellite was built by European aerospace industry and launched by an Ariane 4 rocket. Each star selected for study was visited by the satellite roughly 100 times over four years.

The million bits of information obtained by Hipparcos were radioed to ground stations in Germany, Australia and the United States, making for the largest computation in the history of astronomy. These computations allowed for the creation of a super-accurate frame for the entire sky, identifying shifts in direction of individual stars as the earth orbited around the sun, enabling a star's distance to be measured. The computations also revealed the proper motions of stars across the sky and orbital motions of double stars circling around each other.

Computations from observations generated the Hipparcos catalog of 118,218 stars with the highest precision.

In addition to being named after the early astrometrist of classical times, Hipparcos was also an acronym for High Precision Parallax Collecting Satellite.

Hipparcos was able to observe 24,000 double stars, of which 10,000 were not previously known to double. It also investigated changes in luminosity of 8,000 new variable stars, as well as 4,000 known variables, greatly improving the knowledge of how variable stars behave.

INFRARED SPACE OBSERVATORY (ISO)

ESA's Infrared Space Observatory (ISO) was an astronomical satellite that was operational between November 1995 and May 1998. The 2,400 kg (2.4 ton) satellite operated at wavelengths from 2.5 to 240 microns in the infrared range of the electromagnetic spectrum.

ISO was developed based on the advantage that observing in the infrared offered; that infrared radiation is primarily heat, or thermal radiation, and even objects that we think of as being very cold, such as an ice cube, emit infrared radiation.

Therefore ISO, operating at wavelengths from 2.5 to 240 microns, was able to observe astronomical objects that remain hidden from optical telescopes, such as cool objects that are unable to emit in visible light. Opaque objects, those surrounded by clouds of dust, were another specialty of ISO because the longer IR wavelengths can penetrate the dust, allowing us to see deeper into such clouds.

ISO was able to perform 45 observations per revolution over a period of close to 24 hours, completing more than 900 revolutions and well over 26,000 scientific observations. Its final observation was of emission lines from hydrogen in a hot supergiant star, Eta Canis Majoris, revealing that this star was not ordinary, as previously suspected, but probably surrounded by a disk of matter.

ISO was launched by an Ariane 44P launcher from Europe's spaceport in Kourou, November 17, 1995. It successfully surpassed its initial operational lifetime of 20 months, stretching to more than 28 months.

ISO's highly elliptical orbit had a perigee of about 1,000 km (621 miles), an apogee at 70,500 km (43,808 miles), and a period of almost 24 hours. The lowest parts of the orbit lay inside the earth's Van Allen Belt, which is made up of trapped electrons and protons. Inside these regions ISO's detectors were scientifically unusable due to effects caused by radiation impacts. However, ISO spent nearly 17 hours per day outside the radiation belts, during which all detectors could be operated.

The Science Operations Centre at ESA's Satellite Tracking Station in Villafranca, Spain, was responsible for the control of the satellite. This is also where observations were scheduled. However, for scientific use, ISO also needed to be in continuous contact with a ground station. NASA's station at Goldstone (United States) tracked ISO when it was obscured from Villafranca by the earth.

ISO consisted of the following instruments: a single 0.6 meter (1.96 ft) telescope feeding infrared beams via a pyramidal mirror; an infrared camera, ISOCAM, which covered the 2.5 to 17 micron band with two different detectors, similar to a normal photo camera with the ability to take pictures of the infrared face of astronomical objects at a high resolution in order to distinguish very fine details; a photo-polarimeter, ISOPHOT, to detect the amount of infrared radiation emitted by an astronomical object, operating between 2.5 and 240 microns; the Short-Wave Spectrometer (SWS) covering the 2.4 to 45 micron band, providing valuable information about the little known chemistry of the universe, since many molecules are known to emit copiously in the infrared, finding out the physical conditions of those chemical constituents such as temperature and density; and the Long-Wave Spectrometer (LWS), which operated at the 45 to 196.8 micron band and focused on cooler objects than SWS, being especially useful in studying the physical condition in very cold dust clouds in the space between stars.

ISO found clear links between stars, comets and the earth's origin. In the bright Hale-Bopp comet ISO found the mineral olivine, which is one of the main constituents of the earth's interior. Olivine was also detected by ISO in the dusty disks surrounding young stars, which have been thought to be planetary systems in formation.

ISO saw complex carbon-rich molecules in many parts of the universe, including the huge bubble of organic matter surrounding a young star in the Chamaeleon constellation. It was revealed to be a kind of shell-like structure previously undetected, made primarily of large molecules with hundreds of atoms of carbon and hydrogen, which could provide building blocks for living organisms.

ISO also studied carbon molecules which it found in the atmosphere of the planet Saturn, including the first detection of benzene, which has been best known on Earth as a solvent, but is also the parent of a huge range of molecules used by living organisms.

INTERNATIONAL ULTRAVIOLET EXPLORER (IUE)

The International Ultraviolet Explorer (IUE) was launched in January 1978, with an expected lifetime of three years. After an amazing length of 18 years, the decision was made by IUE partners NASA, ESA and the British government to switch it off.

On average, IUE made one one-hour observation every 90 minutes, around the clock. It was able to intercept ultraviolet light unreachable by telescopes on the ground, encompassing everything from far off Supernovae to approaching comets.

In its observation, IUE spread ultraviolet rays into a spectrum, revealing which wavelengths were strong and which were weak. After 18 years of successful 24-hour operation, IUE was finally shut off on September 27, 1996.

The IUE payload consisted of a telescope with an aperture of 0.45 meters (1.49 ft) and four ultraviolet cameras with a wavelength range of 155 to 310 nanometers.

IUE was designed in a 1.45 m (4.79 ft) diameter hexagonal-prism bus configuration with telescope assembly along the main axis, and fixed solar wings extending from opposing faces.

IUE utilized three-axis control with six gyroscopes, allowing precision pointing to within one arcsec.

Some of the accomplishments made by IUE included the first astronomical satellite in high earth orbit, the first general user UV space observatory, and the world's longest and most productive astronomical space observatory mission lasting 18.7 years.

IUE was the first satellite to allow visiting astronomers to make real-time observations of UV spectra. This made way for the discipline of multi-wavelength astrophysics, where observations with instruments on the ground and in space were coordinated to allow simultaneous measurements over a wide range of the electromagnetic spectrum.

IUE fulfilled many of its original science goals including obtaining high-resolution spectra of stars of all spectral types to determine their physical characteristics; studying gas streams in and around binary star systems, galaxies and quasars at low resolution; interpreting these spectra by cross-reference to high-resolution spectra; observing the spectra of planets and comets; making repeated ob-

servations of objects with variable spectra; and studying the modification of starlight caused by interstellar dust and gas.

In 1993, a supernova event occurred near galaxy M 81 in the constellation of Ursa Major. Twenty-four hours following its discovery, the IUE spacecraft made a spectrum of its ultraviolet light in the central band. It later converted this into a graph of energy which astronomers used to study and judge from the overall shape of the spectrum that gas around the exploding star was radiating at a temperature of 22,500 degrees.

IUE was able to analyze ultraviolet light in a wavelength range from 1150 to 3200 Angstrom units, which were blotted out by the earth's atmosphere. Operating in a range far above the atmosphere, IUE was able to generate spectra revealing intensities at various wavelengths coming from selected sky objects.

IUE was able to unmask the ultraviolet behavior of a large menagerie of different star types and contribute new knowledge concerning galaxies.

IUE was the first space telescope to be turned towards Supernova 1987A. It was able to reveal exactly which star had blown up, to identify chemical elements in the debris, and to discover a pre-existing ring of gas and dust surrounding the star.

IUE also made significant scientific discoveries such as the first detection of sulphur in a comet; the first quantitative determination of water loss in a comet at the rate of 10 tons per second; the first evidence for strong magnetic fields in chemically peculiar stars; the first orbital radial velocity curve for a WF star allowing its mass determination; the first detection of hot dwarf companions to Cepheid variables; the first observational evidence for semi-periodic mass loss in high mass stars; the first discovery of high velocity winds in stars other than the sun; the discovery of starspots on late type stars through the Doppler mapping techniques; the discovery of large scale motions in the transition regions of low gravity stars; the discovery of high temperature effect in stars in the early stages of formation; the first detection of gas streams within and outflowing from close binary stars; the first direct detection of galactic halos; the first observations of extragalactic symbiotic stars; the first detection of the existence of an aurora on Jupiter; the first detection of photos at wavelengths less than 50 nm from any astronomical source apart from the sun; and the creation of the first worldwide astronomical reduced-data archive delivering 44,000 spectra per year at the rate of five spectra per hour to astronomers in 31 countries.

IUE has been the most productive astronomical telescope ever. During 18.7 years of operation it returned 104,470 high- and low-resolution spectra of 9,600 astronomical sources from all classes of celestial objects in the 1150 to 3350 Angstrom (A) UV band.

Everyday Uses for European Space Technology

Technology transfer is the term for using technology, expertise, or facilities for a purpose they were not originally intended by the developers. This implies that technology developed for one sector is then used as a spin-off in a totally different area.

As far as space technology, much of this which lies in the heart of spacecraft and their systems has its origins on the ground. The European space program, much like the United States and others, has invested in converting this technology to "spin-off" that is used here on earth.

Under its Technology Transfer Program, ESA provides opportunities for researchers to generate two-way transfer, both through "spin-off" from space to non-space sectors and "spin-in" of technologies developed in non-space sectors which might be relevant for space. In the last ten years, ESA's Technology Transfer Program has made more than 100 successful transfers of space technologies.

The following are some examples of successful space technologies that have been developed in Europe and Canada over the past few years.

The Hubble Space Telescope's Faint Object Camera (FOC), developed by ESA, has exploited detectors called charge-coupled devices, or CCDs. These are silicon chips made up of arrays of light-sensitive pixels which convert impinging light into an electric charge that can then be used to generate an image. Today, CCDs are found in digital and video cameras, and even the office photocopier. In biomedical applications, they can even be used to observe the movement of living cells.

In another application, technology which emulates our sense of smell is now being used to detect infections. ESA has supported the development of sensors to act as gas detectors on space stations such as Mir based on the sophisticated sense of the human nose.

Two French companies have been helping to improve vehicle safety with space technologies. Messier-Bugatti has produced a novel carbon braking system to use on aircraft such as the Airbus, and it now supplies one third of the world market for carbon composite brakes with more than 100 seats. Similar systems have also been implemented on Formula 1 racing cars, heavy goods vehicles and passenger trains.

Ginger, an ESA technology effort, set out to develop a ground-penetrating radar as part of a proposed program to explore the moon. This same technology is now showing great promise in two life-saving roles — preventing mining accidents, and detecting land mines.

By using portable radars, it is now possible to penetrate the ground and produce images of hidden structures and objects. As a result of the work of Ginger, companies have developed a dedicated ground-penetrating radar prototype to detect cracks in the walls and roofs of mine drifts.

Anti-vibration technology developed from space platforms has been finding wide application in the building construction and instrumentation markets. In space, problems with very small vibrations have been quite noticeable. Since satellite instruments usually focus on small objects at very great distances, any local disturbances become greatly exaggerated.

Sensors have been used to detect unwanted vibrations and, through a control loop, electromechanical actuators cancel them out. As early as 1989, the active damping of a truss structure using piezoelectric actuators was successfully demonstrated, attracting ESA's interest and leading to several collaborations with European aerospace companies and research laboratories.

In the area of applications for mobile devices, the Italian company Space Engineering SpA has been developing techniques to analyze and model electro-magnetic fields from spacecraft antennas and their effects on nearby equipment.

These checks on antenna performance and electromagnetic compatibility, which are critical to avoiding malfunctions in sensitive onboard electronic systems, have led to several space-related projects, including Quickplan, a system designed to fulfill the needs of both radio system developers and environmental agencies. Quickplan has been able to calculate and display radio-frequency field levels across a highly complex urban environment, to indicate both the optimum location of transmitters and the resulting electromagnetic pollution.

Quickplan utilizes multiple maps and a powerful graphical interface to create a three-dimensional image of the territory, with color coding that clearly identifies regions where radio-frequency power levels are above or below the desired threshold. This space technology transfer has provided a powerful aid for radio systems planners to reduce their environmental impact and improve the servicing in Europe.

The need for wireless equipment in manned spacecraft has continued to drive the development of mobile technology on earth. A new wireless communications standard called Bluetooth has been developed by a consortium of leading electronics companies. Bluetooth is a tiny microchip which incorporates a radio transceiver built into a variety of digital devices such as mobile phones, personal digital assistants, printers, fax machines, personal computers, laptops, digital cameras, stereos and headsets. These can be connected together without wires or cables. It is anticipated that in the next few years Bluetooth will be built into hundreds of millions of electronic devices worldwide.

In recognizing Bluetooth's value for space exploration, ESA sponsored Parthus Technologies, an Irish company, to develop a wireless technology based on Bluetooth that could easily be incorporated into a variety of spacecraft equipment.

Future Science Missions

On September 13, 2000, ESA's Science Program Committee (SPC) was presented with the results of studies carried out during the previous three years which carefully defined proposed future mission concepts, identifying the technology needs of four cornerstones of the ESA Science Program.

These cornerstones included Bepi-Columbo, a planetary mission to Mercury; GAIA, an astrometric mission to unveil the origin and evolution of our galaxy; DARWIN, an interferometric mission for the detection and spectroscopic characterization of terrestrial exoplanets; and LISA, a fundamental-physics mission for the detection of low-frequency gravitational waves.

BepiColumbo

BepiColumbo will be a mission to Mercury, the innermost planet of our solar system. Its principle mission will entail characterizing Mercury's internal structure, surface features and composition, and magnetic field and planetary environment. The mission will utilize three scientific elements — two orbiters and a lander.

The Mercury Magnetospheric Orbiter (MMO) will be provided by ISAS of Japan. It will be a small spacecraft which will be placed in an elliptical orbit (400 by 12,000 km or 240 by 7,200 miles) around Mercury. The MMO will be equipped with a range of field and plasma experiments to allow analysis of the magnetospheric physics of the planet.

The Mercury Planetary Orbiter (MPO), a three-axis stabilized spacecraft, will be the second orbital element, and it will be placed in an elliptic polar orbit (400 by 1500 km or 240 by 900 miles). The MPO will carry a range of remote-sensing instruments to study Mercury's surface and interior.

The Mercury Surface Element (MSE) will serve as the lander element which will analyze the planet's chemical and surface properties for a period of at least seven days. Transfer to Mercury will be accomplished by using a combination of planetary swing-bys, solar electric and chemical propulsion.

BepiColumbo's launch has been scheduled for summer 2009.

GAIA

The primary scientific goal of GAIA will be to clarify the origin and evolution of our galaxy. The mission will provide previously unseen positional and radial velocity measurements with outstanding accuracy between 10 µarcsec at 15 mag and 5 km/s (3 mi/s) at 18 mag.

This extremely high rate of accuracy will be necessary in order to make a stereoscopic and cinematic census of close to one billion stars in our galaxy, representing about one percent of the galactic stellar population.

This data, in combination with the astrophysical information for each star that will be provided by the onboard multicolor photometry, will have the precision and depth necessary to address important questions that have been associated with the formation of stars in the Milky Way, referred to as dark matter in our galaxy.

The spacecraft will utilize an onboard propulsion system to reach its final orbit — the L2 Lagrangian point of the sun/earth system, following 200 days of cruising.

For the next five years, the 1700 kg (1020 lb) spacecraft will scan the heavens at a rate of two arcmin/sec, and it will deliver an equivalent science data rate of approximately one Mbps, corresponding to a massive overall data volume of several Terabytes (10^{12} bytes).

GAIA has been scheduled for launch no later than 2012.

DARWIN

The DARWIN (Detection and Analysis of Remote Worlds by Interferometric Nulling) mission will be a multiple-spacecraft mission to perform nulling interferometry in the medium- and far-infrared wavelength bands. The primary objective of this goal will be to detect and spectroscopically characterize terrestrial exoplanets.

DARWIN will consist of six free-flying spacecraft in a hexagonal configuration. Each will be equipped with a 1.5 m (4.95 ft) diameter telescope that will collect incoming photons and then transmit them to a seventh beam-combining spacecraft.

The beam-coupling spacecraft will be located at the center of the satellite formation and equipped with optical benches for both the ruling interferometry and imaging functions.

An eighth spacecraft will be dedicated to the overall management of the constellation, data handling and communication both to and from the earth and the other seven spacecraft.

Formation flying of DARWIN will be achieved by use of a combination of GPS techniques, high-precision laser metrology, and accurate low-thrust electric propulsion. This combination will keep the optical path differences between spacecraft below 20 nm.

DARWIN has been scheduled for launch in 2014.

LISA

Although gravitational waves were predicted at the beginning of the last century by Einstein's theory of general relativity, they have so far eluded actual detection. The Laser Interferometry Space Antenna (LISA) will be the first ESA cornerstone mission in fundamental physics.

LISA will target the detection of tiny changes in relative distance due to the passage of gravitational waves.

DARWIN will be comprised of three spacecraft positioned at the vertices of an equilateral triangle, with sides five million km (three million miles) long. Each spacecraft will contain two proof-masses, which will be kept in a free-fall environment shielded from all forces except gravity.

The mutual position of each proof-mass will be continuously measured by a sophisticated optical system.

The spacecraft configuration will be a giant Michelson-type interferometer with three arms, allowing the proof masses to function as adjustable elements.

Passing gravitational waves will be expected to move the proof-masses only by a fraction of an Angstrom (10^{-10} m), changing the length of the optical path of one arm of the interferometer with respect to the others.

The LISA mission will be a joint venture with NASA, and has been scheduled for launch in 2010.

FINLAND

Tekes, the National Technology Agency of Finland

Finnish space research on spacecraft began with the first manmade satellites that focused on orbital motions in the study of the earth's gravitational field. The International Geophysical Year 1957–1958 led to the establishment of the Committee on Space Research (COSPAR) and the contribution to several ground-based space research instruments including all-sky cameras such as those used today to study the aurora borealis and the space physics behind this amazing phenomenon.

Finland became a member of COSPAR in 1964, although it was not until the mid–1980s that the country began to participate actively in space-borne instrument projects. The first instrument project began in May 1985, with the plasma analyzer, AS-PERA, in the Soviet Phobos mission.

Later in the decade, Finland became an associate member of the European Space Agency (ESA) and a full member of its science program, contributing to astronomy missions such as Spectrum-X-gamma and Radioastron, as well as several projects involving remote sensing of the earth. Finland continues to actively participate in ESA science missions.

Finland has contributed to ESA satellite imaging programs such as Earthnet, providing pre-processing, archiving, and distribution of image data; EOPP, assisting with research and development activities; ERS-1 and 2, assisting with data collection; MSG, pro-

viding hardware and software; ENVISAT, providing hardware and software for the GOMOS observation instrument which detects ozone and other trace gases and high altitude chemical reactions vital to understanding ozone depletion; the Metop satellites series, providing satellite electronics and software development; and EOEP, the Earth Observation Envelop Program.

It has also contributed to ESA telecommunications programs, including ASTP-4 with research and development activities; DRS, providing a ground station for the Artemis satellite developed in Finland; ARETS, providing basic systems specifications; and Galileosat, providing assistance with navigation systems.

With the launch of ENVISAT in 2001, Finland has benefited from its data in management of its forest industry and maritime transportation system through applications of sea ice, snow cover, forest and land use mapping.

The National Technology Agency of Finland (Tekes), established in 1983, is the main organization in Finland responsible for applied and industrial research and development, also focusing on space technology for the nation. Through Tekes, Finnish universities and research institutes, along with industry contractors, have participated in international projects in space science, technology and remote sensing since the mid–1980s. In 1995, Tekes launched two space technology programs: Globe 2000 and Space 2000.

The Globe 2000 program was aimed at developing entrepreneurship in the remote sensing industry while using operative remote sensing techniques and developing remote sensing technologies and methods. Remote sensing has proved to be an effective tool for producing information on the state of the environment affecting Finland, as well as related changes.

The Space 2000 program has concentrated on the technology of space satellites and their ground support equipment. The primary objective of the program has been to increase the opportunities of the Finnish space industry in order to carry out ESA cooperative projects, while allowing Finnish companies to remain competitive.

GLOBE 2000—REMOTE SENSING

Remote sensing has proven to be an effective tool for airborne instruments producing information concerning the state of the environment, as well as changes affecting it. Satellite remote sensing has been especially useful in obtaining data quickly from a wide or distant area.

Since remote sensing data is often part of a knowledge-based service, the technology required to produce this service consists of data acquisition equipment, an efficient data communications solution, a geographic information system, and an application-specific expert system for data interpretation. Remote sensing methods have been utilized in many ways for the information society in Finland.

In conjunction with Tekes, nearly 20 research organizations and groups, as well as several companies in industry, have participated in remote sensing research activities and the utilization of the results.

The Globe 2000 technology program has helped develop the remote sensing industry for operational and commercial applications as well as deepen the cooperation between the participants.

Since 1995, over 50 remote sensing satellites were launched with participation by Finland. They have covered the optical, short-range infrared, infrared, and microwave wavelengths. Satellite images with a resolution of one to two meters (3.28 to 6.56 ft) will become available for civilian use in the near future. Thirty new instruments will be introduced by the program for atmospheric survey alone.

Tekes has been responsible for the shift in the focus of application development from using the data of an individual instruments to using satellite data from many sources.

By implementing operative remote sensing techniques in this program, Tekes has helped the nation of Finland gain considerable economic and commercial benefits as well as benefits related to the monitoring of the state of the environment.

The Globe 2000 technology program has been coordinated with the remote sensing programs of ESA and the remote sensing program of the European Union (EU).

Four types of projects were launched by the Globe 2000 technology program, including companies' product development projects for commercializing remote sensing methods and supporting technology projects; applied technology research projects for obtaining internationally significant new information about remote sensing; demonstration projects for presenting a remote sensing instrument, method, or data set to end users; and operative remote sensing implementation projects during which remote sensing methods with significant economic or commercial value have been implemented.

Under the Globe 2000 program, Finland has been involved in a three-year project concerned with the development of an advanced instrument for environmental research. Two other projects have been related to the processing and application from GOMOS, the ozone instrument on ESA's ENVISAT, which was launched March 1, 2002, and future missions to be organized by the European satellite agency, EUMETSAT.

Other projects under this program have been related to applications in forestry and compiling related satellite data. Two projects have conducted snow monitoring, two others have emphasized sea ice monitoring and classification, and two others have concentrated on coastal and lake water monitoring.

In addition to cooperative work with ESA and EUMETSAT, Tekes has begun work with Space Systems Finland on Finland's own satellite, the Finnish small satellite, FS-1. This satellite will be dedicated to experiments of particular relevance to the Nordic environment, such as magnetospheric research, or observation of forests, snow, ice or the northern ozone hole, and is still currently in the study stages.

In the meantime, Tekes continues to offer supportive services in satellite technology including power systems and computers, onboard software, microwave technology, lightweight composite structures, and X-ray detector technology.

SPACE 2000—SPACE EQUIPMENT TECHNOLOGY

The Space 2000 program began in 1995 shortly after Finland became the fourteenth member state of the European Space Agency. This membership increased the opportunities of Finnish researchers to participate in space research and benefit from the data produced by ESA satellites. It also offered Finnish companies and research institutes an opportunity to provide research services to ESA and to supply subsystems, units and sub-units of satellites systems for launch into space. It was therefore found necessary to establish a Finnish national technology development activity to increase the level of know-how to participate in, and to utilize, ESA programs, and become competitive in the international space markets.

The main focus of the Space 2000 program has been to concentrate on the technology of space satellites and their ground support equipment, meaning earthbound applications.

The initial phase of the Space 2000 program was limited to the flight and ground segments of satellite systems and did not include interpretation of the data collected or transmitted by the satellites.

Finnish companies and research institutes worked on the equipment and related software for the satellite systems. Another focus of the Space 2000 program was the development of core competencies for each company participating in conjunction with Tekes, so that a certain satellite subsystem could be realized sufficiently in relation to size, mass, power consumption, telemetry, schedule, and costs.

Many of the projects were closely related to ESA or NASA's future satellite projects as well as ESA's technology programs. Finnish support work in these areas focused on developing key technologies and processes which were required for a particular project, including the definition and development of science and earth observation instruments.

The largest of these projects was the development and building of the Ozone Monitoring Instrument for the NASA EOS Aura satellite. The Earth Observation System (EOS) Aura is a NASA mission to study the earth's ozone, air quality and climate. This mission has been designed exclusively to conduct research on the composition, chemistry and dynamics of the earth's upper and lower atmosphere, employing multiple instruments on a single satellite. EOS Aura will be the third in a series of major earth observing satellites to study the environment and climate change, and is part of NASA's Earth Science Enterprise. The first and second missions, Terra and Aqua, were designed to study the land, oceans, and the earth's radiation budget. Aura's chemistry measurements will also follow up on measurements which began with NASA'S Upper Atmospheric Research Satellite and will continue the record of satellite ozone data collected from the TOMS missions.

The EOS Aura satellite, instruments, launch, and science investigations will be managed by NASA's Goddard Space Flight Center in Greenbelt, Maryland. The satellite will be launched in January 2004, and operated for five or more years. Scientific investigations will continue throughout the years the spacecraft is in operation and several years afterwards.

Under this program, Finland contributed the Ozone Monitoring Instrument (OMI) to EOS Aura through the Finnish Meteorological Institute (FMI). The OMI will record ozone and other atmospheric parameters related to ozone chemistry and climate. OMI measurements will be highly synergistic with the other instruments on the EOS Aura platform. The OMI instrument will employ hyperspectral imaging in a push-broom mode to observe solar backscatter radiation in the visible and ultraviolet ranges. The earth will be viewed in 740 wavelength bands along the satellite track with a swath large enough to provide global coverage in 14 orbits (one day). The nominal 13 by 24 km spatial resolution can be zoomed to 13 by 13 km for detecting and tracking urban-scale pollution sources. The hyperspectral capabilities will improve the accuracy and precision of the total ozone amounts and will also allow for accurate radiometric and wavelength self calibration over the long term. The expanded wavelength characteristics will provide a number of features including the continuation of global total ozone trends from satellite measurements beginning in 1970 with BUV on Nimbus-4; mapping of ozone profiles at 36 by 48 km, a spatial resolution never achieved before; measuring key air quality components such as (NO_2, SO_2, BrO, OClO), and aerosol char-

acteristics; and distinguishing between aerosol types such as smoke, dust, and sulfates. It will measure cloud pressure and coverage, which provides data to derive tropospheric ozone; map global distribution and trends in UV-B radiation; and measure near real time (NRT) production of ozone and other trace gases.

Finland has also participated in several ESA missions, including Integral, Rosetta, ENVISAT and Galileo. A Finnish company also provided the composite carbon fiber structures for ESA-NASA's XMM telescope tube.

In the future, the main target of Space 2000 will be to increase the opportunities of the Finnish space industry to carry out ESA projects with a content and purpose suitable to the technology of the Finnish space industry, highlighting its expertise in X-ray and gamma-ray astronomy, earth-sun interaction, plasma physics, and planetary science.

FRANCE

Centre National d'Etudes Spatiales (CNES)

The Centre National d'Etudes Spatiales (CNES) was formed in 1961 to explore innovative technology concepts forming the foundation for future systems, and to utilize space in order to achieve maximum benefit from space-based assets.

Today, it remains a strong driving force behind initiatives and proposals of programs led by the European Space Agency (ESA).

CNES's strongest support program has been the development of the Ariane family of launchers, which was headed by the CNES Launch Vehicles Directorate branch on behalf of ESA.

The CNES Launch Vehicles Directorate overseas industrial production of each new launcher, while providing support to ensure maximum reliability, availability, maintain-

ability and safety from production through launch.

Since 1979, Ariane rockets have launched over 140 commercial satellites with an outstanding success rate of 97 percent.

The Guiana Space Center (CSG) located in Kourou, French Guiana, is a CNES technical facility with an exceptionally high launch rate of an average of 15 launches per year.

CNES as an agency provides thorough expertise covering every aspect of space technology, from materials and fail-safe computer systems to robotics and communications.

It has been closely involved in every stage of space program development, including technological research activities, definition of mission specifications or development of systems, monitoring satellite manufacturing by industrial teams, and controlling satellite operations and system exploitation.

CNES has been heavily involved in the development of the new global satellite navigation system, Galileo. Similar in nature to the United States' global positioning system (GPS), Galileo will considerably improve flight safety on transoceanic and transcontinental journeys.

In order to address the needs of its most important commercial space application, satellite telecommunications, CNES has developed the Stentor program. This demonstration satellite will bring new telecommunications services in orbit while providing links to French overseas territories as well as digital transmissions over mainland France.

Since 1982, the Cospas-Sarsat satellites have enabled the rescue of over 14,000 people by rapidly detecting distress signals from emergency beacons on boats, aircraft or land expeditions.

CNES was the first to develop satellites for meteorology and earth observation with its SPOT system, which is recognized today worldwide as a first-class source of earth observation data. The newest version, SPOT 5, will provide increased performance through 2010.

CNES will also be participating in the GMES (Global Monitoring for Environment and Security) initiative designed to support policy decisions in Europe and to meet the needs of future environmental and security challenges. GMES will improve understanding and management of natural resources and climate change while fostering better mitigation and management of natural and human-induced disasters.

Today, Europe's weather forecasters continue to rely exclusively on the Meteosat satellites designed by CNES in 1969.

The French-United States Topex/Poseidon oceanography mission has performed remarkably, allowing ocean tides to be known to within two centimeters (0.8 inches), and the El Niño phenomenon to be detected several months in advance. Jason-1, which was launched in December 2001, has continued to perform with similar capability.

CNES has also developed Proteus, a new standard, modular spacecraft bus that can be re-used for different missions. This spacecraft will carry minisatellites under 1,000 kilograms (2200 pounds), including Calipso, to study clouds and aerosols; MOS, to study soil moisture and ocean salinity, and Corot, to study the inner structure of stars.

Cospas-Sarsat System Diagram — satellite mission in search of salvaging maritime ships. Since 1982, through this program, 14,000 people have been saved. (CNES/Illustrated by David Ducros, 1999)

Jason Oceanographic satellite which was launched December 7, 2001, from a Boeing Delta 2 Rocket in cooperation with NASA. (CNES/Illustrated by David Ducros, 2000)

Space Transportation

CNES has continued to enhance its Ariane launchers with upgrades to Ariane 5. These enhancements, A5 ESC/ESV and A5 ESC-A, have been implemented to improve performance and make Ariane 5 more versatile, with a reignitable solid propellant stage offering compatibility with long ballistic phases.

The agency has been performing qualification tests on a new engine for Ariane 5, Vulcain 2, along with a new flight model of Ariane 5 Evolution's upper cryogenic stage propellant tank.

The first model of the new upper cryogenic stage, ESC-A, underwent readiness for dynamic tests on the upper part of the launch vehicle. A second ESC-A stage underwent implementation tests in the first half of 2002. The maiden flight of the Ariane 5/ESC-A

STENTOR (Satellite of Telecommunications for Experiencing New Technologies in Orbit) in radar wave–absorbing chamber. (CNES/Pascal Le Doarf, 2001)

configuration occurred in August 2002 when it launched the Stentor satellite.

The Ariane 5/ESC-B configuration with a new Vinci engine was derived from the ESC-A stage.

In addition to carrying on its Ariane launcher program, CNES has been conducting studies into the launch systems of the future.

Two possible paths have been explored, including conventional launch vehicles and reusable launch vehicles.

Under conventional launch vehicles, CNES has established the Ariane 2010, initiative which has pursued a variety of research activities in bilateral or multilateral cooperation with other European countries. These in-depth studies have been investigating alternatives to Ariane 5, including liquid boost launchers.

Under reusable launch vehicles, the CNES Launch Vehicle Directorate has begun a new program through ESA called ANGEL (Advanced New-Generation European Launcher). The focus of this program is the proposed experimental "Pre-X" vehicle for the chief purpose of helping Europe acquire expertise in atmospheric re-entry techniques before developing more ambitious demonstration vehicles.

As a part of the future launcher study process, CNES has been looking into other technology demonstrators such as the Pre-X, including a hydrogen turbopump, to be produced at half the cost of the Vulcain 2 turbopump by using highly innovative technology such as fluid bearings. The P80 solid-propellant rocket engine, designed to reduce the cost of Ariane 5 boosters while serving as the Vega launcher's first stage and an experimental Lo_x/Ch_4 engine for reusable launch vehicles are also being studied.

CNES also has a balloon observation program with balloons capable of flying up to 45,000 meters (148,500 feet) above the earth. The agency conducts over 50 balloon launches a year in France and abroad. Scientific applications for use include astronomy, space plasma research, geophysics, and atmospheric studies including a number of stratospheric chemistry experiments.

CNES utilizes different types of balloons and operational services that have been developed by its personnel.

Zero-pressure stratospheric balloons have been designed for gondolas ranging from a few kilograms to over one ton. They have been widely used for short- or medium-duration flights.

Superpressure stratospheric balloons have been used as Lagrange tracers to track the movement of atmospheric masses and to carry chemical experiments. These balloons have served as the only means of exploring all the layers of the stratosphere.

Infrared hot-air balloons have been used for flights lasting several weeks in duration, carrying 50 kilogram (110 pound) gondolas fitted with measuring instruments.

Accomplishments made by CNES's balloon program have included the maiden flight of an infrared atmospheric sounding interferometer (IASI) on a CNES precise-pointing gondola; validation of a telemetry/telecommand system by Inmarsat during flights of infrared hot-air balloons released from Bauru, in Brazil, with the longest flight setting a new record of 71 days aloft; the Escompte campaign to study the boundary layer above Marseille, France, involving 33 balloons, 15 of which were fitted with ozone-measuring instruments; and the maiden flight of the Archeops balloon experiment released from Kiruna, Sweden, during the polar night, with gondola separation several hours later in Russia, marking the first time that operational telecommands and telemetry data was sent from the control center to the balloon via an Inmarsat satellite. Archeops was designed to measure three kilometer fossil radiation anisotropies, a remnant of the Big Bang.

Earth Observation

CNES was responsible for the first satellites designed for meteorology and earth observation. It has since broadened its field of applications and developed new services to improve management of natural resources. It has also been a leading contributor to European and international climate and environmental research programs.

Gamma camera lense for the CNES Stratospheric Balloon Project, Claire, a new instrument to conduct observations in gamma astrophysics. (CNES/Pascal Le Doarf, 2000)

The SPOT (Satellite Pour l'Observation de la Terre) system has been in operation since 1986 and now features four orbiting satellites: SPOT 1, launched February 22, 1986, SPOT 2, launched January 22, 1990, SPOT 4, launched March 29, 1998, and SPOT 5, launched in May, 2002.

Although SPOT 1 and SPOT 2 no longer record data, they continue to collect and transmit data when within range of one of the many direct receiving stations spread over all five continents.

SPOT 4 has offered enhanced mission performance due to a new spectral band in the shortwave infrared (SWIR). Its operational ability has also been expanded by two new-generation 120-gigabit onboard tape recorders to a 10-Gigabit solid-state memory.

SPOT 5 will offer panchromatic images with a resolution of 2.5 meters (8.25 feet). A star tracker, used in conjunction with the DORIS precise positioning system, will provide image

DORIS (Determination of Orbit at Integral Radio-Positioning for Satellite) antenna for land spot four satellite. (CNES Pascal Le Doarf, 1997)

Illustration of SPOT 5 satellite profile. (CNES/ Illustration by David Ducros, 2002)

Helios 1B military satellite before launch December 3, 1999, onboard Ariane four. (CNES/Illustrated by David Ducros, 1999)

location to an accuracy of tens of meters. The satellite has also been equipped with an HRS (high-resolution stereoscopic) imaging instrument designed to acquire stereopair images at the same instant.

The HRS will allow two images to be acquired on the same track, with one telescope facing forward and the other aft. It will provide systematic stereoscopic coverage of a wide area (120 by 600 kilometers or 72 by 360 miles).

Stereopairs are required in order to produce digital elevation models (DEMS), which are files containing a uniform grid of terrain elevation values for a given area.

The resulting three-dimensional imaging has contributed to a number of applications such as cellular telephone network planning, mapping, airport approach simulations and mission planning. This rapidly developing market has been growing at a rate of 15 to 25 percent per year.

France has been working together with Italy and Spain on the Helios program since the launch of Helios 1A in July 1995. The Helios 1B was launched in December 1999.

Helios 2A has been scheduled for launch in the first half of 2004.

The Helios program was established to provide earth observation coverage for the three participating countries.

SPOT 5 has been equipped with a special instrument, vegetation, to provide daily

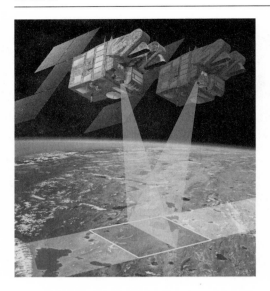

Illustration of SPOT 5 HRS beam to obtain images usable for mapping. (CNES/Illustrated by David Ducros, 2002)

SPOT 5 satellite team at Intespace, Toulouse. (CNES/Patrick Dumas, 2001)

global coverage with a resolution of close to one kilometers. It operates in four spectral bands that were optimally designed to monitor the continental biosphere and crops.

As a part of the first-ever French-Japanese partnership in the space sector, the French multimission POLDER instrument was launched by NASDA aboard the Japanese ADEOS 1 satellite on August 17, 1996.

POLDER has been studying the earth's environment and is the first spaceborne instrument to simultaneously measure the polarization and direction of radiation reflected by the earth's surface and atmosphere.

Another first will come with the launch of SMOS (Soil Moisture and Ocean Salinity), which will measure soil moisture and ocean salinity on a global scale.

Scheduled for launch in early 2006, SMOS is a cooperative project between France and Spain.

CNES will supply the Proteus satellite bus and be responsible for both satellite project management and in-orbit control.

The payload will consist of a microwave interferometry radiometer operating in L band (1.4 GHz), which is being developed by CASA of Spain. Its antenna will consist of three four-meter (13.2 feet) long booms, each equipped with 21 receivers.

The Calipso mission will study the impact of clouds and aerosols on the earth's radiation budget. CNES will continue to work in cooperation with NASA on this mission currently scheduled for launch aboard a Delta 2 rocket in April 2004.

Calipso will provide a unique data set of vertical cloud profiles measured by the first spaceborne backscattering lidar. The satellite will fly in formation with Aqua, NASA's large climatology satellite, with the radar-carrying Cloudsat developed jointly by Canada and the United States, as well as CNES's Parasol microsatellite, which is a part of the POLDER imaging polarimeter.

The resulting space observatory will utilize all active and passive remote sensing techniques available to characterize interactions between radiation and clouds, or aerosols.

The Megha-Tropiques will be a research mission focusing on atmospheric circulation,

Integration of the mechanical thermal STM module for the instrument IASI (Inteferometer Atmospheric of Sounding in the Infrared), and instrument for meterological satellites in the European Metop series.

the water cycle and climate change. Resulting data will help to expand scientific knowledge on the water cycle's role in tropical atmosphere dynamics and processes related to tropical convection.

Megha-Tropiques is a joint mission with the Indian Space Research Organization (ISRO) that has been scheduled for launch in 2006.

The low orbital inclination of 20 degrees will allow the satellite to record repetitive measurements of parameters such as water vapor, clouds, cloud condensation, precipitation and evaporation throughout the day. Megha-Tropiques will also study the role that tropical convection systems play in the energy balance in order to improve the forecasting of cyclones, monsoons and the rainy season.

ISRO will provide the mission's main instrument, Madras, a multichannel microwave imaging device. CNES will provide the radio receivers for Madras, as well as the Proteus satellite bus. It will also be responsible for controlling the satellite once in orbit.

The agency will provide two instruments — Saphir, a 183-GHz radiometer for vertical sounding of water vapor; and Scarab, a scanning radiometer for measuring the global radiation budget.

The Infrared Atmospheric Sounding Interferometer (IASI) will be the key instrument board Meteop, to be launched in 2005. The IASI will help provide meteorologists with accurate temperature and humidity profiles.

CNES will be responsible for the IASI instruments and developing data processing software for the mission. It will be working in conjunction with the European organization for the exploitation of meteorological satellites, EUMETSAT.

Altimetry is important to understanding, modeling and predicting ocean dynamics, a major contributor to ocean studies particularly in relation to climate. Jason-1, a reference altimetry satellite, was successfully launched from Vandenberg Air Force Base, California, on December 7, 2001.

Jason-2, an ocean surface topography

Illustration of Jason and Topex-Poseidon satellites. (CNES/Illustrated by David Ducros, 2002)

Integration of the microsatellite platform Demeter (Detection of Electro-Magnetic Emissions Transmitted from Earthquake Regions), which will study electromagnetic and seismic waves, as well as volcanic eruptions. (Emmanuel Grimault, 2003)

mission (OSTM) is being developed for launch in 2005. It will continue the work of Jason-1.

The DORIS (Doppler Orbitography and Radiopositioning Integrated by Satellite) system was created by CNES with the support of the French space geodesy research group, GRGS, and the national mapping and survey agency, IGN.

The first version of DORIS was flown on SPOT 2 in January 1990. The newest version flew aboard Jason-1.

The DORIS system has provided a set of validated beacon coordinates used in geodesy to study movements of the earth's crust.

CNES worked with the Danish on their Ersted satellite which launched in 1999 to measure the earth's magnetic field. The agency funded the onboard scalar magnetometer developed by the French atomic energy agency (CEA/LETI). The satellite has provided exciting new data concerning the dynamics of the earth's core.

The Demeter (Detection of Electro-Magnetic Emissions Transmitted from Earthquake Regions) is a satellite project in development to study electromagnetic signals associated with earthquakes. It is hoped this satellite will help provide an early warning system to avoid this catastrophe.

Satellite Telecommunications

Satellite telecommunications have been a very important sector to the economic, political, strategic and industrial issues of France. To strengthen this need, CNES in conjunction with France Telecom, and the French defense procurement agency (DGA), conceived the Stentor program in October 1994.

Stentor is a telecommunications satellite designed to qualify the most innovative technologies developed by the Research and Technology Programs division of the project's partners in orbit.

Stentor was launched in August 2002, on the maiden flight of Ariane 5 in its ESC-A configuration. Technological innovations in the satellite payload included a multi-beam, reconfigurable active antenna, high-performance traveling wave tube amplifiers, a transponder to generate digital television bouquets on board, and basic building blocks using MMIC and ASIC technologies for signal processing and radio functions.

Satellite bus innovations include the plasma propulsion sub-assembly, electrical power supply system with high-performance gallium arsenide solar cells and lithium-ion batteries, altitude and orbit control technologies, onboard management, thermal control using capillary fluid loops and a deployable radiator.

Several experiments will be carried out by Stentor in the area of autonomous navigation and in-orbit measurements of the satellite's environment. This will include the Comrad experiment which was designed to measure space radiation.

The European Geostationary Navigation Overlay System (EGNOS) has been established as a part of the GNSS 1 satellite navigation program, designed to develop systems to supplement the United States global positioning system (GPS) and the Russian Glonass systems by increasing their accuracy and availability.

EGNOS will use geostationary satellites to transmit data that will improve the accuracy and reliability of navigation signals from GPS and Glonass all over Europe.

Galileo, Europe's alternative to GPS, will be an independent system based on the GPS system of the United States.

ATF, a future telecommunications project that was initiated in 1999, will provide CNES with the resources needed for engineering future satellite telecommunications system. Under this project, CNES has been developing a simulation environment (ASIMUT) for a satellite constellation project which is a part of a future telecommunications research network.

Argos is a satellite-based location and data collection system that has been in operation since 1978, providing services to ocean-faring yachtsmen. It has also been devoted to scientific studies and environmental protection.

The third-generation version of Argos will fly aboard the Metop 1 satellite in December 2005. Argos 3 will fly on satellites NOAA-N and Metop 2 in 2008 and 2009, and are expected to remain in service beyond 2015.

Cospas-Sarsat, which has been in service for 20 years as of 2002, is a satellite-based humanitarian research and rescue program that has played a vital role in saving over 14,000 lives.

It has been operated in France by CNES and two user organizations, the French civil aviation authority DGAC (Direction Générale de l'Aviation Civile) and the French maritime and seafaring affairs authority DAMGM (Direction des Affaires Maritimes et des Gens de Mer).

In the area of navigation systems, CNES has worked together with healthcare professionals to examine how space systems could be beneficial to telemedicine.

Two key areas were identified — tele-epidemiology, which merges environmental and clinical data; and tele-consultation, to be used in remote areas or for distance consultation of medical experts using a portable telemedicine kit containing a PC, a satellite transmission system via Inmarsat and one or more medical modules.

Several telemedicine networks using space systems were set up to monitor epidemics and to offer medical consultations in remote areas for skin complaints, mothers and young children, and medical emergencies.

These included four remote areas chosen in French Guiana for a satellite link-up with the main hospital in Cayenne in an effort to treat the frequent occurrence of dermatological and parasitic problems. This link has since provided improved management of

Meteosat Second Generation (MSG) satellite. (CNES/Illustrated by David Ducros/Metzo)

patient transfers and facilitated diagnosis and treatment.

In cooperation with the French medical charity, Médecins du Monde, a network has been operating routinely in Cambodia to screen patients and offer an early diagnosis of cervical cancers. Swabs prepared by healthcare officials generate data, which is transmitted to France via an Inmarsat satellite link for analysis.

CNES has designed a remote diagnosis system to be used from a passenger seat on airlines, making long-distance flights able to provide immediate medical assistance when passengers become ill. This system has been used on Airbus A 340–600 flights, and will be offered on the future Airbus A 380.

Tele-epidemiology involves assessing a geographical range where there has been a number of epidemics affecting humans and animals which have been spread by elements sensitive to changes in the environment.

Predictive mathematical models that have been developed to forecast the spread of these outbreaks have used a combination of data from earth observation satellites such as SPOT, Meteosat, and Topex/Poseidon, as well as human and animal clinical data on the particular epidemic.

This technology has been used in Senegal to monitor outbreaks of Rift Valley fever and in French Guiana to monitor outbreaks of hemorrhagic dengue fever. Early-warning networks and a specific-targeted set of portable telemedicine kits were used.

Space Science Programs

France's program to understand the universe has been a core component of the European Space Agency's science program. This has brought CNES a number of cooperative projects with ESA and NASA.

XMM-Newton is a huge X-ray astronomy observatory, weighing four tons and measuring 11 meters (36 feet) high, equipped with three identical 6-meter (20 feet) long telescopes with grazing incidence mirrors. Launched by Ariane 5 on December 10, 1999, its large collecting surface allows for highly sensitive observations that give it a unique ability to explore the distant universe.

CNES contributed to the telescope with a radiation monitor designed to warn the satellite in the event of danger to the other instruments.

COROT is a very high-precision stellar photometry mission which will form part of the CNES minisatellite program built around the Proteus satellite bus. It will follow Jason-1 and Calipso, and has been scheduled for launch in late 2004.

COROT will search for extrasolar planets around nearby stars and study the internal structure of stars by observing their oscillation modes.

CNES is the prime contractor for COROT and has delegated the development and assembly of its subsystems to three laboratories — the Paris Observatory, the Marseille astronomy laboratory, and the space astrophysics institute, IAS of Orsay, France.

In cooperation with NASA and the United States Department of Energy, CNES will work on the GLAST (Gamma-Ray Large

COROT (Convection and Rotation of Inner Stars) astronomy satellite. (CNES/Illustrated by David Ducros, 2000)

Area Space Telescope) mission, a new generation gamma-ray telescope that will identify and study the nature of accelerators of high-energy particles by measuring the spectrum and evolution over time of high-energy gamma radiation between 20 MeV and 300 GeV. GLAST's launch has been scheduled for March 2005.

France will also contribute to the ESA Herschel and Planck-Surveyor mission. Planck will be launched in the year 2007, together with ESA's next infrared and submillimeter space observatory, Herschel Space Observatory. Both satellites will separate after launch to operate independently at a distance of 1.5 million kilometers (932,100 miles) from earth.

Planck will carry a telescope with a primary mirror of 1.5 meters (4.92 feet). The telescope will focus radiation from the sky onto the payload with two arrays of highly sensitive detectors called the Low Frequency Instrument and the High Frequency Instrument. They will measure the temperature of the cosmic microwave background radiation over the whole sky, searching for regions slightly warmer or colder than the average.

The instruments provided by France include SPIRE, PACS, and HIFI, for Herschel; and the HFI instrument for the Planck-Surveyor mission.

The Spectral and Photometric Imaging Receiver (SPIRE) will greatly enhance our understanding of the processes of galaxy and star formation. For most galaxies, from one-third to nearly all of the radiation they emit occurs at far-infrared wavelengths. Ultraviolet radiation emitted by stars is often absorbed by huge clouds of dust grains that surround them. The heated dust then cools by radiating at infrared wavelengths. In order to understand all the processes occurring in a galaxy, it is essential to measure the total energy emitted at all wavelengths. The infrared part of the spectrum accounts for the greatest proportion of the total flux (light) from stars and galaxies, so observations with SPIRE will provide much needed information for a complete study of these objects. SPIRE will make large scale surveys of the sky at high angular resolution and will also measure the flux in several

wavelength bands, giving much needed information on the spectral energy distribution of stars and galaxies. As a result, scientists will have a much better understanding of the global characteristics of galaxies and stars, answering long-standing questions on how galaxies and stars formed.

The Photoconductor Array Camera and Spectrometer (PACS) is an infrared camera and spectrometer. It employs two Ge:Ga photoconductor arrays (stressed and unstressed) and two bolometer arrays to perform imaging line spectroscopy and imaging photometry in the 60 to 210 _m wavelength band. In the photometry mode, it will simultaneously image two bands, 60 to 90 _m or 90 to 130 _m, and 130 to 210 _m, over fields of view of 1.75 by 3.5 arcmin with full beam sampling in each band.

In the spectroscopy mode, it will image a field of about 50 by 50 arcsec, resolved into 5 by 5 pixels, with an instantaneous spectral coverage of ~ 1500 km/s and a spectral resolution of ~ 175 km/s. In both modes background-noise limited performance is expected, with sensitivities (5 sigma in 1h) of 3 mJy or 2.5×10^{-18} W/m^2, respectively.

The Heterodyne Instrument for the Far Infrared (HIFI) will study various aspects of interstellar chemistry based on the principle that understanding the chemical processes in different astrophysical environments is developed by observing many different molecules. The large-scale physical structures and chemical make-up can be mapped out by detecting the emissions from the molecules which form the gases in the interstellar medium. The far-infrared and submillimeter wavebands are the best places to observe these molecules. HIFI has been specifically designed to have the high spectroscopic resolution and sensitivity required to detect and analyze the emissions from a large variety of molecules.

The High Frequency Instrument (or HFI) is an array of 48 bolometric detectors which work by converting radiation to heat. The amount of heat is then measured by a tiny thermometer, which is read out and converted to a real temperature in a computer. The HFI detectors will work in six frequency channels centered between 100 and 857 GHz. They are operated at -272.9°C (only one tenth of one degree above absolute zero). To achieve that temperature a complex system of refrigerators is put onboard the satellite, each of which uses a different technology to provide a successively colder temperature.

France worked on the Swedish ODIN satellite which was launched on February 20, 2001, by a Start 1 rocket from the Russian launch center in Svobodny, France. CNES's contribution to ODIN included the provision of sophisticated altitude control instruments from Sodern, Sagem and Astrium; as well as sending a CNES engineer to work with the Swedish project group, partially funding the launch costs, allowing use of the interspace test facilities in Toulouse, France, and providing an acoustic/optical spectrometer integrated into the main instrument, a submillimeter radiometer, carrying out submillimeter alignment tests.

The Premier program is a CNES Mars exploration program that will prepare for the future Mars sample return mission by completing technical validations of the rendezvous and capturing of a sample container in Mars orbit. It will fulfill a set of scientific goals through the Netlander project as well as a complementary orbital science mission. The Netlander network will consist of four geophysics packages designed to take various measurements after being released onto the surface of Mars.

A precursor orbital mission will be launched in 2007 with these objectives. The main mission will include a direct launch by Ariane 5, scheduled for September 2007, of an orbiter and four Netlanders mounted on the orbiter's cruise stage. It will include the transportation, ejection and positioning of the Netlanders, the orbiter's insertion in Mars orbit, CNES-NASA demonstration of the feasibility of a rendezvous and capture of a sample container in orbit around Mars, and the relaying of Netlander data. The complementary mission will consist of an escape from Mars orbit and flyby of the Vesta asteroid, bringing a Mars atmospheric sample taken during the aerocapture orbit insertion phase back to earth, and the returning of a sample from Phobos, one of Mars' two natural satellites.

French astronaut Claudie Haigneré in training on the Portapress materialize experience inside the International Space Station (ISS) during mission Andromeda. Portapress was a cardiovascular conditioning lab to record respiratory movements over long periods. (CNES/C. Haignere, 2001)

On December 22, 2000, CNES signed an agreement with the Russia space agency, Rosaviacosmos, and RKK Energia to fly a French astronaut to the International Space Station (ISS). The French-Russian crew for the Andromède mission, including Victor Afanassiev, Claudie Haigneré and Konstantin Kozeev, performed this taxi mission in October 2001.

France's astronaut, Claudie Haigneré, trained at Star City, near Moscow. As flight engineer on the mission he assisted the flight commander during approach and docking maneuvers, passed on instructions for the new Soyuz spacecraft, and performed additional tasks, including transferring seats and unloading hardware from Soyuz.

The European ACES (Atomic Clock Ensemble in Space) has been attached to a platform on the outside of the ISS to test the performance of a new type of atomic clock that exploits and depends upon microgravity conditions. CNES's contribution was a laser link for optical transfer of time and frequency, and the laser cooled atomic clock PHARAO.

The scientific objectives of ACES have been based in the fields of atomic physics, with relativity tests designed to measure gravitational redshift, and the search for any drift in the fine structure constant or anisotropy in light propagation.

PHARAO (Projet d'Horloges Atomiques par Refroidissement d'Atomes en Orbite) is a cooled caesium atomic clock using laser cooling to reduce the thermal velocity of atoms to a few centimeters per second, which corresponds to a temperature of about one micro Kelvin. Under microgravity conditions, the atoms remain at these low velocities, while on earth they would increase their speed rapidly due to gravitational acceleration when the lasers are switched off for signal interrogation.

GERMANY

DLR, Germany's Aerospace Research Center and Space Agency

DLR is Germany's aerospace research center as well as its space agency. The agency has participated in joint programs with the European Space Agency (ESA) and conducted its own programs in areas such as radar technology and optical remote sensing, atmospheric physics, data processing and refining, telecommunication and navigation, telemedicine, research under space conditions, robotics, hot structures and materials, and space flight and test infrastructure. It has been particularly interested in projects and missions that have an interdisciplinary focus, such as linking sensor technology and robotics in planet research, or a merger of earth observation, telecommunication and navigation technology in the field of applications.

Experimenting with microgravity, exploring other planets, and observing the earth's environment from outer space have been among DLR's primary space activities.

DLR has conducted research in space with applications usable on earth in medicine, agriculture, mechanical engineering and land surveying. It has also used such cutting-edge methods as telescience, or the operation of test equipment in a space lab by remote control.

DLR has a strong interest in making space flight less expensive and contributing to international cooperative projects in a variety of areas including extraterrestrial exploration, scientific observation of the earth, space transport, application programs, and utilization of the International Space Station.

It has recently signed an agreement with the Russia space agency, Rosaviakosmos, to explore the possibilities of developing manned spaceflight systems and satellite projects. In the future, this cooperation will include the development of environmentally friendly rocket propulsion and research in the field of aeronautics.

DLR has continued to work with Japanese facilities, including NASDA, in space; ISAS in extraterrestrial studies; NAL in aeronautics; and NEDO in combustion research. Projects have examined re-entry, robotics, and microgravity research, as well as new propulsion methods and transport system technologies.

The agency has also been involved in mission planning, satellite operation and remote sensing in cooperation with India.

DLR will continue to work with China on research in aerodynamics, aeroacoustics, structure technology, and materials in relation to space research.

DLR has several institutes devoted to space project development. These include Space Flight Management; Space Operations; Space Propulsion Systems; Space Sensor Technology and Planetary Exploration; and Space Simulation.

The Space Flight Management Institute was commissioned by the government of the Federal Republic of Germany based on the political concept of Raumfahrt — Perspektiven fuer Anwendung und Forschung (Space travel perspectives for application and research).

This division provides space flight support to the ESA, while serving the German space program through the areas of satellite communications, navigation, earth observation, space exploration, research under space conditions, space station development, space transportation systems, and technologies for spaceflight systems.

The Space Operations division has been responsible for future-oriented subjects such as autonavigation, communications, and mission planning.

For autonomous navigation, the focus has been on autonomous onboard orbit determination and the development of a spaceborne GPS receiver for orbit and altitude determination. It has also conducted research into the automation of the operational flight dynamics software, developing systems that are suitable for the operation of satellite formations and constellations.

Communications development has targeted smart ground-based systems for spaceflight automation based on workflow systems, while considering web- and satellite-based communication between the spacecraft and the mission control center.

Planning systems designed by this division, including ATLAS, PLATO and TIMON, will be used for future space flight projects, as well as commercial applications, such as automotive engineering or medical technology.

The Space Propulsion Institute is divided into three key areas — the development of advanced technologies for future transport systems, the operation of large-scale test rings commissioned by European industry, and the continuous development of related measuring, control and process technologies.

This center has been involved in the core components of chemical rocket engines and their characteristic processes, using start-of-the-art test facilities and measuring methods.

In the testing of rig operations, qualification and acceptance tests on engines within the framework of the Ariane launcher program have been conducted. This involves the use of test rigs for upper and main-stage engines.

The Space Propulsion Institute designs and operates facilities for rocket engine altitude simulation under vacuum conditions and for emission control systems. This also includes rocket steam generators which run on oxygen and alcohol as fuel.

The Space Sensor Technology and Planetary Exploration division conducts planetary research on the planets, moons, asteroids, comets, and extra-solar planets. It also studies the infrared and far-infrared range including the birth of stars, and molecular clouds.

The institute develops digital line and matrix sensors in the visible and infrared spectral regions such as cameras and spectrometers, as well as far-infrared sensors, solar sails, microsatellites, and landers.

It has developed a complete digital photogrammetry system for satellite-based or airborne remote sensing experiments.

The advanced space sensor technology can be used for a variety of spin-off applications, including commercial products such as HRSC-AX and ADS40 airplane cameras for remote sensing and photogrammetric airborne imaging applications and the AWFS early warning system for forest fires, traffic analysis, and control systems.

Real-time processing systems are applied in addition to camera technology. The institute has special facilities for developing and testing spaceborne equipment, such as electronics laboratories, clean rooms, vibrating tables, space simulation chambers, and calibration equipment. A central planetary image data archive (RPIF) is available for use by scientists, the press, and the public.

The Space Simulation Institute conducts research and development in the field of solidification research under both laboratory and zero-gravity conditions, as well as the exploration of planetary bodies through the use of in-situ methods.

In collaboration with the Institute of Aerospace Medicine, it performs development and service tasks for user support, and has been responsible for teleoperations methods and science, particularly for the International Space Station (ISS).

Future planetary missions will increasingly make use of landers to look for traces of life on the spot and to better understand the history of planets and the solar system. The institute has concentrated on the development and use of acoustic investigations, automatic drills, and system management of mission landers.

There are several sites where aerospace research is conducted for DLR. These include Lampoldshausen, Köln-Porz, Stuttgart, and Oberpfaffenhofen.

Lampoldshausen

The Lampoldshausen Research Center was founded in 1959 by Professor Eugen Sanger, the famous German spaceflight pioneer, as a test center for liquid rocket propulsion. The center began full operation in 1962, and a year later the Institute of Chemical Rocket Propulsion was established. This center performs high-altitude rocket engine testing and has facilities for testing the third stage of the ELDO launcher.

The center currently takes part in the Ariane launcher program and has a large test facility (PS) for rocket engines with liquid hydrogen and liquid oxygen as propellants, which went into operation in 1990.

Since 1997, the research and operations were regrouped to form DLR's space propulsion unit.

The space propulsion unit concentrates its research on liquid propulsion, using classic rocket engines as well as air-breathing propulsion systems. It studies technical combustion processes with high energy density and high combustion quality.

The unit investigates engine technologies such as atomization, mixing and combustion in hydrogen/oxygen high-pressure engines as well as supersonic combustion ramjets, with an emphasis on the phenomena of injection, heat transfer and combustion stability. The unit also develops models for a better understanding of side load origins and prediction of flow phenomena in thrust nozzles.

There are several test facilities available for development and qualification of the European Ariane launcher, specifically the hydrogen/oxygen main stage VULCAIN engine (100 kN) and the upper stage, AESTUS (27 kN).

P2 Test Facility is used for upper stage engines using storable propellants, with thrust levels up to 30 kN. P3 Test Facility is used for cryogenic hydrogen/oxygen high-pressure rocket combustors with thrust levels up to 1000 kN and a chamber with pressures of up to 100 bar. P4 Test Facility is used for rocket propulsion systems or stages using storable propellants and thrust levels up to 700 kN, or up to 30 kN under vacuum conditions. P5 Test Facility is used for cryogenic hydrogen/oxygen turbopump engines up to 1000 kN thrust. P8 Test Facility is used for investigating the atomization, mixing and combustion of liquid hydrogen and liquid oxygen at combustion pressures up to 300 bar in experimental combustion chambers. Complex P1 is used for small rocket engines using storable propellants with thrust levels from 4 N up to 20 kN and up to 440 N under vacuum conditions, as well as research engines running green propellants.

Köln-Porz

The Köln-Porz Center provides support in the development of new materials and the optimization of propulsion technologies, with emphasis on reducing emission values while increasing performance and reliability. It utilizes large-scale test facilities including wind tunnels such as the European Transonic Wind Tunnel (ETW), and engine and materials testing systems.

A second main focus of the center is spaceflight, encompassing the affects of microgravity on the organisms of humans and on materials revolving in an orbit around the earth. This study involves cross-discipline research through the Institute of Space Simulation, the Institute of Materials Research, the Institute of Aerospace Medicine, the Microgravity User Support Center (MUSC) and the Astronaut Training Center.

The Institute of Propulsion Technology has been devoted exclusively to the improvement of gas turbines in aviation and electric generation by medium to long-term exploitation of the inherent technical potentials.

Major objectives of the institute include turbomachinery research with the verification of propfantechnology, the enhancement of thrust to weight ratio, and the power per unit of the cycle and component efficiency with higher cycle temperatures due to improved cooling concepts.

An important aspect of current combustion research has been the development and testing of new combustor concepts aimed at reducing nitric oxide production in spot-free and stable combustion. Engine noise analysis and reduction, active noise control, exhaust emission analysis and fire safety continue to be other institute objectives.

The Institute of Aerospace Medicine contributes to solving problems encountered by the personnel responsible for the operation of aerospace vehicles. It also conducts basic research on the affects that extreme environmental conditions have on living organisms.

The institute covers the area of telemedicine, which involves remote medical care and diagnosis. This activity was initiated by the necessity of monitoring the vital parameters of astronauts during the course of a space mission from the ground. On earth, this method is ideally suited for the remote monitoring of persons at high-risk for illness, including outpatients such as infants threatened by sudden infant death syndrome or elderly patients in danger of suffering collapse.

Other projects of the institute include using human spaceflight as a tool to solve basic medical questions; providing methods and criteria and conducting studies measuring the stress arising from man and machine systems such as aviation; the psychological and medical selection and monitoring of aerospace personnel; and using basic study problems of gravitation and radiation on biological specimens.

The Institute of Space Simulation provides support to scientists from research establishments and industry in conducting experiments under the special environmental conditions existing in space. This includes microgravity as well as extreme vacuum, temperatures and radiation.

The institute operates the Microgravity User Support Center (MUSC) for space experiments, offering replicas of the experimental facilities used in space that function in the same manner. Here, other conditions found in space, such as those existing on a planet's surface, whether it be Mars or another planet, can also be reproduced through simulation in a special chamber.

The influence of gravity on physical systems, particularly those involving the production of new materials, has been studied in conjunction with German SPACELAB missions D-1 and D-2, during NASA missions, onboard the Russian space station MIR, and on TEXUS rockets.

Future experiments will examine the physical processes on the surface of an artificial comet in preparation for a probe being developed in cooperation with CNES, ASI, and the Max Planck Institute.

The Institute of Materials Research provides support in the field of metallic and nonmetallic structural and high-temperature materials. Its primary objective is to gain new knowledge on the production, processing and characteristics of these materials, particularly for aerospace applications.

The range of the materials examined includes monolithic lightweight construction materials, powder metallurgical materials, fiber composite materials with metal and ceramic matrices, functional materials, and high-strength ceramic materials, as well as thermal insulation coatings and protective coatings against hot gas corrosion operating at high temperatures.

The institute focuses on materials technology, materials analysis of microstructures, materials mechanics, and testing. Materials technology concerns the development or optimization of production processes which lead to new or improved materials, protective coatings, thermal gradient materials, and the economical manufacturing of components.

The institute also participates in the Microgravity User Support Center (MUSC) in experiments investigating crystal growth.

The Astronaut Training Center serves as a training and preparation center for astronauts performing scientific experiments during manned space missions, and works in cooperation with the European Space Agency's astronaut center.

The center played an important role in the SL 1 (1983), D-1 (1985), MIR (1992) and D-2 (1993) space missions. It also provided support to the EAC in the EUROMIR '94 and EUROMIR '95 missions.

It specializes in the training of manned space missions with an emphasis on scheduled experiments and payloads using the SPACE-LAB simulation facility, integrated simulations, and the largest water tank in Europe, in which extravehicular activities can be practiced under conditions similar to those encountered in microgravity.

The Mobility and System Technology division is responsible for investigating complex systems of space transport and terrestrial traffic. It maintains state-of-the-art computing, networking, and software technology which support the analysis, conceptualization, design, simulation, and optimization of these systems.

Activities within the division are focused on analyzing the demand and market for space transport systems, finding the most efficient technology with regard to overall system conditions, and studying operational scenarios taking into consideration interrelationship with the technological, economic and political environment. These activities include microscopic traffic simulations to guarantee a continuing mobility, as well as planning, control, and optimization of traffic systems encompassing the field of telematics; and the advancement and application of the TRANSYS software system featuring conceptual design, optimal analysis, and comparative evaluation for space transport systems such as follow-up models of the Ariane 5 launcher.

Stuttgart

The Stuttgart site was founded at Stuttgart Airport in 1954 and originally headed by Eugen Saenger, one of Germany's leading aerospace pioneers. Today, it is comprised of several institutes which make important contributions to research on renewable energy sources, combustion techniques, design and construction, and high-energy laser systems.

The Institute of Combustion Technology has been concerned with environmental protection and the efficient handling of energy resources. It has made essential contri-

butions to improve the design of aero engine combustors and stationary combustion systems.

Laboratories at the institute are equipped with the most advanced technology needed to fulfill its goals, including shock tubes and flow reactors for chemical kinetic studies in a wide range of temperatures and pressures, gas chromatography, mass spectrometry, and jet-REMPI for chemical analysis. There are several test rigs on hand to stabilize flames from atmospheric to high pressure, with gaseous and liquid fuels, as well as high-performance computers for flame modeling.

The institute's main areas of research include chemical kinetics, laser diagnostics, and combustion modeling.

The Institute of Technical Thermodynamics has concentrated its efforts on efficient and low-emission energy technologies, and on the utilization of renewable energy sources for electric power supply, transport technology and space.

Work applications have included the development of laboratory and prototype models, design and operation of demonstration plants, systems analysis and the assessment of related technologies.

In its electrochemical energy technology research, the institute focuses on fuel cells and electrolysis technology that offer a wide range of solutions for highly efficient and low-emission energy, transportation technologies, and power generation and storage in space.

In the area of solar thermal energy technology, the institute develops solar thermal concentrating technologies for terrestrial and space applications, including technologies for solar thermal power stations, solar dynamic power supply units for space vehicles, high temperature heat exchangers for power plants, and sorption technology for heating and cooling purposes.

The institute also investigates technologies for rational and low-emission energy conversion with energy economy considerations including individual analyses of technological and economical performance, the design of climate compatible energy supply systems, and the analysis of life cycles of new energy technologies.

The Institute of Technical Physics conducts laser research, with priority placed on applications and development of high powered lasers. Research in this area concentrates on laser applications for manufacturing purposes including surface treatment, welding and cladding of steel and light metals using the laser powder technique, and developing systems utilizing interchangeable processing modules.

Laser applications in the field of semiconductor technology emphasize the development of components on the basis of group III nitrides where process-adapted laser radiation has been employed in order to achieve epitaxial layer growth, structural layout, and metalizing of components.

The Institute of Structures and Design focuses on heat resistant lightweight design, structural integrity of composite structures, and cost-efficient automated composite structures.

Basic and applications-oriented investigations have included the study of the characteristic properties of composite materials, design conforming to these properties, production technology, and price-to-performance ratio.

The institute continues to work on the development of manufacturing technologies for fiber ceramics; the development of structural components for transport vehicles, airframes and subfloor of aircraft such as helicopters with the property of absorbing crash engines; automated composite processing with CAD/CIM; high-temperature testing of materials and components at 1600 to 2500°C; and the development of thermal protection systems for reusable space transport vehicles.

Oberpfaffenhofen

The Oberpfaffenhofen site has been responsible for space flight operations, and is made up of several institutes.

The Institute of Radio Frequency Technology has conducted research into the areas of remote sensing and reconnaissance, satellite positioning and navigation, satellite communications and traffic guidance.

In remote sensing and reconnaissance,

the operating range of the microwave radars and radiometers extends from 480 MHz to 240 GHz. The institute developed the concept of the German-Italian radar experiment X-SAR, which flew successfully on two space shuttle missions along with NASA's SIR-C radar. Another mission, the Shuttle Radar Topography Mission, was launched in 1999.

In satellite positioning and navigation, clock synchronization and time dissemination using satellites and global navigation systems are the core activities.

For satellite telecommunications, research has concentrated on antenna technology and propagation measurement and analysis.

The primary goal of traffic guidance has been to design autonomous traffic guidance systems for land, air and sea traffic control, such as a short-range radar network for controlling ground traffic at airports.

The Institute of Communications Technology has been focusing on research into aviation and aerospace applications, including mobile ground communications and communications in space. Primary emphasis in these areas has been placed on digital transmission procedures in radio channels, including optical transmission in space.

Research conducted on the transmission of information in channels subject to fading has led to results which have been applied to marine, aeronautical, and ground mobile radio communications.

The institute continues to contribute to the development and testing of air and space radio communication systems, terrestrial digital mobile radio systems, and digital audio and video broadcasting systems.

Future long-term projects will concentrate on accessing frequency ranges beyond 20 GHz for satellite radio communication and optical communication in space.

The Institute of Optoelectronics focuses on the development and testing of optoelectronic procedures and systems. This has extended to application-oriented research in remote sensing and communications, including mapping of environmental damage to forests and hazardous waste accumulations; stereoscopic imagery for topographical mapping;

trace gas analysis in the upper atmosphere; and laser remote sensing of wind velocity and state of vegetation.

The institute has exhibited particular expertise in developing optoelectronic systems and methods for environmental observation in aircraft and satellite sensor systems, covering activities such as optical sensor technology, laser and lidar procedures, methods of digital image data correction, models and simulation of radiation transmission in the atmosphere and environment, and earth observation remote sensing.

The institute has participated in environmental studies carried out from aircraft as well as from space. A primary example of this has been the optoelectronic stereo and multispectral camera MOMS, which performed successfully during the D-2 mission. A modified version flew for two years as part of the PRIRODA program on the Russian space station MIR.

The Institute of Atmospheric Physics has concentrated on the regional and global investigation of important atmospheric processes, including tropospheric dynamics and transport processes, stratospheric dynamics and chemistry, the effects of pollutants on the atmosphere and their influence on climate, and utilization of data obtained from space observations. Changes in the chemical composition of the atmosphere as well as climate change have been of particular interest.

The institute has equipped research aircraft with instruments to record measurements on turbulence, cloud and aerosol parameters, and the influence of radiation at the boundaries of the atmosphere, the free troposphere and the lower stratosphere.

The Institute of Robotics and System Dynamics focuses on research in control technology, multibody dynamics, sensor and actuator technology, intelligent control systems and human-machine interfaces, with applications to the development of innovative multisensor lightweight robot systems and their remote control and programming for space activities, as well as in the simulation and design of mechatronic systems.

Mechtronics, a central aspect of the institute's study, involves the integration of mechanics, electronics and computer performance on the smallest of scales such as the development of highly sensitive multifinger robot hands, hand integrated simulation, and design optimization computer-aided design technology for complex systems. Three-dimensional simulation graphics are useful tools for this development.

For the first time in the history of space flight, the robot ROTEX carried out prototype tasks in a highly adaptable manner during the Spacelab D-2 mission, in a variety of modes including reprogramming and remote control from the ground. This was a result of work from the institute, which provided scientific and technical contributions for the experiment.

These contributions included multisensor gripper technology and predictive three-dimensional graphic simulation to compensate for signal delays of up to seven seconds. The technology utilized has benefited invasive surgery and telesurgery techniques being used today.

DRL's Remote Sensing Data Center (DFD) located in Oberpfaffenhofen, Bavaria, serves as Germany's national facility for satellite earth observation data. It is responsible for data acquisition, user-oriented processing, archiving, distribution, and promoting applications for remote sensing from space.

DFD has been heavily involved in European satellite-supported navigation activities including the development of algorithms, processes, and code software for data processing and information technologies. It has also been responsible for operating the related processing and distribution systems.

The center also manages ground stations worldwide for German users as well as European and international partners.

The German Space Operations Center (GSOC) is the site of spaceflight projects, maintaining a satellite ground station in Weilheim, a mobile sounding rocket base, simulation facilities, and a control center.

GSOC provides support for ground stations and relay satellites by assisting in the determination of orbit and altitude, predicting the location and velocity of spacecraft, and planning and executing orbit maneuvers.

In ten successful missions from 1989 to 1995, the German Space Operations Center demonstrated its ability to position communications satellites such as the X-ray satellite ROSAT.

Prior to a new scheme for operating small satellites, which was implemented in 1997, all GSOC operations dependant upon the retrieval and soft landing of a space vehicle were determined and tested during preparations for the re-entry mission EXPRESS.

Since the new scheme was implemented with its first satellite, EQUATOR-S, the center's emphasis has shifted to payload operations support which will include future operations for the European contribution to the International Space Station.

GREECE

Institute for Space Applications and Remote Sensing (ISARS)

The Institute for Space Applications and Remote Sensing (ISARS) is one of four research institutes of the National Observatory of Athens (NOA). ISARS was founded in 1955 under the name Ionospheric Institute. In 1990, the institute was renamed to Institute of Ionospheric and Space Research. It was later renamed in 1999 to reflect its expanded activities, which cover a variety of aspects of space research and applications.

ISARS was originally located at the historic site of the Hill of Nymphs near Acropolis and Thission. However, by July 1995, the significant increase of staff and research and development projects made it necessary for the institute to move to new, modern facilities at the NOA campus north of Athens, on mount Pendeli.

The institute is made up of several facilities, including an ionospheric station, satellite receiving stations, and a computer center.

The new fully automated ionospheric station has operated at the Pendeli site since September 2000. Users can access real-time ionogram results of the automatic scaling, preview some recent ionograms and download daily SAO files using an SAO database.

Satellite receiving stations include the NOAA/AVHRR Image Acquisition Station which was manufactured by Telonics, Inc., consisting of a receiving antenna with satellite data from NOAA 12, 14, 15 and 16, and imaging that is archived, pre-processed with radiometric calibration, navigation, and enhancement. They also include the Seawifs Image Acquisition Station, where data is captured on a daily basis with a frequency of one image per day; and the Meteosat Receiving Station, a Dartcom PDUS system, where data is visible in the near–Infrared and also generated as water vapor from the geostationary satellite, Meteosat, on a daily basis with a frequency of two images per hour.

The computer center is equipped with a SUN UltraSparc2, two HP NetServers, and 15 Pentium PCs.

Space Physics

The activities of the space physics research group of ISARS continue to focus on solar and heliospheric physics, interplanetary disturbances, magnetospheric dynamic processes and impacts on the terrestrial atmosphere. The group has been particularly active in investigations of solar atmospheric dynamics, charged particle acceleration mechanisms, space magnetic storms and space weather, magnetosphere-ionosphere coupling, storm-time ring current dynamics, particle propagation in coronal mass ejections, and propagation channels in co-rotating interaction regions.

These investigations have been supplemented by data processing; analysis and interpretation of spacecraft data, both from current and from past missions; the dexvelopment of modeling software for the implementation of mission objectives; and computer simulations of basic physical processes.

In the future, the group plans to engage in the detailed investigation and interpretation of dynamic chains of events observed at the sun, interplanetary space, magnetosphere and terrestrial atmosphere, and their cause-and-effect relationship.

Remote Sensing

The primary goal of the remote sensing group at ISARS has been to collect and fruitfully exploit space derived data and provide information and services to those members of industry, government and the public who are interested in learning about the state of the earth's environment and its dynamics. Current research relates to the study of natural resources and the development of remote sensing systems capable of supporting water management in the Mediterranean.

This research utilizes methodological approaches that permit the integration of newly acquired high-resolution satellite imagery in urban planning and land use mapping. The development of advanced image analysis techniques to process the next generation of high-resolution satellite imagery has been among the main research tasks at ISARS.

Natural hazards are studied in parallel. The use of remote sensing techniques for risk assessment and mitigation is evaluated through specific experiments. The technique of radar interferometry to observe very small changes of the crust due to volcanic and seismic activity in Hellenic territory is currently being tested.

Other research activities at ISARS encompass the use of satellite imagery and in-situ data for assessing the degree of atmospheric pollution over big cities and industrial zones. For the purposes of satellite data collection and distribution, ISARS operates two image reception stations for the NOAA and METEOSAT satellites. The collected data are treated and distributed systematically to the user's community by using commercial, in-house developed software for image processing, archiving and delivery.

Ionospheric Physics

The institute has served as a co-investigator in two major space missions. One was CHAMP, Comparative Studies between Athens Digisonde and CHAMP ionospheric data, in cooperation with the German company, GeoforschungsZentrum Potsdam (GFZ). This featured a comparison of the ionospheric products received from both the Athens Digisonde and the GPS experiment onboard CHAMP for the validation of the method used by GFZ. Another was SWARM, a constellation to study the dynamics of the earth's magnetic field and its interactions with the earth system in conjunction with ESA's Earth Explorer Opportunity Missions.

CHAMP (CHAllenging Minisatellite Payload) is a German small satellite mission for geoscientific and atmospheric research and applications, managed by GFZ. With its highly precise, multifunctional and complementary payload elements consisting of a magnetometer, accelerometer, star sensor, GPS receiver, laser retro reflector, ion drift meter, and its orbit characteristics (near polar, low altitude, and long duration) CHAMP will generate for the first time simultaneous highly precise gravity and magnetic field measurements over a five-year period. This will allow the detection of the spatial variations of both fields and also their variability with time. The CHAMP mission will open a new era in geopotential research and will become a significant contributor to the Decade of Geopotentials.

CHAMP will also perform radio occultation measurements onboard the spacecraft and through the infrastructure developed on ground, becoming a pilot mission for the pre-operational use of spaceborne GPS observations for atmospheric and ionospheric research and applications in weather prediction and space weather monitoring.

CHAMP mission objectives include the provision of highly precise global long-wavelength features of the static earth gravity field and the temporal variation of this field; global estimates of the main and crystal magnetic field of the earth with precision accuracy and the space/time variability of these field components; and a large number of GPS signal refraction data caused by the atmosphere and ionosphere, with good global distribution, which can be converted into temperature, water vapor and electron content.

The CHAMP mission will make contributions to the understanding of earth science with its study of the geosphere, including an investigation of the structure and dynamics of the solid earth from the core along the mantle to the crust, and investigation of interactions with the ocean and atmosphere. It will also study the hydrosphere, providing a more accurate monitoring of ocean circulation, global sea level changes and short-term changes in the global water balance as well as interactions with weather and climate; as well as the atmosphere, providing global sounding of the vertical layers of the neutral and ionized gas shell of the earth and the relationship between weather on earth and space weather.

The CHAMP satellite was launched with a Russian COSMOS launch vehicle on July 15, 2000, into an almost circular, near polar orbit with an initial altitude of 454 km (282 miles). The design lifetime of the satellite system is five years. The 87 degree inclination is the maximum inclination which can be served from the Plesetsk cosmodrome.

The objective of the SWARM mission will be to provide an accurate survey of the geomagnetic field and its temporal evolution, and gain new insights into improving our knowledge of the earth's interior and climate. The SWARM concept consists of a constellation of four satellites in two different polar orbits between 400 and 550 km (248 to 341 miles) altitude. Each satellite will provide high-precision and high-resolution measurements of the magnetic field. Together they will provide the necessary observations for the global high-precision survey of the geomagnetic field that is needed to model its various sources.

Magnetic fields play an important role in physical processes throughout the universe. The magnetic field exerts a very direct control on the electrodynamic environment, on thermospheric dynamics, and possibly even on the evolution of the lower atmosphere. SWARM will provide important new knowledge of the expanding and deepening South Atlantic Anomaly, with its serious implications for low-earth orbit satellite operations. Geographically, the recent decay of the earth's magnetic dipole has been largely due to changes in the field in that region. The geomagnetic field models resulting from this mission will have practical applications in many different areas, such as space weather and radiation hazards as well as furthering our understanding of atmospheric processes related to climate and weather.

SWARM has been tentatively scheduled for launch in 2008.

Telecommunications

The main thrust of the research and development activities of the telecommunications group deals with state-of-the-art satellite and terrestrial wireless telecommunication systems and networks for both fixed and mobile applications. Current emphasis involves projects related to future PCS/UMTS third generation systems for multimedia applications.

The group has been involved with the following projects: satellite systems, including Ka-band (20/30 GHz) GEOs for mobile voice/data system applications and LEOs/MEOs satellite networks for mobile multimedia system applications; terrestrial systems, including smart antennas for PCS/UMTS systems and HF (2MHz) radio systems; and multicarrier and OFDM systems, covering satellite/terrestrial systems, transceiver structures for interference channels, channel measurements, modeling and simulation, CDMA and TDMA capacities, and HDTV transmission over satellite and cable channels.

HUNGARY

Hungarian Space Board/Hungarian Space Office (HSO)

On February 6, 1946, the first successful Hungarian lunar radar experiment resulted in an echo from the moon by experimental radio radar equipment sent back to Hungarian scientists, becoming a first in radar astronomy. Since then, Hungarians have been involved in over fifty years of space research.

Much of that time, Hungary's space program was directly linked to the Soviet space program, but this began to change as a result of thorough redesign in 1990. Recently, the governments of the United States and Hungary have signed a cooperation agreement resulting in significant contributions to NASA and the U.S. space program.

Hungary participated in planetary missions such as Vega probes to Venus and Halley's comet, as well as Soviet Phobos probes to Mars. In 1980, a Hungarian cosmonaut was the first Hungarian to visit the Soviet space station, Salyut-6. Hungarian physicists and engineers produced software and electronic ground support equipment for the Cassini spacecraft to planet Saturn and have also participated in NASA's Stereo Heliophysical mission. The NASA Small Bodies Node and European Subnode, which contain data mainly on comets and asteroids, are functioning at the Konkoly Astronomical Observatory of the Hungarian Academy of Sciences.

Other cooperative efforts with NASA have resulted in a number of accomplishments. In 1984, the Hungarian built thermoluminescent dosimeter (PILLE) flew onboard the Space Shuttle Challenger, and was operated by the first American woman in space, astronaut Sally Ride. The Central Research Institute built it for physics in Hungary. A similar dosimeter was delivered to the International Space Station (ISS) during the STS-102 mission, which was launched on March 8, 2001.

The Passive Dosimeter System (PDS) serves as a flexible and easy-to-use radiation monitor consisting of two kinds of radiation dosimeters and an electronic "reader." The dosimeters can be placed anywhere in the ISS to provide accurate point measurements of the radiation at their locations.

One of the radiation dosimeters is a thermoluminescent detector, or TLD. Each TLD, which resembles a fat fountain pen, contains calcium sulfate crystals inside an evacuated glass bulb. These crystals absorb energy from incident ionizing radiation (protons, neutrons, electrons, heavy charged particles, gamma and X-rays) as the radiation passes through them. This process results in a steady increase in the energy level of the electrons in the crystal.

To read the accumulated radiation dose, an astronaut aboard the ISS removes the crystal-containing dosimeter from its measurement location and places it into the electronic reader. A component inside the reader heats the crystals. As the crystals are heated they emit a glow of light that is proportional to the amount of radiation they have been exposed to. This glow is measured by a photomultiplier tube in the reader. The reader stores the measured dose on a memory card that can be returned to earth for further analysis. After the crystals have emitted all their stored energy, they are ready to begin accumulating a dose again and the TLD is ready to be reused.

The other dosimeter is a set of Plastic Nuclear Track Detectors (PNTDs). The PNTDs are thin sheets of plastic which are similar to the material used for some eyeglass lenses. As heavy charged ions pass through the PNTDs, the surface becomes pitted with tiny craters. When the PNTDs are subsequently returned to earth, the plastic is etched to enlarge the craters. The craters are then counted and their shapes and sizes are analyzed using a microscope. This information is used to improve the accuracy of the radiation dose the TLDs have recorded and to improve the estimate of the biological affects of the radiation.

Understanding the radiation environment on the ISS will help scientists explain experimental results that otherwise might be unaccounted for. The radiation measurements can help scientists determine whether a given effect is due to microgravity, radiation or another cause. The PDS system is a vital part of NASA's laboratory support equipment.

Hungary also supplied electrical ground support equipment for the Cassini Plasma Spectrometer (CAPS), which was launched successfully in 1997.

INDIA

Indian Space Research Organization (ISRO)

The Indian space program's beginnings were driven by the vision of Dr. Vikram Sarabhai, who is considered to be the father of Indian space program.

The Indian Space Research Organization (ISRO) was set up in 1969, with the primary objective of developing space technology and its applications to fulfill various national tasks. Since then, it has established space systems like the INSAT for telecommunications, television broadcasting and meteorological services; and the Indian Remote Sensing Satellites (IRS) for monitoring and managing resources. ISRO has also developed the satellite launch vehicles PSLV and GSLV to place these satellites into orbit.

In June 1972, the Indian government set up the Space Commission and Department of Space (DOS) to serve in conjunction with the Indian Space Research Organization (ISRO). The main objectives of India's space program include development of satellites, launch vehicles, sounding rockets, and the required ground systems.

Experimental phases of the program have included the Satellite Instructional Television Experiment (SITE), Satellite Telecommunications Experiment (STEP), remote sensing application projections, satellites such as Aryabhata, Bhaskara, Rohini, APPLE, and launch vehicles SLV-3 and ASLV.

The Polar Satellite Launch Vehicle (PSLV) has been used for launching IRS satellites, and the Geosynchronous Satellite Launch Vehicle (GSLV) has been used to launch INSAT satellites.

Space science activities have also included SROSS and IRS-P3 satellites and participation in international science missions such as the MST radar.

The Indian Remote Sensing Satellite (IRS) System was commissioned with the launch of IRS-1A in March 1988. The IRS has been under the management of the National Natural Resources Management System (NNRMS), coordinated at the national level by the planning committee of NNRMS.

Under this system, a number of satellites have been launched: IRS-1B in August 1991, IRS-1C in December 1995, and IRS-1D, launched on September 29, 1997. IRS-P3 was launched with IRS-1D by India's Polar Satellite Launch Vehicle (PSLV). IRS-P4, equipped with an Ocean Color Monitor (OCM) and a Multi-frequency Scanning Microwave Radiometer (MSMR), was launched by a PSLV-C2.

IRS-P5, with a very high resolution panchromatic camera for cartographic applications, and IRS-P6, for agricultural applications, have been planned for launch in 2004.

Data received from IRS satellites is processed by the National Remote Sensing Agency, located in Hyderabad. It is then marketed by SI, a United States company, under a commercial contract with the Antrix Corporation of the Department of Space.

Under the Stretched Rohini Satellite Series (SROSS), the 113 kg (250 lb) SROSS-C2 satellite was launched by ASLV-D4 on May 4, 1994, carrying two scientific payloads, a Gamma-Ray Burst (GRB) experiment and a Retarding Potential Analyser (RPA). A similar satellite, SROSS-C, had been launched by ASLV-D3 in May 1992. SROSS-C2 continues to be in service.

The PSLV launched the IRS-1D satellite on September 29, 1997, after successfully completing several developmental flights. On May 26, 1999, a PSLV-C2 launched with the IRS-P4 (OCEANSAT), also carrying two smaller satellites, KITSAT of Korea and TUBSAT of Germany.

The PSLV-C3 launched three satellites on October 22, 2001, including the Technology Experiment Satellite (TES) of ISRO, the BIRD satellites of Germany, and PROBA of Belgium. On September 12, 2002, the PSLV-C4 launched the KALPANA-1 satellite.

The Geosynchronous Satellite Launch Vehicle (GSLV) was built for launching the 2,000 kg (2 ton) class of communications satellites into geosynchronous transfer orbit. It is a three-stage vehicle, consisting of a 129-ton first stage with a solid propellant core motor; four liquid propellant strap-on boosters with 40 tons of propellant each; a second stage with a liquid propulsion system containing 37.5 tons of propellant; and a cryogenic upper stage with 12 tons of liquid oxygen and liquid hydrogen.

The first developmental flight of the GSLV-D1 was completed successfully on April 18, 2001. On May 8, 2003, the second developmental flight, GSLV-D2, was launched with the GSAT-2 satellite.

India's Department of Space manages several space centers, including the Vikram Sarabhai Space Center (VSSC), Liquid Propulsion Systems Center (LPSC), Satish Dhawan Space Center (SHAR), ISRO Inertial Systems Unit (IISU), ISRO Satellite Center (ISAC), Space Applications Center (SAC), Development and Educational Communication Unit (DECU), Physical Research Laboratory (PRL), ISRO Telemetry, Tracking and Command Network (ISTRAC), INSAT Master Control Facility (MCF), National Remote Sensing Agency (NRSA), and the National Mesosphere/Stratosphere/Troposphere Radar Facility (NMRF).

The Vikram Sarabhai Space Center (VSSC) is the lead center for rocket and launch vehicle projects. Its research activities cover avionics, aeronautics, materials and mechanical engineering, solid propulsion and composites, propellants, polymers and chemicals, as well as systems reliability and computer information.

The VSSC Space Physics Laboratory carries out research in atmospheric and related space sciences.

Achievements at VSSC have included the development of sounding rockets and ISRO launch vehicles SLV-3, ASLV, and PSLV.

The Liquid Propulsion Systems Center (LPSC) has been engaged in the development of liquid and cryogenic propulsion stages for launch vehicles and auxiliary propulsion systems for both launch vehicles and satellites. Its activities have related to liquid propulsion stages, cryogenic propulsion stages and control systems for launch vehicles and spacecraft.

Test facilities are located at Mahendragiri in Tamil Nadu, which includes precision fabrication facilities. At this site scientists work on the development of transducers and integration of satellite propulsion systems carried out at Bangalore.

LPSC has worked on the development of liquid propellant stages for PSLV; control systems for SLV-3, ASLV and GSLV; satellite propulsion systems including those for INSAT and IRS; and production of pressure transducers.

The Satish Dhawan Space Center, SHAR, is the main launch center of ISRO, located 100 km north of Chennai. This center processes solid propellant motors and conducts ground tests. It manages launch ranges at Thuma which are also used for sounding rockets.

The ISRO Inertial Systems Unit (IISU) carries out development of inertial sensors, and systems for satellites and launch vehicles covering navigation systems, satellite inertial systems, bearing and space tribology and inertial systems integration and simulation.

Facilities include precision fabrication, assembly, integration and testing.

IISU provided inertial systems for ISRO launch vehicles and satellites, solar array drive assemblies, and scanning mechanisms. It is currently engaged in development of an inertal navigation system for GSLV, and INSAT and IRS satellites.

The ISRO Satellite Center (ISAC) serves as the lead center for satellite technology. Its activities have included digital systems, power systems, communication and microwave systems, spacecraft assembly integration and testing, thermal structures, spacecraft mechanisms, control systems, spacecraft mission planning and analysis, computers and information, systems reliability and space physics. Facilities include fabrication and test facilities for satellite projects.

The center's achievements have included the design and development of 26 satellites to date, including a variety of scientific, communications and remote sensing satellites. Current projects include IRS-P5, IRS-P6, INSAT-3 and G-SAT.

The Space Applications Center (SAC) conducts space applications research and development in satellite communications and remote sensing. It is responsible for designing and building communications, remote sensing and meteorological satellite payloads and satellite communications earth station equipment. Its facilities include mechanical fabrication, electronic fabrication, payload fabrication, MIC fabrication and environmental tests.

The center also operates Delhi Earth Station for satellite communication, which has been responsible for the development of communication and meteorological payloads for INSAT, and camera payloads for IRS satellites. It is currently engaged in the development of INSAT-3 communication and meteorological payloads and cameras for follow-on IRS satellites.

The Development and Educational Communication Unit (DECU) has been involved in the conception, definition, planning, implementation and socio-economic evaluation of space applications. This unit works with users to experiment with innovative space system configurations to meet specific requirements.

Its primary functions include space application experiments and demonstrations, providing communication support for application projects, production of video programs for education and development, and training of TV program production personnel and social science research in application areas on the society-technology interface. It has conducted several space application demonstrations in video productions for socio-economic development.

The Physical Research Laboratory (PRL) serves as a national center for research in space and allied sciences, supported mainly by the Department of Space. Its research programs cover astronomy and astrophysics, planetary atmosphere and aeronomy, earth sciences and solar system studies and theoretical physics. PRL manages the Udaipur Solar Observatory.

The ISRO Telemetry, Tracking and Command Network (ISTRAC) provides mission support to near-earth satellites and launch vehicle missions. It has a network of ground stations at Bangalore, Lucknow, Port Blair, Sriharikota, Thiruvananthapuram and Mauritius, with a multi-mission spacecraft control centre at Bangalore, and is currently supporting IRS-1B, IRS-1C, IRS-1D IRS-P3, IRS-P4 and SROSS-C2 satellites.

ISTRAC also operates the Local User Terminal/Mission Control Center (LUT/MCC) under the international satellite-aided search and rescue program.

The INSAT Master Control Facility (MCF) is responsible for post-launch operations on INSAT satellites including orbit maneuvers, station keeping and on-orbit operations. It is currently supporting on-orbit operations on INSAT-1D, INSAT-2A, INSAT-2B, INSAT-2C, INSAT-2E, INSAT-3B and INSAT-2DT satellites.

The National Remote Sensing Agency (NRSA) is an autonomous institution supported by the Department of Space, responsible for acquiring, processing and supplying data from remote sensing satellites.

NRSA manages the satellite earth-station at Shadnagar, near Hyderabad, for reception of data from Indian remote sensing satellites, U.S. Landsat and NOAA, French SPOT, and microwave data from the European remote sensing satellite ERS.

It also undertakes remote sensing application projects to serve the needs of the users, and runs the Indian Institute of Remote Sensing at Dehra Dun. The center is currently supplying data from IRS-1B, IRS-1C, IRS-1D, IRS-P3 and IRS-P4.

The National Mesosphere/Stratosphere/Troposphere Radar Facility (NMRF) was set up by the Department of Space at Gadanki near Tirupati, with support from the Department of Electronics, Defense Research and Development Organization, Department of Science and Technology, Department of Electronics and the Council of Scientific & Industrial research. It is available for national and international scientists to conduct atmospheric research.

Indian Remote Sensing Satellite System (IRS)

Following previously successful demonstration flights in 1979 and 1981 of Bhaskara 1 and Bhaskara 2 satellites, respectively, India began the development of an indigenous IRS program to support the national economy in the areas of agriculture water resources, forestry and ecology, geology, water sheds, marine fisheries and coastal management.

The Indian Remote Sensing satellites have been the mainstay of National Natural Resources Management system (NNRMS) under the management of the Department of Space (DOS, providing operational remote sensing data services. Data from the IRS satellites is received and disseminated by several countries all over the world, with applications in the areas of urban sprawl, infrastructure planning and other large scale applications for mapping.

Remote sensing applications in the country, under the umbrella of NNRMS, now span such diverse fields as crop acreage and yield estimation, drought warning and assessment, flood control and damage assessment, land use and land cover information, agro-climactic planning, wasteland management, water resources management, underground water exploration, prediction of snow-melt run-off, management of watersheds and command areas, fisheries development, under development, mineral prospecting and forest resources survey.

The first two IRS spacecraft, IRS-1A (March 1988) and IRS-1B (August 1991) were launched by Russian Vostok boosters from the Baikonur Cosmodrome. IRS-1A failed in 1992, while IRS-1B continued to operate through 1999. From their 22-day repeating orbits of 905 km (562 miles) mean altitude and 99 degrees inclination, the two identical IRS spacecraft hosted a trio of Linear Imaging Self-Scanning (LISS) remote sensing COD instruments working in four spectral bands: 0.45–0.52 μm, 0.52–0.59 μm, 0.62–0.68 μm, and 0.77–0.86 μm.

The 38.5-kg (85 lb) LISS-I images a swath of 148 km (92 miles) with a resolution of 72.5 m (238 feet) while the 80.5-kg (177 lb) LISS-IIA and LISS-IIB exhibited a narrower field-of-view, but were aligned to provide a composite 145-km (90 mile) swath with a 3-km (1.86 mile) overlap and a resolution of 36.25 m (119 feet).

Each IRS spacecraft weighed 975 kg, nearly a ton, at launch, with a design life of two and a half to three years. The three-axis stabilized spacecraft was of rectangular design with two narrow solar arrays producing less than one kW electrical power. The Spacecraft Control Center at Bangalore oversaw all spacecraft operations, with the principal data reception station for the remote sensing payload located at Shadnagar. Spacecraft data transmissions have been effected via X-band and S-band antennas at the base of spacecraft.

IRS-1A and IRS-1B were to be joined in 1993 with IRS-1E, the modified IRS-1A engineering model, which had been equipped with the LISS-I and a German Monocular Electro-Optical Stereo Scanner. Unfortunately, however, the spacecraft was lost when its PSLV launch vehicle failed to reach earth orbit.

In October 1994, the PSLV functioned correctly, allowing IRS-P2 to assume an 820-km (509 mile), sun-synchronous orbit. This spacecraft continued to operate until September 1997.

With an 870-kg (1918 lb) mass (slightly

less than IRS-1A and IRS-1B), IRS-P2 carried the LISS-II system with a ground resolution of 32 m (105 ft) across-track and 37 m (121 ft) along-track. The total swath width was 131 km (81 miles), and the CCD array was tuned to four spectral bands between 0.45 and 0.86 am. The spacecraft's solar arrays provided up to 500 W and were linked to conventional nickel cadmium storage.

IRS-P3 was launched by PSLV in 1996 with a German modular electro-optical scanner and an Indian visible–IR scanner.

The Indian Space Research Organization (ISRO) and its commercial marketing arm, ANTRIX Corp. Ltd., successfully launched the IRS-1D earth imaging on September 29, 1997, from Sriharikota, India. The satellite is an identical twin to the IRS-1C, launched in December 1995. The dual use of these satellites has provided 5.8-meter (19 foot) resolution images to customers twice as often as was possible with the IRS-1C.

IRS-1C and IRS-1D introduced a heavier version of satellite, weighing 1,350 kg (1.35 tons), with more capable earth observation platforms. The spacecraft buses were similar to those of IRS-1A and IRS-1B, but with a slightly larger solar array generating more than 800 W.

Both IRS-1C and 1D produced 5.8-meter (19 feet) panchromatic (0.50.75 μm black and white) imagery, which was resampled to five-meter pixel detail. These satellites are also equipped with two-band Wide Field Sensors (WiFS) that cover a 774-square-kilometer (481-square-mile) area in a single image, as well as LISS-3 4-band (0.52–0.59, 0.62–0.68, 0.77–0.86, and 1.55–1.70 μm) multispectral sensors that provide 23.5-meter (77 foot) resolution multispectral coverage.

The 23.5-meter (77 foot) resolution imagery was resampled to produce 20-meter (66 foot) pixel detail. The spacecraft also carried a two-channel (0.62–0.68 and 0.77–0.86 μm) wide-field sensor with 190 m (623 foot) resolution.

The IRS C and D pan sensor sacrificed swath width for its higher resolution. However, it can be pointed off the orbit path which allows two to four day revisits to specific sites. IRS-1C and IRC-1D data can be received and

procured from EOSAT in the United States or in India at the NRSA, Hyderabad.

The Indian Remote Sensing Satellite IRS-P3 was launched with the third test launch of the Indian PSLV on March 21, 1996. It is an experimental mission mainly oriented on earth remote sensing. The launcher and the satellite bus was provided by the ISRO, with a portion of the payload provided by German Aerospace Research.

The payload consists of three instruments, including the WiFS provided by ISRO, the Modular Optoelectronic Scanner (MOS) provided by DLR, and an X-ray astronomy experiment by ISRO.

The Indian X-ray astronomy instrument aboard the satellite consists of two instruments. The Pointed-mode Proportional Counters (PPC) consist of three identical, coaligned, multilayer proportional counters collimated to a two by two degree field-of-view, each with an effective area of 400 square centimeters. The proportional counters are sensitive to 2 to 18 keV photons.

The X-ray Sky Monitor (XSM) is a pinhole camera with one square centimeter opening placed above a position sensitive proportional counter. The instrument has a 90 by 90 degree field-of-view and is sensitive to 3 to 8 keV photons. The viewing axis of the PPCs is aligned with the roll axis of the satellite, while the XSM is offset by 35 degrees in the roll-pitch plane.

The principle objective of the X-ray astronomy instrument is to carry out timing studies of X-ray pulsars, X-ray binaries, and other rapidly varying X-ray sources. The XSM detects transient X-ray sources and monitors the light intensity of bright X-ray binaries.

Stretched Rohini Satellite Series (SROSS)

The Indian Space Research Organization (ISRO) developed the Stretched Rohini Satellite Series (SROSS) for conducting various scientific experiments, as well as for new and novel application-oriented missions. The first two satellites in the series did not make it into orbit due to launch vehicle failures. The third,

SROSS 3 (also known as SROSS C), successfully reached an orbit on May 20, 1992.

Although they decayed rapidly, the orbital parameters were initially: apogee ~ 430 km (267 miles), perigee ~ 255 km (158 miles), and orbital inclination ~ 46 degrees. The satellite spin period was 10.6 seconds. The satellite carried a gamma-ray burst (GRB) experiment and Retarded Potential Analyzer (RPA) payloads. The spacecraft reentered the earth's atmosphere on July 14, 1992. SROSS C2, launched on May 4, 1994, with an Indian Augmented Satellite Launch Vehicle (ASLV-D4), is currently operating at 420 by 620 km orbit with an inclination of 42 degrees.

Onboard the SROSS C, the GRB experiment operated from May 25, 1992, until reentry on July 14, 1992. The instrument consisted of a main and a redundant CsI (Na) scintillator operating in the energy range 20 to 3000 keV. The crystals were 76 mm (main) and 37 mm (redundant) in diameter. Each had a thickness of 12.5 mm.

A burst mode was triggered by the 100 to 1024 keV count rate exceeding a preset limit during a 256 or 1024 millisecond time integration. In this mode, 65 seconds of temporal and two seconds of spectral data prior to the trigger are stored, as well as the subsequent 16 seconds of spectral data and 204 seconds of temporal data. The low resolution data consisted of two energy channels (20 to 100 keV and 100 to 1024 keV) from 65 seconds before the trigger to 204 seconds after the trigger in 256 millisecond integrations. The 20 to 1024 keV rates were also recorded with a two millisecond resolution from one second prior to one second after trigger and a 16 millisecond resolution for one second prior to eight seconds after the trigger. Energy spectra were conducted with a 124 channel PHA. Four pre-trigger spectra and 32 post-trigger spectra were recorded for every burst with a 512 millisecond integration time.

During the mission lifetime, 53 triggers occurred. Most of these, as expected, were false. There were eight candidates for "real" bursts.

The GRB experiments onboard SROSS-C2 were an improved version of the GRB payload flown successfully on the SROSS-C satellite. The improvements consisted of enhancements of the onboard memory and a better measurement of the background spectra after a burst event. These improvements led to the discovery of twelve candidate events detected up to February 15 1995, out of a total of 993 triggers.

Polar Satellite Launch Vehicle (PSLV)

In 1963, India embarked on a program to independently develop its own satellites and launch capability, following the country's successful launch of its first satellite Rohini-1B aboard an SLV (Satellite Launch Vehicle). An improved ASLV (Augmented Satellite Launch Vehicle) flew in 1987. The newer PSLV (Polar Satellite Launch Vehicle) developed by ISRO marks India's third generation of launch vehicles, designed to place the one-ton class geo-observation satellite series (IRS) in polar orbit at an altitude of 900 km (600 miles).

The PSLV is a four-stage launcher measuring 44 meters (144 ft) high with a 2.8 meter (9.18 foot) diameter, and weighing 275 tons, capable of orbiting around a one-ton payload in sun-synchronous polar orbit.

The first PSLV launch (PSLV-D1) occurred on September 20, 1993. Unfortunately, the satellite payload did not achieve orbit due to a guidance system failure.

The first stage is powered by a solid fuel engine (Hydroxyl-Terminated Poly-Butadiene) burning 100 seconds, and provides 3500kN thrust at sea level and 4600kN in vacuum. It is supported by six boosters, each of which deliver 440kN thrust at sea level and 660kN in vacuum.

The second stage is powered by the Vikas engine, which was built under French SEP license, and consumes liquid propellant (Unsymmetrical DiMethylHydrazine and nitrogen tetraoxide). It provides 725kN thrust during a 150 second burn. The third stage is powered by a solid fuel engine (HTPB) providing 340kN of thrust. The fourth stage is protected by a bulb cap with two ergols engines (Peroxyde d'Azote and MonoMethyl-Hydrazine), which burn in about seven minutes.

Geosynchronous Satellite Launch Vehicle (GSLV)

In the 1980s, India began designing the Geosynchronous Satellite Launch Vehicle (GSLV), a Delta-II class medium launch vehicle, with an objective of placing 2.5 metric ton payloads into GTO. The development and launch of the GSLV has been aimed at creating a dense satellite network to meet the country's requirements for telecommunications, earth sounding, environmental monitoring and other systems, as well as India's entrance to the international market of space. The goal of the new launch program has been to launch at least one satellite per year.

Based heavily on the PSLV, early concepts for the GSLV borrowed the six strap-on boosters and first two stages of its core vehicle. A later design suggested replacing the solid strap-on boosters with four liquid units similar to the second stage of the core vehicle. The third stage was to incorporate an indigenous liquid oxygen/liquid hydrogen engine with a thrust of approximately 12 metric tons. Development on this engine was already underway in the late 1980s, and subscale development continued through 1992.

In that same year, India contracted with Russia to buy a liquid oxygen/liquid hydrogen engine (KVD-1/KVD-7.5) developed in the 1970s for the heavy-lift N-1 launch vehicle. The plan, which had been in negotiations since 1988, came under fire from the United States, which considered the transfer of such technology a violation of the Missile Technology Control Regime. Eventually, a compromise was reached which allowed the Russian Federation to supply a limited number of engines to India (seven) without the transfer of critical technologies. The first engine was delivered in 1996 for the inaugural GSLV mission, initially planned for late 1997 or early 1998. Test firings of lower stage GSLV motors began in 1994.

The GSLV is a three stage vehicle. The first stage consists of a 129-ton solid propellant core motor with four liquid propellant strap-ons, holding 40 tons of propellant each. A second stage liquid propulsion system holds 37.5 tons of propellant, and the cryogenic upper stage holds 12 tons of liquid oxygen and liquid hydrogen.

The first GSLV flew in April 2001. ISRO called the launch a success, although space observers pointed out that the rocket deployed its cargo into a lower-than-planned orbit.

On May 8, 2003, India's largest rocket soared skyward on its second test flight, carrying with it an experimental satellite and plans for indigenous access to space for a wide range of payloads. Liftoff occurred from the Satish Dhawan Space Center in Sriharikota, India, along the Bay of Bengal.

Approximately 17 minutes after launch, the rocket deployed its GSAT-2 satellite payload into the targeted egg-shaped transfer orbit with a low point of about 112 miles, a high point of about 22,370 miles and an inclination of 19.2 degrees.

The satellite's final position in orbit will be along the equator at 48 degrees east longitude, or 22,300 miles above the Indian Ocean. The nearly two-ton spacecraft features four C-band transponders and two Ku-band transponders that will be used to conduct communications tests and experiments, as well as a radiation instrument, an electrical charge detector, a spectrometer to look at solar flares and a beacon to study the atmosphere using radio signals.

The second launch of the GSLV followed a number of upgrades to allow an increased payload mass capability to orbit, including propellant loading techniques for the first stage core solid motor, modifications to the liquid-fueled engines on the four strap-on boosters and the second stage, and optimized structural components. GSAT-2 weighed over 500 pounds more than GSAT-1.

A second launchpad has been under construction at Sriharikota to allow for a more aggressive launch pace for ISRO.

ISRO's future satellite launching workhorse, GLSV Mark 3, has begun development. The Rs 2,500-core launch vehicle project will be capable of lifting four-ton class satellites into space, bringing Indian launch capabilities on a par with those of the French space program's Ariane 5.

GSLV Mark 3 or MK-III will be a three-stage vehicle with a 110 ton core liquid propellant stage and strap-on-stage with two solid propellant motors, each with 200 tons of propellant.

This vehicle will launch a series of future earth observation satellites, which include IRS-P6 (RESOURCESAT) planned for launch using the indigenous polar satellite launch vehicle (PSLV).

IRS-P6 will be placed in a sun-synchronous polar orbit of 800 km (497 miles) and will provide service following IRS-1C and IRS-1D, as well as an enhancement of service capabilities in the areas of agriculture, disaster management, and land and water resources with better resolution imageries.

IRS-P5 (CARTOSAT-1) satellite, intended for advanced cartographic applications, has been planned for launch by PSLV between 2004 and 2005. CARTOSAT-2, an advanced remote sensing satellite with a single panchromatic camera capable of providing scene specific spot images for cartographic applications, has been scheduled for launch in 2005. The panchromatic camera will provide more than one meter (3.28 foot) spatial resolution imageries with a swath of 10 km (6.21 miles).

ISRO also plans to launch an all-weather, 24-hour observation capability radar imaging satellite (RISAT) during 2006. RISAT, with a five year mission life, will support and complement the operational remote sensing program by increasing agricultural and disaster applications.

Regional Remote Sensing Service Centers (RRSSC)

In order to serve the need and importance of natural resources management, the Indian government started the National Natural Resources Management System (NNRMS). NNRMS has served as an integrated approach for the management of natural resources, while optimally utilizing the advantages of conventional systems and the information derived through remote sensing. The Department of Space (DOS) overseas NNRMS and all remote sensing related activities.

The DOS established five Regional Remote Sensing Service Centers (RRSSCs) to quickly integrate remote sensing as an integral part of natural resources inventory, monitoring and management. These centers allow remote sensing technology use at a reasonable cost, while obtaining the necessary information on management of natural resources.

These centers are located at Jodhpur (Western Region), Dehradun (Northern Region), Kharaqpur (Eastern Region), Nagpur (Central Region) and Bangalore (Southern Region).

The National Remote Sensing Agency provides facilities for digital image analysis and Geographic Information Systems (GIS); guides and assists users in applications of digital analysis techniques and GIS; develops and demonstrates techniques in new applications areas; and trains scientists of user agencies in remote sensing applications.

RRSSCs also provide visual interpretation of remote sensing data, including interpretation equipment for carrying out field experiments and sample data collection to supplement remote sensing data.

They are actively involved in several remote sensing applications projects catering to national, regional, state, district and locale-specific needs. The centers participate in a number of studies.

The Integrated Mission for Sustainable Development (IMSD) provides locale-specific action plans for sustainable development of land and water resources, which are generated on a watershed basis. This requires integrating thematic information generated by satellite data with collateral and conventional information and socioeconomic input.

The action plans consist of recommendations towards improved soil and water conservation for ensuring enhanced productivity, while maintaining ecological and environmental integrity of the area and region. These plans address identification of sites and areas for surface water harvesting, groundwater recharge, and soil conservation measures by thoroughly checking dams, vegetation bunding, and potential sites for improved and diversified farming systems with fodder, fuel wood plantations, agroforestry, and agro-horticulture.

The National (Natural) Resources Information System (NRIS) is a sample of an IMSD study. It was designed to aide decision-makers at national, regional, state and district levels to plan various developmental activities in a scientific, systematic and timely manner.

The NRIS provides databases of spatial (thematic) and non-spatial data with GIS solutions for decision-making.

An NRIS concept involves biodiversity characterization at the landscape level in order to prepare biological zone maps and establish disturbance gradients for important biodiversity rich areas of the country using remote sensing and GIS.

RRSSCs have been actively involved in the project through database creation and by providing software solutions under image processing and GIS domain.

The Agro-climatic Planning and Information Bank (APIB) is a pilot project from Karnataka in South India, which consolidates large amounts of statistical and spatial information that has been generated by several organizations in order to create a single-window knowledge base for agricultural development. This information will apply specifically to all aspects of farm management that can be implemented by the farmer individually.

The Rajiv Gandhi National Drinking Water Mission is a national mission to create a scientific database for ground water using remote sensing technology. The RRSSCs are involved in the generation of precision products and ground water prospect maps at 1:50,000 scale for the states of Kerala, Karnataka, Andhrapradesh, Madhyapradesh and Rajasthan.

The crop acreage and production estimation uses remote sensing techniques to provide pre-harvest estimates on crop acreage for major crops in various parts of the country. RRSSCs provide software solutions through a package called CAPEWORKS, which is operationally being used in all ISRO workcenters and several state remote sensing centers regularly during the cropping seasons to derive information necessary to crops' acreage.

Watershed related studies allow for the planning and implementation of action plans to improve the land productivity and water resources in a given watershed. RRSSCs mon-itor and evaluate watersheds treated under the NWDPRA scheme using multi-temporal remote sensing data.

The disaster management system on flood damage assessment provides quick and accurate information related to flood and cyclone-related disasters using both remote sensing and GIS techniques. RRSSCs create digital databases for the flood-prone region of Assam and develop information systems for decision-making and effective disaster management, which will be applied to flood-affected areas.

National Remote Sensing Agency (NRSA)

The National Remote Sensing Agency (NRSA) serves as an autonomous organization under the Department of Space (DOS), Government of India (GOI). It is the central point for distribution of remote sensing satellite data products in India and other neighboring countries.

India's remote sensing needs have been served by foreign satellites such as LANDSAT, NOAA, and SPOT. Data reception began from the United States' LANDSAT satellite when an earth station opened at Hyderabad in 1979. In March 1988, the launch of India's first civilian remote sensing satellite, IRS-1A, used two LISS sensors to beam down valuable data that assisted in large scale mapping applications. In August 1991, IRS-1B was launched with greater technological advances.

The PAN and WiFS sensors on IRS-1C, in December 1995, and IRS-1D, in September 1997, further strengthened the scope of remote sensing, with increased coverage and foray into application areas like resources survey and management, urban planning, forest studies, disaster monitoring and environmental studies.

In order to test the launch vehicle program, IRS-P3 and IRS-P4 satellites were launched. IRS-P3 carried an X-ray astronomy payload for space science studies, as well as WiFS and MOS sensors.

A satellite dedicated to ocean applications was launched in May 1999, with OCM and MSMR sensors especially designed for ocean studies.

IRS systems fall under the scope of the National Natural Resources Management System (NNRMS), which is coordinated at national level by the Planning Committee of NNRMS (PC-NNRMS).

Today, IRS data is being used for a wide range of applications, including crop acreage and production estimation, drought monitoring and assessment based on vegetation conditions, food risk zone mapping and flood damage assessment, hydro-geomorphological maps for locating underground water resources, irrigation command area status monitoring, snowmelt run-off estimation, land use and land over-mapping, urban planning, biodiversity characterization, forest survey, wetland mapping, environmental impact analysis, mineral prospecting, coastal studies, and integrated surveys for developing sustainable action plans.

Data from IRS is received at the Hyderabad earth station, a dedicated data reception facility with three independent antennae. The data is processed following several stringent quality checks at various levels. It is then available for supply upon user request on digital or photographic media. SI-EOSAT, a United States company, also receives and markets IRS data worldwide under a commercial contract with Antrix Corporation of the Department of Space.

Payload programming support for IRS-1C and 1D is being provided for the ground stations in a number of countries, including the United States, Alaska, Ecuador, Germany, Spain, Taiwan, South Korea, Saudi Arabia, Abu Dhabi, Thailand, Myanmar and Iran.

IRS-P3 data continues to be received at ground locations in Germany and Spain. IRS-P4 data also continues to be transmitted to stations in Korea, Germany and the United States upon request.

In the future, IRS-P5, equipped with a high-resolution 2.5 meter (8.2 feet) PAN, will be used for cartographic applications, while IRS-P6 will focus on agricultural applications with its sensor. Both satellites have been planned for launch between 2004 and 2005.

NRSA has an earth station at Shadnagar, about 55 km (34 miles) from Hyderabad, to receive data from almost all currently operating remote sensing satellites such as IRS-P4, IRS-1D, IRS-1C, IRS-P3, IRS-1B, ERS-1/2, Landsat-5 and the NOAA series of satellites.

The data is recorded at Shadnagar on High Density Digital Tapes (HDTs), Digital Linear Tapes (DLTs), CD-ROMs or 8mm Exabyte Digital Tapes (DATs), depending on the mission, and archived for providing data products to users.

Indian Remote Sensing (IRS) Satellites are important elements of the NRMS, serving a national goal of providing continuous and operational remote sensing data services for effective management of India's natural resources.

The IRS system became operational on March 17, 1988, with the launch of IRS-1A. The second satellite, IRS-1B, which was identical to IRS-1A, was launched on August 29, 1991, and is still operational. These were operational, first generation remote sensing satellites with two Linear Imaging Self Scanning Sensors (LISS-I and LISS-II) for providing data in four spectral bands, both in visible and near infrared regions, with a spatial resolution of 72.5 m (238 feet) and 36.5 m (120 feet), repeating every 22 days.

Following the success of IRS 1A and 1B, India developed the second generation of remote sensing satellites, IRS-1C and 1D.

IRS-1C was launched on December 28, 1995, and IRS-1D was launched on September 19, 1997. Both the satellites have proven capable of improved spatial resolution, extended spectral bands, stereo viewing, wider swath and faster revisit capability.

IRS-1C and 1D have three cameras, including the Panchromatic camera (PAN), a high resolution camera operating in Panchromatic band with a resolution of swath of 70 kms. PAN camera can be steered up to about 26 degrees across the track to provide stereoscopic data and to improve the revisit to five days in the case of IRS-1C and three days in the case of IRS-1D; the Linear Imaging Self-scanning Sensor (LISS-III) operating in four bands — two in visible, one in near infrared (V/NIR), and one in shortwave infrared (SWIR) range, providing a ground resolution of 23.5 m (77 feet) in V/NIR bands and 70.5 m (231 feet) in SWIR band with a swath of 141 kms (88 miles) and 148 kms (92 miles) in V/NIR and SWIR bands respectively. LISS-III data provides continuity to users who have been accustomed to using IRS-1A/1B LISS-III and Landsat TM data; and the Wide Field Sensor (WiFS), a medium resolution camera with spatial resolution of 188 m (617 feet) operates in two bands with a swath of 810 kms (503 miles). Due to its large swath, WiFS provides a revisit every five days.

Most of the existing missions have been used for land applications. IRS-P4 satellite, also called Oceansat, will primarily cater to oceanographic applications. This satellite was launched by the indigenous Polar Satellite Launch Vehicle (PSLV) on May 26, 1999, into polar sun-synchronous orbit at an altitude of 720 km (447 miles). The satellite has a high repetition rate of every two days. The payload includes an Ocean Color Monitor (OCM), a Multi-frequency Scanning Microwave Radiometer (MSMR), and solid state memory for recording data outside the visibility of a ground station.

The OCM has six spectral bands in the visible and two in the near infrared region of the electromagnetic spectrum. The data collected by this sensor will be optimum for quantitative estimation of ocean primary productivity. The resolution of the OCM will be 360 by 250m (1181 by 820ft). With this resolution, better information on chlorophyll distribution near the coast will be achieved. High radiometric sensitivity and dynamic range are provided to measure the reflectance, varying from 0.7 to 7 percent, from the ocean surface. Four bands (0.545–0.565, 0.660–0.680, 0.745–0.785 and 0.845–0.885 microns) will have a dynamic range covering 100 percent solar reflectance, allowing it to be suitable for land applications including cloud and snow studies.

The MSMR operates in four frequencies and two polarizations. Many geophysical parameters such as sea surface temperature (SST), wind speed over oceans, total water in the atmosphere and others strongly influence the black body radiation from earth's surface. It is therefore possible to estimate a number of such parameters by passive microwave radiometers. Microwave measurements have the

additional advantage of all-weather capability.

IRS-P2 and IRS-P3, launched by India's PSLV on October 15, 1994, and March 21, 1996, respectively, are the first two satellites in the IRS-P series intended as technology demonstration missions. The IRS-P2 is of similar design to IRS-1A and 1B, carrying a modified LISS-II camera.

IRS-P3 has been equipped with a WiFS camera similar to that of IRS-1C, but with an additional band in SWIR. It also carries a Modular Opto-Electronic Scanner (MOS) of the German Space Agency, DLR, and an X-ray astronomy payload. MOS will be useful for developing algorithms for ocean applications.

On August 13, 1988, NRSA signed an agreement with Radarsat International, Canada, for distribution of RADARSAT data products to Indian users. RADARSAT's Synthetic Aperture Radar (SAR) has the capability to penetrate darkness, clouds, rain and haze. It provides solution for acquiring data over dynamic areas like tropical, coastal and polar regions. RADARSAT can acquire SAR data over any part of the world. Data collected by the satellite is either directly transmitted to the local ground stations or to the RADARSAT ground receiving stations in Prince Albert, Saskatchewan or Gatineau, Quebec, Canada.

The satellite is equipped with two on-board tape recorders to record data over areas outside the visibility of the ground stations. RADARSAT provides images in seven sizes known as beam modes. They vary from fine beam mode (50 by 50 km area in 10 m resolution) to scan SAR wide (which covers 500 by 500 km area in 100 m resolution).

RADARSAT also offers a range of incidence angles from 10 to 60 degrees, which can be used to provide more frequent revisit cycles (regular cycle is 24 days), also offering more opportunities to acquire stereo pairs.

NRSA has been acquiring the data from the NOAA series of satellites since 1987.

It has also been acquiring microwave Synthetic Aperture Radar (SAR) data in images from the ERS-1 and 2 satellites from 1992 to present.

National MST Radar Facility (NMRF)

The nationally coordinated Indian Middle Atmosphere Program (IMAP) was put in force during 1982 to 1989, focusing on campaign experiments with ground based, balloon, rocket and satellite based techniques. The IMAP program gave birth to in-depth studies of atmospheric dynamical phenomena by developing a versatile ground based radar technique.

Since then, Indian scientists have carried out research work in the fields of astronomy and astrophysics, solar and interplanetary medium, earth's upper atmosphere and ionosphere, aeronomy and middle atmosphere, and weather and climate phenomena.

The gaseous envelope surrounding the earth is known as the terrestrial atmosphere, which regulates the temperature and provides a shielding affect from harmful wavelengths of the solar radiation, making life on earth possible. The division of the atmosphere is in the form of spherical shells named the troposphere, the stratosphere, the mesosphere and the thermosphere, each characterized by the way temperature varies with height. Statistical description of atmospheric motions over the earth, their role in transporting the constituents of the atmosphere and the transformation of different forms of energy fall under the area of atmospheric dynamics studied at the NMRF.

The MST radar is a state-of-the-art instrument capable of providing estimates of atmospheric parameters with very high resolution on a continuous basis. This study is essential to the understanding of different dynamical processes in the atmosphere. It is an important research tool in the investigation of prevailing winds, wave (including gravity waves) turbulence, atmospheric stability and other mesoscale phenomena.

Scientists at the facility have created a reliable three-dimensional model of the atmosphere over the low latitudes to improve understanding of the climate and weather variations.

INDONESIA

National Institute for Aeronautics and Space (LAPAN), Indonesia

Indonesia's involvement in space is concentrated in the field of remote sensing. The country has worked on various satellite projects, including most recently LAPSAT-1 and LAPSAT-2 equipped with black and white CCD cameras. Since 1976, Indonesia has operated a national GEO telecommunications network based on Hughes, a spin-stabilized spacecraft made in the United States.

Known as the Palapa constellation, Indonesia's telecommunications network consists of three HS-376 class spacecraft located at 108 degrees east, the Palapa B2R, launched in April 1990; Palapa B2P, launched March 1987 at 113 degrees east; and Palapa B4 launched May 1992, at 118 degrees east.

The Palapa spacecraft have an on-station mass of 630 kg and were all launched by United States Delta rockets.

The Palapa B satellites carry 30 6/1 4 GHz transponders, including six spares, to support telecommunications services throughout Southeast Asia. In 1991, the aging Palapa B1 satellite, which was launched in June 1983, was sold to Pasifik Satelit Nusantara (PSN) for use on a new mission to provide commercial services to the Pacific Rim.

Palapa B1 was moved to a new location at 134 degrees between March and May of 1992, remaining in operation through 1994.

In early 1993, a subcontractor, PT Satelit Palapa Indonesia of Jakarta, was established to oversee the follow-up Palapa C satellites. The first Palapa C spacecraft was launched in 1995 to replace Palapa B2P.

The Palapa C series are Hughes' HS-601 spacecraft with 34 active transponders — 24 C-Band with six spares, six extended C-Band with two spares, and four Kuband with two spares. The on-station mass of the satellite at the beginning of life was 1,775 kg, with a design lifetime of at least 12 years.

The Indostar system is another Indonesian satellite, providing direct broadcast television and radio services for Indonesia.

Indonesia's Pasifik Satelit Nusantara (PSN), in cooperation with Thailand and the Philippines, has designed the Asia Cellular Satellite System (ACES) in order to meet the growing demand for hand-held telephone service for Asia. The system is aboard a Garada spacecraft, which was built by Lockheed-Martin.

LAPAN has also recently signed a contract with the Indian Space Research Organization (ISRO). The Memorandum of Understanding (MOU) was signed on April 3, 2002, for the purposes of cooperation in the peaceful uses of outer space.

Cooperation between the two countries in the area of space initially began in 1997, when ISRO signed an MOU with LAPAN for the establishment of a Telemetry, Tracking and Command (TTC) Station for supporting ISRO's missions.

The TTC station, located at Biak in Indonesia, has provided valuable support to Indian Remote Sensing (IRS) satellite missions. It also supported the launch of India's GSLV (Geosynchronous Satellite Launch Vehicle) in April 2001. LAPAN support includes provision of land, logistics and manpower for TTC Station operation.

By signing a second MOU, LAPAN and ISRO plan to expand the scope of cooperation in the areas of space sciences, technology, and related applications.

IRELAND

Space Ireland

Ireland does not have its own independent space agency, but it is an active collaborative participant in the European Space Agency (ESA). Through its Space Ireland, Ireland contributes its technological expertise to a variety of space activities. These include advanced materials, electronics, engineering services, precision engineering, software, space science, and telecommunications.

Irish companies continue to demonstrate a capacity to bring innovative and leading-edge technologies to the space community with highly skilled space scientists and researchers.

In the area of advanced materials, Ireland has contributed to composites testing and magnetic fluids. In electronics and microelectronics, Ireland has provided high-frequency RF components, microelectronics test support laboratories, miniaturized data acquisition and control units, electronic temperature sensors, and optoelectronic devices.

The nation has provided high-precision machined components and subassemblies, electrovalve technologies, and fueling valves.

Ireland has contributed software systems including onboard satellite control software, software testing of ADA and C++, simulation software for fluid dynamics and structural analysis, experimental control software, and software for space mission support.

Ireland has also contributed telecommunications systems, including satellite Internet terminals and services; communications software; satellite network operational support systems; satellite communications and navigation user terminals; IC design, low-profile satellite antennas; satellite multimedia content; and security for satellite networks.

Irish scientific teams have been involved in a number of high-profile ESA science missions, including the Giotto mission to Halley's comet in 1985, the SOHO mission in 1995 to monitor the sun and its effects on the earth's environment, and the gamma-ray astronomy mission, Integral, launched in 2002.

The teams have also collaborated with the United States, Russia, and China on international space science missions, including the long duration exposure facility (U.S.), Phobos I and II to Mars (Russia), and Double Star to the sun (China).

In the future, Ireland will participate in international missions to Mars and Mercury, as well as a mission to test some of the fundamental laws of physics, including those of gravity and general relativity.

Advanced Materials

Providers of advanced materials for space activities through Space Ireland include Composites Testing Laboratory, Ltd.; Trinity College, Dublin; and the University College at Dublin.

Composites Testing Laboratory (CTL), Ltd. specializes in the mechanical characterization of advanced composites materials for the aerospace industry. CTL is fully accredited under the European Accreditation of Laboratories scheme to perform a comprehensive range of standard tests, including tensile, compression, in-plane shear, bearing strength, fracture, compression after impact and fatigue.

The company has also been involved in developing specialized component tests for the aerospace industry and is fully equipped to manufacture one-off test rigs and fixtures.

The Foams Group at the physics department of Trinity College, Dublin has conducted research on materials that can be foamed, which means they can be brought into a mixed-phase cellular structure with solid or liquid cell walls and gaseous cells.

This research has supported the Prodex project for the ESA in developing a highly sophisticated powder-compact foaming route and novel foam imaging techniques using X-ray spectroscopy.

The division also theoretically investigates the degree of homogeneity that can be reached from a hot liquid metal foam that is allowed to cool and solidify, by modeling the competition between the processes of solidification and liquid drainage. Rapid solidification indicates that the foam remains uniform, while drainage redistributes material leading to spatial inhomogeneity. This finding has been confirmed using numerical solutions of the relevant differential equations.

At the University College, Dublin, research has been performed on modeling the effects of gravity on alloy solidification, in order to focus on the effects of microgravity on solidification of metal alloys, and is being carried out with a view to designing experiments to be performed on the International Space Station (ISS). The project involves collaboration with senior scientists and engineers from France, Germany, and the United Kingdom, and the team is working together to investigate the physical differences between solidification of alloys on earth and in space.

The space station will be the only laboratory in which the long-term effects of microgravity can be studied, with experimental apparatus being set up and monitored by a resident crew. Work has started on the development a computer model of solidification of a metal casting, in which gravity can simply be switched on or off, depending on whether one needs to predict the physics on earth or in space, respectively.

Electronics

Companies providing electronics development for Space Ireland programs include ACRA Control, BetaTHERM Ireland, and NMRC.

ACRA Control produces high-performance, cost-effective data acquisition systems for the world aerospace and automotive industries. Products are currently in use in over 25 countries in very demanding applications including flight test instrumentation and operational load monitoring. Customers include Aerospatiale-Matra, Alenia, BAE Systems, Hughes, Lockheed Martin and NASA.

The company produces KAM-500 which is a rugged, miniature PCM data acquisition system with a wide range of plug-and-play modules. It includes programming signal conditioning, A/D conversion and solid-state memory storage.

KAM-500 can be used for both real-time data acquisition and telemetry (single unit or distributed system) and as a stand-alone solid-state recorder. Integrated software provides many advanced functions including automatic system configuration and calibration, on-line data display, and archiving.

Another product developed by ACRA is the SAM/DEC/005, a PCM decom card in PCMCIA format. It is designed for use with notebook PC's for portable PCM applications including pre-flight and launchpad checkout and in-flight data display and archiving.

Since 1994, BetaTHERM has been supplying NTC Thermistor components and probe assemblies to the aerospace and space industries. It has also managed a qualification program for its thermal control products in conjunction with the ESA.

NMRC, established in 1981, conducts research in the areas of optoelectronics, nanotechnology, microelectronics, and ICT/Life sciences.

It has participated in research and development for the ESA since 1982, performing research to customize ionizing radiation dosimeter RadFETs for a range of applications and quantifying the influence of various radiation sources including electrons, protons, and X-rays. NMRC's RadFETs have also been adapted for use in nuclear physics to characterize high-energy particle beams; space dosimetry for use in satellite missions and radiation shielding programs; and the commercial arena for application in the radiation oncology market.

Engineering Services

Engineering service needs have been fulfilled by one sole supplier, Engineering Solutions International Limited (ESIL), which is an engineering services company specializing in computational analysis of engineering components and processes.

ESIL provides services in computer modeling techniques for design, production and manufacturing teams. The company has supported the ESA with hypervelocity impact simulation of satellite debris shields; numerical and analytical assessment of fluid-in-tube dampers for ESA satellites; prediction of transient buffeting of Ariane 5 rocket nozzles; and recommendations on fluid-in-tube damper designs for the agency's PLANCK satellite.

Precision Engineering

Devtec Limited and Hitol supply precision engineering capabilities for Space Ireland.

Since 1988, Devtec has been the design authority for the mechanical supports for the Vulcain Engine of the Ariane 5 launch vehicle. These precision components were designed, developed and qualified at Devtec's facility, close to Dublin Airport. Devtec is currently involved in the Vulcain Mark 2 development, which will provide an additional 30 percent thrust for future launchers.

Devtec, in association with the company's U.S. partner, Marotta Scientific Controls Inc., was responsible for the design, development and qualification of the cold gas thruster module for the tethered satellite system reflight in February 1996, onboard the STS-75 shuttle mission.

Additional space related products and services provided by Devtec include mechanical and structural component design and development; precision manufacturing in high strength alloys (inconel, titanium); fluid control devices for flight and ground applications including, solenoid operated valves, motor operated valves, check valves, pressure regulators, pressure relief valves, latch valves, cold gas thrusters, and electric propulsion feed system components.

Hitol is a design and manufacturing engineering company supplying high precision machined components and sub assemblies to the aerospace industry. The company maintains a state-of-the-art facility to support international space missions.

Software

Skytek in Dublin has been a provider of software services for the European Space Agency. The company developed an application to assist astronauts undertaking complex tasks and procedures on board the International Space Station.

The application known as COReCT (Critical Operations e-based Control Tool) is a Web-based system designed to assist repair and maintenance crews undertaking complex operations. There is currently no generic software application in the marketplace that walks a user through a complex procedure. COReCT performs a number of functions including acting as a mobile resource for personnel engaged in repairs and maintenance; providing a man-machine interface to equipment; acting as a training tool for repair and maintenance; and providing quality assurance.

Space Science

Astrocourier (Ireland) Ltd. is a new company which has been set up to provide low cost commercial access to space for schools, universities, industry, entrepreneurs and enthusiasts. This will be accomplished through the use of two carrier trays, Astrodeck and Astroplate, which can accommodate, respectively, up to 96 or 24 small experimental units. These carrier trays will be located either on the rooftop of the Spacehab module or on the Integrated Cargo Carrier (ICC) in the space shuttle cargo bay. The experiments will spend two to three weeks in space and then be returned to the customers for analysis. The first Astrodeck flight was scheduled for the summer of 2003.

Astrocourier offers complete support assistance with experiment design, development and qualification; integration and de-integration of the experiment with the carrier tray; shipping to and from the launch site; and flight operations and assistance with post-flight analysis.

Astrodeck and Astroplate will be available in both passive versions (Astrodeck I, Astroplate I) and versions offering power and data services (Astrodeck II and Astroplate II).

Astrocourier (Ireland) Ltd. has an American sister company, Astrocourier (USA) LLC, based in Florida near the launch site at Cape Canaveral.

A third product, Astropack, has also been planned, which would allow subscribers access to space-based experiments via the Internet.

The Far-Infrared Terahertz Space Optics Group at NUI Maynooth provides services in the design and modeling of astronomical instrumentation in the far-infrared. The group has been actively collaborating in two separate consortia of scientists and engineers from Europe and the United States involved in the design and development of the Planck Surveyor satellite and the Herschel Space Observatory.

Their contribution has involved the electromagnetic characterization of the unusual telescope configuration of Planck, as well as in the novel horn antenna developments of its HFI instrument.

Company optical models of the system will enable Planck to achieve its challenging main science goal of the full characterization of the cosmic microwave background (CMB).

The NUIM IR/THz Space Optics Group has expertise in the following areas of submillimeter-wave space optical design: horn antenna modeling including specialized profiled horns, partially coherent few-modeled systems, physical optics and polarization analysis of electrically large antennas and telescopes, quasi-optical beam guide analysis, and the development of CAD tools for far-IR optical system design.

The Space Science and Advanced Materials Group has had extensive involvement in space-related research, training and development since the 1980s. Scientific data from large ESA missions and experiments, such as the Infrared Space Observatory, XMM and COMPTEL, have been used to carry out fundamental research on a range of astrophysical topics including the time profiles and spectra of gamma-ray bursts, multi-wavelength behavior of active galactic nuclei and galaxy clusters.

The group has been involved in hardware and software development for the Optical Monitoring Camera (OMC) flown on

ESA's Integral mission. It has continued to be responsible for analyzing and interpreting gamma-ray data obtained by the spacecraft.

The Dublin Institute for Advanced Studies, through the astronomy and astrophysics sections of the School of Cosmic Physics, has participated in almost all Irish space science research activities dating back to collaboration with the University of Berkley in NASA's Apollo program.

The institute also cooperated with ESA's technology center, ESTEC, to build a large passive experiment for NASA's long duration exposure facility mission.

The institute has also helped to construct the digital electronics for the Irish EPONA experiment on the European GIOTTO mission to Halley's comet, as well as related experiments on the Soviet PHOBOS mission to Mars and its moons. In addition to this hardware involvement, the institute has participated in software development for the Infrared Space Observatory mission and has participated scientifically in a number of other missions as well as ESA committees, such as those involving the study of space weather.

Telecommunications

Airtel ATN is an independent publicly quoted company, providing telecommunications products and services since 1993. The company combines its engineering services with its range of software products to deliver tailored data communication solutions for the aviation industry.

Airtel's contributions have included the supply of ATN software to the American Airlines A/C participating in the Eurocontrols Petal IIe program and the ground based communications software for the ARINCís VDL Mode 1 ATN Service; delivery to ESA-ESTEC of a concept project which enables airborne cabins Web access via IP over the ATN; participation in the architectural definition of the GALA phase of the Galileo project, emphasizing the integration of Galileo satellites communication and navigation capabilities with the ATN; participation in the SDLS 2 project where Airtel ATN developed the specification and design of the AES (Airborne Earth Station),

GES (Ground Earth Station) and MES (Master Earth Station or Network Management Center), both on the hardware (antenna, modem) and software side.

Airtel is currently working on the SDLS Demonstrator project, Airtel-ATN, designing and developing the SSNL (Satellite Sub Network Layer) component, which will provide the ATN-AMSS (Aeronautical Mobile Satellite Systems) standardized layer functionality for connecting ATN airborne and ground routers via satellite data link.

Bocom provides systems and solutions for broadcasting of real time multimedia information via existing satellite, terrestrial or cable television networks.

The company provides services to realtime financial information providers, software distributors and television broadcasters. Applications include Internet broadcast; realtime information of financial news, current news, and sports results; multimedia point-of-sale advertising; software distribution; and subscription service networks for games and news.

Ossidian Technologies Ltd. is a private independent company set up in February 1999, dedicated to providing Web-based training on mobile, fixed-broadband and satellite telecommunications technologies. Ossidian courses offer fast, flexible, effective, convenient and inexpensive technical training.

Ossidian's courses focus on telecommunications technologies and engineering, including UMTS, GPRS, WAP, GSM, CDMA, ATM and IP over wireless.

In 2001, Ossidian collaborated with the European Space Agency to develop a series of teleservices Operations Support Systems (OSS) courses including satellite billing and rating; teleservice revenue assurance; rating IP teleservices and teleservices customer care.

Web-Sat Ltd. has developed systems and services to provide bi-directional high speed Internet and VPN access via Satellite.

This low cost solution has provided "always on" Internet service independent of local infrastructure such as telephone lines, ISDN, ADSL etc. The service has also offered an effective permanent two-way circuit resulting in both time and cost savings to the end user. Applications include high speed Internet, file transfer, video streaming, multicasting and interactive multimedia.

Web-Sat technology has been supplied to Canada, North America and Australia, as well as Europe, North Africa, Russia and the Middle East via Eutelsat satellite W3. Part of the core technology developed by Web-Sat has been patented.

ISRAEL

Israel Space Agency (ISA)

In 1960 the Israeli Academy of Sciences and Humanities established the National Committee for Space Research (NCSR), which paved the way for an Israeli space program and official support for space research.

At the time, the NCSR was geared more towards the research of space and education rather then the establishment of an Israeli space program. This meant NCSR accomplished great things in the field of space research while the Israeli space program was practically non-existent. The only notable space program effort during this time was the launch of the Shavit 2 two-stage solid fuel sounding rocket in 1961. This step was part of a small-scale space race between Israel and Egypt that was used to show Israel's superiority over Egypt and to boost the Israeli morale.

The Israeli Space Agency (ISA) was established within the Israel Defense Force of Science and Technology in 1983. It has participated in space activities jointly with the Interdisciplinary Center for Technological Analysts and Forecasting of Tel Aviv University, the National Committee for Space Research of the Israel Academy of Sciences and Humanities, and the Israel Aircraft Industries (IAI).

On September 19, 1988, ISA launched its first satellite, Ofeq-1, by the Shavit, a solid fuel, three-stage rocket. Four other Ofeq satellites were later launched. The observation satellite Ofeq-2 was launched on April 3, 1990. A launch failure occurred on September 15, 1994, which was followed by the successful launch of the Ofeq-3 photo-reconnaissance satellite on April 5, 1995. The launch of Ofeq-4 was unsuccessful on January 22, 1998.

Since then, the Israeli space program has been restricted by a shoestring budget, a costly war and an economic crisis. However, the country had great hope when it achieved the opportunity to send its first astronaut aloft.

Unfortunately, Colonel Ilan Ramon, was aboard the ill-fated space shuttle mission Columbia, STS-107, which broke apart February 1, 2003, during its re-entry into the atmosphere, and he perished, along with six other crew members.

ISA's annual budget of about 50 million dollars has further been diminished as the Israeli government puts priority on waging its war against Palestinian militants and tackling a growing economic crisis.

The agency continues to use its limited funds on developing hardware such as small satellites and satellite-based equipment like remote sensing, global positioning systems (GPS), and propulsion engines. It also benefits from cooperation with national space agencies in the United States, France, Germany, the Ukraine and Russia, as well as from the Israeli space industry, made up of 20 firms it ultimately seeks to promote.

ISA has worked with various experts at Tel Aviv and other universities, but its proposals to undertake projects with Egypt, with which Israel has a peace treaty, continue to be ignored amid regional tension.

It hopes that some of its projects like space cameras and electric boosters designed to change satellite orbits will sell commercially and help to revive a struggling program.

Colonel Ramon's job on the space shuttle Columbia was to work with a camera analyzing dust storms over the Middle East and their links to global warming. ISA hopes to use a similar camera permanently aboard the Space Station.

Recently, ISA has been working on several projects with international partners, including GPS applications for the study of the movement of tectonic plates in a region vulnerable to earthquakes; miniaturizing satellites which will allow more payload for rockets sending them into space; studies on how satellites weather space conditions linked to radiation, vacuum, magnetic storms, and dramatically shifting temperatures; telescopes to join a network run by NASA and the United Kingdom to track new asteroids that may threaten the earth; and remote sensing for agriculture, forestry and fishing.

Satellites

Ofeq 1 was launched on September 19, 1988, by a Shavit launcher from the Palamchim launch site. The 156 kg (344 lb) satellite entered a low earth orbit (LEO) at an altitude of 1150 km (715 miles) with a declination of 43 degrees. It remained in orbit for 118 days, although its expected lifespan was only one month.

Ofeq 2 was launched on April 3, 1990, by the Shavit launcher. It entered a LEO of 1580 km (982 miles) and remained in orbit for 40 days.

Ofeq 3 was launched on April 15, 1995, by the Shavit improved launcher from the Palamachim site. It entered a LEO of 729 km (453 miles) with a declination of 37 degrees, and continues to orbit the earth once every 90 minutes.

Ofeq 3, weighing 189 kg (417 lbs) was designed as a second generation satellite based on the Ofeq 1. It has exceeded its projected life span and operates via an advanced navigation system.

The satellite was publicized as merely a test satellite, like its predecessors. However, it is actually a spy satellite carrying the ERMS CCD with a resolution of up to 2.5 meters (8 ft). Ofeq 3 served as the prototype for the EROS satellite, which now provides 24-hour contact with Israel.

The Earth Resources Observation Satellite (EROS), launched in 1998, was based on the Ofeq 3 satellite and uses its bus. The EROS satellite payload consists of an improved version of the EL-OP ERMS with a resolution of up to 1.5 meters (5 ft). The EROS network will include six satellites in order to achieve full earth cover.

The AMOS (Afro-Mediterranean Orbital System) was built by Israel Aircraft Industries (IAI) at a cost of $250 million. It was launched on May 15, 1996, by an Ariane 44L from Kourou with another satellite (Palpa C2) on board.

AMOS entered its final position above the Gulf of Guinea a week later and is expected to have a lifespan of 10 years, providing coverage of central Europe and the Middle East.

Tauvex, the Tel Aviv University UV Experiment

In early 1988, the Israel Space Agency (ISA) called for academic and commercial research and development groups in Israel to propose a scientific payload for a National Scientific Satellite (NSS) of the OFEQ-class. Among the many proposals submitted, one from Tel Aviv University, to orbit a cluster of small, wide-field telescopes to image astronomical objects in the ultraviolet (UV), was finally selected with the highest priority. This payload is now referred to as TAUVEX, the Tel Aviv University UV Experiment.

TAUVEX consists of a three-telescope array mounted on a single bezel and enclosed in a common envelope. Each telescope has field-flattener corrector lenses. The clear aperture of each telescope is 20 cm.

The systems were designed for imaging the same 0.9 degree field in the space-UV band from 140 nm to 300 nm. The image quality is six to eight arcsec (FWHM), depending on the spectral band.

The filter array consists of a broad-band filter (BBF), which provides a blue cutoff for wavelengths shorter than 200 nm; three intermediate band filters (SF-1, SF-2, and SF-

3) with central wavelengths near 160, 210, and 260 nm respectively, and band passes of approximately 40 nm; and two narrow band filters centered at 150 and 210 nm, with band passes of about 10 nm.

The detectors are photon-counting imaging devices made of a CsTe cathode on the inner surface of the entrance window, a stack of three microchannel plates (MCP), and a multi-electrode anode of the wedge-and-strip type. The typical on-board image integration time will be one hour.

TAUVEX offers obvious advantages in observation such as reduced sky background, a longer observing time per target, and a long-duration mission.

TAUVEX was originally scheduled for launch in June 1991, and has since been postponed to mid-2004.

The TAUVEX imagers will operate on the SRG platform alongside numerous X-ray and gamma-ray experiments. This will be the first scientific mission providing simultaneous UV-X-Gamma observations of celestial objects. The instruments on SRG include the Danish SODART; the JET-X instrument of the U.K., Russia and Italy, which is a 0.2–10 keV imager with 40' FOV and 10–30" resolution); MART, contributed by Italy and Russia, with a coded aperture 4 to 100 keV, an imager with 1° FOV and six-inch resolution; EUVITA from Switzerland, Russia and Canada, with 100–400A°, imagers with 1° FOV and 10" resolution; MOXE, a U.S. all sky X-ray burst detector in the 3–12 keV band; SPIN, a Russian all sky Gamma-ray burst detector in the 10keV to 10MeV band, with 0°.5 optical localization, and DIOGENE, a French and Russian Gamma-ray burst detector.

TAUVEX will be bore-sighted with SODART, JET-X, MART and EUVITA. It will obtain simultaneous imaging photometry of objects in the UV with three independent telescopes, using a combination of filters to accommodate wide, intermediate and narrow spectral bands. During a single pointing it will be possible to change filters, thus more than three UV bands can be used on one observation.

TAUVEX will detect hundreds of faint galaxies in each high latitude field. It is even possible that most faint, high latitude UV sources are galaxies. The data collection of TAUVEX will represent the deepest UV-magnitude-limited survey of a large fraction of the sky.

For the first time, it will be possible to study the physics of accretion disks around black holes and neutron stars, from hard X-rays to near the optical region. Other subjects of study will include the inner regions of QSOs and AGNs, where the physics of the accretion phenomenon, probably powering all such sources, are best studied with simultaneous multi-wavelength observations.

The Meidex Experiment

In 1995, Shimon Peres, who was the prime minister of Israel at the time, and United States president Bill Clinton agreed that an Israeli astronaut would be flown on board a U.S. space shuttle mission. It was also decided that the astronaut would be a payload specialist for an Israeli scientific experiment to be decided by the Israeli Space Agency (ISA) with the approval of NASA.

This mission was a significant landmark to the Israel Space Program in that it would also be an opportunity to perform a full-scale Israeli space scientific experiment. In selecting a mission, ISA had to take into account all the restrictions imposed by a manned flight, namely, short mission duration, the availability of human and financial resources, and the limited time available for the preparation of the experiment.

The MEIDEX experiment was Tel Aviv University's answer to this challenge, choosing the goal of the first Israeli astronaut flight to study the transport of mineral dust in the atmosphere over the Mediterranean Sea and the tropical Atlantic Ocean. This choice was based on the important role which aerosols, especially desert dust, play in weather and climate conditions in many parts of the world and especially in the Middle East. Many Israeli institutions and scientists, in particular at Tel Aviv University, have conducted intensive studies of this topic in past years.

It was intended to complement the

spaceborne remote sensing experiment with ground based and airborne in-situ measurements of aerosol properties by performing a comprehensive study of the chemical, physical and optical properties of desert aerosol transported over the Mediterranean region.

Mission objectives included measurements of the reflective properties of the earth's surface, measurements of the visibility in the atmosphere and spectral observations of sprites above the tops of thunderclouds.

The MEIDEX (Mediterranean Israeli Dust Experiment) project was dedicated to studies of the atmospheric aerosols by means of remote sensing experiment operated by the Israeli astronaut, Colonel Ilan Ramon, aboard the space shuttle Columbia.

The project included remote as well as in-situ measurements of light scattering by desert aerosol particles in six wavelengths starting from near UV to solar IR. The supporting ground based and airborne measurements included optical observations as well as direct sampling.

Colonel Ramon's responsibility was to observe the underlying terrain and identify dust plumes, their location and their extent. He also completed the measurement sequence when flying over dust plumes, over the airplane and the ground observation network, and conducted visibility experiments.

Secondary objectives of the experiment included visibility studies, particularly slant visibility, which is an important feature of atmospheric sciences with many applications. In the study of practical, the oldest and most well-known has been the Koschmieder algorithm for visual contrast. Visibility is basically a systems concept used in the Koschmieder model, such as in an application to human eyesight in daytime.

The problem encountered in finding a visibility range for a given system is that parameterizations have to be developed separately for each application, making it very difficult to translate the results from one application to another or even from radiance data to a visibility criterion.

The visual determination of long-range slant visibility of suitably chosen targets along a shuttle footprint by a trained observer was

therefore considered of great interest, since measurements of the optical depths may be available at many of the targets and, moreover, the latter can be observed along different lines of sight not only by the astronaut but also by the MEIDEX instrumentation.

The choice of targets was determined by the presence along a given shuttle footprint of locations with high visual contrast and linear dimensions of the order of at least several kilometers.

The sea surface albedo was another important area of study. The albedo of the surface below the region of the remote observation was a crucial parameter in the inversion procedure, and was measured directly by instruments aboard the aircraft. It was hoped that the spaceborne part of the MEIDEX experiment would enable study of the sun glint under various meteorological conditions, however, results were lost along with the space shuttle Columbia when it disintegrated during reentry on February 1, 2003.

Shavit Launcher

The Shavit launch vehicle first flew on September 19, 1988, placing the Ofeq 1 engineering technology satellite into LEO. The third flight of Shavit was postponed in early 1994 until 1995. The delay was partly due to budgetary constraints.

Shavit is a small, three-stage, solid propellant booster based on the two-stage Jericho 2 ballistic missile and developed under the general management of Israeli Aircraft Industries (IAI) through its MBT System and space technology subsidiary. Israel Military Industries produced the first and second stage motors, while Rafael was responsible for the third stage motor. The demonstrated payload capacity has been 160 kg (353 lbs) into an elliptical orbit of 207 km (129 miles) by 1,587 km (986 miles) with a highly retrograde inclination of 143.2 degrees. Shavit was originally proposed to launch a U.S. commercial recoverable spacecraft (COMET), requiring a payload of 800 kg (1763 lbs) or more inserted into a low altitude orbit.

The upper stage of the Shavit was designated AUS-51 (Advanced Upper Stage). A more powerful upper stage has been under development by Israeli Aircraft Industries for much larger launch vehicles with a GEO objective. This stage has been named the Cryogenic Transfer Module (CTM), and will burn liquid oxygen and liquid hydrogen to produce a thrust of approximately one metric ton. CTM will be capable of lifting a 2.1 metric ton satellite from a 200 km (124 mile), 28 degree parking orbit to GEO.

Shavit boosters have been launched from an undisclosed site near the Palmachim Air Force Base on the coast of Israel south of Tel Aviv. The facility is also sometimes referred to as Yavne. In order to prevent overflight of foreign territory, Shavits have been launched on a northwest trajectory over the Mediterranean Sea, passing over the Straits of Gibraltar at the west end of the Mediterranean. This procedure significantly reduces the payload capacity of the launch vehicle and severely limits potential operational orbits.

Most recently, the Shavit launcher placed Israel's Ofeq satellites in space including Ofeq 5 that was launched on May 28, 2002. Following its insertion into orbit, Ofeq 5 underwent a series of in-orbit tests to verify its operation and performance.

The satellite carries a remote sensing payload that will enable it to perform high-resolution observation missions for national needs.

Qfeq 5 is a three-axis stabilized, lightweight satellite platform, adapted for high-resolution observation, scientific, or technological payloads. The satellite continues to circle the earth from east to west every hour and a half, at an approximate angle of inclination of 143 degrees.

It was designed to operate at altitudes between 370 and 600 km (230 and 373 miles) above the surface of the earth. Its projected lifetime is four years. Ofeq 5 belongs to the class of small and lightweight satellites. Its launch weight is about 300 kg (661 lbs), has a height of 2.3 meters (7.5 feet) and is 1.2 meters (3.9 feet) in diameter.

The satellite's light weight allows for maximum agility over targets to yield rapid image acquisition. It acquires images in swaths ahead of satellite trajectory, beneath it and lateral to it.

ITALY

Agenzie Spaziale Italiana (ASI)

Italy became one of the first European nations to operate its own earth satellite, which was launched by the United States in 1964. In 1988, the Italian Space Agency or ASI (Agenzie Spaziale Italiana) was established under the Ministry of Universities and Scientific and Technological Research (MURST) and its Undersecretary of Space.

In 1992, ASI underwent a restructuring due to some financial and management problems. Today, it is a relatively small organization with headquarters in Rome. It performs space science research in close cooperation with the University of Rome as well as the National Research Council.

The National Research Council's central division is the Aerospace Research Center, which manages the San Marco space launch facility in the Indian Ocean near Kenya.

Because of limited funding, ASI remains focused on space research; no space or satellite launches have occurred since 1988.

Space Geodesy Center "G. Colombo" (ASI-CGS)

The Space Geodesy Center "G. Colombo" (ASI-CGS) is located near Matera in the Basilicata region of southern Italy. It was started in 1983 to coordinate observational activities linked with several data analysis and scientific research projects in collaboration with many national and international institutions.

CGS manages projects in space geodesy and geodynamics, including satellite laser ranging; the very long baseline interferometry (VLBI); global positioning system (GPS); and the precision range and range-rate experiment (PRARE); remote sensing, including the X-SAR and SIR-C missions, the Italian Processing Archiving Facility (I-PAF), and interplanetary missions; and space automation and robotics, including the Center for Robotics Simulation.

CGS serves as one of the few fundamental geodetic stations in the world due to its utilization of all precise positioning space-based techniques. The CGS high-precision positioning capabilities and the nationwide space geodesy network established by ASI continue to play an important role in the long-term global monitoring of many geodynamic parameters including continental drift, polar motion, and earth's gravity field, as well as on the calibration activities for radar-altimetric missions such as ESA's ERS-1 and the NASA-CNES TOPEX/POSEIDON.

SAO-1 is the satellite laser ranging (SLR) station located at the center that has been in continuous operation since 1983, providing high precision telemetric observations of several satellites equipped with cube-corner retroreflectors. These satellites have included Lageos I and II, Starlette, Ajisai, ERS I and II, TOPEX/POSEIDON, Stella, and Meteor III.

In the near future, the new Matera Laser Ranging Observatory (MLRO), the most advanced satellite and lunar laser ranging facility in the world, will be installed at CGS.

In the early 1990s, CGS extended its operations to the very long baseline interferometry (VLBI) using a 20-m (66 ft) radiotelescope, observing at frequencies of two and eight GHz.

The center also branched out into the use of satellite-based radio positioning techniques comparable to the United States' Global Positioning System (GPS).

In 1996, the center began work on the precision range and range-rate experiment (PRARE), a precision satellite positioning system.

To exploit maximum integration in the field of earth observations, ASI expanded the center's involvement in remote sensing activities in the late 1980s for missions such as ERS-1, ERS-2, X-SAR, SIR-C, and EN-VISAT.

In 1992, CGS opened the Italian ERS Processing and Archiving Facility (I-PAF) to support ERS satellite missions and archive data.

In 1994, CGS supported the X-SAR and SIR-C cooperative missions with the German Space Agency and NASA by providing, processing, archiving and distributing the X-SAR data to the national and international scientific community.

CGS also plans to provide significant contributions in the field of robotics with the ASI Robotics and Automation Facility. It will host the core facility of the distributed national space robotics and automation test facility, and develop a center for robotics simulation.

BeppoSAX (Satellite)

The X-ray astronomy satellite BeppoSAX (satellite per Astronomia X, "Beppo") was named in honor of Giuseppe "Beppo" Occhialini. Beppo, considered to be one of the greatest Italian physicists, along with E. Amaldi and others, played a crucial role in starting the European Space Research Organization, giving an impetus to its scientific program from which the present-day European Space Agency (ESA) still benefits.

BeppoSAX was a joint project of the Italian Space Agency (ASI) with participation of the Netherlands Agency for Aerospace Programs (NIVR). The mission was supported by a consortium of institutes in Italy together with institutes in the Netherlands and the Space Science Department of ESA.

SAX, or Satellite per Astronomia X, is Italian for X-ray astronomy satellite. It was launched on April 30, 1996.

The main scientific objective of BeppoSAX was wide spectral coverage ranging from 0.1 to over 200 keV, with a relatively large area and a good energy resolution, associated with imaging capabilities at a resolution of about one foot in the range of 0.1 to 10 keV.

SAX was composed of a medium energy (1–10 keV) concentrator optics/spectrometer, MECS, with three units — a low energy (0.1–10 keV) concentrator optics/spectrometer, LECS; a high pressure gas scintillation proportional counter (3–120 keV), HPGSPC; and a phoswich detector system (15 to 300 keV), which is made up of two joined scintillators with different decay time constants. By discriminating on the pulse shape, it is possible to distinguish events interacting in either crystal. It also had a PDS, all of which have narrow fields and point in the same direction (Narrow Field Instruments, NFI).

BeppoSAX was also intended to monitor large regions of the sky with a resolution of five feet in the range 2 to 30 keV to study long term variability of sources down to 1 m (3.3 ft) and to detect X-ray transient phenomena. It was designed with two coded mask proportional counters, wide field cameras (WFC) pointing in diametrically opposed directions perpendicular to the NFI. Anticoincidence scintillator shields of the PDS will be used as a gamma-ray burst monitor in the range of 60–600 keV.

BeppoSAX's NFI was intended to observe very wide spectral bodies such as a Seyfert 1 galaxy, namely MCG-6-30-15, in 40,000 seconds with all the spectral components and features detected by several satellites in the past.

With instrument capabilities over a wide energy range, SAX was expected to provide a significant and unique contribution for science involving the exploitation of the wide band in several areas of X-ray astronomy such as compact galactic sources; shape and variability of the continuum of narrow spectral features including iron line and cyclotron lines as a function of the orbital and rotational phases; ultra-soft sources; discovery and study of X-ray transients; active galactic nuclei; spectral shape and dynamics of the variable continuum and of the narrow and broad components from 0.1 to 200 keV in bright objects (soft excess, warm and cold absorption and related oxygen and iron edges, iron line and high

energy bump, high energy cut-off); spectral shape of objects down to 1/20 of 3C273 and up to 100–200 keV; and spectra of high redshift objects up to 10 keV.

It was to study galaxy clusters, particularly spatially resolved spectra of nearby objects, and study temperature gradients and cooling flows. It would also study chemical composition and temperature distribution as a function of redshift; supernova remnants, including resolved spectra of extended remnants; and spectra of magellanic cloud remnants.

The satellite was also to study normal galaxies — spectra from 0.1 to 10 keV of the extended emission; stars — multi-temperature spectra of stellar coronae from 0.1 to 10 keV; gamma-ray bursts — temporal profile with a one msec resolution from 60 to 600 keV; and X-ray counterparts of a subset with positional accuracy less than five feet.

BeppoSAX was scheduled for a minimum lifetime of two years, extendable to four years. It was to perform more than 2000 pointings.

Following its launch, the first SAX scientific instrument was successfully switched on June 3, 1996. Other instruments were switched on consecutively and SAX performed the first observation of a cosmic source on June 24, 1996. Cygnus X-1, a bright black hole in our galaxy, was successfully observed with the narrow field instruments (NFI) and wide field cameras (WFC) of SAX.

Following an onboard synchronization problem between the altitude control computer and the data-handling computer which was resolved later that year, BeppoSAX was able to monitor for gamma ray bursts using the phoswich detector system (PDS) and WFC to monitor transient phenomena.

In 1997, the satellite experienced problems with one of its six gyros. Three gyros were needed to continue normal operations. The observation program was temporarily interrupted and a new safe mode, gyro-less safe mode, was instituted for the satellite.

Gyro problems continued to plague that satellite until the single gyro scientific mode software was installed. Initial data analysis revealed that the accuracy of satellite pointing was closely comparable to when three gyros were in use.

The satellite remained in operations until April 30, 2002, when it was decided to end the mission due to poor and degrading spacecraft conditions and to the rapid orbit decay of all in-orbit operations. BeppoSAX re-entered the atmosphere on April 29, 2003.

Telecommunications and Navigation

Italy has an established tradition in the areas of search and utilization of the high frequency as evidenced with its national programs such as SIRIUS and Italsat. It has also participated in the European programs Olimpus and Artemis.

Following the conclusion of its national telecommunications program Italsat, ASI established a new program, Ex. With Ex came ARTES (Advanced Research in Telecommunications Systems) with satellites Artes 1, 2, 3, 4 and 5 to study new applications and provide multimedia services.

Artes satellites provided data relay transmission once placed in low orbit, operating with radio frequency in S-Band and Ka-Band.

ASI has also been involved with the European Galileo program to expand mobile telephone, television and Internet services to millions of Europeans. Other applications span maritime, earth and aerial operations, communications synchronization, geological prospecting for oil and gas, agricultural management, and large civil engineering projects.

Galileo will consist of a constellation of 30 satellites placed in orbit nearly 24,000 km (14,400 miles) above the earth. This position will guarantee the localization of services on earth with horizontal precision within 10 meters (33 ft).

Shuttle Radar Topography Mission (SRTM)

The Shuttle Radar Topography Mission (SRTM) is an international project with participation of the National Imagery and Mapping Agency (NIMA), NASA, the Jet Propulsion Laboratory (JPL), and the Italian Space Agency (ASI). The primary objective of SRTM is to obtain the most complete high-resolution digital topographic database of the earth.

On February 11, 2000, the SRTM payload was launched aboard the space shuttle Endeavor. SRTM radars swept most of the earth's surface, acquiring enough data during its ten-day mission to obtain the most complete near-global high-resolution database of the earth's topography.

SRTM collected topographic data over nearly 80 percent of the earth's land surfaces, creating the first-ever near-global data set of land elevations.

In order to accomplish this, SRTM was outfitted with two radar antennas. One antenna was located in the shuttle's payload bay, while the other was placed at the end of a 60-meter (200-foot) mast, extending from the payload bay once the shuttle was in space.

Processed SRTM data will be used to meet the needs of military, civil, and scientific user communities. Other uses of this data include improved water drainage modeling, more realistic flight simulators, navigation safety, better locations for cell phone towers, and improved maps for backpackers.

Virtually any project that requires accurate knowledge of the shape and height of the land can benefit from this data. Examples of this include flood control, soil conservation, reforestation, volcano monitoring, earthquake research, and glacier movement monitoring.

SRTM operated by means of radar interferometry, where two radar images are taken from slightly different locations. Differences between these images allow for the calculation of surface elevation or change.

In order to obtain radar images from different locations, the SRTM utilized the two radar antennas placed strategically on the shuttle.

SRTM was launched into an orbit with an inclination of 57 degrees, allowing its radars to cover most of earth's land surface that lies between 60 degrees north and 56 degrees south latitude, amounting to nearly 80 percent of earth's land mass.

The SRTM instrument was made up of three sections — the main radar antenna, the mast, and the outboard radar antenna.

The main radar antenna transmitted the radar pulse and contained special panels which allowed it to receive the returned radar pulse after it was bounced off the earth. It was attached to a structure that was bolted into the payload bay of the space shuttle.

The mast was folded up accordian-style inside a canister that was attached to the side of the main antenna. Once the shuttle was in space and the payload bay doors opened, the mast extended from the canister and unfolded out to 60 meters (200 feet). The SRTM mast was the longest rigid structure ever flown in space.

The outboard antenna was attached to the end of the mast, which was folded along the top of the canister, and the main antenna, while inside the payload bay. After the payload bay doors opened, the outboard antenna was partially swung down before the mast was extended.

Once the mast was fully extended, the outboard antenna was lowered into its operating position. The outboard antenna contained special panels that allowed it to receive the same returned pulse as the main antenna.

When two interferometric radar data sets are combined or interfered, the first product made is called an interferogram. This was accomplished by the SRTM with its two antennas.

The SRTM's main antenna was positioned in the cargo bay of the space shuttle Endeavor. It contained two types of radar types — the C-Band and the X-Band. Both types transmitted and received radar signals.

The C-Band antenna was able to transmit and receive radar wavelengths 5.6 cm (2.24 in) long. During the mission, the C-Band radar, with a swath width of 225 km (135 miles), scanned close to 80 percent of the land surface of earth.

The C-Band data are being processed at the Jet Propulsion Laboratory (JPL) to make a near-global topographic map of the earth.

The X-Band antenna was able to transmit and receive radar wavelengths three cm (1.2 in) in length. With a swath width of 50 km (30 miles), the X-Band antenna will produce topographic maps at a slightly higher resolution than the C-band data, but without near-global coverage.

The mast, named Able Deployable Articulated Mast (ADAM), was built by the AEC-Able Engineering Company, Inc. of Goleta, California. It was a truss structure consisting of 87 cube-shaped sections called bays. Unique latches on the diagonal members of the truss allowed the mechanism to deploy bay-by-bay out of the mast canister to its full length of 60 m (200 ft). The canister housed the mast during launch and landing. It also deployed and retracted the mast.

The mast was deployed and retracted by a motor-driven nut within the mast canister. This nut pulled the mast from its stowed position and into its deployed position. An astronaut inside the space shuttle controlled the mast deployment, which could have also been accomplished manually using a hand-held motor.

The SRTM outboard antenna was attached to the end of the mast and contained both C-Band and X-band radar panels. It transmitted, but did not receive, radar signals.

In addition to the C-Band and X-Band antennas, there were two Global Positioning System (GPS) antennas, Light Emitting Diode (LED) targets, and a corner-cube reflector.

One outboard antenna received radar signals in the C-Band where the radar wavelength was equal to 5.6 cm (2.24 in). The other radar received radar signals in the X-Band where the radar wavelength was equal to three cm (1.2 in).

The GPS antennas were used to gather accurate position information for the space shuttle. The LED targets were used by the target tracker on the Altitude and Orbit Determination Avionics (AODA) to measure the position of the outboard antenna relative to the main antenna. The corner-cube reflector was used by the electronic distance measurement unit on the AODA to measure the length of the mast to with 3 ml (0.12 in).

The AODA system combined the functions of metrology, altitude determination, and orbit determination. Its purpose was to answer questions regarding the length of the mast, direction of pointing, and location.

AODA performed four major tasks — to prove that the mast was safely deployed; to help align the radar antennas so the beams overlapped properly on the ground; to help improve shuttle altitude control system performance so that the mast wouldn't shift too much; and to record mast length, shuttle altitude, and orbit data so the earth's land topography could be determined.

AODA consisted of a flight segment and a ground segment. The flight segment contained all the sensors, electronics, computers, and software onboard the shuttle required for measurements. The ground segment consisted of all the computers, software, and other hardware needed to support mission operations and data processing.

Orbit determination was provided by the GPS. Two GPS receivers developed by JPL's space receiver program were connected to GPS antennas located on the outboard radar antenna.

The SRTM had orientation with two primary components — the altitude relative to the stars and the relative motion of the outboard radar antenna. The altitude was measured by a Star Tracker Assembly (STA) from Lockheed Martin. The STA consisted of a high-performance camera and a computer with an onboard database and a large star catalog.

The Inertial Reference Unit (IRU) manufactured by Teledyne measured altitude changes with extreme precision. The data from the STA and IRU were combined to get an absolute fix of the altitude with respect to the stars by the STA. The output of the IRU was then used to propagate that altitude through time.

The Astros Target Tracker (ATT) was located on the inboard antenna. It tracked three red Light Emitting Diode (LED) targets referred to as the Optical Target Assembly (OTA), which was located on the outboard antenna. These measurements allowed AODA to determine the outboard antenna's relative position.

The AODA Processing Computers (APC) served as the brains of the AODA. The APC was located in the shuttle's crew cabin and consisted of two IBM Thinkpad laptop computers that controlled the ATT, guided antenna alignment, provided AODA status displays, commanded interfaces for the astronaut crew, and recorded the AODA data.

JAPAN

Institute of Space and Astronautical Science (ISAS)

The Institute of Space and Astronautical Science (ISAS) is one of two organizations in Japan, along with the National Space Development Agency of Japan (NASDA), engaged in space-related missions and rocket development.

ISAS works with solid propellants, scientific satellites and the Uchinoura launch site. NASDA works with liquid propellants, application satellites, and the Tanegashima launch center.

NASDA's space activities directly relate to daily life and include the launch and operation of satellites for communications, broadcasting, meteorology, earth observation, and the participation of Japanese astronauts onboard the space shuttle.

ISAS launches scientific satellites and planetary explorers, while conducting research on the activities of the sun, moon, planets and black holes, as well as the origin and evolution of the galaxy. ISAS also uses large balloons to observe the atmosphere around the earth and in outer space.

The Institute's history began in 1955 with the PENCIL rocket launch experiment at the University of Tokyo. Three years later, the University developed a rocket capable of reaching an altitude of 60 km (36 miles). It also joined the International Observation Program by observing wind and temperature of the upper atmosphere.

In 1964, the Institute of Space and Aeronautical Science (ISAS) was founded in the University of Tokyo. Six years later, in 1970, Japan's first artificial satellite, OHSUMI, was launched by an L-4S rocket using solid propellant.

The institute remains devoted to space science, using its scientists and engineers to research and develop solid propellant rockets and scientific satellites.

Since the launch of OHSUMI in 1970, ISAS has sent 25 scientific satellites into orbit. The institute now serves as one of the leading centers of excellence in the world of space science.

Scientific Ballooning

The large scientific balloon serves as one of the flight platforms for scientific observation and engineering research at ISAS. Balloons are launched annually at Sanriku balloon center (SBC), which is the permanent balloon facility of ISAS. Since 1971, more than 250 balloons have been launched with an average of ten to fifteen per year.

There are two types of balloons available — a regular zero-pressure balloon and a newly developed, high-altitude balloon made of extremely thin film.

The zero-pressure balloons can operate up to 200,000 m³ (7,000,000 ft³) in volume and reach an altitude of 35 km (21 miles) or higher, carrying a payload of about 500 kg (1100 lbs).

The volume of the high-altitude balloons has increased each year.

In January 1997, a 120,000 m³ (4,200,000 ft³) balloon ascended to 50.2 km (30.1 miles) with a 10 kg (22 lb) payload.

Balloon scientific observations cover several fields, including cosmic ray physics, infrared astronomy high-energy astrophysics, and stratospheric atmosphere sciences. Engineering experiments for the development of new space technologies are also performed using balloons.

Flight techniques have been developed at ISAS to extend the duration of science observation. The most common are the boomerang balloon and the patrol balloon, which have been applied to science observation at Sanriku.

Another of these methods is the transoceanic flight. Between 1986 and 1988, flights from South Japan (Kagoshima) to China (near Shanghai or Nanjing) were carried out as a cooperative effort between ISAS and Chinese institutions.

Balloon observation is also carried out at foreign balloon bases. In the last ten years, groups of Japanese scientists have transported their scientific payloads to Brazil, Canada, and Norway to conduct balloon observations.

ISAS, in collaboration with the National Institute of Polar Research (NIPR) conducted the Polar Patrol Balloon (PPB) experiment from 1987 to 1993. The objective of PPB was to fly a balloon in a circumpolar wind in order to make observations of an extremely long duration. NIPR and ISAS plan a second PPB program in light of the success of the first.

ISAS developed a high-altitude balloon made with thin Winzen polyethylene film which has been flown for the observation of upper atmosphere and for future improvement of fabrication technology.

This Winzen film balloon has been able to reach an altitude of 40 km (24 miles). In January 1997, one such balloon with a volume of 120,000 m³ (4,200,000 ft³) reached an altitude of 50.2 km (30.1 miles), which was the highest balloon altitude achieved in Japan.

EVAL (Ethylene-Vinyl-alcohol), a new plastic film for balloons, was tested to fabricate balloons of high tolerance to internal pressure, which will be used for long flights. In 1997, a test balloon of 1,000 m³ (35,000 ft³) was successfully flown.

A year before, a new Low Altitude Space Communications System (LASCOS) was completed consisting of a mobile balloon tracking and receiving station and networks connecting them to SBC and ISAS in Sagmihara.

The stations were connected by public telephone lines allowing balloon trajectory monitoring, tele-command transmission operation, and telemetry data acquisition to be accomplished from any computer terminal through LASCOS, which is being used for long range tracking and balloon expeditions.

There are three types of observations performed by scientific balloons. These cover the fields of cosmic rays, geophysics, and infrared observation.

In the study of cosmic rays, measurements of the high-energy cosmic-ray electrons above one TeV provide important information on the sources of cosmic rays and on the propagation in the galaxy.

On September 13, 1996, an emulsion chamber was exposed to cosmic rays at a ceiling altitude of 37.4 km (22.4 miles) for 35 hours to improve the statistical accuracy of the energy spectrum above one TeV.

Analysis of shower events recorded on X-ray films in the chamber enabled the detection of six electrons above 800 GeV and 21 electrons above 400 GeV. The results obtained were consistent with the extension of the spectrum obtained to higher energy. The statistical accuracy of this observation was considerably improved in the 400 to 100 GeV energy range.

ISAS researchers found an indication of LPM (lines per minute) effect for these showers in the energy range higher than 400 GeV from the detailed inspection of the starting points of the first pair of electrons in the observed electron showers.

Since 1995, high-energy cosmic electrons have been measured with a new detection system which was developed for the observation of cosmic-electrons of 10 GeV to 1000 GeV boarding on balloons. The detector consists of a particle track detector made of scintillation fibers and image intensifiers, calorimeter, and a trigger system.

On June 2, 1997, a balloon observation was carried out at SBC and the detector was floated at an altitude of 36 km (21.6 miles) for five hours. During this observation, close to 600 electrons with energy higher than 10 GeV were detected.

The energy spectrum achieved was of the same power law type as those obtained by emulsion chambers.

In the area of geophysics, it was necessary to make clear variations of trace gases in the stratosphere. This was accomplished on June 6 and September 6, 1996, and May 30, 1998, when air samples were collected using a balloon-borne cryogenic sampling system at altitudes between 15 and 35 km (9 and 21 miles).

Stratospheric air samples were also collected using the same sampling system at altitudes between 10 and 28 km (6 and 16.8 miles) over the Scandinavian Peninsula on February 22 and March 18, 1998; and using a grab sampling system at 25.3 km (14.2 miles) on January 22, 1996; at 20.2 and 13.7 km (13 and 8.2 miles) on January 25, 1996; 20 km (12 miles) on January 19, 1997; as well as at 21.6 and 9.9 km (13 and 5.9 miles) on January 22, 1997, at Showa Station, Antarctica. These samples were taken by the National Institute for Environmental Studies and by the National Institute of Polar Research.

The sampled air was analyzed at the Center for Atmospheric and Oceanic Studies (CAOS) of Tohoku University to determine the concentrations of CO_2, CH_4, NO_2, and CO, followed by testing at the Department of Chemistry of the University of Tokyo for halocarbon analysis.

13C value concentration in CH_4 and CO_2 and 14C concentration in CO_2 were also measured at CAOS, the Ocean Research Institute, University of Tokyo, and the Dating and Materials Research Center, at Nagoya University.

Observations using balloon-borne optical ozone sensors aboard thin-film, high-altitude balloons were performed three times at SBC, once in 1996, and twice in 1997. These yielded ozone vertical profiles up to 42 km (25.2 miles), with both seasonal and latitudinal variations.

On September 9, 1997, atomic oxygen and ozone densities were measured simultaneously at altitudes of 38 to 44 km (22.8 to 26.4 miles) by a balloon launched from SBC. Atomic oxygen was detected with the resonance lamp technique, and the ozone was monitored with the solar UV absorption.

Measured O and O_3 density ratios were found to be consistent with the current photochemical theory within experimental errors, suggesting that the cause of the ozone deficit problem exists outside the O and O_3 partition.

A simple, lightweight, two-channel radiometer, the NO_2 sonde, was launched on a lightweight, high-altitude balloon, which was developed to measure solar flux at two wavelengths corresponding to a maximum and minimum of absorption cross section of NO_2. The differential absorption spectroscopic technique was used to obtain a vertical distribution of atmospheric nitrogen dioxide (NO_2).

Infrared observations will be performed by a large X-ray telescope awaiting lift-off at a balloon base in Palestine, Texas. The detector was developed through a collaboration between Japan and the United States for the purpose of obtaining a detailed image of the Crab Nebula.

The BESS Experiment (Balloon-Borne Experiment with a Superconducting Magnet Spectrometer) was established to observe antiproton flux in the cosmic rays. A balloon flight in the summer of 1996 failed, but the instrument was recovered without damage. In July 1997, the balloon was launched successfully from Lynn Lake in North Canada and floated at an altitude of 35 km (21 miles) for more than 20 hours before being recovered at Peace River.

More than 400 cosmic-ray anti-proton candidates have been detected in the energy region from 0.2 GeV to 3.8 GeV. Analysis continues to determine the origin of the cosmic ray anti-protons as well as the upper limit of the cosmic-ray anti-matter. So far, antiprotons have been detected without the contamination of positive electrons and mesons (group of subatomic particles) by the employment of aerosol Cerenkov counters.

Space Science

Since the launch of Japan's first satellite, OHSUMI, the country has continued its launching activities, including satellites, sounding rockets, and balloons, to explore the mysteries of the earth region, the solar system, and the universe. Through its space science program, several areas of study have been covered, including astrophysics, high-energy astrophysics, solar physics, infrared astronomy, radio astronomy, space plasma physics, lunar and planetary science, and basic science.

The high energy astrophysics group at

ISAS is engaged primarily in X-ray astrophysics research through satellite observation. It was recently involved in the operation of the ASCA satellite, formerly named Astro-D, Japan's fourth cosmic X-ray astronomy mission, following previous X-ray astronomy satellites HAKUCHO, TENMA, and GINA. The satellite was successfully launched on February 20, 1993. However, altitude control was lost on July 14, 2000, during a geomagnetic storm, ceasing scientific observations. ASCA reentered the atmosphere on March 2, 2001, after more than eight years in orbit.

ASTRO-E was launched by the M-V rocket from the Kagoshima Space Center of ISAS on February 10, 2000. It carried two focal-lane instruments for soft X-ray observations, and one collimated large-area counter array for hard X-ray. A micro-calorimeter array (X-ray spectrometer) and four identical sets of X-ray CCDs (X-ray imaging spectrometers) were onboard to cover the energy band from 0.5 keV to ~10 keV with imaging capability. The hard X-ray detector was a combination of scintillation detectors and silicon PIN detectors to cover the hard X-ray band from 10 keV to 600 keV.

Immediately following launch, ASTRO-E experienced a malfunction of the first stage motor. The satellite could not pick up the necessary speed for a circular orbit, resulting in mission failure.

The YOHKOH (SOLAR-A) X-ray satellite was designed as an observatory for studying X-rays and gamma-rays from the sun. It was launched from Kagoshima, Japan, with the spacecraft built in Japan, and observation instruments contributed by the United States and the United Kingdom.

The satellite returned excellent data on the very active quiet sun during the sunspot minimum of 1995–1997. These observations included sources of the coronal mass ejections that have been known to cause geomagnetic storms.

YOHKOH, Japanese for Sunbeam, was the second solar mission of ISAS, following HINOTORI's launch in 1981. On December 14, 2001, it suffered a spacecraft failure during the solar eclipse. The spacecraft lost pointing and the batteries discharged. Spacecraft operators were unable to command the satellite to point toward the sun, and the mission was terminated.

SOLAR-B is a follow-up mission to SOLAR-A, consisting of a coordinated set of optical, EUV and X-ray instruments that will investigate the interaction between the sun's magnetic field and its corona. This result is expected to yield an improved understanding of the mechanisms which cause solar magnetic variability and a demonstration of how this variability modulates the total solar output creating the driving force behind space weather.

ISAS will provide the spacecraft, the launch vehicle (ISAS M-V), and major elements of each of the scientific instruments. The spacecraft is being developed by Mitsubishi Electric Corporation (MELCO) and will accommodate three major instruments — a 0.5m solar optical telescope (SOT), an X-ray telescope (XRT), and an EUV Imaging Spectrometer (EIS). The EIS will link the photosphere to the hot corona.

NASA will provide the Focal Plane Package (FPP) for the optical telescope as well as components of the X-ray telescope and Extreme Ultraviolet Imaging Spectrometer (EIS).

The 875-kg (1929 lb) Solar-B spacecraft has been scheduled for launch in the fall of 2005. It will be placed in a sun-synchronous orbit about the earth in order to keep the instruments in nearly continuous sunlight for nine months each year.

The Solar-B, over a lifespan of three years, will provide for the first time quantitative measurements of the full vector magnetic field on small enough scales to resolve elemental flux tubes. The field of view and sensitivity allow for changes in the magnetic energy to be related to both steady state (coronal heating) and transient changes (flares, coronal mass ejections) in the solar atmosphere.

The infrared astronomy group has been engaged in observations covering diffuse infrared emissions by use of balloon and satellite telescopes. The Balloon Infrared Carbon Explorer (BICE) has provided an extensive mapping of the CII line emission, which is the most effective interstellar gas cooling mechanism. This mapping was made in the galactic plane.

Results obtained revealed the distribution of star formation activities throughout the galaxy, along with the discovery that the CII line emissivity in the galactic center is substantially lower than far infrared continuum emission. This means star formation in the galactic center is currently dormant and therefore the UV emission responsible for CII emission is relatively weak.

The first infrared satellite mission utilized the multi-purpose space platform SFU (Space Flyer Unit). A small, cryogenically cooled infrared telescope, IRTS (Infrared Telescope in Space), was onboard the SFU to observe diffuse infrared rays in a wide range of wavelengths from 1.6 to 800 microns.

During four weeks of observation, roughly seven percent of the sky was surveyed, yielding a wide range of data on zodiacal light, interstellar dust and line emissions as well as near infrared and sub-millimeter background radiation. Additionally, more than 20,000 discrete sources were observed during the course of the survey, providing non-biased samples of stellar spectra, specifically of late-type stars.

Another result revealed that infrared band emissions attributable to Poly-Aromatic Hydrocarbon (PAH) are distributed ubiquitously in the galactic plane. This distribution is similar to that of the far infrared continuum emitted by silicate-like dust, which indicates that organic matter is commonly present in interstellar space and the distribution is well-mixed with inorganic matter.

The radio astronomy group at ISAS is responsible for conducting the VLBI Space Observatory Program (VSOP — loosely translated as "Very Superior Old Pale"), the first project dedicated to very long baseline interferometry between a radio telescope in space and arrays of radio telescopes on earth. The VSOP satellite, HALCA, previously known as MUSES-B, is also a translation of the Japanese word *haruka*, meaning far away, as HALCA's elliptical orbit takes it out to an apogee 21,400 km (13,300 miles) above the earth's surface, while exploring the mysteries of the distant universe.

The surface of HALCA's telescope consisted of a fine wire mesh supported by six masts, which were deployed in orbit to create an eight meter (26 ft) diameter reflector. Observations with HALCA have allowed images of celestial radio sources to be made at wavelengths of 18 cm (7.08 in) and 6 cm (2.36 in) with an angular resolution up to three times better than that obtainable from the earth.

HALCA transmitted science data in real-time at a rate of 128 mega-bits per second to the tracking station. Data was recorded at the tracking stations and ground radio telescopes on magnetic tape, and after observation, the tapes were sent to a central processing facility for correlation. Space VLBI data has been processed at three centers: Mitaka, Japan; Socorro, New Mexico; and the Penticton, Canada.

The space plasma physics group primarily focuses on the study of the earth's magnetosphere. The solar wind draws the earth's magnetic field into a long tail on the nightside of the earth, storing energy in the stretched field lines of the magnetotail. Interaction of the solar with the magnetosphere produces diverse phenomena that involve the storage and energization of charged particles. During its most active periods, the tail couples with the near-earth magnetosphere, sometimes releasing energy stored in the tail and activating auroras in the polar ionosphere.

AKEBONO (EXOS-D), was launched on February 22, 1989, by an M-3SII launch vehicle, and was injected into an initial polar orbit of 10,500 (6,524) by 270 km (168 miles). The telemetry data from AKEBONO satellite was received at four ground stations — Kagoshima Space Center (Japan), Showa Base (Antarctica), Prince Albert (Canada) and ESRANGE (Sweden).

The primary scientific objective of the AKEBONO project was to investigate magnetospheric phenomena associated with auroral particle acceleration. AKEBONO has operated continuously for more than 10 years, and all instruments except the auroral imager, whose CCD was degraded after one year's operation due to severe radiation particle flux, remain in good order. It has been anticipated that observation of the full solar cycle will be possible. The data acquired has been reprocessed and archived into the AKEBONO

science database, which is open to all interested scientists.

Major scientific contributions of AKEBONO have included demonstration of particle acceleration by parallel electric field; quantitative study of ion outflow from the polar ionosphere; detailed study of equatorial enhancement of UHR waves; thermal structure of lower plasma sphere; discovery of storm time partial depression of plasma sphere density; and long term variation of radiation belt particles.

On July 24, 1992, the GEOTAIL satellite was launched by a Delta II launch vehicle from Cape Canaveral, Florida. Its primary purpose was to study the structure and dynamics of the tail region of the magnetosphere with a comprehensive set of scientific instruments.

The satellite's orbit was designed to cover the magnetotail over a wide range of distances — 8 Re to 210 Re from the earth. This orbit has also allowed for study of the boundary region of the magnetosphere as it skimmed the magnetopause at perigees.

GEOTAIL has been a joint cooperative project between ISAS and NASA. ISAS developed the spacecraft and provided close to two-thirds of the scientific instruments, while NASA provided the launch and about one-third of the scientific instruments. It has played a major role in the International Solar-Terrestrial Physics (ISTP) program, making available a scientific database for public use and Internet access to view magnetic field and plasma data.

The satellite has exceeded its projected lifetime of three and a half years, surviving an eclipse lasting for 251 minutes without incidence on February 28, 1999.

On January 7, 1985, SAKIGAKE (MS-T5) was launched by an M-3SII-1 launch vehicle from Kagoshima Space Center by the Lunar/Planetary Science group at ISAS. The spacecraft's objective was to test the schemes of the first escape from the earth gravitation for Japan on an engineering basis, while observing space plasma and magnetic fields in interplanetary space.

In August of that year, ISAS launched the second interplanetary spacecraft, SUISEI, which was sent into heliocentric orbit to explore Halley's comet which reappeared in 1985 and 1986. The Lyman-f imager onboard SUISEI observed hydrogen coma activity of Halley's comet and found the rotation period of the nucleus. SUISEI crossed the bow shock generated by the interaction between solar wind and Halley's comet and the phenomena near the shock wave was studied by the onboard plasma analyzer.

A new launch vehicle, M-V, was successfully launched with close to three times higher launching capability than the M-3SII, its predecessor.

NOZOMI (PLANET-B) was launched on July 4, 1998, as the first Japanese Mars orbiter. Its primary scientific objective was to study the Martian upper atmosphere with emphasis on its interaction with the solar wind. The orbiter weighs 541 kg (1192 lb), including the fuel for altitude and orbit control. It will have an orbit around Mars with 150 km (92 mile) periapsis (the point in as orbit closest to the body being orbited) and 15 Mars radaii apoapsis (the point in an orbit farthest from the body being orbited) on its arrival at the red planet. The low periapsis altitude was chosen to probe the ionosphere as low as possible and the relatively large apoapsis distance is to study the night side of Mars where detection of ionospheric ions is expected.

NOZOMI is currently in its heliocentric orbit and scheduled to arrive at Mars in early 2004.

NOZOMI observations fall into five categories, including the magnetic field of Mars, the atmosphere of Mars, plasma in the ionosphere of Mars, pictures, and dust. NOZOMI was designed to precisely measure the Martian magnetic field for the first time. It will investigate the composition and structure of the atmosphere by using ultraviolet remote-sensing detectors as well as a small mass-analyzer to identify ionosphere composition.

NOZOMI was designed to investigate the components, structure, temperature, and plasma waves within the Martian ionosphere with its newly developed detectors, emphasizing previously unobserved regions. A very small onboard camera will take pictures of the Martian weather. Two satellites, Phobos and Deimos, will enable a better understanding of how sandstorms and clouds are generated, while monitoring the growth and retreat of polar ice caps. The spacecraft will also use a dust counter to confirm whether or nor a dust-ring exists along the orbit of Phobos.

In order to obtain these scientific objectives, fourteen instruments were installed on the NOZOMI spacecraft, including the Mars Imaging Camera (MIC), Magnetic Field Measurement (MGF), Probe for Electron Temperature (PET), Electron Spectrum Analyzer (ESA), Ion Spectrum Analyzer (ISA), Electron and Ion Spectrometer (EIS), Extra Ultraviolet Scanner (XUV), Plasma Wave and Sounder (PWS), Low Frequency plasma wave Analyzer (LFA), Ion Mass Imager (IMI), Mars Dust Counter (MDC), Neutral Mass Spectrometer (NMS), and the Thermal Plasma Analyzer (TPA).

The Mars Imaging Camera (MIC) is a visual wavelength camera to take global images of Mars. It can monitor changes of global atmospheric conditions including dust storm growth, change of atmospheric opacity due to dust and thin hazy clouds, change of cloud features, growth and retreat of polar caps, and development and thickness of the polar hood. MIC can also observe the shapes and surfaces of the two Martian satellites, Phobos and Deimos, in great detail.

The Magnetic Field Measurement (MGF) is designed to measure the magnetic field around Mars which, for the most part, still remains unknown. The NOZOMI includes low altitude measurements of the Martian atmosphere which could resolve previous difficulties in regard to the magnitude and structure of the Martian magnetic field.

The Probe for Electron Temperature (PET) will measure the electron temperature of the Martian ionosphere with the primary goal of studying the thermal structure of the Martian ionosphere by continuous observation of electron temperature.

The Electron Spectrum Analyzer (ESA) will measure the electron energy flux in the range of 12 eV to 16 keV, and provide information for studies on the structure of the magnetosphere and ionosphere, as well as information on particle acceleration and wave-particle interaction processes around Mars.

The Ion Spectrum Analyzer (ISA) will measure the ion energy flux in the 10 eV to 16 keV range, and provide similar studies in this range to the ESA.

The Electron and Ion Spectrometer (EIS) will measure the energy flux of high energy particles such as electrons, protons, helium ions and heavy oxygen ions, in the range of 40 keV to 500 keV per charge. The EIS will measure these particles while contributing to the understanding of the acceleration mechanism.

The Extra Ultraviolet Scanner (XUV) will measure the abundance and distribution of helium gas and helium ions in the Martian atmosphere by scanning the scattered extreme ultraviolet sunlight through neutral helium gas and ions. This observation will yield information on the internal activity of Mars such as volcanic or water circulation. It will also give information on the ionization process of helium gas and its escape from the ionosphere to outer space.

The UltraViolet imaging Spectrometer (UVS) will measure the FUV and MUV region from 115 to 310 mm (4.52 to 12.2 in) as well as the hydrogen and oxygen corona around Mars and dayglow emissions such as the CO Cameron band. It will also measure the D/H ratio to study the escape processes and the evolution of the Martian atmosphere.

The Plasma Wave and Sounder (PWS) instrument was designed to observe the structure of the ionosphere by using the topside sounder technique along with the features of plasma waves that are associated with wave-particle interactions. These are the origin of the microprocesses controlling the direct interaction processes of ionospheric plasma with the solar wind plasma.

The Low Frequency plasma wave Analyzer (LFA) was developed to measure Martian plasma waves, having the capability of measuring the wave spectrum in the band from 10 Hz to 32 kHz. Its scientific objectives are to explore the macroscopic plasma environment and boundaries from the solar wind to the ionosphere, as well as microscopic plasma phenomena induced by the interaction

between the solar wind and the Martian atmosphere with its associated moons.

The Ion Mass Imager (IMI), a lightweight ion mass composition instrument, will measure ions with energies between 10 eV and 35 keV per charge, with a 360 degree field-of-view aperture. It will utilize the spacecraft's spin to cover almost the full unit sphere to measure three-dimensional distribution of ions.

The Mars Dust Counter (MDC), a lightweight impact-ionization type dust detector, will determine mass and velocity of a particle. Its primary purpose will be to measure dust particles around Mars and reveal the distribution of the predicted Martian ring, or torus, of dust particles from Phobos and Deimos. It will also measure other particles such as interplanetary dust and other space debris around earth.

The Neutral Mass Spectrometer (NMS), a lightweight quadrupole-type mass analyzer, will measure the composition and density of neutral particles in the upper atmosphere of Mars, providing key information to the study of interactions between the solar wind and the Martian upper atmosphere.

The Thermal Plasma Analyzer (TPA) will measure the characteristics of thermal ions in the upper atmosphere of Mars, such as velocity, temperature, and their compositions. TPA measurements will greatly contribute to the understanding of these mechanisms which play important roles in the interactions between the neutral atmosphere, ionosphere, magnetosphere, and the solar wind.

Although NOZOMI weighs only 541 kg (1192 lbs) including fuel, it will serve as a very high-performance spacecraft.

The Japanese lunar penetrator mission, LUNAR-A, is scheduled for launch in fall 2004 by the M-V launch vehicle from Kagoshima Space Center (KSC). This mission objective will be to study the lunar interior using seismometers and heat-flow probes installed in the penetrators. Two penetrators will be deployed on the lunar surface, one on the nearside, the other on the farside.

The penetrators for the LUNAR-A mission will contain a two-component seismometer and a heat-flow probe, along with other supporting instruments such as a tiltmeter and an accelerometer. The tiltmeter will be used to discern the attitude of the penetrator in the regolith (mantle rock), and the accelerometer is used to judge the depth of the penetrator by integrating the recorded deceleration at penetrator impact.

The LUNAR-A mission will be the first mission dedicated to studying the lunar internal structure.

The MUSES-C is an ISAS space engineering spacecraft launched by the M-V launch vehicle into a transfer orbit toward asteroid 1998SF36 in May 2003, and is scheduled to arrive at the asteroid in the summer of 2005.

The mission objective is to investigate an asteroid known as an earth-approaching type. With this mission, ISAS hopes to establish the technology to bring back samples of an asteroid's surface to earth for sampling and detailed analysis.

MUSES is the acronym for "Mu Space Engineering Spacecraft" or a space engineering spacecraft launched by a Mu rocket, "C" refers to the third. MUSES-A, the first of the MUSES series, was originally called HITEN and was launched by the M-3SII vehicle in 1990, with target technologies such as a swingby using the moon's gravity. MUSES-B, originally called HALCA, was launched by the M-V launch vehicle in 1997, and is currently actively serving in the VLBI (very long baseline interferometry) program to study the radio wave region.

One of the key technologies used by MUSES-C is electric propulsion, which will carry out orbital maneuvers between the earth and the targeted asteroid. This propulsion method uses an electric propulsion engine that first ionizes the propellant, Xenon, by microwave, then accelerates the ions in a strong electric field and expels them at high speed, using the reactionary energy as propulsion.

Basic science research is performed to support the various space programs with rockets, satellite, and balloons, while helping to develop future projects. The Space Atomic Physics section at ISAS performs theoretical studies of atomic and molecular processes and their application to space science and other fields. Researchers in this group also produce databases of cross sections for photoabsorption of atoms and electron collisions with atoms, molecules, and ions, as well as perform observational studies of physical processes in molecular clouds, including the influence of turbulence on cloud hierarchy, formation of new stars, and formation and evolution of protoplanetary disks around young stars.

Research also includes theoretical and observational studies of the origin of small bodies in our solar system including comets, asteroids, and meteorites.

Missions

Since the 1970s, ISAS has conducted a number of missions by the use of satellites and cosmic explorers. Following is a brief history of the most important missions, including future missions.

SHINSEI (MS-F2) was the first Japanese scientific satellite. It was launched on September 28, 1971, by an M-4S-3 launch vehicle from Kagoshima Space Center.

Weighing 66 kg (145.2 lbs), SHINSEI observed solar radio waves, cosmic rays, and ionospheric plasma at an inclination orbit of 32 degrees.

TANSEI (MS-T1) was launched on February 16, 1971, by an M-4S-2 launch vehicle from Kagoshima Space Center. Weighing 63 kg (138.6 lbs), TANSEI demonstrated the performance of a new launch vehicle and studied the space environment after orbit insertion into an inclination of 30 degrees.

DENPA (REX) was launched on August 19, 1972, by a M-4S-4 launch vehicle from Kagoshima Space Center. Weighing 75 kg (165 lbs), the satellite observed plasma waves and plasma density in space at an inclination of 31 degrees.

TANSEI-2 (MS-T2) was launched on February 16, 1974, by an M-3C-1 launch vehicle from Kagoshima Space Center. The satellite weighed 56 kg (123.2 lbs) and was placed in an orbit inclination of 31 degrees. TANSEI-2 successfully proved its performance through a series of engineering tests.

TAIYO (SRATS) was launched on February 24, 1975, by an M-3C-2 launch vehicle from Kagoshima Space Center. The 86 kg (189.2 lb) satellite observed soft X-rays and ultraviolet radiation from the sun while it remained in a 32 degree orbit inclination.

TANSEI-3 (MS-T3) was launched on February 19, 1977, by an M-3H-1 launch vehicle from Kagoshima Space Center. The 129 kg (283.8 lb) satellite, placed at an inclination of 66 degrees, successfully underwent a series of engineering tests.

KYOKKO (EXOS-A) was launched on February 4, 1978, by an M-3H-2 launch vehicle from Kagoshima Space Center. The 126 kg (277.2 lb) satellite observed the density, temperature and composition of space plasma, studied the energy spectrum of auroral electrons, and obtained UV images of Aurora while remaining at an inclination of 65 degrees.

JIKIKEN (EXOS-B) was launched on September 16, 1978, by an M-3H-3 launch vehicle from Kagoshima Space Center. Weighing 90 kg (198 lbs), the satellite observed the electron density and plasma waves at an inclination of 31 degrees.

HAKUCHO (CORSA-b) was launched on February 21, 1979, by an M-3C-4 launch vehicle from Kagoshima Space Center. The satellite, weighing 96 kg (211.1 lbs) observed X-ray sources of space origin, including X-ray bursts and soft X-ray nebulae from an inclination of 30 degrees.

While in orbit, HAKUCHO discovered eight cosmic X-ray burst sources, and observed unusual activity from another burst source, the rapid burster. It also discovered a new X-ray star. Foreign optical astronomers performed an optical survey of this region revealing a globular cluster named Terzan 5.

HITEN (MUSES-A) was launched on January 24, 1980, by an M-3SII-5 launch vehicle from Kagoshima Space Center and placed in an inclination of 30.6 degrees. The satellite performed a series of on-orbit techniques, including swingby, by use of the moon's gravitation. HITEN approached the Moon on April 11, 1993, injecting a tiny lunar orbiter, HAGOROMO, into orbit.

HINOTORI (ASTRO-A) was launched on February 21, 1981, by an M-3S-2 launch vehicle from Kagoshima Space Center and placed into an inclination of 31 degrees. The 188 kg (413.6 lb) spacecraft obtained two-dimensional hard X-ray images of solar flares, and observed X-ray bursts.

TENMA (ASTRO-B) was launched on February 20, 1983, by an M-3S-3 launch vehicle from Kagoshima Space Center and placed into an inclination of 32 degrees. The spacecraft observed X-ray sources from space, including X-ray stars, X-ray galaxies, gamma-ray bursts, and soft X-ray nebulae.

Gas scintillation proportional counters (SPC) onboard TENMA provided a highly effective tool to study cosmic X-ray sources. SPC sensitivity enabled ISAS researchers to trace the 283 sec pulsation from an X-ray pulsar Vela X-1 with a high data quality.

OHZORA (EXOS-C) was launched on February 14, 1984, by an M-3S-4 launch vehicle from Kagoshima Space Center. Weighing 207 kg (455.4 lbs), the spacecraft was placed into an inclination of 75 degrees and observed the earth's upper atmosphere as a part of the International Middle Atmosphere Program (MAP).

SAKIGAKE (MS-T5) was launched on January 7, 1985, from Kagoshima Space Center and placed into a Heliocentric orbit. The 138 kg (303.6 lb) spacecraft tested the schemes of the first escape from earth's gravitation and observed space plasma and the magnetic field in interplanetary space.

SUISEI (PLANET-A) was launched on August 18, 1985, by M-3SII-2 launch vehicle from Kagoshima Space Center and placed into a Heliocentric orbit. Together with other orbiting satellites, VEGA, GIOTTO, ICE, and SAKIGAKE, SUISEI constituted "Halley Armada" to explore Halley's comet when it made its closest encounter with the sun. The 140 kg (308 lb) spacecraft performed Solar Wind Interaction with Halley's comet on March 8, 1986, coming within 150,000 km (90,000 miles) of Halley.

GINGA (ASTRO-C) was launched on February 5, 1987, by an M-3SII-3 launch vehicle from Kagoshima Space Center and placed into an inclination of 31 degrees.

The 420 kg (924 lb) spacecraft observed X-ray sources from space, including black holes, neutron stars, supernovae, active galactic nuclei, and gamma-ray bursts.

YOHKOH (SOLAR-A), ISAS's second solar physics satellite, was launched on August 30, 1991, by an M-3SII launch vehicle from Kagoshima Space Center.

X-ray images taken by YOHKOH currently number several million and are redrawing traditional images of the sun.

The GEOTAIL satellite was launched on July 24, 1992, by a Delta II launch vehicle from Cape Canaveral, Florida. GEOTAIL's primary objective was to study the structure and dynamics of the tail region of the magnetosphere with a comprehensive set of scientific instruments. To meet this objective, GEOTAIL's orbit was set to cover the magnetotail over a wide range of distances from 8 Re to 210 Re from the earth. Selection of this orbit allowed for study of the boundary region of the magnetosphere as it skimmed the magnetosphere at perigees.

In the satellite's first two years, the double lunar swingby technique was used to keep apogees in the distant magnetotail. The apogee was lowered down to 50 Re in mid–November 1994. It was then lowered to 30 Re in February 1995, in order to study substorm processes in the near-earth tail region.

GEOTAIL's current orbit is 9 Re by 30 Re with an inclination of -7° to the ecliptic plane.

ASCA (Advanced Satellite for Cosmology and Astrophysics, formerly ASTRO-D), an X-ray astronomy satellite, was launched on February 20, 1993, by the launch vehicle M-3SýU into an approximate circular orbit of 520 to 620 km (312 to 372 miles). The 417 kg (917.4 lb) three-axis stabilized spacecraft is Japan's fourth X-ray astronomy satellite following HAKUCHO, launched in February 1979; TENMA, launched in February 1983; and GINGA, launched in February 1987.

HALCA (MUSES-B) was launched on February 12, 1997, by an M-V launch vehicle from Kagoshima Space Center and is the first astronomical satellite dedicated to very long baseline interferometry (VLBI). MUSES-B refers to "Mu Space Engineering Satellites."

Since the satellite's successful deployment, the main reflector mesh that is very similar in appearance to a satellite dish, has yielded testing of new engineering technologies such as the two-way communications link between the satellite and tracking stations. HALCA continues to be used for space VLBI observations.

NOZOMI (PLANET-B) is the first Japanese Mars orbiter, which was launched on July 4, 1998. The primary objective of PLANET-B is to study the upper Martian atmosphere with emphasis its interaction with the solar wind.

Weighing 541 kg (1190.2 lbs), including the fuel for altitude and orbit control, NOZOMI is now in its Heliocentric orbit and scheduled to arrive at Mars in early 2004.

MUSES-C, one of ISAS's space engineering spacecraft series, scheduled for launch in 2004, will investigate an asteroid known as an earth-approaching type and bring back samples of an asteroid's surface to earth.

LUNAR-A, the Japanese lunar penetrator mission, has been scheduled for launch in 2004. The mission will focus on the study of the lunar interior using seismometers and heat-flow probes installed in the penetrators. Two penetrators will be deployed on the lunar surface, one on the nearside, the other on the farside.

ASTRO-F, also known as the Infrared Imaging Surveyor (IRIS), is ISAS's second infrared astronomy mission, launched in 2003, and placed into a sun-synchronous polar orbit. IRIS employs a 70 cm (28 in) telescope cooled to 6 K using liquid helium. It was designed for second-generation infrared survey, a survey with much higher sensitivies than those of previous ones. IRIS will investigate formation and evolution of the galaxies, stars, and planets.

SELENE (SELenological and Engineering Explorer) was developed as a joint lunar program between ISAS and NASDA (National Space Development Agency of Japan).

SELENE will be launched by an H-IIA rocket in 2005. Primary mission objectives will be to obtain scientific data of the lunar origin and evolution, while marking the beginning of the development of technology for future lunar exploration.

Planned as the largest mission to the moon after the Apollo program, SELENE will consist of the main orbiting satellite, placed

100 km (60 miles) above the earth into polar circular orbit; and two sub-satellites — the Relay satellite and the VRAD satellite.

The sub-satellites will remain in elliptical orbits of 2400 km (1440 miles) and 800 km (480 miles). The orbiters will be equipped with instruments for scientific investigation of the moon, both on the moon and from the moon.

Japan's fifth X-ray astronomy satellite, ASTRO-EII, has been scheduled for launch in 2005. It will have superior spectroscopic analyzing power along with a very wide energy band, ranging from soft X-rays up to gamma-rays (0.3–600 keV). High resolution spectroscopy and wide-band capability are essential to physically investigate high energy astronomical phenomena such as black holes and supernovae.

ASTRO-EII will improve current knowledge of the physical state of space hot plasma. It will also enable the measurement of Doppler effect in great detail. ASTRO-EII will perform measurements of the emissions from highly accelerated particles, opening a window to the active and heating universe. It will present viable clues to the dynamics of the merging of galaxy clusters, considered to be the greatest collapse of the largest objects in the universe.

The spacecraft will also study the line emission from materials falling into a black hole, contributing to the understanding of the evolution of the universe, as well as the time-space structure under the strong effect of general relativity.

SOLAR-B, the third solar physics satellite of ISAS, succeeding YOHKOH (SOLAR-A), has been scheduled for launch in 2005. The 700 kg (1540 lb) spacecraft will be placed in a polar, sun-synchronous orbit about the earth in order to keep the instruments in continuous sunlight, with no day or night cycling for nine months each year. It will be supplied with 170 kg (374 lbs) of thruster gas to maintain its sun-synchronous orbit for more than two years.

Space Technology

ISAS's space technology research division focuses on the development of near-term missions performing leading-edge observations and interplanetary exploration. Missions have been pursued in the fields of aeronautics, electronics, instrumentation, and the utilization of the space environment and associated basic technologies. The development of new space transportation systems and space power systems is also performed by this division.

The M-V launch vehicle has launched several types of spacecraft, weighing hundreds of kilograms, into interplanetary space, making it possible to explore near-earth planets such as Venus and Mars, as well as the moon.

Through interplanetary mission planning, a number of orbits are analyzed in order to handle delta-V and launch window-limitations, as well as dispersion caused in the launch phase.

In order to accomplish this, ISAS utilizes interactive analysis tools for optimization, lunar, and interplanetary orbits as demonstrated in missions such as NOZOMI (PLANET-B, the Mars orbiter), LUNAR-A (Lunar Penetrator), and MUSES-C (Asteroid sample return).

Space technology also focuses on systems required for space vehicles such as propulsion, flight dynamics and control, structures and materials, aerodynamics and reentry technology, ARTEX (Air Breathing Propulsion System), and reusable space transportation systems.

ISAS has strived to continuously improve its solid propellant rocket technology by conducting extensive research on propulsion mechanisms and performance enhancement.

Achievements in this area have included a numerical technique for analyzing two-phase nozzle flow for specific impulse prediction and nozzle contour design; highly aluminized, high-performance composite propellants, including one with added positive catalyst and higher burning rate; EEC (extendable exit cone) nozzle systems utilizing helical spring extensors for upper stage motors; nozzle-throat-plug type aft-end ignition systems for upper stage motors; and studies on combustion stability, erosive burning, and residual chamber pressure of rocket motors loaded with highly aluminized composite propellants.

In the area of flight dynamics and control, ISAS investigate dynamics and control of space structures, such as launch vehicles, deployable structures, and flexible multibody systems, applying new theories to flight systems.

An example of this is a robust control design which was specifically designed for the altitude control system in ISAS launch systems. The entire system is susceptible to uncertainty in various system parameters such as bending rigidity, aerodynamic parameters, and actuator bandwidth, which may cause the deterioration of flight stability.

For the M-V launch vehicle, the $H\frac{1}{8}$ control theory, a post-modern control theory, has been applied to provide the altitude control system with sufficiently robust stability characteristics. This features a newly established methodology for the application of mathematical theory to large classes of actual systems.

Scientific mission demands require the development and enhancement of structures and materials. In this area, dynamic analysis, estimation of loads and mechanical environments, and improvements to structural verification tests have been studied and applied.

ISAS developed a high-strength, maraging steel for the first and second stage motor casings of the M-V satellite launch vehicle, as well as a filament wound CFRP motor casing for the third stage, and new jettison mechanisms for the half interstage joint and the nose fairing.

ISAS has been working on a CFRP filament wound motor casing with new technologies to improve its payload capability for the second stage of the M-V.

CFRP tri-axial woven fabric for weight reduction in satellites was recently applied to the high gain antenna of PLANET-B. An extendable optical bench with high geometric stability under thermal fluctuation and distribution in orbit is currently under development for ASTRO-E.

Studies of aerodynamics are required for the launch vehicle as well as the reentry and recovery system. In this area, ISAS aerodynamicists have been working on experimental and analytical numerical systems.

Basic research is performed in wind tunnel test facilities and high enthalpy flow experiment facilities at ISAS. Supercomputer-based CFD (computational fluid dynamics) numerical analysis provides a powerful tool for basic research and development of real vehicles.

ISAS has currently been working on the development of technology for hyper-velocity atmospheric entry to a planet and return to earth from interplanetary space.

In high-speed atmospheric reentry flights, many problems remain unsolved concerning aerothermodynamics and thermal protection. Studies into the better understanding of flow characteristics and for TPS material along with in-flight demonstration with flight tools are helping to resolve some of these problems.

For the future, ISAS continues to work on developing new space transportation and innovative propulsion systems. Following the completion of a demonstration study of the cryogenic liquid hydrogen rocket engine in the 1980s, new research on hydrogen-based, air-breathing engines began.

The Air Turbo Ramjet (ATR) engine is a current program at ISAS. ATR consists of a combined cycle system using a turbojet and a fan-boosted ramjet running on liquid hydrogen as a fuel as well as a coolant.

This ATREX (Air-Breathing Propulsion System, or ATR of an expander cycle) has potential for applications such as the fly-back booster of the TSTO (two-stage-to-orbit) spaceplane.

A series of firing tests of a sub-scale model have been completed under static conditions at sea-level. The next stage will be the development of a flight demonstrator.

ISAS has a strong interest in the development of reusable space transportation systems. This includes the building and designing a single-stage-to-orbit (SSTO) vehicle which will be fully reusable, demonstrating higher-performance related technologies, reliable operability, and efficient reusability with capabilities for supporting quick turnaround and continuous abort.

ISAS has currently been testing a small vertical landing vehicle, equipped with a liquid hydrogen rocket engine, performing a series of hardware-oriented exercises to demonstrate the benefit of reusability in future vehicles.

ISAS has applied satellite and spacecraft technologies to current rocket systems and future transportation and utilization systems.

This area has focused on the STRAIGHT project, altitude control of spacecraft, electric propulsion, deployable structures, satellite mission operation, tracking and orbit determination, space environment utilization, and a solar power satellite.

The STRAIGHT (Study on the Reduction of Advanced Instrument Weight) project is aimed at the development of next-generation spacecraft technology. This project involves the development of a new concept in onboard computer architecture, a digital transponder, inflatable deployment mechanisms, data recorders with higher density memory devices, and lightweight star sensors.

Altitude control requirements for spacecraft can vary from one mission to another. ISAS investigates the most appropriate altitude control system for each mission before it is designed. The inclusion of high-performance sensors, both optical and inertial, efficient actuators, and capable onboard computers and electronics are essential.

This technology has also been applied to satellites and planetary probes. Advanced control concepts and new ideas have been explored to solve the problems associated with structural flexibility and large altitude disturbances. Schemes for altitude maneuvers continue to be investigated.

Researchers at ISAS expect electric propulsion (EP) to provide future opportunities for interplanetary missions, as well as lightweight orbit-transfer vehicles (OTV) for near-earth applications.

Activities in this area have focused on the research and development of several types of thrusters and on plasma diagnostics.

In 1995, the first space test of the MPD arcjet onboard the Space Flyer Unit (SFU) was completed. This test was aimed at verifying the propulsive function of the MPD thruster system.

Development of the DC arcjet has emphasized stable operation in a low power range of less than several hundred watts for application to OTV and satellite station keeping.

An ion-thruster developed at ISAS releases a microwave discharge to create plasma, making for a much simplified system in comparison to conventional cruising engines. This engine will be used for an asteroid sample return mission.

ISAS has been studying several concepts for deployable structures in space. A unique concept of a hingeless version of callable longeron extendable masts has been applied to support structures for scientific instruments and to structural members for deployable substructures such as flexible solar arrays.

A planar deployable two-dimensional array membrane structure has been tested onboard an SFU. An articulated extendable mast with high stiffness for the two-dimensional array has been modified for a deployable antenna onboard HALCA.

Concepts for intelligent adaptive structures and inflatable structures for future space systems continue to be studied.

Realtime operations of ISAS spacecraft are directed from the Sagamihara Control Center (SCC). Tracking data and telemetry are transmitted from the remote tracking stations, Usuda Deep Space Center (UDSC) and Kagoshima Space Center (KSC).

The UDSC 64 m (211.2 ft) station is dedicated to tracking deep space probes.

The KSC 20 m (66 ft) and 34 m (112.2 ft) stations are used for low-earth orbit (LEO) satellite tracking.

Orbit determinations for ISAS deep space probes are performed on a weekly basis. Antenna pointing and frequency predicts are transmitted to UDSC for tracking operations.

Commands are generated at SCC and transmitted to spacecraft through the remote tracking stations.

ISAS views the utilization of several aspects of the space environment in orbit as offering precious opportunities for new science and space systems. These aspects include microgravity, extreme vacuum, and high energy particle showers.

In support of these opportunities, ISAS conducts micro-G material processing, life science, and other studies using the space environment.

The Space Flyer Unit (SFU) is an unmanned, reusable space platform dedicated to these space experiments. The SFU has been launched and retrieved using Japan's H-II launch vehicle and the United States' space shuttle.

ISAS has performed seven experiments onboard an SFU, including the material experiment under micro-gravity (MEX), the space biology experiment (BIO); infrared telescope in space (IRTS); two-dimensionally deployable array experiment (2D Array); high voltage solar array experiment (HVSA); space plasma diagnostic package (SPDD); and the electric propulsion experiment (EPEX).

The solar power satellite (SPS) has been proposed to help solve the energy crisis and global environment problems. The SPS working group at ISAS has been conducting research programs for SPS 2000, an SPS Strawman design model which will be used to identify problem areas towards the realization of a practical SPS at the beginning of the next century.

Recent study has included experiments on the survivability of commercial solar cells in the space environment, the development of a new type of compact microwave antenna and amplifier element, system level testing with an electrical functional model, and demonstration of an automatic beam building system for the SPS 2000 truss.

Working group members have conducted field surveys of several equatorial countries receiving microwave power from SPS 2000 in orbit prior to the group's dissolve in 1997 after 10 years of research activity.

Since then, a new broader study group has formed, including researchers from fields outside the scope of space engineering. The new SPS group's mission has been finding realistic approaches to the development of an SPS pathfinder.

Rockets

ISAS has been involved in rocket development since the 1950s. It currently has five types of rockets which are launched from Kagoshima Space Center. One is a satellite launch vehicle, the M-V. There are four other types in the division of sounding rockets: SS-520, S-520, S-310, and MT-135. These rockets continue to support increasing demands in space science.

SATELLITE LAUNCH VEHICLES

ISAS satellite launch vehicles include L-4S, M-4S, M-3C, M-3H, M-3S, M-3SII, and M-V. The L-4S rocket weighed 9.4 tons with a payload capacity of 26 kg (57.3 lbs). The M-4S rocket weighed 43.6 tons with a payload capacity of 180 kg (397 lbs). The M-3C rocket weighed 41.6 tons with a payload capacity of 195 kg (430 lbs). The M-3H weighed 48.7 tons with a 300 kg (661 lbs) payload capacity. The M-3SII weighed 61 tons with a 770 kg (1697 lb) payload capacity, and the M-V which is currently used, weighs 139 tons with an 1800 kg (1.8 ton) payload capacity.

The L(Lambda)-4S rocket was the first rocket used by Japan to attempt to launch a satellite into earth orbit. It served as a demonstration vehicle for satellite insertion into orbit in advance of the Mu project. The L-4S was a four-stage, all-solid propellant system.

In attempting to send the first Japanese manmade satellite into orbit, ISAS faced a number of difficulties. Finally, during the fifth launch trial on February 11, 1970, they succeeded in injecting a 24 kg (53 lb) payload into an elliptical orbit around the earth, with an apogee of 5.140 km (3.19 miles) and a perigee of 350 km (217 miles).

Although the first satellite, OHSUMI, was relatively simple in nature, carrying only accelerometers and thermometers, it marked a significant achievement for the Japanese that would lead to other achievements in satellite launch and development.

SOUNDING ROCKETS

For more than 40 years, ISAS has been developing and launching sounding rockets. These rockets have been dedicated to astrophysical observation, upper atmosphere exploration, space plasma physics, and other types of scientific research. ISAS engineering studies have also been conducted to demonstrate new vehicle systems such as altitude control systems, reentry flight technologies, recovery systems, and new avionics. Microgravity studies are also conducted using sounding rockets for material research and life science.

The MT-135, S-310, S-520, and SS-520 are the current workhorses at ISAS for sounding rocket observations. The MT-135 has a total weight of 0.07 tons with a payload capacity of 6 kg (13 lbs). The S-310 weighs 0.7 tons with a payload capacity of 50 kg (110 lbs). The S-520 weighs 2.2 tons with a payload capacity of 95 and 150 kg (209 and 331 lbs). The SS-520 has a weigh of 2.6 tons with a 140 kg (309 lb) capacity.

ISAS has conducted launch campaigns with the S-310 and S-520 in Antarctica, as well as at the Andoya Rocket Range in Norway for in-situ measurement of Aurora phenomena near the North Pole. The agency plans to conduct an additional campaign on Spitsbergen Island, Norway, with the SS-520 for study of the magnetosphere above that site.

The MT-135 is a small rocket used primarily for sounding phenomena in the middle atmosphere where there is ozone layer depletion. It has been developed since 1963 jointly by ISAS with the University of Tokyo and the Meteorology Agency.

The MT-135 has been devoted to meteorological observations since its maiden flight in July 1964. Although initial flight trials proved to be unsuccessful, subsequent trials yielded success after a series of vehicle improvements. In April 1968, several flights were successfully carried out from Wallops Station, along with U.S. Archus sounding rockets for comparison.

A short time after, the new MT-135P was developed, featuring a motor case that was recoverable after separation using a parachute for maritime safety. The MT-135P is now launched from Ryori Meteorological Station at Sanriku, on a regular Wednesday schedule.

The propellant, consisting of a preformed grain, polyurethane composite with a low burning rate, is loaded and bonded in the case. The chamber is built up by welding tubes made of AISI 4340 steel. An outer edge

of the nozzle is welded to it. The throat insert material is made of graphite, and the exit cone is made of ablative silica-phenoolic FRP.

Each tail fin is a solid titanium plate. The magnesium-alloy tail cylinder is shaped into a boat tail in order to reduce drag during flight. At 95 seconds after liftoff, the rocket separates into a sonde, a nose cone, and a motor case. Seventeen seconds later, the sonde deploys its parachute to begin a slow descent. The sonde observes temperature, wind speed, and wind direction from approximately 60 km (37 mile) altitude, over a period of 90 minutes.

Observation data is reported to the WMO (World Meteorology Organization) and used for long-term meteorological forecasts.

The S-310 is a mid-sized rocket used for carrying a variety of payloads. It is a single-stage sounding rocket, 310 mm (12 in) in diameter, capable of reaching 200 km (124 miles) in altitude. Its predecessor, the S-300, was used for observations in Antarctica, whereas the S-10 reached a 160 km (100 mile) altitude during its first flight in the fall of 1966.

Two out of three flights experienced body trouble, which was later attributed to an unusual increase in the angle of attack due to pitch-roll resonance.

The S-310 spins positively in the atmosphere in order to overcome resonance, avoiding such problems. It also corrects for altitude disturbance by aerodynamic damping. Spin is provided by twisted tail fins which cause 2.8 Hz spin to the body.

Thrust programming has been designed to peak in the early stage, while keeping the thrust level low in the latter half of burning time when aerodynamic forces increase dramatically. With this capability, increased summit altitude is attained, relieving aerodynamic heating by reducing dynamic pressure.

The S-310 chamber is made of AISI 4340 steel. The CTPB composite propellant is single with two axially different wagon-wheel port configurations. A dual-thrust profile is provided since the aftward position of the grain is consumed earlier. Each tail fin is made of a solid titanium plate, and the nose cone is made of FRP.

A yo-yo despinner system in the payload bay is actuated at 50 seconds after liftoff to reduce the spin to one Hz during the observation period.

The first flight of S-310 in January 1975, was successful. Flights continue from Kagoshima Space Center at Uchinoura and Showa Base in Antarctica.

The S-520 is a powerful single-stage rocket optionally equipped with three-axis altitude control and a recovery system. It has a capacity for launching a 100 kg (220 lb) payload above 300 km (18.6 miles) and provides more than five minutes for micro-gravity flight environments.

The S-520 was developed as a replacement for the K-9M and K-10 sounding rockets. It succeeded in doubling the payload capability of the K-9M by applying the use of a high-performance propellant, optimum thrust program, and lightweight structure.

Since its first flight in 1980, the S-520 has proven to be substantially reliable with its simplified flight operation, without the use of staging, settlement of impact-related maritime safety, and providing reduction of launch costs.

The HTPB composite propellant grain is cast and molded in the case similar to the way it was done in the first stage of Mu launch vehicles. The propellant grain is single, giving a dual-thrust profile similar to the S-310s. The forward portion of the grain has a seven pointed gear configuration, providing an initial period of high thrust while the aftward portion, in a simple tubular design, sustains a lower thrust level period.

The nozzle, having an initial expansion ratio of eight to one, is designed to improve the effective specific impulse. The chamber is made of high tensile steel HT-140. The leading edge of the tail fin is made of titanium alloy for weight saving and heat resistance. The fin body is composed of an aluminum honeycomb sandwich plate with GFRP/CFRP (Glass Fiber-Reinforced Plastics/Carbon Fiber-Reinforced Plastics) laminated surface plates.

The nose fairing, made of GFRP, is used to store scientific instruments. Common instruments are stored in the parallel section. An altitude control module or recovery module can be put into the part between the common instruments and the rocket motor as an alternative option.

The SS-520 is a two-stage rocket with a first stage coming from the main booster of the S-520. It has a capacity for launching a 140 kg (309 lb) payload to an altitude of close to 1,000 km (621 miles).

The SS-520 was designed to carry out technological experiments concerning the development of a mini-satellite launch vehicle by adding the third stage on top. The first stage of the rocket is aerodynamically stabilized by use of tail fins similar to those in the S-520.

The second stage is heavier than the head of the S-520, which means the aerodynamic margin is secured more than it has been previously. The entire motor case of the second stage is made of CFRP.

The spin generated in the first stage is succeeded by the second stage. It is utilized in the Rhumb-line control and spin stabilization.

The first flight of the SS-520 occurred in January 1998. In the future, ISAS plans to launch it from Spitsbergen, Norway, to send a payload into the cusp region of the geomagnetosphere.

The ISAS sounding rocket experiments were carried out during the periods of August through September 1996, January through February 1997, August through September 1997, and January through February 1998. Fourteen sounding rockets were launched during these periods, including four MT-135s, three S-310s, two S-520, one SS-520, and four Viper 3A rockets.

As part of an ISAS meteorological study, a series of MT-135 rockets were launched to measure vertical profiles of stratospheric ozone between 18 and 54 km (11 and 34 miles) over Uchinoura, Japan. The ozone sensor consisted of four filter photometers for measuring the solar attenuation in the middle ultraviolet wavelengths during the slow descent of the payload by parachute.

The flights also provided ozone density, temperature, and horizontal wind measurements. The flights have been carried out since 1990 to study the long-term variation of stratospheric ozone density during the August through September season when the stratospheric ozone profile is stable. Estimated accuracy was close to three percent. Results of the twelve flights conducted from 1990 to 1997 revealed a small negative variation between 40 and 45 km (25 and 28 miles). Observed zone profiles were also used for comparison and validation of satellite and ground-based observations.

On January 25, 1998, a coordinated ozone campaign was conducted in order to study chemical and dynamic processes of ozone up to heights of 90 km (56 miles). The campaign commenced with a balloon launch to measure the ozone density up to heights of 42 km (26 miles) after which two U.S.-made Viper-3A rockets were launched in order to measure the neutral wind in the height range of 80 to 100 km (50 to 62 miles) by using chaff. The chaff was not tracked, although a rough wind profile was obtained by using MF radar.

Shortly thereafter, a sounding rocket S-310-28 was launched to measure the ozone density and the relevant atmospheric quantities. Ground-based facilities such as MU radar of Kyoto University, MF radar or Communication Research Laboratory, and other imagers and radiometers for 630 nm, 1380 nm, and 557.7 nm were operated at Kyoto, Yamagawa, and Uchinoura.

Two mm-wavelength heterodyne receivers were utilized in order to get the height distribution of ozone at two sites, Nagoya and Tuskuba, yielding data for analysis.

On January 14, 1997, a foil chaff experiment was conducted at Uchinoura by launching two Viper-3A rockets. The winds observed at the 80 to 100 km (50 to 62 mile) altitudes showed temporal variation of atmospheric waves, while contributing to the validation of wind estimation of the Yamagawa MF radar, located 50 km (31 miles) west of Uchinoura involving the MU radar, 600 km (373 miles) east.

In late August 1996, a rocket/radar/optics campaign called SEEK (Sporadic-E Experiment over Kyushu) was conducted in Kyushu, Japan. SEEK was designed to investigate the mechanism for the generation of quasi-periodic (QP) radar back-scatter from field-aligned irregularities imbedded in nighttime sporadic-E (Es) layers.

SEEK's purpose was to determine in-situ small-scale electrodynamic properties using two sounding rockets and large-scale dynamics, as well as electrodynamics using ground-based sensors. These included various radio and optical instruments deployed in the vicinity of the rocket range.

The sounding rockets, S-310-25 and S-310-26, were launched into the Es layers when the transportable radar detected intense QP echoes. The Es layers were observed to exist in a convergent wind shear region where large electric fields were induced and when active atmospheric gravity waves existed in the mesosphere. However, very little evidence was revealed which positively supported the hypothesis that Es layers were deeply modulated in altitude.

Meteorological observations of wind, temperature, and altitude in the stratosphere and lower mesosphere were carried out by MT-135P rockets during 1996 and 1997 by the Japan Meteorological Agency at the Ryori Meteorological Rocket Observation Station. During this period, thirty rockets were launched each year. Observation data obtained was reported to the World Data Center A (WDC-A) in the United States.

ISAS has used the SS-520 to perform remote sensing of the plasmasphere and magnetosphere from SS-520-1. The SS-520 is a two-stage sounding rocket which was developed in order to meet three objectives — to study the high-altitude ionosphere and the low-altitude magnetosphere, to conduct engineering experiments with high velocities, and to launch an ultra-small satellite with an addition of an upper-stage motor.

The SS-520 was successfully launched on February 5, 1998. It achieved several results, including the discovery of neutral hydrogen atoms over an energy range of 5 to 25 keV at low latitudes by the Energetic Neutral Atom (ENA) instrument, which had been developed to measure faint fluxes of energetic neutral atoms unambiguously under intense noise fluxes of charged ions and photons. The Extreme ultra-violet Plasma Scanner (EPS) observed the resonance scattered 30.4 nm He-

II emission from the plasmasphere, contributing to the study of the structure of the plasmasphere. Also, Lyman Alpha Photometers (LAP), with a hydrogen absorption cell and hydrogen/deuterium absorption cells, successfully measured hydrogen and deuterium lyman alpha intensities of the geocorona as well as the interstellar wind component.

On December 4, 2000, the SS-520-2 rocket was launched from SvalRak (Ny Olsen), Norway, with the ground-based European incoherent scatter radar (EISCAT), a rocket experiment to target cusp position. Cusp refers to the region where ionic heating occurs in the magnetosphere. The area referred to as the polar cusp is the place which is connected with the daytime-side magnetosphere boundary with respect to the magnetism, where the energy of the solar wind plasma pours directly into the upper atmosphere.

Research experiments in the past have revealed that the most likely cause of ionic heating is electrostatic wave motion energized by electric current drive-type plasma instability. However, time and space variations of this phenomenon have proven to be very drastic, therefore, this detail has yet to be confirmed from actual observation results.

EISCAT revealed that there is ion loss from an altitude of several hundred km near the polar cusp. Telemetry reception for the experiment was conducted in three locations — Ny Olsen, Longyearbyen, and Andoya — yielding excellent data. By monitoring EISCAT radar data in realtime, along with solar wind plasma and interplanetary magnetic fields by ACE satellite, it was confirmed that the SS-520-2 rocket actually flew above the cusp.

On January 31, 1998, the XUV Doppler Telescope was successfully launched to observe the XUV sun along with the velocity fields of the two MK solar corona. The telescope was equipped with a Casse-grain multi-layer optics device with an X-ray CCD camera. It was designed with a field-of-view of 45 arcmin, enabling it to cover the entire sun.

Objectives of the XUV mission were to obtain single temperature (1.8 MK) X-ray images of the sun by isolating the specific emission line (Fe XIV line) and to obtain the Dopplegram of the solar corona with two normal incidence telescopes with peak wavelengths slightly shifted toward red and blue from the line. When the line moved between the blue and red windows of the multi-layer mirrors due to the motion of the plasma, the velocity of the map of the 1.8 MK plasma was obtained by subtracting the blue from the red images.

Key technologies employed by the telescope have included a high wavelength-resolution XUV multi-layer optics with an He-II (304) light trap, a tip-tilt secondary mirror to stabilize the X-ray images with accuracy of five arcsec for wide altitude excursion of the rocket body with about 0.5 degrees around the sun, a 512 by 512 X-ray camera, and a semiconductor image recorder located in the reentry capsule.

The XUV Doppler Telescope has thus far yielded very high-quality pure 1.8 MK images of the sun for the first time, leading to extensive analysis of data to detect a high speed associated with reconnection.

National Space Development Agency of Japan (NASDA)

NASDA, the National Space Development Agency of Japan, was established in 1969 to promote Japan's development and utilization of space for peaceful purposes.

The agency develops and launches vehicles and satellites, and also conducts research and experiments on using the space environment while continuing to develop technology for space equipment.

In addition to heavy emphasis on its current launch vehicle, the H-IIA, Japan has also become active in participation with the International Space Station. The country has been developing its experimental module, Kibo, to house research experiments in space.

Japan has a team of astronauts who have participated on the U.S. space shuttle in cooperation with NASA.

The country has also recently developed a variety of space instruments, including a nickel-metal hydride (Ni-MH) battery, which has a longer life and is friendlier to the environment than nickel-cadmium batteries; a 64-bit microprocessing unit (MPU) that enables the production of high-performance, low-cost parts for spacecraft and other space devices; and a packet data transfer component (TDSL) with a data transfer capacity more than 20 times higher than existing systems with a very low weight of just 105 grams (0.37 ounces), 1/2000 the size of these.

NASDA has three main exhibit halls that are open to the public and its installations, much like NASA. These include the Earth Observation Center Exhibition Hall at Ohashi, Hatoyüma-machi, where visitors can experience new aspects of earth as they have never done so before by seeing its images observed by earth observation satellites; the Space Exhibition Hall at Tanegashima Space Center (TNSC), Kumage-gun, Kagoshima, NASDA's largest exhibition facility, displaying launch vehicle technology, a full-scale model of Kibo, and lunar or planetary exploration presentations; and the Exhibition Hall at the Tsukuba Space Center (TKSC), Tsukuba City, Ibaraki, where visitors can study and observe full-scale satellites which were produced for development tests, and another full-scale model of Kibo, the Japanese experiment module for the International Space Station.

Satellites

Over the years, NASDA has been engaged in a number of satellite programs in order to meet a wide range of objectives. Himawari Geostationary Meteorological Satellites (GMS) were a series of satellites designed for weather forecasting. Observation began in 1978, with the latest active model being Himawari No. 5.

The GMS satellites have performed in a geostationary orbit at 140 east longitude, monitoring weather conditions in one link with World Weather Watch sponsored by the World Meteorological Organizations. Observation data has consisted of cloud distribution pictures sent from these satellites for use in many fields, including television and newspaper weather forecasts.

The first GMS satellite was launched July 14, 1977, aboard a Delta launch vehicle from Kennedy Space Center (KSC) in the United States. GMS-2 was launched from Tanegashima Space Center on August 11, 1981, followed by GMS-3 and GMS-4. GMS-5 was launched in 1995.

The Ajisai Experimental Geodetic Satellite (EGS), launched on August 13, 1986, contributed to more accurate mapping capability by utilizing triangular geodetic measurement connecting the space and earth by reflecting sun light. The primary short-range objective of EGS was to test NASDA's H-1, a two-stage launch vehicle, in placing satellites into orbit.

EGS weighed 685 kg (1510 lb) and was equipped with solar ray and laser beam reflectors.

The Midori Advanced Earth Observing Satellite (ADEOS) was the first Japanese large-scale earth observation satellite to acquire global-scale observation data. It was launched by an H-II launch vehicle on August 1996.

ADEOS was designed for monitoring global environmental changes such as maritime meteorological conditions, atmospheric ozone, and gases that promote global warming. It provided a large volume of data containing valuable information on our environment atmosphere, ocean, and land for close to 10 months, until it suddenly lost control on June 30, 1997, due to the structural damage suffered in its solar array panel.

ADEOS included a variety of instruments for consolidated continuous measurement of land, sea and air, including AVNIR (Advanced Visible Near Infrared Radiometer) and OCTS (Ocean Color and Temperature Scanner), both of which were developed by NASA; six kinds of AO (Advanced Observation) sensors, including NSCAT (NASA Scatterometer) and TOMS (Total Ozone Mapping Spectrometer), also from NASA; POLDER (Polarization and Directionality of the Earth's Reflectances), a geosurface reflection measuring device from CNES; IMG (Interferometric Monitor for Greenhouse Gases), a sensor for measuring the greenhouse effect from the Ministry of International Trade and Industry; ILAS (Improved Limb Atmospheric Spectrometer), an improved spectrometer for measuring infrared radiation on the edge of the atmosphere; and RIS (Retroreflector in Space), a retroreflector for measuring laser long light-path absorption between the earth and satellites.

Tropical Rainfall Measuring Mission (TRMM) was a satellite to measure precipitation in tropical areas that was developed as collaborative mission between Japan and the United States. TRMM was launched November 1997, and marked its fifth anniversary in 2002. It was the first space mission dedicated to measuring tropical and subtropical rainfall from space using multi sensors simultaneously.

TRMM included the first spaceborne rain radar, developed by NASDA and the Communication Research Laboratory (CRL), and four other sensors developed by NASA. It was launched by an H-II rocket from NASDA's Tanegashima Space Center and placed in a non-sun-synchronous orbit in order to increase observation over the tropics and vary the satellite local observation time.

Following the successful launch of TRMM, a number of scientific results, such as observations of the three-dimensional structure of rainfall within typhoon clouds and abrupt termination of El Nino, as well as the subsequent development of La Nina, in the early summer of 1998, were fulfilled.

The satellite continues to perform well, and is expected to further contribute to scientific research.

AQUA/AMSR-E Earth Observation System PM is a joint project of the earth observation satellite with the participation of the United States, Japan, and Brazil. The satellite has been acquiring atmospheric and marine data from the space to study water and energy circulation mechanisms on the earth. Aqua will also enable the regular collection of data from broader areas on the earth, especially in the middle of the oceans where it is difficult to set up observation stations, by measuring the earth from the space. This data will be provided to the Japan Meteorological Agency to improve the accuracy of weather forecasts, such as movement of typhoon and cold and warm fronts, and to the Fishery Information Service Center to inform fishing boats of real-time fishing spot conditions.

Japan has the world's largest measuring sensor onboard the satellite, called the Advanced Microwave Scanning Radiometer for EOS (AMSR-E), a microwave radiometer for the observation of geophysical parameters primarily relevant to water on the earth.

It has opened new pages of global map geophysical parameters, which have shown the spatial and temporal change in visualized global mapping. With AMSR-E and AMSR radio sensors, AQUA has been able to measure faint radio waves radiated from the earth's surface and atmosphere by themselves with multiple frequency bands precisely in order to help in the understanding of global water circulation.

MDS-1, the Tsubasa Mission Demonstration Test Satellite-1, is a satellite to verify technologies needed in space in relation to three key objectives — making it faster, less expensive, and more reliable. The satellite was launched February 2002, in order to verify the function of commercial parts in orbit, minimize the use of technology for components, and to measure space environment data such as radiation.

The Kodama Data Relay Test Satellite (DRTS) is a satellite that is currently relaying large volumes of earth observation data. It was launched from an H-IIA rocket at Tanegashima Space Center and will continue to conduct in-orbit demonstration tests to improve existing satellites' data relay functions and performance. It will also expand the data relay area in order to meet the upcoming high level application requirements from spacecrafts.

MIDORI II, the Advanced Earth Observing Satellite II, also known as ADEOS-II, was launched on December 14, 2002. It is a satellite which is expected to take over ADEO's observation mission of monitoring the frequent climate changes occurring in the world, as well as the expansion of ozone holes and global environmental changes and their causes.

The satellite's primary objective is to collect the necessary data for clarifying changes in water and energy circulations, carbon circulation, and ozone in the stratosphere. These data are important for elucidating the mechanisms of global environment changes. In order to achieve this objective, ADEOS-II was equipped with five sensors, including the Advanced Microwave Scanning Radiometer (AMSR) and Global Imager (GLI), which were developed by NASDA. The other three include the Improved Limb Atmospheric Spectrometer — II (ILAS-II) of the Ministry of Environment of Japan, SeaWinds of NASA's Jet Propulsion Laboratory (JPL), and Polarization and Directionality of the Earth's Reflectances (POLDER) of the Center National d'Etudes Spatiales (CNES).

The Advanced Microwave Scanning Radiometer (AMSR) is a sensor that can detect faint microwave natural emissions from the earth's surface and atmosphere. It can observe various types of physical volumes of water (H_2O) such as water vapor distribution on the earth, precipitation, ocean surface temperature, ocean wind velocity, and sea ice concentration. The observation can occur both during day and night hours.

The Global Imager (GLI) is a sensor to acquire the whole global image of solar radiation and infrared light reflected by land, ocean, and clouds. It can measure physical volume of chlorophyll concentration, organic substance, vegetation index and biomass, as well as cloud and ice distributions.

The Improved Limb Atmospheric Spectrometer-II (ILAS-II) is an atmospheric sensor developed by the Ministry of Environment of Japan to monitor and study ozone layers in the stratosphere over the North and South poles. Through continuous measurement of the atmospheric species in the stratosphere, ILAS-II will provide new information on the physical and scientific mechanism of ozone layer depletion, while verifying the effectiveness of counter-measures against depletion, such as the regulation of the use of freon.

SeaWind is a sensor to observe wind direction and velocity over the ocean on a daily basis with a very high degree of accuracy. By performing continuous measurement for a prolonged period of time, SeaWind will contribute to the understanding of the interaction between the atmosphere and ocean, while clarifying the global-scale meteorological system. It will also help contribute to improving

the accuracy of weather forecasts all over the world, and in the tracking of typhoons.

The Polarization and Directionality of the Earth's Reflectances (POLDER) is a sensor to measure polarization, directionality and spectral characteristics of solar radiation reflected by the earth's surface, aerosol in the atmosphere, clouds and oceans. POLDER will send commands to six data collection systems (DCS), such as buoys deployed in the ocean, to make them go under water and rise up to collect observation data such as water temperature, and transmit them to the ground, thus allowing on-the-spot measurement without human presence.

The Advanced Land Observing Satellite (ALOS) is currently under development. It will be one of the world's largest earth observation satellites and is expected to contribute to disaster monitoring and resource surveying as well as mapping and precise land coverage observation.

I-Space

Optical-fiber networks, CATV, the Internet, and digital satellite broadcasting are advanced information technologies (ITS) which continue to bring greater comfort and convenience to our daily lives. With this in mind, making use of "space infrastructure" consisting of several satellites orbiting the earth at an altitude of 36,000 km (21,600 miles) will enable a high-speed transmission of a large amount of data to Japan and the entire Asia-Pacific region. This NASDA space project to establish advanced space infrastructure has been named I-Space.

Advantages of space infrastructure include disaster prediction, quick rescue and recovery in national land management and disaster monitoring; narrowing the IT gap within the Asia-Pacific region as part of the resolution for digital divide; building a safe and convenient network for land, sea, and air transport in Intelligent Transport Systems (ITS); bringing a variety of real topics into classrooms enhancing education and research; and improving quality of life for everyone.

I-Space was designed to explore new and attractive applications while identifying key technologies to build an advanced space communications infrastructure. As part of the program, a number of pilot experiments have been conducted since 2001 on existing commercial satellites.

Pilot experiments serve as a testing base for the necessary applications, key technologies, and practicability of developing satellites. Experiments are conducted with existing satellites, with the experimental results applied to satellite design and future application experiments.

Application experiments are conducted with engineering test satellites (ETS) or wideband internetworking engineering test and demonstration satellites (WINDS). These experiments help to verify the feasibility of future satellite utilizations and serve as a bridge towards practical services.

In the area of national land management and disaster monitoring, I-Space will prove instrumental in creating a disaster information network. It will be integrated around a database of information gathered from disaster sites and earth-observation satellites. The network will provide vital information to rescuers and relief workers.

The space infrastructure has proven to be largely immune to natural disasters and terrorist attacks. It can facilitate information gathering and damage assessment to make prompt and necessary responses.

Image data from earth observation will enhance terrestrial photos taken from helicopters, aircraft, and vehicles, providing central monitoring of every inch of land for fissures and other irregularities.

The ETS will allow bi-directional video transmission with a small, portable terminal. By means of remote learning, students in a classroom will be able to fully experience the dynamic ambience of remote fields. Researchers on remote islands or in the mountains will be able to easily exchange academic data with their peers.

WINDS will provide high-speed transmissions, enabling multi-point teleconferencing and simultaneous transmission of research data to multiple locations. It will also allow the transmission of video images and research data anytime, anywhere, which will significantly promote communications among researchers, educators, and students, increasing efficiency in education and research.

The WINDS satellite will be able to provide a high-quality Internet connection using a small dish of only 45 cm (18 in) in diameter. This will enable users to access the Internet at any time or place by means of wireless communications at speeds comparable to typical ADSL services currently available in urban areas. This will enable easier transmission of local information online in rural areas and help to narrow the digital gap between cities and lower populated areas.

A major goal of I-Space is to build a comprehensive intelligent transport system (ITS) for land, sea and air, integrating the elements of transport with the latest satellite and communication technologies. The electronic toll collection (ETC) system will be extended to handle all kinds of cashless shopping on the move.

Advances in the ITS navigation system may lead to automatic driving, creating a safer and more comfortable traffic environment. Sophisticated use of positioning data will help streamline traffic and logistics, and satellite-based communications will enable fast Internet access from cars, trains, ships, and aircraft.

Through I-Space, NASDA will establish mobile healthcare, a system for providing quality medical services anytime, anywhere. They intend to accomplish this by two different approaches. The first will be to ensure preventative medical care using the mobile hospital, which will be equipped with satellite communications to assist in the performing of medical examinations in "medical divide." While conducting medical checkups, the field staff will be able to consult with doctors in urban hospitals via satellites.

The second approach will focus on in-home care and emergency medicine called mobile telemedicine, which will provide a briefcase-sized, satellite terminal to doctors or nurses who are making house calls or rushing to the scene of an accident, so they can consult with specialists in urban hospitals via satellite while examining patients. These types of mobile healthcare may significantly reduce medical costs while improving the patients' quality of life.

Three satellites will comprise I-Space, including the ETS-VIII, WINDS, and the Quasi-Zenith satellite system.

NASDA's ETS-VIII follows its previous satellite bus/mission satellites ETS-I through ETS-VII.

ETS-VIII will be one of the largest geostationary S-band satellites in the world and is currently under development. It will conduct several in-orbit experiments in Japan and surrounding areas to verify mobile satellite communications functions while making use of a small satellite handset similar to a mobile phone.

ETS-VIII is expected to add to the efficiency of communications, broadcasting, and global positioning. An example of this will be the provision of quick and accurate directions given to an emergency vehicle by transmitting traffic control information via satellite in the event of a disaster.

WINDS will be a geostationary S-band communications satellite providing ultra-high-speed data communications. It will provide wider coverage, broadcasting capability, and immunity to terrestrial disasters to Japan as well as Asia-Pacific regions.

The satellite will carry high-gain antennas and a high-speed asynchronous transfer mode (ATM) switch to enable fast Internet access for households equipped with a small dish antenna.

The Quasi-Zenith satellite system will consist of at least three identical satellites, configured to allow at least one of them to remain positioned at a higher elevation angle near Japan's zenith.

With the system, RF transmission will not be obstructed by tall buildings or mountains. One of the satellites will remain near zenith over Japan at all times. Problems such as RF connection loss or signal degradation caused by building blockage, multiple paths and rainfall will occur less frequently, increasing reliability for mobile data communication and broadcasting.

Japanese Experiment Module (JEM) "Kibo"

Japan is among 15 countries participating in the International Space Station (ISS), including Russia, Canada, the United States, and 11 European nations. Six laboratories have been scheduled to be put into operation, including Japan's Kibo.

As Japan's first manned facility in space, Kibo is expected to remain in service for many years. It has passed through the testing stage and will soon enter the final stage of development.

Japanese astronauts have been busy training to work on the laboratory which, in the microgravity of space, will provide an excellent environment for experiments and research in the natural sciences. It will also expand the value of space as a creative venue for education, the arts, and business.

At 400 kilometers (240 miles) above the earth, ISS will provide a space environment with many features not found on the earth's surface, including microgravity, a high vacuum, excellent visibility, and cosmic rays. The Japanese experiment module (JEM) will be one of the experimental modules that will be attached to the ISS.

Also known as Kibo, JEM will have equipment that can be used both inside and outside the module. The pressurized module will have the same constant air pressure (one atm), humidity and temperature as a laboratory on earth. Kibo will be manned by astronauts in regular clothing.

Kibo's exposed facility will be unique among the ISS's modules, serving as the staging area for long-term space experiments as well as earth and astronomical observations.

Kibo will contain the Superconducting SubMillimeter-wave Limb Emission Sounder (SMILES) to make space-based observations of short waves (submillimeter waves) emitted in the stratosphere not only by ozone, but by trace gases such as chlorine and bromine that are destroying the ozone layer.

Since space offers an excellent 360-degree viewing environment for making observations without interference from the atmosphere, the Monitor of All Sky X-Ray Image (MAXI) will be mounted on Kibo to make X-ray observations of space, to examine the phenomena beyond our galaxy and map the distribution of the galaxies.

MAXI will be the world's largest wide-angle camera that will also be used to solve the questions of evolution as well as the origin and structure of the universe.

With Kibo, it will be possible to perform microgravity experiments by growing large single crystals, or by mixing two substances that have never been mixed on earth.

Kibo's crystal growth equipment will enable the production of larger, protein crystals than can be obtained on earth, which will help scientists develop new medicines and understand disease mechanisms.

Experiments conducted in the lab's advanced furnace for microgravity experiments with X-ray radiography (AFEX) will lead to the development of new materials such as innovative alloys and superpure semiconductors.

In anticipation of an age of long-term residence in space, the study of the effects in the space environment, such as microgravity and radiation on plants, animals, and humans, becomes critical.

The cell cultivation equipment on Kibo will be used to study the basic phenomena of life in space using the cells of plants, animals, and microorganisms.

Kibo's exposed facility platform will house space-based experiments for future technology development in robots, communications, and energy.

The Space Environment Data Acquisition Equipment-Attached Payload (SEDA-AP) will be used aboard Kibo to measure phenomena in space such as plasma and radiation. The results will then be used for technological development and experiments. This research will allow continued progress on the development of optical communications technology that will be able to transmit high-density images and massive amounts of experimental data to earth in an instant.

JEM will consist of seven major instruments, including the experiment logistics module pressurized section; the pressurized module; the experiment logistics module exposed section (palette); the remote manipulator system robotic arms; the exposed facility (platform); the air lock; and the inter-orbit communication system (ICS).

The experiment logistics module pressurized section will be used to store experiment materials and will be kept at the same air pressure as on earth. Kibo will have a special storage room capable of holding up to eight racks which can be taken to the lab when necessary.

The pressurized module will serve as the main facility of Kibo where the microgravity conditions of space will be utilized for a variety of experiments. This module's 23 racks will include 11 on the ceiling, floor, and side walls for devices needed for Kibo's operation, including electricity, air conditioning, communications, and robotic arm manipulation equipment.

The remaining 12 racks, including two in the storage room, will be for experiments. Two windows on the platform side will allow the astronauts to check the conditions outside the module which can accommodate up to four people.

The experiment logistics module exposed section (palette) will be used to store up to three experimental apparatuses on the exposed facility. It will be removable from the main module and can be transported by the space shuttle back to earth after experiments. Robotic arms will be used to move the equipment from the palette to the platform.

The remote manipulator system (robotic arms) will consist of two six-jointed robotic arms that astronauts will manipulate from inside the module to operate test equipment for outside experiments.

The main arm will be used for moving large equipment. The small fine arm will be used for more delicate operations and can be attached to the main arm.

The exposed facility (platform) will be used to conduct experiments with direct exposure to space. It will be a high vacuum environment with a wide field of view that will provide an excellent environment for earth and astronomical observations as well as for developing space technology.

The platform will come with power generations and cooling functions along with 10 apparatuses to perform experiments. It will be transported to space by the U.S. space shuttle and Japanese H-IIA rockets and then placed in position by Kibo's robotic arms.

The air lock will serve as a passageway for objects to be moved between the interior and exterior of Kibo.

The inter-orbit communication system (ICS) will be a two-way communication system linking Kibo with the Tsukuba Space Center via the Kodama data delay test satellite. Data will be transmitted at a rate of 50 Mbps and received at three Mbps.

Astronauts who will work aboard Kibo have been training at NASDA's Tsukuba Space Center, where there are actual scale models of Kibo's pressurized module, experiment logistics module pressurized section, remote manipulator system, and air-lock.

This training will help prepare the astronauts to perform experiments, communicate with ground stations, operate the equipment, and take immediate action in emergency situations.

Using a huge water tank at the center, astronauts have been simulating weightlessness as practice for extravehicular activity (EVA) from Kibo.

Rocket Launch Vehicles

Over the years, NASDA has developed a wide variety of its own rocket launch vehicles. These have included the N-I, N-II, H-I, J-I; experimental vehicles such as the Automatic Landing Flight Experiment (ALFEX), High Speed Flight Demonstrator (HSFD), the GX; the H-II, and H-IIA.

The H-II became the first 100 percent made-in Japan liquid oxygen and hydrogen launch vehicle. Up until its development, Japan had established a long history of building large-sized vehicles and implementing satellite launches with American technological assistance.

The H-II was capable of launching a two-ton geostationary satellite into orbit. However, its LE-7 engine proved to be problematic, resulting in the postponement of the flight for two years, until it was successfully launched in February 1994.

Unfortunately, after five consecutive launches of H-II without incident, the rocket suffered two subsequent failures, ending operations.

NASDA rebounded from this disappointment with the H-IIA, incorporating enhanced features and increased reliability.

N-I, N-II

The N-I was a three-stage launch vehicle based on imported technology from the United States Delta rocket.

It was used during seven launches from 1975 to 1982 for launching experiments, communications, broadcasting, meteorological and earth observation satellites.

The N-I had an overall length of 32.57 m (107.5 ft), weighed 90.4 tons, and operated by means of a radio guidance system.

The N-II was a three-stage follow-up vehicle to the N-I, which was also based on imported technology from the United States Delta rockets. It was also used for launching experiments, communications, broadcasting, meteorological, and earth observation satellites.

The N-II made a total of eight launches between 1981 and 1987. It had an overall length of 35.36 m (116.7 ft), a total weight of 135.2 tons, and operated by means of an inertial guidance system.

H-I, J-I

The H-I was a three-stage launch vehicle used for launching up to a 550 kg (1210 lb) payload into orbit. Its first stage and strap-on boosters were identical to those of the N-I. The second-stage engine, LE-5, and propellant, as well as the third stage solid propellant rocket motor and inertial guidance system were all direct Japanese technology.

The H-I made nine successful launches from 1986 to 1991. The rocket was 40.30 m (133 ft) in length, weighed 139.3 tons, and utilized an inertial guidance system.

The J-I was a project vehicle initiated as a three-stage solid propellant launcher for smaller satellites. It was designed with the ability to launch a one-ton satellite into low earth orbit (LEO).

The J-I was incorporated with the solid rocket booster (SRB) of the H-II developed by NASDA, and the upper stage of the M-35 II rocket developed by the Institute of Space and Aeronautical Science (ISAS).

Development on the J-I was suspended, pending design re-evaluation, in December 2001.

EXPERIMENTAL VEHICLES

The purpose of the Automatic Landing Flight Experiment (ALFLEX) was to establish the basic technology for automatic landing of the proposed HOPE spaceplane.

It was designed to return and land experiments from space as a part continued research into the development of orbiting planes like HOPE.

In this experiment, a test vehicle of the HOPE configuration was released from a helicopter traveling at a high altitude. Following the release, the test vehicle captured the approach path, landing automatically on the runway.

ALFLEX was successfully conducted 13 times between July and August of 1996.

ALFLEX weighed 760 kg (1672 lb) and had a length of 6.10 m (20.1 ft), with a span of 3.78 m (12.5 ft).

HYFLEX, or hypersonic flight experiment, was another flight test of future HOPE technology in testing orbital planes. It was designed to provide experience to the Japanese in the design, manufacture, and flight operation of a hypersonic lifting vehicle, as well as to record flight data in the hypersonic speed range.

The surface of HYFLEX was covered with double carbon, ceramic tiles, and flexible insulator, comparable with the proposed HOPE design.

The HYFLEX utilized a system with temperature and pressure sensors as well as reflectometers.

It was launched by a J-I launch vehicle in February 1996, and collected useful data while in flight before splashdown into the ocean. However, it was not successfully recovered.

The Orbital Re-entry Experiment (OREX), also called Ryusei, was a launch project the Japanese used to establish their initial research into the prospects of developing an orbital plane.

In February 1994, the OREX vehicle was launched and inserted into orbit by an H-II rocket. The vehicle collected experimental data during re-entry, transmitted after re-entry, and then splashed down in the Central Pacific Ocean.

There were several objectives of OREX in relation to acquiring data related to atmospheric re-entry, including aerodynamic heating data during re-entry; heat-resistant structural data during re-entry; communications blackout data during re-entry; and GPS navigation data during re-entry and in orbit.

The OREX vehicle had a blunt-cone shape. The vehicle's front, which was subjected to aerodynamic heating during re-entry, was constructed of double carbon material and ceramic tiles.

Still under development is the GX launch vehicle, a mid-size, two-stage liquid launch rocket to be operated by Galaxy Express Corporation, a conglomerate of private space and aeronautical launch companies.

A full-scale model of the GX's LOX (liquid oxygen) composite cryogenic tank will be tested before 2005.

The second stage engine will be loaded with a liquid natural gas (LNG) propellant, the first of its kind in the world. LNG is considered relatively expensive, and is most commonly known for its use as utility gas, but it also has potential power that is equivalent to liquid hydrogen.

The HSFD project, or high speed flight demonstrator, was established in an effort to test safe, reliable transportation systems for access to space. HSFD has been undergoing tests since 2002. It was designed to acquire data during the transonic flight phase that will help to refine system design tools and methodologies for controlling flight of re-entry vehicles with limited handling qualities.

The second phase, or HSFD 2, will be performed in cooperation with the French space agency, CNES. In early June 2003, several stratospheric balloon flights from the Kiruna launch base in Sweden commenced in order to perform drop tests from an altitude of 30 km (18 mi) on a flight prototype developed by Japan's National Aerospace Laboratory (NAL) and NASDA.

The flight prototype was a 500 kg (1100 lb) quarter-scale model of NASDA's Hope plane. Tests required the prototype to be released in free fall with analysis focusing on the transonic flight phase between 10 and 20 km (6 and 12 miles), at which time it reached a speed of Mach 1. The flights ended with soft parachute landings cushioned by air bags.

H-II, H-IIA

The H-II launch vehicle is the primary workhorse of Japan's space program, with the capability to launch a two-ton class satellite into geostationary orbit. It is a two-stage rocket that was entirely developed with Japanese technology. The H-II was also designed to launch payloads into low and medium-altitude orbits, and for an even greater economy, the rocket can simultaneously launch two geostationary satellites weighing about one ton each.

The first stage of the H-II has a large, high-performance liquid oxygen/liquid hydrogen engine known as the LE-7. The LE-7 was newly developed for the H-II launch vehicle and offers propulsion of approximately 110 tons in a vacuum. The H-II second stage uses the LE-5A engine which is a reignitable engine offering higher performance and reliability than the LE-5 engine developed for the H-I launch vehicle. The guidance system of this engine employs an inertial guidance method.

Since 1994, there were a total of seven successful H-II launches. In 1998 there was the unsuccessful injection of a satellite by vehicle No. 5. Vehicle No. 7 launch was cancelled, with another failure of No. 8 in 1999.

The first stage of the H-II is comprised of a core vehicle equipped with the LE-7 engine and two solid rocket boosters (SRBs). The LE-7 runs on liquid hydrogen and liquid oxygen with 86 tons of thrust at sea level. The SRBs are polybutadiene composite solid propellant boosters with 158 tons of thrust each at sea level.

The guidance and control of the first stage is performed by the hydraulically steerable nozzles of the LE-7 engine. Control of the SRBs is performed by the inertial guidance computer (IGC). The first stage is equipped with two auxiliary engines to aid in altitude control.

The second stage of the H-II is equipped with the LE-5A liquid hydrogen/liquid oxygen engine. The LE-5A engine is an improved LE-5 engine, which was originally developed for the second stage of the H-I launch vehicle. It provides 12 tons of thrust in a vacuum.

The guidance and control of the second stage is performed by the hydraulically steerable nozzle of the LE-5A engine. The stage's reaction control system is controlled by the IGC.

The guidance and control system of the H-II utilizes a strapped-down inertial guidance and control approach. This system consists of the inertial measurement unit (lMU) which uses three ring laser gyros and the IGC. The inertial guidance and control system enables the H-II launch vehicle to automatically correct errors and to maintain the planned orbit without commands from the ground station.

The payload firing of the H-II protects the payload from the severe launch environment and from contamination on the ground.

A spin-off vehicle from the H-II is the H-II Transfer Vehicle (HTV) which is currently under development by NASDA. HTV will be one of the orbital transfer vehicles designed to carry supplies to the International Space Station (ISS). It will be launched by H-IIA launch vehicle to enable transport of cargo and equipment to the ISS and disposal of non-recoverable equipment devices, used clothing and wastes.

The history of the H-II actually dates back to 1970 when Japan decided to import rocket technology from the United States in the form of Delta rockets. When Japan originally began launching satellites for communications or meteorology, the country had no sufficient and reliable means of launch transport. Thus, the country entered into an agreement with the United States requiring it to get permission every time Japan launched a foreign satellite.

Japan developed the strong need to have its own rocket launch technology in order to perform national space activities without any restrictions.

The first launch vehicle with a practical satellite onboard was the N-I, with its maiden flight in 1975. However, N-I technology was primarily based on U.S. technology. The body of the vehicle was based on Thor-Delta launch vehicle of Douglas, but a Japanese-made liquid engine, LE-3, was used for the second stage, utilizing a similar shape to that of the Thor-Delta, while the guidance control system was different.

However, primary satellite users at the Meteorological Agency, Japan Telegraph and Telephone Public Corporation, and the Japanese Broadcasting Corporation, were not satisfied with the capability of N-I. It was not considered suitable to meet the growing needs and growing sizes of satellites which had increased to 300 kg (661 lb). The N-I was only capable of launching 130 kg (286 lb) to 36,000 km (22,370 mi) geostationary orbit.

The Japanese went to work on developing the N-II in order to meet the increasing satellite size needs up to 350 kg (772 lb). The N-II was followed by the H-I, which was heavily based on the technology of the Delta launch vehicle. The H-II brought the goal of the first 100 percent made-in-Japan rocket vehicle that was capable of lifting a two-ton payload into geostationary orbit.

The H-II evolved into the H-IIA with the critical LE-7A liquid engine. The LE-7A weighs 1.7 tons with a 1074 kN thrust in a vacuum, in comparison to the GE90 turbo fan engine of General Electric Co., Ltd, in the United States, which is used for a Boeing 777 aircraft. The GE90 weighs seven tons and has only a 382 kN thrust.

The H-II is roughly the same height as a 17-story building. It performs inertial guidance flight with its onboard electronic equipment. Inertial guidance is an automatic function used by the H-IIA to correct the flight path according to its scheduled trajectory. It accomplishes this by sensing its position and acceleration during flight.

The H-IIA has two SRBs which are 2.5 meters (8.2 ft) in diameter and 15.2 meters (50 ft) in height.

The total weight of the H-IIA is approximately 285 tons including propellants, liquid oxygen and liquid hydrogen, and helium for pressurization. In comparison, other launch vehicles, such as the Ariane 4 of Europe, weighs 460 tons, and the Proton of Russia, weighs nearly 1,000 tons.

The relative light weight of H-IIA has added to its high rate of performance. In addition to SRBs, it also has SSBs, or solid support boosters, which are small propellant boosters for supporting H-IIA acceleration. A group of two or four can be attached to the rocket for adjusting its launch capability.

NASDA's Astronauts

NASDA has a team of experienced Japanese astronauts who have participated, or will participate, in U.S. space missions. These include Mamoru Mohri, Chiaki Mukai, Takao Doi, Koichi Wakata, Soichi Noguchi, Satoshi Furukawa, Akihiko Hoshide, and Naoko Sumino.

Mamoru Mohri received a doctorate in chemistry from Flinders University of South Australia in 1976 and has published over 100 papers in the fields of material and vacuum sciences. He holds the title of diplomatic pilot.

Chiaki Mukai is a medical doctor, also holding a doctorate in physiology from Keio University School of Medicine, Japan. She is also certified as a cardiovascular surgeon. From 1987 to 1988, Mukai was a visiting scientist at the Division of Cardiovascular Physiology, Space Biomedical Research Institute, NASA Johnson Space Center.

In 1985, Mukai participated as one of three Japanese payload specialist candidates for the first material processing test (Spacelab-J), which flew aboard space shuttle mission STS-47. She also served as a back-up payload specialist for the Neurolab mission, STS-90.

As the first Japanese woman to fly in space, and the first Japanese astronaut to fly twice, Mukai has logged over 566 hours in space.

She participated in the space shuttle STS-65 Columbia mission from July 8 to 23, 1994, consisting of 82 investigations of space life science including human physiology, space biology, radiation biology, and bioprocessing, as well as investigations of microgravity science including material science, fluid science, and research on the microgravity environment and countermeasures.

Mukai was also aboard the space shuttle

STS-95 Discovery mission from October 29 through November 7, 1998, assisting in investigations on space flight and the aging process.

Takao Doi received a doctorate in aerospace engineering from the University of Tokyo in 1983, and has published over 40 papers on the topics of chemical propulsion systems, electric propulsion systems, fluid dynamics, and microgravity.

In 1985, Doi worked for NASA's Lewis Research Center as a National Research Council research associate. He was a mission specialist on STS-87 from November 19 to December 1997, becoming the first Japanese astronaut to perform an EVA, or spacewalk.

Doi, working with Navy Captain Scott, participated in two spacewalks. The first was a seven hour and 43 minute spacewalk to manually capture a Spartan satellite and to test EVA tools and procedures for future space station assembly. The second spacewalk lasted five hours and was used to perform additional space station assembly tests.

Kochi Wakata is a multi-engine and instrument-rated pilot who has successfully logged over 1,100 hours in several types of aircraft. Wakata flew aboard STS-72 Endeavor from January 11 to 20, 1996, as the first Japanese mission specialist. During the mission the crew retrieved the Space Flyer Unit, launched from Japan 10 months earlier; deployed and retrieved the OAST-Flyer; and performed two spacewalks to demonstrate and evaluate techniques for future assembly of the International Space Station (ISS).

Wakata also flew aboard STS-92 Discovery from October 11 to 24, 2000. During the mission, the seven member crew attached the Z1 truss and Pressurized Mating Adapter 3 to the ISS using Discovery's robotic arm.

Soichi Noguchi received his education in aeronautical engineering and completed two years of astronaut training at NASA's Johnson Space Center. He has been scheduled for space shuttle mission STS-114 and will be the second Japanese astronaut to visit ISS.

Satoshi Furukawa received a doctorate in medicine from the University of Tokyo in 1989, as well as a doctor of philosophy in Medical Science in 2000. He will be assigned to a future mission for ISS.

Akihiko Hoshide received a master of science degree in aerospace engineering from the University of Houston and worked for two years at NASDA's Nagoya office on the development of the H-II rocket. Hoshida was a member of the STS-72 crew and was selected by NASDA to participate in a future mission to ISS.

Naoko Sumino, NASDA's youngest astronaut, was actually born in Matsudo City, China. She received her education in aerospace engineering and was involved in the system integration of the Japanese Experiment Module (JEM). From June 1998 through March 2000, Sumino was involved in the development of the ISS centrifuge, a life sciences experiment facility. Sumino will also participate in a future upcoming mission to ISS.

MALAYSIA

Space Science Studies Division (BASKA)

The Space Science Studies Division (BASKA) was initially called the Planetarium Division in the Prime Minister's Department in 1992. In 1993, its name was changed. BASKA serves as the center of space science and technology for the country of Malaysia. It is responsible for providing leadership in space science by making available expertise as well as research and educational facilities; assisting the government in forming a national space policy for Malaysia; playing an active role in international activities related to space science and technology, including space laws and regulations; monitoring space activities in Malaysia; producing the official national almanac; managing the national planetarium; and promoting the national planetarium as a tourist attraction and leading educational institution.

National Planetarium

The construction of the national planetarium began in 1990 and was completed in 1993. A test launch for the public began in May 1993, and it was officially opened by the prime minister, YAB Dato' Seri Dr. Mahathir Mohamad, on February 7, 1994.

In July 1995, following one and a half years of smooth operation, planetarium operation was transferred to the ministry of science, technology and environment.

The National Planetarium Observatory is located at Kuala Lumpur, the capital city of Malaysia, 370 ft above sea level. The main instrument inside the dome is a 35 cm (one in) Celestron C-14 Schmidt-Cassgrain telescope on the German equatorial mounting.

The observatory serves as a basis for research in many fields of astronomy such as photometry, spectrometry, astrometry, CCD imaging, and solar observation. The most important detector is the STAR 1 CCD camera from Photometrics Ltd., which uses UV-enhanced coating Thomson TH 7883 CCD chip (384 by 576 pixels) and cools down to –45 degrees Celsius.

The observatory has been used mainly for astronomy and astrophysics education as well as for certain astronomical research. Differential photometry and image processing techniques have been used to overcome light pollution problems in the city. The telescope has been used by universities, schools, and the general public.

Sunspot observation began at the national planetarium in 1996. The observation occurs between 10 A.M. and 12 noon every working day. The number of groups and spots visible on the sun's surface are counted and their positions noted each day since 1998. Be-

ginning in 1999, sunspot positions have been recorded through photography to ensure a more accurate result.

The Merdeka Sundial was built in 1957 and originally housed in Taman Tuanku Abdul Rahman (TTAR). In 1997, the sundial was moved to the national planetarium grounds.

The Merdeka Sundial is unique in comparison to other sundials, as it provides information on local mean time (LMT), date and month, earth revolution, and analemma.

The sundial has incorporated the time and zone adjustments for the peninsular during the time GMT + 7.5 hours. The sun moves significantly from time to time between + 23.5 to -23.5 declination. Dates and months are determined by referring to the mosaic tiles and horizontal lines on the sundial's plate. The gnomon also points to zodiac drawings which match zodiac constellations at a specific time on the sundial's plate.

It is possible to know the earth's revolution by observing the different shadow positions from one constellation to the next, giving the period of earth's movement around the sun in a given year.

Analemma refers to a curve in the form of an elongated eight marked with a scale, drawn on a globe of the earth to show the sun's declination and the equation of time for any day of the year formed by plotting the sun's actual daily position at noon, or mean solar time, for a year.

A verification on the time precision of the Merdeka Sundial was performed in 1999. This verification was important to ensure proper usage of the sundial.

The Star 1 CCD camera, or Charge Coupled Device, is a light detector semiconductor with a sensitive electrical charge recorder aimed towards light photons. An important component in the camera is the CCD chip which provides light-sensitive photosit.

Star 1 CCD applications began in 1999. This verification was important to ensure proper usage of the sundial. Star 1 CCD applications include photometry, spectroscopy, and astrometry.

Photometry is used to measure the brightness of sky objects and requires use of the CCD, software, and standard filter. Spectroscopy involves the study of the chemical compound of sky objects and elements. It requires the use of the CCD, software, and a spectrograph. Astrometry is the study of the position and mechanics of celestial bodies and requires the CCD and software.

Remote Sensing Applications

Remote sensing in Malaysia was first used for forestry applications in the 1970s. Since then, the use of remote sensing data has become widespread. The country established a national resource and environmental management program coordinated by MACRES (Malaysia Center for Remote Sensing) in order to fully utilize remote sensing and related technologies such as geographic information systems (GIS) and satellite-based positioning in the country.

The program covers three subsystems: a satellite-based information extraction subsystem; a spatial modeling subsystem utilizing GIS and an expert system; and a decision-making subsystem.

The country continues to develop technology in agriculture, forestry, geology, hydrology, the environment, coastal zones, marine biology, topography, and socio-economic applications.

Achievements in these areas have included the development of remote sensing and GIS applications for the monitoring of forest fires, the monitoring of water catchment areas, the detection of change of forested areas, and the development of a database and decision-making application tools for the system of national resource and environment management.

Southeast Asian countries have been frequently affected by the smoke haze caused by forest fires and the open burning of agricultural wastes. In 1997, the haze episode lasting from July to October was the worst environment disaster recorded in recent years.

This episode resulted in substantial economic loss as well as significant health implications in Malaysia and other neighboring countries.

As a result, a total fire management plan was instituted integrating remote sensing and GIS technologies in order to assist the government in providing an operational system for forest fire management.

This plan was made up of three components — an early warning system, a detection and monitoring system, and measures and procedures for mitigation. The plan includes an early warning system aimed at producing maps that indicate areas which are susceptible to forest fires.

Earth observation satellites such as the French Systéme Pour l'observation de la Terre (SPOT), or Land Spot Observation System, and the U.S. National Oceanic and Atmospheric Administration (NOAA), along with ground surveillance, have provided near real-time information on the exact locations and extent of forest fires and open burning.

Research in remote sensing applications is also carried out by universities such as Universiti Teknologi Malaysia (UTM, Malaysia Technological Institute); Universiti Putra Malaysia (UPM, Malaysia Putra University), and Universiti Kebangsaan Malaysia (UKM, Malaysia Kebangsaan University).

Remote sensing user agencies include the Malaysia Agriculture Research and Development Institute (MARDI) and the Forest Research Institute of Malaysia (FRIM).

Research at the UTM Department of Remote Sensing encompasses the areas of bathmymetry (the science of measuring the depths of oceans and seas), seabed features, vegetation index mapping, sea surface temperature, sea grass mapping, landslide-prone area study, oil slick studies, and land use mapping.

The UPM Center for Remote Sensing and Geographic Information Systems has been researching a pavement management system, a road accident information system, coastal zone management, irrigation resources, and environmental changes.

At FRIM, remote sensing for forestry applications include forest inventory, mapping, rehabilitation, and monitoring.

Past research at MARDI has included crop surveillance and a land resource inventory. The agency has recently conducted research activities in spatial modeling for regional agricultural development and the characterization of plant species.

Meteorology

There are six meteorological satellite ground stations in Malaysia operated by the Department of Meteorology. These include a high-resolution picture transmission station, three medium data utilization stations, and two secondary data users stations, which receive and process data from NOAA geostationary meteorological satellites (GMS).

Meteorological satellite data and image processing has been used to support operational weather forecasting, weather warning and other applications, including cloud type identification, cloud top estimation, weather system detection, monitoring cloud system evolution, detection of forest fires, smoke plumes and hazes, as well as vegetation index to assess crop yield.

Malaysia has also extended meteorological applications to volcanic ash cloud detection and discrimination, post-flood assessment, rainfall estimation, and oil slick detection.

Telecommunications

In the field of telecommunications, Malaysia has followed an open policy in regards to collaboration in science and technology. The country has cooperative agreements in satellite technology with Brazil, India, the Republic of Korea, Russia, South Africa, the United Kingdom, Northern Ireland, and the United States. It has also pursued similar collaboration with Australia, France, Germany, Italy, Japan, and Singapore.

It participates in the Association of South-East Asian Nations (ASEAN) in the training and development of remote sensing, as well as contributing to the strengthening of existing networks between ground receiving stations for satellite data reception and distribution in the region.

ASEAN nations continue to work together in the monitoring and prevention of haze. Cooperative projects have been pursued with the European Space Agency/European Union, Canada, China, Japan, and the United States.

Malaysia's first regional satellite was MEASAT (Malaysia East Asia Satellite), designed to provide optimum coverage of the East Asian region.

The MEASAT system consisted of two high-powered HS376 spacecraft built by Hughes Space and Communications Company.

On January 13, 1996, MEASAT-1, an advanced hybrid 12 C-Band and 5 Ku-Band payload satellite, was launched from Kourou, French Guiana, by Arianespace.

It was placed at an orbit of 91.5° E with its C-Band covering a major part of East Asia including the Philippines, Cambodia, parts of southern China, Hong Kong, Taiwan, the Lao People's Democratic Republic, Malaysia, Myanmar, Singapore, Thailand, Vietnam, Northern Australia, Guam, and Papua New Guinea.

On November 14, 1996, MEASAT-2 was launched, serving up to four 72 MHz C-band and nine 48 MHz Ku-Band transponders. It was placed into an orbital inclination of 148° E to provide reliable C-Band broadcasting and telecommunications services to East Asia, Eastern Australia, Guam, and the United States via Hawaii.

The Ku-Band capacity of the MEASAT system has offered reliable direct-to-user broadcasting services over eastern Australia, India, Indonesia (Sumatra and Java), eastern and western Malaysia, the Philippines, Taiwan, and Vietnam. It has allowed for point-to-point and point-to-multipoint services within its coverage.

Telemetry tracking and control for MEASAT was provided by the MEASAT satellite control center in Pulau Langkawi, an island located off the northwest coast of the Malaysian peninsula.

Malaysia's third satellite, MACSAT (Multiple Access Communications Satellite), will be launched in 2004. It will be the first Malaysian satellite to orbit the earth at the equator.

MACSAT was designed as a NEGO (Near Equatorial Low Earth Orbit) satellite to provide data on many applications including research and development.

The satellite will pass over any given spot on the equator more frequently than polar satellites, while providing constant data streams. It will also be used for other applications such as disaster response, oil spills, marine ecosystems, water resources, and mapping of terrain.

MACSAT's projected lifespan is three years.

TiungSAT-1 Satellite Program

TiungSAT-1 was Malaysia's first microsatellite, built in collaboration with the University of Surrey, United Kingdom, and Northern Ireland. It was named after a variety of a singing mynah bird. It was launched into orbit September 2000, onboard a Dnepr launch vehicle from the Baikonur Cosmodrome in Kazakhstan, and placed into a 650 km (404 mile), 64 degree inclination, low earth orbit (LEO).

The satellite was successfully activated on its first transit over Malaysia, just seven hours after launch, from the ground station installed in Kuala Lumpur.

The launch onboard Dnepr was significant in that it is the second commercial use of the demilitarized SS18 intercontinental ballistic missile. The first was for the launch of Surrey's UoSAT-12 minisatellite in April 1999, when Surrey was the sole payload for the Dnepr rocket.

The 50 kg (110 lb) TiungSAT-1 microsatellite provided 80 m (262 ft) resolution multispectral earth imaging, 1.2 km (0.75 mile) meteorological earth imaging, digital store-and-forward communications, and a cosmic-ray energy deposition experiment.

TiungSAT-1 provided information on earth resources, land use and environmental haze pollution, as well as weather patterns, including hurricane warnings for Malaysia.

The satellite carried onboard a cosmic energy deposition experiment, consisting of three large area PIN-diode detectors in telescopic arrangement, and brass shielding with aluminum housing.

TiungSAT-1's earth imaging system consisted of a wide angle camera (WAC) for meteorological imaging with a spectral band ranging between 0.81 and 0.89 μm, a CCD area array sensor with 1024 by 1024 pixels, and 4.8 mm (0.188 in) optics. It also contained a narrow angle camera (NAC) for multi-spectral earth imaging with three cameras — green band (0.5–0.59 μm), which was plant vigorous and water body sensitive; red band (0.61–0.69 μm), which was useful for vegetation, soil and geological boundary identification; and the near infrared (0.81–0.89 μm), which showed good visualization for oil/crop and land/water contrast.

The satellite also housed a digital signal processor with data transfer experiment, operating a VHF scanner under 140 to 150 MHz (10 MHZ bandwidth), and a built-in FSK decoder able to detect signals from pre-set signal strength thresholds within the selected band. The DSP was capable of processing audio transmission for rebroadcast.

Malaysian Center for Remote Sensing

The Malaysian Center for Remote Sensing (MACRES) was officially established in August 1988, and became fully operational in January 1990. The agency's objective is to lead Malaysia in the areas of remote sensing space technology applications for development.

The center is equipped with facilities for satellite image processing and geographic information system (GIS). A satellite ground receiving station for direct remote sensing data reception is also in the process of being built.

MACRES continues to develop remote sensing, GIS and related technologies through research for operational use in environment and resource management, to thoroughly support the needs of the country.

The agency consists of two major programs — research and development and operations. The research and development program conducts research on applications in remote sensing and related technologies in all sectors of the management of environmental resources. It also conducts research in spatial analysis and modeling in geographic information system (GIS) environments as well as research for hardware and software development in user, ground, and space segments of remote sensing and related technologies.

The operations program manages a user service center for remotely sensed data. It also manages and maintains in-house hardware and software systems and is responsible for the operation and management of satellite remote sensing ground receiving stations, as well as a national remote sensing information center.

MACRES manages several projects including the National Resource and Environmental Management (NAREM) Program; AIRSAR PACRIM; Total Forest Fire Management Plan (TFFMP); Satellite Image Map (SIM); and the Microwave Remote Sensing System.

The National Resource and Environmental Management (NAREM) Program was established to develop an operational national resource and environmental management system using remote sensing and its related technologies. NAREM consists of the NASAT, NAMOS, and NADES sub-systems.

NASAT is a satellite based information extraction sub-system. NAMOS focuses on using geographic information system and expert system techniques for modeling in the spatial domain. Development of spatial models allows for the production of derived composite thematic layers useful for decision making. NADES is a decision making tool for integrated development planning, utilizing resource, environmental, socio-economic, and policy information.

MACRES has been inputting data into NAREM from various sectors — agriculture, forestry, geology and mineral, fishery and marine, coastal zone management, environment, topography and socio-economic. These data are sourced from existing databases in user agencies or generated from satellite data, and cover the coastal area of Selangor, stretching from Sabak Bernam to Sepang. The objective of data management has been to develop the spatial database for coastal environment sensitivity zoning (CESZ) against oil spill pollution.

CESZ covers two main areas — coastal land resource and shoreline sensitivity zoning. Values compiled by CESZ have been derived from ecological, socio-economic, geomorphology and oceanography factors, providing useful information for managing oil spill threats. To date the project has established the coastal land resource database and generated a land eco-system map.

In participation with NASA and CSIRO of Australia, Malaysia established the AIRSAR PACRIM program, with the main objective of acquiring polarimetric AIRSAR and interferometric TOPSAR data for use in topographic mapping, forest canopy analysis and mapping, volcanic and tectonic research, geological research and archaeology. This data has been used for research into terrain analysis, land use and cover change detection, forest density monitoring, coastal zone information extraction and enhancing understanding of local geological formation.

Data analysis yielded has been applied toward developing a technology for operational precision geo-coding of SAR data using interferometric algorithm; developing a SAR backscattering model for crop yield and timber harvest predictions; developing an algorithm for fractal analysis of multi-polarised SAR data for reliable land use and cover classification; using general techniques for SAR analysis for geological and topographical applications; modification of existing models for marine, coastal and environmental studies to suit local conditions; acquiring programming knowledge and skills in the IDL (interactive data language) environment for algorithm development to improve SAR processing techniques through research attachment at NASA-JPL; and acquiring advanced SAR processing and analysis knowledge and skills in specific areas of expertise through national and regional workshops.

Two airborne SAR imaging missions occurred on November 25, 1996, in East Malaysia over three study sites (Kucing, Samarahan and Kinabalu), and on December 3, 1996, in Peninsular Malaysia over four sites (Muda Merbok, Kuala Trengganu, Pulau Tioman and Cameron Highland). The Muda Merbok site was only imaged 15 km (9.32 miles) due to operations difficulties. Fieldwork in the four sites of the peninsular was also conducted simultaneously during data acquisition, with the consideration of required real-time data to fulfill research requirements.

Southeast Asia countries continue to be frequently affected by smoke haze caused by forest fires and open burning of agricultural wastes. The haze episode of July through October 1997, was one of the worst environmental disasters recorded in recent years in the region. As a result, Malaysia declared an environmental emergency in Sarawak when the air pollution index (API) reached 839, far exceeding the dangerous level of 500. In response to this, MACRES initiated a Total Forest Fire Management Plan (TFFMP) utilizing remote sensing and GIS technologies to assist responsible authorities in managing the disaster.

The primary objective of TFFMP has been to provide an operational system for an integrated management of forest fires and haze. TFFMP consists of three major components — early warning, detection and monitoring, and mitigation measures.

The early warning component has been aimed at producing maps of areas susceptible to forest fires. The detection and monitoring component has been carried out through the use of earth observation and meteorological satellites, such as SPOT and NOAA, to provide near real-time information on the exact locations and extent of forest fires to the coordinating authority. The mitigation measures have involved interagency activities carried out through a Forest Fire Management Coordination Centre (FFMCC) to mitigate forest fires.

Active fires from either forest fires or the burning of agricultural wastes can be detected by the NOAA satellite and the high spatial resolution SPOT satellites. These fires have normally been associated with burnt scares with a streak of smoke plumes arising from the fire that also indicates the direction of the wind. Detection of forest fires at an early stage is essential when the size of fire is still small and hence easy to control. The accuracy and frequent passage of SPOT-1, SPOT-2 and SPOT-3 satellites increase the chance of detecting such active fires.

The Satellite Image Map (SIM) project was initiated by MACRES in 1997 and continues in collaboration with the Department of Surveying and Mapping Malaysia (JUPEM). The objectives of the project have been to establish an efficient technique and effective procedure for operationalization of SIM production, and to establish a digital satellite image map database that contains both remote sensing images and related vector information.

SIM consists of an ortho-rectified satellite image overlaid by selective corresponding topographic, thematic and cartographic information manipulated in geographic information system (GIS) environment. In addition to topographical data, transportation and hydrological network, and administrative boundaries, cartographic information such as a projection grid, orientation legend and annotation are also incorporated. The projects also utilize the global positioning system (GPS) techniques to establish a National Standard Ground Control Point (GCP) required for geometric correction of satellite images. The project began with the pilot study area of Selangor before its full implementation to cover the whole country.

The project uses image and GPS processing, GIS and cartographic operations. The final product of SIM will be maps of 1:50,000 scale, equivalent to the format of topographical maps currently produced by JUPEM.

The SIM, containing both enhanced remotely sensed data and vector information, will be used to complement the current topographical maps which only have vector information. The project will eventually lead to the development of remote sensing image, national remote sensing GCPs, and vector databases, which will allow the production of maps at any scale as requested by users.

Since its establishment, MACRES has focused on airborne and spaceborne measurements. This involved plans to set up a microwave remote sensing laboratory that will be equipped with the bistatic microwave anechoic chamber and mobile scatterometer to investigate and enhance the understanding of physics of remote sensing in line with national efforts to attain full capabilities in space technology. The project is being put in force in collaboration with the Multimedia University (MMU), for which the development of anechoic chamber and mobile scatterometer was contracted through a consultancy agreement signed on December 29, 1999.

An anechoic chamber will be constructed at the Multimedia University. The chamber will operate from 30 MHz through 18 GHz. The types of measurements that can be performed in this facility will include EMC tests, antenna measurement, radar cross-section measurement, evaluation of RF transceivers, calibration of scatterometer and research topics such as biological effect due to RF radiation.

A ground-based C-band scatterometer system was built at the Multimedia University. The system consists of a full polarimetric FM-CW radar, which has the capability to determine the complete backscattering matrix of a natural target. This system will be used to conduct in situ backscatter measurements from earth terrain such as vegetation fields, forest and soil surfaces. The system's operating frequency is 6 GHz, with a bandwidth of 400 MHz. A 100ns delay line was incorporated into the hardware system for internal calibration. External calibration is accomplished by using a 12-inch conducting sphere.

The system will be mounted on a boom truck so that the antenna can be erected to a sufficient height for the scattering measurements of natural resources on the field. An antenna fixture will enable the change of wave incidence angle. The mechanical connection will be designed to enable the scatterometer be elevated to a one hundred foot vertical height and capable of transmitting and receiving electromagnetic (microwave) signals.

The boom is rigidly mounted on to a truck and its base is connected to a gearing system as to allow circular 360° motions or positioning as required. The telescopic boom extension motion is provided by the truck's diesel engine and its uniform motion is controlled manually. Lifting of the boom is done by hydraulic arm and operating angle is between 0 to 90°.

The maximum vertical height of the boom will allow the withstanding of wind force, and its vibration will be reduced to a minimum so as not to contribute to or amplify unacceptable errors in scatterometer readings. The boom was built using a material that will not cause signal interferences, or its magnetic properties would be reduced to a minimum acceptable value.

The telescopic boom weight at full length must be balanced by a counterweight if necessary to ensure it does not topple the truck when taking turns or become entrapped by its own dead weight when operating on soft ground. The scatterometer is securely hinged at the top of the boom and to a geared motor and is easily position at any inclination or depression angle of 0 to 70° by a remote control button, whereas the telescopic boom base can be rotated through 360°.

THE NETHERLANDS

Space Research Organization Netherlands (SRON)

The Space Research Organization Netherlands (SRON) is part of the Netherlands Organization for Scientific Research (NOW). It was established as a national center of expertise for the development and exploitation of satellite instruments in astrophysics and earth system science. It also acts as the Dutch national agency for space research as well as the country's national point of contact for ESA programs.

The selection of these main areas of research by SRON was based on various experimental space science investigations performed during the 1970s and '80s.

SRON's divisions include astrophysics — High Energy Astrophysics Division (HEA) and Low Energy Astrophysics Division (LEA); earth oriented science (EOS); and research and development — the Sensor Research and Technology Division (SR&T) and the Engineering Division.

Astrophysics

X-ray and gamma-ray astronomy began in the early 1960s with the advent of spaceborne instrumentation. The development of IR space astronomy followed later in response to the demanding requirements of cryogenically cooled sensors in space. SRON has been involved in these fields from their very early stages.

It has acquired specific knowledge in sub-fields such as cosmic X-ray timing, in particular transient and burst phenomena, X-ray spectroscopy, X-ray imaging, wide-field gamma-ray imaging and spectroscopy, and IR photometry/spectroscopy.

Related missions BeppoSAX, CHANDRA, and XMM-Newton continue to be operational and produce scientific data. The COMPTON observatory has been taken out of orbit, although its data is still available.

The astrophysics division of SRONG produces technology related to imaging proportional counters, X-ray optics, X-ray defraction gratings, scintillation counters, IR detectors, IR filters, cryogenic techniques, instrument electronics, mechanics, and instrument calibration.

Two new, world-class, X-ray observatories in space, CHANDRA and XMM-Newton, have begun to set the stage in X-ray astrophysics. SRON will contribute in a major role in the data analysis of these missions. For the first time, X-ray spectrometers with sufficient sensitivity and resolving power to perform detailed plasma diagnostics of the hottest matter in the universe will allow study of nearby stellar objects, as well X-ray spectroscopy of compact extragalactic objects and clusters of galaxies.

SRON's astrophysical activities are concentrated in the divisions of High Energy Astrophysics (HEA) and Low Energy Astrophysics (LEA).

HIGH ENERGY ASTROPHYSICS DIVISION (HEA)

The High Energy Astrophysics Division (HEA) at SRON is responsible for the design, development, and building of space instruments for X-ray and gamma-ray astrophysics. It is also responsible for carrying out scientific data analysis in support of missions in collaboration with astronomy groups at universities in the Netherlands.

HEA has been involved in a number of projects since the beginnings of X-ray and gamma-ray astronomy, including the Astronomical Netherlands Satellite (ANS), COS-B, EXOSAT, the Wide Field X-ray Camera in the KVANT module on the Mir space station (COMIS/TTM), COMPTEL, the Compton Gamma-ray telescope on the COMPTON GRO spacecraft, the Wide Field X-ray Cameras on BeppoSAX, the Low Energy Transmission Grating on Chandra (formerly AXAF — the Advanced X-ray Astrophysics Facility) which was launched July 23, 1999, the Reflection Grating Spectrometer on XMM launched on December 10, 1999, and the development of the spectroscopic plasma code SPEX in preparation for the data analysis of X-ray spectrometers.

The X-ray Multi Mirror (XMM) mission is the second of four cornerstone projects of ESA for its long-term program, Horizon 2000. The XMM payload consists of three co-aligned high throughput telescopes with a FOV (field of view) of 30 arcmin and a spatial resolution of close to 16 arcsec. Imaging CCD detectors were placed in the focus of each telescope.

Behind two of the three telescopes, nearly half of the X-ray light is utilized by the reflection grating spectrometers (RGS). The RGS instruments are capable of achieving high resolution power (150 to 800 in the first spectral order) over a range from 5 to 35 Ångstrom (first order). The effective area peaks around 15 Ångstrom (first order) at about 150 cm^2 for the two spectrometers.

The design was incorporated with an array of reflection gratings placed in the converging beam at the exit of the X-ray telescope. The grating stack defracts the X-rays to an array of dedicated charge coupled device (CCD) detectors which have been offset from the telescope focal plane.

The Advanced X-ray Astrophysics Facility (AXAF), which was recently renamed

CHANDRA, is the third observatory in the series of Great Observatories in the NASA program, following the Hubble Space Telescope and the Compton Gamma-Ray Observatory. CHANDRA was equipped with a Wolter-Type I high-resolution telescope, two insertable gratings, the Low-Energy Transmission Grating (LETG) and the High-Energy Transmission Grating (HETG), as well as two imaging detector systems. The LETG was developed by SRON in cooperation with the Max Planck Institute fuer Extraterrestrische Physik (MPE) in Garching.

The scientific objectives of the wide field camera (WFC) instrument on the BeppoSAX satellite include the monitoring of large, but selected, regions of the sky for cosmic X-ray transient sources which will allow for follow-up studies with higher-sensitivity narrow-field instruments on BeppoSAX and other platforms; and the performing of spatially-resolved simultaneous monitoring of compact X-ray sources in crowded fields with high sensitivity.

The instrument was designed with two identical wide field cameras that are active at few keV photon energies (or about 1 to 10 Angstrom). The field of view of each camera was made at an unprecedented large size for an astrophysical X-ray telescope — 40 by 40 degrees squared. The cameras point in opposite directions, and together they cover seven percent of the sky. However, due to low earth orbit (LEO), the earth blocks the field of view of either camera for a few tens of percents of the time.

BeppoSAX was launched into a low-earth, low-inclination orbit on April 30, 1996, from Cape Canaveral Florida. Scientific operations commenced in July 1996, following an instrument check-out period. Observations were ceased during May and August 1997, in order to implement a one-gyro mode after four of the six gyros had failed. Normal operations resumed shortly thereafter.

COMPTEL was the Gamma-ray Compton telescope onboard the NASA Compton Gamma-Ray observatory (CGRO), and named the second of NASA's Great Observatories. Compton, weighing 17 tons, was the heaviest astrophysical payload ever flown at the time of its launch in April 1991, onboard the space shuttle Atlantis. On June 4, 2000, its orbit was safely ended and it re-entered the atmosphere.

The Imaging Compton Telescope (COMPTEL) utilized the Compton effect as well as two layers of gamma-ray detectors to reconstruct an image of a gamma-ray source in the energy range 0.75 to 30 million electron volts (MeV). It had a field of view of approximately one sterradian, an angular resolution of the order of one degree and a spectral resolution of 6–10 percent. Gamma-rays from active galaxies, radioactive supernova remnants, and diffuse gamma-rays from giant molecular clouds were studied with COMPTEL.

COMPTEL's upper layer of detectors were filled with a liquid scintillator which scattered an incoming gamma-ray photon according to the Compton effect. This photon was then absorbed by NaI crystals in the lower detectors. The instrument recorded the time, location, and energy of the events in each layer of detectors which made it possible to determine the direction and energy of the original gamma-ray photon and reconstruct an image and energy spectrum of the source.

SRON contributed to the building of COMPTEL and provided calibration and data analysis after launch. The institute developed the database-driven analysis system, COMPASS, for the processing and analysis of COMPTEL data. SRON continues to maintain all COMPTEL data in an online tape archive.

SPEX (SPEctral X-ray and UV modeling, analysis and fitting) is a software package developed at SRON for the analysis and interpretation of cosmic X-ray spectra. It was designed with options for spectral modeling, fitting, graphical display and output.

The coded mask imaging spectrometer, or the COMIS/TTM instrument, was built for the Mir space station in cooperation with the Soviets and the United Kingdom's University of Birmingham. The COMIS detector and its electronics were built by SRON, while the coded aperture and star sensor were built by the University of Birmingham. COMIS took only four years to complete and cost less than one million dollars to the Dutch tax-payer. It remained in operation for 12 years.

COMIS was a part of the first module of the Mir space station which was launched in 1986. The first module, called Kvant, was launched in April 1987, containing a station altitude control system and an astrophysical observatory called Roentgen. It consisted of four experiments that covered the medium and high X-ray regime part of the electro-magnetic spectrum between 2 and 800 keV. COMIS was the only imaging instrument on-board Mir.

Observations with COMIS officially began in June 1987. A few months earlier, a rel-atively nearby supernova went off. This super-nova, SN1987a, was only a distance of 170,000 light years away. It was the first time such a su-pernova could be observed with modern tech-niques, but unfortunately COMIS was unable to detect SN1987a.

A few months later, a malfunction oc-curred in the high-voltage control of COMIS. As a result, no scientific data could be ex-tracted. Although COMIS was not meant to be repaired in flight, the Soviets made two at-tempts to replace its flight detector through EVA (extravehicular activity). The first repair attempt was made on June 30, 1988, but was unsuccessful. However, the second, on Octo-ber 20, was a success. The next day, observa-tions on COMIS resumed.

In November 1989, observations with Kvant were suspended temporarily because the Mir station needed to be reconfigured with two additional modules, Kvant-2 and Kristall. These reconfigurations took nearly a year. When an attempt was made in October 1990, to resume observations, it was discovered that the revised station cost too much energy. In-stead of only using the gyroscopic flywheels, rockets were now necessary to aid in the re-orientation of the station. This problem was remedied within a year's time and operations resumed in early 1992.

The scientific objectives of COMIS/ TTM were to monitor selected regions of the sky for cosmic X-ray transient sources; per-form spatially-resolved simultaneous moni-toring of compact X-ray sources in crowded fields with high sensitivity; gain experience in

constructing multi-wire position-sensitive proportional counters in preparation for Bep-poSAX; and gain experience in data handling from a coded aperture camera in preparation for the same mission.

SRON has provided support in the area of interferometry for ESA's Darwin mission, which will be capable of detecting earth-like planets orbiting nearby stars. Darwin will an-alyze their atmospheres and the capability to sustain life as we know it. It will also carry out an ambitious astrophysics program aimed at understanding the formation and evolution of planets, stars, active and normal galaxies.

SRON, along with the Leiden Observa-tory and the Technical University of Delft, has been involved in the conceptual design of the mission which has been scheduled for launch in 2014.

LOW ENERGY ASTROPHYSICS DIVISION (LEA)

The Low Energy Astrophysics Division (LEA) has been involved in the construction and operation of instruments which have been designed to perform astronomical observa-tions from planes, balloon platforms, and satellites in the infrared and sub-millimeter spectral range. This range covers from 2.5 to 1000 μm.

Several types of detection techniques are used by LEA in order to observe such a large spectral range. These include infrared IRAS, infrared (ISO-SWS), sub-millimeter, submm (Herschel-HIFI), submm (ALMA), and submm (Champ+).

The infrared (IRAS) technique has pro-vided support to two of the instruments of IRAS (Infrared Astronomical Satellite) which were built by SRON. These instruments are the low resolution spectrometer (LRS) and the chopped photmetric channel (CPC).

The infrared (ISO-SWS) technique has provided support to the ISO (Infrared Space Observatory), which was launched in No-vember 1995. One of the four instruments on-board ISO was built by SRON and the Max-Planck Institut fuer Extraterrestrische Pysik in Garching — the Short Wavelength Spectrom-eter (SWS).

Following a very successful lifetime of 28 months, which was 10 months longer than expected, ISO ceased operations. Most of the instruments stopped functioning without cooling to near the absolute zero, except for the shortest wavelength band of SWS. With this single functioning band, ranging from 2.2 to 4 μm, an additional survey of 250 stars was performed. This was accomplished in addition to the 9000 observations that had already been performed by ISO of stars, planets, galaxies, dust and nebulae.

The sub-millimeter technique covers the smallest wavelength down to a few millimeters. SRON currently utilizes this technique for the detection of electromagnetic radiation of 300 GHz (1 mm) to three THz (100 μm). It belongs to one of the few groups in the world that can make low-noise sub-millimeter mixers at the highest level frequencies.

Submm techniques developed at LEA have also been important for stratospheric research, as the concentration of certain molecules that play a crucial role in the destruction of ozone can only be measured in the submm wavelength range. Together with the EOS division and a group from the University of Bremen, an airplane observation program was performed. Recently, a similar program to perform such measurements from a balloon platform, together with a German (DLR-IMK) and United Kingdom group (RAL), was started.

The submm (Herschel-HIFI) technique was established in support of ESA's Herschel mission, which has been scheduled for launch in 2007. SRON has been responsible for the designing of one of Herschel's three instruments, the Heterodyne instrument for the far infrared. It will provide two of Herschel's mixers, in bands three and four (800–1120 GHz), which will be based on a new, complicated design where NbTiN and AlN layers have to be used for an optimal result.

SRON will also provide the cryogenic focal plane unit (FPU) subsystem. This will be a very complicated opto-mechanical box with many functions, weighing 50 kg (110 lb), containing optics, mixer assemblies, diplexers, straps, coatings, and EMC suppression circuits for seven mixer bands. The complete warm electronics to control the FPU will also be designed by SRON.

The submm (ALMA) technique enables SRON to develop receivers for the frequency range of 620 to 720 GHz.

The submm (Champ+) technique was applied to the APEX telescope of Germany in Chili, which has served as a precursor telescope to the ALMA array, an array instrument of the Max Planck Institute. This will be upgraded to Champ+ with two sets of array elements (each set consisting of seven mixers) becoming operational at 650 to 850 GHz.

From the end of 1995 through April 1998, the Infrared Space Observatory (ISO) gathered spectroscopic data in the infrared. One of the instruments for ISO was built by SRON in collaboration with MPE-Garching and KU-Leuven, the short wavelength spectrometer (SWS). The satellite ceased operations following 28 months of successful observations.

The Infrared Astronomical Satellite (IRAS) was a joint project of the United States, the United Kingdom, and the Netherlands. The IRAS mission performed an unbiased, sensitive, all-sky survey at 12, 25, 60 and 100 microns. In detecting close to 350,000 infrared sources, IRAS increased the number of catalogued astronomical sources by about 70 percent.

IRAS discoveries included a disk of dust grains around the star Vega, six new comets, and very strong infrared emissions from interacting galaxies as well as wisps of warm dust, referred to as infrared cirrus, which could be found in almost every direction of space. IRAS also revealed for the first time the core of our galaxy, the Milky Way. The satellite's design and survey strategy were maximally optimized for reliable detection of point sources. Pointed observations, known as additional observations, or AOs, were also performed, along with regular survey observations.

IRAS was equipped with a low resolution spectrometer (LRS), a slitless spectrometer sensitive from 7.5 to 23 microns with a resolving power in the range of 20.

One of the largest and most ambitious projects in ground based radio astronomy for the next millennium is ALMA, (Atacama Large Millimeter Array), a millimeter and submm wave interferometer made up of 64 antennas, to be built in the Atacama desert in northern Chile. This project, a collaboration between Europe and the United States, has presented major technical challenges for the design and construction of various components. A key feature of this future observatory will be receivers in the millimeter and sub-millimeter wave regime. The instrument will be equipped with 10 frequency bands, ranging from 30 GHz to about 950 GHz. A total of 1200 receivers will be needed for the final array scheduled for completion around 2009.

SRON will be contributing to ALMA with the development of high frequency mixers using superconducting mixer elements.

HIFI, the Heterodyne instrument for the far infrared, will be one of the three instruments for the Herschel Space Observatory. HIFI will provide continuous coverage over the range of 480 to 1250 GHz in five bands and 1410 to 1910 GHz in two additional bands.

Earth Oriented
Science Division (EOS)

The Earth Oriented Science Division (EOS) at SRON is focused on two main lines of research — atmospheric composition and chemistry and gravity field and ocean circulation. This research supports SRON's interest in atmospheric composition and chemistry while building on the experimental track record in spectroscopy from the astrophysics program.

The division's major programs are the SCIAMACHY/ENVISAT, scheduled for operations between 2001 and 2005; the GOCE Earth Explorer, planned for launch in 2004; and a yet unnamed atmospheric chemistry mission.

Beyond 2005, SRON will be broadening the scope of its atmospheric science line by extending the diagnostics to far-infrared and sub-millimeter spectroscopy for the study of atmospheric trace gases.

EOS has been involved in several key programs, including SCIAMACHY, directed at the development of ENVISAT detector modules, calibration, and data retrieval;

GOME, and research support for GOME-2 (ERS-2) and METOP satellites; ASUR, a sub-millimeter pilot experiment in collaboration with the University of Bremen; the High Tc Bolometer Detector and an OH-retrieval study PIRAMHYD; and GOCE, which is exploration of opportunities in the fields of Gravity and Ocean Topography.

SCIAMACHY, the scanning imaging absorption spectrometer for atmospheric chartograpy, is a joint project of the Netherlands and Germany, with participation by Belgium, for global atmospheric measurements. It was launched on March 1, 2002, onboard the ESA ENVISAT-1 polar orbiting platform. SCIAMACHY has been equipped with a high resolution (0.2 to 0.4 nm) spectrometer to observe transmitted, reflected and scattered light from the atmosphere in the UV, visible and near infrared wavelength regions over the range of 240 to 1750 nm, and in two selected regions between 1.9 and 2.4 micron. The instrument's main purpose is to allow small optical absorptions (as small as 0.02 percent in some regions of the spectrum) to be detected.

SCIAMACHY was designed to measure both tropospheric and stratospheric abundances of a number of atmospheric constituents, which play a part in ozone break-off or, the greenhouse effect. These includes species in the troposphere, including ozone, O_3, O_4, N_2O, NO_2, CH_4, CO, CO_2, H_2O, and aerosols and, in polluted conditions, SO_2; and in the stratosphere, including ozone, NO, NO_2, NO_3, CH_4, CO_2, H_2O, ClO, OClO, BrO, aerosols, stratospheric clouds, and possibly, HCHO and CO.

The Global Ozone Monitoring Experiment (GOME) is a high-resolution (0.2 to 0.4 nm) spectrometer on board ESA's ERS-2 satellite which was launched in April 1995.

It measures the spectrum from 240 to 800 nm, while scanning ground pixels of 40 to 320 km (25 to 200 miles) long and 40 km (25 miles) wide, around nadir. GOME's main objective is to provide high-accuracy global ozone columns, with the anticipated measurement of other trace gases such as NO_2, and of O_3 profiles.

ASUR (Airborne Sub-mm SIS Radiometer) successfully performed measurements of CIO, HCI, N_2 and O_3 during the SESAME (Second Stratospheric Arctic and Midlatitude Experiment), an atmospheric study which used novel SIS (Superconductor-Insulator-Superconductor) detector technologies developed at SRON's LEA division, operating in the frequency bands ranging from 626 to 686 GHz.

PIRAMHYD (passive infrared atmospheric measurements of hydroxyl) was established by SRON to measure the stratospheric hydroxyl radical. Its forward model consists of an atmospheric model in which atmospheric parameters can be specified allowing the radiation transport in the far-infrared close to the OH-lines to be completed; and an instrument model with the most important parameters of the instrument being modeled as a function of wavelength. The combination of these two give spectra as a function of path through the atmosphere, where in a satellite, it serves as a function of tangent height.

The SFINX (SRON Fabry-Perot interferometer experiment) is an instrument currently in development by SRON that will serve as a demonstration model for a possible satellite-borne OH monitor. SFINX will cover the wavelengths between 65 and 90 microns, and with a spectral resolution in excess of 6000. It will be well capable of detecting the radiation emitted by rotational transitions of lightweight molecules and radicals.

SFINX will fly as a piggy-back instrument onboard the MIPAS-B2 (Michelson interferometer for passive atmospheric sounding, balloon version 2) stratospheric balloon gondola in cooperation with the Institut fuer Meteorologie und Klimaforschung (IMK) of the University of Karlsruhe.

Measurement of stratospheric OH with a Fabry-Perot is an instrument SRON has been developing in collaboration with the Smithsonian Astrophysical Observatory to measure the far-infrared emission of stratospheric OH. The chosen design allows for minimal demands on satellite resources as it is lightweight. It will consist of a telescope, followed by a slit system to select a strip of space to view. The vertical resolution will be obtained by measuring in limb geometry at grazing incidence in the atmosphere.

The Fabry-Perot interferometer will select the wavelength, followed by a defraction grating to block other orders of the Fabry-Perot. A high Tc superconductor bolometer is being developed at SRON which can operate at temperatures of ~80 K and will not require liquid helium cooling, which would otherwise limit the operational time of the instrument.

GOCE (Gravity Field and Steady-state Ocean Circulation Explorer) is an ESA mission which will be the first dedicated gravity field mission of ESA. Its emphasis will be to explore the earth's gravity field and to examine its oceans' circulation.

Research and Development

The research and development division of SRON focuses on the development of enabling technology for the high and low energy astrophysics and earth system science programs. It has been used as a strategic tool for SRON in the creation and optimal use of space flight opportunities.

The research and development division consists of two main lines — research and development of the technology for a cryogenic X-ray imagine spectrometer, and research directed towards the next generation of heterodyne instrumentation to contribute to future missions in astrophysics as well as the field of atmospheric composition and chemistry.

This division complies with the requirements for the design, fabrication, assembly, and testing of space-flight instrumentation to support sensor research and development, as well as performance simulations, dataprocessing and scientific analysis.

Research and Development activities at SRON are concentrated in the divisions of sensor research and technology (SR&T) and engineering (ED).

SENSOR RESEARCH & TECHNOLOGY DIVISION (SR&T)

Responsibilities of the sensor research and technology division (SR&T) cover the development of enabling technology to support SRON's high energy astrophysics (HEA), low energy astrophysics (LEA), and earth observation science (EOS) divisions. This enabling technology includes detection systems, spectrometers, and imaging systems of superior performance.

In support of the HEA division, SR&T has been developing an imaging low Tc microcalorimeter designed to reach an energy resolution less than 2eV at E=1 keV, with the application of X-ray spectroscopic sensors for X-ray astronomy expected after 2008, and a low temperature superconducting hot electron bolometer mixer (LTS-HEBM) for 1.0 to 2.5 THz with a noise temperature of nearly 2000 K for applications to sub-millimeter astronomy and future space and airborne atmospheric chemistry missions emphasizing the detection of OH radicals.

Since 1990, the sensor research and technology division (SR&T) has been involved in the research and development of a next generation of devices for the spectroscopic detection of X-ray photons.

X-ray astronomers have come up with the definition of next generation X-ray observatories as being dedicated to the study of cosmological aspects of hot matter in the universe.

As a result, SRON has designed a cryogenic X-ray sensor, or imaging cryogenic X-ray spectrometer, with a high spectral resolution, aiming for 5 eV FWHM for photons of 6 keV and 2 eV at 1 keV; close to 100 percent detection efficiency over the energy range 0.5 keV < E < 10 keV; spatial resolution (32 by 32 pixels); and relatively high counting rate capability (100 cts/s/pixel and 4000 cts/s for the array).

The baseline design for the detector is an array of pixels.

In consideration of the imaging cryogenic X-ray spectrometer design, two different approaches were considered. One approach was to make use of an intrinsic one-dimensional or two-dimensional spectrometer where the deposited energy would be sensed by two or more thermometers and the position would be derived from the relative signals. The advantage given would have been a largely reduced complexity of the electronic readout.

SRON decided on the second approach, which was to utilize an array of single pixels that would allow the advantage of an optimized energy resolution and good counting rate capability. With this approach, the number of channels to readout could be reduced by the use of multiplexing techniques.

The design of an array of micro-calorimeters was actually a copy and paste process of an optimized single pixel design.

SRON initiated the low Tc superconducting bolometer mixer development due to the fact that the development of sub-millimeter receivers had become an active research field. In this field, the frequency range of interest is between 300 and 3000 GHz, referred to as terahertz technology.

The main applications of sub-millimeter receivers are for astronomical and aeronomical observations. There have also been other applications in earth-remote-sensing, high temperature plasma diagnostics, high-definition radar, and future telecommunications.

Yet another application of sub-millimeter receivers has been in the atmospherical chemistry studies where spectral lines of atmospheric trace gases such as O_3, N_2O, HCl, and ClO can be best studied. Successful measurements in the sub-millimeter range have been conducted at different flight altitudes and at different locations by airborne missions. In light of increasing interest in the studies of environmental and global climate change, it is expected that in the near future more and more research projects will be organized for this application.

All these applications require high spectral resolution instrumentation which can only be provided in a practical way by using heterodyne detection techniques. These have been shown to perform very well at radio and microwave frequencies. The principle of heterodyne-mixing is based on the multiplication of two incoming signals. A relatively high-power local oscillator signal with frequency fLO is multiplied with a low-power signal with frequency fS. The mixing element converts this signal at high frequency fS down to a signal of relatively low frequency. The relatively low frequency, also known as the intermediate frequency, is usually around a few GHz and is further amplified with a cryogenic GaAs high electron mobility transistor

(HEMT) amplifier and analyzed with a radio spectrometer.

A hot electron bolometer (HEB) is a device in which the resistance responds to the change of the electron's temperature when it absorbs incident radiation. A traditional bolometer consists of a heat-sensitive detection element mounted inside a heat sink and physically supported by a thermally conductive physical supporter. The supporter is specifically chosen to provide a conducting path between the detection element and the heat sink, but no electrical path.

There are several advantages of HEB mixers, including that its upper-frequency limit will not be set by the superconducting energy gap and it can be operated at frequencies of several THz; it can be operated near the quantum noise limit, resulting in a low noise temperature; the mixing process requires low LO power and will be ~10 to 100 nW; it is possible to reach an IF bandwidth as large as 10 GHz; and the RF impedance will be resistive and therefore no integrated tuning structure would be needed, simplifying the RF circuits.

The microstructures section develops fabrication methods for sensors in the SR&T division. In this section, thin layer and microlithography activities are carried out in support of SRON projects.

Sensors developed in this section have included an imaging X-ray micro-calorimeter, using a low Tc transition edge sensor (TES) with an energy resolution of < 4eV for 6 keV X-rays, targeting a future resolution of < 2 eV @ E = 1 keV and the development of an array of calorimeters. Other sensors were a sub-millimeter/IR spiderweb bolometer, also using a low Tc TES; a high temperature superconducting bolometer for use at 85 um; and superconductive tunnel junctions, a development line which was discontinued at the end of 1997.

The clean room facility forms an essential infrastructure for space projects at SRON. It is here that the assembly of highly sophisticated electronic circuitry, fine mechanical parts, and optical equipment occur in an environment where dust level, temperature, humidity, and static electricity are carefully controlled.

The facility includes temperature control (19 to 21 °C +-0.5 °C), humidity control (35 to 60 percent), standard clean conditions of Class 1000 (US Fed. standard 209 d), ultraclean conditions in restricted areas, Class 10 (laminar down flow), controlled luminosity and color, and services providing special gasses, ultra pure water, and disposal of exhaust fumes.

ENGINEERING DIVISION

The engineering division is made up of the mechanical, electrical, and quality control sections. The mechanical design and realization section performs structural analysis and cryogenic design, as well as mechanical fabrication and assembly. The electrical section designs and builds scientific instruments for investigation and integration. It also performs systems engineering, digital electronics experimentation, and simulation of satellites and ground stations through expanded testing. The product and quality control section ensures workmanship standards, while performing quality control and product assurances.

NORTH KOREA

North Korea Rocket Technology

While North Korea, whose capital is Pyongyang, does not officially have a national space program, it has been heavily involved in the development and exploitation of space technology. Unfortunately, throughout most of its history, the country has applied this technology to less than peaceful purposes and military weaponry.

On August 31, 1998, North Korea launched the first medium-range Taepo-Dong 1 ballistic missile from the northeastern part of the country. After flying over the Japanese island of Honshu, the rocket landed in the high seas off the Sanriku Coast of Japan.

Neighboring countries were alarmed by the test launch, suspecting North Korea's motives as a show of force to mark the installation of Kim Jong-II as the new leader of the secretive Stalinist state.

That same year, North Korea launched an artificial satellite named Kwangmyong-song-1 aboard a Taepo-Dong 1 multi-stage rocket. Reported by the country as an effort to promote scientific research, the satellite broadcast revolutionary hymns into space.

North Korea continues to develop and test its rocket technology.

Nodong

A redesign of SCUD technology in North Korea led to the SCUD-D, most commonly known in the country as Nodong-1.

Nodong-1 has a potential range of 1,000 to 1,300 km (600 to 780 miles) and a payload capacity of 700 to 1,000 kg (420 to 600 lbs).

The highest range covers a wide array of cities from Tokyo to Taipei. The highest extreme of ranges of the Nodong has been estimated to be between 2,000 and 4,000 m (6,600 and 13,200 ft).

A prototype of the one-thrust chamber Nodong was spotted on a launch pad in May 1990. However, test flights did not begin until May 1993, with a successful launch 500 km (300 miles) into the Sea of Japan. During this flight test, the Nodong-1 reached a high altitude with warhead separation demonstrated.

Propulsion tests commenced in 1994 in North Korea, Pakistan, and Iran.

The U.S. Department of Defense made it known that it suspected North Korea was continuing to make and field Nodong missiles in recent years that have been capable of striking American forces in Japan.

Technical and financial problems have continued to plague the program, although there have been miscellaneous unconfirmed reports of Nodong sightings.

The single-stage missile incorporates an SS-N-4, Isayev S-2, 713 M engine with a single large combustion chamber. The Iranian Shehab-3 and Pakistani Ghauri-II closely compare with this design.

The 15,200 to 16,000 kg (15.2 to 16 ton) Nodong runs on a mixed fuel of 20 percent gasoline and 80 percent kerosene.

The Nodong warhead is very much like a bullet fired from a rifle barrel. If the barrel happens to be grooved to spin up the bullet along its longitudinal axis, it tends to fly through the atmosphere to its target more smoothly and accurately. However, if the barrel is not built with this capability, the bullet will tumble uncontrollably about its center of gravity throughout its flight in the atmosphere to its target. This tumbling will reduce the accuracy of the projectile.

To date, North Korea has deployed over 300 Nodong medium-range and nearly a thousand SCUD-B and C short range missiles.

Hwasong 5/SCUD-B

In 1969, the North Korean government received Frog-7s and 60-km (36 mile) range Frog-5 tactical rockets from Russia, formerly the Soviet Union. Around the same time, North Korea developed chemical projectile warheads for the Frog-5 and Frog-7A.

The country received SCUD-B missiles from Egypt in mid–1976 in return for its assistance to Egypt in the Yom Kippur War.

North Korea now produces its own SCUDS, which were exported to Iran during the Gulf War. It also provided some assistance to Egypt in establishing that country's production of a SCUD clone.

SCUD-B missiles, referred to in North Korea as Hwasong 5s, have a range of 285 to 330 km (171 to 198 miles). They are equipped with one thrust chamber, operate with one stage, and run on a combined fuel of 20 percent gasoline and 80 percent kerosene.

Hwasong 6/SCUD-C

In 1988, a program to modify the North Korean version of the SCUD-B began. The updated version, SCUD-PIP (Product Improvement Program), or SCUD-C, achieved a longer range than its predecessor by a reduction of payload and extension of the length of the rocket body to increase the propellant by 25 percent.

Officially named Hwasong 6, the missile was designed with a 500 km (300 mile) range and a weight ranging from 700 to 800 kg (1,540 to 1,760 lb).

Successful test firings were completed in June 1990. Later that year, Iran received delivery of a number of the missiles, while soliciting North Korea's assistance in setting up its own assembly and manufacturing facility.

Hwasong 6/SCUD-C missiles run with one thrust chamber, one stage, and a fuel-mix of 50 percent Triethylamine and 50 percent Xylidine/T-1 kerosene.

Taepo-Dong 1 (TD-1)/ Paeutudan-1

North Korea has successfully developed a missile designated the Taepo-Dong 1 (TD-1) or Paeutudan-1. On August 31, 1988, completely without advance warning, the country launched a space booster based on Taepo-Dong technology from a missile test launch pad in eastern North Korea near Taepodong.

The missile consisted of two stages with a solid propellant third stage added. The Nodong-derived first stage booster pummeled into the Sea of Japan, while its SCUD-B-derived second stage fell into the waters off the Sanriku coast.

The TD-1 consists of either two stages with an estimated range of 2,000 to 2,200 km (1,200 to 1,320 miles) or three stages with a range of either 2,200 to 2,672 km (1,320 to 1,603 miles) or 2,200 to 2,896 km (1,320 to 1,737 miles), and a 700 to 1,000 kg (1,540 to 2,200 lb) warhead.

If a third stage has been added, it probably consists of a small ellipsoidal solid motor.

Taepo-Dong 1 can carry a payload ranging from 50 to 100 kg (110 to 220 lbs) and runs on a mixed fuel of 20 percent gasoline and 80 percent kerosene.

Taepo-Dong 2 (TD-2)

The Taepo-Dong 2 (TD-2) is a two or three stage missile with an estimated range of 3,650 to 3,750 km (2,190 to 2,250 miles) in the two-stage version and a 700 to 1,000 kg (1,540 to 2,200 lb) payload.

North Korea has given other names to the missile including Nodong 3, Hwasong (Mars)-2, and Moksong (Jupiter)-2.

Development on Taepo-Dong 2 began in 1987. It was widely believed TD-2 was designed as a defense against the United States.

In its three-stage version, Taepo-Dong 2 has a maximum range between 4,650 and 6,200 miles. At the greatest extreme, the missile could reach all major American cities on the West Coast, including Los Angeles, San Francisco, and San Diego, and possibly as far east as Chicago.

North Korean engines use highly corrosive and highly toxic storable propellants and can only undergo one test firing before they require tearing down, cleaning and reassembling for future firings, installation on launch vehicles for a flight test, or missile deployment.

Taepo-Dong 2 runs on a mixed fuel of 20 percent gasoline and 80 percent kerosene.

Kwangmyongsong-1

On August 31, 1998, North Korea launched its first artificial satellite, Kwangmyongsong-1, from Musudan-ri, Hwadae County, North Hamgyong Province. The satellite was launched by a Taepo-Dong 1 (TD-1) rocket comprised of a Nodong 2 first stage with a SCUD-class second stage.

The satellite was placed into an orbital inclination near 41 degrees, four minutes and 53 seconds following launch.

The satellite was equipped with sounding instruments and was reported to be designed to promote scientific research by the North Korean government.

A Russian space observation center spotted the satellite, which was transmitting revolutionary national hymns shortly after launch praising the late North Korean leader Kim-

II-Sun and his son, as well as the political heir, Kim Jong-II. The hymns broadcast were the "Song of General Kim II Sung," "Song of General Kim Jong II," and Morse signals for "Juche Korea" in 27 Mhz.

NORWAY

Norwegian Space Center (NSC)

The Norwegian Space Center (NSC) is responsible for coordinating all Norwegian space-related research with international partners such as ESA and NASA. It also provides administrative and project support for the country's participation in these projects. NSC headquarters are located in Oslo.

The center has been heavily engaged in space science projects, the majority of which utilize sounding rockets launched from Andoya Rocket Range. The rocket range also offers services to scientists around the world wishing to study phenomena in the middle or higher polar atmosphere.

Andoya Rocket Range

Andoya Rocket Range (ARR) is the launch center for NSC and is located in northern Norway. ARR operates ALOMAR, a unique atmospheric research facility, and also offers launches of sounding rockets from Svalbard (SvalRak).

ARR is the world's northern-most permanent launch facility for sounding rockets and scientific balloons. All scientific-related balloon and rocket operations for Norway are conducted here. The ranged has conducted 698 rocket launches to date.

The range is located at 69° North and 16° far North of the Arctic Circle. This particular high-latitude location provides ideal conditions for studying a variety of atmospheric and ionospheric phenomena using balloons, rockets, aircraft, and ground-based instruments.

ARR has a launch capacity for rocket configurations up to 20 metric tons. It is equipped with wide-band mobile and stationary telemetry stations, with a slant-range system for tracking purposes.

Since the range has a large impact area, a wide variety of launch directions and rocket configurations can be used on site without the need for guidance systems.

The launch site on the arctic archipelago, Svalbard, provides unique conditions and support for rocket studies of the dayside polar cusp, cleft and cap. It is located at 79° North, making it ideal for scientific exploration of the dayside aurora, as well as processes in the magnetospheric boundary layer.

ARR also operates the ALOMAR observatory, which houses a network of ground-based lidars, radars and spectrometers providing information on the dynamic and photochemical processes in the middle atmosphere. These measurements are accomplished with rocket and balloon launches or satellite passes.

Rockets can be launched from ARR without guidance or flight termination-systems, which saves money while increasing the net payload weight for scientific purposes. Payloads are easily recoverable from the Norwegian Sea by ship or helicopter, with recovery sites at either Andoya or Spitzbergen. The type of recovery vessels used depends on missions and user requirements.

Large balloons, greater than 100 m3 (3531 ft3), are launched in cooperation with other space organizations. Launches of scientific balloons from Spitzbergen at 78° North can result in circular flights driven by the systemic circulation of high altitude winds around the North Pole.

The combination of high geographic and

geomagnetic latitude at ARR is ideal for scientific exploration of the dayside aurora and processes in the magnetospheric boundary layer. Sounding rockets can be launched directly into the polar cap, as well as perpendicular to the earth's magnetic field.

Telecommunications

Telecommunications continues to be a dominant sector in Norway, accounting for nearly two-thirds of its space activities. Norwegian space companies Telenor and NERA have been major players in satellite development.

Alcatel Space Norway has continued to perfect its SAW filters, moving towards the achievement of higher frequencies in the two GHz and greater bandwidths. The company has contracted with Hughes of the United States to supply SAW modules for the Asia Pacific Mobile Telephone (APMT) satellites.

THOR SATELLITES

Norway's Thor I, the country's first television and communications satellite, was deorbited on January 7, 2002, after 12 years of service. It was placed into orbit by a Delta-II rocket launched from Cape Canaveral on August 17, 1990. The Thor satellites, I, II, and III, are Boeing 376s.

Thor II was launched in May 1997, to target the Nordic region and northern Europe in its service. It operates with a 15 Ku-band transponder capacity and was manufactured by Boeing Satellite Systems, with an expected lifetime of 12 years.

The Thor III was launched in June 1998, to service the Nordic region as well as central and eastern Europe. It is operating with a transponder capacity of 14 Ku-band and has an expected lifetime of 12 years.

Satellite Navigation

Norway has been using satellite navigation for a number of years in a variety of applications such as shipping, the fishing industry, private boating, and oil drilling. Norwegian companies participating include Navia

Seatex, Navia Aviation, Fugro-Geoteam and Simrad, which is a part of Kongsberg Maritime.

The country has benefited from Europe's Global Navigation Satellite System 1 and 2 (GNSS-1 and GNSS-2) programs. In conjunction with the GNSS-1 program, the European Union (EU) and European Space Agency (ESA) worked with Eurocontrol establish the European Geostationary Navigation Overlay System (EGNOS), which is a regional support system to improve the accuracy and integrity of the existing global positioning system (GPS). Seatex and the Norwegian Mapping Authority have also been active participants in EGNOS, with delivery of its test bed and reference stations.

Norway will also be participating in the future satellite navigation system, Galileo, scheduled for development and implementation during 2004 and 2008. Seatex will collaborate with the Norwegian University of Science and Technology to develop Galileo's software. Seatex has also been active in the EU GALA project to implement Galileo's architecture, performance and coverage, including coverage at northern latitudes, which are very relevant to Norway in management of its geological features.

Earth Observation

Earth observation has proven to be particularly useful to Norway, which has large, territorial waters. The ability to observe marine and polar operations in near real-time is critical.

Programs through NSC have supported the establishment of cost-effective services based on data obtained from the detection of the Coastguard and Norwegian Navy ships; oil detection for the State Pollution Control Authority (SFT) as well as oil companies, allowing for the monitoring of oil spills in high priority areas of Norwegian territorial waters; and ice monitoring for users who operate in ice-infested waters in conjunction with the Norwegian Meteorological Institute, the Norwegian Polar Institute, and the Nansen Environmental and Remote Sensing Center.

NSC has found several ways in which

satellite data can be useful in environmental research and management. Five sectors within this area have been identified, including the conservation and utilization of biological diversity; ocean and water pollution; climactic changes, air pollution and noise; international environmental cooperation and support in relation to polar regions; and maps and geographical data.

SvalRak Sounding Rockets

Norway has been using scientific sounding rockets for studies of the middle atmosphere and the ionosphere. These rockets are launched from Andoya Rocket Range in northern Norway and from Svalbard.

SvalRak is the newest type of Norwegian sounding rocket which is being launched from Spitsbergen's Svalbard facility to study certain aspects of the energy exchange between the earth and the sun, particularly phenomena in the magnetospheric polar cleft. The location of Svalbard makes it ideal for the study of the dayside aurora against a dark sky.

SvalRak rockets are currently launched in campaigns every two years. The program, thus far, has been an operational and scientific success.

The launch site at Svalbard provides unique conditions for rocket studies of the dayside polar cusp, cleft, and cap due to its prime location at the arctic. Svalbard is located 79 degrees North and is ideal for scientific exploration of the dayside aurora and magnetospheric boundary layer process.

Polar orbiting satellites at Svalbard are launched for earth observations, telecommunications, and other scientific missions. Data received is stored on tape recorders and transmitted to the ground when the satellites pass over a ground station. This data is received and downloaded directly in real time.

The ground station at Svalbard is also unique because it covers all 14 daily passes of polar orbiting satellites, making it very cost-effective for a satellite owner or operator. At this latitude, one station provides complete coverage and two stations are no longer needed to provide full coverage.

The SvalSat ground station became operational in 1997. NASA was the first customer and continues to use it for earth observation satellites (EOS). NASA installed one 11 m (36 ft) S-X band antenna system. A second, large antenna system was installed by Kongsberg Spacetec and Lockheed Martin.

In 2000, the European meteorological organization, EUMETSAT, began using Sval-Sat as the site for its EPS satellites.

New Projects

The Norwegian Space Center supports a number of projects which provide services for satellite owners, as well as users of satellite data, and new tools for scientists at Andoya Rocket Range. These projects include Mini Dusty, MIDAS, the Hotel Payload Project, and the development of unmanned aerial vehicles (UAVs).

The reduction of scientific payloads for sounding rockets has been studied at NSC. Cheap, small meteorological rockets can be more easily used for studies of the middle atmosphere. A series of these small instrumented rockets has been developed at the University of Tromso. These rockets are currently being launched from Andoya Rocket Range and Svalbard. The project requires the development of several small payloads with different sensors for a variety of measurements.

MIDAS is an ambitious German-Norwegian project in which a standardized payload with recovery unit has been launched 15 times over a five-year period.

The Hotel Payload Project will help reduce costs for scientists working with sounding rockets. This is the proposal in which a standard platform for payloads using newly-designed rocket motors will be used.

Norway has an interest in the development of UAVs, or unmanned aerial vehicles, which are known to play an important role in surveillance as well as atmospheric research. Services based on the use of UAVs will be offered to scientists at Andoya Rocket Range in the near future.

PAKISTAN

Space and Upper Atmosphere Research Commission (SUPARCO), Pakistan

The Space and Upper Atmosphere Commission, known as SUPARCO, of Pakistan was established in 1961 and is a national organization with a high degree of autonomy. SUPARCO's programs include the development and launch of sounding rockets and satellite applications in the field of remote sensing and communications, and is headquartered at the Arabian Sea port of Karachi in southern Pakistan.

Pakistan's space program began by building its own rocket launching facility at Sonmiami. In 1962, Pakistan entered into the space age by launching a rocket, Rehbar-1, followed by Rehbar-II launched June 11, 1962. Rehbar flights were for the purpose of acquiring meteorological data pertaining to wind velocity and direction at an altitude of 50 to 80 miles.

SUPARCO's meteorological sounding rocket program continued with the firing of three Skua rockets in March and April 1973, to conduct experiments of stratospheric winds and temperature measurements. Through launching a series of sounding rockets, SUPARCO achieved its objectives of in situ measurements in the upper atmosphere. The space research and technology program was further expanded by developing necessary ground facilities for tracking rockets and satellites and acquiring telemetry and other scientific data from weather, earth resources surveying, radio amateur and navigational satellites.

Fabrication of ground receiving system for the ATS-6 satellite in 1975–76 enabled the agency to gain experience in integrated electronics used in telecommunications, time and frequency standards and digital processing systems. Beacon satellite studies using ATS-6

radio beacon data were carried out, and vertical incidence ionospheric soundings continued to be made from Karachi and Islamabad at regular intervals.

In 1980, as part of an operational satellite system, development of a Direct Broadcasting Satellite Receiving System (DBSR) and fabrications of a small experimental satellite was commenced. For low earth orbit practical applications two tracking, telemetry and telecommand ground stations were set up at Lahore and Karachi. This was followed by the design and development of Pakistan's first experimental satellite, Badr-1, which was successfully launched in July, 1990. Badr is named after the Urdu language word for new moon.

Badr-1, or Badr-A, was launched as a piggyback payload aboard the Chinese Long March 2-E launch vehicle. Badr-1 was inserted into an orbit of 205 km by 990 km, lasting a short five weeks, though successfully completing store and dump message tests. Badr-2, or Badr-B, was developed and is ready for launch from Baikonur cosmodrome in Kazakhstan on a ZENIT-2 rocket.

When SUPARCO began launching sounding rockets in 1962, it fired small sounding rockets on suborbital flights from launch pads at Sonmiami Beach flight-range which is 36 miles west of Karachi. During the 1970s, SUPARCO developed the ability to fabricate rocket motors from raw materials at a solid-propellant manufacturing plant.

By the early 1980s, SUPARCO announced plans for the development of the Hatf-1 and Hatf-2 surface-to-surface ballistic missiles. Solid propellant production facilities were enlarged by 1987 to support this effort. Tests of the Hatf-1 and Hatf-2 were announced in April 1989, and the Hatf-2 was displayed publicly during a Pakistan Day Joint Services Parade later that year.

In July 1997, Pakistan launched an enhanced version of its Hatf missile in a test carried out as part of SUPARCO's continued development of rocket motor technology. The Hatf-3 had a range of 800 kilometers (500 miles).

In addition to developing launch vehicles, SUPARCO engaged in the study of remote sensing satellite applications for earth resources survey with seven proposals created and forwarded to NASA for monitoring ERTS-B data. In 1973, SUPARCO initiated its remote sensing applications program for earth resources and environmental monitoring using Landsat data acquired through NASA.

Later, in 1976, a portable Landsat ground receiving station was set up near Rawalpindi which provided extensive coverage of Pakistan for a period of 12 months. The station operated under a collaborative arrangement between SUPARCO and NASA. In 1989, SUPARCO established its own satellite ground receiving station at Rawat, near Islamabad, for reception of earth resources data from different satellites including United States' Landsat and NOAA, and the French SPOT satellite series. Using this data, a number of demonstrative and pilot studies in different fields have been carried out for the benefit of different data user agencies in Pakistan.

These remote studies include flood mapping, wetlands mapping, forest cover mapping, vegetation cover in Pakistan, waterlogging and salinity, coastal landform mapping, general land use and land cover mapping, population and housing census in Pakistan, and mapping of urban and rural sprawl.

On November 11, 2001, Pakistan's second satellite, Badr-2, was successfully injected into earth orbit from the Russian Cosmodrome at Baikonur, Kazakhstan. The satellite was launched with a main Russian meteorological satellite, Meteor3-M, onboard a Zenith-II launch vehicle, in collaboration with the Russian aviation and space agency. It is orbiting the earth in a near circular sun-synchronous orbit.

Badr-2 weighs 70 kilograms and is expected to have an operational life of two years. Orbiting at a height of around a thousand kilometers, it passes over Pakistan between ten and fifteen minutes during each orbit. Badr-2 is expected to decrease Pakistan's reliance on other nations for plotting its topography, natural resources and other physical characteristics. Such data can be used to formulate policies relating to land and water use, agriculture, and conservation of the environment and of natural resources.

SUPARCO intends to also use data gathered by Badr-2 for defense purposes and is currently in the process of developing its satellite launch vehicle in the hope of helping other developing countries launch their satellites.

PERU

National Aerospace Research & Development Commission (CONIDA) of Peru

The National Aerospace Research and Development Commission (CONIDA) of Peru signed a cooperation agreement with the Indian Space Agency and a similar agreement with the Space Agency of the Russian Federation. In signing these agreements, CONIDA hopes to establish closer links with space agencies in other countries through international cooperation and technical assistance programs that will make it possible to make use of new knowledge in this area and the latest advances in space technology.

CONIDA is currently designing a series of small satellites that will in the future receive financial and technical assistance from these space agencies.

The CONIDA Center for Space Studies

provides advanced training courses for public and private sector professionals in different aspects of remote sensing technology, digital processing of satellite images, geographic information systems (GIS) and global positioning systems (GPS).

Through its radioastronomy laboratory, CONIDA is implementing several projects for studying the galaxy and the sun. These include solar explosions type III, solar rays in 2800 Hz, solar corona region, magnetic field monitoring, sun-earth connection, artificial model for observing the solar corona, and variable stars in the galaxy.

The project with the most importance is variable stars in the galaxy, which will study star variables and engage in star detection in an effort to achieve a better understanding of the galaxy. Star classification, identifying pulsar modes, and studying variations that indicate the color in cataclysmic stars are also critical aspects to this project.

Another project with high priority is the sun-earth connection, which will study the relationship between the earth and the sun relative to the rest of the planetary system. The hypothesis here is based upon the fact that the earth is permanently bombarded with particles and electromagnetic radiation. The effects of ultraviolet rays (UVs) will also be examined.

THE PHILIPPINES

Philippine Space Agency

The emphasis of the Philippine Space Agency is on the infrastructure of a constellation of telecommunications satellites hovering above earth. Earth observation, through environmental satellites, has made it possible to mitigate and plan better ways of preserving dwindling and fragile resources, whose loss was brought about by societal progress and development. These resources are indeed critical to the Philippines.

In the Philippines, a wide array of space technologies, including satellite remote sensing and geographic information systems (GIS), satellite meteorology, satellite communications, environmental and disaster monitoring systems and others, have been used comprehensively to provide information needs for an environmentally sound and sustainable development planning process, and to assist in poverty alleviation. These technologies have gained increasing acceptance and have contributed significantly and cost-effectively to promoting social and economic development in the Philippines. The Science and Technology Coordinating Council-Committee on Space Technology Applications (STCC-COSTA), through a combined

synergy with other government agencies and the private sector, has initiated a number of research and development projects on space technology applications.

Following the Action Plan on Space Applications for Sustainable Development in Asia and the Pacific which was implemented at a September 1994, conference, the Philippines developed new space policy guidelines, including political commitment for the promotion of space applications at the national level and integration of space technology with development planning; stress on intersectoral, regional and international cooperation, training and education, scientific research and development, and information services; and allocation of adequate resources on a regular basis for those activities and institutional arrangements for national coordination. This program has since been referred to as the National Space Applications Program.

Since its inception in the early 1990s, STCC-COSTA has been able to implement a number of research and development projects, mostly in remote sensing and GIS, and has hosted and coordinated several international workshops and conferences. However, a concrete national framework and strategy for space technology applications research and development still has to be laid down.

The National Space Technology Applications Program is in the process of addressing the areas that will be the focus of scientific and technological efforts in all aspects of space technology use and development in the Philippines. It is part of a series of measures that will be pursued to achieve the common vision of the Philippines to become a knowledge-based economy in the medium term (1999–2004). The program emphasizes the development and utilization of superior space technologies to a level of competitive advantage and is intended to run in parallel with the currently outlined national and regional programs which include the National Science Technology Agenda and the Regional Space Applications Program for Sustainable Development.

In the areas of remote sensing and GIS technology, the Philippines has been involved in a number of applications for more than two decades. STCC-COSTA had humble beginnings and was an offshoot of the Philippine/Australian remote sensing project in the early 1990s. The increasing role of remote sensing became apparent in 1992, and thus paved the way for the creation of the National Coordinating Council for Remote Sensing, which was converted into STCC-COSTA in 1995.

Several projects have been initiated by the Philippines in collaboration with international organizations and agencies. One of the earliest major projects spearheaded by STCC-COSTA was the Commission on Environmental Cooperation between the ESA and the Association of Southeast Asian Nations (ASEAN); a natural resource and environment management project. This project aimed to enhance local capability in processing data from ERS-1 and the Advanced Very High Resolution Radiometer (AVHRR) sensor. This included equipment upgrading as well as training of technical personnel from the Philippine Atmospheric, Geophysical and Astronomical Administration (PAGASA) and the National Mapping and Resource Information Authority (NAMRIA).

The country has also joined the ASEAN/Australian project on topographic mapping using remote sensing technologies with NAMRIA as the lead implementing agency.

A milestone project entered into by STCC-COSTA is the Pacific Rim mission (PACRIM) of NASA. Phase I of the Philippines NASA-AirSAR was funded by the Department of Science and Technology with technical assistance from the NASA Jet Propulsion Laboratory and the University of New South Wales, Australia. The development objective of this project was the promotion of the use of airborne synthetic aperture radar (AirSAR) data for various applications relating to natural resource management and development planning. Five research studies are being implemented by six government agencies and a private firm or three study sites. Phase II activities of the project, which are under way, are concerned with information processing and extraction, interpretation and map generation for the selected sites.

The land use and land cover change project was completed in 1997 as an activity financed by the International Geosphere-Biosphere Programme, the Global Change System for Analysis Research and Training, the South Asian Regional Cooperation countries and ASEAN. The project established the methodologies for identifying parameters of change in land use and land cover that could be used in the development of a model for predicting such change using socio-economic factors.

Two other projects made use of Advanced Earth Observing Satellite (ADEOS) data. These projects, entitled "Monitoring Lahar using ADEOS data" and "Chlorophyll study of the Lingayen Gulf using ADEOS," were funded by the National Space Development Agency (NASDA) of Japan through RESTEC and ESCAP. These projects were implemented by the University of the Philippines Training Center for Applied Geodesy and Photogrammetry and the Marine Science Institute respectively.

When struck by of El Nino, the Philippines suffered from forest and brush fires, in particular on the island of Palawan. There was difficulty in obtaining clear and useful images that would indicate the stricken areas. Despite this predicament, analysis of archived satellite images was undertaken in order to assess the original vegetative cover of the affected areas and to present the results and their possible impact to decision makers for policy and strategy formulation. To strengthen the Philippines' commitment towards regional study, a legislative bill was passed to promote modernization of natural resource and environmental management using space technology, known as the NAMRIA Modernization Bill.

In the mid–1990s, through the cooperation of large private telecommunications and broadcasting firms, the Agila I and II satellites were launched into orbit. Agila I was ill-fated, and followed by the launch of Agila II. The Agila fleet consists of telecommunications satellites that were launched to address the burgeoning demand of the telecommunications and commercial broadcast industries in the Philippines. The Agila II satellite has a large ground footprint, making access by neighboring Asian countries available. To date, Agila II is one of the most formidable satellites of its class in the region.

Agila II, the first high-powered telecommunications satellite, built by Space Systems/Loral (SS/L) for the Mabuhay Philippines Satellite Corporation, was successfully launched into orbit in August aboard a Long March 3B rocket from the Xichang satellite launch center. The Agila satellite reinforces SS/L's dominance in the emerging domestic and international market for advanced high-powered broadcast satellites. The satellite has more than nine kilowatts of total telecommunications satellite in service in the Asia-Pacific region. The high-powered spacecraft will allow the Mabuhay Philippines Satellite Corporation to transmit more than 190 channels of high-fidelity digital programming to cable companies and home satellite dishes and to handle more than 50,000 simultaneous two-way telephone conversations.

The Agila satellite operates 30 C-band transponders at 27 watts and 24 Ku-band transponders at 110 watts that are combinable to 12 high-power transponders at 220 watts. The satellite features the largest number of active transponders of any satellite in the region and has a high power-to-mass ratio, making it one of the most efficient satellites in the in-

dustry. Agila II has an expected service life of over 12 years.

In addition to designing and manufacturing the satellite, SS/L provided satellite control ground station equipment in Subic Bay, the Philippines, and has trained the Mabuhay Philippines Satellite Corporation personnel to operate the satellite after completion of on-orbit testing. SS/L will conduct the on-orbit testing from its mission control center located in Palo Alto, United States, and from the Mabuhay Space Center in Subic Bay.

The Agila II design uses SS/L's flight-proven three-axis, body-stabilized FS-1300 bus, tailored to accommodate the required communication payload. The modular design and construction of the FS-1300 platform supports reliable long-life operation with an integral bipropellant propulsion system to place the satellite on station. A three-axis momentum bias system accurately maintains altitude stability on-orbit throughout the satellite's life. Deployable solar arrays supplemented with high-energy nickel–hydrogen batteries provide uninterrupted electrical power to the spacecraft.

SS/L is a full-service provider of commercial communications satellite systems and services, including launch services, insurance procurement and long-term mission operations from its mission control center in Palo Alto. SS/L currently has a total backlog of more than 80 spacecraft. In addition to building Agila, the company is the prime contractor for the Globalstar low earth orbit satellite system and the builder of INTELSAT, N-STAR, APSTAR, Telstar, M2A and CHINASAT communications satellites, audio-radio satellites for CD radio, direct broadcast satellites for TCI/Tempo, MCI, PanAmSat and L-STAR, the latest series of weather watch satellites, the Geostationary Operational Environmental Satellite (GOES) and the Japanese MTSAT, the next-generation Japanese air traffic control and weather watch satellite.

Other areas of continued research and development in the area of space applications include a topical cyclone forecasting and warning research system; a severe weather forecasting and warning research system; a quantitative precipitation and flood forecasting research program; a long-range weather forecasting program; a climate/agro-meteorological applications and climate change research program; a hazard analysis, environmental impact assessment and disaster management/mitigation research program; and an astronomical research program.

These programs are aimed at improving the meteorological and hydrological studies in particular, with respect to severe weather, tropical cyclone and flood forecasting and warning. The programs will also enhance the agency's competence in the monitoring and prediction of El Nino and La Nina, specialized weather services for agriculture, marine meteorology and oceanography, aviation meteorology, climate change and global warming issues, disaster preparedness and mitigation and astronomy and space science.

POLAND

Polish Academy of Sciences — Space Research Center (SRC)

The Space Research Center (SRC) of the Polish Academy of Sciences was established in 1977. It has since been involved in activities covering the design, preparation, and development of space experiments through international cooperative programs. These programs include the constructing of scientific instruments, performing satellite observations and solar/ionospheric observations, and conducting space research in the areas of space physics, remote sensing, and solar physics.

During the period of 1977 through 1997, SRC developed, built, and prepared 39 instruments for launch, including 19 for suborbital flights and 20 for satellite missions.

The institute's first experiments were launched using Russian VERTICAL rockets within the INTERCOSMOS cooperative program. However, the last rocket experiment was launched in 1992 using a NASA Terrier Black Brent rocket.

The first satellite experiment used two instruments which were developed by SRC and launched in 1986 aboard the IONOSONDE mission (Cosmos-1809). Other missions utilized the Phobos 1 and 2, as well as the Vega and Mars-96 space probes. The Mars-96 was deployed on the MIR space station. A thermal sensor developed by SRC is currently a part of the payload onboard Huygens, which is on its way to Saturn and its satellite Titan. This mission is a feature of the international NASA/ESA planetary mission CASSINI.

The institute has also been actively involved in the construction of many unique ground-based experiments such as the KOS inosonde, a laser range meter, a microwave soil dampness tester, and a spectrometer to measure visual reflective characteristics of natural objects.

SRC has recently participated in the building of a network to contribute to knowledge of the earth and its space environment. This system, called EUREF (European Reference Frame), is a European fundamental geodetic reference global positioning system (GPS), featuring a Polish unified geodetic network.

The Polish network has 358 nodes with coordinates measured using centimeter accuracy. It facilitates practical applications within a common reference system while also providing a means of scientific research.

SRC has also developed a model of the ionosphere above Europe which has been used to provide state-of-the-art heliogeophysical prediction services both nationally and internationally through the International Space Environment Service (ISES).

SRC has been using this model for geodynamics and laser observations of satellites, providing data and analysis which has enabled the discovery of short-term oscillations of the earth's pole and perturbations of its rotation in relation to their correlation to geophysical phenomena. In addition, rocket and satellite experiments have provided SRC with extensive knowledge on the electromagnetic environment of the earth as well as the discovery of its antropogenic conditioning.

SRC has a program on the investigation of space plasma in which experiments on the interaction of modulated electron beams with plasma give information on the excitation and propagation of plasma waves. These discoveries have contributed to the field of plasma physics by enhancing knowledge of the upper atmosphere.

Studies of the scintillation of electromagnetic waves emitted by earth's satellites have allowed for the developing of a picture of turbulence in the ionosphere which is an important factor in the model of this region and allows for predictions of electromagnetic wave propagation conditions.

This research has also covered the prediction of the existence of thin current sheets during magnetic storms in the polar regions of the terrestrial magnetosphere. It has also yielded the discovery of a new plasma population in the inner magnetosphere referred to as a warm shell of the plasma sheet.

SRC also conducts experimental and theoretical studies of the solar corona, where the plasma temperature is a very hot millions of kelvins. It also uses instruments to collect and analyze the X-ray spectra of solar flares which make it possible to determine the chemical composition of solar plasma and provide a better understanding of the processes of energy deposits in the solar corona.

SRC participated in the first in situ detection of neutral interstellar helium atoms on Ulysses as well as the interpretation of helium pickup ion data from AMPTE/IRM, where the existence of the neutral helium cone, which was predicted by theoretical studies conducted by SRC, was experimentally confirmed.

Theoretical models of planetary magnetotails were also developed, allowing for predictions on the shapes of these plasma forma-

tions, and the experimental confirmation of models for earth and Jupiter.

SRC has also contributed to investigations of subtle effects in cometary motion. For the first time, during the Halley's comet campaign, a cometary nucleus and its activity were observed. SRC used this information to develop a model of non-gravitation forces affecting the cometary motion for inclusion in orbital studies.

Several motion models of periodic comets were constructed, including the Wirtanen comet for the ESA Rosetta mission in which SRC will participate.

The year 2000 marked the 30th anniversary of the first launch of a Polish-made scientific instrument.

Other achievements of the institute have included the development of a new time-dependent three-dimensional MHD model of interaction of the solar wind with the totally ionized interstellar wind in the presence of a non-negligible, arbitrarily directed interstellar magnetic field. This model predicts deviations of the heliospheric structure from axial symmetry when the magnetic field is not aligned with or perpendicular to the flow direction.

The institute developed a method of comparing multi-channel GPS observations which was applied to compare eight caesium clocks operating in Poland. As a result of this research, a new Polish national atomic time scale (TAPL) was developed as a weighted average of time scales from the eight clocks. The stability of these clocks combined has proven to be better than the stabilities of the individual clocks used by an order of magnitude.

The TAPL system requires use of an algorithm deployed in a numerical program which was developed in cooperation with the International Bureau of Measures and Weights (BIPM) in Paris.

Remote Sensing

There are several ongoing projects in the remote sensing department of SRC. These include PFS, the investigation of the surface and atmosphere of Mars during the Mars Express mission; HIFI, the control block for the local oscillator for the Heterodyne instrument for

Herschel; VIRTIS, modeling of optical effects from gas, dust and the surface of the Wirtanen comet for the ROSETTA mission; IBIS, the electronic block for the anti-coincidence system of the gamma telescope for the INTEGRAL mission; and WIZJER, a system in ISTOK-1, which was an experiment used for the orbital station aboard MIR.

The Planetary Fourier Spectrometer (PFS) experiment is a part of the Mars Express payload which was launched by the European Space Agency on June 2, 2003. Its mission is to answer questions about the Martian surface related to water erosion by studying the chemical composition and the atmosphere of Mars from a circumplanetary orbit. The study will be based heavily on the fact that absorption or emission bands in the infrared spectra make invaluable "fingerprints" for an unambiguous identification of chemical species.

A number of spectral bands of various compounds fall into the range of sensitivity of PFS. Their detection will enable the solving of a wide set of scientific problems concerning the surface and atmospheric composition of Mars.

There has been a strong interest in water on the surface of Mars and its present low-pressure, low-temperature conditions which cause its state of instability. The discovery of sedimentary deposits, particularly carbonates, might indicate that very different climactic conditions may have existed on the planet in the past. It is possible that the average abundance of carbonates within the globally mixed Martian regolith could be very low. Therefore, the search for this kind of material on Mars would be successful only if it was conducted along those areas of the planet where large carbonate deposits are thought to be present, as allowable by the PFS.

The remote sensing department developed several subsystems of the PFS instrument, including a pointing device or scanner, Module S FM, which allows the PFS to receive radiation from Mars or from in-flight calibration sources; and the power supply block with a DC/DC converter, Module P FM.

The HIFI (Heterodyne instrument for the far infrared) spectrometer is one of three scientific instruments which will be placed on the Herschel space observatory which is scheduled for launch in 2007. Herschel will study the origin of stars and galaxies while searching for water in space. It will help contribute to our understanding of the formation of our own solar system through detailed observations of comets and transneptunian objects, of which very little is known.

Herschel will be the first space observatory to cover a major part of the far-infrared and sub-millimeter waveband from 100 to 625 microns.

SRC contributed to the construction of HIFI's modules, including an optical input block containing detectors, mixers, and pre-amplifiers; a local oscillator working in temperatures to about 100 K or –173C; an output block containing intermediate frequency amplifiers and spectrometers; and a HIFI control unit for instrument control, communications with satellites and transmission of scientific data.

VIRTIS (Visible and InfraRed Thermal Imaging Spectrometer) is devoted to the study of the comet 46P/Wirtanen for the ESA Rosetta mission by imaging spectroscopy. It will study the cometary nucleus and its environment as well as the nature of solids on the surface. It will also identify various gaseous species and physical conditions of the coma. VIRTIS will provide characterizations of asteroids.

SRC built the Veto Electronics Box (VEB) as a part of the anti-coincidence electronic system for the telescope IBIS (imager onboard INTEGRAL satellite) onboard the INTEGRAL (International gamma ray laboratory) mission for ESA. The anti-coincidence system reduces the noise level of the instrument while enhancing its sensitivity. The VEB block issues the final veto signal used by other subsystems of the telescope to prevent detectors from making a false count. The VEB block also serves to power, control and monitor 18 photomultiplier blocks from anti-coincidence system and to calibration. INTEGRAL was launched on October 17, 2002, on a PROTON rocket from Baikonur, Russia.

WIZJER was developed for the international earth remote sensing experiment ISTOK-1 to assist in providing a spectral analysis in infrared range (4 to 16 micrometer) to investigate desintegration of dust aggregates (CH_4, SO_2, N_2O) and the spectral features of the earth's atmosphere.

In 1996, WIZJER was launched into orbit on PRIRODA, a module that docked with the Russian orbital station Mir.

SRC contributed to WIZJER with a digital television camera and a scientific program experiment. The primary goal of the experiment was to investigate the earth's atmosphere and surface, conducting measurements with spectral instruments.

WIZJER was a digital image processing camera incorporated with the infrared spectrometer mounted on the common platform. The instrument developed by SRC consisted of two parts — the camera and the electronic box. The first block was installed outside Mir and the second was installed inside the station. The instrument weighed 9.5 kg (21 lbs) and consumed 13 W in power.

RESIK

RESIK is the first X-ray spectrometer designed to perform the systematic study of solar plasma composition for a number of species including both low and high FIP elements. RESIK, Rentgenowsky Spektrometrs Izognutymi Kristalami, was built with the primary purpose of determining elemental composition of active region and flare plasma, and determination of differential emission measures (DEM).

It was launched on July 31, 2001, and equipped with two main units — two spectrometers, A and B, with supporting front-end electronics placed on the satellite instrument payload; and a control unit with telemetry interface, including a computer system within the sealed compartment.

RESIK is a Bragg crystal spectrometer which was a part of the CORONAS-F solar observatory payload, one of the satellite observatories devoted to solar physics. CORONAS-F is a follow-up satellite to the CORONAS-I satellite launched in 1994.

RESIK, consisting of channels spanning ten different spectral bands in 1.1 Å to 6.1 Å range, has two position-sensitive double proportional counters to aid in the observation of active solar flare plasmas.

RESIK is a cooperative project between SRC, IZMIRAN in Russia, the Mullard Space Science Laboratory (MSSL), the Rutherford Appleton Laboratory (RAL) in the U.K., and the Naval Research Laboratory (NRL) in the United States. Its diffraction elements include two quartz and two silicon monocrystals working in first, second, and third order.

The instrument's objectives include the determination of relative and absolute coronal abundance in the upper limits of elements with atomic numbers Z = 13 ffl 30; studies of variability of the coronal composition in time and between different structures of the corona with investigations of possible solar cycle effects; the investigation of ionization state of solar high temperature plasma components; the verification of atomic theory for ionization balance calculations; the investigation of possible local non–Maxwellian velocity distribution of electrons; and investigations of the spectrum shape close to ionization limits of individual ions and the relative intensities of higher members of H- and He- like resonance line series.

ROMANIA

Romanian Space Agency (ROSA)

The Romanian Space Agency (ROSA) was established in 1991 as an independent public institution under the management of the Ministry of Research and Technology, also referred to as the Ministry of Education and Research. The goals of ROSA are to promote and coordinate the development of national efforts in space while promoting international cooperation.

ROSA's activities cover basic space science research, space structures, technologies, microgravity, communications, education, earth observation, and remote sensing applications, as well as life sciences and medicine.

The agency participates in international space missions and develops new basic and advanced space research projects. It also continues to develop spin-off space technology to stimulate the national economy.

The primary focus of space infrastructure projects applies to hazards monitoring, global information systems, and the use of microsatellites.

Space Science

Studies in space science include those on meteorology and climate through the National Institute on Meteorology and Hydrology. Other studies focus on the earth's surface and tectonic movements in conjunction with the Institute of Geodynamics of the Romanian Academy.

ROSA contributed to the onboard computing system for the PRIRODA remote sensing experiment which was placed onboard the Mir space station.

Space studies conducted through the Astronomical Institute of the Romanian Academy have included the earth-moon system, planets and small bodies of the solar system, satellite dynamics in the observation of the upper terrestrial atmosphere, and observations of space telescopes.

Space studies conducted by the Institute for Space Science have included the use of onboard mass spectrometers for the study of atmospheric composition and dynamics, the study of the earth's magnetosphere using satellite data processing, the launching of magnetometers through international cooperation, and contributions to the EQUATOR-S, FAST, and CLUSTER magnetometry and space plasma projects of ESA, as well as participation in their PLANK and SPORT projects.

During the total solar eclipse of August 11, 1999, ROSA participated in the NOTTE project to study solar neutrino oscillations.

It has also contributed in the area of satellite dynamics with a fluidic accelerometer for use onboard satellites, as well as methods to utilize optimal singular control in space dynamics.

The agency has explored fundamental physics possibilities in space through discrete space-time structure and applications of the theory of categories to gravity; and theoretical researches in general relativity, including spin-offs for NASA's Gravity Probe-B.

Microgravity and Life Science

In the area of microgravity and life science, ROSA has coordinated the study of magnetic fluids in microgravity, studied the mechanism of heat transfer in nucleate boiling of magnetic fluids under microgravity conditions, performed GRL studies of the magnetic fluids composites within a microscopic inner rotation of the nonmagnetic phase in magnetic liquid, proposed experiments for future missions with small payloads ranging between 0.5 and 0.9 kg (1.1 and 1.9 lb) for microsatellites, studied human and animal physiology under microgravity conditions and radiation, studied cellular behavior in microgravity, and performed experiments on the influence of magnetic liquids on plants and cells.

Space Applications

ROSA has operated the Cheia Intelsat ground station with two 32-m (105 ft) antennas since 1977, developed a VSAT communications system, participated in the Italian Space Agency's SHARED telemedicine project since 1998, and served as a local dealer for satellite systems such as ORBCOMM, Globalstar, Iridium, and ICO.

In the area of earth observations, the agency has designed applications for improving natural resources management, cartography, land use, and environmental protection. It has also applied imagery from optical and radar high-resolution satellites such as Landsat, Spot, IRS, ERS, and Radarsat to local land management.

The agency designs satellite image processing algorithms, studies space imagery for applications to forestry and hydrology, and operates a receiving station for the NOAA-14 and NOAA-15 satellites.

ROSA has conducted studies on the precision and stability of satellite global positioning systems, developed onboard GPS systems and prepared second-generation satellite navigation and positioning system proposals for the European Commission's Fifth Framework Research and Development Program.

The agency continues to market the commercial use of global positioning techniques to companies that are now using digital mapping, cartography, and geographic information systems on a regular basis.

Aerospace and Spin-Off Technology

ROSA developed a platform for flexible orientation along with an onboard computer to maintain the remote sensor for the ISTOK experiment of the Mir space station. It also designed a stabilized platform with positioning precision of a tenth of a second of an arc in order to transport a neutrino oscillations detection experiment during the total solar eclipse from August 1999.

The agency has also developed a series of small, unmanned aircraft to use for experiments and to teach space science and technology applications.

Other experiments have the measured and monitored electromagnetic pollution, tested vacuum leakage for helium cryostats with mass spectrometers, and developed rotary vacuum seals for chemical industry and crystal growth equipment.

Institute for Space Sciences

The Institute for Space Sciences began its activities in 1954. It has since focused on cosmic space physics, covering all experimental and theoretical concepts including equipment development, experiments in cosmic space, data processing and interpretation, theoretical research, and cosmic space utilization. The institute also participates in international cooperative programs emphasizing earth studies.

ISS research concentrates specifically on magnetometery and cosmic plasmas, planetary atmospheres, astrophysics and cosmic rays, gravitation, celestial mechanics and microgravity.

Its research groups include theoretical physics; astrophysics and mathematical physics, covering atomic and molecular physics in cosmic space, quantum field theory, dynamical systems, statistical physics and non-equilibrium statistical mechanics; the kinetic theory of the simple gas and reactive kinetic theory; equilibrium statistical mechanics including phase transitions and exactly soluble models; cosmology, covering cosmic background radiation and non-accelerator high energy astrophysics with cosmological relevance; and cosmic rays and nuclear astrophysics, including properties of cosmic rays and accelerated particles, detectors development for corpuscular, X-ray and gamma-ray cosmic radiation.

Studies in fundamental and advanced technological research in space magnetometry and plasmas focus on the development of special computational and treatment techniques for satellite data processing. In this area, electromagnetic wave propagation studies are conducted, as well as the study of structures induced by the geomagnetic field into near-earth plasma.

Related achievements in this research have included the placement of several space magnetometers onboard seven satellites. These were of the SG-R type for measurements of the earth's magnetic field from circumterrestrial orbits; the development of an onboard computing device for the infrared remote sensing spectrometer ISTOK-1 and for the complex remote sensing experiment PRIRODA onboard the Mir space station; for prototypes for process control systems designed for embarked experiments; for prototypes for the command processors of unmanned flying micro-objects; for firmware and software development tools for microprocessors; for the development of software for neutron spectroscopy data processing onboard the MARS 96 mission; and for the development of software for satellite magnetometry data processing.

Fundamental and advanced technological

research in gravitation, microgravitation, and space dynamics has focused on gravitation, including theoretical methods for the investigation of gravitation and space-time structures; microgravity, including advanced and applied research in high sensitivity inertial sensors, and low-g statistical and dynamical accelerometers; and celestial mechanics, or the study of the trajectories of cosmic objects.

Achievements in these areas have included an experimental model of low-g accelerators, magnetic liquid devices, high-resolution inertial sensors with magnetic fluids, high sensitivity biaxial inertial sensors, and high sensitivity biaxial inertial sensors for monitoring the geophysical laboratory of the Institute of Geodynamics, Bucharest.

National Institute on Aerospace Research

The National Institute on Aerospace Research began its activities in aerodynamics, flight dynamics, and aerospace system design in 1950. Its main specializations include complex aerodynamic testing at subsonic, transonic, and supersonic speeds; the design, manufacture and testing of aerospace systems; flight quality synthesis and quality assurance through analysis; software development for aerospace applications; design and manufacturing of ultra-light aircraft and hot air balloons; and maintaining the Romanian Aeronautics and Space Information System, a space data information network.

Areas of space specialization for the institute include projects to define missions and build payloads for sounding rockets and small scientific and technological satellites; experimental studies to promote the conversion of military rockets for civilian scientific uses; physics studies under microgravity conditions; and the development of spacecraft systems for missions to Mars.

The National Institute on Aerospace Research "ELIE CARAFOLI" conducts research into aerospace and aeronautical fields, including general aerodynamics, flight and systems dynamics, aerospace structures, aeroelasticity, resistance of materials applicable in aeronautics, and aerospace propelling systems. Applied research and technological development covers aerospace technologies and materials; electronic mechanical-hydraulic and pneumatic equipment, experimental models in the aeronautical and aerospace fields, and testing benches and installations, platforms and pilot stations, laboratory apparatus, devices and tools for the aeronautical industry.

Astronomical Institute

The Astronomical Institute began its activities in 1908 and became a part of the Romanian Academy in 1990. The institute conducts studies on terrestrial and space-based astronomy and astrophysics including solar physics, stellar physics, large scale structure of the universe, celestial mechanics, meridian and photographic astronomy, reference systems and reference frames, CCD astrometry, earth's rotation, Solar X and UV radiations, solar total irradiance, coronal mass ejections, solar proton events, high speed plasma streams, solar wind, international observation programs of variable stars from space and on the ground, observational data processing from satellites, solar systems experiments such as ESA's Rosetta, and the upper atmosphere of the earth and planets.

A recent project on solar activity and its consequences in the periterrestrial medium was completed by the institute in 2002. Results yielded analysis of the solar flare on July 14, 2000, including morphology and magnetic field of the active region, dynamics and radiation of the flare and of its effects on space missions; estimation of the energy emitted in solar flares which were intended to improve empirical methods for solar activity prognosis; study of biological effects of solar and geomagnetic phenomena; and possible effects of solar activity on earth's rotation.

Studies in 2002 dealt with torsion oscillations in the solar corona; variations of the differential rotation with the solar cycle; differential rotation of filaments; the distribution of solar flares between 1976 and 2001, north-south asymmetry and distribution in the butterfly diagram; contribution of the energy emitted by solar flares to the variation of the total solar irradiance; ionization and recombination states for the superthermal-electron population that emits X-rays in solar flares; and high-speed plasma streams in the solar wind where distribution serves as a function of the sectorial structure of the interplanetary magnetic field and periodicity as a function of their source.

Institute of Geodynamics

The Institute of Geodynamics began its basic and advanced research into projects related to earth monitoring in 1962. These projects cover geodynamics, advanced methods in seismic monitoring and forecasting, high precision inclinometry for terrestrial tides measurements, and geophysical tomography, which is a method of producing a three-dimensional image of internal structures by the observation and recording of the differences in the effects on the passage of waves of energy impinging on those structures.

Gravitational Researches Laboratory

The Gravitational Researches Laboratory began its basic and advanced research activities in 1977. The laboratory conducts research into general relativity and space-time structure, celestial mechanics, magnetic fluids research and applications, inertial sensors, microgravity experiments, space-time structure and solar system experiments, and magnetofluidic thermal transfer including the development of magnetofluidic membranes.

RUSSIA

Soviet Space Program

Russia, formerly part of the Soviet Union (the USSR), has given the United States stiff competition in the space arena for nearly 50 years. It has made a number of space firsts, including the first artificial earth satellite, Sputnik; the first non-human space traveler, Laika, the dog; the first man in space, Yuri Gagarin; the first woman in space, Valentina Tereshkova; and the world's first space station, Salyut. The Russians have managed to be a definitive force in the field of space exploration in spite of doing so through troubled economic and political times.

At first, the Soviet space program was believed to be a series of political stunts in an attempt to show the rest of the world Communist superiority. However, one of its greatest rocket designers, Sergei P. Korolev, persevered in his quest to conquer space in spite of living under the tyrannical rule of Stalin, and in spite of not receiving proper credit at the time for his many accomplishments.

As a part of Korolev's efforts, the Soviet space program was comparatively simple in contrast to that of the United States, which was highly technological and sophisticated. Korolev's design bureau used simple materials, such as stainless steel instead of aluminum and titanium, to build their space vehicles. Glushko designed simple, but more powerful, rockets that ran on kerosene and liquid oxygen (LOX). Both designers also utilized simple rocket engines rather than the large, complicated engines used by the Americans.

Soviet rockets were launched by the military, and it was often thought that they were launched strictly for military purposes, as opposed to the exploration of space. In addition, rockets had to be launched in frigid and inclement weather or during extremely hot summers. They operated both near the Arctic Circle and in the sand-blown areas of Kazakhstan.

The Soviets relied on the same basic rocket designs for many years and enhanced their program through frequent launch efforts. The Americans had far fewer launches as a whole.

The Soviet space program was, for years, very secretive, operating under a cloak of propaganda. In contrast, the American space program was very open, and every failure was instantly noted around the world.

The Russians cleverly used their rocket designs for many purposes. An example of this is the Vostok capsules that were converted from manned vehicles to their primary reconnaissance spacecraft, thus replacing the human with a camera. This effort became known as ELINT, Earth Resources and Interplanetary Spacecraft, until it was replaced by a Soyuz-based design.

Korolev was instrumental in the Soviets' drive to the moon. Following the successful Luna program, which resulted in the first unmanned lunar landing, Korolev started the Vostok and Voskhod programs to prove that human spaceflight was possible. These vehicles were also intended to allow soft-landings on the moon's surface to ensure that a cosmonaut would not sink into the planet's dust which accumulated over billions of years of meteorite impacts. Another objective of this effort was to develop a huge booster to provide the enabling technology which would allow the cosmonauts to reach the moon.

It turned out the most difficult of these objectives was the latter. Although the N-1 vehicle was designed to launch 40 to 50 metric tons (88,000 to 110,000 pounds) into earth orbit, it would not succeed in its purpose in the long-run, to carry the Soviets to the moon.

Korolev worked with great dedication on the N-1 project, however, Nikita Khrushev assigned another designer, Vladimir N. Chelomei, the task of developing a spacecraft capable of launching at least one cosmonaut on a circumlunar mission. Chelomei developed a new three-stage vehicle with a hypergolic propellant consisting of nitrogen tetroxide and unsymmetrical dimethylhydrazine.

Glushko designed the first stage consisting of an RD-253, while Kosberg developed the second and third stages with RD-468 and RD-473 engines. This vehicle became known as the Proton booster, which was capable of placing 20 metric tons into orbit. Chelomei's Proton rocket could place one cosmonaut on a circumlunar voyage aboard the Luna Korabl, LK-1.

However, a feud began between Korolev and Glushko about what type of fuel to use for the N-1 vehicle. Glushko wanted to employ hypergolic fuel, while Korolev wanted to use either kerosene and liquid oxygen (LOX) or liquid hydrogen (LH2) and LOX. Lighter engines and propellant storage tanks were among the advantages for hypergolic fuel, while the primary disadvantage was launchpad safety in the event of fuel leaks.

Korolev insisted upon the LOX and hydrocarbon mixture and Glushko resigned himself from the N-1 program, setting back the N-1 and leading to the loss of powerful political support in the government for Korolev. Korolev sought help from an experienced aircraft engine designer, Nikolai D. Kuznetsov, who was not experienced in designing rocket engines. The result was an N-1 design which contained simple LOX and kerosene engines for all three stages. An alternative decision was made to include a number of small engines rather than two or three larger and more powerful ones in the various stages.

In 1963, Korolev started work on the design of the Soyuz vehicle for the human lunar mission with a target date of 1967 or 1968 for a manned moon landing. The needed capacity for the N-1 by 1964 became 92 metric tons into low earth orbit, which called for more main engines. The N-1's payload structure would only allow two cosmonauts to go to the moon and only one cosmonaut could land on the lunar surface. It was because of this limitation that Korolev required his rocket design bureau to develop LH2 and LOX engines for all three N-1 stages. In October 1964, Premier Khrushchev was removed from office by a coup, costing Korolev a strong government ally.

The Soviet human lunar program was then divided into two phases, L-1 and L-3. L-1 was assigned to be the human circumlunar mission flown by a Proton launcher. L-3 would be the actual landing of cosmonauts on the moon accomplished by an N-1.

In 1965, Korolev started a new robotic exploration project of the moon, but his attempts at launching a soft lander for exploration failed as Lunas 5, 6, 7, and 8 either missed or crashed into the lunar surface. However, in spite of these failures, valuable experience was gained in spacecraft guidance.

Chelomei's Proton vehicle was successfully launched on July 16, 1965, and on November 2, 1965, but since Chelomei had spacecraft design difficulties, Korolev persuaded the government to allow him to use his design for the circumlunar program.

Shortly thereafter, a medical mishap would keep Korolev from achieving further triumph. He died on January 14, 1966, from a botched hemorrhoid operation. His doctor had found tumors in Korolev's intestines and continued to operate without help, medical supplies, or blood. Korolev was granted a hero's funeral with his accomplishments revealed, finally, to all, and buried in the Kremlin Wall.

Following Korolev's death, Luna 9 made a successful soft landing on the moon's surface and returned the first historical pictures. Lunas 10, 11, and 12 successfully orbited the moon and returned photographs of potential landing sites. Luna 13, the final probe of 1966, landed on the moon, took surface photographs, and analyzed soil samples.

Chelomei persuaded the government to resume the design of the lunar missions. His capsule was tested in late 1966 and would be used for both the L-1 and L-3 programs. A successful launch was made with a Proton vehicle tested in low earth orbit. On April 8, 1967, a second test failed, but the engineers readily identified the problem and there was hope to launch a cosmonaut around the moon by the end of the year.

These hopes were abruptly halted on April 23, 1967, when Cosmonaut Vladimir Komarov was launched aboard a brand new vehicle called Soyuz-1. Komarov made 18 successful orbits, but when his parachutes tangled, the capsule pummeled to earth, killing Komarov.

Komarov's death brought the Soviet human space program to a complete standstill. Shortly thereafter, two other Protons failed and the lunar program started to appear like a hopeless endeavor. This was followed by seven Zond missions toward the moon, with only one success.

In January 1968, Soviet cosmonauts began training for the L-3 lunar landing program. Yuri Gagarin, the first man in space, was favored to win an early L-3 mission. Hopes for that would be dashed as well, when on March 22, 1968, at 10:41 A.M., Gagarin crashed the Mig-15 he was flying. The Soviet Union had lost its greatest space hero.

Zond 5 was launched on September 14, 1968, as the fifth unmanned launch in the L-1 circumlunar program. The spacecraft carried small animals, insects, and a tape recorder which transmitted a cosmonaut's voice to test radio reception from the distance of the moon. It flew around the moon and then, due to a human error, landed in the Indian Ocean.

The era of Soviet human spaceflight resumed again on October 26, 1968, when Soyuz 3 was launched with Cosmonaut Georgiy Beregovoy at the controls. The mission proceeded according to plan with Soyuz 3 rendezvousing with an unmanned Soyuz 2, but no docking. Beregovoy gave viewers a television tour around the new Soyuz spacecraft, and then returned to earth following a week's mission.

On November 6, 1968, a Proton rocket launched Zond 6 to within 2,420 km (1,503 mi) of the moon's surface. It was fortunate that the mission was not manned as there were equipment failures onboard, including a gasket and a parachute failing to open during landing.

Other Zond flights followed with another Zond failure on January 20, 1969, along with its Proton booster. Following NASA's successful Apollo 11 moon landing, Zond 7 successfully orbited the moon and returned. The last flight, Zond 8, flew successfully around the moon, but landed in the Indian Ocean instead of on Russian soil.

The Soviets did not give up on pursuing a manned moon landing, and continued with their L-3 program in 1968 with the development of the lunar lander (LK), the lunar orbiter (LOK), and the N-1 rocket. It was intended that cosmonauts would spacewalk from the LOK vehicle to the LK vehicle and perform their landing. After the mission had been completed and the rendezvous was accomplished, the cosmonauts would perform an EVA with the moon samples from the LK to the LOK and head back to earth.

Soyuz 4 launched on January 14, 1969, with Cosmonaut Vladimir Shatalov, and was followed the next day by the launch of Yevgeni Khrunov, Aleksei Yeliseyev, and Boris Volynov in Soyuz 5. Two days later, the two spacecraft docked. Khrunov and Yeliseyev, who wore special lunar space suits, depressurized the orbital module on Soyuz 5 and transferred, one at a time, to Soyuz 4. The three cosmonauts landed on January 17, followed by Soyuz 5 on January 18. During the mission, the LOK to LK and back transfer had been successfully tested. The next important test to follow was that of the N-1.

By this time, the N-1 had grown tremendously in stature, with a diameter of 56 feet, a height of 340 feet, and a weight of nearly six million pounds. The vehicle was made up of two main sections: the 200 foot three-stage booster rocket and the 140 foot faring, which contained the L-3 lunar complex.

The 92-foot first stage had a lower diameter of 56 feet and an upper diameter of 33 feet. It contained 30 NK-33 engines which had been developed by Kuznetsov. Twenty-four of the N-1's engines were placed around the first stage's base, while six engines remained in the middle of the craft. Each engine was capable of delivering 340,000 pounds of thrust, and with a combination of all thirty engines, the rocket delivered over 10 million pounds of thrust. The first stage had a burn time of 110 seconds.

The N-1's second stage had a base of 33 feet, an upper diameter of 25 feet, and a height of 66 feet. It had eight engines with a total of three million pounds of thrust, and a propellant mix of kerosene and LOX. Kuznetsov designed the NK-43 engine for the second stage, which had larger nozzles to take advantage of the higher altitude operating environment. It had a burn time of 130 seconds.

The N-1's third stage had a height of 42 feet, a lower diameter of 25 feet, and an upper diameter of 20 feet. Its four NK-39 engines burned kerosene and LOX. The thrust was 360,000 pounds with a burn time of 300 seconds. The third stage was the stage responsible for placing the entire L-3 complex into a 220 km (137 mi) low earth orbit.

The N-1 was also designed by Korolev

with an engine operation control system, or KORD, to be used in the event that a single engine failed. If one engine failed, the KORD would immediately reduce the thrust on the engine diametrically opposed to the failed one. The KORD would then increase the burn time to make up for the lost thrust and to use up fuel. The L-3 complex had been programmed to reach low earth orbit if two first-stage engines failed or if one second-stage engine failed. If a third-stage engine happened to fail, the three remaining engines could be gimbaled to compensate for the unsymmetrical thrust.

Set on top of the N-1 was the L-3, stage which was made up of four separate parts: two rocket stages, the lunar orbiter and the lunar lander. The first rocket stage, a Kuznetsov NK-31 liquid kerosene and LOX engine, performed the translunar injection. The second rocket stage performed midcourse corrections and the lunar injection orbit.

On February 21, 1969, the first test of the N-1/L-3 vehicle was conducted at Tyuratam. The spacecraft launched around midday Moscow time, and within seconds, the KORD system shut down engines 12 and 24. At 66 seconds, an oxidizer line leading into one of the engines erupted due to acoustic vibrations, and a fire broke out. Seventy seconds into flight, the KORD system shut everything down and the escape tower jettisoned its payload. It turns out this failure had occurred because Korolev and his successor Mishin had decided not to test the 30 engines in a test stand due to expense and program delays. Only single engine tests were performed and the actual KORD system never underwent any tests.

On July 3, 1969, another attempt was made to launch the N-1/L-3 mission. A metal object fell into the number eight oxidizer pump, causing its engine to explode. The remainder of the engines in the first stage were shut down as they were already on fire. The rocket, which had lifted briefly, fell back onto the launching pad and exploded. Oddly enough, the emergency escape system functioned perfectly, protecting the L-1.

On July 13, 1969, a four-stage Proton vehicle launched Luna 15 to the moon. The intent of the mission was to perform a soft landing on the lunar surface, gather a soil sample, and return to earth before Apollo 11. However, when the spacecraft attempted to land on the moon on July 21, it smashed instead into the Sea of Crisis at about 480 km/hr.

The Soviets tried again on September 12, 1970, successfully landing Luna 16 on the moon's equator to gather a 101 gram (3.56 ounce) soil sample, and returned it to earth on September 24, 1970.

On November 10, 1970, Luna 17 landed in the moon's northern hemisphere roughly 2,500 km (1,553 mi) from the Luna 16 site. Two ramps were sent down from the vehicle, and the first Lunar rover Lunokhod 1 was released. The eight-wheeled vehicle traveled for 11 months over a course of 10 km (6.21 mi), recording more than 25,000 photographs and conducting lunar soil tests at 500 separate sites.

Even though the Soviets had found success with their lunar landers and orbiters through November of 1972, the massive N-1 never appeared to be flyable. In a June 27, 1971, launch attempt, the N-1 began to experience severe roll control problems and by 51 seconds the vehicle was completely out of control. The KORD system shut down the engines, which had not been malfunctioning, and the vehicle was destroyed.

When the Americans announced the end of the Apollo program in 1972, the Soviets made plans to set up a modest base on the moon and carry out much more extensive explorations. However, these plans were contingent upon the operation of the N-1. The next flight occurred on November 23, 1972, with a liftoff as planned and all systems functioning, until 90 seconds after launch when the six central core engines shut down. The abrupt shut down of fuel flow caused pressure which ruptured the fuel lines. A fire erupted, exploding the first stage 107 seconds into the launch.

As a result, Soviet engineers tried to develop a plan to follow through with the separation and ensure continuation of the rocket launch even with a malfunction such as that experienced with the November launch, but the government would not allow the program to continue.

On January 8, 1973, the lunar rover Lunokhod 2 landed inside the crater LeMonnier. This success allowed Soviet designers to obtain invaluable experience in remote operator techniques.

Mishin, unfortunately, became another victim of the struggling Soviet space program. He had already been under intense fire for the Soyuz 10 failure and the Soyuz 11 fatal accident, which was followed by the failure of two Salyut launches and the trials and tribulations of the N-1. In May 1974, Mishin was dismissed, with Valentin Glushko resuming his position.

Glushko's first act was to cancel the N-1 program and destroy the components, resulting in the moon program being placed on hold again. Glushko concentrated his efforts on the new Soviet heavy lifter, Energia, and the new space shuttle, Buran.

The development of Buran was influenced by the Russian need to return various spaceloads back to earth from space such as photos, research materials, satellites, and samples of products manufactured in space. Another strong motivator in its design was the need on the part of the Soviets to build reusable vehicles to save money.

A reusable rocket plane would be capable of accelerating and lifting a rocket through hypersonic flight. The first stage would push the plane from the ground and a second manned stage would push the winged spacecraft into orbit.

At first sight, it may be easy to compare the Soviet Buran to the U.S. space shuttle. However, there are some differences. The Energia uses all liquid propellant boosters, in contrast to the shuttle which uses solid rocket boosters to obtain the necessary thrust. The Buran did not have main engines within its fuselage, which would have allowed a greater payload mass to be lifted into orbit. Both shuttle systems were equipped with their own autonomous guidance systems.

Development on the Energia Buran began in the mid–1970s, with the primary organization responsible being NPO Energia, headed by Valetin Glushko. Glushko's designer-in-chief was Boris Gubanov who oversaw the program. The Energia consisted of a first stage, with four modules surrounding the second stage. Each module contained a four m (13 ft) diameter engine which ran on liquid oxygen and kerosene. Each engine had a thrust at sea level of close to 1.7 million pounds. A new Soviet launcher evolved from this technology, called the Zenit or SL-16.

The Energia's second stage was eight meters (26 feet) in diameter, with four engines, which operated on liquid oxygen and liquid hydrogen. Each of these engines had a thrust of 333,000 pounds.

The entire vehicle had a total height of 60 meters (200 feet) and a combined thrust of 8.1 million pounds.

The first flight of Energia was on May 15, 1987. It started off flying normally except for a bad circuit in the mockup payload which prevented the last stage from reaching orbital velocity. Computers controlled everything at the complex including fueling of the spacecraft.

The second flight of the Energia included the Buran vehicle which was launched on November 15, 1988. Buran was built to carry the Mir space station or any one of its payload modules, which would have allowed the modules to be returned to earth for refurbishment or updating.

The Buran was 36.4 m (119.4 ft) long, 16.5 m (54.1 ft) tall on its landing gear, and had a wingspan of 23.9 m (78.4 ft). It consisted of three compartments — the nose, the payload compartment and the tail. The crew compartment was located in the nose and housed room for two pilots and three work stations for flight engineers, docking, and manipulator arm control. The lower deck held the living areas with a pantry, recreation and hygienic facilities. The control equipment and the airlock were also located in this area. Reaction jets, radio antennas and pneumatic equipment were also located in the spacecraft's nose.

The payload bay was located in the Buran's midsection and was 4.7 m (15.5 ft) in diameter and 18.3 m (60 ft) long. The bay was built to accomodate payloads of up to 66,000 pounds (30 metric tons). The payload bay was covered by two large doors which were opened upon reaching orbit. A remote manipulator arm was available for use by the crew to handle payloads.

Buran's tail compartment contained the orbital maneuvering system which used liquid oxygen and kerosene for fuel. Three auxiliary power units (APUs) operated the craft's aerodynamic surfaces and a drag chute was also stored in the tail section.

The spacecraft was covered with 38,000 individually shaped thermal tiles for thermal control, and was designed with carbon-carbon coating for the nose and leading edges of the wings.

Buran utilized a microwave landing system which allowed the spacecraft to touchdown 3.5 m (12 ft) off centerline and 80 m (260 ft) from the halfway point of the runway. When Glushko died in 1989, support for the Buran program began to fade away, until it was finally cancelled in 1994.

Sputnik

History was forever changed with the launch of Sputnik I by the Soviet Union on October 4, 1957. The world's first artificial satellite was roughly the size of a basketball, weighing a mere 183 pounds, and it took 98 minutes to orbit the earth on its elliptical path. Sputnik's launch brought in a new age of political, military, technology, and scientific developments, also marking the start of the space age and the United States — USSR space race.

In 1952, the International Council of Scientific Unions decided to establish July 1, 1957, to December 31, 1958, as the International Geophysical Year (IGY), due to the fact that scientists knew that the cycles of solar activity would be at a high point during these times. Then, in 1954, the council adopted a resolution calling for artificial satellites to be launched during the IGY to map the earth's surface.

In July 1955, the United States announced plans to launch an earth-orbiting satellite for the IGY and began soliciting proposals from government research agencies to undertake its development. In September 1955, the Naval Research Laboratory's Vanguard proposal was selected to represent the United States during the IGY.

However, the launch of Sputnik changed everything by catching the world's attention and the American public off-guard. Its size was far more commanding than Vanguard's intended 3.5 pound payload. The American public also feared that the Soviet's ability to launch satellites translated into the capability to launch ballistic missiles that could carry nuclear weapons from Europe to the United States.

Then, without warning, the Soviets struck again, launching Sputnik II on November 3, which carried a much heavier payload, including a dog named Laika.

By this time, the U.S. Defense Department responded to the political uproar caused by Sputnik by approving funding for another U.S. satellite project, the Explorer, which was headed by the great rocket scientist, Wernher von Braun.

On January 31, 1958, the United States made its own satellite statement with the successful launch of Explorer I, which carried a small scientific payload that eventually discovered the magnetic radiation belts around the earth, named after principal investigator James Van Allen. The Explorer program then continued with a series of ongoing lightweight, scientifically useful spacecraft.

The Sputnik launch also led directly to the creation of the National Aeronautics and Space Administration (NASA) following the passing by Congress of the National Aeronautics and Space Act, most commonly referred to as the Space Act. NASA was officially established October 1, 1958, from the National Advisory Committee for Aeronautics (NACA) and other governmental agencies.

Sputnik was twenty-two inches round with four spring-loaded antennae, and was the first manmade object to orbit the earth.

Sputnik, translated, means traveler. It carried a battery-operated radio transmitter that repeatedly beeped as it circled the globe.

On January 4, 1958, after 92 days in orbit, Sputnik I re-entered the earth's atmosphere and burned up. Sputnik II remained in orbit for 162 days before re-entering the atmosphere and burning up. Its canine cargo,

Laika, had died after 10 days in space when the oxygen supply onboard was depleted.

Sputnik 3 was launched on April 6, 1960. It was a conically-shaped vehicle measuring 3.57 m (11.7 ft) by 1.73 m (5.7 ft), powered by solar panels embedded around the base of the main body. Several antennas protruded from the bottom, sides and top of the craft. An onboard instrumentation package had both vacuum tubes and solid-state technology. The payload returned data for two years.

Soviet Lunar Missions: Luna and Zond

The Soviet's lunar program had 20 successful missions to the moon, achieving a number of lunar firsts including the first probe to impact the moon; the first flyby and image of the lunar farside; the first soft landing; the first lunar orbiter; and the first circumlunar probe to return to earth. The Soviets launched two successful series of Soviet probes — the Lunar, consisting of 24 lunar missions, and the Zond, consisting of five lunar missions.

The Luna 1 mission was launched January 2, 1959. It was the first spacecraft to reach the moon, and the first of a series of Soviet automatic interplanetary missions to be successfully launched in the direction of the moon. The Luna craft was sphere-shaped with five antennae extended from one hemisphere. Instrument ports protruded from the surface of the sphere and there were no propulsions systems on the Luna 1 spacecraft itself.

It was presumed that Luna 1 was intended to impact the moon because of its high velocity and design package of various metallic emblems with the Soviet coat of arms.

On January 2, 1959, Luna 1 separated from its 1,472 kg (1.47 ton) third stage after reaching escape velocity. The third stage, which was 5.2 m (17 ft) long and 2.4 m (7.87 ft) in diameter, traveled along with the spacecraft.

On January 3, a large one kg (2.2 lb) cloud of sodium gas was released by the spacecraft, leading an orange trail which was visible over the Indian Ocean with the brightness of a sixth-magnitude star, allowing astronomers to track the spacecraft. It also served as an experiment on the behavior of gas in outer space.

Lunar 1 passed within 5,995 km (3,725 mi) of the moon's surface on January 4 after 34 hours of flight. It then went into orbit around the sun, between the orbits of earth and Mars.

The spacecraft was equipped with radio and tracking transmitters and a telemetering system, along with five different sets of scientific devices for studying interplanetary space, including a magnetometer, a Geiger counter, a scintillation counter, and a micrometeorite detector.

Measurements obtained during the mission provided new data on the earth's radiation belt and outer space, including the discovery that the moon had no magnetic field and that a solar wind, a strong flow of ionized plasma from the sun, streamed through interplanetary space.

Luna 2 ("Lunik" 2) was launched on September 12, 1959. It crashed two days later onto the rim of the crater Autolycus, showing that the moon possessed little or no magnetic radiation. It was the first spacecraft to land on the moon, impacting the lunar surface east of Mare Serenitatis near the Aristides, Archimedes, and Autolycus craters. Thirty minutes later, the final stage of Luna 2 also impacted the moon.

Luna 3 was launched October 4, 1959, and weighed 278.5 kg (612.7 lb). It was an automatic interplanetary station, equipped with radio communication and telemetering systems, a television system with an automatic film processing unit, a set of scientific instruments, systems for orientation relative to the sun and moon, solar cells for electric power supply, and a temperature control system. The spacecraft was controlled by radio command from earth and launched on a trajectory that bent over the moon (closest approach to the moon was 6,200 kilometers or 3,850 miles) to be stabilized while in optical view of the far side of the moon.

On October 7, 1959, the onboard television system obtained a series of photographs that were developed on the spacecraft. The photographs were scanned and then radio transmitted to ground stations in facsimile form on October 18, 1959, as the spacecraft returned near earth in a barycentric orbit.

The photographs were supposed to be re-transmitted at another point close to earth, but this was not performed. The result was a series of very indistinct pictures which, through computer enhancement, a tentative atlas of the lunar farside was generated.

The mission was to obtain photographs of the lunar surface as the spacecraft flew by the moon, with the added goal of getting photographs of parts of the moon not seen well, or which were never seen from the earth, such as the limb and far side of the moon. This was to gain knowledge of the characteristics of the unseen hemisphere of the moon.

Luna 4 was launched on April 2, 1963, and was the USSR's first successful spacecraft of their second generation lunar program. The spacecraft was first placed in an earth orbit and then in an automatic interplanetary station, rather than being sent on a straight trajectory toward the moon, before being rocketed in a curving path towards the moon. Luna 4 achieved the desired trajectory but missed the moon by 8336.2 km (5,180 mi) on April 5, 1963, and entered a barycentric 90,000 by 700,000 km (55, 926 by 434,980 mi) earth orbit.

While the intended mission of the probe was not known, it was speculated the probe was designed to land on the moon with an instrument package based on the trajectory, and on the later attempted landings of the Luna 5 and 6 spacecraft. Coincidentally, at the time, a lecture program entitled "Hitting the Moon" was scheduled to be broadcast on Radio Moscow at 7:45 P.M. the evening of April 5, but was cancelled.

Luna 5 was launched on May 9, 1965. It had been designed to continue the investigations of a lunar soft landing. However, the retrorocket system failed, and the spacecraft impacted the lunar surface at the Sea of Clouds.

Luna 6 was launched on June 8, 1965, and was intended to travel to the moon, but, because a mid-course correction failed, it missed the moon by 159,612.8 km (99,183.4 mi).

Lunik, or Luna 7, launched October 4, 1965, was intended to achieve a soft landing on the moon. However, due to premature retrofire and cutoff of the retrorockets, the spacecraft impacted the lunar surface in the Sea of Storms.

Luna 8 was launched on December 3, 1965, with the intended mission of achieving a soft landing on the Moon. Unfortunately, the retrofire was late, and the spacecraft impacted the lunar surface in the Sea of Storms. The mission was able to complete the experimental development of the star-orientation system and ground control of radio equipment, flight trajectory, and other instrumentation.

Luna 9, launched January 31, 1966, was the first spacecraft to achieve a lunar soft landing and to transmit photographic data to earth. The automatic lunar station that achieved the soft landing weighed 99 kilograms (218 pounds). It was a hermetically sealed container with radio equipment, a program timing device, heat control systems, scientific apparatus, power sources, and a television system.

The Luna 9 payload was carried to earth orbit by an A-2-E vehicle, and then conveyed toward the moon by a fourth stage rocket that separated itself from the payload. Flight apparatus separated from the payload shortly before Luna 9 landed.

On February 3, 1966, after landing in the Ocean of Storms, the four petals, which formed the spacecraft, opened outward and stabilized the spacecraft on the lunar surface. Spring-controlled antennas assumed operating positions, and the television camera rotating mirror system, which operated by revolving and tilting, began a photographic survey of the lunar environment. Seven radio sessions, totaling eight hours and five minutes, were transmitted, as were three series of television pictures. When assembled, the photographs provided a panoramic view of the nearby lunar surface. The pictures included views of nearby rocks and of the horizon 1.4 kilometers (.9 miles) away from the spacecraft.

The purpose of the mission was to obtain information on the characteristics of the lunar surface. These characteristics included the amount of cratering; structure and size of craters; the amount, distribution, and sizes of ejecta; and mechanical properties of the surface such as bearing strength, cohesiveness, compaction, etc. Determination and recognition of processes operating to produce the lunar surface features also were among the objectives of the Luna 9 onboard equipment.

Luna 10 was launched on March 31, 1966, towards the moon from an earth-orbiting platform. The spacecraft entered lunar orbit on April 4, 1966. Scientific instruments onboard included a gamma-ray spectrometer for energies between 0.3 and 3 MeV, a triaxial magnetometer, a meteorite detector, instruments for solar-plasma studies, and devices for measuring infrared emissions from the moon and radiation conditions of the lunar environment. Gravitational studies were also conducted. The spacecraft played back to earth the *Internationale* during the twenty-third congress of the Communist Party of the Soviet Union. Luna 10 was battery powered and operated for 460 lunar orbits and 219 active data transmissions before radio signals were discontinued on May 30, 1966.

The onboard instrumentation of Luna 10 included a triaxial fluxgate magnetometer with a dynamic range of -50 to +50 gammas. No independent altitude determination system was included, so only the magnitude of the magnetic field and the components parallel and perpendicular to the spin axis were determined. The magnetometer was located at the end of a boom 1.5 meters (5 feet) from the spacecraft surface.

The sampling rate of the vector magnetic field occurred once every 128 seconds. The accuracy of the measurements was estimated from in-flight data to be nine gammas for the component parallel to the spin axis and 2.5 gammas for the component perpendicular to the spin axis, yielding a residual error of 10 gammas for the magnitude.

Luna 10 measured the magnetic field of the moon intermittently for two months.

Luna 11 was launched on August 24, 1966, towards the moon from an earth-orbiting platform and entered lunar orbit on August 28, 1966. The objectives of the mission included the study of lunar gamma- and X-ray emissions in order to determine the moon's chemical composition; lunar gravitational anomalies; the concentration of meteorite streams near the moon; and the intensity of hard corpuscular radiation near the moon. A total of 137 radio transmissions and 277 orbits of the moon were completed before the batteries failed on October 1, 1966.

Luna 12, or Lunik 12, was launched October 22, 1966. It was launched towards the moon from an earth-orbiting platform and achieved lunar orbit on October 25, 1966. The spacecraft was equipped with a television system that obtained and transmitted photographs of the lunar surface. The photographs contained 1100 scan lines with a maximum resolution of 14.9 to 19.8 meters (49 to 65 feet). Pictures of the lunar surface were returned on October 27, 1966. The number of photographs is not known. Radio transmissions from Luna 12 ceased on January 19, 1967, after 602 lunar orbits and 302 radio transmissions.

Luna 13 was launched December 21, 1966, towards the moon from an earth-orbiting platform and accomplished a soft landing on December 24, 1966, in the region of Oceanus Procellarum. The petal encasement of the spacecraft was opened, antennas were erected, and radio transmissions to earth began four minutes after the landing.

On December 25 and 26, 1966, the spacecraft television system transmitted panoramas of the nearby lunar landscape at different sun angles. Each panorama required approximately 100 minutes to transmit. The spacecraft was equipped with a mechanical soil-measuring penetrometer, a dynamograph, and a radiation densitometer for obtaining data on the mechanical and physical properties and the cosmic-ray reflectivity of the lunar surface.

The goal of the mission was to obtain information on the characteristics of the lunar surface. These characteristics included the amount of cratering; structure and size of craters; the amount, distribution, and sizes of ejecta; and mechanical properties of the surface such as bearing strength, cohesiveness, compaction, etc. Determination and recognition of processes operating to produce the

lunar surface features also were among the objectives of this photographic experiment. Spacecraft transmissions terminated before the end of December 1966.

On April 7, 1968, the Luna 14 spacecraft was launched and entered lunar orbit on April 10, 1968. The spacecraft instrumentation was similar to that of Luna 10 and provided data for studies of the interaction of the earth and lunar masses, the lunar gravitational field, the propagation and stability of radio communications to the spacecraft at different orbital positions, solar charged particles and cosmic rays, and the motion of the moon. This flight marked the final flight of the second generation of the Luna series.

Luna 15 was launched on July 13, 1969, and crashed on the moon on July 21, 1969, at Mare Crisium, 17°N lat., 60°W long. It was believed to have been intended as a sample-return mission, similar to Luna 16, 20, and 24.

Luna 16 launched September 12, 1970, and landed on the moon on September 20, 1970, at Mare Fecunditatis, 0.68°S lat., 56.30°E long.

Luna 17 landed on the moon on November 17, 1970, following its launch on November 10. It landed at Mare Imbrium, 38.28°N lat., 325.00°E long, and placed a Lunar Rover, Lunokhod 1.

Luna 18 was launched on September 2, 1971, and made lunar impact at latitude 3.57 N, longitude 50.50 E on Mare Fecunditatis.

Luna 19 was launched on September 28, 1971, and entered lunar orbit on October 3, 1971, returning images of the moon.

Luna 20, launched February 14, 1972, landed on the moon on February 21, at Mare Fecunditatis, 3.57°N lat., 56.50°E long, performing a lunar sample return to earth February 25, 1972.

Lunik 21, or Luna 21, launched January 8, 1973, and landed on the moon on January 15 at Mare Serenitatis, 25.51°N lat., 30.38°E long, releasing Lunar Rover — Lunokhod 2.

Luna 22 launched on June 2, 1974, and entered lunar orbit around June 3, returning images.

Luna 23, launched on October 28, 1974, was intended to return a lunar sample to earth. It was launched by a Proton SL-12/D-1-e booster. However, the spacecraft was damaged during landing in Mare Crisium (Sea of Crises). The sample collecting apparatus could not operate, and no samples were returned. The lander continued transmissions for three days following landing.

In 1976, Luna 24, which was launched on August 14, landed several hundred meters away and successfully returned samples.

The Zond series of lunar and planetary spacecraft began as a Soviet attempt to reach Mars that later evolved into a series of tests for what was to be the Soviet manned lunar program, carrying film return capsules, scientific instruments, and in a few cases, small animals.

Zond 1 was actually designated as a Venus, or Venera, spacecraft. It was launched on April 2, 1964. Contact with Zond 1 (zond is the Russian word for probe) was lost roughly one and a half months following launch.

Zond 2 was an automatic interplanetary station launched from a Tyazheliy Sputnik (64-078A) vehicle in earth parking orbit towards Mars to test spaceborne systems and to carry out scientific investigations. The probe carried a descent craft and other instruments, including a magnetometer probe, television photographic equipment, a spectroreflexometer, radiation sensors (gas-discharge and scintillation counters), a spectrograph to study ozone absorption bands, and a micrometeoroid instrument. The spacecraft had six experimental low-thrust electrojet plasma-ion engines which served as actuators of the altitude control system and two solar panels to provide power.

Zond 2 followed a curving trajectory towards Mars to minimize the relative velocity. The electronic ion engines were successfully tested shortly after launch under real-space environment conditions over the period December 8 through 18, 1964. One of the two solar panels failed, so only half of the anticipated power was available to the spacecraft. After a mid-course maneuver, communications with the spacecraft were lost in early May 1965. The spacecraft flew by Mars August 6, 1965, at a distance of 1500 km (932 mi).

Zond 3 was launched July 18, 1965, from a Tyazheliy Sputnik (65-056B) earth orbiting platform towards the moon and interplanetary space. The spacecraft was equipped with a television system that provided automatic in-flight film processing.

On July 20, during lunar flyby, 25 good quality pictures were taken of the lunar farside from distances of 11,570 to 9,960 kilometers (7,190 to 6,190 miles). The photos covered 19 million square kilometers (7.3 million square miles) of the lunar surface. Photo transmissions by facsimile were returned to earth from a distance of 2.2 million kilometers (1.4 million miles) and were retransmitted from a distance of 31.5 million kilometers (19.6 million miles) which proved the ability of the communications system. After the lunar flyby, Zond 3 continued space exploration in a heliocentric orbit.

Zond 4 was launched on March 2, 1968. It flew successfully until a reentry failure caused mission controllers to destroy the vehicle in earth's atmosphere.

Zond 5 was launched September 14, 1968, from a Tyazheliy Sputnik in earth parking orbit to make scientific probes during a lunar flyby and to return to earth. On September 18, 1968, the spacecraft flew around the moon with the closest distance of 1,950 kilometers (1,212 miles). High-quality photographs of the earth were taken at a distance of 90,000 kilometers (56,000 miles).

A biological payload of turtles, wine flies, meal worms, plants, seeds, bacteria, and other living matter was included in the flight. On September 21, 1968, the re-entry capsule entered the earth's atmosphere, braked aerodynamically, and deployed parachutes at 7 kilometers (4.35 miles). The capsule splashed down in the Indian Ocean and was successfully recovered, serving as a precursor to manned spacecraft.

Zond 6 was launched November 10, 1968, on a lunar flyby mission from a parent satellite in earth parking orbit. The spacecraft carried scientific probes including cosmic-ray and micrometeoroid detectors, photography equipment, and a biological payload, and was also a precursor to manned spaceflight. On November 14, Zond 6 flew around the moon at a minimum distance of 2,420 kilometers (1,504 miles).

Photographs of the lunar near and farside

were obtained with panchromatic film. The mission's objective was to photograph the lunar surface, particularly areas missed by earlier missions, and to overlap with better photography those areas that had been previously covered. Each photo was 12.70 by 17.78 centimeters (5 by 7 inches) with some of the views allowing for stereo pictures. The photos were taken from distances of approximately 11,000 kilometers (6,835 miles) and 3,300 kilometers (2,050 miles). On November 17, 1968, with controlled reentry of the spacecraft, Zond 6 landed in a predetermined region of the Soviet Union.

On August 7, 1969, Zond 7 was launched towards the moon from a mother spacecraft on a mission of further studies of the moon and circumlmunar space to obtain color photography of the earth and the moon from varying distances, and to flight test the spacecraft systems.

On August 9, 1969, earth photos were obtained. Two days later, the spacecraft flew past the moon at a distance of 1984.6 kilometers (1,233.2 miles) and conducted two picture-taking sessions. Zond 7 reentered the earth's atmosphere on August 14, 1969, and achieved a soft landing in a preset region south of Kustanai.

Zond 8 was launched on October 20, 1970, from an earth orbiting platform, Tyazheliy Sputnik, towards the moon. The planned objectives were investigations of the moon and circumlunar space, and testing of onboard systems and units. The spacecraft obtained photographs of the earth on October 21 from a distance of 64,480 kilometers (40,070 miles).

The spacecraft transmitted flight images of the earth for three days. Zond 8 flew past the moon on October 24, 1970, at a distance of 1,110.4 kilometers (690 miles) and obtained both black and white and color photographs of the lunar surface. Scientific measurements were also obtained during the flight. Zond 8 reentered the earth's atmosphere and splashed down in the Indian Ocean on October 27, 1970.

Vostok

The Vostok spacecraft was used to launch the first man in space, with a modified design later used for the Voskhod program. The Vostok spacecraft had a service module and a manned cabin which separated from each other during reentry. The service module housed chemical batteries, orientation rockets, the main retro system and support equipment. The manned cabin contained the radios, life support equipment, instrumentation and ejection seat. There also were three small portholes to see out into space. Television transmissions and radio communication could be maintained throughout each flight.

In the USSR, the first studies of how to put a man in space began before the first satellite was ever launched. They started in June 1956, when Soviet designers Sergei Korolev and Konstantin Feoktistov began conceptualizing a spacecraft that could send a person to space and return him home safely. In January 1958, work commenced on this spacecraft, called Vostok, and its third stage. The following November, the Vostok program was officially accepted by the Council of Chief Designers.

The Vostok spacecraft had some striking differences from later manned space vehicles in that it had no maneuvering capabilities and required cosmonauts to parachute to safety at the end of a flight. The Soviets managed to conceal the fact that the first cosmonauts did not land in their spacecraft for some time from the Fédération Aéronautique Internationale (FAI), the world's air sports federation, because manned landing was required in order to be eligible for a variety of world space records.

In March 1960, cosmonaut candidates began training, and the original group of official cosmonauts was selected in May. The group included Anatoly Kartashov, Yuri Gagarin, Andriyan Nikolayev, Pavel Popovich, Gherman Titov and Valentin Varlamov, but further regrouping occurred before the final Vostok missions. The final prime crew selections for Vostok one through six included Yuri Gargarin, Gherman Titov, Andriyan Nikolayev, Pavel Popovich, Valery Bykovsky, and Valentina Tereshkova.

Oddly enough, during the first Vostok flight, Yuri Gagarin was not permitted to operate the controls, perhaps due to the concern of how Gagarin would be able to work in space since the effects of weightlessness had only been tested on dogs up until that time. The mission instead was actually controlled by ground crews, and an override key was provided in case of emergency.

On April 12, 1961, Gagarin lifted off from Baikonur Cosmodrome, Kazakhstan. His spacecraft, which weighed 4,725 kg (4.72 tons) was launched from Baikonur Cosmodrome. His mission lasted one hour, 48 minutes, and ended with a landing in Kazakhstan, approximately 26 kilometers (16 miles) southwest of Engels. Gagarin had completed one earth orbit, and this was accomplished 25 days prior to the first U.S. suborbital manned flight by Alan Shepard.

Other Vostok missions allowed the cosmonaut to manually control the spacecraft and also featured scientific and biomedical experiments and earth photography.

Vostok 3 and 4 launched within one day of each other. Vostok 5 and 6 were also launched relatively close, within two days of each other. The spacecraft flew in similar orbits, but did not have the ability to rendezvous and dock.

Vostok 6 featured the first woman in space, Valentina Tereshkova, who was also the first woman commander.

The Vostok program was canceled in 1964, when the Soviet space program's focus shifted towards the Voshhod program and the prospect of sending multiple travelers into space on one spacecraft.

Vostok 2 was a 4,731 kg (4.73 tons) spacecraft, also a Vostok-K, launched August 6, 1961, from Baikonur, lasting 25 hours and 18 minutes. The craft was commanded by Gherman Titov.

Vostok 3 was a 4,722 kg (4.72 ton) spacecraft which was launched from Baikonur on August 11, 1962. The flight lasted three days, 22 hours, and 22 minutes and was commanded by Andrian Nikolayev.

Vostok 4 was launched a day later. It was a 4,728 kg (4.73 ton) craft commanded by Pavel Popovich, with a flight duration of two days, 22 hours, and 56 minutes.

Vostok 5 was commanded by Valery Bykovsky and launched on June 14, 1963. The spacecraft weighed 4,720 kg (4.72 tons) and the flight lasted four days, 23 hours, and seven minutes.

Vostok 6 was launched on June 16, 1963, and weighed 4,713 kg (4.71 tons). It was commanded by Valentina Tereshkova, the first woman in space. The mission lasted two days, 22 hours, and 50 minutes.

In 1964, the remainder of the Vostok missions were cancelled and the Soviets concentrated on their new goal of launching three astronauts in one spacecraft and performing the first space walk. A modified design of Vostok was used for the Voskhod program.

Voskhod

The Voskhod spacecraft were developed during nine months in 1964. They were adaptations of the single man Vostok spacecraft and were meant to accomplish flights with up to three crew members, as well as being used for spacewalks well in advance of the U.S. Gemini program.

Voskhod served as the first spacecraft capable of transporting more than one traveler and was designed with the removal of ejection seats, the escape tower, and the cosmonauts' space suits, which could have been potentially dangerous. However, there was a backup solid retrorocket package mounted on the nose of the spacecraft.

The 5,320 kg (5.32 ton) Voskhod 1 was flown by three cosmonauts, Vladimir Komarov, the pilot; Boris Yegorov, a physician; and Konstantin Feoktisov, a scientist. The launch occurred on October 12, 1964, from Baikonur Cosmodrome at Kazakhstan.

The mission tested the in-flight potential and cooperation of a group of cosmonauts with specialists in different branches of science and technology. It also served as an opportunity to perform scientific physio-technical and medical-biological research in space. Live television pictures were broadcast of the crew in flight.

Land recovery of the vehicle was made possible by a rocket package suspended above the capsule in parachute lines, which ignited just prior to impact in order to cushion landing.

The crew landed following the completion of 16 orbits of the earth, 24 hours and 17 minutes after they had launched.

On March 18, 1965, Voshkod 2 was launched with two cosmonauts, pilot Pavel Belyayev and co-pilot Alexei Leonov. The Voskhod 2 spacecraft had a dry mass of 5,682 kilograms (5.68 tons).

During this mission, the first spacewalk occurred, performed by Leonov. Since the spacecraft had an extendable airlock, the main cabin air did not have to be evacuated when Leonov exited the craft. He performed the extra-vehicular activity (EVA) in a space suit with life support equipment in his backpack and was recorded by an externally-mounted television camera, as well as his own handheld camera. Leonov's EVA lasted 20 minutes, although it had been planned for a shorter length of time. His spacesuit became stiff, which made it difficult for him to reenter the spacecraft. Leonov was forced to let air leak out of his suit in order to squeeze back inside.

Other problems occurred during the mission when the cosmonauts could not properly reseal the primary hatch, resulting in the flooding of the cabin with pure oxygen by the environmental control system and creating a fire hazard. Later, a malfunction of the automatic orientation equipment forced the crew to manually control the re-entry.

Following a mission lasting 26 hours and 16 orbits, Leonov and Belyayev landed, touching down north of their target in a pine forest. It took a while for the ground crew to locate them. Once they were found it took a day to chop through the forest and recover them on skis.

Originally, five Voskhod missions were planned, yet only two were actually flown. Following the death of top Soviet spacecraft designer Sergei Korolev in late 1966, the program was cancelled and the Soviets shifted their attention to the development of Soyuz spacecraft and lunar landing technology.

Soyuz

Soyuz is the Russian word for union. The Russian Soyuz launch vehicle evolved out of the original Class A — ICBM designed by Sergei Korolev and his OKB-1 design bureau, which is now called RSC Energia. From the early 1960s until today, the Soyuz launch vehicle has been the backbone of Russia's manned and unmanned space launch fleet.

Soyuz is the longest serving manned spacecraft in the world. It was originally conceived by Korolev as a means to accomplish the Soviet goal of exploring the moon. Following the termination of the moon race, which had been won by the Americans, Soyuz spacecraft continued to ferry Russian crews to the Salyut orbital station, and also performed several solo flights as well as the historic docking with the U.S. Apollo spacecraft during the Apollo-Soyuz mission in 1975.

The Soyuz spacecraft was different from the preceding Vostok in that it was three-manned, rather than one, and could conduct active maneuvering, orbital rendezvous, and docking, features which were necessary for a flight around the moon and for lunar exploration.

An earlier version of Soyuz was designated the L1 for circumlunar flight onboard a Proton rocket. L1 became most commonly known as Zond. Other versions of Soyuz followed.

The first test flight of Soyuz occurred in 1966 with varied results. Problems were encountered which were not entirely fixed in time for the flight of Soyuz-1 on April 23, 1967, with Vladimir Komarov. The mission was planned for an orbital rendezvous and docking with the second Soyuz which was scheduled to follow Soyuz-1.

However, problems with Soyuz-1 in flight forced cancellation of the second mission, and Soyuz-1 ended with a disaster during landing that would set the Soviet lunar program back 18 months.

While in flight, one of the solar panels failed to deploy and stayed wrapped around the service module. In addition, the spacecraft only received half of its allotted solar power. An attempt was made to maneuver the spacecraft, which was unsuccessful due to interference of the reaction control system exhaust with the ion flow sensors that were a primary method of the spacecraft's orientation.

Soviet space officials made the decision to bring Komarov back to earth. A successful re-entry was made with proper deployment of the drag chute. However, the main parachute did not deploy due to a failure of a pressure sensor. When Komarov released the reserve chute, it became entangled with the drag chute. The spacecraft crashed into a field at a high speed, killing Komarov.

The Soviets followed Soyuz-1 with a series of unmanned missions. Manned missions eventually resumed in October 1968.

In 1971, a three-seat Soyuz was used to deliver two crews to the first Salyut space station. Yet another space disaster hit the Soviets when the first Salyut crew returned from orbit. The Soyuz-11 crew, Georgi Timofeyevich Dobrovolsky, Viktor Ivanovich Patsayev, and Vladislav Nikolayevich Volkov, died during the sudden depressurization of their re-entry capsule. This was caused by a pressure equalization valve which had jerked loose at the jettison of the Soyuz Orbital Module.

The valve was not supposed to open until the capsule had reached an altitude of four km (2.48 mi). The three crew members had not worn spacesuits. Following the disaster, Soyuz spacecraft were redesigned to carry two crew members, but wearing spacesuits. The new two-manned spacecraft then continued to ferry crews to the Salyut stations.

In 1980, the first version of the Soyuz T flew on a manned mission. From 1986, the modified Soyuz TM delivered crews to the Mir space station until it was taken out of commission. Modifications to the Soyuz TM included the introduction of a new weight-saving computerized flight-control system and an improved emergency escape system, which would allow increasing the crew back up to three while they could still be protected with pressure suits.

The Russian space company, RKK Energia, also developed another version of the Soyuz craft, referred to as Soyuz TMA, which removed the height limitations of the crew members onboard, and as a result, allowed use

of the spacecraft as a lifeboat for the International Space Station (ISS). If the station's main computer failed, the crew could use the spacecraft for power and life support. Production of the TMA spacecraft was stalled by the failure of the Russian government to make payments to RKK Energia by the end of the 1990s. The TMA had been developed as a result of a U.S.-Russian cooperative program, but NASA, which had requested the upgrades, also refused to pay for their development until Russia had insured the production of the spacecraft.

During its history, over 1,500 launches have been made with Soyuz spacecraft to orbit satellites for telecommunications, earth observation, weather and scientific missions, as well as manned flights.

A Soyuz vehicle is considered a three-stage launcher with a lower portion consisting of four boosters in the first stage and a central core in the second stage; an upper portion consisting of the third stage, payload adapter and payload fairing; and liquid oxygen and kerosene for propellants in all three stages.

The Soyuz spacecraft has three main components — the large spherical section at the front which is the orbital module; the bell-shaped section in the middle, which is the landing module; and the cylindrical section at the rear, which is the instrument module.

The orbital module is used for storage during launch as well as a workshop and living area for the cosmonauts during flight. The landing module is a crew cabin used during launch and re-entry. It is the only part of the Soyuz that returns to earth. The instrument module contains the main spacecraft systems, including propulsion, heating, cooling, and communications. The solar panels provide electric power for the spacecraft. The docking devices prepare the spacecraft for linking into larger structures and transferring crews from the shuttle-craft to space stations such as the Salyut and Mir.

Since 1967, more than 100 cosmonauts have flown in Soyuz spacecraft on a variety of earth-orbiting missions.

Salyut

In the 1960s, the United States and the Soviet Union were engaged in a race to the moon. After the Americans won this race with the Apollo moon landing in July 1969, the Soviets decided to shift their focus to a goal that was more within their reach: placing space stations in earth orbit.

In 1971, the Soviets became the first to launch a working space station into orbit with Salyut. In 1986, they became the first to launch a permanently occupied space station, Mir.

When the Soviets lost the moon race, they immediately began to fear that the Americans would achieve yet another first in space by launching Skylab into orbit and claiming the world's first space station. The Soviets rushed to develop a military space platform called Almaz, which was formally approved in 1967. Since a chief goal of the station was to evaluate the effectiveness of human spying from space, Almaz was supported by the Soviet military.

But, like other Soviet programs, Almaz fell behind schedule. Korolev's design bureau stepped in with a viable solution. It promised that if it were given the hull of an Almaz station, which had been built by another entity, it would equip the hull with systems and electronics from the Soyuz ferry spacecraft and have a small station ready for launch in time to beat Skylab.

The Soviet government agreed with the proposition and approved the new project in February 1970. The project was named the Long-Duration Orbital Station (DOS). DOS would remain as an example for nearly all Soviet space station designs to come in the following decades.

In April 1971, the Soviets succeeded in launching the first DOS, which was formally named Salyut, or Salyut 1. Salyut was meant as a "salute" to the first Soviet cosmonaut, Yuri Gagarin. The station was 16 meters (52 feet) long and made up of two primary sections. It weighed nearly 19 tons and had a single docking port on its front end to receive Soyuz crew spacecraft. Crews could stay aboard Salyut for nearly a month, conducting experiments.

Salyut's first crew was unable to enter the station. However, in June 1971, the second crew, consisting of Soyuz 11 members, became the first to enter a space station and dwell in it. Cosmonauts Dobrovolksy, Volkov, and Patsayev spent 24 days onboard the station, conducting experiments and making the historic point that humans could remain in orbit for relatively long periods of time. Unfortunately, on their return to earth on June 30, 1971, a valve aboard the Soyuz ferry failed. All the air escaped from the capsule within seconds and all three cosmonauts were killed.

The Soviets did not meet with much success in the following years when they launched DOS 2 and 3, in 1972 and 1973, respectively.

In 1975, NPO Energia successfully launched DOS 4, which became known publicly as Salyut 4. Two crews visited the station, with the second remaining for more than two months.

Salyut 2, 3, and 5 flew as Almaz stations between 1973 and 1977. These were primarily geared toward the purpose of conducting military experiments.

In September 1977, DOS 5 was launched, which became known as Salyut 6. It was an improved version of the DOS concept with two docking ports and new life support systems that could maintain life for as long as six months at a time.

Cosmonauts Romanenko and Grechko became the first crew to board Salyut 6, spending 96 days in space and breaking the world endurance record which had been set previously by the American Skylab 4 crew four years before. The Soviets also introduced an expendable cargo spacecraft known as Progress, which had been based on Soyuz technology.

Other cosmonauts to follow Romanenko and Grechko spent 140, 175, 185, and 75 days aboard the station between the years 1978 and 1981. During that period, 18 Soyuz and 12 Progress vehicles successfully docked at the station with no major fatalities or failures. The station also hosted guest cosmonauts from several Communist countries including Poland, East Germany, Hungary, Vietnam, Cuba, Mongolia, and Romania.

In 1982, Salyut 7 was launched with similar success, hosting five crews for short periods between 1982 and 1986. These crews carried cosmonauts from France and India, as well as the second Soviet woman cosmonaut, Svetlvana Savitskava.

During these missions, several spacewalks were conducted to perform repairs, as well as the dramatic rescue mission of Soyuz T-13, which successfully revived Salyut 7 following a series of notable failures. The longest duration for a crew aboard the station became 237 days.

The launch of Mir (Russian for "peace" or "community") or DOS 7 in 1986 brought in a new era of space station.

The Space Race

The space race was a competition between the United States and the USSR (Union of Soviet Socialist Republics) in space exploration and technology, with particular emphasis on a race between the two nations to land a human being on the moon. For over a decade, the United States and the Soviet Union were engaged this heated competition, which began in 1957 when the Soviet Union launched the first artificial satellite, Sputnik. The Soviet leader, Nikita Khrushchev, and the American presidents Dwight Eisenhower, John Kennedy, Lyndon Johnson and Richard Nixon, all agreed that conquering outer space was of critical importance to proving their respective countries' scientific superiority and showing their military strength.

Soviet Premier Khrushchev wanted to prove that communist technology was superior to that of the Americans, and President Kennedy wanted to beat the Soviets to the moon. In a speech on the prospects of sending astronauts to the moon in 1961, Kennedy said, "No single space project in this period will be more impressive to mankind, or more important for the long-range exploration of space. And none will be so difficult or expensive to accomplish."

The space race came on the heels of the Cold War which began in 1945 with the end of World War II. In actuality, the Cold War was an intense competition for military leadership, rather than a real war. It was a stiff political battle in which the main disagreement was the scope of the participating countries' governments; the USSR was communist, while the United States was run democratically.

In the mist of the Cold War, both nations believed that the other was trying to expand their form of government using unfair methods. The nations differed dramatically in that the Soviets tried to tightly control areas they felt were strategically imporant, and in contrast, the United States attempted to convince other nations to be independent and demoncratic in nature.

The atmosphere of distrust and misunderstanding between the two countries started the Cold War, leading to the development of more dangerous weapons. At the time, no satellites or highly sophisticated methods of surveillance existed, so the only way information could get out was by what spies and spy planes learned. This created a great deal of fear in both countries.

On October 4, 1957, the Russians shocked the world by launching Sputnik, the first man-made object in space. Sputnik was launched from Baikonur Cosmodrome by an A-1 rocket and orbited the earth every 96.2 minutes at 18,000 mph for 57 days, just prior to burning up in the earth's atmosphere upon re-entry.

In particular, the United States was greatly taken by surprise because it had no idea that the Russians had the capability to launch a rocket of that size and power, in this case 98 feet high with over 100,000 kg (100 tons) of thrust.

It was widely believed in the United States that if the Soviets could launch a satellite into space, they could therefore launch ICBM (Inter-Continental Ballistic Missile). Fears also existed that with this new technology, the Soviets could launch a rocket with a nuclear payload and target it to the United States, killing millions of citizens. The United States had little capability to stop such a missile other than by using B-52s, which would have had very little effectiveness.

To exacerbate matters, Sputnik was very noisy in its presence, continuously transmitting loud beeps.

The United States rebounded from the shock of Sputnik by encouraging more advances in rocket and aerospace technology. However, they could not stop the Soviets from launching yet another satellite into space. This time, it weighed over 10 times more than what the United States was capable of putting into space at that time. Sputnik 2 weighed nearly 1,100 lbs (0.5 tons) and carried a dog named Laika, translated as "little barker," along with advanced scientific equipment. Laika survived the mission until her life support was depleted.

In 1958, the United States formed the National Aeronautics and Space Administration, most commonly known as NASA, making its role in the space race official.

NASA went on to develop the Vanguard project, which was America's first program to develop rockets for launch into space. Although the first launch vehicle was designed in 1956 for the Navy, lack of funding prevented the project from proceeding. Vanguard used a three-stage rocket with liquid propellant in its first two stages, and a slow-burning solid propellant for the final stage.

Vanguard was designed with the capacity to travel from the United States to the USSR as well as to propel a satellite into space. However, only one test flight was made prior to the launch of Sputnik. Following Sputnik's launch, the United States poured more money into the program and conducted more tests until the first fully completed Vanguard rocket was made available.

On December 6, 1957, Vanguard 1 TV-3BU was launched, exploding three feet after take-off.

Project Orbiter began around the same time as Vanguard. This project was led by German rocket scientist, Wernher von Braun, using a Redstone rocket as a foundation for a four-stage launch vehicle with a satellite top.

In January 1958, a Jupiter C rocket launched the Explorer I, weighing 31 pounds, into orbit, thus becoming America's first object in space. Onboard sensors discovered the Van Allen radiation belts surrounding the earth. The success of Explorer I enabled the Americans to catch up in the space race.

Other highlights of the space race included the launch of Luna 2 by the Soviets in September 1959, becoming the first space probe to hit the moon. The launch of Vostok 1 in April 1961, with Soviet Cosmonaut Yuri Gagarin becoming the first person in space and the first person to orbit the earth; in May 1961, Alan Shepard, Jr. became the first U.S. astronaut in space, riding the tiny Freedom 7 capsule during a sub-orbital flight lasting 15 minutes; in February 1962, John Glenn, Jr. was launched on a

Friendship 7 capsule and became the first U.S. astronaut to orbit the earth, orbiting it 3 times in 4 hours and 55 minutes; and in June 1963, the first woman in space, Soviet cosmonaut Valentina Tereshkova, was launched aboard a Vostok 6 capsule.

These events clearly led up to sending a man to the moon. The Soviets tested lunar landings with their Luna probes, which were designed to orbit and sometimes crash into the moon. These probes also took photographs of the moon's surface. It was also a Luna probe that made the first soft landing.

The United States followed suit by sending unmanned probes to the moon, commencing with the Ranger series, which was the first U.S. attempt to gain close up photos of the moon's surface. Between 1961 and 1965, the United States sent nine Rangers to the moon. Unfortunately, the first six failed, never making their destination.

Between 1966 and 1968, the United States sent another series of probes into space, the Surveyors, with the objective of successfully landing and taking off from the moon, and also recording images from the moon's surface.

These unmanned missions gave each country sufficient information on the moon to begin developing a manned mission to it. At this point, the United States was greatly behind the USSR in the moon race. The Americans made a desperate effort to beat the Soviets by launching the multi-billion-dollar Apollo 11. Apollo 11 was launched using the mega-rocket, Saturn 5, which was 363 ft.

The mission was manned by Neil Armstrong, the commander; Michael Collins, the command module pilot; and Edwin "Buzz" Aldrin, Jr., the lunar module pilot. It was launched on July 16, 1969. The lunar module, the Eagle, landed on the moon and Neil Armstrong stepped out, making his famous declaration, "It's one small step for man, and one giant leap for mankind." He became the first man to step on the moon.

The mission lasted eight days, three hours, 18 minutes, and 35 seconds, with the astronauts remaining on the moon for 21.6 hours, before splashing down on earth on July 24, 1969.

By being the first to land on the moon, the United States had become the winner of the space race, proving that it was a more technologically advanced country that the USSR.

In July 1975, the Soviets and Americans got together on a cooperative space project named the Apollo-Soyuz test project, which was the first international manned spaceflight. It was designed to test rendezvous and docking systems of both the American and Soviet spacecraft. The Apollo spacecraft, specifically Apollo 18, was nearly identical to the one that orbited the moon. The Soyuz spacecraft, which was introduced in 1967, was used by the Soviets for the project. The module which served as an airlock between the two spacecraft was designed and built by NASA.

The Apollo crew consisted of Thomas P. Stafford, Vance D. Brand, and Donald "Deke" K. Slayton. The Soyuz crew was made up of Valeriy Nikolayevich and Alexei Arhipovich Leonov.

Fifty-two hours following the launch of Soyuz, the Apollo spacecraft docked with the Russian spacecraft. The Apollo-Soyuz crews worked together on a series of experiments over the two days they were linked. The Soyuz spacecraft then returned to earth 43 hours following separation. The Apollo spacecraft remained in space for an additional six days.

The success of this joint mission enhanced space relations between the two countries, which would lead to future cooperation on Mir and the International Space Station.

Sergei P. Korolev — Soviet Space Mastermind

Sergei Pavlovich Korolev was born on December 30, 1906, in the city of Zhitomir in present day Ukraine. In 1916, Sergei's parents divorced, and a year later Sergei's mother remarried. In 1917, the year of the Bolshevik Revolution in Russia, the family moved to Odessa, which is a major port city in Ukraine.

In 1922, as the city was still recovering from the civil war, Sergei Korolev passed qualifying exams for a senior year at the Odessa construction professional school. By that time, he had already developed an interest in aviation. Two years later, in 1924, Korolev was admitted to the Kiev Polytechnic Institute, where he joined a group of glider enthusiasts. In another two years, Korolev transferred to Moscow's Bauman High Technical School, MVTU, the best engineering college in Russia, comparable to MIT in the United States.

Korolev graduated from MVTU in 1929 and joined the Central Aero and Hydrodynamics Institute, TsAGI, in 1931. He later co-founded the Moscow rocketry organization GIRD (Gruppa Isutcheniya Reaktivnovo Dvisheniya, Group for Investigation of Reactive Motion). Like the VfR (Verein fuer Raumschiiffahrt, Society for Spaceship Travel) in Germany, and Robert H. Goddard in the United States, the Russian organizations were testing liquid-fueled rockets of increasing size by the early 1930s.

In Russia, GIRD lasted only two years before the military, seeing the potential of rockets, replaced it with RNII (Reaction Propulsion Scientific Research Institute). RNII developed a series of rocket-propelled missiles and gliders during the 1930s, culminating in Korolev's RP-318, Russia's first rocket-propelled aircraft. Unfortunately, before the aircraft could make a rocket propelled flight, Korolev and other aerospace engineers were thrown into the Soviet prison system from 1937 to 1938, during the peak of Stalin's purges.

Korolev ended up spending months in transit on the trans–Siberian railway and on a prison vessel at Magadan, which was followed by a year in the Kolyma gold mines, the most dreaded part of the Gulag. Stalin soon recognized the importance of aeronautical engineers in preparing for the impending war with Hitler. He retrieved the incarcerated Korolev, as well as other technical personnel, to provide help for the Red Army by developing new weapons.

A system of sharashkas, or prison design bureaus, was set up to exploit the jailed talent, including Korolev. Korolev was saved by the intervention of senior aircraft designer Sergei Tupolev, who was also a prisoner, when he requested his services in the TsKB-39 sharashka. Fllowing the war, Korolev was released from prison and appointed chief constructor for development of a long-range ballistic missile. As Korolev was preparing for the first launch of the R-11 rocket on April 1, 1953, he received approval from the Council of Ministers for development of the world's first intercontinental ballistic missile (ICBM), the R-7.

In order to concentrate on development of the R-7, Korolev had his other projects spun off to a new design bureau in Dnepropetrovsk, headed by Korolev's assistant, Mikhail Kuzmich Yangel. This marked the first of several design bureaus, some later competing with Korolev's, that would spinoff once Korolev had perfected a new technology. It was Korolev's R-7 ICBM that launched Sputnik 1 October 4, 1957.

Korolev's intelligence, dedication to the prospects of rocket technology, managerial abilities and almost mythical skills in decision-making helped make him the head of the first Soviet rocket development center, which is known today as RKK Energia. He has merited the most credit for turning rocket weapons into an instrument of space exploration and making the Soviet Union the world's first space-faring nation.

During the early 1960s, Korolev campaigned to send a Soviet cosmonaut to the moon. Following the initial reconnaissance of the moon by the lunar missions, Luna 1, 2, and 3, Korolev established three largely independent efforts aimed at achieving a Soviet lunar landing before the Americans. The first objective, answered by Vostok and Voskhod, was to prove that human space flight was possible. The second objective was to develop lunar vehicles which would soft-land on the moon's surface to ensure that a cosmonaut would not sink into the dust accumulated by four billion years of meteorite impacts. The third objective, and the most difficult to achieve, was to develop a huge booster to send cosmonauts to the moon.

In 1962, Korolev's design bureau began work on the N-1 launch vehicle, a counterpart to the American Saturn V. This rocket was targeted to be capable of launching a maximum of 110,000 pounds into low-earth orbit. The project ran through 1971 before cancellation, although the N-1 never made a successful flight.

On January 14,1966, Sergei P. Korolev died from a botched hemorrhoid operation which could have been partly attributed to his weakened immune system caused by years in the prison system. It is ironic that only after his death were his accomplishments acknowledged by his country. He was allowed a hero's burial within the Kremlin wall.

Cosmodromes — Baikonur and Plesetsk

Russia has recently been planning the development of two new cosmodromes, with the goal of discontinuing the use of Baikonur in Kazakhstan as a satellite launch site. The country has currently been paying in the area of $115 million per year in rent for Baikonur.

Plans are being made to use the Plesetsk cosmodrome in Russia's far north as an alternative to Baikonur for major launch projects.

Russia made the decision to pull out of Baikonur as a result of long-standing tensions with Kazakhstan over satellite program management. Baikonur was built in the 1950s in the Soviet Republic of Kazakhstan, and difficulties have arisen since 1991 when the territory became a newly independent state with the fall of communism.

In 1994, Russia and Kazakhstan signed an agreement recognizing the central Asian republic's territorial claim on Baikonur and establishing that Russia would pay $115 million per year for its use. However, in the wake of two launch accidents of Proton rockets in July and October 1999, relations between the two countries deteriorated. Kazakhstan accused Russia of damaging the environment and banned Proton launches from Baikonur for several months. This contributed to the delay of the dispatching of the key International Space Station (ISS) module, Zvezda.

Baikonur

In the mid–1950s, Soviet designers required a test site for the first intercontinental ballistic missiles, R-7 and winged Burya, they were developing. They needed a new test site, since the existing proving ground in Kapustin Yar on the Volga River would not allow for fitting the flight range of missiles exceeding 1,000 to 1,500 km (621–932 mi). The new test range required radio-control developers which would deploy an array of guidance antennas, allowing for an unobstructed view of the rocket over hundreds of miles during the powered phase of the flight.

Sergei Korolev was key in making the decision to establish the new test range location. He and his men tried moving to the Stavropol region, west of the Caspian Sea, an area of soft climate and popular resorts, where the booster stages would fall into the Caspian Sea. This site choice was reportedly ridiculed by Ryazansky, the man who was in charge of flight control system development, and Korolev informed his deputies to seek another location.

On March 17, 1954, the Soviet of Ministers USSR issued a decree assigning the Ministry of Defense, Ministry of Medium Machine Building, Ministry of Defense Industry, Ministry of Radiotechnical Industry, and Ministry of Aviation Industry to conduct a search for a new test site for long-range missiles. They were to find this location by January 1, 1955, and report their proposals to the government by March 1, 1955. The search commission was lead by Vasili Voznuk.

After trying several locations, with Korolev's insistance on choosing a site as far south as possible in order to increase the range of the missiles with the assistance from the earth's rotation, a site was located at Tyuratam

junction, a sparsely populated and remote region which was linked to industrial centers of Russia by the Kazakhastanskava railroad, later renamed Western-Kazakhstan railroad.

Building at the site began in March 1955. By the end of July 1955, more than three thousand military construction workers were erecting facilities around Tyuratam. On July 28, the first train with military test personnel for the range arrived. Also in July, a communications link between Tyuratam and supply bases in Moscow and Tashkent had been established. A survey team from Moscow hammered markers into the ground around the future launch pad, although excavations did not begin until September 15, 1955.

A pair of 1,000 cubical-meter reservoirs and a pair of 3,000 cubical-meter reservoirs were built along the road to the launch complex, farther north. Three 3,000 cubical-meter underground water tanks were also built just south of the launch pad.

Military units were sent to the area and by the end of 1955, 20 military units had been deployed.

The Soviets tried their best to conceal activities at Tyuratam once the launch area had been completed, and the center remained a top-secret site for decades. Although Yuri Gagarin's Vostok 1 flight took off from Pad 1 at the center and opened the era of manned spaceflight on April 12, 1961, it was official policy at the time by the Soviet ideologists not to confirm any unwelcome information on Soviet affairs, no matter how widely known and well-proven, particularly if this information came from the West.

As a cover, in an official telegram to the Federation Aviation Sport Commission of the Central Aero-club of the USSR, it was claimed that Vostok was launched from "Cosmodrome" located near Baikonur, registering on the date of July 18, 1961.

Subsequently, the village of Baikonur was chosen as the "cover-up site" for the first manned launch by several Russian officials, including Vladimir Barmin, the designer of the launch complex for the R-7 missile.

The actual town of Baikonur, was located 300 km (186 mi) northeast of Tyuratam, was picked because it was the first identifiable location downrange from the launch site. It was reported that experiments with nuclear blasts in the upper atmosphere were launched from the area, and the name Cosmodrome Baikonur began to appear in the Soviet press.

Baikonur has since been known around the world as the launch site of Russia's space missions until the collapse of the USSR in 1991, however, its primary purpose was to serve as a test site for liquid-fueled ballistic missiles.

It has 11 assembly building and nine launch complexes with 15 launch pads for space boosters, as well as an oxygen and nitrogen-producing plant; three fueling facilities with only one active since the mid–1990s; a power station; 600 energy-converting stations; 92 communication sites; two airports; 470 km (292 mi) of railways; 1,281 km (796 mi) of roads; and 6,610 km (4,107 mi) of communications lines.

The center encompasses 6,717 square kilometers (2,593 square miles) and consumes 600 million kilowatt/hours of electric power annually.

Baikonur is actually divided into three regions, which were formerly ruled by the launch and processing facilities of the major players in Soviet rocketry—Sergei Korolev, Mikhail Yangel, and Vladimir Chelomei. These regions include the central region (Korolev area); the right flank (Yangel area); and the left flank (Chelomei area).

Baikonur began with the construction of the R-7 ICBM launch complex, which was developed at Korolev's OKB-1 design bureau. This region became known as Korolev's area when Baikonur's test facilities began sprawling east and west from the original launch complex.

After serving as a test complex, the R-7 facilities located in the central region of the range were converted into space launch sites. In the 1960s and 1970s, when the manned lunar and Energia-Buran programs were in process, the Korolev area grew significantly.

The right flank area refers to the eastern section of Baikonur Cosmodrome, which has also been known as the Yangel area. Several generations of ballistic missiles and space launchers developed by Mikhail Yangel's design bureau had been tested there since 1960. These included the R-16, different versions of the R-36, MR-UR-100, R-36M, and R-36M2 ballistic missiles. Early tests of the Cosmos-1 booster and all launches of the Zenit-2 rocket occurred on right flank launch pads.

The left flank, or Chelomei area, located on the west side of Baikonur Cosmodrome, was where several generations of ballistic missiles and space launchers developed by Vladimir Chelomei's OKB-52 design bureau were tested. These also included the UR-200 and several generations of UR-100 ICBM. Launch pads and processing facilities for the OKB-52-designed Proton rocket are also located on the left flank.

Other test facilities at Baikonur have been designated with numbers used in conjunction with the word *Ploshadka*, which means the construction site or launch pad in Russian. Launch pads at Baikonur are most commonly referred to as pushkovaya ustanovka (launching device) along with their own numbering system.

Tyuratam is the only site that can launch satellites directly into retrograde orbits due to range safety restrictions at other launch sites.

Baikonur supports a variety of launch vehicles, including Proton-K, Rokot, Soyuz-U, Molniya-M, Tsyklon-2, and Zenit. Eight launch pads were operational in 1994, two were being overhauled, and three Energiya launch pads were no longer in use. Baikonur has served as the origin of all manned and man-related (space stations and re-supply ships), lunar, interplanetary, high-altitude navigation, and GEO missions.

Plesetsk

Plesetsk Cosmodrome is the world's busiest spaceport. Over 1250 launches have taken place since 1966, which is greater than combined launch totals from all other nations. Plesetsk is located at 62.8 degrees latitude, which enables high inclination, polar, and highly elliptical orbits. Many military satellites have been launched from Plesetsk.

Pletsetsk Cosmodrome is located in northwestern Russia, about 400 miles northeast of St. Petersburg (formerly Leningrad).

The 1762-km (680 mi) square cosmodrome has been supported by the adjacent town of Mirny. It has served as primarily a military launch facility, to deliver most (if not all) polar orbiting sensor payloads, and many Molniya orbit payloads.

From its northern latitude (~63 degrees N), space missions have been restricted to orbital inclinations between 63 and 83 degrees. The high inclination of the Molniya communications satellites is a natural result of an eastward launch from Plesetsk. The site is on Russian soil and the launch flight profile does not pass over any other countries during the boost phase. The requirements for coordination with other countries are minimal and there are launch pads for the SL4, SL6, SL8 and SL-14 space launch vehicles. The extreme northern latitude of the Plesetsk facility has provided Russia with valuable experience in the conduct of extreme cold weather launch operations and launch vehicle design.

Four launch vehicle types are used at Plesetsk — Kosmos-3M, Soyuz/Molnlya, Tskylon-3, and Start. Kosmos-3M can be launched from any of three launch pads including Complexes 132 left and right and 133. Soyuz/Molniya launch vehicles are supported by three active pads, Complexes 16 and 43 left and right, while a fourth pad, Complex 41, is in mothballs. The Tsyklon launch facilities include two active launch pads, Complexes 32 left and right. Start launches, which began in 1993, are conducted by the Strategic Missile Forces instead of the Military Space Forces from the fixed RS-12M launch facilities at site 158.

In 1957, the Cold War entered a new phase, as it was the first time the USSR could target U.S. territory with nuclear-tipped missiles. Soviet designers had also begun testing the R-7 missile in Tyuratam, and the military was looking for places to deploy the new weapon.

Since the shortest path for missile attack against North America extended across the Arctic Ocean, it became clear that the launch pads needed to be located as far north as possible to enable maximum use of the missiles' flight range. Future launch sites also needed to be accessible by railroad, which was the only means to transport R-7 stages, while being remote enough to maintain maximum secrecy.

A Military of Defense search team chose the village of Plesetsk, located in the Archangel Region, 800 km (497 mi) north of Moscow, as the location of the first operational base for the R-7 missile.

In February 1957, the first military construction crews arrived at Plesetskava railroad station and were met by a harsh blizzard along with cold temperatures of–45°C. Other units followed.

By 1960, U.S. intelligence had placed Plesetsk high on its list of suspected ICBM sites. It became a primary surveillance target following Francis Gary Powers' reconnaissance flight on May 1, 1960, resulting in the famous U-2 incident. In August of that year, following numerous previous failures, the Corona spacecraft delivered the first photos of Plesetsk. Even though the quality of the photos was low, railway lines not previously found on Germany military maps from World War II were revealed.

A Soviet government commission officially declared the first launch pad in Plesetsk operational in December 1959, for the R-7 missiles. On December 17, 1959, the Soviet government created Strategic Missile Forces, RVSN, within the Soviet Army, within days following the completion of the Plesetsk launch complex. Two additional R-7 launch pads at Site 3 in Plesetsk were commissioned on July 15, 1961, and processing time for an R-7 launch ranged between seven and eight hours, as opposed to the 12 to 16 hours it would have taken to launch from any of two pads at Tyuratum.

On September 16, 1963, the Soviet of Ministers USSR issued a resolution approving a merger of a future test range to be used for solid-fueled ballistic missiles and high-inclination orbits for space launches and the existing ICBM base in Plesetsk.

Three silos for solid-fueled RT-2 ICBMs became the first test facilities to be built at Plesetsk, and by October 3, 1968, 25 launches of RT-2 ICBM had been conducted from the range. A total of 142 RT-2 would eventually fly from Plesetsk, and between January 16, 1970, and January 1972, there were also 51 modified RT-2P missile launches.

On March 17, 1966, the first satellite was launched from Plesetsk, which was announced as Cosmos-112 and was carried aloft by the Vostok-2 booster. The spacecraft belonged to the first-generation of the Zenit spysat which had been previously launched from Tyuratam. On April 6, the second-generation Zenit (Cosmos-114) blasted off from Plesetsk onboard the Voskhod booster.

A group of students and their physics teacher, Geoffery Perry, noticed the higher than usual inclination of these two spacecraft, which was 73 degrees. The group had been monitoring trajectories and analyzing radio signals from the satellites, and closer evaluation of the satellites' ground tracks suggested that they originated in Northwestern Russia.

October 14, 1966, Cosmos-129 was launched, and on November 3, 1966, the discovery of Plesetsk was officially announced. Since then Plesetsk has been known publicly in the West. However, oddly enough, the Soviet Union did not acknowledge the existence of the launch site in Plesetsk until 1983.

In 1965, south of the original R-7 pads, the construction of the R-12 launch complex began, which was later called Raduga, or Facility 133. Facility 133 was used for the first time on March 16, 1967, to launch a new version of the R-12 booster designated 11K63 or Cosmos-2. On May 15, 1967, the Cosmos-3M also began flying from Plesetsk.

Around 1968, Plesetsk became a testing ground for the early efforts to create mobile ICBMs. Twelve launches of the RT-20 (SS-X-15) mobile system were conducted. Eight launches reportedly resulted in failures, after which the project was terminated. On March 14, 1972, testing of the new mobile ICBM Temp-C (also known as SS-16 and RS-14) started in Plesetsk and it was conducted by a test unit led by Lt. Colonel N.V. Mazyarkin.

By 1976, 35 launches were made during the course of the intensive test program, and although in 1974, Leonid Brezhnev and President Ford promised not to deploy SS-16 missiles during the Vladivostok summit, U.S. satellite imagery later revealed what appeared to be up to 200 solid-fueled SS-16s deployed near Plesetsk under camouflage netting.

Construction of a highly-automated launch complex for the Tsyklon-3 (11K68) booster started at Site 32 in 1970. It was designed by the Transmash design bureau which was led by chief designer V.N. Soloviev. It included two pads called left start and right start. The first launch pad was used on June 24, 1977, to launch Cosmos-921.

After six years of Cosmos-3M launches, a routine launch was planned for 1:32 A.M. on June 26, 1973. During launch preparation, a sensor malfunction occurred and the fuel tank was overfilled. On-duty personnel drained part of the fuel and refueled the launcher, at which point the fuel tank developed a leak and 15 seconds before the liftoff, the launch sequence was automatically suspended. The launch was canceled and the more than 40-member launch team tried to deactivate the vehicle.

At 4:18 and 4:20 A.M. two crews of 13 people were dispatched to the launch pad, and at 4:22 A.M. a dual explosion shook the complex, followed by a fire. Seven people were killed at the spot, 13 were injured, and two of those later died in the hospital. No announcement of the tragedy was made at the time, and its victims were buried in a mass grave in Mirny. A special memorial to the victims of the accident was dedicated in 1974.

On March 18, 1980, while dozens of military technicians worked on the pad during the fueling of the Vostok-2M launcher with the Tselina satellite, a devastating explosion incinerated the rocket, killing 50 people. The victims of the tragedy were buried within the limits of the town of Mirny, by the same memorial where the nine people who had died in the 1973 Cosmos explosion were buried. The official investigation of the cause of the disaster blamed the ground personnel for breaking fire safety rules, although most people refused to believe that was the case.

Later, according to a post–Cold War Russian source, the results of investigation were proved wrong when on June 23, 1981, a similar disaster was miraculously averted at the last second in Plesetsk. A new investigation pinpointed a valve made of materials which on contact with hydrogen peroxide could cause an explosive chain reaction. Those outside Russia would not learn about either accident until the end of the 1980s.

From January 1982 to April 1985, testing of the railroad-based RT-23 (RS-22) missile was conducted at Plesetsk, which was followed by the testing of modified RT-23 UTTKh system designed for both railroad and silo launchers. The railroad-based system was tested between February 27, 1985, and December 22, 1987. Eight underground pads of two different types were constructed in Plesetsk for a silo based version along with fortified control bunker and modified measurement complex. Twenty launches of the missile were made between July 31, 1986, and September 23, 1988.

In spite of being in a better politico-economic position than Baikonur, Plesetsk was unable to escape financial problems of the economic transfer in the 1990s. More than 1,500 spacecraft have been launched from the site, although, in the wake of the reduction in defense spending, space launches at Plesetsk fell from 47 in 1988 to six in 1996. The site has also faced environmental problems in the areas of failing booster stages, which had to be addressed.

Testing of strategic weapons has also continued in Plesetsk since the 1990s. The Mobile ICBM Topol M (RS-12M2) was launched there for first time on December 20, 1994, with two more launches conducted in 1995 and 1996 and another on July 8, 1997.

The Soviet N-1 Moon Rocket

When the space race began, there was no rocket that had been developed which was powerful enough to send a man to the moon and back. The contest between the Americans and the Soviets was to develop a super heavy-lift booster, or moon rocket. Ultimately, the United States succeeded with the behemoth Saturn V, while the Soviet counterpart, the N-1, never made it into space.

The N-1 was the largest of a family of launch vehicles following the previous Soviet ICBM-derived launchers that were in use prior to 1960.

It was intended to launch Soviet cosmonauts to the moon, then Mars and Venus, as well as to place huge military stations into orbit.

The N-1 project was started later than work on the Saturn V and was characterized by lack of funds, low priority, and ongoing political and technical struggles between its chief designers Korolev, Glushko, and Chelomei.

There were four launches of the N-1, resulting in complete failure and cancellation of the project just five years after Apollo landed on the moon.

Prior to the development of the N-1, the Soviets tried to develop launchers and ICBM's using thermal nuclear propulsion. In a decree of January 30, 1956, the future of Soviet spaceflight was mapped out to include a number of objectives, including a one-week flight of a manned spacecraft by 1964; an unmanned reconnaissance satellite by 1970; a rocket capable of 12-ton escape velocity payload by 1970; a rocket with a 100-ton low-earth orbit payload, capable of placing two to three men on the moon; and orbiting of satellites of 1.8 to 2.5 tons by 1958.

Korolev's team began work on nuclear launchers and missiles in June of 1958. Competing engine designs were submitted by both Bondaryuk and Glushko. The Bondaryuk engine used a mixture of ammonia and alcohol, while the Glushko engine operated on ammonia alone.

Utilizing these designs, a Super Rocket was developed with a lift-off mass of 2,000 tons and a payload of 150 tons. This was considered to be an antecedent of the N-1. Both first and second stages were later adopted for the N-1 in conical or *raketov* form. The first stage was comprised of a Kuznetsov NK-9 cluster of engines, each having a thrust of 52 tons.

The second stage had a total thrust of 850 tons from four nuclear engines. This nuclear propulsion configuration was later abandoned for the more conventional chemical propulsion that provided nearly equivalent performance at less developmental, safety, and environmental risk.

Until 1989, the existence of the N-1 booster was never admitted by the Soviets.

"N" stands for Nosital, which means carrier in English.

Sergei Korolev's Answer to the Saturn V

In a January 1960 letter to the central committee of the Communist Party, Sergei Korolev, who later served as the N-1's chief designer, proposed an aggressive plan for the Community Conquest of space, asking that the Soviet design bureau make a broad swift assault on space research; stating that a new rocket between 1,000 and 2,000 tons in gross lift-off mass and a 60 to 80 ton payload must be developed at the earliest possible date; that advanced propulsion systems — nuclear, LOX/LH2, low thrust liquid, ion, and plasma engines — and correction rockets be developed as quickly as possible; and that new automatic and radio guidance systems be developed to meet these objectives.

The N-1 heavy-lift rocket was proposed to be developed with a 40 to 50 ton payload by 1963.

Korolev and his team of scientists and engineers began to move forward with plans to design rockets larger than the Soyuz. Their ultimate goal was a 60 to 80,000 kg payload to LEO.

The Korolev bureau decided to develop two different boosters; one with a payload of 40 to 50,000 kg (40 to 50 tons), called the N-1, and the N-2, a 60 to 80,000 kg (60 to 80 ton) booster. The Soviet government did not provide solid funding or support initially, resulting in a delay of the N-1 project until 1965.

Meanwhile, Glushko, chief rocket engine designer, who was Korolev's rival, promoted a lunar rocket in 1960 and received government approval for large rocket engines and for large boosters in the same year. However, because of his continuing disputes with Korolev, significant funding for large engines for lunar rockets did not emerge until 1966.

In the same period, the UR-700, using Glusko's 600,000 kg (600 ton) thrust engines, was given the go ahead for production by then-Premier Nikita Khrushchev. Korolev protested a series of boosters by another rival, Chelomey, featuring the UR-200 with a payload of 3 to 4,000 kg (3 to 4 tons) and the UR-500 with a 20,000 kg (20 ton) payload. The UR-700 was intended to follow with a payload of 90 to 130,000 kg (9 to 130 tons).

Korolev used his influence with individuals within the government and party to protest Chelomey's project, resulting in the termination of the UR-700 based primarily on concerns over technical problems with Glushko's large engine design and the danger of using toxic propellants associated with it.

Following the cancellation of the UR-700, Korolev finally received approval for his N-1 rocket. In 1961, he proposed to use an N-1 booster with a 75,000 kg (75 ton) payload to carry two cosmonauts to the moon, but was rejected.

Korolev later tried to pitch his N-1 for use in military applications including global reconnaissance, anti-satellite, antiballistic missile, and interceptor spacecraft used to rendezvous with, examine and neutralize enemy satellites, and as nuclear anti-satellites. However, the military did not support his attempts.

In July 1962, M.V. Keldysh, head of the Soviet Academy of Sciences who chaired a commission studying the feasibility of Korolev's proposed N-1 project, issued a report recommending that the N-1 payload be increased to 75,000 kg (75 tons), which Korolev had asked for initially in 1961.

This new report served to fuel a long-standing argument between the Soviet Union's lead chief designers, Korolev and Glushko, over the best method for propulsion of the large booster.

Korolev wanted to develop a hydrogen-oxygen propellant like the United States was using for the Saturn rocket family, while Glushko favored the use of oxygen-flourine.

Soviet deputy V. Mishin cited Glushko's published views on propellants in his paper "Chemical Sources of Power," saying "liquid oxygen is nowhere near the best oxidizer, and liquid hydrogen will never be of any practical use in rocket equipment." This belief was later proved wrong by NASA when it used hydrogen-oxygen rocket propellants, finding them highly practical for upper stages in conventional multi-stage rockets.

The final decree authorizing N-1 to go into production was issued in September 1962, with the first flight planned for 1965. Although Korolev now had authorization to produce the rocket, he still lacked military support for a payload to launch it.

In September 1963, Korolev submitted plans for space projects in the period between 1965 to 1975. He had hoped to appeal to the Soviet leadership for a manned lunar landing program.

Korolev presented five spacecraft that would perform reconnaissance, do a landing on the moon, and then explore its surface, including the L1, L2, L3, L4, and L5.

The L1 project had the objective of sending two men on a circumlunar flyby trajectory. It would consist of a 7K manned spacecraft, a 9K rocket spacecraft, and an 11K tanker. The L1 would also have six modules: the descent capsule (SA), the equipment module (AO), the propulsion module (AO), the living module (BO), the rendezvous electronics module (NO), and the docking unit (SU).

The L2 project objective was to land a remote-controlled self-propelled rover on the surface of the moon. It would also conduct scientific research on the lunar surface and allow the selection of a favorable landing point for later manned flights. An onboard television would send back panoramic television pictures. The L2 rover would be nuclear-powered and equipped with a radio beacon for precision landings. It would investigate cosmic ray flux, the relief of the lunar surface, the magnetic fields of the moon, the mechanical properties of the lunar soil, and solar insulation at the surface.

The L3 would be designed to make a direct lunar landing using the earth orbit rendezvous method. The 200-ton spacecraft would require three N-1 launches to place it in low earth orbit.

The L4 was a planned lunar orbiter research spacecraft to take two to three cosmonauts into lunar orbit for an extended survey and mapping mission. With a total mass of 75 tons, it would be placed into orbit in a single N-1 launch.

The L5 would be a heavy lunar self-propelled craft used for extended manned reconnaissance of the lunar surface. Traveling at a maximum speed of 20 km/hr, it would provide living accommodations for three cosmonauts and 3,500 kg (3.5 tons) of provisions.

Ultimately, the L3 project was decided upon, which would utilize the same lunar orbit rendezvous technique to achieve moon landing as chosen for the Apollo moon program.

In 1963, Korolev began production on the N-1 using kerosene as fuel for the N-1 because he was under too much pressure to try and develop a hydrogen-based engine from scratch. Korolev chose to use the Kuznetsov factory at Kuybyshev for the production site, a region comprised of 28 related factories and departments that had also been responsible for the production of the Soyuz booster.

By April 1963, the conceptual design for the N-1 and its lunar landing payload were underway. Korolev continued pushing his plan for a lunar mission through 1964.

Korolev followed through with work on the N-1, increasing its payload to 90,000 kg (90 tons) by 1965, with plans to further increase it to 130,000 kg (130 tons).

Construction of the N-1 launch complex Raskat, began in 1964. Located in Tyuratam, Russia, the construction efforts employed a total of 35,000 military workers at its peak.

The Raskat N-1 complex consisted of two launch pads at site 110, a command post 103, an administrative building 20, and a huge tank farm for storage of massive quantities of liquid oxygen and kerosene to fuel the N-1. An assembly building was added, capable of housing two assembled boosters.

Diesel locomotives running on two rail lines 18 meters (59 ft) apart pushed the grant erector with the N-1 to the launch pad, where the rocket was installed in a vertical position. A rotating service structure allowed access to the rocket.

Components for the N-1 were built at Kuznetsov factories and Korolev maintained supervision over the entire project until his untimely death on January 14, 1966, during surgery.

The N-1 project draft was finalized in mid–1966.

Deputy Chief Designer Vasily Mishin

took Korolev's place and was in charge of finishing the development of the N-1. A funding shortage had forced Korolev to order all-up testing of the N-1, which was also used by NASA for testing the Saturn V. Mishin followed through with this policy, which was in place in part due to the looming cost of building giant rockets and assembling their various stages. Kuznetsov lacked facilities for extensive ground testing of the N-1's stages due to cost constraints. In comparison, NASA was able to perform all-up testing of the Saturn V using a network of test stands across the United States for repeatedly firing engines and stages.

Only individual engine tests or small engine clusters were performed on the N-1 before being assembled onto the booster and readied for flight. This complicated prelaunch preparations, during which engines were shipped to Baikonur for installation because they required major work for integration into the stage. Thus, the lack of extensive ground testing led to the failure of the N-1 program.

Production began in 1966 on the L3 lunar orbiter and lander spacecraft, and more test stands and launch complexes were erected for the N-1.

By 1968, most of the N-1 infrastructure was in place. The booster stood vertically on the launch pad, which was set over three flame ducts. A 140-meter (459 ft) tail rotating service tower stood to one side of the booster, which would be rotated 180 degrees away from the pad during launch.

A 100-meter (328 ft) tall fueling tower sat at the side of the rail lines next to the booster. Four 183-meter (600 ft) towers protected the booster, fueling and service towers from lightening.

The completed N-1 consisted of five stages, including 30 NK-33 LOX/kerosene engines with 10.1 million lbs of total thrust; eight NK-43 LOX/kerosene engines with 3.1 million lbs of total thrust; four NK-39 engines with 360,800 lbs of total thrust; one NK-31 engine with 90,200 lbs of total thrust, acting as the trans-lunar boost stage; and one engine with 19,200 lbs thrust, acting as the lunar orbit insertion and initial lunar descent stage.

The first stage, Block A, was powered by 30 Kuznetsov engines burning a liquid oxygen and kerosene mix. Mass of the stage fuel-loaded was 1,875 tons, empty it was 25 tons with a burn time of 125 seconds. The estimated cost of development was $600 million.

The second stage, Block B, was powered by eight NK-15V Kuznetsov engines burning a liquid oxygen and kerosene mix. The mass grew from its original capacity of 440 tons to 540 tons in 1962 to accommodate more propellant. Empty mass was equivalent to that of Block A, 35 tons. The burn time was 120 seconds. Total thrust generated in vacuum increased from 1,4040 tons to 1,431,68 tons.

The third stage of the N-1 was powered by four Nk-18 engines burning a fuel mix of liquid oxygen and kerosene. The third stage, Block V, had a loaded mass of 185 tons with an empty mass of 10 tons. The burn time during orbital insertion was 370 seconds. Total thrust generated in vacuum was 164 tons.

The Failure of the N-1

After years of political and engineering disputes and funding difficulties, the first N-1 was launched with an L3 spacecraft on February 21, 1969.

The first flight-ready N-1 had been installed on the launch pad as early as May 7, 1968, but had to be returned when cracks were found in the first stage. It was rolled out again in mid–January 1969, after a brief test period.

As mission N1-3L began to rise into the sky, 68.7 seconds after the launch, small metallic particles lodged in the gas generator turbine of engine 2. This caused rising high frequency oscillation, leading to engine component fatigue and dislodging from their mounts. Propellants leaked from an oxidizer pipe, starting a fire in the tail compartment.

All engines were shut down and the rocket was destroyed by range safety 1.3 seconds later. It was later determined that heat and vibrations of the first stage's 30 engines had caused damage to the rocket.

Following the failure, Mishin called for test firing of all engines and stages, but this mandate was not followed through with and funding was never provided.

The next mission, N1-5L, was launched just two weeks before the Apollo 11 moon landing, from launch Pad 110R. The N-1 booster lifted off thunderously rising 100 meters (328 ft), failing just 0.25 seconds after lift-off when an oxygen pump exploded. A fire ignited and the KORD engine monitoring system reacted, shutting down all engines and causing the booster to fall back onto the pad. A fire resulting from the heavy impact caused by the N-1 striking it and exploding with the force of a small nuclear bomb heavily damaged the launchpad.

As a result of this failure, substantial modifications were made to the N-1, delaying further launch attempts for two years. The commission investigating the failure concluded that the engines would need to be redesigned with filters to prevent ingestion of metal splinters and shavings into the turbine machinery, the launch vehicle trajectory required modification so that it would move away from the launch pad as soon as it cleared the tower, and the KORD logic would need to be modified to prevent unnecessary engine shutdown.

It took three years to rebuild Pad 110F and by September 24, 1969, an N-1 was erected to test the launch pad interfaces. This N-1 was placed without a payload. Another N-1 was installed on the pad May 18, 1970, also without a payload.

Attempts were being made to design more powerful versions of the N-1 to launch heavier payloads to the moon.

In winter of 1970, the third N-1 booster for launch, 6L, underwent engine tests in the static test stands. It was then rolled out to the secondary launch pad that was damaged in the second launch attempt in March or April. It was reported that the launch was also attempted before July 1971, but was aborted while still on the launch pad due to engine failure during the engine start sequence.

The N-1-6L, when launched, rose from the pad, making the new evasive maneuver to move away from the pad. The launch vehicle developed a pitching roll of 10 degrees and veered out of control in the roll axis. The engines were shut down and the booster fell back onto the pad, causing significant damage and failure at 50.1 seconds.

In spite of three catastrophic failures, the Soviets still held onto the hope of reaching the moon with the N-1. However, the fourth and final launch attempt would not prove to be a success.

On November 23, 1972, N1-7L blasted off from the pad early in the morning. The first stage engine bay had been redesigned with a smaller diameter of 15.8 meters (52 ft) and the kerosene pipeline covers on the first three stages were sharpened at the top.

When the rocket reached the 90 second mark, there was a failure of the liquid oxygen tank caused by a 250mm (9.84 in) line. A fire developed in the tail section, the engines started to explode and the entire first stage shut down after 107 seconds, six seconds before the second stage. The escaped rocket was destroyed by range safety command to prevent impact outside of the launch corridor.

Chief Designer Mishin called for the construction of two new N-1s, Vehicle No. 8L and 9L, to be launched in 1974, with the goal of a lunar landing in an unmanned mode.

However, Mishin was relieved from his post after delivering a detailed report to Brezhnev on the falling behind of space technology with the United States.

Mishin was replaced by V.P. Glushko, who was heavily favored by Brezhnev to head the Korolev Bureau. Glushko incorporated the bureau, along with other entities, into the NOP Energia and suspended work towards future launches of the N-1.

Mishin and others appealed to congress to launch the two improved boosters, but failed to get support. Mishin later blamed underfunding ($4.5 billion compared to Apollo's $24 billion), lack of cooperation between design bureaus, lack of ground testing and failure to grasp the significance of President Kennedy's challenge for the failure of the N-1 program.

The N-1 failed due to unreliability and thrust instability of the 30 Nk-33 Kuznetsov engines in the first stage. It also failed because of lack of cooperation amongst its leading designers, Korolev and Mishin competing with Glushko and Chelomei.

The remaining N-1s were destroyed with payload shrouds and tank bulkheads used as carports, storage sheds, and sun shelters. Since then, denials concerning the N-1 program or that the Soviets attempted to reach the moon continue to exist.

General Data for the N-1

Total Mass:	5,914,170 lb
Liftoff Thrust:	9,712,799 lb
Total Length:	251 ft
Total Cost:	$600 million

The structure of the sixth scientific directorate responsible for the testing of the N-1 moon rocket in Baikonur included First Department led by Mark Berezin, responsible for ground equipment; Second Department led by Vladimir Mishenko, responsible for propulsion; Third Department led by Vitaly Romanenko, responsible for the overall launcher and flight control system; Fourth Department led by Gennady Rakitin, responsible for measurement; coordination office, led by Vladimir Ovchinnikov; political directorate, led by Vasily Borodin; and the Communist Party committee, led by Lev Rutsky.

MIG 105-11— Early Space Shuttle

The MIG 105-11 EMSA (experimental passenger orbital aircraft) was an experimental prototype built to pave the way for the future Soviet space shuttle. It was designed to assess handling, abandon-orbit, and landing procedures. EPOS began as a project of Aerocosmic system Spyral, or spiral program, which was commenced in 1965 under the supervision of leading designer G. E. Lozino-Lozinsky in the design bureau of A. I. Mikoyan.

The project included two wide-fuselage aircraft, which were linked aerodynamically, and a clean horizontal takeoff/landing system for multiple use. The orbital airplane was supposed to take off from a mother ship at an altitude of 28 to 30 km (17 to 19 mi).

Two scaled (1:3 and 1:2) unmanned models were flown during rocket launches to test heat screens.

There were also three Analog 105 aircraft, built to evaluate subsonic handling during landing, testing supersonic (105.12) and hypersonic (105.13) behavior.

Unlike the Soviet space shuttle Buran, EMSA, or EPOS in Russian, employed flexible scale plate armor made up of many steel plates, which hung on special ceramic bearings. This design allowed all plates to be kept in place in a wide range of high temperatures. It was also considerably less expensive than space shuttle Buran's quartz-based skin.

The spiral space system consisted of an orbital spacecraft, which was the MIG 105, along with a rocket booster and supersonic aircraft carrier, which was the Tupolev, Article 50. Following completion of its orbital mission, the spacecraft was designed to reenter earth's atmosphere with the wings set at a 60-degree angle, serving as the vertical stabilizers.

In 1971, the testing program carried out under the spiral project was joined by scale 1:3 and 1:2 EMSA models manufactured by LII Institute and code-named Bor.

Technical program difficulties forced the first flight of the MIG 105-11 to be delayed until October 11, 1976. The vehicle took off from an old dirt airstrip near Moscow, flying to an altitude of 560 m (1,837 ft), and then landing at the Zhukoskii flight test center 19 km (12 mi) away.

Also in 1976, the USSR established a Buran Space Aircraft Program to encourage the development of new aircraft.

A year later, on November 27, 1977, the first air-drop launch from a Tu-95K was completed from an altitude of 5,000 m (3 mi), with a landing on skids on a beaten-earth air strip. The eighth and final flight of the EPOS was made in September 1978, which resulted in a hard landing and the write-off of the aircraft.

The first and last flights were made by test pilot A. G. Festovets. The eighth flight was considered sufficient to characterize the spaceplane's subsonic aerodynamic characteristics and airbreathing systems.

Although the spiral program had terminated, all efforts and experience gathered when working on it were not in vain, as they were widely used in the development of the Energy-Buran multipurpose spacecraft system, which launched on November 15, 1988.

Yuri Gagarin Cosmonaut Training Center

The Soviets made the decision to construct a cosmonaut training center on January 11, 1960. In 1968, it was named for the first man in space, Yuri Gagarin, shortly after his tragic death in a plane crash. Following the collapse of the Soviet Union on May 15, 1995, the Russian government established the Russian State Scientific-Research Center of Cosmonaut Training, which was also named after Yuri Gagarin. It was placed under the authority of the Russian Ministry of Defense (Air Force) and the Russian Space Agency. In addition to training Soviet and Russian cosmonauts, the Gagarin Cosmonaut Training Center (GCTC) at Star City had trained 25 international crews by April 1, 1996, including astronauts from 17 countries.

Like NASA's astronaut training center at Johnson Space Center in Houston, Texas, the GCTC offers high-tech training facilities including integrated simulators for the Soyuz spacecraft and the Mir space station modules; a neutral buoyancy laboratory for extra-vehicular activity training consisting of a 5,000 cubic meter (176,580 ft³) water tank; a II-76 MDK aircraft "flying laboratory" for the simulation of microgravity; and both large (TsF-18) and small (TsF-7) centrifuges, for the simulation of G-loads during launch.

The GCTC also offers survival training for many possible landing situations, including mountains, woodlands, marshes, deserts, oceans and in the Arctic region. From 1961 through October 2002, there have been 379 people who have trained at GCTC, 195 of which were cosmonauts who had actual space flights.

During training, every cosmonaut has been required to pass three stages, including general space training; group training; and mission/crew training. A cosmonaut must pass a mission training stage before each new mission. More than 500 cosmonauts have passed the final training or mission training stage.

Cosmonauts

Cosmonauts are the Russian equivalent of U.S. astronauts. There have been a number over the years, including several women. This section features brief biographies and information on missions completed.

Victor Mikhailovich Afanasyev, a colonel in the Russian Air Force, also served as a test cosmonaut at the GCTC. He was born in Bryansk, Russia and is considered a hero in the Soviet Union. From 1970 to 1976, Afanasyev served in the Air Force fighting troops as a pilot, senior pilot and aircraft flight commander. He went on to attend the test pilot training center and serve as a test pilot and senior test pilot at the State Research/Test Institute named after Valery Chkalov.

Afanasyev has a Class 1 military test pilot certification and has logged over 2000 flight hours in more than 40 different aircraft.

In February 1989, Afanasyev trained for a space flight aboard the Mir orbital station as the Mir-7 mission backup crew commander. He went on to log 175 flight days during his first space flight (December 2, 1990, to May 26, 1991) as the Mir-8 mission crew commander. The mission included joint flight with a Japanese and British crew member. Afanasyev performed four EVAs totaling 20 hours and 55 minutes.

From January 8 to July 9, 1994, Afanasyev participated in a space flight aboard the Soyuz-TM-18 transport vehicle and Mir orbital station as the Mir-15 mission crew commander.

From October 1996 to January 1998, Afanasyev trained for the Mir-25 mission as a backup crew commander. In March 1998, he underwent training as the Mir-27 mission primary crew commander. From February 20 to August 28, 1999, he participated in a 189-day space flight aboard the Soyuz-TM transport vehicle and Mir orbital station, and performed three EVAs.

In all, Colonel Afanasyev has logged over

545 days in space and seven EVAs totaling 38.55 hours. He has merited a Class 1 cosmonaut certification, and will be serving on the ISS Taxi-1 backup crew.

Nikolai Mikhailovich Budarin has been a test cosmonaut of the Russian space company RSC Energia. He was born in Kirya, Chuvashia (Russia). He has also been awarded the title Hero of Russia.

In addition to being an engineer and lead engineer at RSC, Budarin was enrolled in the ENERGIA cosmonaut detachment as a candidate test cosmonaut in February 1989.

Between September 1989 to January 1991, he underwent a complete basic space training course at the Gagarin Cosmonaut Training Center and passed a state examination, qualifying as a test cosmonaut.

From February 1991 to December 1993, he completed an advanced training course for the Soyuz-TM transport vehicle and the Mir station flight. From June 27 to September 11, 1995, Budarin served as a board engineer of the nineteenth long-term expedition launched by the space shuttle and landed by the Soyuz TM-21 transport vehicle.

From January 28 to August 25, 1998, he participated in a space mission as a board engineer of the twenty-fifth long-term expedition aboard the Mir orbital station. Budarin went on to log over 161 days in space as Expedition-6 flight engineer aboard the International Space Station between November 23, 2002 to May 3, 2003. The Expedition-6 crew launched on STS-113 space shuttle Endeavour and then returned to earth on Soyuz TMA-1.

Vladimir Nikolaevich Dezhurov is a lieutenant colonel test cosmonaut who resides in Star City, Russia. He was born in Yavas settlement, Zubovo-Polyansk district, Mordovia. Dezhurov was awarded three armed forces medals.

In March 1994, Dezhurov underwent flight training as commander of the prime crew of the Mir-18 mission. The crew launched from the Baikonur Cosmodrome in Kazakhstan on March 14, 1995, aboard a Soyuz-TM-21 transport vehicle and completed a 115-day flight on July 7, 1995. Dezhurov has lived and worked aboard the International Space Station where he serves as a member of the Expedition-3 crew.

Yuri Pavlovich Gidzenko is a colonel with the Russian Air Force, as well as a test cosmonaut of the Yuri Gagarin Cosmonaut Training Center. He was born in the village of Elanets, Nikolaev region, and has the special honor of being Hero of the Russian Federation.

Gidzenko is an instructor of general parachute training, and has personally made 145 parachute jumps.

From March 1994 to October 1994, he trained for a space flight as a back-up crew commander, which was the seventeenth Primary Expedition/Euro-Mir-94 Program.

From November 1994 to August 1995, Gidzenko attended training for a space flight aboard the Soyuz TM transport vehicle/Mir orbital complex as the Expedition 20 Primary Crew Commander of the Euro-Mir-95 Program. Gidzenko served aboard Mir from September 3, 1995 to February 29, 1996, and logged 180-days in space.

Gidzenko served aboard the Soyuz transport vehicle/ISS/space shuttle from October 31, 2000, to March 21, 2001, and logged an additional 140 days in space.

Alexander Yurievich Kaleri is a test cosmonaut of the Energia Rocket/Space Corporation (RSC) who was born in Yurmala, Latvia. He has the honor of being Hero of the Russian Federation, as well as a pilot-cosmonaut.

In 1979, Kaleri began training at the Energia Rocket/Space Corporation. He has participated in developing design and technical documentation and full-scale tests of the Mir orbital station. In April 1984, he was selected as the Energia RSC cosmonaut candidate.

Following completion of training and evaluation at the Gagarin Cosmonaut Training Center (1985–1986), Kaleri became qualified for flight assignment as a test pilot, and went on to log 22 flight hours piloting the L-39 training aircraft.

From April 1 to December 9, 1987, Kaleri took a training course for a spaceflight aboard the Mir orbital station as a backup crew flight engineer of the Mir-3 long-duration mission.

From March 17 to August 10, 1992, he participated in a 145-day flight aboard the Soyuz-TM transport vehicle and the Mir orbital station. The mission included an eight-day joint flight with German cosmonaut Klaus-Dietrich Flade (Mir-12 program) and a twelve-day joint flight with French cosmonaut Michel Tognini of the Antares program. Kaleri performed two space walks.

Between August 17 to March 2, 1997, Kaleri participated in a 197-day flight aboard the Soyuz-TM transport vehicle and the Mir orbital station as the Mir-22 mission flight engineer, which included joint flights with NASA-2, 3 and 4 astronauts, a French astronaut and a German astronaut.

During the period April 4 to June 16, 2000, Alexander Kaleri performed his third spaceflight aboard the Soyuz-TM-30 transport vehicle and the Mir orbital station as the Mir-28 mission flight engineer.

Alexander Kaleri has logged a total of 416 days in space and four EVAs. He has been assigned to the ISS 5 backup crew as a crew commander.

Elena V. Kondakova was born in Mitischi, Moscow region, and has been made a Hero of Russia.

In 1980, Kondakova started to work in RSC-Energia completing science projects, experiments and research, and then was selected as a cosmonaut candidate by RSC-Energia's main design bureau and sent to Gagarin Cosmonaut Training Center to start the course of general space training in 1989.

From January through June of 1994, she underwent training for the seventeenth main mission and Euromir-94 flight as a flight engineer of the prime crew. October 4, 1994, through March 22, 1995, she participated in her first flight on board the spacecraft Soyuz TM-17 and the orbital complex Mir as a flight engineer of the seventeenth main mission, spending 169 days in space, including five days with NASA astronaut Norman Thagard. The mission also included a month-long joint flight with German astronaut Ulf Merbold.

May 15 to 24, 1997, she was a mission specialist on STS-84, NASA's sixth shuttle mission to rendezvous and dock with the Russian Space Station Mir. The mission lasted nine days, five hours and 20 minutes. Kondakova has logged over 178 days in space.

Dmitri Yurievich Kondratyev is a lieutenant colonel in the Russian Air Force and a test-cosmonaut candidate of Gagarin Cosmonaut Training Center. He was born in Irkutsk.

As a senior pilot in the air force, Kondratyev has flown six different types of aircraft, including Yak-52, L-29, L-39, MiG-21, MiG-29 and Su-27. He has logged over 600 hours of flight time and is a Class 1 Air Force pilot. Kondratyev has recently been assigned to the ISS 5 backup crew as a flight engineer.

Oleg Dmitievich Kononenko is a test cosmonaut of RKK ENERGIA who was born in Chardzhow, Turkmenia, which was part of the USSR until 1991.

In 1996, Kononenko was selected as a test cosmonaut candidate to the Cosmonaut Corps of the Samara Central Design Bureau. From June 1996, to March 1998, he attended basic training and qualified for flight assignment as a test cosmonaut in March 1998. In October 1998, he attended test cosmonaut advanced training for a space flight to the International Space Station (ISS). In January 1999, he was assigned to the RKK ENERGIA Cosmonaut Corps as a test cosmonaut, and has recently been assigned as a flight engineer of the Taxi-3 backup crew.

Mikhail Borisovich Kornienko is a test cosmonaut of the Energia Rocket/Space Corporation (RSC) who was born in Syzran, Kuibyshev region, Russia.

In October 1995, Kornienko started working at the Energia Rocket/Space Corporation (RSC) as an engineer. He was assigned with developing technical documentation for cosmonaut primary and backup crew tests and training, and took part in EVA tests in simulated zero-gravity at the hydrolab and at the Selen dynamic stand. He also participated in testing the Energia RSC booster production on the testing ground.

In 1998, Kornienko was selected as a test cosmonaut candidate and later qualified as a test cosmonaut. He has recently been assigned to the ISS-8 backup crew as a flight engineer.

Valery Griorievich Korzun is a colonel with the Russian Air Force who was born in Krasny Sulin. Korzun was awarded six Air

Force medals and is certified as a test cosmonaut.

From September 1989 through September 1992, he trained for space flight as part of the test cosmonauts group. Between October 1992 and March 1994, he underwent extensive training as Commander of the Soyuz TM rescue spacecraft. He also trained as a group member for flight onboard the orbital complex Mir from March 1994 to June 1995.

Korzun served as deputy director of the 27KC crew flight training complex as crew communication supervisor from March 1994 to January 1995. As as a first class military pilot, Korzun has logged 1473 hours in four types of aircraft. He is also an instructor of parachute training, and has completed 377 parachute jumps.

In August 1996, Korzun completed training as commander for the Mir-22/ NASA-3 and Cassiopia which were sponsored by the French space agency CNES. In early March 1997, Korzun returned to earth after completing a 197-day flight onboard the Mir space station. His mission included joint flights with NASA/Mir 2, 3 and 4 astronauts, as well as astronauts from France and Germany. While in flight, Korzun performed two space walks totaling 12 hours and 33 minutes.

Korzun also served as a member of the Expedition-Five crew which was launched on June 5, 2002, aboard STS-111, and docked with the International Space Station on June 7, 2002. He performed two EVAs during his six-month stay aboard the space station. The Expedition-Five crew, consisting of one American astronaut and two Russian cosmonauts, returned to earth on December 7, 2002, aboard STS-113. With total combined flights, Korzun logged 184 days, 22 hours and 14 minutes in space, including two EVAs totaling nine hours and 46 minutes.

Oleg Valerievich Kotov is a licensed medical doctor, and a lieutenant colonel in the Russian Air Force. He was born in Simferopol. He was selected as a cosmonaut candidate in 1996. From June 1996 to March 1998, he completed a course of basic training for spaceflight, and in March 1996, he received a test cosmonaut qualification.

In May to August 1998, Dr. Kotov trained for a flight on the Soyuz and the Mir station as a backup crew member to the Mir-26 mission. Since October 1998, he has been doing advanced training for ISS flights, and has recently been assigned to the ISS-6 backup crew as a flight engineer.

Konstantin Mirovich Kozeev is a test cosmonaut of the Energia Rocket/Space Corporation (RSC) who was born in Kaliningrad which is now known as Korolyev, Moscow region, Russia.

In March 1991, Kozeev was employed by the Energia RSC as a technician, and later was promoted to engineer and test engineer. He was assigned with developing technical documentation for tests and training in simulated zero-gravity in a pool, in an airplane and at a dynamic stand, and has also participated in tests and training as an operator and an EVA specialist.

In 1996, Kozeev was made a member of the Energia RSC cosmonaut corps as a test cosmonaut candidate. He began training on the ISS cosmonaut group and has recently been assigned to the ISS Taxi-2 mission primary crew as a flight engineer.

Sergei Konstantinovich Krikalev was born in Leningrad, Russia, which has since been renamed St. Petersburg. He was a member of the Russian and Soviet national aerobatic flying teams, and received championships of Moscow in 1983, and of the Soviet Union in 1986.

He was awarded the title of Hero of the Soviet Union, the Order of Lenin, the French title of L'Officier de la Légion d'Honneur, and the new title of Hero of Russia for his flight efforts. He was also awarded the NASA Space Flight Medal for the years 1994 and 1998.

In 1981 he joined NPO Energia, the Russian industrial organization responsible for manned space flight activities. There, he tested space flight equipment, developed space operations methods, and participated in ground control operations. In 1985, when the Salyut 7 space station failed, Krikalev worked on the rescue mission team, developing procedures for docking with the uncontrolled station and repairing the station's onboard system.

Krikalev was selected as a cosmonaut in 1985 and completed his basic training in 1986.

He was briefly assigned to the Buran shuttle program.

In early 1988, he began training for his first long-duration flight aboard the Mir space station, which included preparations for at least six EVA's, installation of a new module, the first test of the new Manned Maneuvering Unit (MMU), and the second joint Soviet-French science mission.

On November 26, 1988, Soyuz TM-7 was launched, with Krikalev as flight engineer, Commander Alexander Volkov, and French Astronaut Jean-Loup Chretien. The previous crew, consisting of Vladimir Titov, Musa Manarov, and Valeri Polyakov, remained on Mir for another twenty-five days, marking the longest period a six-person crew had been in orbit.

When the crew returned to earth, Krikalev, Polyakov, and Volkov continued to conduct experiments aboard the Mir station. In light of the delayed arrival of the next crew, the three cosmonauts continued to prepare the Mir for a period of unmanned operations before returning to earth on April 27, 1989.

In April 1990, Krikalev began preparing for his second flight as a member of the backup crew for the eighth long-duration Mir. In December 1990, Krikalev began training for the ninth Mir mission, which included training for 10 EVA's.

On May 19, 1991, Soyuz TM-12 launched with Krikalev as flight engineer, Commander Anatoly Artsebarsky, and British astronaut Helen Sharman. Sharman returned to earth with the previous crew after one week. Krikalev and Artsebarsky remained on Mir and conducted six EVA's to perform a variety of experiments and some station maintenance tasks.

Krikalev agreed to stay on Mir as flight engineer for the next crew, scheduled to arrive in October because the next two planned flights had been reduced to one. On October 2, 1991, the engineer slot on the Soyuz-13 flight was filled by Toctar Aubakirov, an astronaut from the Soviet republic of Kazakhstan, who had not been trained for a long-duration mission.

Franz Viehbok, the first Austrian astronaut, returned with Artsebarsky on October 10, 1991. Commander Alexander Volkov remained on board with Krikalev, and after the crew replacement in October, Volkov and Krikalev continued Mir experiment operations and conducted another EVA before returning to earth on March 25, 1992.

In October 1992, NASA announced that an experienced cosmonaut would fly aboard a future space shuttle mission, and Krikalev was one of two candidates named by the Russian Space Agency for mission specialist training with the crew of STS-60. In April 1993, he was assigned as prime mission specialist.

On February 3, 1994, Krikalev flew on STS-60, which was the first joint U.S./Russian Space Shuttle Mission. During the eight-day flight, the crew of the Discovery conducted a wide variety of materials science experiments on the wake shield facility and in the Spacelab, and performed earth observation and life science experiments.

While onboard, Krikalev conducted significant portions of the Remote Manipulator System (RMS) operations. Following 130 orbits of the earth in 3,439,705 miles, STS-60 landed at Kennedy Space Center, Florida, on February 11, 1994. Krikalev had successfully logged an additional eight days, seven hours, and nine minutes in space.

From December 4 through 15, 1998, Krikalev flew on STS-88 Endeavour, the first International Space Station assembly mission. The mission was accomplished in 185 orbits of the earth in 283 hours and 18 minutes.

On October 31, 2000, Krikalev was a member of the Expedition-1 crew which launched on a Soyuz rocket from the Baikonur launch site in Kazakhstan, successfully docking with the station on November 2, 2000. The Expedition-1 crew prepared the inside of the orbital outpost for future crews. They left the station with the STS-102 crew, undocking from the station on March 18, and landing at the Kennedy Space Center, Florida, on March 21, 2001.

After completing his fifth space flight, Krikalev logged more than one year, five months and 10 days in space, including seven EVA's.

Yuri Valentinovich Lonchakov is a lieutenant colonel with the Russian Air Force who was born in Balkhash, Dzhezkazkansk region. He has served as a second crew commander, crew commander, squadron senior pilot, and aviation brigade commander in the navy. He flew several types of aircraft, including Yak-52, L-39, Su-24, A-50, L-29, Tu-134 and Tu-16. Lonchakov has logged over 1400 hours of flight time and is a Class 1 Air Force pilot. He is also a paratroop training instructor who has successfully completed 526 jumps.

In December 1997, Lonchakov was selected as a test cosmonaut candidate of the Gagarin Cosmonaut Training Center Cosmonaut Office.

He participated on the STS-100 Endeavour from April 19 to May 1, 2001, which was the ninth mission to the International Space Station, during which the crew successfully delivered and installed the Canadarm2 Robotic Arm supplied by the Canadian Space Agency. Lonchakov traveled 4.9 million miles in 186 earth orbits and logged 283 hours and 30 minutes in space.

Yuri Ivanovich Malenchenko is a colonel with the Russian Air Force. He was born in Svetlovsdsk, Kirovograd Region, Ukraine. Malenchenko was awarded the Hero of the Russian Federation medal and the National Hero of Kazakhstan medal.

Malenchenko was the commander of the backup crew for Mir 15. From July 1 to November 4, 1994, he served as commander of Mir 16 with Musabayev, Polyakov, Kondakova, Victorenko, and Ulf Merbold. Malenchenko controlled the first manual docking of Progress during the flight.

He has also served on the crew of STS-106 from September 8 to 20, 2000. The STS-106 crew was charged with preparing the International Space Station for the arrival of the first permanent crew. Malenchenko worked with his fellow astronauts and cosmonauts to deliver more than 6,600 pounds of supplies, and installed batteries, power converters, a toilet and a treadmill on the space station.

Malenchenko and Ed Lu performed a six hour and 14 minute space walk in order to connect power, data and communications cables to the Zvezda service module and the space station. Malenchenko has logged over 137 days in space, including three EVA's totaling over 18 hours.

As Expedition-7 commander, Malenchenko has served aboard the International Space Station. His two person crew launched from Baikonur Cosmodrome, Kazakhstan, on April 25, 2003, aboard Soyuz TMA-2 and docked with the ISS on April 28, 2003.

Yuri Ivanovich Onufrienko is a colonel and test cosmonaut who resides in Star City. He was born in Ryasnoe, Zolochev district, Kharkov region, Ukraine. Onufrienko is a Hero of Russia and was awarded with two armed forces medals. He was also named a chevalier in the French Honor Legion.

He has over 800 flight hours and has flown the L-29, SU-7, SU-17 (M1-4), and L-39 aircraft.

From February 21 to September 2, 1996, Onufrienko served as commander on Mir-21. One month later, he and Yuri Usachev were joined aboard by NASA's Shannon Lucid. During his time on Mir-21, he performed numerous research experiments and participated in six EVAs. He and Yuri Usachev were joined by French cosmonaut Claudie Andre-Deshays following the departure of Shannon Lucid.

Onufrienko also served as commander on ISS Expedition-4, which was launched on December 5, 2001, aboard STS-108 and docked with the International Space Station on December 7, 2001. During a six and a half month stay, the crew performed flight tests of the station's hardware, conducted internal and external maintenance tasks, and developed the capability of the station to support the addition of science experiments.

Onufrienko logged 12 hours and 2 minutes of EVA time in two separate spacewalks. On June 19, 2002, the Expedition-4 crew returned to earth aboard STS-111, with Endeavour landing at Edwards Air Force Base, California.

Gennady Ivanovich Padalka is a colonel with the Russian Air Force who was born in Krasnodar, Russia. He was awarded the Star of Russian Federation Hero and the title of Russian Federation test cosmonaut.

Padalka is a first class pilot who has flown six types of aircraft and logged 1500 hours. He is an instructor of general parachute training, and has performed more than 300 parachute jumps.

From August 28, 1996, to July 30, 1997, he trained for space flight on the Soyuz-TM transport vehicle/Mir orbital complex as a commander of the backup crew for Mir 24/NASA-5.

From October 1997 to August 1998, Padalka attended a space flight training mission aboard the Soyuz-TM/Mir orbital complex as a primary crew commander as part of the Expedition 26 Program.

From August 13, 1998, to February 28, 1999, he served aboard the Soyuz-TM-28/Mir orbital complex as the Expedition 26 crew commander, and logged 198 days in space.

Padalka was recently assigned as station commander of the ISS Expedition-9 crew.

Alexander Fedorovich Poleschuk is an RSC ENERGIA test cosmonaut who was born in Cheremkhovo, Irkutsk region, Russia. He currently resides in Moscow, Russia. Poleschuk was awarded the title of Hero of the Russian Federation.

Poleschuk has worked for RSC Energia as a test engineer since 1977, where he was occupied with perfecting repair and assembly techniques performed during space flights. He has had extensive experience in test work under simulated weightlessness conditions. From January 24 to July 22, 1993, he participated in a 179-day space flight to the ISS with Gennady Manakov and performed two EVAs totaling nine hours and 58 minutes. He also assisted in testing the androgynous peripheral docking subassembly of the Kristall module.

From October 1994 to March 1995, he trained as backup flight engineer for the Soyuz TM-21 transport vehicle and Mir Station eighteenth primary expedition flights. Poleschuk will participate in future International Space Station flights.

Roman Yurievich Romanenko is a major with the Russian Air Force. He was born in Schelkovo, Moscow region. Romanenko has logged over 500 hours of flight time onboard L-39 and Tu-134 aircraft, and is a Class 3 Air Force pilot.

In November 1999, Romanenko was qualified as a test cosmonaut and continues to train for future missions.

Valery Victorovitch Ryumin was born in the city of Komsomolsk-on-Amur in the Rus-

sian far east. He has been decorated twice as Hero of the Soviet Union, and has been awarded other Russian and foreign decorations.

From 1958 to 1961, Ryumin served in the army as a tank commander. Since 1966, he has been employed at the RSC Energia, holding the positions of ground electrical test engineer, deputy lead designer for orbital stations, department head, and deputy general designer for testing. He has helped to develop and prepare all orbital stations, beginning with Salyut-1.

In 1973, Ryumin joined the RSC Energia cosmonaut corps, and has since become a veteran of three space flights, logging a total of 362 days in space.

In 1977, he spent two days aboard Soyuz-25. Ryumin spent 175 days aboard Soyuz vehicles and the Salyut-6 space station, and in 1980, he spent 185 days aboard Soyuz vehicles and the Salyut-6 space station.

From 1981 to 1989, Ryumin served as flight director for the Salyut-7 space station and the Mir space station. He also served as the director of the Russian portion of the Shuttle-Mir and NASA-Mir program.

Ryumin participated in the STS-91 Discovery June 2 to 12, 1998, mission, which was the ninth and final Shuttle-Mir docking mission. The STS-91 mission accomplished 154 earth orbits, traveling 3.8 million miles in 235 hours and 54 seconds.

Salizhan Shakirovich Sharipov was born in Uzgen, Oshsk region, Kirghizia. He has logged over 950 hours flying time, with experience flying on MIG-21 and L-39 aircraft.

In 1990, Sharipov was selected by the Gagarin Cosmonaut Training Center (GCTC) to become a cosmonaut candidate. In 1992, he completed general space training and became a cosmonaut.

Sharipov has flown one mission and has logged over 211 hours in space. He served as a mission specialist on the crew of STS-89 from January 22 through 31, 1998, which was the eighth Shuttle-Mir docking mission. The crew transferred more than 8,000 pounds of scientific equipment, logistical hardware and water from space shuttle Endeavour to Mir. The mission lasted eight days, 19 hours and 47 seconds, traveling 3.6 million miles in 138 orbits of the earth.

Sharipov has been assigned as flight engineer for ISS Expedition-10 scheduled for launch in 2004.

Oleg Ivanovitch Skripochka is a test cosmonaut with RSC Energia. He was born in Nevinnomysk, Stavropol region. He worked as an engineer on RSC Energia's project bureau on the development of transport and cargo vehicles between August 1993 and August 1997. He is currently training for future missions.

Anatoly Yakovlevich Solovyev is a pilot and cosmonaut who resides in Star City and was born in Riga. He was awarded the Order of Lenin, the Gold Star medal, the Order of the October Revolution, the Order of the Friendship of Peoples, and six armed forces medals. He is a test pilot third class and a test cosmonaut.

From 1979 to 1984, Solovyev underwent training for a flight aboard the Soyuz-T transport vehicle and the Salyut-7 and Mir orbital stations as part of a group. In 1987, he was the commander of a backup Soviet-Sylian crew for a mission that visited the Mir station.

In 1988, Solovyev participated in his first flight, which lasted nine days. From February 11 to August 9, 1990, Colonel Solovyev performed a long-duration stay of 179 days aboard Mir.

Gennady Mikhailovich Strekalov is a test cosmonaut and the department head at RSC Energia. He resides in Kaliningrad, Moscow region, and was born in Mytishohi, Moscow region, Russia. Strekalov was awarded three Orders of Lenin, two Gold Star medals, and the Order of People's Friendship.

As an engineer at RSC Energia, Strekalov was involved in experimental investigations and testing of space technology. He also participated in mission control for flights of scientific research vehicles belonging to the Academy of Sciences.

In January 1974, he began training as a crew member for a mission aboard the Soyuz spacecraft as a flight engineer and, in 1976, was part of the backup crew of the Soyuz of the Soyuz-22 mission.

From November 27 to December 10, 1980, Strekalov completed an experimental mission aboard the Soyuz T-3 spacecraft. During the flight, the crew accomplished a docking of the Soyuz T-3 spacecraft with the Salyut-6 Process-11 orbital complex.

From April 20 through 22, 1983, he flew aboard the Soyuz T-8 spacecraft as part of a crew comprised of V. G. Titov, G. M. Strekalov, and A. A Screbrov.

He participated in a third space mission from April 3 through 11, 1984, aboard the Salyut-7 orbital scientific-research complex as part of an international Soviet-Indian crew comprised of Yu. V. Malishev, G. M. Strekalov, and R. Sharma of India.

His fourth mission occurred from August 1 through December 10, 1990, when he served as flight engineer of the seventh primary expedition to the Soyuz-TM-10 station and the Mir orbital scientific-research complex as part of a crew comprised of G. M. Manakov and G. M. Strekalov. At the completion of the fourth flight, Strekalov accumulated 153 days in space.

Maxim Victorovich Suraev is a major with the Russian Air Force and a test cosmonaut with the Gagarin Cosmonaut Training Center. He was born in Chelyabinsk. Suraev has logged over 500 hours of flight time in aircraft such as the L-39 and Su-27 (Flanker).

In December 1997, he was selected as a test cosmonaut candidate of the Gagarin Cosmonaut Training Center Cosmonaut office.

Vladimir Georgievich Titov is a retired colonel with the Russian Air Force and a former cosmonaut. He was born in in Sretensk, in the Chita region of Russia.

Titov was awarded the title of Hero of the Soviet Union, and was a recipient of the Order of Lenin in the years 1983 and 1988. Also in 1988, the French awarded him the title of Commandeur de la Legion d'f Honneur. In 1990 he, along with Manarov, were awarded the U.S. Harmon Prize — the first Soviet citizens to win the Award — in recognition of their world endurance record.

Titov has flown 10 different types of aircraft and logged more than 1,400 hours flying time, and holds the qualifications of military pilot, first class, and test pilot, third class.

Vladimir Titov was selected to join the cosmonaut team in 1976, and in September

1981 was paired with Gennady Strekalov. The two men served as the backup crew for Soyuz T-5 in 1982 and Soyuz T-9 in 1983.

Titov served as commander on Soyuz T-8 and Soyuz T-10 in 1983. He also flew on Soyuz TM-4 in 1987 and was a member of the STS-63 crew in 1995, as well as the STS-86 crew in 1997. He has logged a total of 18 hours, 48 minutes of EVA, and has spent a total of 387 days, 52 minutes, 18 seconds in space.

On April 20, 1983, Titov made his first space flight, as commander of Soyuz T-8. He was next assigned to command Soyuz TM-2. He and his flight engineer, Alexander Serebrov, were scheduled for a long-duration flight onboard Mir 1.

However, six days prior to launch, doubts surfaced about Serebrov's health, and they were replaced by the backup crew.

Titov continued training for a long-duration mission. In April 1987, he was teamed with Musa Manarov.

On December 21, 1987, Titov took on his next assignment as the commander of Soyuz TM-4. Working with Musa Manarov and Anatoli Levchenko, he linked up with the orbiting Mir 1 space station and her crew. Romanenko, Alexandrov, and Levchenko returned to earth handing over the space station to Titov and Manarov after performing some joint work. The two men completed a long program of scientific experiments and observations, and played host to the visiting Soyuz TM-5 and TM-6 missions.

Following the end of the Soyuz TM-6 visit, one of its crew, Dr. Valeri Polyakov, remained on board with Titov and Manarov.

On February 26, 1988, the two cosmonauts carried out an EVA lasting four hours and 25 minutes. They removed one of the sections of the solar panel and installed a new one. They also installed some new scientific experiments and removed samples of material that had been left exposed to open space, and inspected the Progress 34 spacecraft.

On June 30, 1988, they made an attempt to repair the Roentgen X-ray telescope, which had not been designed for repair or replacement. Their bulky gloves made removing the small bolts very difficult, and as a result, they

required 90 minutes instead of the 20 allocated. When a special wrench they were using suddenly snapped, the EVA had to be aborted. The two men returned inside the Mir, having spent five hours, 10 minutes in open space.

On October 20, 1988, repairs were successfully completed, and the X-ray telescope resumed operations. Titov and Manarov returned to earth after a mission lasting 365 days, 22 hours, 39 minutes, setting a new record by surpassing one year in space for the first time.

From February 2 to 11, 1995, Titov was a mission specialist aboard the Orbiter Discovery, on STS-63, which was the first flight of the new joint Russian-American Space Program. During the mission, a rendezvous was performed with the Russian Space Station.

From September 25 to October, 1997, Titov served on the crew of STS-86 Atlantis which was NASA's seventh mission to rendezvous and dock with Mir. During this mission there were several highlights, including the exchange of U.S. crew members Mike Foale and David Wolf, the transfer to Mir of 10,400 pounds of science and logistics, and the return of experiment hardware and results to earth.

Titov and Scott Parazynski performed a five hour, one minute spacewalk during which they retrieved four experiments first deployed on Mir during the STS-76 docking mission, tethered the Solar Array Cap for use in a future Mir spacewalk to seal any hole found in the hull of the damaged Spektr module, and evaluated common EVA tools which may be used by astronauts wearing either Russian or American-made spacesuits. The mission was completed in 169 orbits in 10 days, 19 hours, 21 minutes.

Titov currently works for Boeing, Moscow.

Valery Ivanovich Tokarev is a colonel with the Russian Air Force and a test cosmonaut. He was born in the town of Kap-Yar, Astrakhan region, and currently resides at Star City, Moscow region. Tokarev has been awarded the title Hero of the Russian Federation as well as other orders and medals of Russia.

Tokarev is a First Class Air Force Pilot

and a First Class test pilot, with experience flying 44 types of airplanes and helicopters. He has also performed tests of fourth-generation carrier-based aircraft and vertical/short takeoff and landing jets (SU-27K, Mig-29K, Yak-38M, SU-25UTG), as well as bomber and missile navy fleet jets (SU-24M).

Tokarev flew on Discovery STS-96 from May 27 to June 6, 1999. During the 10-day mission, the crew delivered four tons of logistics and supplies to the International Space Station in preparation for the arrival of the first crew to live on the station. The mission was accomplished in 153 earth orbits, and traveled four million miles in 235 hours and 13 minutes.

Tokarev was recently assigned to the Expedition-8 crew, a long-duration flight to the International Space Station.

Sergei Yevgenyevich Treschev is a cosmonaut of the RSC Energia. He was born in Volynsky district, Lipetsk region of Russia.

Treschev participated participated as a test operator during tests of the ground-based complex (transport vehicle/Mir core module/KVANT-2 module docked configuration) to optimize the life support system.

From June 1997 to February 1998, Treschev trained as a flight engineer for the Mir station backup Exp-25 crew.

From June 1999 to July 2000, he trained as a flight engineer for the Soyuz-TM backup ISS contingency crew.

Treschev was a member of the Expedition-5 crew launched on June 5, 2002, aboard STS-111. The mission docked with the International Space Station on June 7, 2002, and Treschev performed one EVA during his six-month stay aboard the space station. On his first flight, Treschev logged 184 days, 22 hours and 14 minutes in space, including an EVA totaling five hours and 21 minutes.

Mikhail Tyurin was born in Kolomna, Russia, which is about 50 miles of Moscow. In 1993, he was selected to begin cosmonaut training.

In 1998, Tyurin trained as a flight engineer for the Expedition-3 crew. He also served as a backup crew member for the first ISS mission. Tyurin served as a member of the Expedition-3 crew onboard the International Space Station.

Yury Vladimirovich Usachev was born in Donetsk, Rostov on Don region, Russia. He was awarded both the Hero of the Russian Federation and the Pilot/Cosmonaut medals following his first space flight in 1994. After his second flight in 1996, he was awarded the Order of Service to the Country, Level III. He was also named a Chevalier in the French Honor Legion, and NASA awarded him the NASA medal for Public Service, as well as the NASA Space Flight Medal.

Usachev was a member of the backup crew for the Mir-13, 14 and 19 missions. From January 8, 1994 to July 9, 1994, he served as board engineer on Mir, and from February 21 to September 2, 1996, he again served as board engineer on Mir-21. One month later, he and Yuri Onufrienko were joined on the station by NASA's Shannon Lucid.

He next flew on STS-101, which was the third shuttle mission devoted to International Space Station (ISS) construction.

On March 8, 2001, he was the commander of the Expedition-2 crew which launched on March 8, 2001, aboard STS-102 Discovery and successfully docked with the International Space Station on March 9, 2001. The Expedition-2 crew lived and worked aboard ISS for 163 days. On August 22, 2001, they returned to earth with the crew of STS-105 on the shuttle flight delivering the third Expedition crew. Usachev has logged over 670 days in space and has participated in six EVAs.

Fyodor Nikolayevich Yurchikhin, Ph.D., is an RSC Energia test cosmonaut who was born in Batumi, Autonomous Republic of Ajara in Georgia. He worked as a controller in the Russian Mission Control Center and held the positions of engineer, senior engineer, and lead engineer, eventually becoming a lead engineer for Shuttle-Mir and NASA-Mir programs.

In August 1997, he was selected in the RSC Energia cosmonaut detachment as a cosmonaut candidate. In November 1999, he was qualified as a test cosmonaut and in January 2000, he began training in the test cosmonaut group for the ISS program.

In October 2002, Yurchikhin flew aboard STS-112 and logged a total of 10 days, 19 hours, and 58 minutes in space.

Sergei Zaletin is a lieutenant colonel of the Russian Air Force and a test cosmonaut. He was born in the town of Tula.

In 1983, Zaletin graduated from the Borisoglebsk Higher Military School of fighter pilots. He is a First Class Air Force Pilot and instructor. He is also a flight commander, and has logged a total of 1,400 hours flying L-29, L-39, MIG-21, MIG-23, and SU-17 aircraft.

In 1990, Zaletin joined the cosmonaut corps. He served as the backup crew commander for the twenty-sixth Mir expedition in 1998.

Russian Space Agency (RKA)

The Russian Space Agency (RKA) was established following the break up of the former Soviet Union (USSR) and the dissolving of the Soviet space program. RKA utilizes technology and launch sites that belonged to the former Soviet space program. It currently manages Russia's civilian space program, including all manned and unmanned flights.

A recent major program of the agency was the Mir space station which de-orbited in March 2001, following a successful 15 years in orbit.

The agency is currently involved in development of the International Space Station (ISS). A previous program was the Soviet shuttle Buran.

The prime contractor used by RKA is the Energiya Rocket and Space Complex. Energiya developed the Soviet's powerful Energiya booster, which was used to propel the shuttle Buran into space.

Military Space Forces (VKS) serves as the military counterpart of the RKA. VKS controls Russia's Plesetsk Cosmodrome launch facility. It shares control of Baikonur Cosmodrome with RKA. The two entities also share control of the Gagarin Cosmonaut Training Center.

While Buran was an entirely new venture for RKA, the idea of a spaceplane in Russia is not new. It had been previously conceived by such rocketry greats as K. Tsiolkovsky and F. Tsander. Sergei Korolev and his affiliates at the Reactive Research Institute, RNII, had worked on the RP-318 rocket glider, which was equipped with a rocket engine.

German rocket great Eugene Sanger, along with mathematician Irene Bredt, came up with the idea of a flying bomber which would be capable of attacking New York, following a rocket-powered launch, and a gliding reentry into the atmosphere over the Altantic Ocean, during World War II. Following the war, both the United States and the USSR obtained copies of Sanger and Bredt's plans, using them as a basis for further research.

The U.S. Air Force began work on the Dyna-Sour project, which was a manned glider to be launched into orbit on top of the Titan-3 rocket that would land on a runway like a glider. The USSR's Vladimir Chelomei, chief of the OKB-52 design bureau, became one of the first in the country to push for the idea of a manned winged orbiter.

Also in the USSR, the Mikoyan design bureau had begun work on developing a small reusable spacecraft, referred to as Spiral, in the mid–60s, which would be launched on the back of a hypersonic aircraft and capable of reaching Mach 6, or six times the speed of sound. Following separation from the carrier aircraft, Spiral would then be powered by an attached rocket stage.

In the '70s, the United States began work on the space shuttle as a target to replace its previous fleet of existing rockets while lowering the cost of launching satellites. The Russians, however, when learning of the plans, thought the United States was preparing a new carrier for nuclear weapons and military purposes. As a result, they began a similar project headed by NPO Energia in the Kaliningrad area of Moscow — the development of Energia-Buran around 1976.

Buran, which means snowstorm in Russian, became the largest and most expensive project in the history of the Soviet space program. The construction of the shuttles began in 1980, and the first full-scale Buran was rolled out in 1984. Five additional scale-models were built, and 24 test flights were conducted. Buran was designed to make 100 flights and carry a crew of four, including a pilot, co-pilot, and two cosmonauts who were trained for extravehicular activity (EVA) and payload maintenance.

The Soviet shuttle made its first and only orbital launch, unmanned, on November 15, 1988, being carried into orbit by the specially designed Energiya booster. There had been no software installed on the CRT displays, and the life support system onboard was not yet tested. The shuttle made two earth orbits prior to returning.

Following the first flight, the project was suspended due to lack of funds and an unstable political situation in the Soviet Union. Designs for two additional orbiters, Ptichka (the little bird), and another unnamed, were scrapped, and the project was terminated in 1993.

Mir

Russia's Mir space station was the world's first permanent residence in space. From 1986 to 1999, it was occupied by cosmonauts almost continuously.

Mir remained in orbit for 15 years and re-entered the atmosphere in a fiery descent in March 2001. The majority of the 130-ton outpost burned up over the South Pacific between Australia and Chile. It is believed that 30 tons of the station may have survived re-entry through the earth's atmosphere to splash into the ocean.

Mir was made up of an original core module plus five modules added on over the years. The oldest part of Mir stayed aloft more than 5,000 days. A small 19-ft. astronomy observatory module called Kvant-1 was sent up and attached to the station in 1987, followed by a 19-ton expansion module as big as the Mir core itself, Kvant-2, which was sent to the station in 1989, and relieved station overcrowding by doubling its size.

In 1990, the Kristall module was launched, which was the same size as Kvant-2 and the original Mir. Spektr was sent up in 1995, followed by Priroda in 1996.

Russia's initial planning had included sending up and linking six 43-ft. Mir clones to form one 250,000-lb. six-pointed star, 85 to 90 feet in diameter. Just prior to deorbiting, the Mir complex weighed a total of 130 tons. Mir's six modules were arranged in a "T" shape, creating a complete spacecraft about the size of railroad car.

It orbited 225 miles above the earth and was 98 feet wide and 85 feet long.

Mir began as the design of an improved model of the Salyut DOS-17K space station, which had been authorized as part of the third generation of Soviet space systems on February 17, 1976, by an official decree. It was originally planned as two stations (DOS-7 and DOS-8), which would be equipped with two docking ports at either end of the station and an additional two ports at the sides of the forward small diameter compartment.

However, by the time of the draft in August 1978, this plan had evolved to the final Mir configuration of one aft port and five ports in a spherical compartment at the forward end of the station. Prior, it was planned that the ports would provide docking positions for seven-ton modules derived from the Soyuz spacecraft which would use the Soyuz propulsion module, but would be equipped with long laboratory modules in place of the descent module and orbital module.

Subcontractor work began in the summer of 1979, with drawings being released in 1982 and 1983. The Russians developed new systems for the station including the Salyut 5B digital flight control computer and gyrodyne flywheels (taken from Almaz), and the new Kurs automatic rendezvous system, Altair satellite communications system, Elektron oxygen generators, and Vozdukh carbon dioxide scrubbers.

Early in 1984, work on Mir came to a halt in order to shift resources into getting the space shuttle Buran into flight testing. Later in the spring, Valentin Petrovich Glushko, chief Soviet space designer, took the office of the Central Committee's Secretary for Space and Defense, and ordered the orbit of Mir in time for the twenty-seventh Community Party Congress, scheduled for the spring of 1986.

Static and dynamic test models of the station were completed by the end of 1984, and the ground test model of the station was delivered in December.

Unfortunately, a major problem occurred

with the station. It ended up one ton heavier than designed due to the final weight of the electrical cabling. The Russians tried removing most of the experimental equipment; however, it still exceeded the performance of the Proton booster to the planned 65 degree inclination orbit. In January 1985, the decision was made to use the same 51.6 degree orbit as Salyut, although this would reduce photographic coverage of the Soviet Union.

More problems arose with the development of the new software for the Salyut 5B computer, which lead to the decision to launch Mir with the old analogue Argon computer from Salyut DOS-17K, meaning the digital computer would have to be installed later in orbit.

Mir was shipped to Baikonur in April 1985, with 1100 of the 2500 cables needing reworking based upon previous testing of the ground test model at Khrunichev. It was rolled out several months later in October.

Two launch attempts were made, the first on February 16, 1996, which was unsuccessful due to very low temperatures and the failure of spacecraft communications; and the second succeeded on February 20.

The original core component of Russia's Mir space station weighed 42,000 lbs. and was 43 feet long with a diameter of 13 feet. Five modules were added to that core in orbit after the core was launched in 1986.

Mir was more like a home than the earlier Salyut space stations. It had a larger, more-palatable galley, several recreation facilities, a bigger bathroom with a nicer shower, and private compartments for crew members.

The Mir core contained an operations area and a living area. The living area had crew quarters, a galley and a personal hygiene area. Each crew member had his or her own cabin with a chair, a sleeping bag and a porthole. The personal hygiene area had a toilet, a sink and a shower, and the galley had a table, cooking elements and trash storage.

The operations area served as the control area for the Mir complex. It was here the crew could monitor and command core systems, science equipment and facilities, and the piloting station.

Inside, the station was very much like home in that the habitable areas all had distinct floors, walls and ceilings, including carpet on the floor, colored walls and a white ceiling with fluorescent lighting.

Mir had four compartments, including the working, transfer, intermediate, and assembly compartments. Each compartment was pressurized except for the assembly compartment. A small airlock was installed for experiments, for the release of satellites, or refuse. The station was equipped with its own orbital maneuvering engines.

Mir had an extensive array of earth observation instruments, along with sixteen major systems within its modules. These included, in the Mir core, an EFO-1 electronic photometer for studies of atmospheric aerosols and dust; a Haselblad camera; a KATE-140 topographic camera (50-m resolution); a MKS-M multi-band spectrometer (0.4-0.9 micrometers); a Spektr-256 multi-band spectrometer (256 channels in visible and infrared); and a Terra impulse photometer for the study of atmospheric optical emissions. In the Kvant 2 module, the systems included AFM-2 for study of the atmosphere and pollutants; Gamma 2 video spectropolarimeter; ITS-7D spectrometer; KAP-350 topographic camera; MKF-GMA multi-spectral camera (0.5–0.9 micrometer, 10–15 m resolution); and MKS-M2 multi-band spectrometer. The Kristall Module contained a Priroda 5 multi-purpose high resolution (5 m) camera.

On March 23, 2001, Mir was deorbited, breaking up in the atmosphere. Some highlights of the station include: May 1991— Helen Sharman, a chocolate researcher for a candy company who had won a contest to become the United Kingdom's first astronaut, visits Mir on a privately financed trip; February 1999 — a Progress supply vessel separates from Mir unfurling a giant banner of foil, which Russian researchers intended for use to shine sunlight on Arctic cities during dark winters; March 1995 — cosmonaut Valery Polyakov sets a record of 438 days in space; April 1996 — ten years after its construction in space began, Mir station is completed with the arrival of a module named Priroda; February 1997 — during a routine ignition, an oxygen-generating canister bursts into flames forcing the two cosmonauts on board, Vasiliy Tsibliev and Alexander Lazutkin, to put on gas masks and put out the fire; June 1997 — the same cosmonauts, Tsibliev and Lazutkin, faced deadly danger again during a docking test when a cargo ship crashed into Mir, marking the worst collision ever in space with an impact which created a hissing air leak, which the two miraculously located and sealed off; November 1998 — NASA puts pressure on the Russian space agency to bring Mir down from orbit because of concerns over the aging station's safety, also, a Proton rocket ferried the first segment of the new International Space Station Alpha to orbit — the Russian module Zarya; August 1999 — Mir's twenty-seventh crew lands back on earth with no replacement crew sent up; June 2000 — cosmonauts Alexander Kaleri and Sergei Zaletin travel up to Mir to become the last two persons to live on the old station, they returned to earth following a two-month stay; October 2000 — as the first Alpha crew prepares to fly to the new International Space Station, Russia decides to bring Mir down in March 2001; February 2001 — Mir completes 15 years in orbit, surpassing its planned life of less than five years; March 2001 — Mir falls to earth in a fiery descent as the Russians command the old station to a lower orbit.

Crew members were ferried to Mir using the Soyuz-TM spacecraft as well as the U.S. space shuttle. Mir was visited by over 100 cosmonauts and astronauts during its 15 years in orbit. Forty-three space travelers called the station home, while 59 others visited the station for less than one month. Sixteen remained on Mir for multiple, long-duration missions.

Demonstrator-2

In July 2002, a Russian nuclear submarine launched a prototype of a European-Russian inflatable space vehicle that could be used to return payloads or people back to earth from space.

The Demonstrator-2 landed in Kamchatka 30 minutes after being blasted off from underwater in the Barents Sea. It was sent into orbit on a converted Volna SS-N-18 intercontinental ballistic missile (ICBM). Volna is the civilian designation for the R-29 RL Russian submarine-based ballistic missile.

The project was a joint effort between Russian space officials, the European Space Agency, and the German-based Astrium, a unit of the European Aeronautic Defense & Space Co.

The Demonstrator-2 prototype was a 2.6-foot diameter sphere. Upon its release, its two sail-like panels — one 7.6 feet high, the other 12.5 feet high — inflated one inside the other, and then drifted back to Earth. By inflating in the atmosphere, the Demonstrator was designed to reduce speed and perform a soft landing.

The inflatable reentry technology used by the Demonstrator, known as IRDT, was originally developed by the Khimki-based NPO Lavochkin design bureau for a Martian lander, the Mars-96 project. The same technology was later adapted for use in low-earth orbit and tested in three different configurations during two launches in 2000 and 2001. An experimental payload, called Demonstrator, was the only case of a successful return to earth. In 2000, the Fregat upper stage was believed to have successfully reentered the atmosphere using the IRDT, however, the search for the stage in the landing area yielded no results. In 2001, attempts to return a solar-sailing spacecraft failed.

The Demonstrator-2 launch was made specifically to test the vehicle's inflatable braking system.

However, the craft went missing in Russia's far east peninsula of Kamchatka four days following its launch.

Rockets

The Molniya, or SL-6, or A-2E Type booster, was identical to Soyuz except it was designed with an additional Block-L upper stage for use on missions in space and for orbit launches. The rocket's upper stage was slightly smaller than the Vostok stage and measured two m (6.56 ft) in diameter by two m (6.56 ft) long. Molniya weighed 1,260 kg (1.26 tons) empty.

The Block-L stage was powered by a restartable oxygen-kerosene propellant engine.

In the late 1960s, a new version was developed called Molniya M which was capable of launching nearly two tons into orbit.

The first launch of Molniya-M was on February 19, 1970, with an additional third stage powered by a liquid oxygen-kerosene combination.

The Soyuz, SL-4, or A2 Type vehicle, was used for Soyuz spacecraft. It was made up of an R-7 with a new Block-1 or Venus upper stage, replacing Vostok's Block-Ye upper stage. Soyuz was first used on November 16, 1963, to launch Cosmos 22, the first second-generation reconnaissance satellite.

There have been three major variations of Soyuz, including Soyuz-M, Soyuz-U, and Soyuz-U2. A different type of rocket engine was used for Soyuz-M in comparison to Soyuz-U. The Soyuz-U2 utilized a special type of kerosene propellant engineered to increase payload capacity. In 1996, the vehicle was pulled from service because the propellant was so expensive to make.

On December 27, 1971, the first launch of Soyuz-M occurred. The first launch of Soyuz-U was on May 18, 1973.

There are two Soyuz-U launch pads in operation at the Baikonur Cosmodrome, and three additional at the Plesetsk Cosmodrome.

Kosmos-3M, or SL-8, or C Type, is a small Russian launch vehicle which was originally derived from the R-14 medium range ballistic missile. It consists of an R-14 first stage and a restartable second stage.

In the 1970s, the Kosmos-3M launched the Soviet anti-satellite (ASAT) weapon during test flights. It also launched space plane tests for BOR during the 1980s, which was a part of the development of the Soviet space shuttle.

The first launch occured on May 15, 1967, and was designated Kosmos 158.

Kosmos-3M is a two-stage booster that burns unsymmetrical dimethylhydrazine (UDMH) and uses nitric acid (N2O4) as the oxidizer. The first stage uses two RD216 main engines or 11 D614, and the second stage runs with a single, restartable 11 D49 main engine. The second stage also utilizes an independent propulsion system for coast and spacecraft deployment purposes. The Kosmos-3M

launcher is only used for LEO (low-earth orbit) missions and can carry a 1,500 kg (1.50 ton) payload into a low altitude.

The Start rocket was derived from the RT-2PM Topol intercontinental ballitic missile, and was converted due to the signing of the Start 1 treaty, which allowed all participants to have the right to convert their ICBMs (intercontinental ballistic mísiles).

The Start-1 or RS-12M consists of four solid-propellant stages, and has a diameter of 1.8 m (5.9 ft) and a height of 22.7 m (74.4 ft).

It was first launched from Plesetsk Cosmodrome on March 25, 1993. The rocket has a 550 kg (1,212 lb) LEO payload capacity.

In addition, Start-1 has a small post boost propulsion system or PBPS which is powered by a nitrogen gas generator in order to enhance orbit injection and placement.

In the 1990s, Start-1 had three successful launches to orbit, including, the March 25, 1993, launch of the EKA-1, a 573-lb Russian experimental communications satelite; and the March 4, 1997, launch of the communications satellite, Zeya-1, which was used for navigation and geodesy tests from a sun-synchronous orbit. The satellite was also known as Mozhaets, as it was designed by students of the Mozhaiskiy Military Space Engineering Academy. On December 24, 1997, Start-1 launched the Early Bird civilian earth resources and photo-imaging satellite for the United States agency, Earth Watch, located in Longmont, Colorado. The Early Bird satellite failed four days after being placed in orbit due to underpower voltage of the onboard power system.

The Rockot, SL-19, or M1 Type, was built with a payload capacity of close to 1.9 metric tons for LEO. Rockot translated means rumble or roar in Russian. It is a three-stage rocket, with all three stages running on UDMH and N_2O_4.

Rockot is 3.4 m (11.2 ft) long with a 2.2 m (7.2 ft) diameter. Its first and second stages were derived from the retired stages of the RS-18 intercontinental ballistic missile. One of its stages is referred to as the Breeze stage. This stage has a high performance storable liquid engine.

Rockot successfully performed three test flights, including two during December 1990 and 1991, and a third, launching an amateur radio satellite, called Radio-ROSTO RS-15, on December 26, 1994.

Another launch on May 16, 2000, carried the dummy satellites, Simsat-1 and Simsat-2.

Following an integrated test failure on December 22, 1999, during which a control system error switched on power, setting off explosive bolts and jettisoning the rocket's payload, the Rockot was fitted with a larger payload fairing, and the booster re-tested.

On May 16, 2000, the first oficial launch of Rockot occurred with two dummy satellites onboard, which were placed into LEO.

The payload fairing, whose elements fell into the launch tower during the incident, was damaged beyond repair and had to be replaced. Following the incident, Eurockot made a decision to use an entirely new booster for the first demonstrational flight from Plesetsk and use a modified Breeze-KM upper stage instead of the original Breeze-K. The concern about the reliability of the launcher prompted this switch, according to Eurockot.

The Zenit rocket is a medium lift booster with a first stage that was used for the Energia booster strap-ons. Flight testing for Zenit began in 1985, and it has since been used strictly for the launch of ELINT satellites.

Zenit-2 evolved during the mid–1970s with a weight of 15 tons, and a satellite payload capacity of 16 tons for LEO. Zenit-2 became Zenit-3 once a Block-D stage was added, and can launch 4,500 kg (4.5 tons) to GTO.

A LOX-kerosene mix serves as propellant, providing 804,000 kg (804 tons) of thrust for the first stage, and 93,000 kg (93 tons) of thrust for the second stage.

The Zenit provides a highly automated launch infrastructure, which allows it to be launched within 90 minutes of reaching the launch pad. It was originally developed during the mid–1970s and it is the only large rocket to be developed by the former Soviet Union, other than the unsuccessful N-1.

The rocket utilizes an RD-171 engine in its first stage, which is the most powerful engine ever flown. It has been equipped with high-pressure staged-combustion turbopumps which provide higher sea-level specific impulse than any other type of LOX/kerosene engine.

On June 21, 1985, the first orbital launch of Zenit occurred. Other tests were performed with Kosmos designations.

On October 4, 1990, shortly following launch, a Zenit failed due to an explosion of the first stage. Zenits were planned for use to carry payloads to the International Space Station (ISS). However, these plans have not been fulfilled.

The Zenit is still in operation, although rather limited, to carry government payloads.

SAUDI ARABIA

Space Research Institute, Saudi Arabia

Recently, Saudi Arabia established the Space Research Institute at King Abdulaziz City for Science and Technology in an effort to focus its interest in developing space technology. The objectives of the institute include technology transfer through aerospace systems, numerical simulation, laser applications, remote sensing, and geographical information systems; receiving and processing of satellite imagery and raising public awareness of aerospace technology; and high performance computing, laser technology, data collection techniques and applications.

To accommodate these objectives, the institute is split into various divisions including the commercial office, the Saudi Center for Remote Sensing (SCRS), the Aeronautic Technology Center (ATC), the Satellite Technology Center (STC), the Numerical Studies Center

(NSC), and the Laser Application Center (LAC). Key projects engaged in by the institute cover the Satellite Technology Project, Numerical Studies Project, the transfer of the Laser Ranging data to CDDIS, an on-site analysis in cooperation with NASA, the Laser Radar Project, RADARSAT and ERS-1C satellite data receiving in cooperation with outside agencies, a Space Atlas for Saudi Cities, a joint study with Japan using the new generation of radar satellite, PALSAR, another joint effort with Japan to study earth resources, a data elevation model with drainage, and the implementation of a new operating system of the Remote Sensing Center.

To support the Saudi interest in advanced research activities in earth observation and the study of earth's resources, the Saudi Center for Remote Sensing (SCRS) was established in 1986 as a division of the Space Research Institute. The responsibilities of SCRS include data reception and distribution to various users, promoting the use of satellite data and building a rich data archive. In sup-port of this effort, SCRS signed a number of agreements to receive satellite data from various satellites.

Currently, SCRS receives and distributes satellite images from the Land Remote Sensing Satellite (Landsat), SPOT-1, SPOT-2 and SPOT-4, RADARSAT, the Indian Remote Sensing Satellite (IRS-1C and IRS-1D) and National Oceanic and Atmospheric Administration (NOAA) satellites. The coverage area of the SCRS reception ground station extends to a radius of 2,700 km, with about 23 million km^2 of surface area coverage. The ground station is capable of simultaneously receiving multiple satellites and it is fully automated for satellite tracking reception. With the recent upgrading of its reception and image analysis and processing capabilities, SCRS is now considered one of the leading centers worldwide.

On September 26, 2000, two microsatellites, SaudiSat 1A and 1B, developed and built by the Space Research Institute, were launched successfully by a Russian launcher.

SOUTH KOREA

Korean Aerospace Research Institute (KARI), South Korea

On October 10, 1989, the Korean Aerospace Institute, known as KARI, was created as part of the strong technological basis for the Republic of Korea. KARI was established as a leading Korean research institute to promote advanced aerospace research activities, and is in charge of advancing the level of Korean aerospace research to the world, helping to create a very competitive aerospace marketplace in Korea.

$4.8 billion dollars to date has been allocated to Kari with aircraft, aerospace, and satellite technologies as the main focus areas. The research areas in aircraft technology include aerodynamics, structural mechanics, aeropropulsion, flight dynamics and control, and aircraft systems. In aerospace technology, space launchers, space propulsion systems, satellite buses, and space tests are research areas under study at the institute. In satellite technology, the institute is performing mission analysis and developing core parts of a satellite system, such as electrical power, telemetry, and command and control subsystems, as well as setting up ground tracking and control stations.

In the area of aerodynamic research, KARI is engaged in performing theoretical and computational flow analysis and comparing the results with wind tunnel experimental data. This involves working with subsonic wind tunnels and scale models of mid-class commuter airplanes specifically designed to study the effects of wakefield flow patterns.

In the field of aeropropulsion, Kari is in the process of establishing in-house technologies needed to develop gas turbine engines. The use of computer simulation models to predict detailed flow patterns and a three-dimensional laser doppler velocimetery, which consists of a turbine blade cascade wind tunnel set up, a 100 lb thrust gas turbine engine, and a spin and burst rotating test machine, is highly beneficial in this area of study.

For flight dynamics and control, researchers are using research and development flight simulators and unmanned airships to test alternative designs of auto-pilot systems equipped with robust flight control mechanisms.

The aerospace technology division carries out research on the development of sounding rockets and integration of satellites with related technologies. It is most active in the development of the KOREASAT satellite and its launcher as well as performing structural, thermal control, and environmental tests for the KITSAT satellite.

The sounding rocket was built in 1993 with the capability of reaching an altitude of 70 to 75 km (43 to 47 mi) with a payload capacity of 150 kg (331 lb), allowing for 50 kg (110 lb) as a scientific purpose. The length and weight of the rocket are 6.7 meters (22 feet) and 1.3 tons. It was designed to collect data at ozone and ionosphere layers over the Korean Peninsula.

KARI's space propulsion research involves the development of solid and liquid apogee kick motors for placing a satellite in geostationary orbit and providing sufficient thrust for orbit control. For the sounding rocket, the thrust of the solid rocket motors can accommodate a weight of 10 tons for liftoff.

South Korea broke into the satellite industry with the launch of the country's first two spacecraft — KITSAT 1, launched on August 10, 1992, and KITSAT 2, launched on September 26, 1993. The United Kingdom's Surrey Satellite Technology Ltd. (SSTL) microsatellite design was used as the basis for the two spacecraft which were launched on European Space Agency (ESA) Ariane booster flights.

KITSAT 1 weighed 50 kg (110 lb) and carried two CCD cameras for earth photography in a 1,300 by 1,400 km (808 by 870 mi) orbit inclined 66 degrees to the equator. KITSAT 2 was inserted into an orbit of 795 by 805 km (494 by 500 mi) at an inclination of 98.7 degrees, carrying two CCD imaging systems.

For satellite development, KARI places great emphasis on the design of the satellite bus system in order to assure the proper operation of the satellite in the space environment. The space test group conducts integration, assembly, and environmental tests of satellites for independent checks. This group uses a thermal vacuum test chamber, the satellite vibration test device, and the satellite physical measurements device. The satellite center will expand to conduct development and qualification tests on future scientific and communications satellites.

The KOMPSAT-1 is a major satellite program established for the purpose of earth remote sensing. The KOMPSAT system performs several functions related to earth applications including cartography of the Korean peninsula, worldwide ocean color monitoring, and space environment monitoring.

The system is made up of a single satellite in a sun-synchronous low earth orbit and a dedicated mission ground station, KGS, located in Taejon. KOMPSAT-1 has an expected lifetime of three years at an altitude of 685 km (426 mi) and is 53 inches in diameter, with a height of 98 inches.

The KOMSAT payload consists of an EOC for cartography data used to develop stereo images of Korean territory which can allow for 1/25,000 scale mapping for land use and planning; an OSMI, which is a multispectral imager generating six color ocean images; a space physics sensor which includes high energy cosmic particles measurement; an IMS (ionosphere measurement sensor) for measuring densities and temperature of electrons in the ionosphere and monitoring the ionospheric irregularities of the KOMPSAT-1 orbit for characterization in the space environment; and an HEPD (high energy particle detector) used to characterize the low altitude high-energy particle environment and to study the effects of radiation environment on microelectronics such as a single event upset.

SPAIN

Center for the Development of Industrial Technology (CDTI)

The Center for the Development of Industrial Technology (CDTI) is a Spanish public organization under the Ministry of Science and Technology, which also serves as Spain's space agency.

Since 1986, CDTI has been the official representative in Spain's cooperative programs through the European Space Agency (ESA). It manages the participation of Spanish industry in the diverse range of international space programs and projects.

Programs in which CDTI has participated include Hispasat 1A, 1B, 1C, 1D and Amazonas satellites, Eumetsat, and the Egnos satellite navigation program which is under ESA sponsorship.

In 2001, CDTI was given management of the Spanish communications satellite Spainsat/xtar by the Ministry of Defense. CDTI has also recently become involved in Europe's Galileo satellite navigation system program.

National Space Program

The National Space Programme (NSP) is part of the National R&D&I Plan (2000–2003) designed to promote space research and development in Spain and to respond to the needs of the Spanish space sector by strengthening its technological position and increasing its participation in international space activities.

The goals of this program include the promotion of international cooperation with Spanish industry; the strengthening of existing technological capabilities in Spain to encourage business and science cooperation in the Spanish space sector; and the promotion of the development of innovative and techno-logically advanced products to stimulate new markets and new applications.

NSP projects and activities are divided into four focus areas — the technological development of subsystems and equipment for small platforms, including minisatellites and microsatellites; the development of transportable instruments and experiments for the observation of the earth and use in the areas of microgravity and space science; and the development of competitive subsystems and applications in telecommunications, navigation and satellite teledetection.

Hispasat, Eumetsat, Spainsat

CDTI coordinates the industrial and technological aspects of space programs with Spanish participation by virtue of collaboration agreements with other departments of administration and national entities, including Hispasat S. A., for industrial returns associated with its telecommunications satellites; the National Meteorological Institute for the industrial participation of Spain in the European organization, Eumetsat; and the Ministry of Defense for the project on military communications by satellite, Spainsat/xtar.

Hispasat S.A. manages the construction and operation of the Hispasat satellites. The Hispasat 1A, 1B and 1C are currently in operation, and the HSA 1D satellite will soon be sent into orbit. All of these satellites monitor above Spanish territory. Hispasat S.A. will also been implementing the AMAZONAS project, a telecommunications satellite that will be located over Brazil.

Eumetsat is a European organization which operates, maintains, and exploits meteorological satellite systems. Germany, Austria, Belgium, Denmark, Spain, Finland, France, Greece, Ireland, Italy, Norway, the Netherlands, Portugal, the United Kingdom, Sweden, Switzerland and Turkey are among the organization's member countries.

The CDTI was officially appointed Industrial Focal Point of Spain in Eumetsat as a result of a collaborative agreement signed with the National Meteorological Institute (INM), the Spanish representative of Eumetsat. This agreement has assigned CDTI to promote the participation of Spain in the construction and exploitation of the meteorological exploration satellites Meteosat Second Generation (MSG) and Eumetsat Polar System (EPS).

In light of increased developments in the accuracy of numerical weather prediction, the need for more frequent and comprehensive data from space has led to the current work on the Meteosat Second Generation (MSG) system. Meteosat Second Generation will be a significantly enhanced follow-up system to the current generation of Meteosat. It has been designed in response to user requirements and will serve the needs of "nowcasting" applications and numerical weather prediction, in addition to providing important data for climate monitoring and research.

The new satellites will be spin-stabilized like the current generation, but with many increased design improvements. The more frequent and comprehensive data collected by MSG will also aid weather forecasters in the swift recognition and prediction of dangerous weather phenomena such as thunderstorms, fog and explosive development of small but intense depressions which can lead to devastating wind storms.

The MSG space segment is made up of three satellites being manufactured by a European industrial consortium led by Alcatel Space Industries, France, under the management of the European Space Agency (ESA). It was responsible for the development of the first satellite and has acted on behalf of Eumetsat as procurement agent for MSG-2 and MSG-3 satellites. The MSG satellites are expected to provide operational service to users for at least 12 years. Plans are being made for the procurement of a fourth MSG satellite which would allow an increased duration of the operational service.

The Eumetsat Polar System allows for a series of satellites to observe meteorological, climatological and environmental features of the earth and transmit regional data to user stations throughout the world, while storing global data for central facilities in Europe for further processing and distribution.

The Eumetsat Polar System (EPS) was designed as an integrated end-to-end data system to serve user needs on a continuous basis. EPS will be implemented with three Metop satellites to be flown commencing in 2005, at which time, supporting ground facilities will become operational.

Central facilities will include spacecraft command and control, data reception and processing of global data, generation of products at application centers, and data exchange from corresponding satellites of the United States. The Metop satellites will broadcast regional data to user stations around the world.

The Metop satellite system has been designed to remain operational for at least 14 years. It will be comprised of several major elements, including three Metop satellites, developed in cooperation with the European Space Agency (ESA); satellite and mission control functions from Eumetsat headquarters in Germany; reception of global data at a high latitude station in Europe; exchange of equivalent satellite data from NOAA satellites within the United States; pre-processing data and generating standard global products at Eumetsat headquarters; generation of specialized products at application centers within Europe known as Satellite Application Facilities (SAF); and the continuous direct broadcast of instrument data from the Metop satellites in orbit.

Real-time data access to EPS data will be accomplished by the Metop satellites, which will broadcast two data streams continuously to user stations throughout the world. This will enable users to receive local data in real-time from the satellites each time they pass overhead or close to the station.

The two data streams will be coordinated with those of the NOAA satellites, although transmission details will differ. Metop will use a state-of-the-art packaged data transmission standards conforming to the recommendations of the Consultative Committee for Space Data Systems (CCSDS), while NOAA satellites will use their current transmission standards.

The Metop High Resolution Picture Transmission (HRPT) system will provide data for large-scale user stations and carry data from all Metop instruments, including those provided by the United States. However, it will not be compatible with the system of the same name currently being flown on NOAA satellites.

The Low Resolution Picture Transmission (LRPT) system will provide data for relatively small user stations and will serve as a long-term replacement for the analog Automatic Picture Transmission (APT) system currently used on NOAA satellites using digital technology.

In cooperation with Hisdesat S.A., the Spanish Ministry of Defense has contracted the American company, LORAL, for the future telecommunications defense satellite, Spainsat.

CDTI will be responsible for coordinating the satellite program with Gerencia de Cooperación Industrial, a Ministry of Defense company, to offer Spanish industry the chance to access the American market in satellite implementation.

Alcatel Espacio

Alcatel Espacio is the Spanish subsidiary company of Alcatel Space which has designed, developed, and manufactured communications equipment and subsystems for satellite platforms and payloads since 1988. It has also participated in more than 50 satellite programs and remains heavily devoted to the supply of space hardware for satellite and spacecraft applications.

In 2001, Alcatel joined Galileo Sistemas y Servicios (GSS), a company which was established to promote participation of Spanish industry in the European Galileo satellite program.

Alcatel Espacio specializes in TTC and data transmission subsystems, including, S and X band TTC transponders and transceivers, S-Band TTC spread spectrum transponders, S-Band high power amplifiers, UHF to X Band transmitters and receivers, BPSK/QPSK modulators, C/Ku Band TTC transmitters and beacons, and TTC subsystems. It also supplies passive microwaves, including Ku, X and Ka band input multiplexers (IMUX), filters, diplexers and other passive devices from S to Ka band, and microwave assemblies including distribution units.

Alcatel Espacio manufactures 9342 DVB onboard processors, digital processing and modules and subsystems, onboard handling units, including remote terminal units (RTU), payload interface units (PIU), control electronic equipment including antenna pointing mechanism electronics (APME), and solar array drive electronics.

It has contributed S-band transponders to the ATV (automated transfer vehicle) and Japanese HTV transfer vehicle for supplying the International Space Station (ISS). Alcatel Espacio will also be providing similar units to the Galileo navigation system.

It has supplied S-band TTC transponders to a variety of European Space Agency science missions, including XMM, INTEGRAL, SOHO, CLUSTER, HERSCHEL and PLANCK, ROSETTA, and MARS EXPRESS.

The company has built S-band transponders for earth observation satellites designed for both civil and military applications. These include Envisat, Metop, Spot 4 and 5, and Helios 1 and 2.

The S-band TTC transponders have been a key product of Alcatel Espacio with over 100 flight models supplied for a variety of programs.

Another key product of Alcatel Espacio has been the L, C, X and Ku band transmitters which contribute to the modular architecture of their digital transponders.

Alcatel Espacio has developed BPSK and QPSK modulators for the following satellite programs: Artemis, Meteosat Second Generation (MSG), Proteus, and Metop.

It supplies microwave filters and input multiplexers (IMUX). The microwave filters have been used for the GLOBALSTAR satellite system. The Ku band IMUX has been used to incorporate dielectric resonator technology within passive radiofrequency systems, covering more than 500 channels for a variety of commercial applications. Alcatel Espacio has recently extended the dielectric resonator technology to the X and K bands.

Nearly one hundred onboard data handling units have been supplied to European space programs. Onboard data handling equipment has been developed for satellites such as SOHO, Spot 4 and 5, HELIOS 2, and XMM.

Alcatel Espacio supplied remote terminal units (RTUs), avionics interface units (AIUs), solar array drive electronics (SADE), for ROSETTA and MARS EXPRESS, and will supply units for VENUS EXPRESS.

It has also provided antenna pointing and control systems for Artemis, Envisat, and Seasat.

SWEDEN

Swedish Space Corporation (SSC)

The Swedish Space Corporation (SSC) is the state-owned entity of Sweden that manages the European Space Research Organization (ESRO). ESRO was founded by Belgium, Denmark, France, the Netherlands, Italy, Switzerland, Spain, the United Kingdom, Sweden and Germany in March 1964. The aim was to establish a coordinated program for peaceful space research, combined with advanced research technological development, and to support European industry in the member countries. Esrange, a subsidiary, was built by ESRO and inaugurated in 1966. Esrange maintains a focus in airborne systems, satellite operations, space systems, and rocket launch sites. Many rocket projects were executed between November 1966 and June 1972, primarily by ESRO. However, the ESRO member states also carried out rocket projects from Esrange on a national basis.

The first sounding rocket launch occurred on November 19, 1966. Between November 1966 and July 1972, there were 152 rocket launches. Subsequently, the program's focus shifted to launching satellites. Now the launch rate for rockets is approximately 10 per year.

Esrange has been managed by the Swedish Space Corporation, which has been headquartered in Stockholm since July 1, 1972. The rocket and balloon activities are coordinated and financed by the Esrange Andöya

Special Project (EASP) within the European Space Agency. The member states of ESA/EASP are France, Germany, Switzerland, Norway, and Sweden. In 1974, Esrange completed construction on a launch facility for scientific balloons. This facility has been regularly upgraded to enable launchings of 1,000,000 m³ (35.3 ft³) balloons. Since 1978, Esrange has played an important role in various satellite projects. There are a number of ground segments for the support of national and international spacecraft programs now in operation.

Esrange mission assignments for sounding rockets and balloons encompass two main objectives — support of the sounding rocket and balloon programs of the member state of ESA/EASP, and operation of ground based scientific instrumentation.

Esrange is located in northern Sweden above the Arctic Circle at a latitude of 67° 53¢N, long 21° 04'E. The town within closest proximity to the range is Sweden's principal mining town, Kiruna. Kiruna has a population of 25,000 and is a half an hour away from the range by car.

There is an extensive network of ground based scientific instrumentation in northern Scandinavia. Some of the main facilities located in the vicinity of Esrange include the Swedish Institute of Space Physics (IRF) where phenomena in the atmosphere and magnetosphere are studied, and the atmospheric research program which is a new program financed by the Environmental and Research Institute (MRI) in Kiruna.

Another important installation is European Incoherent Scatter Facility (EISCAT) made up of a system of stations at Tromsö (Norway), Kiruna (Sweden) and Sodankylä (Finland). North of Kiruna, in Abisko, is a climate research center, which provides possibilities for scientific research in arctic regions and location of ground based instrumentation.

The Esrange facilities are located in an area of 20 km² (7.7 mi²) about 40 km (25 mi) east of Kiruna. The main building area is located in the Vittangi river valley. Close to the main building area is the area for balloon launchings, including two buildings for operations control and payload preparation. Located further east is the tundra region. This area is divided into three zones, A, B, and C, with a total area of 5,600 km² (2162 mi²). Zone A, the impact area for boosters, can be extended when rockets with long-range boosters are launched. Zones B and C are impact areas for second and third stages as well as payloads. Zone C is not allowed for use during the period of May 1 to September 15. The nominal impact point normally chosen is situated 75 km (46.6 mi) north of the launch pads. The impact area for balloons covers the northern parts of the main building which was erected between the years 1964 and 1965. It has four stories with a total floor area of 3,930 m² (42,302 ft²). The basement is used as storage for spare parts. It also contains mechanical, electrical and carpentry workshops. For staff and guests there is a sauna and showers. The ground floor houses offices for Esrange administration and technical facilities, a front desk, a switchboard, a canteen, two conference rooms for 15 and 30 people, and a lounge.

The first floor has offices for operational staff, the operations center for sounding rockets and rooms for timing, telemetry and scientific instruments (Scientific Center). In an annex on the same floor there are offices and guest rooms. The top floor has a large conference room for 80 people as well as staff offices. The main building area also includes a warehouse with a total area of 490 m² (5274 ft²), warm and cold garages for cars and accommodation buildings with 93 single rooms of different standards, showers and kitchens.

Esrange has a typical continental climate with cold winters and warm summers. The precipitation and humidity are relatively low all year. Snow begins in late September, and by mid–October, the ground is normally covered and the lakes are frozen. The 24 hour temperature tends to fall below 0° C in early October and stays below that until the beginning of May. During the coldest months, December, January and February, the average temperature is normally around -15°C. However, a low of -48° C has been recorded. During winter the temperature at the radar hill is generally 10°C higher than in the valley.

By the end of May the snow and ice disappear. Summer temperatures are in the 10° to 18°C range, rising occasionally to 30°C.

Typical balloon flight times at the ceiling in October are three to five hours, and in November one to four hours. The wind velocity varies and even in December, January, and February there are normally some days with winds permitting flight times of one to two hours at the ceiling over Scandinavian territory.

During the winter period the wind direction normally varies between 250° and 290°. There is, on average, one sudden stratospheric warming period every winter. The length of such a period can be more than one week, and the high altitude wind then is very unpredictable. During these periods the wind direction can turn as much as 180° and wind velocities normally decrease. The high altitude winds start decreasing in early March and turn to an easterly direction by 20 to 30 of April. The turn-around time in spring is more difficult to predict than the turn-around in August. Generally, wind velocities are higher in April than in August and the wind direction is rather unstable before the turn-around.

About five to ten hours of flight time at the ceiling can be expected in April. After the turn-around the wind velocity increases to a maximum of 100 km/h on the 20 to 25 of June; after that the velocity rapidly decreases. The wind direction remains stable between 80° to 100° during the summer period.

By the end of July the wind velocity is normally 20 km/h at 30 km altitude and 30 to 40 km/h at 35 km. By placing the ceiling of the balloon on the right level long flight times can be achieved. The turn-around to westerly winds regularly occurs between the 20th and 30th of August. The wind is low (5to 20 km/h) during the whole of August, and flight times of 20 to 60 hours' duration above Scandinavia can be expected if the right days are chosen. The result from the high altitude wind measurements at Esrange during the period 1972 to 1984 are presented as 12 average wind profiles.

Rocket Facilities

The SSC has designed sixty sounding rocket vehicles since the early 1970s. These vehicles have been used for auroral studies, atmospheric physics, astrophysical observations and microgravity research both within the Swedish national space program and as part of the microgravity research program of the European Space Agency.

The rocket facilities are located in a 1000 m (3280 ft) area east of the main building. All operations that are required, from storage to preparation, assembly, integration, testing and launch of rockets with complicated payloads, are performed in this area. Three hundred, eighty-nine rockets have been launched from Esrange from November 1966 to April 1999.

This hall has a floor area of 10.5 by 20 m (34.4 by 65.6 ft) and a height of 3.9 m (12.8 ft) except for the central portion, which has a higher ceiling to allow vertical assembly of long payloads. There is a single rail electric gantry crane for payload handling.

In the rocket assembly portion there are two motor assembly halls. These halls are referred to as Centaure Assembly and Skylark Assembly for the type of motors which are assembled in them.

This hall has a floor area of 32.4 by 10 m (106 by 32.8 ft) and a height of 4.4 m (14.4 ft). Most of the floor is taken up by two Centaure launchers with heating systems and the rails to move the launchers.

There are facilities to connect both launchers to their respective launch and payload desks in the blockhouse so that motors

and payloads can be completely checked out without being taken out to the launch pad. The access door is 3.98 m (13 ft) high and three m (9.8 ft) wide.

The Skylark Assembly hall has a total floor area of 36.0 by 10.5 m (118 by 34.4 ft) and a height of 4.5 m (14.8 ft). Two weighting balances, 0 to 1000 kg (1 ton), are permanently mounted in the south end of the hall. Space in the northern end of this hall is made available to visiting teams for rocket motor preparation. The access door is 4.05 m (13.2 ft) high and 4.52 m (14.8 ft) wide.

There are four laboratories available for advanced chemical work. These laboratories are equipped with gas, sinks, fume hoods, laminar airflow cupboards — horizontal or vertical — refrigerators, deep freezes, and lockable cupboards to store poisonous materials. One chemical laboratory is equipped with gas, sinks, and a fume hood. Another electronic laboratory is reserved for the launch crew.

There is a blockhouse to accommodate the large amount of ground check out equipment. Here, the floor area is 8.0 m by 7.5 m (26 by 25 ft). Payload cables running from the MAXUS building, the SKYLARK tower, and the MRL launcher end in this room. The power supply includes 2 * 7 KVA, 220 V, 50 Hz of steady power (UPS).

The rocket launchers are two Centaure railborne launchers. In preparation for each countdown, the launchers are brought out to the launch pads where control cables are connected and the launchers elevated. The vehicles can be covered by a styrofoam tunnel and heated by oil burners and are remotely controlled and monitored from the launch consoles in the blockhouse. The launchers are equipped with a seven m (23 ft) long military Nike rail overslung.

The following types of rockets have been launched from these launchers: Centaure, Nike-Apache, Nike-Tomahawk, Nike Orion, Black Brant VC, Super Loki.

The Skylark tower is a 30 m (98 ft) long three-rail launcher that is permanently heated. It was built for Skylark rockets as well as other three-fin rockets such as the Nike-Orion, NIKE-BBV, and Terrier-BBV.

The temperature in the launcher building

is controlled. The launcher was constructed so that the rocket stands elevated and positioned in azimuth ready for launch, with the building closed. Just prior to launch, the roof and blast doors are opened. If a hold should occur following the opening of the building it can be closed and the temperature rapidly brought back to what is desired to protect the motor and payload. The launcher elevation and azimuth, and the building roof and blast doors can be controlled locally or remotely from the blockhouse. The launch console monitors the azimuth and elevation angles, roof and blast door positions, and tower temperature. Power outlets are available at the payload platform.

The MRL 7.5K launcher is an 11.3 m (37 ft) long single rail underslung beam launcher stored in a protective house with removable roof. For each countdown the roof is removed and the beam is elevated and turned to its launch position. During a launch standby, the vehicle is protected by means of a styrofoam tunnel and heated by oil burners. The launcher is remotely controlled and monitored from the launch console in the blockhouse.

The following types of rockets have been launched from this launcher: Orion, Nike-Orion, Taurus-Orion, Nike-Black Brant V, Terrier-Black Brant V.

The complex for the MAXUS/ARIES launcher was originally built for the ARIES sounding rocket. In 1990, it was rebuilt to accommodate launches of the CASTOR 4B as well as the ARIES rocket motors. The launcher itself has a very simple stool support with retractable locking devices that secure the motor in windy conditions.

The vehicle is protected by a movable house 23 m (75 ft) high and with a floor area of 8 m by 10 m (26 by 33 ft). The building is kept heated, and the temperature is controlled to a temperature of 20 ± 2°C. The temperature gradient between top and bottom of the vehicle is less than 1.5°C. An electrically operated gantry crane can be used over the entire floor area. The maximum length of vehicle that can be handled is 16 m (52 ft). There are three work platforms at heights of 11.4 m (37 ft), 14 m (46 ft) and 16.6 m (54.4 ft) above the floor which are accessible by means of an

elevator. Umbilicals are connected through a 15 m (49 ft) high tower with platforms for ground support equipment. These platforms are equipped with remotely operated power outlets. Shortly before launch the house is rolled 30 m (98 ft) away from the launch pad and the rocket locking devices are retracted by remote control from the blockhouse.

The Nike launcher is a single beam overslung military launcher with an electrical jackscrew elevating mechanism. The launcher elevation and azimuth are only controlled locally. The launcher is located to the east of the Skylark tower.

The following types of rockets have been launched from this launcher: Black Brant III, Nike-Apache, Nike-Cajun, Nike-Tomahawk, Petrel, and Skua.

The MAN launcher can be used with both over- and underslung with rail lengths of 11700 mm (38.4 ft) and 10700 mm (35 ft) respectively. The launch pad is located between the MAXUS and the MRL launchers.

The RAG launcher is also a property that can be equipped with different types of launch tubes for smaller rockets such as the Super Loki family or radar test rockets. The RAG launcher is situated to the east of the MRL launcher.

A cold storage, 10 by 16 m (32.8 by 52.4 ft), is 50 m (164 ft) south of the payload assembly hall main entrance. This is used for long term storage of launch support equipment, and temporary storage of user's equipment.

Balloon Facilities

Three hundred, twenty scientific balloons have been launched from Esrange, the largest of which was 625,000 m³, with the heaviest payload 865 kg. The balloon launch area is 150 m south of the main building. A large oval field, about 400 by 200 m, is required for release of large balloons. Two buildings for preparation, assembly, integration and testing are located at the north edge of the field.

Balloons are launched using either the dynamic or auxiliary balloon technique. Balloon payloads are commanded to land on

Nordic or Russian territory. Balloons can stay afloat for several days in the vicinity of Esrange when launched in the turn-around period.

Recovery of the balloon payloads by helicopter is a standard procedure. Homing receivers mounted in the helicopter together with flight train beacons allow immediate recovery. Esrange instrumentation supplies ATC radar transponders mandatory for balloon flights, homing beacons, and a complete telemetry and telecommand system for balloon piloting and science data transfers.

The preparation buildings include the Chapel building, which holds 180 m² (1,937 ft²) of floor area. The balloon payload assembly hall occupies 100 m² (1,076 ft²). To support payload handling, a crane of 1000 kg (one ton) lifting capability is run along the top of the ceiling which also allows loads to be carried two m outside the entrance door. One room is used as an operations and communications center, which is equipped with a wind monitoring and recording system, flight command control equipment, and all necessary communication equipment. Another 30 m² (323 ft²) in area is used as a storage for launch support equipment.

The Cathedral building is another preparation building designed for payload handling. The floor area is 375 m², 300 m² of which is payload preparation area. The hall is equipped with an overhead traveling crane with a lifting capability of 3200 kg (3.2 tons), lifting to a maximum height of seven m (23 ft). The payload preparation area floor is heated and equipped with under pressure air vents to prevent dust accumulation.

Handling equipment is necessary for the launch of heavy balloons. Balloons with a volume of 625,000 m³ (22,072,500 ft³) and payloads weighing up to 865 kg (1,097 lb) have been launched from this facility.

The launch field is covered with fine gravel, a surface which allows traffic with heavy cranes and lorries. At the center of the field a cavity is located, containing electrical power, ground cable, public address loudspeakers, and a telephone line.

Science Facilities

A key aspect of the impact area are the three major observation centers. They are located close to the launch area, under the predicted apogee and at the nominal impact point. All sites can accommodate personnel and equipment for long observation periods. Communication is maintained by means of mobile telephones.

The scientific center in the main building is the center for the scientific observations. Data from the scientific instruments enable scientists to survey the scientific situation. A heated observation dome provides observation of the sky. Users can install their own instruments on special platforms and data is routed to the scientific center through a permanent cable network. Telemetry data from the payload are also displayed in the scientific center. These facilities are critical to supporting launch decisions.

The downrange station is below the predicted apogee, approximately 25 km (15.5 mi) north of the launch area. Equipment and personnel must be transported by air as they are no roads to the location. Building power is generated by on-site diesel-driven motor generators.

Measured data is forwarded to the scientific center. Each user is allocated a display console where experiment data and other data can be accessed. The display console consists of an intercom, a word selector and display, a chart recorder, a serial data distributor, and power outlets. There are five units available.

There are a number of ground based instruments of many types that are used to support sounding rocket and balloon borne experiments. The results are available in the scientific center for immediate access.

There are two other major scientific facilities located near Esrange. The Swedish Institute of Space Physics is a center for magnetospheric studies. EISCAT (European Incoherent Scatter Facility) has a headquarters and receiving station in Kiruna for ionospheric studies. These scientific institutions offer unique opportunities for coordinated studies.

Esrange geophysical information services

(EGiS) is a support facility for display, manipulation, archiving and retrieval of data that is generated from scientific ground instruments. Data is available, according to user's choice, on DAT, CD-ROM or via Internet FTP. Data from Esrange instruments is collected continuously. Other data is collected in accordance with the user's requirements. Archived data is stored for ten years.

Range magnetometers are used to record the variations in the three components of the earth's magnetic field. They are situated in a small wooden hut 300 meters northwest of the main building. The display facilities are located in the scientific center.

A photometer measures specific spectral lines in the auroral emission. Instrument data is displayed locally in the scientific center. Various sky locations can be examined through use of a remote controlled pointing mechanism. Spectral line intensity is measured as well as background emission intensity. The background emission is then subtracted to derive the absolute intensity of the examined spectral line. The instrument at Esrange is owned by the Max-Planck Institut für Aeronomie in Katlenburg-Lindau, Germany.

The relative ionospheric opacity meter measures the galactic noise hitting the surface of the earth. Depending on conditions in the ionosphere, this noise is partially absorbed. The reduced noise power received relative to that of a quiet day is a measure of the ionospheric opacity. Two riometers at a fixed frequency are used. Location and configuration of the instruments were chosen to minimize effects of earth rotation and radio frequency interference. The output from the riometers is displayed in the scientific center.

Four Faraday transmitters are installed near the launch area. These transmitters are used to emit linearly polarized RF energy into the ionosphere. In using rocket-borne receivers to measure the change in polarization direction versus height, it is possible to determine the electron density in the ionosphere.

The Esrange Mesosphere Stratosphere Troposphere Radar (EMSTP) is an instrument which provides information on the dynamic state of the atmosphere, including winds, waves, turbulence and layering from the tro-posphere to the lower mesosphere ranging from one km to 110 km (0.621 to 68 mi) in altitude. The radar consists of a large array of YAGI-antennas with associated electronic equipment and is operated in cooperation with the Swedish Institute of Space Physics.

There are ground measurement observation sites available for use by scientific groups at Esrange for ground-based measurements. These include a number of types of mobile huts, caravans and rooms for installation of users' instruments.

A ground observation site is located atop a hill 485 meters (1,591 feet) above sea level. This site has rooms supplied with a viewing window for vertical sky observations.

The Kiruna Esrange Optical Platform System (KEOPS) is located on another hilltop 530 meters (1,738 feet) above sea level. This site is useful for optical observations, with a minimum of disturbing background light. It is intended for fully remotely controlled instruments to further minimize manmade light interference. An optical fiber system links the KEOPS to the Esrange main building.

There is a DigiCora instrument which is an automatic rawinsonde set designed for accurate measurement of upper-air pressure, temperature, relative humidity, and winds up to altitudes of 40 kilometers (25 miles). The measured data is processed automatically in standard meteorological formats. A wide range of optional equipment and programs allows the system to be configured to many different weather service and research applications. The DigiCora system is also equipped to receive special ozone sensor data.

The Vaisala Radioactivity Sonde features a NSS 13 radioactivity sensor with two Geiger-Müller tubes, for gamma and beta radiation, connected to a standard Vaisala series RS 80 radiosonde. The Radioactivity Sonde records standard PTU data in addition to radioactivity data.

Wind measurements are important factors in determining launch settings. A rocket trajectory is to a large extent dependant upon the wind situation at the launch instant. During the early part of the flight, rocket velocity is relatively low, and therefore easily affected by wind pressure. To reduce these effects, the launcher settings are carefully monitored and corrected depending on the wind situation.

The most important wind measurement facility is a tower 100 m (328 ft) high. This tower carries equipment for measurement of wind direction and velocity at several height levels. Winds above 100 m (328 ft) are measured using balloons in combination with radar tracking, or by theodolites, instruments used to measure vertical and horizontal angles. Wind data are processed and launcher settings are changed if necessary. Visual instruments which provide an overall view of the current situation are located in the operations center.

Instrumentation

The instrumentation section is responsible for operation and maintenance of the telemetry, timing, communication, tracking and scientific functions for Esrange. This section also provides flight hardware for balloons. Most of the equipment and personnel are housed in the main building, except for the tracking division which works in a separate building.

The telemetry station can be operated simultaneously for different missions, using RF downlinks in P, S, or L-band. This station also houses equipment for demodulation and recording of PCM, FM and television signals. Flight data are presented in real time or post-flight, using a variety of media and formats.

The P-band tracking equipment consists of two tracking systems with the antennas on the roof of the main building. Single channel and three-channel monopulse systems provide accurate target tracking. The received RF signals are routed to data receivers and/or distributed to the user.

The L/S band tracking equipment consists of a versatile tracking system for SHF frequencies and is located on the roof of the main building. An acquisition aid is used to minimize the risk of losing track of fast moving targets. Full coverage of the hemisphere ensures uninterrupted data from balloon-borne payloads. Polarization diversity improves the quality of tracking and data reception. RF signals, LHCP and RHCP, are routed to the telemetry station for further distribution.

The DLR L/S band tracking equipment has a DLR tracking antenna which can be used for telemetry data acquisition. This system is capable of receiving, demodulating, processing and recording the telemetry data.

There is an S/X band tracking equipment station with a ETX satellite antenna for high altitude rocket flights. The antenna can be controlled from the telemetry station and RF/IF signals are routed to the telemetry station via optical links.

Tracking receivers for the stations are flexible and easily configured for a specific task by means of plug-in modules. Pre- and post-detection polarization diversity combination is used whenever possible. Frequency demodulators are standard, but phase demodulators can also be accommodated. Wide bandwidth television signals can be received and demodulated.

Data extraction is accomplished by means of composite signals and output from receivers which are further processed in FM or PCM equipment. Two systems for PCM signals and one complete system for IRIG FM-signals are available for this purpose.

PCM decommutation is provided by high performance bit synchronizers which are housed to regenerate and decommutate PCM data, using two independent systems. Users have access to buffered outputs including data, clocks and all necessary control signals.

All vital signals from measurement are recorded on magnetic tape in real time. Timing signals, local multiplex and voice communication are also included for reference purposes. Two recorders are used simultaneously to ensure that no data is lost. A standard configuration with 10 DR and four FM tracks provides maximum data capacity, and tape copies with other configurations can be produced.

Telescience capability is available from Esrange via remote laboratories all over the world. To accomplish this, data, television signals and telecommands are transferred between Esrange and remote sites by terrestrial telecommunication links or broadband satellite links.

There is a television center with two TM stations that receive the transmitted television signals in two polarizations. An operator chooses the best signals for recording and further distribution to the blockhouse and the scientific center. S-VHS video recorders are used for recording. The television center is owned by MBB/ERNO in Germany.

A frequency plan for Esrange is based on a permission issued by the Swedish authorities on a yearly basis. All technical data including frequency, output power and bandwidth must be submitted to Esrange at least two months before expected start of use for all transmitters that are to be used.

Trajectory determination is accomplished by different systems used to determine trajectories and payload impact locations with an efficient, thoroughly tested recovery organization available.

Located at Esrange is a DLR MPS -36 radar. This system can be used for tracking of different payloads upon special agreement and is capable of tracking in both skin and transponder mode.

In a ranging system, flight trajectory can also be given by the autotracking telemetry antennas. The slant range to the rocket is determined with doppler measurements on the received PCM data. A highly stabilized oscillator is needed for the payload PCM encoder. Pointing angles are given by the antenna control systems. These parameters and timing information are then used for trajectory estimations. At elevations below 10°, the accuracy is degraded due to ground reflections and atmospheric conditions.

The geographical layout of Esrange along with its activities require high performance communication systems for voice and data. A general public address system connected to loudspeakers both indoors and outdoors is the primary source for voice communication.

All stations involved in measurement activities are equipped with at least one intercom unit with a loudspeaker and a microphone or a headset. There are eight separate communication loops dedicated for special purposes. Any of these loops can be accessed by front panel switches. If several loops must be monitored, special units are available to mix the sound from all selected loops into one loudspeaker.

A "go/no go" system is utilized, as reports on status of the systems involved are time critical. The operations officer, who is responsible for the coordination of all activities, has an immediate survey of the current situation. Each station is equipped with a control panel where a red light corresponds to "no go," i.e. system failure or the equivalent. A green light indicates "go," i.e. everything is under control.

There is a video messaging system through which general information to all stations is distributed via a local video system. A large number of video monitors are installed at Esrange. The basic information passed includes universal time and relative time (countdown time). Short messages can also be displayed.

External communications are possible by means of dedicated communication to and from Esrange via the public telecommunication networks using ISDN, Internet or other suitable methods.

Timing is accomplished as reference frequencies and time code signals are generated in a central facility. The system is synchronized to international standards, which are continuously monitored to ensure that synchronization is maintained at all times. A no-break power system is used to guarantee high system stability. The available signals are distributed to the user via the cable network. All time codes generated are synchronized in universal time and reference frequencies are synchronized to the station reference.

A ground to space transmitter system provides telecommand service. This system is primarily used for flight termination, in case a failure develops in the rocket-borne guidance system; flight commanding and maneuvering of payloads flown on rockets or balloons; and termination of balloon flights over land area, in case the payload must be recovered.

For flight termination, the frequency 448 MHz is used. For payload commands, 449.95 MHz is used. The two transmitters use separate power amplifiers and antennas. The transmitters can be configured as a redundant system using a priority scheme. For high altitude rockets, a 24 foot parabolic dish

(ESC) can be connected, to achieve higher EIRP.

A ESC UHF antenna system is used for telecommand. Antenna pointing is performed under computer control, to predicted angels or to actual angles delivered from tracking antennas.

Modulating signals can be accomplished using a payload command transmitter with signals from the user's ground equipment, connected via the cable system to the modulator.

The Esrange Balloon Service System (EBASS) comprises a flight hardware system for balloons and provides a complete telemetry and telecommand system. All ground based and flight equipment is field proven. The system includes all necessary functions to perform GPS position determination, cutdown on command and cut-down by timers, and top valve and ballast machine operations for balloon piloting. There are also three fully transparent bidirectional serial data channels available. An instrument designed for computer control and monitoring can be linked via the airborne unit from the ground station to the balloon payload in a very simple manner.

An air traffic control transponder is required by all balloons with payloads heavier than five kg (11 lb) for safety reasons. Special units meeting the ATC requirements are available that can be attached to the balloon flight train. A unit consists of a styrofoam box containing a transponder, electronics, batteries and external antenna.

Homing beacons are helpful and are used to support successful recovery operations. Special units can be attached to the balloon flight train. A unit consists of a styrofoam box containing a beacon transmitter, batteries and external antenna.

The power system at Esrange is a five-wire, three-phase 50 Hz system. The phase to phase voltage is 400 VAC -6 percent +10 percent, 50Hz +-2Hz, phase to neutral voltage is 230 VAC -6 percent +10 percent, 50Hz +-2Hz. The system neutral is separated from safety ground in the local distribution systems. Neutral and safety ground are connected only at one point, the main. Power transformers must have separate primary and secondary windings. It is possible to supply 110 VAC 50 Hz power at certain locations. Backup power is installed in the main building (800 kVA), the launching area (300 kVA) and the radar hill (300 kVA). No-break-power (UPS) is installed in the main building (70 kVA; 20 minutes), launching area (30 kVA; 20 minutes), and radar hill (5.0 kVA; 20 minutes).

Operations

For every project planned from Esrange, a project manager is appointed as the Esrange contact for the range user. The project manager is responsible for the campaign planning, coordination, countdown procedure, and operations at the range. Esrange officials are responsible for flight control and flight safety of all vehicles that are flown from Esrange.

Esrange provides launching opportunities any time of the year, any time of day, within the measure of Swedish Laws. The long-term scheduling of the Esrange launching program is carried out by the secretariat of the Program Advisory Committee situated at ESA Headquarters in Paris. A revised schedule is issued every second month.

Assembly and preparation of rockets and balloons for operational support is normally done by Esrange personnel. Assembly, preparation and checkout of payloads, which is normally executed by the range user, must adhere to the ESM regulations.

Recovery of rockets and balloon payloads is standard operating procedure at the range. The land impact area makes Esrange very suitable for all kinds of flights for necessary recovery. The open landscape allows smooth payload landing with minimal impact damage. After impact, the payloads seldom drag in the recovery parachute due to the presence of prevailing low winds.

Balloon payloads are recovered all over northern Scandinavia and northern Russia. Recovery operations are very likely to be successful provided that payloads are equipped with proper homing devices. All other parts without beacons, such as motor cases, nose cones, etc., are recovered as soon as they have been located. Helicopter support from expert pilots makes it possible to maintain a very high probability for successful recovery. Equipment to support recovery, ATC transponders and homing beacons, can be supplied by Esrange instrumentation.

Safety

As a rule, Swedish safety regulations and laws apply for work at Esrange. The Work Environment Act contains the basic provisions concerning occupational safety and health questions in Sweden. This act is a general act of law which is broadened by special rules and regulations in different fields, for example explosives, inflammable materials, toxic materials, and electrical facilities. The specific safety rules and regulations that apply for work at Esrange are defined in the Esrange Safety Manual (ESM), which is available on site at Esrange. The following general safety information is lined out.

The safety organization at Esrange is based on the following main functions: the general manager for Esrange Division is responsible for implementing the range safety policies and criteria. The head of launch services is responsible for conducting the operations in accordance with the ESM.

The head of launch team is responsible for all handling of explosives at Esrange and is also responsible for ground safety in the launching areas during count-down and build-up of a campaign. The head of launch team is appointed superintendent for explosives at Esrange. During operations, the responsibilities are delegated to personnel conducting the actual operational tasks. There are certain areas that must be closed for safety reasons. Only authorized personnel will have access to these areas.

The road to the rocket launching area is closed near the main building with a remotely controlled road block. Authorized personnel gain access by using a special badge. Within the launching area there are additional restricted areas that require proper authorization.

The road to the balloon launching area is also closed near the main building with a remotely controlled road block. Authorized per-

sonnel gain access by using a special badge. The buildings at the north edge of the balloon launching area are not restricted.

There is no access to the roof of the Esrange radar station without permission from the radar team leader due to the health risk arising from RF radiation. There is also a nonpermitted area around the DLR radar. During transmission of this radar, a blue flashing warning-light is activated.

No Access signs are situated above the doors to the operations center and scientific center. When these signs are illuminated, only authorized personnel have access.

Flight safety main objectives are to minimize injuries to personnel, damage to property and the probability of impact outside the range boundaries. Each vehicle flight is planned to optimize the probability of the success of the flight objectives and to minimize the element of risk. Swedish Space Corporation policy requires that the risk associated with each launch at Esrange is controlled so that the hurt risk (risk of personal injury) never exceeds one in a million. In order to implement this policy, every vehicle launched from Esrange is categorized into Category A and Category B vehicles.

Category A vehicles do not have a control or guidance system, have a demonstrated vehicle reliability, and have an impact dispersion such that the hurt risk criteria are fulfilled.

Category B vehicles are vehicles that cannot be classified Category A. They are required to have a destruct system. When launching a Category B vehicle, a Safety Operations System (SOS) is established to control the mission risk. A flight safety plan includes flight limits marking the areas in which the vehicle under certain conditions should be destroyed.

The nominal impact point used is Az: 350°, at a distance of 75 km (46.6 mi) during the period from September 16 to April 30, when zones B and C are permitted impact areas. During summer, the nominal impact point is selected in Az: 350°, at a distance of 60 km (37.2 mi), when only zone B is a permitted impact area. This minimizes the hurt risk and the probability of impacts outside the range boundaries. Some exceptions can be made for rockets with low dispersion and demonstrated reliability.

Launchings of large stratospheric balloons can take place from Esrange or some other place in northern Sweden under the supervision of Esrange safety personnel. All balloons are filled with helium gas and released by range personnel. Stratospheric balloons are required to carry all equipment necessary to fulfill air traffic control and Esrange safety requirements. Impact and recovery in Scandinavia is normal, but permission for impact and recovery in northern Russia can also be arranged.

Any explosives to be brought to Sweden require an import license issued by Swedish authorities. Dangerous equipment is defined as all equipment containing micro-organic, explosive, pyrotechnic, poisonous, corrosive, or radioactive materials. Esrange requires notification when an experiment with dangerous material found listed in the book *Handbook der gefährlichen Güter* (Himmel Springer-Verlag, Berlin, Heidelberg, New York) is proposed.

The Odin Satellite

Odin, the Swedish small satellite project for astronomical and atmospheric research, is a low-cost satellite with a combined astronomy and atmospheric research (aeronomy) mission. The Odin project is the result of cooperation between space agencies and scientists in Sweden, Canada, Finland and France. The main objective of the astronomy mission will be to study star formation and early solar systems. The main objective of the atmospheric research mission will be to study ozone layer depletion mechanisms and extent.

The Odin payload is comprised of a 1.1 meter (3.6 ft) Gregorian telescope with a submillimeter and millimeter radiometer and an optical spectrograph. These wavelengths contain spectral lines of, among others, O_2 and H_2O molecules which are absorbed by the earth's atmosphere. These wavelengths can only be observed from space.

The telescope is fixed to the spacecraft body so it may be moved and pointed in the desired direction through stabilization of the

The Odin satellite for astronomical and atmospheric research. (Swedish Space Corporation)

entire spacecraft body. To accomplish this, the altitude control system (ACS) features three-axis stabilization with high accuracy, both for inertial pointing towards celestial targets and scanning of the earth atmosphere. A double control system cannot be used for Odin since it is a low-cost, low-profile system. Instead, it performs the earth pointing portion of the mission with inertial reference, using star trackers and gyros as main sensors. Actuators are reaction wheels and magnetic coils.

The Swedish Space Corporation (SSC) is prime contractor for the spacecraft and has the overall responsibility for the design, development and testing. The main sensors, star trackers and gyros are provided by France, together with technical support from CNES, the French space agency. The Canadian Space Agency (CSA) has provided a test facility and performs testing of the ACS on a system level. The altitude control and determination computer (ACDC) hardware and software are provided by Saab Ericsson Space AB (SE) under a contract to SSC.

Following a 1994 feasibility and design study, conducted by Swedish Space Corporation (SSC) and the scientist groups behind the Odin proposal, the Swedish National Space Board (SNSB) gave the final go-ahead for the development and launch of Odin. The launch occurred in February 2001.

The scientific goals of Odin were established by a group of scientists from the participating countries, called the Odin Science Team. The main part of the project cost is carried by Sweden, and the Swedish National

Space Board (SNSB) has the overall project responsibility, supported by CSA of Canada, TEKES of Finland, and CNES of France. The Swedish Space Corporation is charged with the implementation of the project.

Odin is designed to observe hundreds of individual molecular clouds in our own galaxy as well as assemblies of giant molecular clouds in other galaxies.

Other topics for astronomical study by Odin are the composition of comets, the composition and dynamics of the atmospheres of Jupiter and Saturn, shells surrounding dying old stars which provide matter to the interstellar medium affecting the next generation of stars, and the search for previously unobserved molecules in the galaxy.

Atmospheric research is another mission Odin will accomplish. Since the discovery in 1985 of the ozone hole over the Antarctic, extensive measurement and study have led to a fairly good understanding of its origin. The ozone depletion is caused by catalytic chemical reactions by halogen atoms like chlorine, released from manmade chlorofluorocarbons (CFC). The large increase in the concentration of active chlorine (ClO and Cl) is caused by heterogeneous chemical reactions on polar stratospheric cloud particles. Similar but smaller disturbances can also be seen over the Arctic and even at lower latitudes.

On a global scale the depletion process involves atmospheric transport phenomena, variations of ozone chemistry at different altitudes, and large natural variations. Determination and geographical mapping of key components will be provided by Odin in order to build better models. Transport and breakdown of CFCs occur over a long period. Odin will monitor the peak disturbance during a period when few other atmospheric research satellites are active.

The Odin payload is made up of several instruments, which include the following:

The main instrument, the radiometer, is a 1.1 m (3.6 ft) diameter radio telescope with heterodyne receivers in five bands, four around 500 GHz frequency and one at 119 GHz. Most of the molecules and atoms of the scientific objectives can be covered by the 500 Ghz bands. The 119 GHz receiver is dedicated to studies of molecular oxygen. A mechanical cooler will be used to cool mixers and amplifiers down to around 100 K which will increase the sensitivity. The radio signals are analyzed in hybrid autocorrelation spectrometers, used in conjunction with an acusto-optical spectrometer.

To supplement the radiometric measurements, the aeronomers need an optical split spectrograph covering UV to IR wavelengths, used for studies of aerosols and additional molecules and atoms.

The radiometer, also referred to as SMR (sub-millimeter radiometer), covers atomic and molecular transitions of aeronomical and astrophysical interest from CI, ClO, 1_2CO, 1_3CO, NO_2, N_2O, H_2O_2, HO_2, $H_2{}^1{}_6O$,

Moon research is another activity of Sweden's space programs. Here is the moon probe SMART-1 in orbit. (Swedish Space Corporation)

Close-up of SMART-1 probe. (Swedish Space Corporation)

$H_2^{18}O$, H_2S, CS, NO, N_2O, HNO_3, NH_3, H_2CO, O_3 and O_2. The spectral line shapes are used in the aeronomical retrieval process and for astronomical dynamics studies.

The telescope itself is a dual-reflector concept operating as an offset Gregorian system with a carbon fiber composite structure used to maintain stability against thermal loads. The deviation from the mathematical shape is 10 micrometer RMS, taking into account the total affect of the surface roughness, the inaccuracies in the manufacturing process, and the thermoelastic deformation.

The Odin optics system consists of combinations of mirrors, grids and meshes. The signal coming from the telescope is routed to the receivers, split and filtered by optics made up of diplexers and sideband filters based on tunable polarizing Michelson interferometers.

All data-handling on the Odin platform is performed by the Odin System Unit (OSU). The OSU contains several processing units which include the ACDC, which carries out the altitude determination and control. The sensors and actuators of the ACS are connected to dedicated interface processors responsible for the communication with the onboard communication network. The ACDC receives sensor data and sends actuator commands through this onboard communication network.

The altitude control system of Odin is based on sensors and actuators with good flight heritage. The two star trackers from France provide the ACS with high accuracy star direction information. The star trackers are mounted on the telescope structure with angular separation of 40 symmetrically around the telescope line of sight. This configuration allows one star tracker to face the sky while the telescope is directed towards the earth limb for aeronomy observations. The three gyro pack, also from France, provide high accuracy angular rate information. Each gyro package gives two axises information so all three ensure a six to three redundancy.

The four reaction wheels from the United States, with four Nms capacity each, are the main actuators for the altitude control. Three of them are mounted orthogonally. The fourth is mounted iso-angular to the other three, serving as backup. Three magnetorquers (electromagnetic coils, from SSC and ACR, Sweden) are used to dump momentum from reaction wheels and for the detumble emergency mode.

Three coarse sun sensors from Matra Marconi Space, France, and two fine sun sensors contributed by ACR, Sweden, provide coverage around the entire spacecraft and give an accurate value of the sun angle within a 76 top-angle cone around the spacecraft z-axis, perpendicular to the solar panels. Two SSC contributed three-axis magnetometers provide altitude information of lower accuracy to the ACS.

The primary objective of Odin is to perform detailed studies of the physics and the chemistry of the interstellar medium by observing emission from key species. There are several types of objects being targeted for observation. These include giant molecular clouds and nearby dark clouds which will help to improve our understanding of the chemistry and the cooling processes of the interstellar medium and the conditions for star formation in particular, by measuring lines from oxygen and water molecules. Additional bodies to be targeted will be protostars; comets, including the outgassing of water, the size of active regions and density estimates; planets, particularly Jupiter and Saturn; and also to concentrate on the physics and chemistry of the deep atmosphere, circumstellar envelopes with studies of the dynamics and chemical composition of outflows, and nearby galaxies with estimates of star formation activity from observations of CO and H_2O.

The research in aeronomy will address scientific problem areas in the stratosphere and mesosphere by making measurements of various trace species. Scientific goals will include stratospheric ozone science to study the geographical extent of and mechanisms responsible for ozone depletion in the ozone hole region and to study dilution effects and possible heterogeneous chemistry even outside of the polar regions due to sulphate aerosols. Mesospheric ozone science will also be used to establish the relative role of odd hydrogen chemistry and the effects of ordered and turbulent transport and corpuscular radiation.

Summer mesospheric science will be examined to establish the variability of mesospheric water vapor including an assessment of the required fluxes for aerosol formation in the polar mesosphere.

Coupling of atmospheric regions will be used to study some of the mechanisms that provide coupling between the upper and lower atmosphere, for example, downward transport of aurorally enhanced NO with its effects on ozone photo chemistry and the vertical exchange of minor species such as odd oxygen, CO and H_2O.

The Odin spacecraft is designed to serve both astronomy and aeronomy. For aeronomy the spacecraft follows the earth's limb, scanning the atmosphere up and down from 15 to 120 km (9 to 75 mi) at a rate of up to 40 scans per orbit. When observing astronomical sources, Odin is continuously pointing towards the object for up to 60 minutes.

Odin will operate in unexplored bands of the electromagnetic spectrum, around wavelengths of 0.5 mm (0.02 in) and 3 mm (0.11 in). These contain emission lines from important molecules such as water vapor, molecular oxygen, ozone and carbon monoxide. The lines will be used as tools to study processes in the earth's atmosphere and in astronomical objects. Information on the atmosphere will come from spectral lines at ultraviolet and optical wavelengths. Major scientific issues relate to star formation processes, interstellar chemistry and atmospheric ozone balance.

Odin is equipped with an antenna with type offset shaped Gregorian, a diameter of 1.1 meters (3.6 ft), a surface 10 μm rms, and material CFRP skins on honeycomb.

It also features an optical spectrometer. This instrument has four wavelength bands and views the limb through optics separate but aligned with the sub-millimeter antenna.

Odin's radiometer has one receiver at a wavelength of 3 mm (0.11 in) and four in the sub-millimeter band (1 - 0.5 mm), and type single side band heterodyne receivers with frequencies of 118.25 — 119.25 GHz, 486.1 — 503.9 GHz, 541.0 — 580.4 GHz, bandwidth 100 MHz to 1 GHz, resolution 0.1 MHz to 1 MHz, and sensitivity 1 K in 1MHz with S/N=5 after 15 min.

Odin has a type three-axis stabilized with reaction wheels, star trackers and gyros, a mass of 250 kg (551 lb) with a 170 kg (375 lb) bus and 80 kg (176 lb) payload, 340 W of power from deployable fixed arrays, a storage exceeding 100 Mbyte in solid state memory, and operates by way of a sun-synchronous circular orbit at a 600 km (373 mi) altitude with ascending node at 18:00, and has a minimum two year lifetime.

Swedish National Space Board

The Swedish National Space Board (SNSB) is a central government agency under the Swedish Ministry of Industry, Employment and Communication, responsible for national and international activities involving space and remote sensing.

SNSB conducts research in space or at high altitudes in the atmosphere. It also ensures extensive international cooperation through Sweden's membership in the European Space Agency (ESA)

Earth Observation

The SNSB has several programs in remote sensing. As a member state of ESA, Sweden has participated in the development of the earth observation satellites ERS-1, ERS-2, and ENVISAT, as well as the meteorological satellites Meteosat, MSG (Meteosat Second Generation), and Metop.

Sweden has its own Global Monitoring for Environment and Security (GMES), which involves the use of earth observation satellites.

In cooperation with France and Belgium, Sweden participates in the Spot program which is a high-resolution space optical imaging system started in 1977.

The program consists of a series of earth observation satellites. The first, Spot 1, was launched in February 1986, with the final one, Spot 5, launched in May 2002.

Spot imagery has been key in applications to forestry, agriculture, mineral exploration, local and regional planning, environmental monitoring, navigation, and production of maps for developing countries.

Sweden has also been a participant in the vegetation program, a program consisting of an instrument to perform continuous, regional and global tracking of the continental biosphere and crops which was placed aboard Spot 4 and 5. The instrument continues to provide daily coverage of the entire globe with an accuracy of roughly one km (0.621 mi). It was specially designed to track vegetation, with emphasis on agricultural production, forestry, and surveillance of the land environment worldwide.

Data supplied by the vegetation instrument has proven to be valuable for community applications such as common agricultural policy, environmental management, and developmental aid.

The Swedish satellite Odin was launched in February 2001. Odin is unusual in that it combines two scientific disciplines on a single spacecraft. It has an astronomy mission to study star formation and the early solar system, as well as an aeronomy mission to study the mechanisms behind the depletion of the ozone layer and the effects of global warming.

Since Sweden is a country that is dominated by forestland, forest resource inventory is another major remote sensing application. Nearly 55 percent of the country is covered by forests, or 227,000 km² (87,647 mi²). The Swedish National Board of Forest is one of the major users of remote sensing data in Europe. Data is used for detection of change and forest monitoring.

GMES

GMES was started in 1998 by the European Commission in cooperation with several space agencies, in order to apply knowledge-supporting technologies in earth observation and information more efficiently to environmental management and security.

The primary long-term goal of GMES is to put into force a distributed information system which will lead to the efficient provision of environmental data, information and knowledge, and contribute to the sustainable management of the global environment.

Sweden has extensive knowledge which has been applied to the GMES program as a result of nearly thirty years of experience with developing and promoting the use of remote sensing and earth observation technology for environmental purposes.

Under the GMES, Sweden established the Global Land Cover 2000 program within a national program, Global Monitoring. Through this program, priority is given to activities supporting various user needs in monitoring the environment.

Global Land Cover 2000 is a joint worldwide effort to produce a land cover map for the entire globe. The overall objective of the GLC2000 project is to provide a harmonized land cover database. The Swedish company Metria Miljöanalys is responsible for the Baltic Sea region, including parts of eastern Europe, as well as part of Germany and Norway.

Astronomy

The Swedish National Space Board (SNSB) has been involved in a wide range of astronomy and astrophysics activities which are carried out by research groups at astronomical observatories in Sweden as well as at Chalmers University of Technology and the Royal Institute of Technology.

The Swedish Institute of Space Physics in Kiruna and Uppsala has active programs focusing on the development of instruments for research on plasma phenomena in the solar system.

SNSB has also contributed Swedish hardware to the ESA missions Rosetta, Cassini/Huygens, Mars Express, and Venus Express.

Lund University contributed to the ESA Hipparcos mission, a satellite equipped with the first space experiment dedicated to the highly accurate measurements of star positions, distance, and space motions, which was launched August 1989 and terminated August 1993. The satellites yielded more than three years of high quality star measurements and accomplished all scientific goals.

Sweden's latest scientific satellite, Odin, has opened up new opportunities for knowledge in microwave astronomy, studying atomic and molecular transitions with the on-board 1-meter (1.09-yard) telescope.

Groups at Onsala Space Observatory, Chalmers University of Technology, and Stockholm Observatory build part of the satellite's radiometer. These groups will also be using experience acquired from work on Odin for ESA's upcoming Herschel mission, which will study the origin of stars and galaxies, search for water in space and help us to understand the formation of our own solar system through detailed observations of comets and of the poorly known transneptunian objects. Herschel is scheduled for launch in February 2007.

Space Physics

Space physics research in Sweden is carried out using small satellites in earth orbits. The Swedish Viking mission in 1986 was dedicated to plasma physics. The tradition continued with other satellites to study the magnetosphere including Freja, Astrid-1 and Astrid-2.

Swedish space plasma physicists have built instruments for measurement of electric and magnetic fields, plasma densities and energetic neutral atoms. They have been using these instruments to perform scientific analysis in international space projects including Ulysses, Phobos, Planet-B, Cassini/Huygens, Rosetta, Mars Express, Interball, Polar, Equator-S, and Cluster.

The space physics group studies the solar driver of space weather, as well as solar activity in collaboration with Stanford University in California for the SOHO project to explore the sun. They also study climate changes and have been developing a real-time forecast service of space weather and effects using knowledge-based neurocomputing for ESA's space weather program study.

The group also studies satellite anomalies, in conjunction with ESA, and effects of geomagnetic induced currents on power systems in cooperation with the Swedish power industry and ESA.

In Project Solar Activity, the space physics group studies how solar magnetic ac-tivity can be modeled and predicted with intelligent hybrid systems (IHSs) using SOHO data. Predictions obtained are used to study the effects of low earth orbiting (LEO) satellites as well as the study of sun-climate and weather relations.

Project Satellite Anomalies is a cooperative venture with ESA in which the study of satellite anomalies can be predicted from the space weather state using neural networks.

Project Radio Communications Conditions has been used to study how radio communication conditions can be predicted from the space weather state using neural networks.

Project Global and Local Magnetic Field Variations involves study of how the solar wind energy is transferred and dissipated within earth's magnetosphere and ionosphere.

Project GIC is where geomagnetically induced currents and their effects on electric power systems and gas pipeline systems are studied and predicted using neural networks.

Atmospheric Research

The Swedish National Space Board has been conducting atmospheric research utilizing altitude balloons, sounding rockets, and satellites.

Odin, which has been in orbit since February 2001, with a 1.1 m (43.3 in) telescope, has been making regular limb-scanning observations of the upper atmosphere between 20 and 100 km (12.4 to 62.1 mi). Three-dimensional maps of several trace gas abundances, such as those important to ozone depletion, have been extracted from these observations.

In December 2001, the Hygrosonde 2 sounding rocket was launched from Esrange rocket range in Sweden to validate observations from Odin. Balloons launched from France and Sweden were also used to validate Odin data at lower altitudes.

Two sounding rockets, NLTE (Non-Local Thermodynamic Equilibrium), were launched from Esrange in March 1998, to study the heat budget and effects of non-local thermodynamic equilibrium in the upper mesosphere and lower thermosphere.

A series of balloons, or Skerries, were launched from Esrange to study climate effects on the stratosphere. These balloons measured concentrations of CFCs (chlorofluorocarbons), water vapor, and ozone.

The atmospheric research program at the Swedish Institute of Space Physics has been conducting studies of the energy balance, dynamics, electrodynamics, and chemistry of the troposphere, stratosphere, and lower thermosphere.

Long-term and solar-cycle changes have been monitored in the middle and upper atmosphere in order to determine how solar activity influences temperature, winds, electric currents, and minor constituents, while allowing possible anthropogenic influences to be determined. Measurements are performed primarily by radar, with some use of ground-based and balloon-borne measurements of atmospheric electric fields and currents.

A survey of nacreous clouds in the Kiruna area of Sweden has been conducted in order to determine whether nacreous clouds have changed in appearance or prevalence over the past few decades, and also, what the relationship is between nacreous clouds, seen by the eye or photographed, and polar stratospheric clouds seen by lidar.

Trace gas measurements and environmental monitoring have been the focus of the Descartes Project to extend the measurement technique to a larger number of trace species; monitor the presence of CFCs and other long-lived anthropogenic tracers in the stratosphere; and to use long-lived anthropogenic species as tracers of atmospheric motion with special emphasis on comparison with atmospheric models. Another research project is the Fourier transform infrared spectrometry which has been operated in collaboration with the Institut für Meteorologie und Klimaforschung in Karlsruhe, Germany, and the Solar Terrestrial Environment Laboratory in Nagoya, Japan. The spectrometer records solar and lunar absorption spectra throughout the year, while covering the spectral interval from 600 to 5000 cm-1 (2 to 17 µm) in the middle infrared.

This research has also covered the study of chemical ozone depletion by observation of key species — O_3, $ClONO_2$, HNO_3, HCl, NO_2; profile retrieval to detect dynamical changes; transport studies of chemical tracers;

satellite validation; details of the ozone formation process by isotopic studies in ozone; and water vapor isotopic studies.

Polar stratospheric cloud (PSC) studies have been performed in an effort to understand stratospheric ozone chemistry using passive ground-based optical instruments which measure scattered or direct sunlight to study PSCs and their impact.

Studies have been conducted using active ionospheric modification experiments to make experimental and theoretical studies of the processes in the polar summer middle atmosphere, leading to the existence of strong radar echoes from the mesopause heights called PMSE.

Two joint PMSE and heating experiments were performed during the summer of 1999 and 2001 to show that ionospheric heating leads to a decrease of PMSE power. By studying PMSE response on heating, information on processes in the mesosphere was obtained, yielding an understanding of PMSE generation.

Another method of ionospheric modification based on the creation of artificial periodic irregularities was applied for estimation of electron diffusivity on mesospheric heights during PMSE events.

Astroparticle Physics

The astroparticle physics group KTH Kungliga Tekniska Högskolan at the Royal Institute of Technology in Stockholm has been conducting a series of balloon campaigns, referred to as Caprice, for flux measurements of rare cosmic ray particles. They have also recently been engaged in the preparation of hardware for the international satellite project, Pamela, which will measure fluxes of anti-matter and neutral atoms.

The primary activity at KTH has been preparations for the ATLAS experiment, which will probe collisions in the TeV energy range at the LHC (large hadron collider) particle accelerator located at CERN, the European Laboratory for Particle Physics. The LHC will collide protons in the multi-TeV energy region and provide the potential for fundamental discoveries concerning the basic interactions of nature. These energies have been believed to produce conditions prevailing in the universe some 10^{-12} seconds after the Big Bang. The LHC experimental program will begin in approximately 2006.

ATLAS will explore the fundamental nature of matter and the basic forces that shape our universe. It is the largest collaborative effort ever attempted in the physical sciences with the participation of 2000 physicists from more than 150 universities and laboratories in 34 countries.

The astrophysics group has been contributing to both detector development and physics simulations for ATLAS. Detector work includes the electromagnetic presampler which will search for the Higgs boson for supersymmetry of heavy W- and Z-like objects as well as the compositeness of fundamental fermions, which require stringency in the ability of the detector to measure the energy of outgoing particles.

The electromagnetic presampler will be an essential part of the liquid argon electromagnetic calorimeter system for reaching the required performances that will allow for the exploration of the large spectrum of expected new physics. It will provide a measurement of the energy of the shower, and of the upstream of the electromagnetic calorimeter, which will allow for the correction of energy loss inside the inner detector.

Another KTH contribution will be high voltage supplies for the liquid argon calorimeters which will involve simulations of the ATLAS experiments to study the possibility of detecting supersymmetry, a theory of the standard model of physics, which describes our knowledge of the particles and forces that make up the universe. It is a quantum mechanical theory that incorporates electromagnetism with the weak and the strong nuclear interactions, for example, the forces between charged particles, particles in the nuclei of atoms, and the forces between the quarks, respectively. It does not include the forth-fundamental force, gravity, since no one has managed to find a way that this can be done. Unifying gravity with quantum mechanics is one of the motivating factors behind the string theory.

The KTH group on X-ray imaging has been developing several different detector systems with multiple applications, focusing on medical imaging. These include gaseous detector based digital imaging which was invented for detecting photons of a wide range of energy (keV to MeV). Two technologies are used, one based on the GEM (gas electron multiplier), and the other on capillary plates. The imager has a pixelized electronic readout system. One potential application is treatment verification of cancer patients in radiation therapy through a portal imager. A semiconductor based digital imaging detector is a photon counting detector system that is a scanned-slit imaging device based on silicon strip readout. A challenging application for this detector will be as a microdose mammography system.

Refractive X-ray optics will be a new type of reflective lens for hard X-rays with potential applications in crystallography or X-ray microscopy. The group has also developed a proportional chamber with CsI, an ultraviolet detector which could be used for fire detection, and a silicon track detector which has been used to correlate observed flashes with tracks.

The astroparticle physics group has been working together with the Swedish Institute for Space Physics in developing artificial intelligence and neural network techniques to control and operate a small nano-satellite, HUGIN. This satellite is low weight, less than five kg (11 lb), designed for quick turnaround times for scientific projects at universities.

Another satellite project is being developed in collaboration with AmSat-SM, called VICTORIA. It is a spin-stabilized, sun-pointing satellite in a sun-synchronous orbit that will carry a simple answering machine and a slow scan television (SSTV) repeater for radio enthusiasts.

It will serve two purposes as a technology demonstrator and as a satellite for education. It will carry memory chips for studying single event upsets as well as a particle detector.

Astrobiology

Research in astrobiology has been conducted by a network recently formed in Sweden called SWAN. A current project involves the microanalysis of microfossils on earth in preparation for ancient earth studies and a sample return mission to Mars. This has been referred to as the Tomas Hode Research Project.

Astrobiology involves a wide range of disciplines to promote the search for extraterrestrial life. One of the central problems in this area involves how to distinguish between the remains of living things from non-biological structures in rock.

The Tomas Hode Project has been designed to develop methods and concepts to aid in the detection and assessment of ancient microfossils on earth, to eventually include samples returned from Mars. The project will involve the development and application of methods to use in the characterization of isotopic and structural composition of individual microfossil-like objects. It will employ a variety of methods, both proven and unproven, while testing their limits and capabilities.

These methods will include ion microprobe mass spectrometry, nuclear microprobe Rutherford backscattering, and Raman spectroscopy. They will be used primarily for space research, and possibly other research areas in the future if successful.

Human Spaceflight

Research in human spaceflight encompasses the study of physiology in microgravity. Researchers at the Karolinska Institute in Solna near Stockhom have conducted studies into this area as well as in hypergravity, in which a human centrifuge is used. Another group has been studying the effects of gravity on the function of lungs and the cardiovascular system. Also under development is exercise equipment to counteract the loss of muscle mass and bone minerals during prolonged spaceflight.

A new project at the Department of Physics, located at the Royal Institute of Technology, has a simulation for the radiation environment on the International Space Station which estimates radiation doses astronauts will receive under certain conditions.

Material Sciences in Microgravity

All microgravity research in Sweden has been carried out in conjunction with ESA microgravity programs, which have offered Swedish researchers opportunities to engage in parabolic aircraft flights, sounding rockets experiments, and manned flights in cooperation with the United States and Russia.

As a part of materials science research, Sweden has conducted studies into the understanding of the formation of non-aqueous foams in such processes as distillation. A research group based at the Institute for Surface Chemistry has taken advantage of the fact that transient foams have increased stability in microgravity due to reduced drainage of the fluid.

At the Institute for Surface Chemistry and the Royal Institute of Technology, work has commenced on the development and use of metallic foams.

Swedish Satellites

Sweden has had a very strong satellite program, including six satellites — Viking, Freja, Astrid 1, Astrid 2, Odin, and Munin.

The Viking satellite was launched February 22, 1986, and terminated in May 1987. Its purpose was the investigation of plasma physics and the auroral phenomena.

The 286 kg (630 lb) Viking was launched as a piggyback payload on the Ariane 1. It conducted a series of very successful magnetospheric research studies until May 12, 1987.

The instrument carried experiments to measure electric fields, magnetic fields, charged particles, waves, and auroral images. These experiments were supplied by several cooperative partners including Canada, Denmark, France, Norway, the United States, and Germany.

Viking was developed based on the fact that northern Scandinavia is among the most favorable places on earth to measure phenomena related to the coupling of energy between the sun and outer space with the lower atmosphere and ionosphere. This is due to the auroral zones serving as focal points for this energy deposition which can reach 10^{11} watts.

The auroral regions cover a dynamic and complex system of plasmas that interact with magnetic fields and electric currents. The Viking program was aimed at understanding large-scale phenomena, such as plasma convection, global current systems, and auroral morphology, as well as small-scale and microphysical problems, including particle acceleration processes, wave-particle interactions, shock structure, fine-structured currents, and auroral kilometric radiation (AKR). Viking was specifically designed to perform high-resolution measurements of electric fields, magnetic fields, energetic particles, plasma waves, and ultraviolet emissions. Its orbit was chosen to sample the auroral plasmas at intermediate altitudes (1-2 RE) that were not usually explored by satellites, and where key mechanisms responsible for the acceleration of auroral particles were present.

The Freja satellite was launched in October 1992, and completed its mission in October 1996. It was a cooperative project between Sweden and Germany to perform high-resolution measurements in the upper ionosphere and lower magnetosphere.

Freja was a magnetospheric satellite launched as a piggyback payload on Long March 2C from the Jiuquan Satellite Launch Center in China, weighing 256 kg (564 lb).

The Astrid 1 satellite was launched January 1995, terminating in May 1995. It was a small spin-stabilized satellite weighing only 27 kg (60 lb), and carried an energetic neutral atom analyzer, an electron spectrometer, and two UV imagers for imaging the aurora. The platform was designed and developed by the Swedish Space Corporation's Space Systems Division, and the payload was developed by the Swedish Institute of Space Physics.

The neutral particle imager, PIPPI (prelude in planetary particle imaging) was Astrid's main instrument. PIPPI was the first dedicated instrument to measure the neutral particle flux from the ring current. The instrument consists of two cameras. The SSD camera used solid-state detectors to resolve the energy of detected particles, and the MCP camera used a technique where incoming neutrals cause charged secondary particles to be emitted from a graphite target. The secondary particles were then detected by a microchannel plate (MCP). Both cameras featured deflection systems which rejected charged particles up to an energy of 140 keV.

The electron spectrometer EMIL (electron measurements, both in-situ and lightweight) consisted of a swept-energy toroidal electrostatic analyzer and a microchannel plate (MCP) detector. The instrument measured the electron distribution at 62.5 ms or 125 ms resolution.

The UV imaging photometers, MIO (miniature imaging optics), were mounted in the satellite spin plane. One observed Lyman alpha-emission from the earth's geocorona, and the other observed auroral emissions. Each photometer consisted of optics mounted in a stainless steel tube with a ceramic channel electron multiplier in the opposite end.

Astrid 2 was launched piggyback on a Kosmos 3M rocket from Plesetsk on December 10, 1998. On July 24, 1999, contact was lost with the satellite during a passage and several attempts to regain contact were unsuccessful.

Astrid 2's mission was to perform high-resolution E-field and B-field measurements in the auroral region, electron density measurements, high resolution measurements of the electron and ion distribution functions, and ultraviolet auroral imaging and atmospheric UV-absorption measurements.

It utilized a spin-stabilized, sun-pointing platform and weighed less than 30 kg (66 lb).

Odin is a cooperative satellite project between Sweden, Canada, Finland, and France which was launched February 2001. It consists of an astronomy mission to study star formation and the early solar system, and an aeronomy mission to study the mechanisms behind the depletion of the ozone layer and the effects of global warming.

The primary instrument on Odin is an advanced radiometer using a 1.1 m (43.3 in) telescope, which is used for both the astronomy and aeronomy missions. It was designed to work in essentially unexplored frequency bands (486-580 GHz and at 119 GHz) with an unsurpassed sensitivity and spatial resolution.

The aeronomy mission of the payload

contains a spectrograph, named OSIRIS (optical spectrograph and infrared imaging system). OSIRIS has provided simultaneous observations in two channels; a UV/Visible channel with a passband of 280–800 nm, and an IR channel with a total passband of 30 nm, centered on 1.27 microns.

Odin was built as three-axis stabilized satellite, capable of switching between astronomy and aeronomy modes. It can be focused on astronomical targets for hours with an accuracy of 15 arc seconds, or it can scan the limb of the earth's atmosphere at various speeds between 10 and 120 km (6.21 and 75 mi) altitudes, 40 times per orbit, with a reconstructed accuracy of 1.2 arc minutes. The entire satellite points towards the targets.

Odin was placed into a 600 km (373 mi) sun-synchronous, terminator orbit by a Russian START-1 rocket on February 2001.

Munin was launched in November 2000, as a student project to collect data on the auroral activity on both the northern and southern hemispheres. It was named after one of the God Odin's ravens in Nordic mythology,

"The ravens Munin and Hugin flew out and brought back news from every corner of the world. Sitting on the God Odin's shoulders, they whispered all the news in his ears. Munin represented the memory and Hugin the intelligence ... and they were his embodied soul...."

The scientific objective of Munin is to collect data on the auroral activity on both the northern and southern hemispheres, so that a global picture of the current state of activity can be made available on-line. The data acquired by Munin will then serve as an aid to the prediction of space weather.

The satellite has a passive attitude control system, using a magnet and oscillation dampers. Silicon solar cells and a Li-Ion battery provide the needed power. The satellite uses the UHF-band for the up- and downlink to the ground station located at the institute in Kiruna. Digital signal processors perform instrument control, data compression and telemetry formatting, while serving as a software modem.

TAIWAN (REPUBLIC OF CHINA)

National Space Program Office, Taiwan

The National Space Program Office was established in the Republic of China (informally known as Taiwan) in 1990 for the purpose of exploring and developing space technology. Prior to this, the nation had a poor foundation in space science and technology; therefore, the primary objectives in establishing the Space Program Office were to form the basic framework and technology for space systems, and to utilize this foundation in implementing various types of space missions.

These missions have thus far entailed applying space technology in the areas of basic science, communications, environmental pro-

tection, resource exploration, transportation, agriculture, fisheries and coastal protection; and have lead to the establishment of a space industry producing satellite components, ground satellite communications systems and satellite data applications. These technologies have included systems integration, large project management and quality assurance and reliability, and have been transferred to the industrial sector in an effort to upgrade industries.

In the early 1990s, the ROC adopted a long-range plan for acquiring technologies related to developing and operating spacecraft. The National Space Program Office was subsequently established to oversee a 15-year program which envisioned the launch of three LEO spacecraft with foreign assistance.

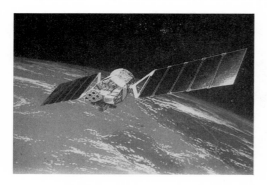

The first NSPO satellite mission named ROC-SAT-1 was initiated in 1994 as a means to build Taiwan's space program infrastructure. The ROCSAT-1 satellite was successfully launched on January 27, 1999, to carry out three scientific research missions: ocean color imaging, experiments on ionospheric plasma and electrodynamics, and Ka-band (20–30 GHz) communications experiments. (National Space Program Office, Taiwan)

ROCSAT-1 satellite ready for launch. (National Space Program Office, Taiwan)

ROCSAT-1 (i.e., Republic of China Satellite 1) is a low-earth orbiting satellite jointly developed by TRW of the United States with a resident team of NSPO engineers. It was launched on January 27, 1999, into an orbit of 600 kilometers altitude and 35 degrees inclination. ROCSAT-1 was devised to carry out three scientific research missions — ocean color imaging, experiments on ionospheric plasma and electrodynamics, and experiments using Ka-band (20–30 GHz) communication payloads.

With the ROCSAT-1 project, NSPO aimed to build the infrastructure for the space program in Taiwan and to gain experience for space systems engineering. Because the focal point of the ROCSAT-1 program has been developing a spacecraft bus, NSPO dispatched a team of engineers to join the development effort at TRW. Through on-site training, NSPO engineers have learned to independently design, manufacture, assemble, and test spacecraft bus.

The ROCSAT-1 craft has a weight of 395 kg (871 lb) with a hexahedron shape, and was placed in a circular earth orbit with an altitude of 600 km (373 mi) and an inclination of 35 degrees. The ROCSAT-1 has a two year mission life with a design life of four years.

The ROCSAT-1 has five spacecraft components: an onboard computer, a remote interface unit, an S-band antenna, a filter/diplexer, and a solar array panel assembly. There are three onboard payload instruments — the ocean color imager (OCI), the ionosphere plasma and electrodynamics instrument (IPEI), and the experimental communications payload (ECP).

Three science teams consisting of faculties and researchers from major national universities have taken the lead to analyze the ROCSAT-1 experimental data. Through September 2001, the OCI science team at National Taiwan Ocean University has processed more than 7,000 OCI images, which have been utilized for oceanography studies by institutions around the world. More then twenty organizations in Taiwan have applied for OCI image data. In addition, the OCI 865nm channel data have been analyzed by the science team to deduce the aerosol optical depth, a measure of the number of particles in the air, during the dust storm season from March to May in China. The OCI science team has used the OCI data to publish numerous articles about atmospheric correction algorithms, the OCI radiometric characterization, and features of ocean color and aerosol optical depth around Taiwan.

The IPEI science team at National Central University has been examining the ROCSAT-1 observations of equatorial anomaly and plasma bubbles over Taiwan and its equatorial neighborhood. They also used the IPEI measurements to study mid-latitude ionospheric density irregularities during magnetic disturbances. The coincident observations of large ion depletion events by ROCSAT-1 and DMPS satellites together with Millstone Hill ISR ground radar have been analyzed to investigate space weather effects during major magnetic storms.

Amazingly, the IPEI instrument has detected an ionospheric density hole above Brazil during the Bastille Day event, the biggest magnetic storm event which happened on July 14, 2000. During this event, an extensive two-dimensional profile of ionospheric density hole has been measured in situ for the first time by a satellite. The IPEI science team has also collaborated with the MU radar of Japan, ISR of Peru and U.S. Air force Geo-

One of the two NSPO Telemetry Track and Command stations is located at Tainan, ROC. This station provides the RF links between the remote ground system and satellites via S-band. The station receives ROCSAT-1 data six times a day. (National Space Program Office, Taiwan)

physical Laboratory to perform radio beacon and ionospheric experiments.

Three Ka-band communication experiments using the ROCSAT-1 experimental communication payload (ECP) have been conducted. The first experiment conducted by the science team of National Tsing Hua University was directly broadcasting digital television signals via ROCSAT-1. The science team of National Cheng Kung University has employed the transportable and fixed ground terminals to transmit video and audio signals to ECP for direct broadcast experiments, and to receive 19.5 GHz beacon signals from ECP for propagation experiments.

Finally the science team of National Central University has conducted an experiment to measure the propagation of Ka-band signals and their rain attenuation effects in Taiwan. The main objective was to investigate satellite-signal characteristics at Ka-band over Taiwan area. This experiment would be used to determine various attenuation effects of Ka-band propagation due to rain particles, clouds, water vapor content, melting hydrometers, and atmospheric refractivity fluctuations.

The ROCSAT-2 program involves the use of a satellite for earth remote sensing and for observing upper atmospheric lightening. The remote sensing mission will take satellite-imaging data for fulfilling Taiwan civilian needs. The land images could be used to monitor the environment and resource throughout Taiwan, the offshore remote islands, Taiwan Strait, and its surrounding ocean. Under international cooperation agreements, ROCSAT-2 may obtain earth environment images over other regions.

The phenomenon of upper atmospheric lightening will be investigated using an imager, which will be the first scientific instrument to observe the phenomenon from a satellite. This can be particularly useful since Taiwan is an island prone to natural disasters brought on by typhoons during the summer months. Therefore, timely availability of remote sensing data is critical for Taiwan in the aftermath of these disasters.

NSPO is developing an Image Processing System (IPS), an integrated hardware and software system that provides full capabilities for the reception, archival, cataloging, user

The ka-band antenna located at National Chung Kuang University is the ground segment for ECP on-board ROCSAT-1. (National Space Program Office, Taiwan)

The ROCSAT-2 program is to develop a satellite for earth remote sensing and for observing upper atmospheric lighting. The remote sensing mission is to take satellite-imaging data for fulfilling ROC civilian needs. The land images could be used to monitor the environment and resources throughout Taiwan, the offshore remote islands, Taiwan Strait, and its surrounding ocean. Under international cooperations agreements, ROCSAT-2 may obtain earth environment images over other regions. The phenomenon of upper atmospheric lighting will be investigated using an imager, which will be the first scientific instrument to obeserve the phenomenon from satellite. (National Space Program Office, Taiwan)

query, and processing of remote sensing image data. IPS will receive the remote sensing image data from NSPO's X-band antenna system (XAS), which could receive downlink data from ROCSAT-2 at a high rate up to 320 Mbps. IPS will include four subsystems — data ingestion subsystem, data management subsystem, data processing subsystem, and planning and scheduling subsystem.

The ROCSAT-2 spacecraft and its remote sensing instrument are currently being built by the prime contractor Astrium Company of France. Astrium has developed a spacecraft bus named LEOSTAR 500 XO for small satellites from which the ROCSAT-2 platform is derived. NSPO is developing the upper atmospheric lightening imager through a joint collaboration program with University of California at Berkeley, Tohoku University in Japan, and National Cheng Kung University. NSPO will integrate and test the satellite system after developed.

NSPO is responsible for designing, analyzing, manufacturing, and testing the satellite primary structure. So far the design and analysis tasks have been completed. A joint team of two local companies, Taiwan Aerospace Cooperation and Aerospace Industrial Development Corporation, have been manufacturing the hardware. The completed structure will be tested at NSPO facilities. By producing the ROCSAT-2 thermal control sub-system, NSPO is advancing all the core technologies in satellite thermal design, thermal analysis, thermal hardware manufacturing, and thermal testing. In the development of ROCSAT-2 electrical subsystems, NSPO engineers have assisted Astrium in reviewing and testing the design.

ROCSAT-2 has a weight of 764 kg (1,684 lb) including payload and fuel. It is of a hexahedron shape, and will orbit at an altitude of 891 km (554 mi) in sun-synchronization. The ROCSAT-2 will have a mission life of five years and is scheduled for launch in 2003.

The ROCSAT-3/COSMIC spacecraft consists of six LEO micro-satellites, of which each comprises a spacecraft bus integrated with payload instruments. Each micro-satellite carries an advanced version of the JPL-developed GPS receiver (Gox), which will measure the propagation time of a radio signal from a GPS satellite to a ROCSAT-3/COSMIC satellite. When the radio signal passes obliquely through earth's atmosphere, the ROCSAT-3/COSMIC will measure the amount of radio occultation, which will be used to infer the density, temperature, and moisture of the atmosphere at various heights.

In addition to the GPS receiver, each ROCSAT-3/COSMIC spacecraft will carry two secondary instruments: a tiny ionosphere photometer (TIP) and a tri-band beacon (TBB) transmitter. These will provide two-dimensional measurements of electron density, an important aspect of the upper atmosphere. These readings will complement the primary GPS receiver so that three-dimensional fields of electron density between 90 and 750 km (56 and 466 mi) can be inferred.

When stowed for launch, each ROCSAT-3/COSMIC cylindrical spacecraft, roughly one meter in diameter by 25 centimeters (9.84 inches) deep, will weigh about 65 kilograms (142 lb) with payload and fuel. The spacecraft will be launched into a low earth orbit with an altitude of approximately 700 km (435 mi), and with an inclination ap-

A view of ROCSAT-2 model under construction. (National Space Program Office, Taiwan)

proximately 72 degrees. At deployment, the satellite's two hinged sides, each with solar panels, will extend outward. Orbit-raising maneuvers will be performed to place satellites into six prescribed orbital planes, which are separated by approximately 24 degrees in their longitudinal ascending nodes.

The ground segment consists of S-band antenna ground stations for both uplink and downlink. The main satellite control station will be located in Taiwan, and another two stations, mainly for data collections and command back-up, will be located in Fairbanks, Alaska, and Kirura, Sweden. A Republic of China analysis and archive center will be set up in the ROC central weather bureau, as a mirror site of COSMIC data analysis and archive center (CDAAC) in UCAR. Together they will deliver the processed data to users in near real-time for both researches and operational demonstration studies.

THAILAND

GEO-Informatics and Space Technology Development Agency (GISTDA), Thailand

Thailand inaugurated its first national GEO communications network between the years 1993 and 1994 with the launches of

Thaicom 1 on December 18, 1993, and Thaicom 2 on October 8, 1994, by Ariane boosters. The spacecraft, based on Hughes HS-376L series, are operated by the Shinawatra Satellite Company of Bangkok under a lease arrangement with the Thai government. Both Thaicom satellites are stationed at 78.5 degrees E with ten C-band and two Ku-band transponders. The 630 kg (1,388 lb) spacecraft have a design life of at least 13 years.

Thailand's Remote Sensing Center of the National Research Council of Thailand (NRCT) has been engaged in remote sensing technology and applications as the primary Landsat provider to local and international users since 1981. The Thailand Landsat Ground Station is located in the Lad Krabang district of Bangkok with its data acquisition radius covering 17 countries of South Asia and Southeast Asia.

NRCT, in cooperation with the National Space Development Agency of Japan, built a second ground receiving station in the same compound for regional data acquisition. The two tracking facilities currently acquire data from the remote sensing satellites such as Landsat, Spot, ERS, MOS, JERS-1, and IRS-1C.

As part of a governmental restructuring policy, Thailand Remote Sensing Center merged with the GIS division of the Ministry of Science, Technology and Environment (MOSTE) to form Thailand's new space agency, GEO-Informatics and Space Technology Development Agency (GISTDA).

GISTDA's mission is to provide remote sensing data and geo-informatics data to benefit the country of Thailand as a whole, and in addition, carry out the research and development in space technology and geo-informatics.

GISTDA's objectives include development of space technology and geo-informat-ics applications for the benefit of the general public; the development of a satellite database and a derived natural resources information center; providing data services relating to space technology and geo-informatics; providing technical services and developing human resources in satellite remote sensing and geo-informatics; and researching and developing other activities related to space technology, including the development of small satellites for a natural resources survey.

Applications for satellite data are in the areas of agriculture, forestry, environment, disaster, and urban planning. In agriculture, the satellite data received can be used to study plantation, particularly in cash crops such as annual and quarter-annual rice, palm oil, rubber, pineapple, manioc, sugar cane, maize, and sunflower. These data are pooled and classified for each type of cash crop and used to efficiently forecast and appraise the production, and also to study and trace the coastal agriculture. In the field of forestry, satellite data received can be used to study an entire forestry area and survey the change, particularly in rain forest and fertile land, or even deforestation. These data are pooled and employed as a plan to protect and to resurrect the forestation. Satellite data can be used to monitor both the environment and natural disasters such as landslides, floods and forest fires. It can also be used in urban planning, whether in provincial, regional or national studies of topography.

UKRAINE

National Space Agency of Ukraine (NSAU)

The National Space Agency of Ukraine (NSAU) was established in 1992, following the break-up of the Soviet Union. Once the Ukraine became an independent nation, it adopted its first state space program commencing in 1993.

As part of this new program, in 1995, a monumental cooperative venture was formed between Russia, the United States, and Norway. SDO Yuzhnoye and Yuzhny Machine-Building Plant became a central part of the internationally known Sea Launch project.

That same year, the launch of the first Ukrainian satellite, Sich-1, occurred from the Plesetsk Cosmodrome in Russia.

In 1996, the National Academy of Science of Ukraine — National Space Agency of Ukraine (NASU-NSAU) Space Research Institute was established. The Yevpatoria National Space Facilities Control and Test Center was also established.

1996 marked the adoption of the Law of Ukraine on Space Activities by Parliament.

In 1997, SDO Yuzhnoye along with its Russian partners began development of the Dnepr launch vehicle, which was based on the intercontinental ballistic missile RS-20 (or SS-18 "Satan" according to NATO classification).

Later that year, in November, Leonid Kadenuk became the first Ukrainian astronaut, joining Space Shuttle Mission STS-87.

NSAU has continued to be involved in a number of pinnacle space activities, including the Russian Zenit launcher, which was built in the Ukraine. In March 1999, the first test launch of Zenit-3SL was performed with a mockup satellite onboard. The launch vehicle's payload had been designed to simulate the mass properties of a 4,500 kg (9,900 lb) commercial spacecraft. A precise, controlled flight profile was executed by DemoSat, enabling one of the most highly instrumented test missions ever flown.

The vehicle's first commercial launch occurred in October 1999, carrying an American Direct TV-1R communications satellite. The 3,450 kg (7,600 lb) payload was successfully placed into Geosynchronous Transfer Orbit (GTO).

Several months earlier, in April 1999, the Dnipro launcher delivered the United Kingdom satellite UoSAT into orbit.

In July 1999, a Zenit-2 launched Okean-O, a Ukrainian-Russian satellite.

Dnipro achieved a record in September 2000, successfully delivering five small satellites into orbit, including SaudiSat-1A and SaudiSat-1B of Saudi Arabia, UniSat, MegSat of Italy, and TiungSat of Malaysia.

There have been a number of successes of the Sea Launch project in which the Ukraine has participated. On July 28, 2000, the 3,659 kg (8,067 lb) PanAmSat, PAS-9 satellite communications satellite was launched into geosynchronous transfer orbit (GTO). Less than two months following, the satellite supported the broadcast of the Summer 2000 Olympics.

On October 20, 2000, the 5,108 kg (5.108 ton) Thuraya-1 communications satellite was launched as the heaviest commercial payload. It was also placed into GTO to provide regional mobile telecommunications services to 99 countries in the Middle East, Europe, India, Africa, and Central Asia.

The XM-2/Rock satellite was launched on March 18, 2001, and is the most powerful commercial communications satellite in orbit. The 4,666 kg (4.67 ton) satellite remains one of two spacecraft to transit state-of-the-art digital audio radio programming directly to cars, homes, and portable radios throughout the continental United States.

On May 8, 2001, the XM-1/Roll, companion twin spacecraft to Rock, was launched, to complete the Rock and Roll constellation for XM Satellite Radio. The XM-1/Roll weighs 4,672 kg (4.672 tons).

Earth Remote Sensing

Earth remote sensing is one of the primary objectives for the National Space Agency of Ukraine. A critical aspect of this program area has been the development of the Ukrainian space program's earth monitoring space system, Sich. The Sich project has been coordinated to perform earth data reception in optical and radio-frequency bands of electromagnetic range from sensors, for placement on airspace carriers.

The creation of a DSE (distant scanning of the earth) closed-loop system for Sich consists of space and ground segments, as well as program-technical facilities for airspace data processing and thematic analysis, to provide data acquisition independence for the Ukraine, while fostering the continued development of space technologies.

As a part of the Sich program, the successful launches of spacecrafts DSE Sich-1 on August 31, 1995, and Ocean-0 on July 17, 1999, became the first and second stages of the earth monitoring space system.

NSAU has also encouraged international cooperation on the Sich program due to limited financial ability. This cooperation has been instituted in conjunction with the Committee of the Earth Observation from Satellites (CEOS) with the principles of free distribution of data concerning solution of operative tasks on hydrometeorology, breakdown situations, and the commercial usage of high-recognition ability data for the solution of a wide range of tasks.

A stipulation of this international cooperation has been the utilization of foreign spacecraft over Ukraine territory, including that of NOAA, Meteosat, and TERRA, in the near future.

Sich has allowed the regular transmission of earth receiving data in different bans of electro-magnetic range due to regular spacecraft launches of micro-satellites such as DSE; an increase of the active exploitation term of spacecraft during orbit between five and seven years of guaranteed working lifetime; and the creation of research samples of spacecrafts and onboard equipment allowing for consideration of world progress in utilization.

Sich provides regular reception of DSE data in a variety of spectral ranges, since Sich spacecraft are launched to polar and gelio-synchronous orbits. Sich-1M spacecraft supply data reception in the optic, IR and SHF ranges, while Sich-2, double-utilization spacecraft, supply high-quality data reception in the optic range. In the future, development will expand to the radiolocation earth observation system, Sich-3.

In addition to Sich, other projects in earth remote sensing have included Project Environment, Project Monitoring, and Project Sounding.

Project Environment was created to develop a ground segment for the National Earth Observation space system, Sich, that will provide receiving in all bands of radio waves L, S, and X, with rates up to 128 Mbit/sec, as well as accumulation, front-end processing, and distribution of airspace information. The center has been designed to function on a 24-hour basis for reception, archiving, and operative data processing.

Project Monitoring was created to set up technical complexes and automated work places for airspace data processing and thematic analysis. Specifically, the program will create highly-effective workplaces of space data receiving and processing based on new technologies and provide space data users with these workplaces. It will also expand scientifically applied space data usage, while increasing the airspace DSE data export potential.

Between 1999 and 2001, Project Monitoring information was processed and distributed from several spacecraft including Ocean-0, Sich-1, Resource-01, NOAA, Spot, and ERS, with a total number of 1,131 snapshots for archiving by the Pyroda State Research and Production Center.

Project Sounding was created to provide scientific and methodic support to the Distant Scanning of the Earth (DSE) program, which requires complex, scientific, and systematic procedures, and the expansion of international cooperation in airspace data for scientifically applied usage.

Under this project, outgoing data for elaboration of technical tasks for new and modernized production is handled, as well as the coordination of international scientific applied programs for data usage resulting from the Sich system of spacecrafts.

Accomplishments achieved included the testing of the Ocean-0 spacecraft prior to its launch in 1999; the release of the second edition of the atlas Ukraine from Space, comprised of decoded snapshots of Ukraine territory obtained from the Sich spacecraft; and a program of scientific experiments conducted during the mission of Ocean-0.

Space Scientific Research

Space scientific research at NSAU encompasses a number of projects. The Koronas-F project is a goal to develop a scientific program in which Ukrainian institutions participate in the processing and interpretation of data received from ground network and Koronas-F spacecraft. These spacecraft are a part of the structuring of a Difos airborne specialized photometer.

Koronas-F is an international project

supported by utilization of the Ukraine's space platform and Cyclone LV spacecraft's scientific equipment system. It is intended for research of atomic and collective (plasma and hydromagnetic) processes proceeding in active sun, and is also based on complex measuring in wide range of electromagnetic waves, which vary from gamma to radio-frequency regions, and for the measuring of streams of electrons, protons, neutrons and solar origin nuclei.

The project's scientific objectives include the exploration of transfer of energy from the sun's interior to its surface; energy storage in upper atmosphere and its liberation during solar non-stationary phenomena; research of powerful dynamic processes of the active sun (sun-spots, solar flares, plasma emissions); the study of characteristics of solar cosmic rays speeded up in solar flare processes and other active phenomena, their emergence condition, dissemination in interplanetary magnetic field and influence on the earth's magnetosphere; and the study of the sun's interior seismology based on global rippling observation.

The Koronas-F project requires the utilization of devices which enable it to register solar electromagnetic radiation in whole frequency range varying from radio waves to X and gamma radiation. This experiment will allow for the study of high-energy electromagnetic radiation characteristics that were observed by Russian GAMMA-1 and American SMM and GRO COMPTON satellites for some solar flares.

The Difos airborne specialized photometer, determined for measuring in three wave ranges — 550 nanometers, 750 nanometers with pass band of 100 nanometers, and also 400–1100 nanometers — was developed. Countries that have participated include Russia, Ukraine, Germany, France, Great Britain, the United States, Georgia, and Poland.

The Poperedzhennya project has focused on conducting comprehensive experiments to study the fundamental processes in earth's ionosphere and magnetosphere, with the aim of searching for precursors of natural disasters including earthquakes of high magnitude.

The primary scientific objective of the project has been to perform detailed measuring of ionosphere plasma parameters from spacecraft as a method of obtaining synchronous data of ground observations, with special emphasis on the seismic, while developing complex formulas on the interconnection of seismic processes and ionospheric phenomena.

The Ukraine had been working in cooperation with Russia, Hungary, Poland, the United States, and the Czech Republic on this project, which has been temporarily suspended.

The Interball Project began in the 1970s with the aim of studying solar-terrestrial relationships and the interaction of separate earth magnetosphere areas; more specifically, the interaction between solar wind and the earth's magnetosphere.

The project has also covered the study of physical properties, their dynamics and processes of transfer of power, mass and impulse from outside to inside; and the study of active processes in magnetic power tubes of polar and auroral zones and their influence on earth's atmosphere and auroras.

The Interball project includes the use of two principal spacecrafts, or probes, and two sub-satellites, to create a tetra-system on orbits of different altitude. For Interball-1, the tail probe's orbit was chosen to provide accurate measurements of the magnetospheric tail up to 30 earth radiuses, or 193,000 km (119,930 mi), as well as in the solar wind and near the magnetospheric boundary from sun side. The tail probe was launched into orbit on August 3, 1995, from the Russian Plesetsk Cosmodrome.

The spacecraft was stabilized in space by a circulating round axis which was directed towards the sun within a time interval of approximately two minutes. During a short distance, it was accompanied by the Czech Magion-4 sub-satellite, allowing for simultaneous measurement and the provision of spatial and time changes of measured parameters. The maximum distance between the sub-satellite Czech-Magion 4 and the satellite Interball-1 was 100 km (62 mi).

The auroral probe, Interball-2, was placed in orbit 20,000 km (12,428 mi) from earth. It was designated for the exploration of processes in the polar cap and auroral zones in coordination with the tail probe, Interball-1. Interball-2 was launched on August 29, 1996, with a distance to its Czech accompanying satellite, Magion-5, of 1,000 km (621 mi).

In October 2000, the tail probe, Interball-1, entered the atmosphere, ending the mission. The auroral probe has continued to operate and perform measurements.

The International Space Station project has been implemented in cooperation with several counties, including the United States, Russia, Japan, Canada, Brazil, and various members of the European Space Agency, including, Italy, Denmark, Norway, Belgium, the Netherlands, France, Spain, Germany, Sweden, and Switzerland.

ISS is being constructed as a large scientific laboratory in space for conducting research. The Ukraine has been limited in its participation by scientific, technical and economic constraints, and has therefore formed direct cooperation agreements with Russia and the United States, without becoming an official partner. As part of this agreement, the Ukraine will be able to perform scientific and technological experiments onboard ISS.

NSAU has been granted full membership in the international strategic group for planning of space experiments in the field of life sciences. It will also observe the work of the international strategic group for planning of space experiments in the field of microgravitational sciences.

The Ukrainian research program onboard of the International Space Station (ISS) will encompass scientific and technological research between the National Space Agency of Ukraine and the National Academy of Sciences. This research will cover the fields of space biology, biotechnology, and medicine.

Ukrainian research units onboard the ISS will include a biolaboratory to perform biological experiments in conjunction with the Kholodniy's Botanical Institute of the NASU; a greenhouse for conducting research on plants under space conditions, again with the Kholodniy Institute; a zoomodule, for conducting research on the influence of spaceflight factors and their effects on organisms' functioning and aging; and a biomedcontrol area for experiments on the medical monitoring of astronauts and the biological control of the ISS environment, in conjunction with the Gerontology Institute of the AMSU (Academy of Medical Sciences of Ukraine).

Other experiments onboard ISS conducted by the Ukraine will cover the areas of space technology and the science of materials. These will include material experiments on the creation of new materials and technologies and their production onboard the ISS with the Frantecevich Institute of Science of Materials and the Paton Electric Welding Institute; degradation, for the investigation of the degradation process of materials in space with the Frantcevich Institute of Science of Materials; and diagnostics, for the diagnostics of the space station's frames in conjunction with the Paton Electric Welding Institute.

In addition, the study of physiochemical processes under microgravity conditions will be performed in the Penta-Complex, focusing on the influence of microgravity on physiochemical processes in fluidic environment, with the Verkina Physicotechnical Institute of Low Temperatures of the NASU; and morphosis, to conduct research on the crystallization of materials and composites under conditions of microgravity with the Kurdjumov's Metalophysics Institute.

Astrophysics and extraterrestrial astronomy experiments will be performed in the Konkurs unit, where research will be conducted on the fundamental processes of the sun using a sun-oriented telescope at the main astronomic observatory of NASU, and the sun's oscillation exploration at the Crimea Astrophysics Observatory.

Earth and near-space exploration studies will be performed on the following units: Inframon, to monitor the earth's upper atmosphere with the main astronomic observatory of NASU; Prostir, to monitor the earth's ionosphere with the Radioastronomic Institute of NASU; Poverhnja, to perform earth and ocean remote sensing with the Institute of Geological Sciences of NASU; and Otochennja, for exploration of gaseous and plasma medium around the ISS using contact methods, with the Institute of Technical Mechanics of NASU.

The Russian-Ukrainian project Interball-Prognoz focuses on developing a system to monitor and forecast space weather and to find the cause-and-effect relationships in an interplanetary environment, particularly solar wind, the magnetosphere, and ionosphere of earth.

Interball-Prognoz includes use of a high-apogee satellite and a group of three low-orbiting spacecraft.

The Spektr-UF project has been established with the goal of building an international space observatory that will be able to receive direct images and spectrum of point and spatial objects, chemical composition and structure of stellar atmospheres, physical conditions and movement of weak stars, as well as distant stellar systems.

The Crimean Astrophysical Observatory will develop the unique T-170 telescope with a diameter of 1.7 meters (5.6 feet) for astrophysical observations of Spectr spacecraft in the 110-150 nanometer wave range. The observatory will be equipped with this telescope, a receiving equipment system consisting of spectrometers of different resolution, a spectropolarimeter, and a direct image camera in the 120–350 nanometer spectral range sections. The direct image camera will be very effective for the study of physical properties of different space objects — stars, quasars, galaxies, and interstellar material, which are impossible for observation from the earth's surface because they are fully absorbed by the earth's atmosphere.

The Variant Project will focus on the exploration of the ionosphere's reaction to influence from the magnetosphere and solar wind (from above), as well as from earth (from below). It will include the direct measurement of electric current and electromagnetic field distri-bution in ionosphere plasma; creation of a database on the solar-terrestrial relationship; and the statistical examination of faint display of ionosphere seismic effects and their selection by ionospheric perturbation of heliophysical nature.

Scientific goals of the project include the exploration of global distribution of longitudinal electric currents in polar ionosphere; structure of large-scaled electric fields and convective moves of ionospheric plasma; the comparison of satellite explorations and ionosphere remote sensing data obtained by radars of Super DARN system; the research of wave processes in polar cusp plasma; the registration of ionospheric phenomena caused by seismic and volcanic activity, and the research of anthropogenic factors' influence on ionosphere; the exploration of interaction of subsonic waves and ionosphere plasma with combined experiments with ground acoustic waves source; and active experiments on ionospheric plasma parameters modification by using powerful radiation of airborne radar.

Although previous satellite experiments such as Bulgaria-1300, S33, GEOTAIL, FAST, and Interball have studied these areas, a number of questions still remain unanswered. These questions focus on the division of currents on the day surface of the auroral ionosphere, the electrodynamic processes in polar cusp plasma highly disturbed by the influence of particles and solar wind fields, and the spatial pattern of ionospheric convection, which also depends on orientation and size of interplanetary magnetic field.

The project will also run electromagnetic experiments onboard Sich remote sensing satellites.

UNITED KINGDOM

British National Space Center (BNSC)

The British National Space Center (BNSC) was formed in 1985 to help Britain obtain the best scientific and economic value out of national and international activities in space. It is a voluntary partnership of government departments and research councils with an interest in the development or exploitation of space technologies.

The BNSC is also a founding member of the European Space Agency (ESA), with nearly 60 percent of the U.K.'s civil space expenditure put into ESA ventures.

The BNSC has centered its activities in areas with the highest comercial potential. These include earth observation, satellite communications and navigation. Other projects encompass space science in the hopes that its pursuit will lead to scientific, environmental, and economic advances in the future.

Satellite Navigation and Communications

The United Kingdom will play an active role in the development of Galileo, the new European civilian satellite navigation system.

The ESA's Galileo will provide continuous service with navigation signals for life safety applications such as air traffic control, road, rail and maritime navigation. It will also assist in search and rescue operations and ambulance tracking for major incident control. Galileo will become operational in 2008.

Telecommunications and broadcasting have been the most profitable applications of space technology in the U.K. The sector represents 78 percent of all U.K. space industry turnover.

The BNSC's SATCOM program has been helping U.K. companies develop innovative technology and applications to better compete in an increasingly electronic and mobile environment.

The BNSC has also contributed to ESA's advanced research in telecommunications systems (Artes) program.

The Artes 3 program assists small and medium-sized companies in bringing innovative satellite-based concepts to market, while focusing on multimedia and information infrastructures.

BNSC has also supported ESA's Artes 1 program, covering basic studies and investigations, as well as the Artes 4 program, an ESA and industry telecoms partnership.

U.K. companies ESYS Ltd. and Ortivus Ltd. provide ambulance monitoring systems in remote areas using satellite technology through the Artes 3 program.

Mobimed is a mobile patient information and monitoring system which uses radio or GSM cellular technology to relay vital information about the patient being transported in an ambulance to the hospital. This enables specialists to monitor the condition of the patient and advise appropriate action.

In remote areas of the U.K. without full GSM or radio coverage, ESYS Ltd. devised the SECOM (satellite enhanced coverage of mobimed) system. SECOM allows the unit to switch automatically to a GlobalStar Satellite phone once leaving an area of GSM coverage.

In 2001, testing of the combined GSM and GlobalStar operation of Mobimed was successfully completed. The system is now being installed on ambulances in Wales.

New Technology

British scientists and engineers have been continuing to work together in an effort to make space technology more cost effective and help to transfer these technologies to other industries.

Through the BNSC's National Technology Program, advances have been made in telecommunications satellites, satellite power systems, and the software used in satellites for controlling them from the ground.

As a part of the National Technology Program, AEA Technology developed the original lithium-ion battery technology that is now mass-produced for use in Japanese camcorders. AEA also used the Japanese batteries in spacecraft where high capacity and reduced size is vital for power supplies.

The U.K. company Logica developed the fault-tolerant onboard software for ESA's Huygens probe as well as the supporting avionics systems used to communicate between Huygens and NASA's Cassini mission to Saturn. Logica has continued to support the mission by providing training and fault investigation services to the European operations team.

The Bristol-based Science Systems Ltd. has been developing software for satellite ground control and data processing stations, specifically ESA missions.

Surrey Satellite Technology Ltd. (SSTL)

has specialized in the development of tiny satellite technology. The company's first nano-satellite, SNAP-1, was launched in 2001, and weighed only six kg (13.2 lb).

SNAP-1 was equipped with a GPS (global positioning system) which was developed in the U.K. The system allows for the inspection of other spacecraft in orbit. The satellite's tiny space GPS receiver will also be used on the Enterprise module of the International Space Station (ISS).

In the future, BNSC's National Technology Program plans to implement a satellite subsystem based on micro and nano technology (MNT) which will be cheaper to launch, and can be used in large numbers to create a swarm effect and broaden observational uses.

BNSC has been funding facilities at Rutherford Appleton Laboratory (RAL) in Oxford, which manufactures and tests MNT devices.

Earth Observation

The BNSC has been heavily involved in Envisat, the European Space Agency's earth observation satelite which was launched March 1, 2002. Envisat has been performing a check of global health by providing vital information about global warming, climate change, and the depletion of the ozone layer. It is the world's largest and most advanced earth observation satellite.

The U.K. government invested nearly $600 million into the Envisat program. One of the ten main instruments onboard the satellite, the advanced along track scanning radiometer (AATSR), was funded and developed by the U.K.

Twelve U.K. firms participated in the design and construction of Envisat, with Astrium UK serving as the prime contractor.

In addition to providing new observations of our land, atmosphere, ice caps and oceans, Envisat will complete a 15-year dataset of much-needed observations of our changing environment.

The satellite will monitor the oceans, ice caps, vegetation, and the atmosphere, taking just 100 minutes to circle the earth.

Through regular observations, Envisat

will enable scientists to detect minute changes occuring on earth, which will provide support to future environmental policies. The U.K. also has strong participation in ESA's earth explorer program consisting of two types of missions — core and opportunity. Core missions will directly respond to scientific issues which have been brought up as areas of public concern.

The first mission will be GOCE (gravity field and steady-state ocean circulation mission) to study the earth's gravity field and ocean circulation. GOCE has been scheduled for launch in early 2005.

The first opportunity mission, Cryosat, will be led by the U.K. and is scheduled for launch in 2004.

Cryosat will determine variations in the thickness of the earth's continental ice sheets and marine ice cover. The primary objective of the mission will be to test whether sea ice is thinning due to global warming by providing climate researchers with data that has previously never been obtained from these uninhabited regions. A highly sensitive indicator of climate change globally has been alterations in sea ice thickness.

To continue the emphasis on British strength in earth observation, the BNSC established the Newton (new technologies for observational needs) program. This program will also maximize the economic benefits gained from the development of earth observation technology, while fostering partnerships between engineers and scientists in the U.K. space sector as well as internationally.

ENVISAT

Envisat was launched on February 28, 2002, by ESA and is the world's most advanced earth observation satellite. It is intended to give scientists a crucial understanding of global warming, depletion of the ozone layer, and environmental change.

U.K. and European scientists and engineers worked together on Envisat with a heavy investment from the U.K. government.

Envisat continues to orbit the earth every 100 minutes, monitoring the oceans, ice caps, vegetation, and the atmosphere on its journey.

By the conclusion of March 2002, Envisat had already begun sending back its first images. At the same time, ESA began to test the onboard instruments and the processes used to transmit data back to earth.

A crucial instrument, the medium resolution imaging spectrometer (MERIS) which was designed to observe ocean color, is capable of measuring the concentration of phytoplankton and detecting chlorophyll concentrations of less than 1/10,000,000 of a gram per liter.

Envisat's first MERIS observation clearly revealed an extensive phytoplankton patch on the Mauritanian coast of West Africa. A study in this area showed that northeast trade winds bring deep and nutrient-rich water up to the surface, feeding phytoplankton in a process referred to as upwelling. The intensity of the upwelling is directly affected by changes in climate, signifying dramatic consequences for marine ecosystems, fisheries and the local economy, all of which will be continuously monitored by MERIS.

Other intial images returned by Envisat included those of the Antarctic Peninsula, where ice shelves can reach a thickness of 300 meters (990 feet) along the 1000 kilometer (600 mile) stretch. The onboard advanced synthetic aperture radar (ASAR) was designed to observe these ice shelves. Observation of this area is crucial as the Antarctic Peninsular has experienced extensive atmospheric warming over the last 50 years, causing an increase in temperature by an average of 2.5°C.

Thirteen U.K. companies made key contributions to the development and construction of Envisat.

Astrium UK was Envisat's lead contractor, developing a radar to study waves, as well as a radiometer to measure sea temperatures.

Bae Systems developed eight infrared detectors used to measure air temperature, pressure and trace gases in the upper atmosphere.

CODASciSys plc. designed a simulator for testing flight procedures, onboard software updates and operator training.

COM DEV Europe Ltd. provided an ultra-high strength amplifier for output of infrared detectors.

ESYS plc. has been contracted to help bring Envisat's data to end users.

Infoterra developed the Envisat archive facility and will also operate the U.K. Processing and Archive Facility.

Logica UK Ltd. designed the ground segment.

Marconi Applied Technologies supplied imaging components to collect data on atmospheric chemistry, the oceans, and land surfaces.

Nigel Press Associates will distribute data to end users.

QinetiQ has been involved in coordinating data distribution and processing, with an emphasis on advanced synthetic aperture radar (ASAR) data.

Rutherford Appleton Laboratory designed and developed the radiometer and will also coordinate promotion to end users.

SIRA Electro-Optics Ltd. delivered the electro-optical subsystems for the ozone monitoring instrument GOMOS, which will measure ozone concentration changes and provide data to as many as 360 ground-based stations.

Vega Space Systems provided technical management support for the satellite radiometer, and has also been responsible for electrical integration and testing of Envisat's payload.

MOSAIC

The MOSAIC (micro satellite applications in collaboration) is a small satellite program which was started by the BNSC in 2000. Its initial phase will continue through 2004, supporting three U.K. small satelite projects.

The BNSC developed the MOSAIC program based on the philosophy that small satellites can help to drive down the cost of access to space for government as well as commercial users.

The MOSAIC program has been implemented to encourage industry to invest in small satellite missions with special emphasis in satellite communications, the largest and most rapidly expanding market for space products.

The program was announced in December 1999, by U.K. Space Minister Lord Sainsbury and in July 2000, the winners of the first round of the MOSAIC funding were announced at a press conference held at Farnborough International Air Show. The three winners included TOPSAT, Disaster Monitoring Constellation (DMC), and GEMINI.

The TOPSAT mission is being conducted by QinetiQ, which was formerly the Defense Evaluation Research Agency (DERA). Top U.K. space scientists and engineers from QinetiQ are developing an innovative low-cost satellite system which will provide rapid delivery of highly detailed images of earth. This will be accomplished by providing relatively high-resolution imagery direct to the local user form a low-cost, small satellite.

The TOPSAT mission will consist of an advanced optical camera that can form images of the earth at 2.5 m (8.25 ft) resolution, integrated with a micro-satellite that can deliver this imagery direct to a mobile ground station.

The TOPSAT system will allow users to gain the practical experience of operating a small 120-kg (264-lb) imaging satellite and the ability to explore its applications in operational situations.

The satellite is expected to be operational from 2004. It will provide data for commerical and research purposes including forestry and habitat mapping, crop monitoring, environmental change, and disaster monitoring.

Unique and innovative aspects of TOPSAT's design will include off-axis optics developed under the U.K. science program, which will provide wide-field images without distortion or aberration. TOPSAT will also be designed with the latest in rapid-pointing technologies to allow time-delayed integration (TDI) imaging, which will be implemented by manuevering the entire platform.

The disaster monitoring constellation (DMC) is sponsored by Surrey Satellite Technology Ltd. (SSTL). The program was proposed on the basis that every year, natural and manmade disasters result in devastation around the world, causing loss of life, widespread human suffering, and devastating economic losses.

While existing satellites observing the earth may provide images of disaster areas, they are not best equipped to monitor such events. Images from these satellites can be infrequent, with the delivery of critical images taking months, due to periodic cloud cover and conflicting tasks that are performed by the satellite. Since the onboard instruments of these satellites are designed to meet many user requirements, these images are also expensive to generate.

SSTL, in conjunction with its partners, has proposed a network of micro-satellites to provide imaging on a daily basis while offering an affordable solution to the problem of disaster assessment and monitoring from space.

GEMINI is another program being administered by SSTL to develop a low cost small geostationary communication satellites to support a wide range of services such as telephone, television, and radio communications.

SSTL will utilize commercial off-the-shelf technologies as a means of achieving cost-effectiveness. The satellite will provide a modest number of channels while ensuring a wide range of services which have been tradionally offered by satellites in geostationary orbit. GEMINI will offer these services at a significantly lower price, making them affordable to developing nations.

Space Science

The U.K. has funds allocated to ESA and other international space science missions through the Particle Physics and Astronomy Research Council (PPARC).

Three of the eleven instruments carried by each of the four identical satellites making up the ESA Cluster mission to study the sun's effects on the earth were led by British research teams. The U.K. also operates the Cluster Science Operations Center.

Cluster sent back significant data in November 2001, when matter ejected from the sun collided with the earth's magnetic field, exposing the Cluster satellites to the full blast of the supersonic wind. Cluster's onboard instruments recorded the effects of the blast on the boundary of the magnetic field, the magnetopause. These results will aid in the prediciton of how such dramatic changes could affect the earth in the future.

ESA's XMM-Newton spacecraft, the

most sensitive X-ray observatory ever to fly in space, yielded exciting results while observing a spiral galaxy 100 million light years from earth. It found that its central black hole seemed to be allowing energy to escape, rather than pulling all the energy into it as anticipated.

An international team of astronomers found an extremely powerful X-ray emission from the galactic center, which they theorized must have been energy escaping from the black hole.

Another ESA probe, Huygens, carried by the Cassini spacecraft, has continued on its seven-year journey to Saturn where it is expected to arrive in 2004. It will then investigate the planet's rings as well as its magnetosphere and smaller icy moon.

When Huygens lands on the surface of Saturn's moon, Titan, it will utilize U.K. flight software, including the decent systems and parachutes.

U.K. scientists contributed to eight of the 18 instruments on Huygens and Cassini.

In December 2003, the U.K.-built Beagle 2 lander will become the next craft to land on Mars, as part of ESA's Mars Express Mission.

Beagle 2 will explore the possibility of whether conditions for life on Mars exist, or have ever existed. The lander was developed by an academic-industry team in the U.K. led by the Open University and Astrium plc.

BNSC has also provided the heliospheric imager instrument for NASA's small explorer mission, the Solar Terrestrial Relations Observatory (STEREO).

STEREO will consist of two spacecraft to observe the coronal mass ejections, eruptions on the sun that eject matter into space, and the resulting interaction of that matter with the earth.

In August 2005, Solar-B, a joint U.K./U.S./Japan mission, will be launched. Solar-B is a solar optical telescope that will be placed into sun-synchronous orbit an an altitude of 600 km (360 mi) which will allow for long-term viewing for eight months each year (short eclipses will limit viewing for four months of the year).

The probe will help to provide an understanding of the relationship between the solar photosphere, the thick glowing gas which represents the surface of the sun; and the corona, the thinner gas that extends millions of kilometers into space. The U.K. has been constructing several components for Solar-B's imaging spectrometer.

The U.K. has also played an active role in the long-term planning of the future of space exploration under ESA's Aurora Program. Aurora has been targeted at examining how existing technologies should be furthered to fill gaps in Europe's expertise, while setting realistic technological goals for the next 30 years of space exploration.

The Aurora program will include the development of autonomous, intelligent robots to return samples to earth from Mars and asteroids. Its longer-term objective will be to investigate possibilities for human exploration of the solar system.

Life and Physical Sciences

BNSC actively participates in ESA's microgravity program, EMIR-2X, which focuses on the study of several processes in the life and physical sciences by removing the effects of the gravitational pull felt on earth.

While the U.K. has not taken part in experiments that have been performed on the International Space Station, it has independently researched the weightless environment of space.

U.K. scientists have also performed studies of the thermophysical properties of metals, with particular emphasis on molten. Results from these experiments could further development in the casting of components that are either very large, made up of unusual alloys or made with unusual properties.

BNSC will also participate in a new microgravity program, ELIPS (European program for life and physical sciences) and applications onboard the International Space Station. This program was approved at ESA's Ministerial Council, held in Edinburgh in November 2001.

The primary objective of ELIPS will be to maximize the benefits to society that can be gained from using ISS, while setting up a framework for European activity in micro-gravity experiments.

Near Earth Objects

Near earth objects (NEO) applies to asteroids and comets whose orbits bring them close to earth. NEOs become potentially hazardous when they come within 0.05 AU (7.5 million kilometers or 4,500,000 miles, equivalent to 20 times the distance between the earth and the moon) of the earth, and when they are at least 150 meters (495 feet) in diameter. Although there are many asteroids and comets in the solar system, only a small percentage are considered to be NEOs.

Recently, 443 potentially hazardous asteroids were spotted, although more are being discovered. There are also nearly 1,000 near earth asteroids greater than one kilometer (0.6 mi) in diameter, and 100,000 with diameters larger than 100 meters (330 feet).

Small NEOs enter our atmosphere frequently, but the earth's atmosphere provides protection causing them to burn up or explode at high altitudes.

Larger NEOs strike from once a century to once every ten thousand years, depending upon their size.

Impacts can cause blast waves and injection of dust into the atmosphere as well as tsunamis and electromagnetic changes in the atmosphere.

The U.K. has been taking the risk to life and property from NEOs very seriously. It has a strong track record in astronomy and sky surveys which can contribute to international efforts to study NEOs. U.K. industry also produces key technologies, such as imaging chips, whch are necessary in examining NEOs.

In 2000, the U.K. started a Near Earth Objects Task Force which prepared a report on how the U.K. could best contribute to an international effort on NEOs.

As a result of the report, several actions were identified by the U.K. These included a review of how U.K. telescope facilities can be utilized to identify and monitor potentially hazardous NEOs, which has been undertaken by the Particle Physics and Astronomy Research Council (PPARC); and the establish-ment of a new U.K. facility for the public and media at the National Space Science Center in Leicester, to provide information and education on NEOs.

The U.K. is leading a steering committee within the Global Science Forum of the Organization for Economic Cooperation and Development (OECD) to promote an international discussion and action forum on the potential threat from near earth objects.

The U.K. has also been working with fellow UN members in an effort to strengthen the international coordination of activities related to near earth objects, which was recommended by the Vienna Declaration of the Unispace III UN Space Conference.

Space Debris

BNSC has been very concerned with the proliferation of space debris. Currently, there are over 9,000 items of space debris orbiting the earth larger than 10 cm (3.93 in). In an effort to address this prevalence, BNSC has been working with international agencies to encourage industry leaders to consider how a spacecraft will de-orbit or re-orbit at the end of its useful life before another satellite is launched.

The term space debris applies to any man-made object in orbit around the earth that no longer serves a useful purpose. This applies to upper stages of launch vehicles, derelict spacecraft, and debris that has been released during spacecraft manuevers. Space debris results from spacecraft exploding or colliding, expent solid rocket motors, or small particle impacts.

Debris remaining in orbits below 600 km (373 mi) usually falls back to earth within ten years, while any debris left at 800 km (497 mi) can often stay there for decades or longer.

The BNSC has been concerned with space debris posing a threat to operational spacecraft by the increase in orbital population which has been predicted over the coming years. It is possible that an object with a mass of one g (0.0353 oz) which is traveling at a speed of eight kilometers (4.34 mi) can easily damage a satellite. Heavier objects can completely shatter a satellite, causing potentially huge revenue losses.

The BNSC has encouraged discussions on the issue at the United Nations, in an effort to standardize policy across all countries. It has also become an active member in the Inter-Agency Space Debris Co-ordination (IADC) group to help establish global agreements on the disposal of satellites.

In the U.K., companies which are involved in launching, operating or buying a launch for space objects are required to obtain a license. This licensing procedure requests that satellite operators demonstrate that they have considered how they will dispose of their satellite once it has reached the end of its operational life.

Other organizations in the U.K. have programs on space debris. The Astronauts Research Group at Southampton has an established research program on orbital debris which focuses on modeling activities and the development of software tools to assess debris impact and protection for orbiting systems. Studies conducted in the past have included constellation satellite systems, tether systems, and the International Space Station (ISS).

The Hypervelocity Impact Laboratory at the University of Kent has a two-stage light gas gun which has been used to study hypervelocity impact. The gun's speed ranges between one and seven and a half km s^{-1}, with projectiles between 100 microns and 4.3 mm (0.169 in) in diameter, which are typically glass, nylon, aluminum, and steel.

The gun is fired several times daily, with targets cooled at low temperatures and connected to power supplies or data-logging equipment during an impact.

QinetiQ's space debris group has been defining the current space debris environment and its long-term evolution. The group assesses collision risk to operational systems, such as satellite constellations, while developing new techniques for evaluating the long-term endurance of spacecraft and maximizing their protection from debris.

The Chilbolton Radar Facility is a ground-based facility for observing space objects at a modest cost. The facility consists of a 25-meter (82 ft) fully steerable radar dish operating at S band, which is located near Andover and managed by the Rutherford Appleton Laboratory.

Century Dynamics develops software used for modeling space debris and hypervelocity impact effects. The software, called AUTODYN, is used by NASA, ESA, and QinetiQ, as well as other agencies and contractors worldwide.

Century Dynamics also conducts research into numerical methods, fragmentation, and material modeling, and has been heavily involved in the design and analysis of the ISS shielding system.

U.K. Space Industry and Exports

The U.K. space industry encompasses several fields, including satellite communcations, hyperspectral radars, battery technologies, and electronic propulsion.

The U.K.'s endeavors in space began in 1957, with the successful launch of the Skylark sub-orbital rocket. Skylark became the world's longest continuously running launch program by 2000, with the number of launches reaching over 450.

In 1962, the first U.K. satellite was launched. Another launch of the British-built satellite, Prospero, followed in 1971 on the British Black Arrow rocket.

In 1974, Skynet 2B was launched, becoming the world's first operational military satellite and the first communcations satellite to be built outside the United States or USSR.

Today, the U.K.'s most important space sector is telecommunications and broadcasting, which together represent 78 percent of all U.K. space industry turnover.

U.K. companies remain very active in space activities, manufacturing their own satellites as well as their accompanying instruments, the controlling software, and data analysis systems to enhance data returned to earth.

The U.K. space industry also manufactures synthetic aperture radar instrumentation, innovative small satellites, and satellite software.

An example of this was ESA's earth observation satellite, Envisat, and its onboard instrument, ASAR, which was designed to monitor oil pollution and locate new submarine sources of oil, as well as measure waveheights and frequencies.

The British also contributed another instrument to Envisat, the AATSR instrument, to provide accurate measurements of global sea surface temperatures.

The U.K. has also been a world leader in the satellite communications industry. Astrium, the U.K./French/German company, has been the prime contractor for more than 50 communications satellites, including IN-TELSAT.

The UK has been active in developing commerical services from earth observation data, including the monitoring of crops under the common agricultural policy, to provide early warning of pollution from oil slicks and signal propagation for the mobile phone industry.

It is also interesting to note that U.K. insurance companies have begun to use remote sensing data for claim assessment purposes.

U.K. companies remain active in the development of microsatellites which are less than 50 kg (110 lb), helping to drive down the cost of access to space for government as well as commercial users. These systems have been exported within Europe and the United States as well as Africa, the far East, and South America.

U.K. companies have also supplied needed instruments and equipment to the International Space Station (ISS). The British firm Bede Scientific Instruments provided X-ray diffraction equipment for the space station. Polyflex Aerospace manufactured equipment for the automated transfer vehicle (ATV), and Raytheon Systems Ltd. will supply 95 DC-DC converters for Boeing's solid state power controller module in the ISS human research facility rack.

Beagle-2 Lander for Mars Express

Beagle-2, the lander for Mars Express, is an important British achievement that involved U.K. academics and industry, including the Open University, the University of Leicester, and the industrial prime contractor, Astrium Ltd.

More than 60 U.K. organizations participated in the development of the Mars Express lander. Astrium, Ltd. served as the prime contractor, providing mechanical systems such as the lander structure, antenna, solar panel substrate, and probe back cover. It also provided the lander's electrical systems, specifically common electronics and harness.

Astrium Ltd. designed, developed, and manufactured the instrument arm, main hinge, solar panel hinges, clamp board, and the main parachute.

Systems Engineering and Assessment Ltd. (SEA) installed the lander with the main processor and the electrical ground support equipment (EGSE). The processor will gather all the information and prepare it for transfer to the Mars Express orbiting satellite for relay back to earth. The processor, working in extremely low power, will control all the instruments on the Beagle.

CodaSciSys developed the lander's software, which will be responsible for opening up the lander once it lands on the Martian surface. The software will also trigger the deployment of the solar arrays and a small mirror so that images may be taken before the arm is deployed.

AEA Technology provided the batteries for the Beagle-2 lander and the orbiter, Mars Express. The lithium-ion batteries are lighter and more compact than traditional nickel-cadmium batteries.

QinetiQ developed the communications package for both Beagle 2 and Mars Express. It also built the transceivers, an RF link between Beagle 2 and Mars Express, as well as a baseland unit.

The lander's energy consumption will only be 60 W, which is less than a normal household lightbulb. The transmitter will only use five W.

Rutherford Appleton Laboratory (RAL) performed thermal testing of the lander to simulate the conditions the probe will encounter on its mission to Mars. The tests were conducted in special chambers in which the temperature, pressure, and gaseous composition were tightly controlled.

RAL also contributed a multi-layer insulation (MCI) blanket for Beagle 2 to provide passive thermal control of the lander.

Roke Manor Research built the Beagle 2's radar altimeter and trigger to deploy the airbags at the correct altitude, enabling the probe to land safely.

The device will calculate the altitude from the strength of the pulse it has transmitted when it is reflected back to the orbiter.

The ASPERA instrument was built by the Mullard Space Science Laboratory and the Rutherford Appleton Laboratory (RAL) to study how the solar wind interacts with the atmosphere.

The high super resolution stereo color imager is a stereographic camera designed by the University College London and the Open University to photograph the surface of Mars within two meters' (6.56 ft) detail.

MARSIS, the subsurface sounding radar altimeter, a contribution of the Universities of London and Bristol, will map the distribution of water and ice in the upper portions of the Martian crust using techniques that are similar to oil prospecting on earth.

Beagle 2 was named after the HMS Beagle that took Darwin around the world in the 1830s. It will be catapulted into the Martian atmosphere at a speed of more than 20,000 km/h (12,428 mi/h) when Mars Express arrives at the red planet.

Bibliography

Ahola, K., H. Koskinen, and J. Lahtinen, eds. *Space Research in Finland*. Report to COSPAR 2000, Helsinki 2000.

Alexander's Gas and Oil Connections. "Saudi Arabia to Launch Satellite for Oil Exploration." January 10, 2003.

Aussenwirtschaft, Austria Export. *Aviation and Space Technology*, Number 91, 1998.

Australian Academy of Science: Australian Space Research 1996–1998. Report to the Committee for Space Research (COSPAR), Australian National Committee for Space Science.

Australian Academy of Science: Australian Space Research 1998–2000. Report to the Committee for Space Research (COSPAR), Australian National Committee for Space Science.

Austrian Space Agency (ASA). "Space Activities in Austria 2000." July 2000.

_____. "Space Research in Austria 2000–2001." Report to the Committee for Space Research (COSPAR), Austrian Academy of Sciences, 2002.

Austrospace. "Austrian Space Technologies — Selected Examples." 2000.

British National Space Centre (BNSC). *BNSC in Europe*. Department of Trade and Industry, August 2002.

_____. *Community Report to the British National Space Centre*. "Astrobiology in the U.K. — Scientific Status and Goals." October 1999.

_____. "Earth Observation Applications." Department of Trade and Industry, August 2002.

_____. "Envisat." Department of Trade and Industry, August 2002.

_____. "Future Launches and Missions." Department of Trade and Industry, August 2002.

_____. "Galileo." Department of Trade and Industry, August 2002.

_____. "MOSAIC Small Satellite Programme." Department of Trade and Industry, August 2001.

_____. "Near Earth Objects." Department of Trade and Industry, August 2002.

_____. "Satellite Communciations." Department of Trade and Industry, August 2002.

_____. "Satellite Navigation." Department of Trade and Industry, August 2002.

_____. "Space Debris." Department of Trade and Industry, August 2002.

_____. "Space: U.K." May 2003, Issue 10.

_____. "Technology." Department of Trade and Industry, August 2002.

_____. "United Kingdom Space Strategy 1999–2002: New Frontiers." BNSC Information Office, August 1999.

_____. "UK Draft Space Strategy 2003–2006 and Beyond." January 2003.

_____. "UK Space Activities 2002." June 2002.

Burrough, Bryan. *Dragonfly: NASA and the Crisis Aboard Mir*. New York: Harper Collins, 1998.

Canadian Space Agency. "Space for Canadians." Government of Canada, 1999.

_____. "Space Technologies: Investing in Our Future." 2002.

_____. "The Canadian Space Program: A New Era for Canada in Space." 1999.

Centre National d'Etudes Spatiales (CNES). Annual Report 2001.

Centro para el Desarrollo Tecnológico Industrial. Perspective CDTI Digest #20. July 2003.

_____. CDTI Annual Report. 2001.

_____. CDTI Annual Report. 2000.

_____. CDTI Annual Report. 1999.

Chernard, S. "Malaysia's Fast-Growing Economy." *Via Satellite*. June 1995. 38–46.

Chinese National Space Administration. *Aerospace China*. Volume 2, Spring Issue, 2001.

_____. *Aerospace China*. Volume 2, Summer Issue, 2001.

_____. *Aerospace China*. Volume 2, Autumn Issue, 2001.

_____. *Aerospace China*. Volume 2, Winter Issue, 2001.

_____. *Aerospace China*. Volume 3, Number 1, 2002.

_____. *Aerospace China*. Volume 3, Number 2, 2002.

_____. Annual Report. 2000.

Clark, Phillip. "North Korean Launches." World-wide Satellite Launches, September 5, 1998.

_____. *The Soviet Manned Space Program: The Illustrated History of the Men, the Missions and the Spacecraft*. New York: Orion Books, 1988.

Comisión Nacional De Actividades Espaciales (CONAE). Comisión Nacional De Actividades Espaciales (CONAE) Report. 2002.

Cooperative Research Centre for Satellite Systems (CRCSS). Cooperative Research Centre for Satellite Systems (CRCSS) Report: Innovation from Satellite Services. 2002.

_____. Cooperative Research Centre for Satellite Systems (CRCSS) Annual Report 2001–2002.

_____. Cooperative Research Centre for Satellite Systems (CRCSS) Annual Report 2000–2001.

_____. Cooperative Research Centre for Satellite Systems (CRCSS) Annual Report 1999–2000.

_____. Cooperative Research Centre for Satellite Systems (CRCSS) Annual Report 1998–1999.

_____. Cooperative Research Centre for Satellite Systems (CRCSS) Annual Report 1997–1998.

Czech Board for Space Activities (CBSA). "Space in the Czech Republic." 2002.

Czech Space Agency. National Report of the Czech Republic for Unispace III Conference. 2001.

Da Valle, Laura. *L'Agenzia Spaziale Italiana. The Italian Space Agency and Its Role in National Space Politics: Organization and Planning*. The Italian Space Agency. December 2002.

Danish Space Research Institute (Dansk Rumforskningsinstitut) Annual Report 2002.

David, L. "India's Space Program Picks Up the Pace." *Aerospace America*. August 1995. 32–35, 45.

David, Leonard. "China Appears Ready for Shenzhou-3 Test." *Space News*. January 9, 2002.

_____. "China Launches Shenzhou-3 Test Flight." *Space News*. March 25, 2002.

_____. "China Orbits Shenzhou-4 as Nation's Space Strategy Evolves." *Space News*. December 29, 2002.

_____. "DLR Research Enterprise: Goals and Strategies." Cologne, November 1999.

Elliman, Wendy. *Focus on Israel: Israel in Space*. Israel Ministry of Foreign Affairs. January 2003.

Enterprise Ireland. "Space Ireland." 2002.

European Space Agency. "Europe in Space — An Overview on ESA Activities." 1997.

_____. ESA Bulletin, No. 49. February 1987.

_____. ESA Bulletin, No. 56. November 1988.

_____. ESA Bulletin, No. 71. August 1992.

_____. ESA Bulletin, No. 84. November 1995.

_____. ESA Bulletin, No. 86. May 1996.

_____. ESA Bulletin, No. 87. August 1996.

_____. ESA Bulletin, No. 88. November 1996.

_____. ESA Bulletin, No. 102. May 2000.

_____. ESA Bulletin, No. 103. August 2000.

_____. ESA Bulletin, No. 104. November 2000.

_____. ESA Bulletin, No. 105. February 2001.

_____. ESA Bulletin, No. 106. June 2001.

_____. ESA Bulletin, No. 108. November 2001.

_____. ESA Bulletin, No. 109. February 2002.

_____. ESA Bulletin, No. 111. August 2002.

_____. ESA Bulletin, No. 112. November 2002.

_____. ESA Bulletin, No. 114. May 2003.

_____. "European Launchers for the World." 1999.

_____. "Preparing for the Future: Space Technology Transfer Activities in Austria." Vol. 10, No. 2. August 2000.

German Aerospace Center (Deutsche Forschungsanstatt fuer Luft-und Raumfahrt e. V).

_____. "Köln-Porz." May 2000.

_____. "Lampoldshausen." March 2000.

_____. "Oberpfaffenhofen." October 1998.

_____. "The Profile." April 2002.

_____. "Stuttgart." June 1999.

Gertz, Bill. "China Assists North Korea in Space Launches." *The Washington Times*. February 23, 1999.

Getsov, P. *Bulgarian Space Studies — Past, Present, and Future*. Space Research Institute of the Bulgarian Academy of Sciences.

Hall, Rex, ed. *The History of Mir: 1986–2000*. London: The British Interplanetary Society, 2001.

Harvey, Brian. *Russia in Space: The Failed Frontier*. London: Springer-Praxis, 2000.

Hungarian Space Office. *Space Activities in Hungary: 50 Years*. Budapest, 1996.

Hussain, Syed Shakir. *Natural Hazards Monitoring in Pakistan*. Pakistan Space & Upper Atmosphere Research Commission (SUPARCO), 2001.

Indonesia National Institute of Aeronautics and Space (LAPAN). Annual Report. 2002.

Indian Space Research Organization (ISRO) Annual Report 2002–2003. Government of India, Department of Space.

"Israel Missile Update 2000." *The Risk Report*. Vol. 6, No. 6, November–December 2000.

"Israel Space Agency Aims High Despite Low Budget." Spacedaily. July 18, 2002.

"Israel to Continue Space Program." *World Tribune.com*. February 3, 2003.Jupp, David L. B. 14th CEOS Plenary 2000, Rio de Janeiro, Brazil Member Report by CSIRO on behalf of Australia. CSIRO Office of Space Science & Applications.

Kiernan, T. "South Korea, China to Create Joint Satellite Project." *Space News*. January 31–February 6, 1994. 16.

_____. "South Korea Seeks Economic Stimulus From Satellites." *Space News*. September 14–20, 1992. 28.

Lee, Y. "South Korea, Taiwan Gear Up To Enter Satellite Era." *Space News*. Sept. 24–30, 1990. 7.

Linder, Craig. "China Ready for Second Pilotless Spacecraft Launch." Space.com. July 5, 2000.

Matsumoto, T., and Shibai, H., eds. *Mid- and Far-Infrared Astronomy and Future Space Missions. Proceedings of the International Workshop held at the Institute of Space and Astronautical Science April 17 and 18, 2000.* The Institute of Space and Astronautical Science, Report SP No. 14, December 2000.

National Environment Research Council. "Planet Earth." Spring 2003.

National Institute for Space Research, Brazil (INPE). CBERS: China-Brazil Earth Resources Satellite. 2002.

_____. HSB: Humidity Sounder for Brazil — A Brazilian Contribution to Advance the Knowledge of Earth's Weather and Climate. 2002.

_____. Lit 2000. Instituto Nacional De Pesquisas Espaciais.

_____. National Space Activities Program. 2002.

_____. Satélites SCDs (SCDs Satellites). 2002.

_____. SCD-2: The Second Brazilian Data Collection Satellite. 2002.

National Space Agency of Ukraine. National Space Agency of Ukraine Bulletin #1. Kyiv. January–March 2001.

National Space Development Agency of Japan. NASDA Report, No. 127. January 2003.

_____. NASDA Report, No. 128. February 2003.

_____. NASDA Report, No. 129. March 2003.

_____. NASDA Report, No. 130. April 2003.

_____. NASDA Report, No. 131. May 2003.

_____. NASDA Report, No. 132. June 2003.

_____. NASDA Report, No. 133. July 2003.

_____. NASDA Report, No. 134. August 2003.

_____. NASDA Report, No. 115. January 2002.

_____. NASDA Report, No. 116. February 2002.

_____. NASDA Report, No. 117. March 2002.

_____. NASDA Report, No. 118. April 2002.

_____. NASDA Report, No. 119. May 2002.

_____. NASDA Report, No. 120. June 2002.

_____. NASDA Report, No. 121. July 2002.

_____. NASDA Report, No. 122. August 2002.

_____. NASDA Report, No. 123. September 2002.

_____. NASDA Report, No. 124. October 2002.

_____. NASDA Report, No. 125. November 2002.

_____. NASDA Report, No. 126. December 2002.

_____. NASDA Report, No. 103. January 2001.

_____. NASDA Report, No. 104. February 2001.

_____. NASDA Report, No. 105. March 2001.

_____. NASDA Report, No. 106. April 2001.

_____. NASDA Report, No. 107. May 2001.

_____. NASDA Report, No. 108. June 2001.

_____. NASDA Report, No. 109. July 2001.

_____. NASDA Report, No. 110. August 2001.

_____. NASDA Report, No. 111. September 2001.

_____. NASDA Report, No. 112. October 2001.

_____. NASDA Report, No. 113. November 2001.

_____. NASDA Report, No. 114. December 2001.

_____. NASDA Report, No. 91. January 2000.

_____. NASDA Report, No. 92. February 2000.

_____. NASDA Report, No. 93. March 2000.

_____. NASDA Report, No. 94. April 2000.

_____. NASDA Report, No. 95. May 2000.

_____. NASDA Report, No. 96. June 2000.

_____. NASDA Report, No. 97. July 2000.

_____. NASDA Report, No. 98. August 2000.

_____. NASDA Report, No. 99. September 2000.

_____. NASDA Report, No. 100. October 2000.

_____. NASDA Report, No. 101. November 2000.

_____. NASDA Report, No. 102. December 2000.

_____. (NASDA). "New Space Ventures in the 21st Century." March 2003.

_____. "International Space Station (ISS)." January 31, 2003.

_____. "i-Space: A Breakthrough in Space Technology will Bring IT Society Much Closer to Us." 2003.

_____. "Japanese Experiment Module" 'Kibo.'" January 31, 2003.

National Space Program Office Taiwan ROC. Annual Report. 2001.

Norwegian Space Centre. "The Envisat Satellite — Monitoring the Global Environment." 2002.

_____. Annual Report. 1997.

_____. Annual Report. 1998.

_____. Annual Report. 1999.

_____. Annual Report. 2000.

_____. Annual Report. 2001.

Office for Outer Space Affairs. "International Cooperation in the Peaceful Uses of Outer Space, Malaysia." National Activities of Malaysia, 1999.

_____. "International Cooperation in the Peaceful Uses of Outer Space, Peru." National Activities of Peru, 2000.

_____. "International Cooperation in the Peaceful Uses of Outer Space, Philippines." National Activities of Philippines, 2000.

_____. "International Cooperation in the Peaceful Uses of Outer Space, Saudi Arabia." National Activities of Saudi Arabia, 2000.

Piso, M. I. *Network of Space Science and Technology Capacity Building Institutions in Central Eastern and South-Eastern Europe.* United Nations Office for Outer Space Affairs, Vienna, Austria, 1997.

Polish Academy of Sciences/Space Research Center (SRC). Annual Report. 2000.

_____. Annual Report 2001. Warsaw 2002.

_____. Intellectual Capital Report 2002. Warsaw 2002.

Polityuk, Pavel. "Ukraine, Brazil Sign Commercial Space Launch Deal." Space.com. November 18, 1999.

Ray, Justin. "First Greek Satellite Launch Performed by Atlas 5 Rocket." *Spaceflight Now.* May 14, 2003.

"Report: China to Use Robots in Space Exploration." *Space News.* October 17, 2000.

Riccitiello, R. "Kitsat-A Launch is First Step for Korean Space Program." *Space News.* August 24–30, 1992. 10.

Romanian Space Agency (ROSA). National Paper of Romania. Proceedings UNISPACE III UN World Conference on the Exploration and Peaceful Uses of Outer Space, Vienna, August 19–31, 1999.

SatBytes. "Did North Korea Launch a Satellite?" 2003.

Saudi Press Agency. "Third Saudi Satellite." July 18, 2002.

"Sea Launch Date is Set." Space.com August 31, 1999.

Sheikho, K.M. "Features Extraction for Ground Water Exploration Using Landsat and JERS-1 Images." Middle East Research Center, Ain Shams University, *Earth Series*, Vol. 11, 1997. 225–223.

Sietzen, Jr., F. "The Shenzhou Effect: Giving a Lift to China's Commercial Space?" Space.com. December 7, 1999.

South Movement. "North Korea Successfully Launches Musical Satellite." September 4, 1998.

Space Research Institute Graz, Austrian Academy of Sciences. Annual Report. 2001.

Space Research Organization Netherlands (SRON). Annual Report. 2000.

_____. "SRONG. Space Research in the Netherlands." 2000.

Swedish National Space Board. "The Swedish National Space Board." 1992.

_____. "International Evaluation of Astronomy and Astrophysics." 2000.

_____. "International Evaluation of the Swedish Remote Sensing Programme." 1999

_____. "Space Research in Sweden 2000–2001. Report to COSPAR." 2002.

_____. "Space Research in Sweden 1998–1999. Report to COSPAR." 2000.

_____. "Swedish Research." 2002.

_____. "The Odin Satellite's Sharp Eyes in Space." 2002.

_____. Annual Report. 1999.

_____. Annual Report. 2000.

_____. Annnual Report. 2001.

_____. "Designing, Launching and Operating Space Systems." 2001.

_____. "25 Years: 1972–1997." September 1997.

Thailand Remote Sensing Center. "Remote Sensing in Thailand." 2002.

"The Multi-Purpose Space Rocket Complex 'Zenit.'" GLAVKOSMOS. 1989.

"Ukrainians Plan to Add Muscle to Zenit Rockets." *Space News.* June 14–20, 1993. 2.

United Press International (UPI). "North Korea Offers to Give Up Missiles for Space Technology." July 20, 2000.

Voice of Malaysia. January 13, 1995.

Watanabe, T., K. Suzuki, and K. I. Oyama, *Observation of Stratospheric Ozone* with *MT-135 Rockets in 1990–1999.* Institute of Space and Astronautical Science Report, No. 679. March 2001.

Index